# Writing for Life

## PARAGRAPH TO ESSAY

D. J. Henry

Daytona Beach Community College

PEARSON Longman

New York San Francisco Boston
London Toronto Sydney Tokyo Singapore Madrid
Mexico City Munich Paris Cape Town Hong Kong Montreal

## Dedication

*To my foremost teacher, my mom, Mary Maxine Powell*

**Longman Publishers**
**Acquisitions Editor:** Matthew Wright
**Development Editors:** Mika de Roo, Katharine Glynn
**Marketing Manager:** Thomas DeMarco
**Senior Supplements Editor:** Donna Campion
**Production Manager:** Ellen MacElree
**Project Coordination:** Nesbitt Graphics, Inc.
**Cover Design Manager:** Wendy Ann Fredericks
**Cover Designer:** Dorling Kindersley
**Cover Photos:** *from left to right:* Gary Pearl/Getty Images Inc.—Photographer's Choice; L.M. Crowhurst/OSF/Animals Animals; © Jamie Grill/Blend Images/Corbis and © Dorling Kindersley; and Blend Images Photography/Veer
**Photo Research:** Linda Sykes
**Manufacturing Manager:** Mary Fischer
**Printer and Binder:** Courier Kendallville
**Cover Printer:** Coral Graphic Services

**DK Education**
**Managing Art Editor:** Anthony Limerick
**Designers:** Ann Cannings and Ian Midson
**Design Director:** Stuart Jackman
**Publisher:** Sophie Mitchell

For permission to use copyrighted material, grateful acknowledgment is made to the copyright holders on page 722, which is hereby made part of this copyright page.

Cataloging-in-Publication Data on file at the Library of Congress



Please visit our website at http://www.ablongman.com/studyskills

ISBN 13: 978-0-321-39231-2 (student ed.)
ISBN 10: 0-321-39231-0 (student ed.)
ISBN 13: 978-0-321-41367-3 (instructor's ed.)
ISBN 10: 0-321-41367-9 (instructor's ed.)

2 3 4 5 6 7 8 9—CRK—10 09 08

# Detailed Contents



## Getting Ready to Write

Part 1

## Using Patterns of Organization to Develop Paragraphs

Part 2

## Part 3

## Writing an Essay

## Part 4

## The Basic Sentence

## Part 5 Writing Clear Sentences

## Part 6 Recognizing and Avoiding Errors

Part 7

# Punctuation and Mechanics

OKLAHOMA CITY
← Civic Ctr Music Hall
← Municipal Crt/Police
← Museum of Art
P
↑ OKC Nat'l Memorial

# Reading Selections



Part 8

# Preface

Writing requires confidence and courage. Every word that flows from mind to paper reveals something about who we are in that moment—our depth of thought, our mastery of language, our ability to connect to others. Our students have a gut-level understanding of the risks posed by writing, particularly in the writing classroom where assignments can seem artificial, and grades, editing marks, and high-stakes exit exams often infuse the writing experience with great anxiety. In a few short weeks, students need to master text structure, improve vocabulary, comprehend writing situations, develop a writing process, grasp grammar rules, change life-long habits, and find their voices.

As their guides and mentors, we writing teachers need a systematic curriculum that engages students with high-interest activities that cultivate success and that fosters deep growth as quickly as possible. *Writing for Life* offers a consistent approach that addresses the complex needs of the developing writer and communicates the power and importance of writing in everyday, college, and work situations. *Writing for Life* guides students step by step through writing instruction while showing them how to take responsibility for their learning.

*Writing for Life* is the culmination of over two decades of experience and education. In 1984, when I first volunteered to serve as a reader for Florida's College Level Academic Skills Test (CLAST), a state-wide exam, I had no idea what invaluable lessons I would learn about writing, the teaching of writing, and the assessment of writing. My motivation was to learn what I could about the test to better prepare my students. During the early years of my twenty-plus-year involvement with state-wide assessment, I began experimenting with portfolio assessment. Analyzing and using the scoring rubric dramatically improved my own abilities to write well, and I was eager for my students to experience the same kind of radical improvements in their own writing. Consequently, I began to write rubrics and create reflective questions that helped students to self-assess and take control of their learning. I quickly learned that they faced barriers that went beyond writing concepts and skills, so my lessons, rubrics, and reflective questions expanded to include learning styles, behavioral patterns, and habitual attitudes. Their improvement was amazing and encouraging!

My experiences with the CLAST exam and then later with the Florida Basic Skills Exit Exam, along with my growing understanding of authentic assessment, prepared me for my work with two key federally funded Title III grants at Daytona Beach Community College.

The first grant established the college's developmental program that included reading, writing, math, and student success. I acted as the portfolio consultant and facilitated the development of a comprehensive classroom portfolio assessment system for each of the four disciplines. Together, my colleagues and I learned about how to use writing to learn; we raised our awareness about various learning styles and pedagogical approaches; and we deepened our understanding of the connection between reading, writing, and learning in various disciplines. During the second grant, I served as Curriculum Revision Director. My role was to research best practices; offer instruction to professors about reading and writing in their content areas; and facilitate the revision of curriculum to incorporate meaningful, realistic reading and writing assignments in content areas. I learned much about what is expected of our students once they exit our developmental programs. These important lessons are the foundations of ***Writing for Life***. I love to write and I love to teach, but, most of all, I love to see students succeed. The following series of purpose statements best summarizes my mission in ***Writing for Life.***

- ***Writing for Life*** *is a highly motivational book geared to actively engage students and inspire their confidence in their own success.*
- ***Writing for Life*** *empowers students to identify and overcome barriers and to take responsibility for their learning.*
- ***Writing for Life*** *establishes, illustrates, and reinforces the connection between effort and improvement.*
- ***Writing for Life*** *fosters understanding and nurtures growth.*
- ***Writing for Life*** *clearly explains, demonstrates, and reinforces writing concepts, skills, and applications.*
- ***Writing for Life*** *illustrates the power of writing in life.*

On a final and most important note, if I could speak directly to every student who holds this book, I would offer the following encouragement. Writing well is a learned behavior, and you can learn most anything you put your mind to. Always remember, every minute you spend learning to write is an investment in yourself and your future. You're worth the effort. A great writer named Emerson once said, "Look to yourself and do good because you are good." Emerson expresses great faith in and respect for our individual abilities. I share his faith and have great confidence in *your ability* to master writing for life. You *can* do it—you can *write for life!*

Sincere wishes for your success,
D. J. Henry

▼ "What's the Point" Photographic Organizer feature

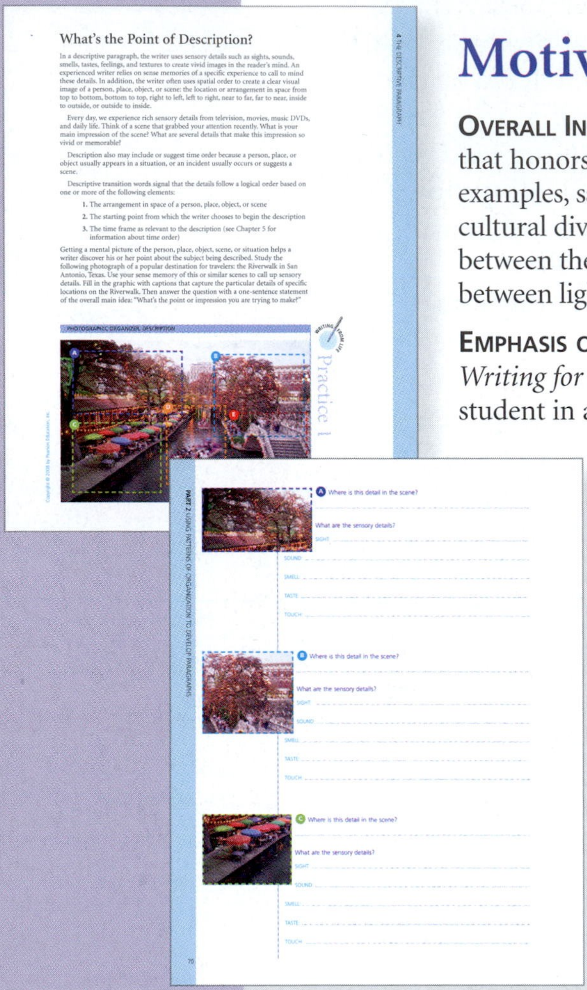


# Features of the Book

## Motivational

**Overall Instructional Voice** establishes a clear, direct, respectful tone that honors adult learners. Topics and language used in instruction, examples, sample writings, and practices reflect issues of high interest and cultural diversity and sensitivity. As Mark Twain said, "the difference between the right word and the almost right word is the difference between lightning and the lightning bug."

**Emphasis on Active Learning** is embedded in instruction throughout *Writing for Life*. For example, every chapter begins by engaging the student in active learning through an activity called "What's the Point?" By answering this question, students learn to preview the chapter and set a purpose for learning about the writing concept or skill. Other active learning activities include "My First Thoughts," "One Writer's Response," "A Writer's Journal," "Writing Workshop," chapter reviews, and numerous writing prompts.

**Emphasis on the Process** is also embedded in instruction throughout the textbook. Many of the activities that emphasize active learning also emphasize the writing process. Directed thinking activities encourage students to actively self-assess how well they handle the writing process as they prewrite, draft, revise, and proofread their work. Students are also guided to think about how to apply what they are learning to improve their writing. For example "A Writer's Journal" records a student's thinking about his or her writing process during a particular assignment.

## Engaging

**High-Interest Topics** such as tattoos, stress, obesity, eating disorders, pop culture icons, fashion, movies, music, relationships, natural disasters, heroes, and current events engage student interest and foster self-expression.

**Innovative Visual Design by Dorling Kindersley (DK)**

"THROUGH THE PICTURE, I SEE REALITY.
THROUGH THE WORD, I UNDERSTAND IT."

Inspired by these words from Swedish lexicographer Sven Lidman, the founders of Dorling Kindersley (DK) set out in the 1970s to develop a new kind of book—a book that would appeal to both the "show me" people and the "tell me" people. At the heart of "the DK look" is the principle that every page needs to appeal to both visual and verbal learners. The signature element is the vivid photograph silhouetted on white, wrapped by expository text blocks. The words and the pictures illuminate one another in what DK calls a "lexigraphic" design approach. In this approach, pages are less linear than in traditional books: a reader has quick access to any idea. Ideas come alive in a way that captures the imagination of a generation brought up in a visual age. DK's design approach combines the best qualities of images and words to create a unique synthesis. Readers are invited to enter the page on many levels and to interact with the flow of information by letting their eyes be their guides.

► DK has been a part of the Penguin Group since 2000. Today, working with Pearson Education, DK begins a new chapter as it sets out to reimagine the educational textbook for U.S. college students.

**Visual Learning Activities** such as photographic organizers in Chapters 4–12 introduce and facilitate writing assignments; concept maps, charts, graphs, and annotated examples enable students to "see" the concept clearly.

**Self-Assessment Tools and Guides** include reflective questions, behavior and attitude surveys, guidelines, checklists, scoring rubrics, and journal entries, complete with examples and explanations. For example, Chapter 3 "Understanding the Paragraph" introduces and explains a scoring guide for a paragraph and then is followed by a practice that asks students to score a set of paragraphs using the scoring guide. These activities transfer the responsibility of learning and assessment of learning to the student.

## Foundational and Comprehensive

**The Writing Situation** is explained and illustrated in Chapter 2 in discussions and engaging activities about how the relationships among topic, audience, and purpose impact the creation of a piece of writing. Writing prompts for paragraphs and essays are fully developed and realistic writing situations based on everyday life, college life, and working life. These writing prompts stimulate role playing and critical thinking skills and illustrate the importance of *writing for life*.

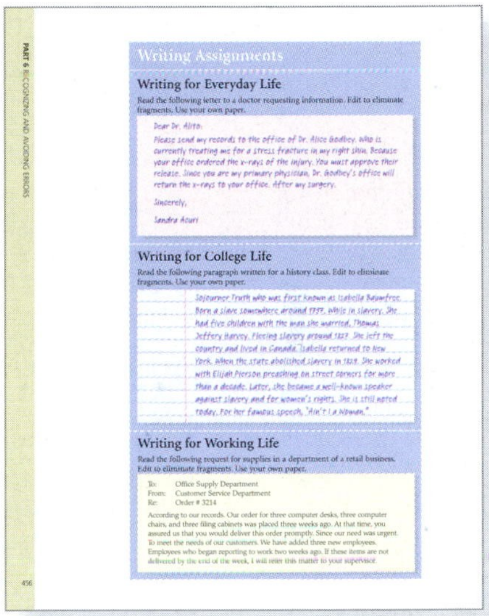

PART 6 RECOGNIZING AND AVOIDING ERRORS

Writing Assignments

Writing for Everyday Life

Read the following letter to a doctor requesting information. Edit to eliminate fragments. Use your own paper.

Dear Dr. Alito:

Please send my records to the office of Dr. Alice Godbey, who is currently treating me for a stress fracture in my right shin. Because your office ordered the x-rays of the injury. You must approve their release. Since you are my primary physician, Dr. Godbey's office will return the x-rays to your office. After my surgery.

Sincerely,

Sandra Acuri

Writing for College Life

Read the following paragraph written for a history class. Edit to eliminate fragments. Use your own paper.

Sojourner Truth who was first known as Isabella Baumfree. Born a slave somewhere around 1797. While in slavery. She had five children with the man she married, Thomas Jeffery Harvey. Fleeing slavery around 1827. She left the country and lived in Canada. Isabella returned to New York. When the state abolished slavery in 1828. She worked with Elijah Pierson preaching on street corners for more than a decade. Later, she became a well-known speaker against slavery and for women's rights. She is still noted today. For her famous speech, "Ain't I a Woman."

Writing for Working Life

Read the following request for supplies in a department of a retail business. Edit to eliminate fragments. Use your own paper.

To: Office Supply Department
From: Customer Service Department
Re: Order # 3214

According to our records. Our order for three computer desks, three computer chairs, and three filing cabinets was placed three weeks ago. At that time, you assured us that you would deliver this order promptly. Since our need was urgent. To meet the needs of our customers. We have added three new employees. Employees who began reporting to work two weeks ago. If these items are not delivered by the end of the week, I will refer this matter to your supervisor.

456

▲ "Writing Assignments" feature

**The Writing Process** lays the foundation of ongoing instruction; the writing process is introduced and illustrated in Chapter 2 with a two-page spread of a four-color graphic with explanations of the entire writing process: Prewriting, Drafting, Revising, and Editing. Then, systematic instruction guides the student step by step through the writing process as individual assignments are modeled and fulfilled throughout the textbook. Grammar lessons have been designed to illustrate the use of the writing process to produce a polished draft. For example, in Part 2, every chapter about using patterns of organization to develop paragraphs includes lessons labeled "Effective Expression." "Grammar in Action" sections show students how to use the revising and proofreading phrases to polish word choice, sentence structure, and mechanics. Appropriate writing process icons appear throughout the textbook as signals to guide students through the writing process of particular assignments. "Workshop: Writing Step by Step" sections in every modes chapter and in Chapter 13 ("Understanding the Essay") give students a full walk-through of the entire writing process, and show, realistically, how processes and patterns weave together in real writing situations.

**Text Structure** is covered extensively at every level, including word, sentence, paragraph, and essay levels. Lessons systematically guide students to consider the types and structures of words, phrases, and sentences; patterns of organization; levels of ideas; traits and function of a main idea; major supporting details; minor supporting details; parts of the paragraph; and parts of the essay. Writing prompts encourage students to adapt text structure to realistic writing situations.

**Grammatical Concepts** are comprehensively covered in an approach that combines an illustrated handbook with intensive practice. Examples are clearly annotated visuals with color-coded highlights that make key concepts jump off the page. Concepts and rules are further defined, explained, and illustrated with charts and graphs. Mastery is encouraged through ample practice and proofreading applications. "Grammar in Action" boxes in each rhetorical modes chapter offer specific advice on correcting common errors that are likely to arise in the context of a particular rhetorical pattern.

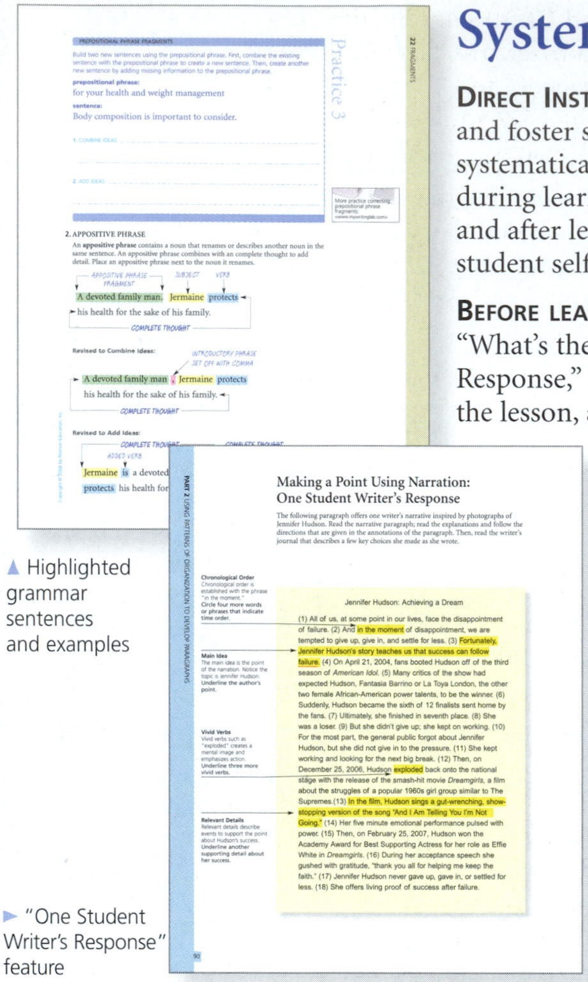


▲ Highlighted grammar sentences and examples

► "One Student Writer's Response" feature

# Systematic

**Direct Instruction** follows a logical order to best ensure comprehension and foster student ownership of the material. Each lesson moves systematically through three distinct phases: before learning activities, during learning activities, and after learning activities. Before, during, and after learning activities make excellent portfolio entries that foster student self-assessment.

**Before learning activities** that prepare students to learn include "What's the Point?," "My First Thoughts," "One Student Writer's Response," and "A Writer's Journal." These activities set the purpose of the lesson, activate critical thinking, and engage the student.

**During learning activities** emphasize understanding concepts and developing skills. Labeled "Understanding the Point," "Developing Your Point," or "Applying the Point," this phase of the lesson offers direct instruction, examples, explanations, checklists, charts, graphics, practices, and workshops.

**After learning activities** test students' abilities to recall and apply what they have learned. After learning activities include chapter reviews, writing assignments, and reflective-critical thinking activities.

# Chapter Features in Part 1

## Getting Ready to Write

Part 1 motivates students to become active learners who assume responsibility for their individual learning, who reflect upon their progress, and who can and will improve their writing skills.

**What's the Point?** is a motivational teaching strategy that addresses the basic question on most students' minds: *Why do I need to know this?* The question and the instructional answer establish the student writer's purpose for studying the chapter. In Chapter 1, "Prepare to Learn about Writing," the activity asks students "What's the Point of Preparing to Learn about Writing?" In Chapter 2, the activity asks "What's the Point of the Writing Process?" Both activities offer a series of photographs that illustrate possible answers. In each chapter, students answer "What's the Point…?" by writing captions for each photograph and then stating their answers to this motivational question in one sentence.

▼ "What's the Point?" feature

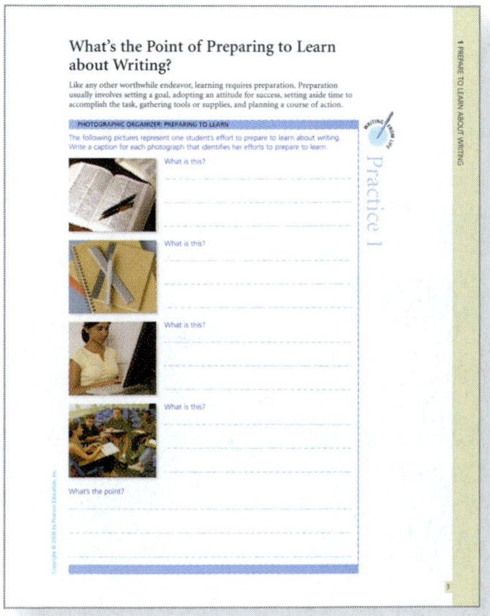


**Making a Point: One Student Writer's Response** offers example responses to the questions "What's the Point of Preparing to Learn about Writing?" in Chapter 1 and "What's the Point of the Writing Process?" in Chapter 2.

**Preparing Yourself to Learn about Writing** in Chapter 1 teaches students to evaluate their attitudes, generate a study plan, and create a portfolio that helps them "to track growth … organize work … and think about" their learning and their writing. Simple and easy-to-follow advice guides students to use checklists, reflective questions, and journal entries as they think about their writing and what they are learning.

**UNDERSTANDING THE POINT: Assessing the Writing Situation** and **Understanding the Point: Using the Writing Process** in Chapter 2 offer direct, step-by-step instruction for two topics: "The Writing Situation: Topic, Purpose, and Audience" and "The Writing Process: Prewriting, Drafting, Revising, and Proofreading." Colorful graphics, relevant photographs, explanations, examples, checklists, and interactive practices enhance learning.

# Chapter Features in Part 2

## Using Patterns of Organization to Develop Paragraphs

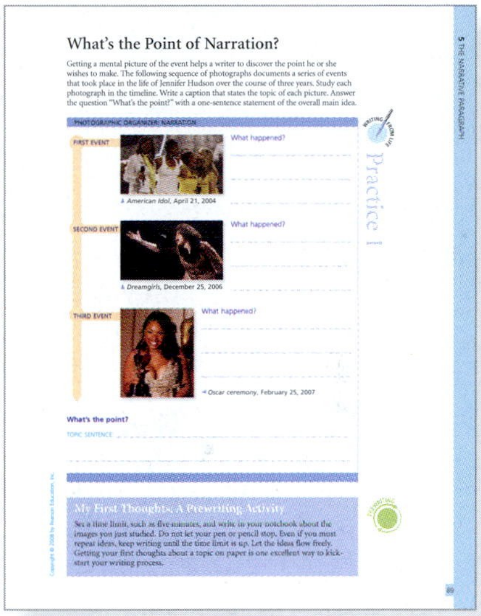
What's the Point of Narration?

Getting a mental picture of the event helps a writer to discover the point he or she wishes to make. The following sequence of photographs documents a series of events that took place in the life of Jennifer Hudson over the course of three years. Study each photograph in the timeline. Write a caption that states the topic of each picture. Answer the question "What's the point?" with a one-sentence statement of the overall main idea.

PHOTOGRAPHIC ORGANIZER: NARRATION

FIRST EVENT — What happened?
American Idol, April 21, 2004

SECOND EVENT — What happened?
Dreamgirls, December 25, 2006

THIRD EVENT — What happened?
Oscar ceremony, February 25, 2007

What's the point?
TOPIC SENTENCE

Practice 1

My First Thoughts: A Prewriting Activity

Set a time limit, such as five minutes, and write in your notebook about the images you just studied. Do not let your pen or pencil stop. Even if you must repeat ideas, keep writing until the time limit is up. Let the ideas flow freely. Getting your first thoughts about a topic on paper is one excellent way to kick-start your writing process.

5 THE NARRATIVE PARAGRAPH

89

▲ "Photographic Organizer" feature

Part 2 offers comprehensive, step-by-step instruction about the structure of a paragraph and how to develop paragraphs using the various patterns of organization. Chapter features are designed to engage students, foster active learning, and improve writing skills.

**WHAT'S THE POINT?** is a motivational teaching strategy that addresses the basic question on most students' minds: *Why do I need to know this?* The instructional answer defines a particular pattern of organization and explains its relevance to the student's everyday life, college life, and working life.

**PHOTOGRAPHIC ORGANIZERS** activate the thinking process, introduce and illustrate a pattern of organization, and stimulate prewriting activities. A set of photographs is arranged in a concept map that illustrates the structure of a particular pattern of organization. A series of reporter's questions ask students to create captions for each of the images, immediately engaging the student in the prewriting phase of the writing process. This chapter-opening activity sets the foundation for follow-up activities that guide the student through the entire writing process.

**MY FIRST THOUGHTS** sustains student engagement in the writing process by prompting a brainstorming session in response to the photographic organizer. Students may choose to use this prewrite as part of a formal writing assignment in the Workshop and Writing Assignment sections of the chapter.

**MAKING A POINT: One Student Writer's Response** is a twofold model of writing and thinking about writing. This section first offers a model writing sample based on the photographic organizer. Students immediately see the relationship between a particular writing prompt and a piece of writing. Each writer's response is annotated with direct instruction about the main idea, supporting details, logical order, and effective expression. The annotations also include directed thinking activities that actively engage students to provide additional (personal) annotations.

**THE WRITER'S JOURNAL** is a "think-aloud" that models reflective thinking about a piece of writing; this journal entry functions as the second part of "Making a Point." The Writer's Journal captures the thinking of the writer of the paragraph featured in "One Student Writer's Response." These writing journals teach students to "think aloud" about their writing. The journals record the barriers, the decisions, and the improvements made by writers as they moved through the writing process. The Writer's Journal serves as a model of student engagement—showing students how to create "think-alouds" about their own writings throughout the semester.

**DEVELOPING YOUR POINT** presents direct instruction that includes explanations, examples, and practices to enhance student understanding about how to develop an idea using a particular pattern of organization. Instruction focuses on four core

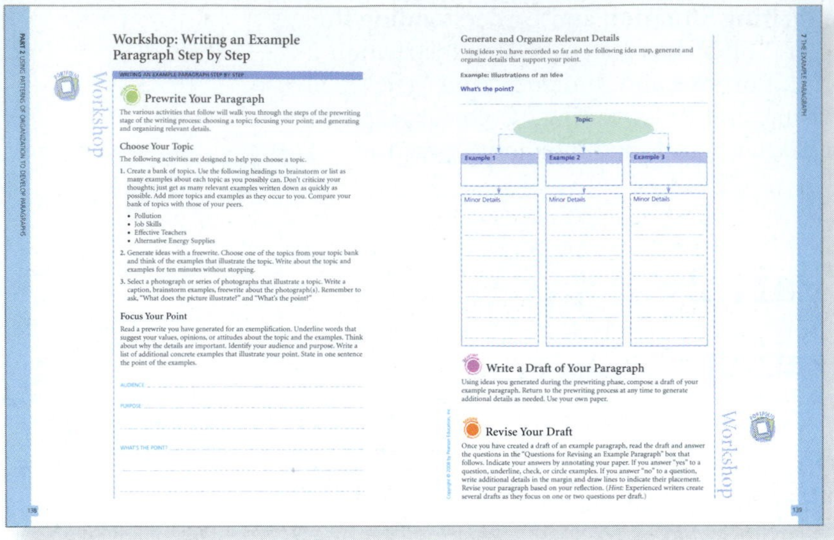


▲ "Workshop" feature

areas: Main Idea, Logical Order, Relevant Details, and Effective Expression. Direct instruction includes a practice that illustrates the use of the pattern of organization in an academic course as in Chapter 4, Practice 6 "Using Description in Your Academic Course."

**Workshop: Writing a Paragraph Step by Step** guides students one step at a time through the writing process from prewriting to editing, and each phase is highlighted with a writing process icon (based on the graphic introduced in Chapter 2), so students know what they are doing at each point in the process, how they are to do it, and why it is important. Activities include choosing a topic, stating a main idea, generating and organizing ideas, revising for effective expression, and editing to polish.

**Grammar in Action** directly addresses some of the most commonly occurring errors in student writing. A specific common error is discussed in the context of a particular pattern of organization. In the last phase of the step-by-step instruction of the Workshop, students study a grammatical concept and then proofread and edit a sample piece of writing to ensure correct application of the concept. The correlation among chapters and grammar concepts are as follows:

| | | |
|---|---|---|
| Chapter 4 | Descriptive | Dangling and Misplaced Modifiers |
| Chapter 5 | Narrative | Unnecessary Shifts in Verb Tense |
| Chapter 6 | Process | Eliminating Run-on Sentences |
| Chapter 7 | Example | Using Commas in a Series |
| Chapter 8 | Classification | Eliminating Comma Splices |
| Chapter 9 | Comparison/Contrast | Commas after Introductory Elements |
| Chapter 10 | Definition | Commas with Nonessential Information |
| Chapter 11 | Cause/Effect | Commonly Confused Words |
| Chapter 12 | Persuasion | Consistent Use of Viewpoint |

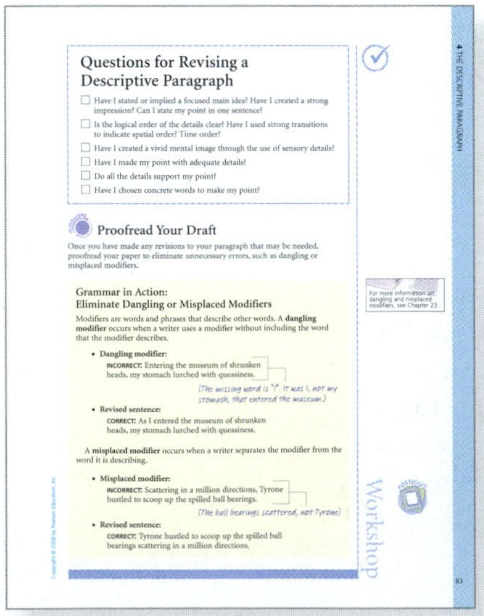


▲ "Grammar in Action" feature

**Review of the Writing Process** offers a fill-in form that students can tear out and use to guide them through their writing process as they respond to a writing assignment. Highlighted with the icons that indicate each phase of the writing process, the form can also help students generate a journal entry about their writing experience. The activity also serves as a chapter review.

**Writing Assignments** are presented in fully developed prompts that create realistic writing situations. The writing prompts direct students to consider audience and purpose as they employ the full writing process. The first prompt "Considering Audience and Purpose" offers students the opportunity to build upon the photographic organizer and "My First Thought" activities that opened the chapter. Additional assignments provide topics and situations relevant to "Everyday Life," "College Life," and "Working Life."

# Chapter Features in Part 3

## Writing an Essay

Part 3 teaches students how to transfer what they have learned about writing paragraphs to writing essays. Students learn how to use patterns of organization to develop points that need several paragraphs of support. Several core features continue in this section:

**WHAT'S THE POINT?** engages the student and establishes the student's need to know the information by asking "What's the Point of an Essay?", "What's the Point of Effective Introductions, Conclusions, and Titles?", and "What's the Point of Using Patterns of Organization to Develop Essays?"

**MAKING A POINT** illustrates and encourages critical thinking and active learning through the use of annotations, student writing samples, and interactive practices.

**DEVELOPING YOUR POINT** offers direct instruction, including explanations, annotated examples, student writing samples, and practice.

**WORKSHOP** is a step-by-step guide that shows students how to apply the instruction to their personal writing process.

**WRITING ASSIGNMENTS** continue to present fully developed writing situations that reflect everyday life, college life, and working life scenarios.

**HIGH-INTEREST VISUALS** include four-color annotations, graphic organizers, concept maps, outlines, checklists, and photographs to stimulate interest, clarify concepts, and facilitate student responses.

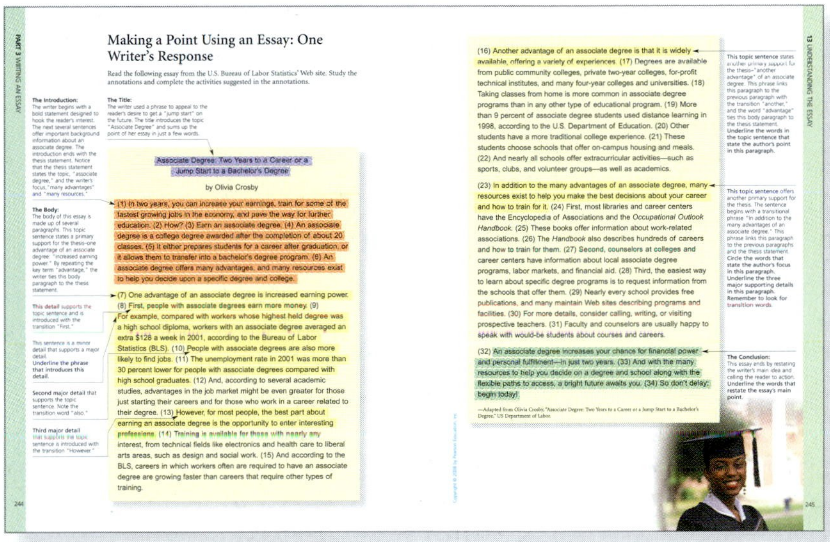
PART 3 WRITING AN ESSAY

Making a Point Using an Essay: One Writer's Response

Read the following essay from the U.S. Bureau of Labor Statistics' Web site. Study the annotations and complete the activities suggested in the annotations.

**The Introduction:** The writer begins with a bold statement designed to hook the reader's interest. The next several sentences offer important background information about an associate degree. The introduction ends with the thesis statement. Notice that the thesis statement states the topic, "associate degree," and the writer's focus, "many advantages" and "many resources."

**The Title:** The writer used a phrase to appeal to the reader's desire to get a "jump start" on the future. The title introduces the topic "Associate Degree" and sums up the point of her essay in just a few words.

Associate Degree: Two Years to a Career or a Jump Start to a Bachelor's Degree

by Olivia Crosby

(1) In two years, you can increase your earnings, train for some of the fastest growing jobs in the economy, and pave the way for further education. (2) How? (3) Earn an associate degree. (4) An associate degree is a college degree awarded after the completion of about 20 classes. (5) It either prepares students for a career after graduation, or it allows them to transfer into a bachelor's degree program. (6) An associate degree offers many advantages, and many resources exist to help you decide upon a specific degree and college.

**The Body:** The body of this essay is made up of several paragraphs. This topic sentence states a primary support for the thesis–one advantage of an associate degree: "increased earning power." By repeating the key term "advantage," the writer ties this body paragraph to the thesis statement.

**This detail** supports the topic sentence and is introduced with the transition "First."

This sentence is a minor detail that supports a major detail. **Underline the phrase that introduces this detail.**

**Second major detail** that supports the topic sentence. Note the transition word "also."

**Third major detail** that supports the topic sentence is introduced with the transition "However."

(7) One advantage of an associate degree is increased earning power. (8) First, people with associate degrees earn more money. (9) For example, compared with workers whose highest held degree was a high school diploma, workers with an associate degree averaged an extra $128 a week in 2001, according to the Bureau of Labor Statistics (BLS). (10) People with associate degrees are also more likely to find jobs. (11) The unemployment rate in 2001 was more than 30 percent lower for people with associate degrees compared with high school graduates. (12) And, according to several academic studies, advantages in the job market might be even greater for those just starting their careers and for those who work in a career related to their degree. (13) However, for most people, the best part about earning an associate degree is the opportunity to enter interesting professions. (14) Training is available for those with nearly any interest, from technical fields like electronics and health care to liberal arts areas, such as design and social work. (15) And according to the BLS, careers in which workers often are required to have an associate degree are growing faster than careers that require other types of training.

244

(16) Another advantage of an associate degree is that it is widely available, offering a variety of experiences. (17) Degrees are available from public community colleges, private two-year colleges, for-profit technical institutes, and many four-year colleges and universities. (18) Taking classes from home is more common in associate degree programs than in any other type of educational program. (19) More than 9 percent of associate degree students used distance learning in 1998, according to the U.S. Department of Education. (20) Other students have a more traditional college experience. (21) These students choose schools that offer on-campus housing and meals. (22) And nearly all schools offer extracurricular activities—such as sports, clubs, and volunteer groups—as well as academics.

This topic sentence states another primary support for the thesis–"another advantage" of an associate degree. This phrase links this paragraph to the previous paragraph with the transition "another," and the word "advantage" ties this body paragraph to the thesis statement. **Underline the words in the topic sentence that state the author's point in this paragraph.**

(23) In addition to the many advantages of an associate degree, many resources exist to help you make the best decisions about your career and how to train for it. (24) First, most libraries and career centers have the Encyclopedia of Associations and the *Occupational Outlook Handbook*. (25) These books offer information about work-related associations. (26) The *Handbook* also describes hundreds of careers and how to train for them. (27) Second, counselors at colleges and career centers have information about local associate degree programs, labor markets, and financial aid. (28) Third, the easiest way to learn about specific degree programs is to request information from the schools that offer them. (29) Nearly every school provides free publications, and many maintain Web sites describing programs and facilities. (30) For more details, consider calling, writing, or visiting prospective teachers. (31) Faculty and counselors are usually happy to speak with would-be students about courses and careers.

**This topic sentence** offers another primary support for the thesis. The sentence begins with a transitional phrase "In addition to the many advantages of an associate degree." This phrase links this paragraph to the previous paragraphs and the thesis statement. **Circle the words that state the author's focus in this paragraph. Underline the three major supporting details in this paragraph. Remember to look for transition words.**

(32) An associate degree increases your chance for financial power and personal fulfillment—in just two years. (33) And with the many resources to help you decide on a degree and school along with the flexible paths to access, a bright future awaits you. (34) So don't delay; begin today!

**The Conclusion:** This essay ends by restating the writer's main idea and calling the reader to action. **Underline the words that restate the essay's main point.**

—Adapted from Olivia Crosby, "Associate Degree: Two Years to a Career or a Jump Start to a Bachelor's Degree," US Department of Labor.

13 UNDERSTANDING THE ESSAY

245

"Making a Point" feature

# Chapter Features in Parts 4 to 7

## Grammatical Instruction

Student motivation, always vital, seems to be even more crucial when it comes to mastering grammatical concepts. Unfortunately, too many times, grammar instruction is met with apathy and dread. Grammar has purpose. It's worth the effort to learn it. The purpose of instruction is to foster confidence and mastery. The core features of this text—designed to inspire and motivate—have been adapted to match the nature of instruction for grammatical concepts.

**WHAT'S THE POINT?** offers a real-life situation to illustrate the importance of grammar in various communication situations. Each chapter begins with a scenario depicted in a photograph and a related piece of writing that illustrates the grammar concept in action. Students are asked to reflect upon the situation and the importance of the grammar concept under study and then to answer the question: *What's the point of learning about...?*

**UNDERSTANDING THE POINT** reinforces the need to know by offering a student response to the opening activity as a think-aloud that models critical thinking. These activities model effective learning practices.

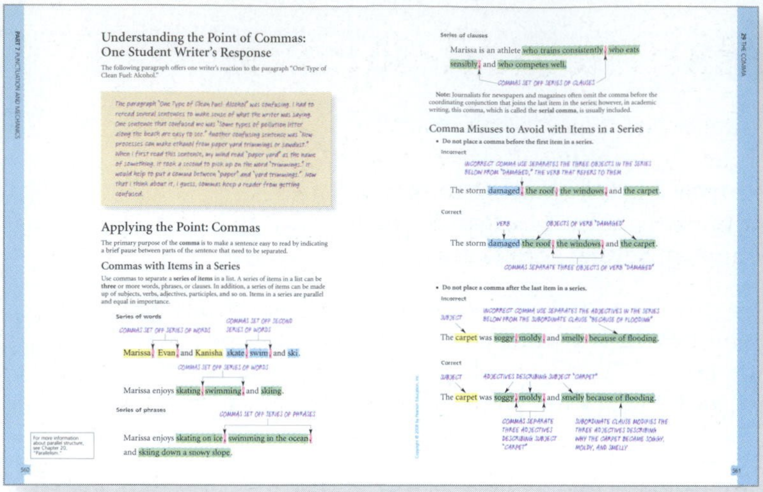
Understanding the Point of Commas: One Student Writer's Response

Applying the Point: Commas

Commas with Items in a Series

Marissa, Evan, and Kanisha skate, swim, and ski.

Marissa enjoys skating, swimming, and skiing.

Marissa enjoys skating on ice, swimming in the ocean, and skiing down a snowy slope.

Marissa is an athlete who trains consistently, who eats sensibly, and who competes well.

Comma Misuses to Avoid with Items in a Series

The storm damaged, the roof, the windows, and the carpet.

The storm damaged the roof, the windows, and the carpet.

The carpet was soggy, moldy, and smelly, because of flooding.

The carpet was soggy, moldy, and smelly because of flooding.

▲ Visual Instruction and "Applying the Point" feature

**Applying the Point** offers direct instruction that includes definitions, explanations, annotated examples, and ample practice to foster mastery of the grammatical concept.

**Visual Instruction** offers annotated visuals with color-coded highlights that make key concepts jump off the page. Concepts and rules are further defined, explained, and illustrated with charts and graphs.

**Writing Assignments** are exercises in proofreading and editing writing samples that reflect realistic writing situations in everyday life, college life, and working life.

**Academic Learning Log** is an end-of-chapter activity that tests students' comprehension of the chapter's instruction. Most questions test students' literal comprehension through fill-in-the-blank prompts. However, the two final questions test students' abilities to transfer what they have learned to their own writing with the questions "How will I use what I have learned?" and "What do I still need to study?"

# Part 8

## Reading Selections

We know that reading enhances our ability to write well. Therefore, the major emphasis in Part 8 is the connection between reading and writing. As in other sections, students are guided to think about the importance of what they are learning and how they are applying what they are learning as writers.

**What's the Connection Between Reading and Writing?** This opening activity offers an attitude and behavior survey that asks students to reflect about their individual reading and writing experiences.

**Understanding the Connection Between Reading and Writing** This section explains the benefits a writer gains from reading, illustrates in a chart the similarities between reading and writing, and offers a practice that models the connection between reading and writing.

**Applying the Point: The Connection Between Reading and Writing** This section emphasizes the thinking processes students can use to make the connection between reading and writing. Students learn how to annotate a text, summarize a text, and read like a writer.

**Nineteen Reading Selections** offer high-interest essays, both contemporary and classical, as models of effective writing. Topics cover a wide range of subjects including poverty, the environment, Hip-Hop music and censorship, horror movies, personal style, growing up, growing older, and culture. The tone and purpose of these essays vary from entertaining humor to biting persuasion and include distinctive voices such as Maya Angelou, Rachel Carson, Nikki Giovanni, Dave Barry, and E. B. White. Students are directed to annotate the text and maintain a vocabulary journal of new or difficult terms they encounter as they read. Discussion questions and writing prompts encourage a careful reading of each essay and stimulate meaningful student responses.

**After Reading Discussion Questions: Meaning, Structure, and Expression** focus student attention on four basic traits of an essay: Main Idea, Relevant Details, Logical Order, and Effective Expression.

**Thinking Prompts to Move from Reading to Writing** offer two fully developed writing situations based on the reading. These prompts ask students to consider audience and purpose as they form a response to what they have read.

# Developmental Writing Instructor Resources

Pearson Longman is pleased to offer a variety of support materials to help make teaching developmental English easier on teachers and to help students excel in their coursework. Many of our student supplements are available free or at a greatly reduced price when packaged with a Longman writing textbook. Contact your local Pearson sales representative for more information on pricing and how to create a package.

**_Writing for Life,_ Annotated Instructor's Edition (AIE / 0-321-41367-9)**

The Annotated Instructor's Edition (AIE) is a replica of the student text, with answers to exercises included for ease of use. Ask your Pearson sales representative for ISBN 0-321-41367-9.

**_Writing for Life_ Instructor's Manual (0-321-41368-7)**

The Instructor's Manual, prepared by Rebekah Rios-Harris of Cedar Valley Community College, features various approaches and suggestions for incorporating the material in *Writing for Life* throughout your course. The manual follows the chapters of *Writing for Life* chronologically, beginning with an overview of each chapter. Each chapter contains the following sections: Topic Talk (sharing writing topics), The Creative Classroom (activity possibilities), Teaching Tips (offering suggestions), and Reality Check (taking the challenges with the triumphs). The manual has you, the instructor, at the heart of its development. Its purpose is to help you take the wealth of information from the text and discover unique teaching strategies to possibly utilize in your course. You will find that the manual has much to offer while, at the same time, encouraging uniqueness and creativity on the part of the instructor. ISBN 0-321-41368-7.

**_Writing for Life_ Test Bank (0-205-52081-2)**

The Test Bank, prepared by Michael Haddock of Florida Community College at Jacksonville-Kent Campus, features 10-question quizzes for each chapter (Multiple-Choice and True & False), 20-question pre- and post-tests for the entire book (True & False and Multiple-Choice), 10-question Grammar in Check review quizzes for each topic covered in the text (Multiple-Choice), and a 20-question Review Quiz for each part (Multiple-Choice and True & False). The quizzes are designed to test the student's holistic understanding of key concepts rather than simple memorization of terminology. Whenever possible, emphasis is placed on the use of sample sentences that require kinesthetic interaction with the material rather than simple definition answers. ISBN 0-205-52081-2. Computerized Test Bank (ISBN 0-205-61691-7).

**Printed Test Bank for Developmental Writing (Instructor / 0-321-08486-1)**

Features more than 5,000 questions in all areas of writing, from grammar to paragraphing through essay writing, research, and documentation.

**Electronic Test Bank for Developmental Writing (Instructor / CD 0-321-08117-X)**

Features more than 5,000 questions in all areas of writing, from grammar to paragraphing through essay writing, research, and documentation. Instructors simply choose questions from the electronic test bank, then print out the completed test for distribution OR offer the test online.

**Diagnostic and Editing Tests, Tenth Edition (Instructor / ISBN 0-205-53642-5)**

This collection of diagnostic tests helps instructors assess students' competence in standard written English to determine placement or to gauge progress. Electronic / ISBN: 0-205-59867-6 MYTEST; ISBN: 0-321-49895-X; TESTGEN.

**The Longman Guide to Classroom Management (Instructor / 0-321-09246-5)**

This guide is designed as a helpful resource for instructors who have classroom management problems. It includes helpful strategies for dealing with disruptive students in the classroom and the "do's and don'ts" of discipline.

**The Longman Guide to Community Service-Learning in the English Classroom and Beyond (Instructor / 0-321-12749-8)**

Written by Elizabeth Rodriguez Kessler of University of Houston, this monograph provides a definition and history of service-learning, as well as an overview of how service-learning can be integrated effectively into the college classroom.

# Multimedia Offerings

**MyWritingLab (www.mywritinglab.com)**

MyWritingLab is a complete online learning system with *better* practice exercises to make students better writers. The exercises in MyWritingLab are progressive, which means that within each skill module, students move from literal comprehension to critical application to demonstrating their skills in their own writing. The 9,000+ exercises in the system do rehearse grammar, but they also extend into the writing process, paragraph development, essay development, and research. A thorough diagnostic test outlines where student have not yet mastered the skill, and an easy-to-use tracking system enables students and instructors to monitor all work in MyWritingLab. See information at the beginning of this book for more details! (www.mywritinglab.com<http://www.mywritinglab.com>)

# Developmental Writing Student Supplements

**Longman English Tutor Center Access Card (VP: 0-201-71049-8 or Stand Alone: 0-201-72170-8)**
Unique service offering students access to an in-house writing tutor via phone and/or email. Tutor available from 5:00 p.m.–12:00 a.m., Sunday through Thursday.

**The Longman Writer's Journal (Student / 0-321-08639-2)**
Provides students with their own personal space for writing and contains helpful journal writing strategies, sample journal entries by other students, and many writing prompts and topics to get students writing.

**The New American Webster Handy College Dictionary, Third Edition (Student / 0-451-18166-2)**
A paperback reference text with more than 100,000 entries.

**ESL Worksheets, Third Edition (Student / 0-321-07765-2)**
These worksheets provide ESL students with extra practice in areas they find the most troublesome. Diagnostic tests, suggested writing topics, and an answer key are included.

**Eighty Practices (Student / 0-673-53422-7)**
A collection of ten-item exercises that provide additional practice for specific grammatical usage problems, such as comma splices, capitalization, and pronouns.

**What Every Student Should Know About Practicing Peer Review, (Student / 0-321-44848-0)**

**Learning Together (Student / 0-673-46848-8)**
This brief guide to the fundamentals of collaborative learning teaches students how to work effectively in groups.

**Longman Editing Exercises (Student / 0-205-31792-8; Answer Key: 0-205-31797-9)**
Fifty-four pages of paragraph editing exercises give students extra practice using grammar skills in the context of longer passages.

**100 Things to Write About (Student / 0-673-98239-4)**
This brief book contains over 100 individual writing assignments, on a variety of topics and in a wide range of formats, from expressive to analytical writing.

**What Every Student Should Know About Researching Online (Student / 0-321-44531-7)**

**What Every Student Should Know About Citing Sources with APA Documentation (Student / 0-205-49923-6)**

**What Every Student Should Know About Citing Sources with MLA Documentation (Student / 0-321-44737-9)**

**What Every Student Should Know About Avoiding Plagiarism (Student / 0-321-44689-5)**

**What Every Student Should Know About Portfolios (Student / 0-205-57250-2)**

**What Every Student Should Know About Study Skills (Student / 0-321-44736-0)**

**The Oxford American Desk Dictionary and Thesaurus (ISBN 0-425-18068-9)**
From the Oxford University Press and Berkley Publishing Group comes this one-of-a-kind reference book that combines both of the essential language tools—dictionary and thesaurus—in a single, integrated A-to-Z volume. The 1,024 page book offers more than 150,000 entries, definitions, and synonyms so you can find the right word every time, as well as appendices of valuable quick-reference information including signs and symbols, weights and measures, presidents of the United States, U.S. states and capitals, and more.

**The Oxford Essential Thesaurus (ISBN 0-425-16421-7)**
From Oxford University Press, renowned for quality educational and reference works, comes this concise, easy-to-use thesaurus—the essential tool for finding just the right word for every occasion. The 528-page book includes 175,000 synonyms in a simple A-to-Z format, more than 10,000 entries, extensive word choices, example sentences and phrases, and guidance on usage, punctuation, and more in the exclusive "Writers Toolkit."

# State-Specific Supplements

## For Florida Adopters

**Thinking Through the Test: A Study Guide for the Florida College Basic Skills Exit Test, by D.J. Henry**
FOR FLORIDA ADOPTIONS ONLY. This workbook helps students strengthen their reading skills in preparation for the Florida College Basic Skills Exit Test. It features both diagnostic tests to help assess areas that may need improvement and exit tests to help test skill mastery. Detailed explanatory answers have been provided for almost all of the questions.

## Available Versions:

**Thinking Through the Test**
A Study Guide for the Florida College Basic Skills Exit Tests: Reading and Writing, Without Answers, Third Edition 0-321-38740-6

**Thinking Through the Test**
A Study Guide for the Florida College Basic Skills Exit Tests: Reading and Writing, With Answers, Third Edition 0-321-38739-2

**Thinking Through the Test**
A Study Guide for the Florida College Basic Skills Exit Tests: Writing, With Answers, Third Edition 0-321-38741-4

**Thinking Through the Test**
A Study Guide for the Florida College Basic Skills Exit Tests: Writing, Without Answers, Third Edition 0-321-38934-4

**Writing Skills Summary for the Florida State Exit Exam, by D. J. Henry (Student / 0-321-08477-2)**
FOR FLORIDA ADOPTIONS ONLY. An excellent study tool for students preparing to take the Florida College Basic Skills Exit Test for Writing, this laminated writing grid summarizes all the skills tested on the Exit Exam.

**CLAST Test Package, Seventh Edition (Instructor/Print ISBN 0-321-01950-4)**
These two, 40-item objective tests evaluate students' readiness for the Florida CLAST exams. Strategies for teaching CLAST preparedness are included.

## For Texas Adopters

**The Longman THEA Study Guide, by Jeanette Harris (Student / 0-321-27240-4)**
Created specifically for students in Texas, this study guide includes straightforward explanations and numerous practice exercises to help students prepare for the reading and writing sections of the THEA Test.

**TASP Test Package, Third Edition (Instructor / Print ISBN 0-321-01959-8)**
These 12 practice pre-tests and post-tests assess the same reading and writing skills covered in the Texas TASP examination

## For New York/CUNY Adopters

**Preparing for the CUNY-ACT Reading and Writing Test, edited by Patricia Licklider (Student/ 0-321-19608-2)**
This booklet, prepared by reading and writing faculty from across the CUNY system, is designed to help students prepare for the CUNY-ACT exit test. It includes test-taking tips, reading passages, typical exam questions, and sample writing prompts to help students become familiar with each portion of the test.

# Acknowledgments

The publication of a text like this requires the effort and sacrifice of many people. I would like to begin with a heart-felt expression of appreciation for the Longman Pearson English team. ***Writing for Life*** has afforded me the opportunity to work with and learn from a talented group of people. I thank the editorial team for giving me the opportunity to partner with Dorling Kindersley (DK), whose design so beautifully appeals to visual and verbal learners. I would like to specifically thank Anthony Limerick from DK for his hard work on this project. Matt Wright, Acquisitions Editor, is a wonderful partner to whom I am indebted and grateful for his enthusiastic support and active involvement throughout this process. I have been fortunate to work with a team of talented, insightful, and gracious developmental editors including Mika DeRoo, Katharine Glynn, and Janice Wiggins. The Pearson commitment to excellence provided me with the opportunity to also work with Katherine Grimaldi, whose keen touch polished the text.

I would like to also acknowledge the production team for ***Writing for Life*** beginning with Kathy Smith from Nesbitt Graphics, Inc., who served as copyeditor and project coordinator, and Genevieve Coyne, proofreader. I am also grateful to Ellen MacElree, Production Manager. I would also like to acknowledge the great debt I owe to several of my colleagues at Daytona Beach Community College: Dustin Weeks, Rhodella Brown, and Sandra Offiah-Hawkins. As Tennyson's tribute in "Ulysses" extols, these are "souls that have toiled, and wrought, and thought with me." Their influence and support has made me a better person, teacher, and writer.

Finally, I would like to gratefully recognize the invaluable insights provided by the following colleagues and reviewers. I deeply appreciate their investment of time, energy, and wisdom.

**Nina Bannett**
*New York City College of Technology CUNY*

**Kathleen Beauchene**
*Community College of Rhode Island*

**Nicholas Bekas**
*Valencia Community College*

**Kay Blue**
*Owens Community College*

**Randy Boone**
*Northampton Community College*

**Brad Bostian**
*Central Piedmont Community College*

**Patricia Bostian**
*Central Piedmont Community College*

**Kathy Britton**
*Florence Darlington Technical College*

**Tracy Brunner**
*Broward Community College*

**Cheryl Cardoza**
*Truckee Meadows Community College*

**Terry Clark**
*Kennedy-King College*

**Kennette Crockett**
*Malcolm X College*

**Marianna Duncan**
*Angelina College*

**Cynthia M. Dunham-Gonzalez**
*Seminole Community College*

**Marie G. Eckstrom**
*Rio Hondo College*

**Margot A. Edlin**
*Queensborough Community College, CUNY*

**Laurie Esler**
*Southern Wesleyan University*

**Cathy Fagan**
*Nassau Community College*

**Robert Ficociello**
*SUNY Albany and Middlesex Community College*

**Catherine Fraga**
*Sacramento State University*

**Deborah Fuller**
*Bunker Hill Community College*

**Paul T. Gallagher**
*Red Rocks Community College*

**Lois Garrison**
*Tacoma Community College*

**Tom Ghering**
*Ivy Tech Community College of Indiana*

**Judy Haisten**
*Central Florida Community College*

**Denise Haley**
*Bunker Hill Community College*

**Cynthia Halstead**
*Broward Community College*

**Beth Hammett**
*College of the Mainland*

**Greg Hammond**
*New Mexico Junior College*

**Ken Holliday**
*Southern State Community College*

**Richard Johnson**
*Kirkwood Community College*

**Peter Kearly**
*Henry Ford Community College*

**Helene Kozma**
*Housatonic Community College*

**Joseph Marshall**
*Villa Julie College*

**Charlene McDaniel**
*Cincinnati State Technical and Community College*

**Judy McKenzie**
*Lane Community College*

**David Merves**
*Miami Dade College, North Campus*

**Jack Miller**
*Normandale Community College*

**Dave Moutray**
*Kankakee Community College*

**Andrea Neptune**
*Sierra College*

**Julie Nichols**
*Okaloosa-Walton College*

**Jay Peterson**
*Atlantic Cape Community College*

**Dawn Pickett**
*Blinn College*

**Diane L. Polcha**
*Tulsa Community College, Southeast Campus*

**Brian L. Reeves**
*Tomball College*

**Charlotte Teresa Reynolds**
*Indiana State University Southwest*

**Leigh Ann Rhea**
*Calhoun Community College*

**Doug Rigby**
*Lehigh Carbon Community College*

**Sara Safdie**
*University of California, San Diego*

**Rebecca Samberg**
*Housatonic Community College*

**Albert C. Sears**
*Silver Lake College*

**Sharon Shapiro**
*Naugatuck Valley Community College*

**Deneen Shepherd**
*St. Louis Community College, Forest Park*

**James Suderman**
*Okaloosa-Walton College*

**Holly J. Susi**
*Community College of Rhode Island*

**Nanette Tamer**
*Villa Julie College*

**Thomas Treffinger**
*Greenville Technical College*

**Sharisse Turner**
*Tallahassee Community College*

**Cynthia M. VanSickle**
*McHenry Community College*

**Linda VanVickle**
*St. Louis Community College–Meramec*

**Kymberli G. Ward**
*Southwestern Oklahoma State University*

**Margie Wilkoff**
*St. Petersburg College*

**Rachael Williams**
*West Georgia Technical College*

**Jilani Worsi**
*Queensborough Community College*

PART 1

# Getting Ready to Write

# 1 Prepare to Learn about Writing

**Chapter Preview**

- What's the Point of Preparing to Learn about Writing?
- Making a Point about Preparing to Learn about Writing: One Student Writer's Response
- Preparing Yourself to Learn about Writing

In countless situations in life, preparation is essential to success. Even a trip to the grocery store requires some planning in order to get all the items needed to feed a family and run a household in the most economical way. A careful shopper may create a menu, check the pantry and make a list of what is needed, read the ads for sale items, or clip coupons. Think of another situation or task that requires preparation. What kind of preparation might be needed to successfully complete the task?

Writing is an essential life skill, and learning to write well allows you to express yourself, influence others, succeed in college, and compete in the job market. By starting your academic career with this writing course, you are preparing for success. You are laying a sturdy foundation for writing for life. If you are like many others, you may have a few qualms about writing, but take heart! With the right attitude and a study plan, you *can* learn to write well. Get ready to learn about writing!

# What's the Point of Preparing to Learn about Writing?

Like any other worthwhile endeavor, learning requires preparation. Preparation usually involves setting a goal, adopting an attitude for success, setting aside time to accomplish the task, gathering tools or supplies, and planning a course of action.

WRITING FROM LIFE

Practice 1

**PHOTOGRAPHIC ORGANIZER: PREPARING TO LEARN**

The following pictures represent one student's effort to prepare to learn about writing. Write a caption for each photograph that identifies her efforts to prepare to learn.

What is this?

What is this?

What is this?

What is this?

What's the point?

# Making a Point about Preparing to Learn about Writing: One Student Writer's Response

The following paragraph records one student's efforts to prepare to learn about writing. As you read the paragraph, underline specific steps he took that you might use as well.

Prepared to Learn

(1) I began preparing to learn about writing even before the class began. (2) My first step was choosing a teacher. (3) I had heard that Professor Rickles was an excellent teacher, and RateMyProfessor.com verified what I had heard. (4) On the first day of class, he handed out his course syllabus which listed the books and materials I needed; later that day, I bought everything he required, and I brought everything I needed with me to every class. (5) Right away, Professor Rickles put us in small groups so we could get to know each other by working together. (6) I found three people who wanted to learn as much as I did so we formed a study group. (7) We helped each other a lot throughout the whole semester. (8) If one of us was sick, we made sure he or she got the notes and assignment for that day, and we read each other's papers to make sure they made sense and didn't have any careless errors. (9) I also used a daily planner to record assignments and set aside time to study and write. (10) I arrived a few minutes early when possible, so that when class began, I was prepared to get to work. (11) I have to admit I had to work on my attitude. (12) I was so shy and afraid of sounding silly that asking questions in class was really hard, so for a while, I stayed after class to ask my questions, but eventually, I gained enough confidence to ask them during class. (13) I also had to learn how to deal with Professor Rickles' comments on my papers. (14) I worked so hard on each essay, yet for a long time, my papers came back to me with grades and edits that showed I still needed to improve. (15) It took a while for my hard work to pay off, but I was determined to succeed. (16) I am proud to say, all my preparation and hard work paid off. (16) Not only did I earn an "A," but I also improved my ability to write.

# Preparing Yourself to Learn about Writing

As you prepare to learn about writing, take some time to evaluate yourself as a student writer. Think about your attitude, how you can become an active learner, your relationship with your teacher, your study plan, and how you will track your growing writing abilities. The more you think and the more you prepare, the more likely you are to learn about writing and to become an effective writer.

## The Attitude of Learning

### Use Positive Self-Talk

Many people have negative thoughts going through their minds that constantly repeat "I can't" phrases: "I can't write...... I can't spell...... I can't understand...... I just can't do it. Never have; never will!" Often these negative attitudes are the result of a prior negative event. A basic step to success is changing that script in your head. You have an amazing ability to learn, so tell yourself that you *can*. Replace "I can't" thoughts with "I can." Then, take steps to prove that you can. For example, instead of believing "I just can't spell," think, "I can use a spell checker," or "I can make a list of words I often misspell and memorize their correct spellings." Success begins in your mind!

### Be an Active Learner

Come to class. Be on time. Sit where you can see—and be seen. Take notes. Ask questions. Do your work—on time! Make connections between assignments. Apply what you learn. Seek help. Find a study partner. Take responsibility for your own learning. The more you do, the more you learn!

### Trust Your Teacher

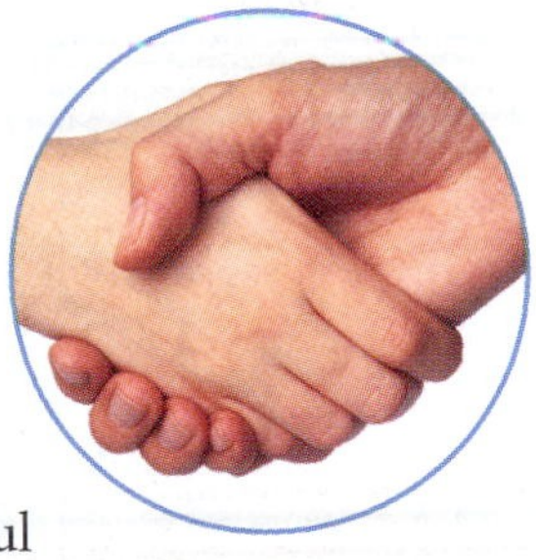

One of the toughest tasks in a writing class is getting and accepting feedback on your writing. Many of us take the teacher's feedback as a personal rejection. Some of us become defensive. Teachers have the hard job of pointing out our errors so that we can correct them. Think of feedback as a service to you. You wouldn't want to go to a job interview with spinach in your teeth or walk into a restaurant with your zipper down, would you? Likewise, you don't want your writing to present your second best self to your reader. So accept feedback as helpful advice. Take note of those errors, study the rules, and revise your work. Turn feedback into an opportunity to learn!

## Practice 2

### THE ATTITUDE OF LEARNING

Read the following reflection written by a student that records how she feels about writing and why. On a separate sheet of paper, write a letter to her, giving her advice to help her overcome her anxiety.

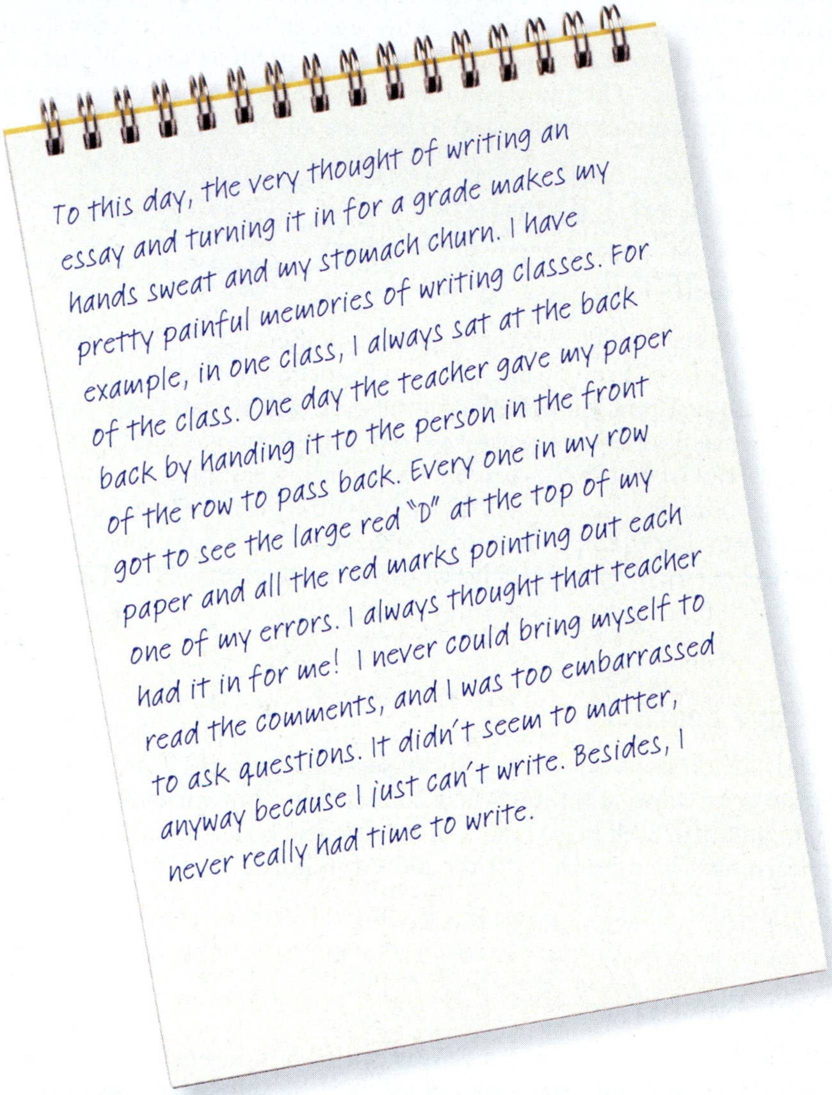
To this day, the very thought of writing an
essay and turning it in for a grade makes my
hands sweat and my stomach churn. I have
pretty painful memories of writing classes. For
example, in one class, I always sat at the back
of the class. One day the teacher gave my paper
back by handing it to the person in the front
of the row to pass back. Every one in my row
got to see the large red "D" at the top of my
paper and all the red marks pointing out each
one of my errors. I always thought that teacher
had it in for me! I never could bring myself to
read the comments, and I was too embarrassed
to ask questions. It didn't seem to matter,
anyway because I just can't write. Besides, I
never really had time to write.

## Practice 3

### THE ATTITUDE OF LEARNING

Reflect upon your own attitude and needs. Write your response to the following questions.

**A.** Explore your own feelings about writing: What have been your prior writing experiences? Were they positive or negative? Why? What are your feelings about writing?

B. In what areas of writing do you know you need to improve? Coming up with a topic? Generating details? Organizing ideas? Word choice? Spelling? Punctuation? Others?

Practice 3

# Create a Study Plan

A vital part of preparing to learn about writing is creating a study plan.

## Gather Your Tools

Foster success by preparing a place without distractions so you can study. Equip that space with all the tools you will need ahead of time to study. Both writers and students in general need the following: reference materials such as your textbook, a dictionary, a thesaurus, magazines, newspapers, and other reading materials of interest to you; pens (blue or black ink), pencils, and paper; a stapler and 3-hole punch. Optional items include a computer and a printer. In addition, you need a 3-ring binder to house the teacher's syllabus, handouts, assignments, class notes, textbook notes, and lab work. Be sure that you bring your textbook, binder, pens, and pencils to class every day.

## Set Goals

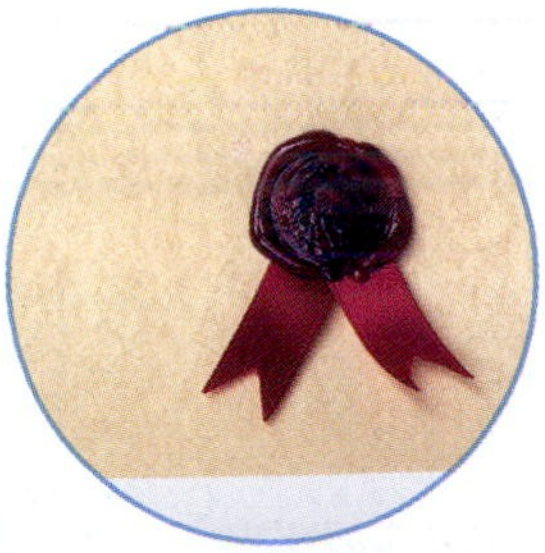

Students who set goals reduce stress, improve concentration, and increase self-confidence. Use the following guidelines to set effective goals. Aim high: Demand your best effort. Be realistic: Strive for balance to avoid burn out. Write goals down: Recording goals makes them clear and important. Be specific: Instead of writing, "Stop procrastinating," write, "Study English on Monday, Tuesday, and Wednesday evenings between 7 and 9 o'clock." Be positive: Instead of writing, "Don't make stupid comma errors," write, "Use commas properly." Set priorities: Rank goals based on need so you can pace your work. Set daily goals based on larger goals: Break a larger goal such as "Understand how to use semicolons" into a series of steps such as "Study the rule, take notes, and do the exercises; then proofread my paper for proper use of semicolons."

## Take Action

Turn your goals into action steps by setting up a time schedule for your study. The following study plan is easy to use, flexible, and will help you set long-term, intermediate, and short-term goals.

| SAMPLE STUDY PLAN | |
|---|---|
| Long-Term Schedule: | Record ongoing weekly commitments such as job hours, class meetings, church, and so on, for the entire semester. |
| Intermediate Schedule: | Make a short list of the events taking place and the tasks to be completed in your class (or classes) this week. Make a fresh list each week, as these activities will change from week to week: Writing assignment Tuesday; Math quiz Tuesday; Chapter 3 in English by Wednesday; Chapter 7 in math by Friday. |
| Short-Term Schedule: | On an index card every morning (or the night before), list your daily schedule. Be specific! Then, carry this card with you and cross off each goal as you accomplish it. Monday: 9:00–9:30 Revise writing assignment; 12:00–12:30 Review math for quiz; 3:30 Return books to library; 7:00–9:00 Read first 30 pages of Chapter 3 for English. |

## Practice 4

### CREATE A STUDY PLAN

Rewrite the following goals so that they are more specific. Be sure to use positive statements. Share your answers with your class or in a small group.

**1.** GOAL: Get an education.

REWRITE OF GOAL: ______________________

______________________

**2.** GOAL: Pass the class.

REWRITE OF GOAL: ______________________

______________________

**3.** GOAL: Manage my time.

REWRITE OF GOAL: ______________________

______________________

Practice 5

CREATE A STUDY PLAN

Evaluate your level of preparation for learning about writing.

**1.** Describe your study space and the tools you use to study. In what ways could you improve your study space?

---

**2.** Rate your readiness to learn about writing. Describe your plan or set up a study plan that includes long-term, intermediate, and short-term goals.

---

# Create a Portfolio of Your Work

To ensure that you learn about writing and to develop writing skills, you need to track your strengths, your needs, and your growth. A portfolio enables you to organize your work and think about what you are learning.

## What Is a Portfolio?

A portfolio is a collection of all the work you do as a writer organized in a notebook or in an electronic folder. Your portfolio shows your hard work and your growth because its contents document how much time and effort you put into thinking about your writing. A portfolio allows you to assess your own strengths, needs, and goals. A portfolio requires that you use critical thinking skills to become a better writer.

More on writing portfolios: <www.mywritinglab.com>

## What Should I Include in My Portfolio?

Your portfolio may include class notes and activities, textbook notes and exercises, grammar tests, lab activities, reflective journal entries, prewrites, drafts, revisions, edited drafts, and polished copies of your writing. By collecting and organizing your work, you are better able to reflect upon your strengths and needs. As a result, you are able to set specific goals as a writer. For example, you may find that as a writer you need to better manage your time, so your portfolio may include a study plan that includes learning goals and a study schedule. The practices you have already completed for this chapter are excellent portfolio entries. Throughout this book, you will find many activities, practices, and workshops designed to help you think about your writing. All are excellent entries for your portfolio.

## What Is a Reflective Journal Entry?

A reflective journal entry is an informal piece of writing in which you analyze some aspect of your work as a student writer. For example, you may write a journal entry that lists and responds to the feedback that your teacher gave on a piece of your writing. In each of the chapters about writing paragraphs, you will read a writer's journal that records this kind of thinking.

# Reflective Journals

## Critical Thinking Questions

To deepen your critical thinking about the feedback, your reflective journal entry also answers the following questions:

- ☐ What steps did I take to write this piece? Did I prewrite, write, revise, and proofread? Do I need to spend more time on any one step?
- ☐ Which of my errors are proofreading errors? What steps will I take to catch these proofreading errors on my next piece of writing?
- ☐ Which of these errors results from the need to study a certain rule? Where in my textbook is this rule found? How much time do I need to learn this rule? How will I study this rule (take notes, complete exercises)?

By writing reflective journal entries, you can track and overcome your writing barriers.

## What Is the Best Way to Set Up My Portfolio?

Many students purchase a 3-ring binder large enough to hold their entire semester's work, and tabbed dividers to section off different types of study and writing tasks for class, lab, and homework. Be sure to date and label all work.

All work that is turned in for feedback should include the following information: At the top of the first page and flush with the left margin, place your name, your professor's name, the course name or number (include the section number if the course has multiple sections), and the date you're turning in the paper, each on a separate line with double-spacing throughout.

Iama Writer

Dr. Richards

ENC 001: Section 32

September 24, 2007

All independent work that is created for your notebook or portfolio should be labeled with the date and by the type of work:

Oct. 9, 2007

Reflective Journal Entry for Narrative Paragraph

Oct. 10, 2007

Comma Splices, Chapter 21, pp. 422–437

Oct. 12, 2007

The Process Paragraph, Class notes

The point of labeling is to help you see and discuss your strengths and needs as they occur in real time.

## Practice 6

CRITICAL THINKING

Rate yourself as a critical thinker on a scale of 1 through 6. 1 equals weak; 4 equals average; 6 equals excellent. Explain why and give examples.

CRITICAL THINKING RATING: ____________

REASONS AND EXAMPLES: ______________________________

## Practice 7

THE PORTFOLIO

Write an email to a classmate who missed class. Explain the portfolio process. Explain how portfolio assessment will improve critical thinking.

# Academic Learning Log

QUESTIONS FOR PREPARING TO LEARN

To test and track your understanding of what you have studied, answer the following questions.

**1.** What are some of the materials and supplies needed by a writing student?

**2.** What are the three attitudes of learning discussed in this chapter?

**3.** What three general steps can you take to create a study plan?

**4.** What is a portfolio?

**5.** What is included in a portfolio?

**6.** What is a reflective journal entry?

# 2

# Thinking Through the Writing Process

## The writing process has four stages: prewriting, drafting, revising, and proofreading.

### Chapter Preview

- What's the Point of the Writing Process?
- Making a Point about the Writing Process: One Student Writer's Response
- Understanding the Point: Assessing the Writing Situation
- Understanding the Point: Using the Writing Process

Writing develops, records, and communicates your thoughts to other people. Careful writers rely on the writing process to discover, organize, and record information in response to a specific writing situation.

# What's the Point of the Writing Process?

The following photographs document some of the situations in which we use writing in our everyday, college, and working lives. Write a caption for each picture that includes a reason for writing well in that situation. Then, state the point of writing well.

WRITING FROM LIFE

Practice 1

PHOTOGRAPHIC ORGANIZER: REASONS TO WRITE

**What's the point of writing well?**

## My First Thoughts: A Prewriting Activity

PREWRITING

Set a time limit, such as five minutes, and jot down in your notebook your thoughts about the importance of writing. Do not let your pen or pencil stop, even if you must repeat ideas, keep writing until the time limit is up.

# Making a Point about the Writing Process: One Student Writer's Response

The following paragraph is one writer's response to the question "What's the point of writing?"

*Writing can increase our academic, personal, and economic power. Of course, writing is necessary to succeed in college, yet writing is also important outside the classroom. For example, if I have strong writing skills, I am much more likely to get a job, promotions, and higher pay. In addition, writing allows me to express myself in everyday life. For example, I am really worried about forest fires started by careless campers. A well-written letter to the editor might make just one person think about campfire safety. And a thank you note allows me to express my appreciation for someone who has supported me; it's a way of giving back. Really, writing is thinking on paper. Writing allows me to think, remember, organize, record, learn, and share ideas.*

## Understanding the Point: Assessing the Writing Situation

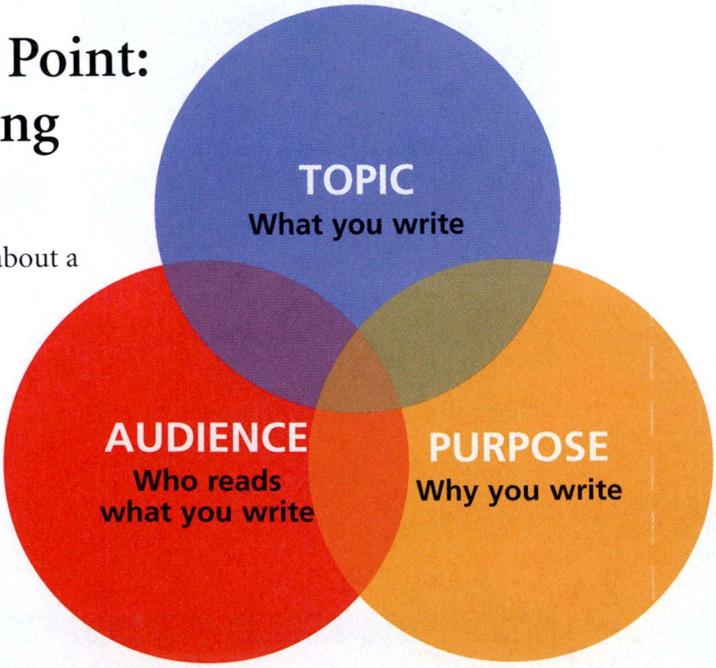


When you write, you develop a point about a topic to fulfill a purpose for a specific audience. To develop your point, you need to think about two aspects of writing: the writing situation and the writing process.

A piece of writing develops in response to a specific **writing situation** that is composed of the **topic** (your subject), the **purpose** for writing (your goal), and the **audience** (your reader).

### The Topic: What You Write

When writing about situations in our personal lives, we may choose to compose a letter of complaint to a business or an email to a friend. Often in these circumstances, the topic of our writing naturally emerges from our need to communicate. However, when writing for college, many of us face writer's block in our search for a topic. You can break through writer's block by building a topic bank for college writing.

Use the following thinking guide to generate a bank of topics.

## The Writing Situation Step by Step:

### Topic

Build a bank of topics by listing ideas in a special section in your notebook. Use the following prompts to create several lists:

- ☐ The major topics of importance in a specific course (such as biology, psychology, history)
- ☐ Interesting or important current events
  - ☐ Topics most covered in magazines and newspapers
  - ☐ Controversial topics from television (such as news and talk shows)
  - ☐ Topics about which you want to learn more
  - ☐ Topics about which you feel deeply
  - ☐ Hobbies and personal interests
- ☐ Share your lists with your classmates; use discussion to generate more ideas.
- ☐ Review and expand your list on a regular basis.

As you continue to build your bank of general topics, read, read, and read some more. Read newspapers, magazines, and textbooks for additional topics. Many textbooks provide writing topics at the end of sections or chapters; in addition, headings and subheadings of chapters or sections are excellent sources of topics for your writing.

## Practice 2

TOPICS

Rank the following topics **1** through **5** to reflect your interest in each one, with **1** representing the least interesting topic and **5** representing the most interesting topic. Then, write a few sentences that explain the reasons for your ranking.

...... The United States' invasion of Iraq

...... The effect of hurricanes or other natural disasters

...... The differences between men and women

...... The benefits of technology

...... Important lessons learned in life

--------------------------------------------------------------------------------

--------------------------------------------------------------------------------

--------------------------------------------------------------------------------

Practice 3

**TOPICS**

Skim a newspaper, a magazine, and a textbook and write a list of five topics from each one. Then, share your list with your class or in a small group.

TOPICS FROM A NEWSPAPER: ______________________________

______________________________

TOPICS FROM A MAGAZINE: ______________________________

______________________________

TOPICS FROM A TEXTBOOK: ______________________________

______________________________

More help with topics for writing: <www.mywritinglab.com>

## The Purpose: Why You Write

Good writing focuses on a goal or purpose. Your writing will flow much more easily when you write with purpose. The following chart presents four basic purposes for writing.

| | |
|---|---|
|  **Informative** When writing informatively, your purpose is to share, explain, or demonstrate information. **EXAMPLE:** An **informative essay** that explains the steps of photosynthesis to your reader; a paragraph that answers an exam question about the major causes of stress. |   **Persuasive** When writing persuasively, your purpose is to change your reader's opinion or call your reader to take action. **EXAMPLE:** An **argumentative essay** that convinces your reader to begin a physical fitness program; a letter to the editor that argues in favor of a law that requires the use of seatbelts. |
|  **Expressive** When writing expressively, your purpose is to share with the reader your personal opinions, feelings, or reactions to a topic. **EXAMPLE:** An **expressive piece**–a poem, short story, or personal essay, for example–that expresses your anger about 9/11. |  **Reflective** When writing reflectively, your purpose is to record your understanding about what you have experienced or learned. **EXAMPLE:** An **informal essay** that explores what you think is significant about a current event; a journal entry that discusses the strengths of a paper written by you or a peer. |

Use the following thinking guide to identify your purpose in writing.

# The Writing Situation Step by Step:

## Purpose

- ☐ Annotate the lists of topics in your topic bank to indicate possible purposes for each topic: Beside each topic write I for informative, P for persuasive, E for expressive, or R for reflective.
- ☐ Generate four sets of topics based on different purposes for writing, using "The Writing Situation: Step by Step: Topic" box on page 17 to guide your thinking.
- ☐ Select one topic for each of the four purposes and complete the following statements:
  - ☐ This topic will inform the reader about...
  - ☐ This topic will persuade the reader to...
  - ☐ This topic will express...
  - ☐ This topic will reflect upon...

## Practice 4

**PURPOSE**

State the purpose of each of the following topic sentences. Discuss with your class or in a small group how a writer's purposes may be combined in certain situations.

**1**. My experience and education make me an excellent candidate for this job.

---

**2**. Adult stem cell research should be funded by the government.

---

**3**. The gentle breeze, the lapping water, and the dappled shade soothes the human soul.

---

**4**. Eating disorders fall into several categories based on their symptoms.

---

**5**. Based on my unit exam, I need to review the following topics.

---

Practice 5

PURPOSE

For each of the following topics, write a sentence that states a purpose you may have for writing about this subject. Discuss your answers with your class or in a small group.

1. Drug testing

2. Relaxation techniques

3. Job hunting

4. Global warming

More help with purposes for writing: <www.mywritinglab.com>

## The Audience: Who Reads Your Writing

When we take part in a conversation, we know exactly to whom we are speaking, and we adjust our tone, word choice, and examples to match the situation. For example, contrast how you talk with a friend to how you talk with the dean of your college. Audience has the same impact in the writing situation.

Assume that you have chosen to write about the topic of marijuana. What main points do you want each of the following audiences to consider about this drug? Use the blanks below each picture to record your ideas.

Use the following thinking guide to identify your audience.

## The Writing Situation Step by Step:

### Audience

- ☐ Choose a specific topic and purpose for writing.
- ☐ List the traits of your audience that are relevant to your topic and purpose:
  - ☐ Age
  - ☐ Gender
  - ☐ Education level
- ☐ If you are writing for a general audience of mixed traits, identify the main traits most relevant to your topic and purpose.
- ☐ Identify three or four points about the topic of most interest to a specific audience.
- ☐ Choose several key words to describe your topic and hook the interest of a specific audience. Use a thesaurus to find the words best suited for your audience.

## Practice 6

AUDIENCE

Based on your first thoughts about the audiences represented by the four pictures on pages 20–21, write a brief response to the following questions. Then, discuss your answers with your class or in a small group.

- What are the most important traits of each audience represented by the pictures?
- Did your main points differ based on the audience? Why or why not?
- Will your word choice or examples differ based on the audience?
- Why or why not?

## Practice 7

AUDIENCE

Each of the following four pieces of writing appeals to one of the audiences depicted by the photos on pages 20–21. Write the letter of the piece of writing in the picture of its audience.

A. Scientists funded by the National Institute on Drug Abuse (NIDA), a federal government agency, have found that the damage to the brain's thinking abilities that results from smoking marijuana can last up to 28 days after an individual last smoked the drug.

B. Marijuana use today starts at a younger age—and more potent forms of the drug are available to you. Marijuana use is a serious threat—do not use it!

C. Under the influence of marijuana, you can forget your best friend's phone number, watch your grade point average drop like a stone, or get into a car accident.

D. Welcome to the Mothers Against Drugs speaker series. During today's speaker panel, we'll investigate the fascinating facts about marijuana. You may have heard it called pot, weed, grass, ganja, or skunk, but marijuana by any other name is still a drug that affects the brain.

When student writers are asked "Who is your audience?" most reply, "The teacher." Of course, the teacher is your immediate audience, and you must carefully consider his or her expectations. However, many teachers understand the value of writing to a real-life audience. College is preparing you for success in life. You are learning to write for life.

## Practice 8

### TOPIC AND AUDIENCE

The following writing prompts apply an academic topic to real audience.

Write the name of the college course(s) for each prompt and describe the traits of each audience. Discuss your answers with your class or in a small group. Talk about how each audience affects the writer's choice of words and details.

**1.** Write a letter to the editor of a newspaper that compares the war in Iraq to the Vietnam War.

COURSE(S): ______________________

AUDIENCE: ______________________

______________________

______________________

**2.** Write a report for the school board that explains the benefits of smaller class sizes.

COURSE(S): ______________________

AUDIENCE: ______________________

______________________

______________________

**3.** Write an email to a classmate explaining the five steps for problem solving.

COURSE(S): ______________________

AUDIENCE: ______________________

______________________

**4.** Write a memo to a new, young employee at a fast food restaurant that explains how the cost of his insurance is based on his age.

COURSE(S): ______________________

AUDIENCE: ______________________

______________________

More help with audience: <www.mywritinglab.com>

# Understanding the Point: Using the Writing Process

Writing is a process that comprises a series of phases or steps. The process approach focuses on the writer, the way writing is produced, and how the writer can improve his or her personal writing process. The process approach is recursive; the writer may loop or combine any of the stages at any point during the writing process. The key outcome at the end of the process is a published piece of writing. Throughout each stage, think about the relationships among your topic, purpose, and audience.

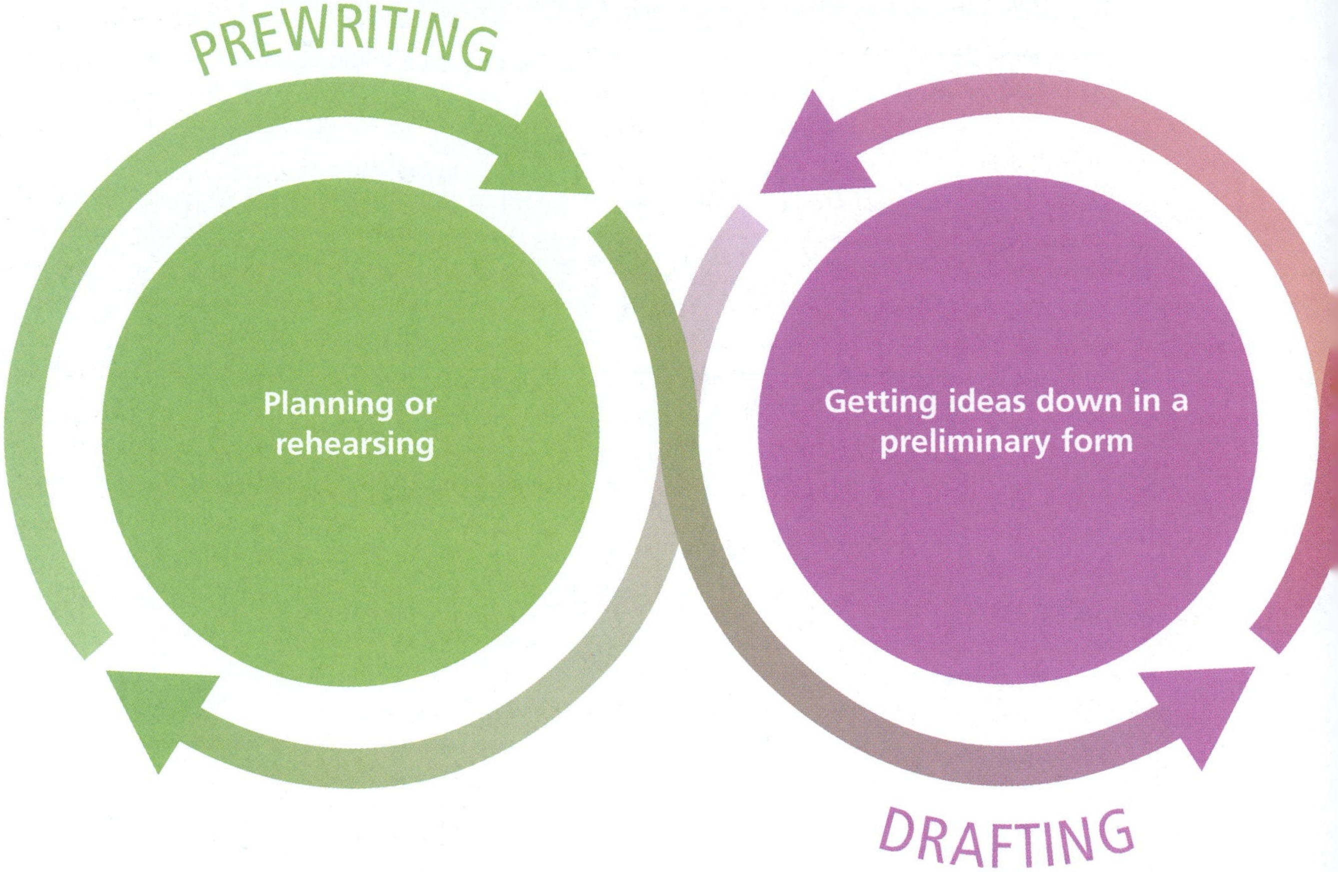


## PREWRITING

During the prewriting stage, you create a plan for your piece of writing.

This phase of writing is made up of the following steps:

- Decide on a topic.
- Determine your purpose for writing.
- Gather information.
- Generate details by using clusters, lists, and freewrites.
- Organize details into an outline.

The rest of this chapter covers specific prewriting techniques.

## DRAFTING

During the drafting stage, you create a draft of your writing.

This phase may include the following steps:

- Decide on audience.
- Choose format (such as an essay or a letter).
- Create introduction, body, and conclusion for longer pieces.

Chapters 3-12 guide you through the entire writing process as you learn how to write paragraphs.

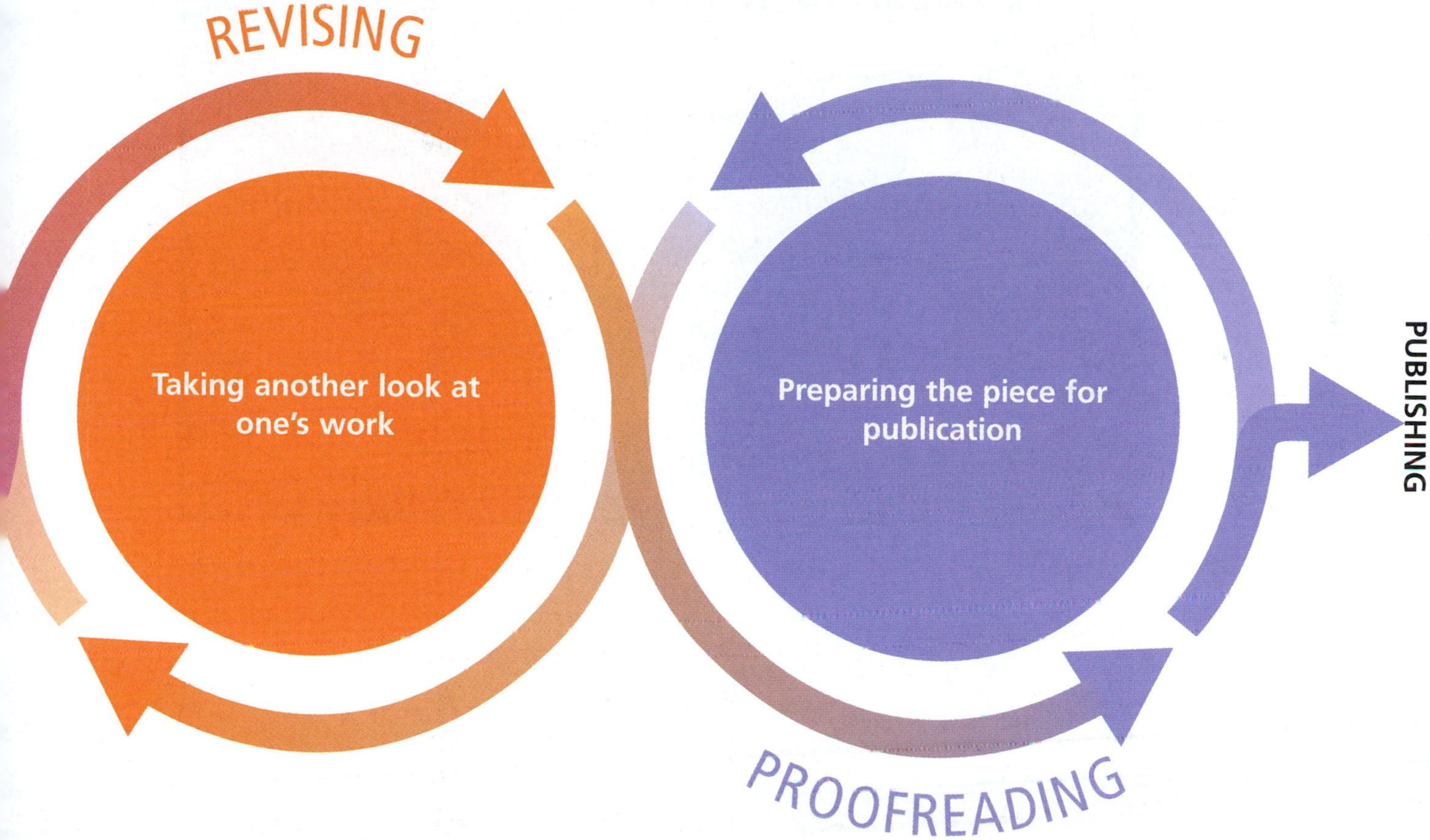


## REVISING

During the revision phase, you fine tune the ideas in your essay. After you have written a draft, allow some time to pass so that you can see your writing with fresh eyes.

This phase includes the following steps:

- Delete details that are not relevant.
- Add details to ideas that need more support.
- Reorder ideas for clarity.
- Insert transitions between details for a smooth flow of ideas.
- Replace vague or weak words with vivid, strong words.
- Write a new draft if necessary.

Part 5 covers specific skills to consider while revising.

## PROOFREADING

During the editing phase of the writing process, you polish your draft so your reader will not be distracted or confused by careless errors.

This phase includes correcting errors such as:

- fragments
- run-ons
- shift in tenses
- spelling
- punctuation

Part 6 covers the skills to consider during editing.

## Prewriting

Carefully examine the cartoon. Then, in the space provided, write a few sentences explaining your understanding of what prewriting is.

What is prewriting?

In general, writing occurs long before you pick up your pen or your fingers touch the keyboard. **Prewriting** includes reading, listening, discussing, and thinking about your topic before you write a rough draft, capturing your prewriting thinking on paper. It allows you to explore ideas and plan your strategies without worrying about polishing them.

Have you ever stared at a blank piece of paper with a blank mind, unable to think of how to start a writing task? Or, have you ever had so many ideas that they jumble up in chaos so that you can't even begin to write? Finding those first few words to put on paper can grind a writer's thinking process to a complete halt.

If you face these problems, take heart, you are not alone! Even the best writers face writer's block now and then. Although no cure-all for writer's block exists, prewriting fuels thinking, triggers the writing process, and fires past the block. Experienced writers have learned to spend time thinking about what they are going to write before they begin drafting.

> **Prewriting** is the act of generating, exploring, developing, and roughly organizing ideas. Prewriting can help you choose a topic, narrow a topic, and put details related to a topic in logical order.

The rest of this section guides you through six prewriting techniques:

- Asking Questions:
  The Reporter's Questions
  The Reflective Questions
- Freewriting
- Keeping a Journal
- Listing
- Concept Mapping
- Outlining

As you write for life, try out each one. Combine a few to stretch your thinking. Experiment with all of them. Discover which one(s) best suit you as a writer or in a particular writing situation.

## Asking Questions

Asking questions helps you identify a topic and develop details about it based on thoughtful insights. Asking and answering questions helps you discover both what you already know and what you need to learn about the topic. Your goal as a writer is to share a point or main idea about a topic. Usually, a main idea or point is made up of the topic and the writer's opinion about the topic. Two types of questions enable you to explore topics and your opinions about those topics: the reporter's questions and reflective questions.

### THE REPORTER'S QUESTIONS

To describe a newsworthy event, effective reporters gather the facts by asking six basic questions:

- Who?
- What?
- When?
- Where?
- Why?
- How?

At first, the answers to these questions may help you identify and narrow a topic that grabs your interest; once you have narrowed your topic, these questions also yield many details of support for your topic.

# Practice 9

**TOPIC AND AUDIENCE**

Assume that you are reporting on the power of propaganda. Discuss the following advertisement for Trim Spa, a weight-loss product, featuring Anna Nicole Smith as a powerful example of propaganda. Use the reporter's questions to brainstorm your first thoughts.

Who is the intended audience of the poster?

..............................................................................

..............................................................................

..............................................................................

..............................................................................

..............................................................................

Why is Smith effective in this advertisement?

..............................................................................

..............................................................................

How are women portrayed in this ad?

..............................................................................

..............................................................................

..............................................................................

## THE REFLECTIVE QUESTIONS

Reflective questions also help you discover your purpose for writing by revealing your attitude toward a topic. By using these questions to reflect, identify, and add your opinion about a topic to your writing, you can also narrow a writing topic that is too general. For example, although the topic in Practice 9 was the power of propaganda, not everyone believes that propaganda is a positive force. For the purposes of narrowing this particular general topic—the power of propaganda—the following questions might help you identify your opinions about it:

- Why do some believe propaganda is negative?
- Why do some believe propaganda is transforming?
- In what ways do I agree or disagree with these opinions?
- How can I best express my point about the power of propaganda to someone with whom I disagree?

Answering these questions before writing will also guide you to make logical decisions about which details to select and highlight when you do begin to write.

When you are ready to explore ideas about a topic on paper, the following thinking guide can help you use questions as a prewriting technique.

# The Writing Process Step by Step:

## Prewriting by Asking Questions

Use the reporter's questions to identify a topic, purpose, and audience.

- ☐ What?
- ☐ Why?
- ☐ Who?

Use the reporter's questions to generate details about the topic.

- ☐ When?
- ☐ Where?
- ☐ How?

Use reflective questions to identify attitudes and generate additional details about the topic.

- ☐ What is my attitude or feelings about this topic?
- ☐ What is my audience's attitude or feelings about this topic?
- ☐ Why is this topic important?
- ☐ How will my audience respond to my point?
- ☐ How can I make this topic interesting and relevant to my audience?

### Practice 10

**QUESTIONING**

Assume you are reporting on the 9/11 attack on the World Trade Center. Using the box "The Writing Process Step by Step: Prewriting by Asking Questions," write a list of questions to identify your point and generate details. Share your ideas with the class or in a small group.

---

---

---

More help with prewriting:
<www.mywritinglab.com>

### Practice 11

**QUESTIONING**

Ask questions to brainstorm your first thoughts about one of the following topics:

- Road Rage ______
- Graffiti ______
- Drug Abuse ______
- Positive Thinking ______
- Workplace Stress ______

## Freewriting

During **freewriting**, you record your thoughts as they stream through your head. The key to this brainstorming strategy, like all prewriting activities, is to turn off the critic inside your head. At this point, no thought is wrong, off base, or silly. The idea is to warm up your thinking muscles, flex your creativity, and set your ideas free. Use the following thinking guide to use freewriting as a prewriting technique.

# The Writing Process Step by Step:

## Prewriting by Freewriting

- ☐ Set a time limit, such as ten minutes, and write whatever comes to mind as fast as you can without stopping at all.
- ☐ If you get stuck, write the same word or phrase until a new idea comes along; do not stop writing. Do not worry about wording, organization, or grammar; later in the writing process, you will organize and polish your ideas—tell that critic inside your head to pipe down for now.
- ☐ When the time limit is up, read what you wrote and underline interesting ideas.
- ☐ Use one of the ideas you underlined as a starting point for a focused freewrite. A **focused freewrite** occurs when you freewrite about a specific topic you have chosen or been assigned.

## Practice 12

FREEWRITING

Read the following two freewrites. Discuss with your class or in a small group how ideas develop using freewriting and focused freewriting. What are the advantages of freewriting? What are the disadvantages?

*Well it is time for another writing assignment, and the teacher said we could choose our own topic, but I don't know what to write I always have a hard time coming up with topics writing is so hard I know I am a terrible at this but I need to find a topic not write about not finding a topic let's see what can I write about? It is so cold in here I can't think think think think think think well wats going on in the news oh, what about all the missing and abused children and the how child molesters are everywhere. Things seem to be getting worse all the time. Pretty depressing. I think things ar worse now than when I was growing up. My hometown was so safe no one locked their doors they didn't have too. We spent hours roaming the neighborhood on our bicycles, swimming in Lake Martha, enjoying being a kid. Now small towns seem as dangerous as crime ridden big cities.*

**Focused Freewrite**

*We spent hours roaming the neighborhood on our bicycles, swimming in Lake Martha, enjoying being a kid. There were about 20 of us kids pretty close in age who lived in my neighborhood, so we always had someone to play with or fight with, and we did both passionately. Our neighborhood was surrounded by orange groves, so we all learned at a pretty young age how to throw and dodge rotten oranges in our on-going orange wars. My brother earned the reputation of the best warrior. He could throw an orange further and straighter than any one any time. The best wars ended with a bike race to Lake Martha to rinse off the sticky juices and dirt that clung to us. I can still hear the ice cream truck's merry music and feel the hot sand beneath my feet as we dashed from the waters edge to catch the ice cream man as he rounded the corner during his afternoon route. Life seemed so simple, so safe, so fun.*

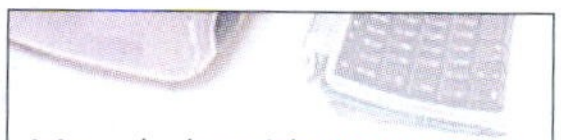

More help with prewriting.
<www.mywritinglab.com>

Practice 13

FOCUSED FREEWRITING

**Step 1**: Choose one of the following topics and freewrite for five minutes. Feel free to ask and answer questions before you begin freewriting.

- Peer Pressure
- Useful Technology
- Eating Disorders
- A Role Model

**Step 2**: Read your freewrite and highlight ideas. Write a focused freewrite for an additional five minutes using the idea(s) you highlighted.

## Keeping a Journal

Many people keep a **journal** to record how they feel about the events of their daily lives, current events, or life in general. A journal allows the writer to explore experiences in a personal way and store them in a private place. Some writers use a spiral notebook; others use a diary or a pre-made journal. The point is to create a specific place where you can record and review your private thoughts and personal experiences. Journal entries are often freewrites with the main purpose of getting ideas onto paper, but they may take on different creative forms, such as a letter or a poem. Many writers use journals as a place to practice their writing and experiment with language. The key to keeping a journal is to write on a regular basis. Writing and reflecting on what you have written on a consistent basis leads to a deeper understanding of yourself and your world—and improves your writing!

Use the following thinking guide to use journaling as a prewriting technique.

# The Writing Process Step by Step:

## Prewriting by Journaling

- ☐ Create a section in your notebook for journal entries or buy a spiral notebook, diary, or pre-made journal that you will use only for journal writing.
- ☐ Commit to writing in your journal on a regular basis for the next two weeks. Select a time of day that you can write in your journal, such as during your lunch break or at the end of your day. Set a time limit for each journal entry such as fifteen minutes.
- ☐ Ask and answer reflective questions and the reporter's questions to stimulate your thinking.

Use the following topics to get started:

- ☐ Record events, images, or scenes of interest to you; write as many details as you can.
- ☐ Record a favorite memory; explore why that memory is so important.
- ☐ Write a brief autobiography.
- ☐ Recount a news event and your reactions to it.
- ☐ Write a letter to yourself or someone else, giving advice about a particular matter.
- ☐ Vent about something that really bothers you.
- ☐ Reread a previously written journal and develop an idea in greater detail.

## Practice 14

**JOURNALING**

Read the following journal entry. Identify the academic courses that are relevant to the personal experiences recorded in the journal. Discuss with your class or in a small group the ways in which the ideas in the journal entry might be developed for an essay in each course.

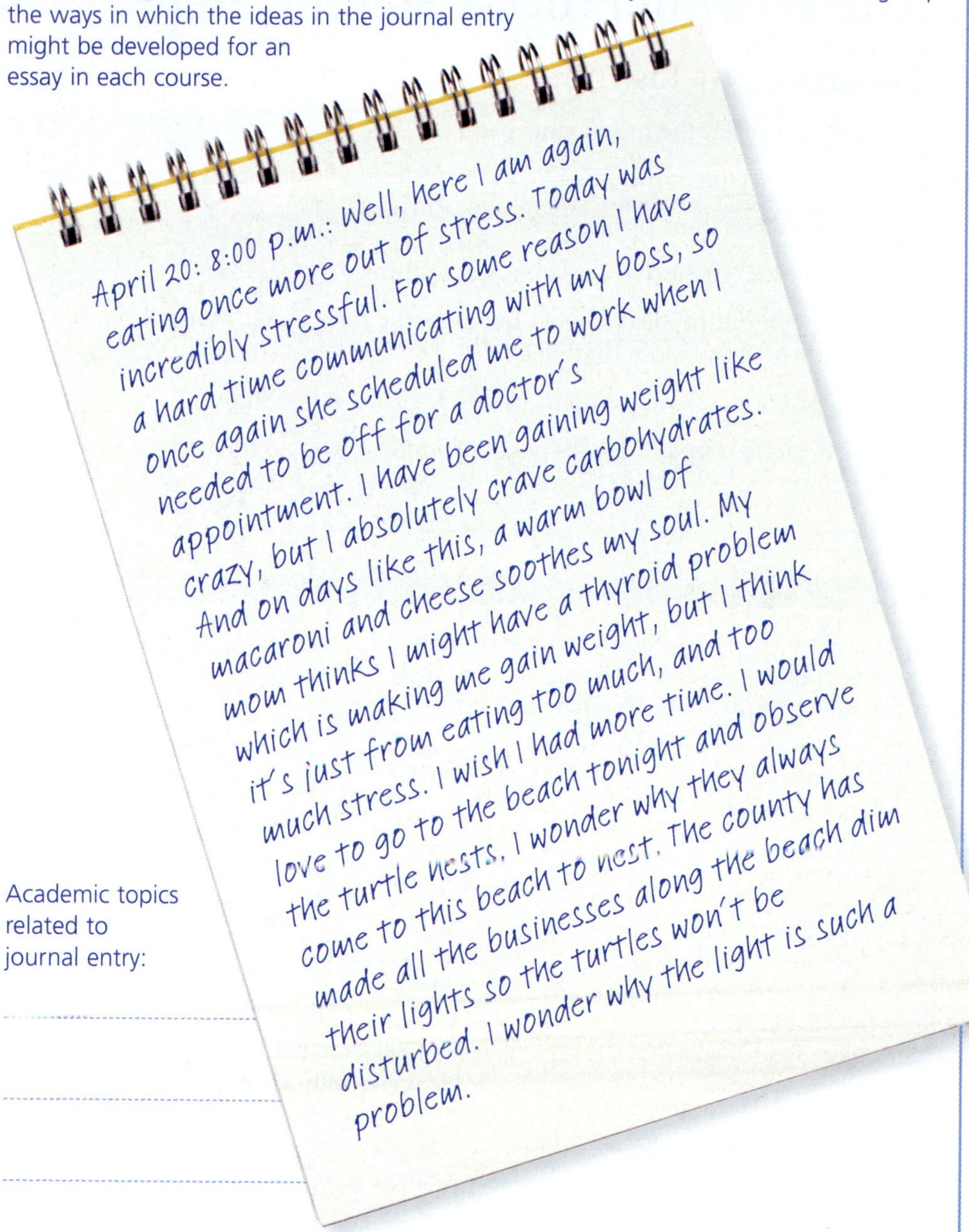
April 20: 8:00 p.m.: Well, here I am again, eating once more out of stress. Today was incredibly stressful. For some reason I have a hard time communicating with my boss, so once again she scheduled me to work when I needed to be off for a doctor's appointment. I have been gaining weight like crazy, but I absolutely crave carbohydrates. And on days like this, a warm bowl of macaroni and cheese soothes my soul. My mom thinks I might have a thyroid problem which is making me gain weight, but I think it's just from eating too much, and too much stress. I wish I had more time. I would love to go to the beach tonight and observe the turtle nests. I wonder why they always come to this beach to nest. The county has made all the businesses along the beach dim their lights so the turtles won't be disturbed. I wonder why the light is such a problem.

Academic topics related to journal entry:

---

---

---

More help with prewriting: <www.mywritinglab.com>

## Listing

A common way to brainstorm ideas is to **create a list.** If you have a free choice of topics, then create a topic bank: List ideas about which you want to learn more or topics about which you already know something and enjoy discussing. To create a list of topics for an academic course, look at the table of contents, the index, and the glossary of your textbook. Use these resources to create a list of topics based on what you will be studying throughout the semester. If you already have a topic, then create a list of everything that comes to mind as you think about your topic. Write your list as quickly as you can. Just as in freewriting, quiet your inner critic. Once you make a thorough list, then you can organize your ideas.

Use the following thinking guide to use listing as a prewriting technique.

# The Writing Process Step by Step:

## Prewriting by Listing

- [ ] Write a topic at the top of your page.
- [ ] List ideas as quickly as possible in the order that they occur to you.
- [ ] Use words or short phrases.
- [ ] List all ideas that occur to you; reject nothing.
- [ ] If you run out of ideas, choose one idea you have already recorded and begin a new list about that idea.
- [ ] Review your list and group ideas into logical relationships.
- [ ] Label each group of ideas as possible points of development for a piece of writing.

## Practice 15

LISTING: PREWRITING FOR AN ACADEMIC COURSE

The following lists are based on the table of contents of two textbooks. Identify the academic courses to which each list is related. Then, brainstorm a list of additional writing topics based on an idea from each list.

COURSES: ______________________

______________________

______________________

COURSES: ______________________

______________________

______________________

**List 1**

Mass Media and Politics
The Power of the Media
Sources of the Media
People in Politics
Stars of the News Broadcasts
Bias in the Media
Freedom versus Fairness

**List 2**

Basics of Good Health
Managing Mental Health
Coping with Stress
Eating Smart
Maintaining Proper Weight
Keeping Fit
Controllable Health Risks

**New Lists of Additional Ideas**

______________________

______________________

______________________

______________________

______________________

**New Lists of Additional Ideas**

______________________

______________________

______________________

______________________

______________________

## Practice 16

### LISTING: PREWRITING FOR BUSINESS WRITING

Assume you have just been given two weeks notice because your company is downsizing and eliminating your job. To locate job opportunities, take the following steps:

**Step 1**: Go to the classified section of your local newspaper and make a list of available jobs in your area.

**Step 2**: Choose one of the advertised positions and list the skills needed to compete for the job.

**Step 3**: List the skills you already possess that qualify you for the job.

**Step 4**: List the skills you need to acquire to qualify for the job.

**Step 5**: Repeat steps 2 through 4 for each of the jobs you listed in Step 1.

More help with prewriting:
<www.mywritinglab.com>

## Concept Mapping

**Concept mapping**, also known as **clustering** or **webbing**, creates a visual picture of the relationships among the ideas you generate. Think of what you already know about a map. Someone can tell you how to get somewhere, but it is much easier to understand the directions when you can see how each road connects to other roads by studying a map. Likewise, a concept map shows how a topic connects to supporting details—how each idea connects to another idea, how the main idea connects to supporting details. Sometimes, as you use a concept map, the idea that first occurred to you might be a great example for a supporting detail. Rarely do ideas occur to us in a logical order. Concept mapping helps a writer figure out the logical order of ideas. Chapters 4 through 12 will show you how to adapt concept maps to specific writing situations and thought patterns.

Use the following thinking guide to use concept mapping as a prewriting technique.

# The Writing Process Step by Step:

## Prewriting by Concept Mapping

- [ ] Draw a circle in the middle of your page and write your topic in the circle.
- [ ] Write a word that relates to the topic, circle the word, and connect it to the topic circle with a line.
- [ ] Repeat this process so that a set of major supports radiate out from the topic circle.
- [ ] Write a word that relates to one of the major supports, circle it, and connect it to that major support circle.
- [ ] Repeat this process for each of the major supports to create clusters of minor supports.

## Practice 17

MAPPING

The writer of the following paragraph used a concept map to brainstorm ideas. Read the paragraph. Then, recreate her concept map by filling in the appropriate blanks with ideas from her paragraph. Discuss how the concept map differs from her final draft.

According to *Merriam-Webster's Collegiate Dictionary*, a role model is "a person whose behavior in a particular role is imitated by others." In other words, a role model is anyone who has influence over us. A role model can be anyone including celebrities, such as actors, athletes, or politicians or plain folks, such as teachers, parents, and friends. Role models can be positive or negative. For example, a positive role model possesses several traits. A positive role model reflects an ideal, such as courage or honesty, has an upstanding reputation, and uses his or her influence for the greater good. In contrast, a negative role model negates an ideal by being cowardly or dishonest, has a damaged reputation, and uses his or her influence for selfish gain. Still, ideals such as courage, cowardice, honesty, and dishonesty are often a matter of opinion. For example, many thought Tom Cruise acted as a strong role model when he spoke out against the psychiatric profession. He claimed that vitamins and exercise, not therapy and drugs, are the best treatments for postpartum depression. He even condemned Brooke Shields as a role model for relying on drug therapy for her postpartum depression. However, many others saw his criticism as an unfair attack that damaged his reputation in their eyes. In the end, a role model actually reflects our own values.

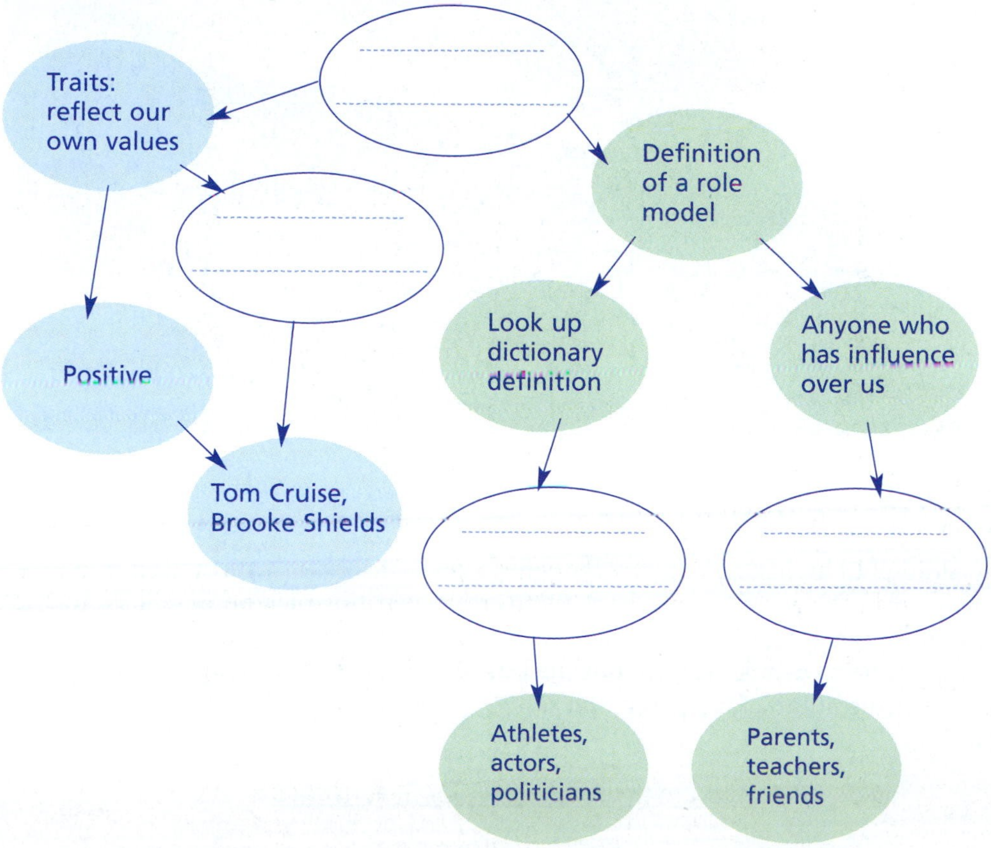


Practice 17

## Practice 18

MAPPING

Using your own sheet of paper, create a concept map to brainstorm ideas for one of the following topics. Use circles and arrows to show your flow of ideas. Or feel free to use ideas generated in a freewrite during Practices 11 and 13.

- Road Rage
- Graffiti
- Positive Thinking
- Workplace Stress
- Gang Violence
- Legalizing Marijuana
- Eating Disorders
- A Role Model

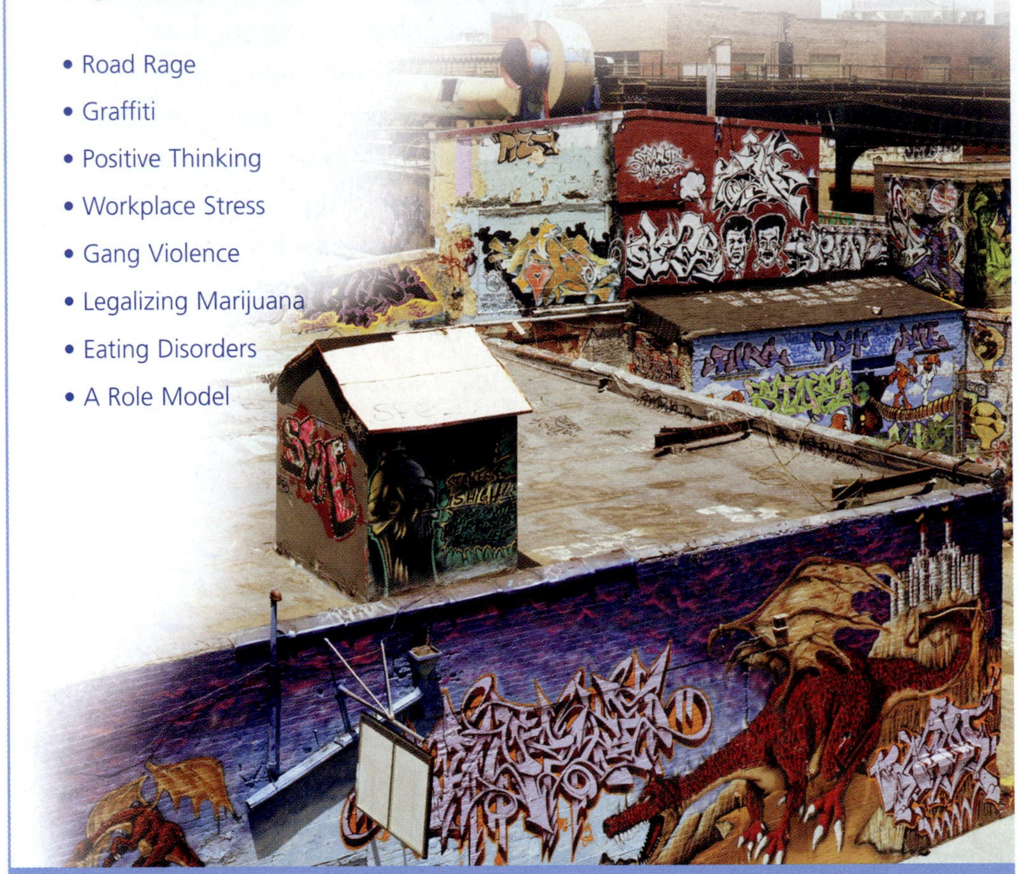

More practice with prewriting: <www.mywritinglab.com>

## Outlining: A Writing Plan

In addition to brainstorming first thoughts, a prewrite also organizes ideas into a writing plan. A concept map is one way to create a writing plan because it shows the flow of ideas among the topic, major details, and minor details. An outline is another way to create a writing plan. An **outline** lists ideas in blocks of thought, as shown in the following outline for a paragraph.

Main Idea Statement: Topic Sentence

A. Major supporting detail
  1. Minor detail
  2. Minor detail

B. Major supporting detail
  1. Minor detail
  2. Minor detail

C. Major supporting detail
  1. Minor detail
  2. Minor detail

Use the following thinking guide to use outlining as a prewriting technique.

# The Writing Process Step by Step:

## Prewriting by Outlining

- ☐ Create an outline from other prewriting activities such as freewrites, lists, and concept maps.
- ☐ List and identify each item with Roman numerals, capitalized letters, Arabic numerals, and lowercase letters, in that order, to show the flow of ideas, as illustrated below:

  I. Main Idea

  A. Major supporting detail

  1. Minor supporting detail

  2. Minor supporting detail

- ☐ Place a period after each numeral or letter.
- ☐ Capitalize each item.
- ☐ For topic outlines, state each item with a word or phrase.
- ☐ For sentence outlines, state each item as a complete thought.

Practice 19

**OUTLINING**

The following reflection and concept map was created by a student during the prewriting phase of an assignment. Complete the outline with ideas from the concept map.

**Laura's First Thoughts:**

*I am going to write about the topic "My Ideal Mate," and my classmates are my audience. I am going to focus my topic by discussing three traits of an ideal mate and how my boyfriend is a perfect example of an ideal mate. My purpose is to let the reader know what a great boyfriend I have.*

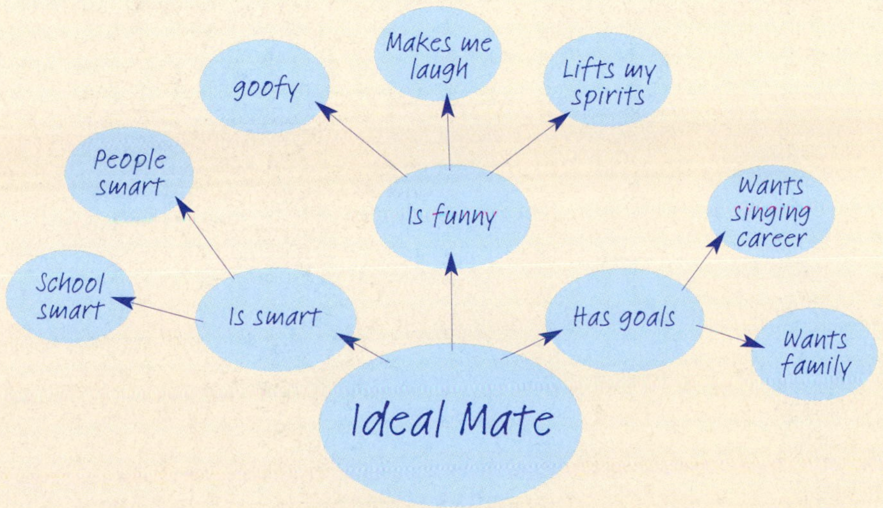


*Main Idea Statement: My boyfriend Kelly is my ideal mate.*

Practice 19

**A.** ........................................

**1.** He excelled in high school and college.

**2.** ........................................

**B.** Kelly is funny.

**1.** ........................................

**2.** He keeps me laughing.

**3.** ........................................

**C.** ........................................

**1.** He is working towards a singing career.

**2.** ........................................

Practice 20

CREATING A WRITING PLAN

Choose your own topic or select one of the following topics. Identify your audience and purpose. Then, generate major and supporting details using the outline. Use the reporter's questions *who? what? when? where? how?* and *why?* to produce details.

- A place everyone should visit at least once
- A famous person who is an excellent role model for youth

TOPIC: ........................................

AUDIENCE: ........................................

PURPOSE: ........................................

........................................

........................................

........................................

TOPIC SENTENCE: ........................................

........................................

........................................

........................................

A. ..............................................................

1. ..............................................................

2. ..............................................................

B. ..............................................................

1. ..............................................................

2. ..............................................................

C. ..............................................................

1. ..............................................................

2. ..............................................................

Practice 20

More practice with prewriting: <www.mywritinglab.com>

# Drafting

The **drafting** stage of the writing process may include several tasks depending on the writing situation. An essay or letter may require the drafting of an introduction, a main idea, supporting details, and conclusion. A stand-alone paragraph may require only a main idea and supporting details.

> **Drafting** is putting your ideas into sentences and paragraphs.

## Compose a Main Idea

For more information on thesis statements, introductions, and conclusions, see Chapters 13 and 14.

The **main idea statement** for an essay is called a **thesis statement.** The main idea statement for a paragraph is called a **topic sentence.** In general, the main idea sentence presents a topic and the point you are making about the topic, as in the following example:

TOPIC

Hip-Hop music has four unique elements including rapping or MCing, DJing, breakdancing, and graffiti.

WRITER'S POINT

The writer's point focuses the topic "Hip-Hop music" into the narrowed subject "four unique elements of Hip-Hop music." With this statement, the writer narrowed the subject by stating the opinion "unique" and focusing on the details that will be discussed: "four unique elements."

Use the following thinking guide to draft a piece of writing.

# The Writing Process Step by Step:

## Drafting

- ☐ Write your main idea in a complete sentence.
- ☐ As you write a thesis statement or topic sentence, assert a point rather than announce your topic. Avoid the following announcements:
  - "I am going to write about…"
  - "My paragraph (or essay) is about…"
  - "My topic is…."
- ☐ As you write your first draft, do not worry about issues such as spelling and grammar.
- ☐ Generate major and minor details to support your main idea.
- ☐ As you write, include new ideas as they occur to you without self-criticism or editing yourself before you have a complete draft; this first draft does not need to be perfect. You will use the revision process to evaluate details for logic and relevance once your draft is complete.
- ☐ Use the first draft to discover how your ideas flow and fit together.
- ☐ Resolve to write multiple drafts to produce your best work.

Practice 21

STATING THE MAIN IDEA

Complete the following set of exercises about main idea statements. Discuss your work with your class or in a small group.

**A.** Read the following main idea statements. Underline the subject once and underline the writer's point twice.

**1.** Space exploration benefits society in three ways.

**2.** Three specific exercises reduce the effects of stress.

**3.** Misusing over-the-counter drugs can be just as dangerous as using illegal drugs.

**4.** Eating disorders harm the body, mind, and spirit.

**B.** Revise the following main idea statements so they are more effectively expressed. Identify the hint you used to revise each one.

**5.** I am going to write about how the automobile costs too much, pollutes the environment, and traps us in isolation.

_______________________________________________

_______________________________________________

**Hint:** _______________________________________

_______________________________________________

More help with drafting:
<www.mywritinglab.com>

6. The annoying and rude manners of people while talking on cell phones in public places.

---

---

**Hint:** ______

---

7. Minimum wage is a controversial issue.

---

---

**Hint:** ______

---

Practice 21

## Write a Draft of Your Paragraph

Writing a draft of a paragraph or essay is the result of careful thought based on prewriting activities. Creating a first or rough draft allows you to get a working copy of your ideas that can be improved upon during the revision process.

Practice 22

COMPOSE A TOPIC SENTENCE AND A DRAFT

**Step 1.** Choose a topic from a previous practice exercise, and compose a main idea statement. (Remember that your **main idea statement** is also called a **topic sentence** if you are writing a paragraph. If you are writing an essay, your main idea statement is also called a **thesis statement**.)

**Step 2.** Write a draft using your own paper.

AUDIENCE AND PURPOSE: ______

---

TOPIC: ______

---

WRITER'S POINT: ______

---

MAIN IDEA STATEMENT (topic sentence or thesis statement): ______

---

## Proofreading

Once you have revised your paragraph, take time to carefully proofread your work. Publishing a clean, error-free draft proves you are committed to excellence and that you take pride in your work. Many student writers struggle with common errors, and every writer has her or his own pattern or habit of careless errors. To create a polished draft, a writer masters the rules of writing and edits to eliminate careless errors.

> **Proofreading** is preparing your work for publication. Proofreading is correcting errors in punctuation, capitalization, mechanics, grammar, and spelling.

Use the following thinking guide to proofread a piece of writing.

# The Writing Process Step by Step:

## Proofreading

- ☐ Allow some time to pass between revising and proofreading.
- ☐ Read your work one sentence at a time from the *end* to the *beginning*. Reading your work from the end to the beginning allows you to focus on each sentence.
- ☐ Read again from the beginning with a cover that you slide down the page as you read so you focus on one sentence at a time.
- ☐ Use a highlighter to mark mistakes.
- ☐ Proofread more than once; focus on one type of error at a time.
- ☐ Proofread for the types of errors you commonly make.
- ☐ Use word processing spell checkers carefully (they don't know the difference between words such as there, their, or there).
- ☐ Use a dictionary to double check your spelling.
- ☐ Have someone else read over your work.

## Practice 25

PROOFREADING

The following draft by a student writer reveals her struggle with two common errors: pronoun agreement and subject-verb agreement. The box below sums up the rules for pronoun agreement and subject-verb agreement and includes a few sentence examples that are correct. Read the rules and examples in the box, and then use them as a guide to correct the same kind of errors in pronoun agreement and subject-verb agreement in the student's draft.

**Pronoun Agreement**

If a noun is singular (*I, you, he, she,* or *it*), then the pronoun that refers to the noun must be singular. If a noun is plural *(we, you, they),* then the pronoun that refers to the noun must be plural.

More help with proofreading:
<www.mywritinglab.com>

### Subject-Verb Agreement

If a subject of a sentence is singular, then the verb and object of the verb must be singular. If the subject of a sentence is plural, then the verb and object of the verb must be plural.

**CORRECT:**

SINGULAR NOUN — SINGULAR PRONOUN

The runner pins her number to her jersey.

SINGULAR SUBJECT — THIRD PERSON SINGULAR VERB (ADD "–S") — SINGULAR OBJECT

**CORRECT:**

PLURAL NOUN — BOTH PLURAL PRONOUNS

The runners pin their numbers to their jerseys.

PLURAL SUBJECT — THIRD PERSON PLURAL VERB — BOTH PLURAL OBJECTS

**Student draft**

The Bride to Be

(1 ) In a traditional wedding, the center of attention revolves around the bride. (2) Although brides vary in temperament and style, most often they fall into three common types: bridezilla, coldarella, and bellaella brides. (3) First, the bridezilla is the typically testy, irritated and acerbic bride. (4) The best known trait of a bridezilla is the tendency to have high voltage temper tantrums. (5) For example, they cannot settle a single, simple issue without blowing off the handle and making something out of nothing. (6) The second type of bride, coldarella, is also known as a runaway bride. (7) Though she may come across as calm and understanding, deep down they are repressing all their bottled tension. (8) A runaway bride often smiles until the day she skips town and leaves the man of her dreams waiting at the altar. (9) The third and best bride is the bellaella bride, the beautiful bride. (10) Her inner beauty makes them the most delightful ones to be around. (11) She loves the intrinsic details and although she wants everything to be perfect, they don't fuss if it is not. (12) This bride is gentle, easy going, and understanding. (13) She doesn't fret over unexpected circumstances. (14) This bride is the bride to be and the bride to marry!

Practice 25

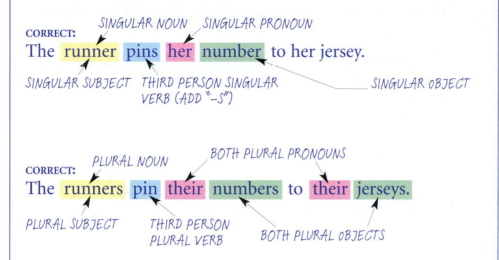

# Academic Learning Log

PORTFOLIO

## THINKING THROUGH THE WRITING PROCESS

To test and track your understanding of what you have studied, answer the following questions.

1. A piece of writing develops in response to a specific situation that is composed of the ______, the ______ for writing, and the ______.

2. The four basic purposes for writing are ______, ______, ______, and ______.

3. The four phases of the writing process are ______, ______, ______, and ______.

4. The writing process is ______: any step can be repeated as necessary.

5. Several prewriting techniques are ______, ______, ______, ______, and ______.

6. Drafting is putting your ideas into ______ and ______.

7. Revising is ______ your work through the eyes of your reader.

8. Revising is reworking your draft for ______, ______, ______, and ______.

9. Proofreading is preparing your work for ______.

10. Proofreading is correcting errors in ______, ______, ______, ______, and ______.

PART 2

# Using Thought Patterns to Develop Paragraphs

# 3 Understanding the Paragraph

**Chapter Preview**

- What Is the Point of a Paragraph?
- Developing Your Point Using a Paragraph
- Workshop: Analyzing the Effectiveness of a Paragraph

## A paragraph is a well-planned sequence of sentences coupled together.

All of us have had some experience reading, writing, or studying paragraphs. What do you already know about paragraphs? What are the traits of a paragraph?

A paragraph allows a writer to express clearly and powerfully one main idea about a narrowed subject. A well-written paragraph can express a valid consumer complaint, a compelling reason to be hired, a sincere apology to a loved one, or a concept tested by a written exam in a college course.

# What Is the Point of a Paragraph?

A paragraph is a well-thought-out chunk of information. A writer narrows a topic into a focused main idea, selects enough relevant details to support the main idea, and organizes these supporting details in a logical flow of information.

## Three Levels of Information in a Paragraph

The following flow chart shows the three levels of information within a paragraph.

**Subject**
- A narrowed topic

**1 Main idea**
- Is often stated as a topic sentence
- Explains the author's one main point about the subject
- Is a more general statement than any of the supporting details

**2 Major detail**
- Explains the main idea
- Provides primary support to the main idea
- Is more general than a minor detail

**3 Minor detail**
- Explains a major detail
- Provides secondary support to the main idea
- Is the most specific idea in the passage

WRITING FROM LIFE

Practice 1

**PHOTOGRAPHIC ORGANIZER: LEVELS OF INFORMATION**

Study the following outline based on an article that was published in the journal *Dermatology Nursing* about types of tattoos. In the blanks, identify each piece of information as the narrowed topic, main idea, major supporting detail, or minor supporting detail.

Four Types of Tattoos ____________

There are four major types of tattoos: traumatic, amateur, professional, and cosmetic.

____________

**A.** Traumatic ____________

**1.** Cause: accidental embedding of colored material, which leaves pigment after healing ____________

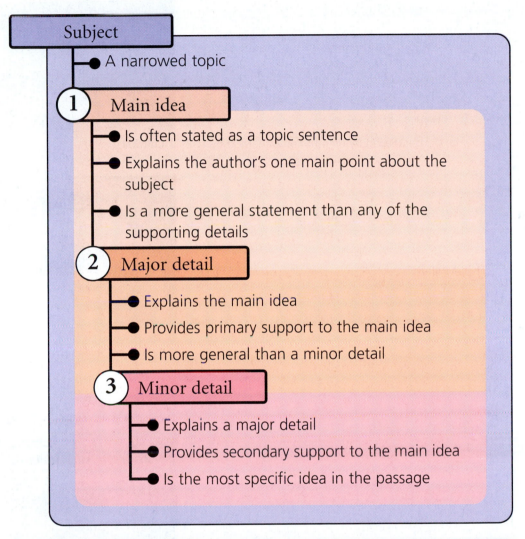

2. Examples: motorcycle rash, "graphite tattoo" from a puncture injury with a pencil

______________________

B. Amateur ______________________

1. Cause: placed by the person being tattooed or by a friend with little experience

______________________

2. Example: boyfriend's name; gang tattoo

______________________

C. Professional ______________________

1. Cultural ______________________

a. Cause: placed by time-honored method by members of certain cultural groups

______________________

b. Example: Samoan tattoos

______________________

2. Modern ______________________

a. Cause: placed by "tattoo gun" by experienced, paid artists

______________________

b. Example: Tattoo parlors

______________________

D. Cosmetic ______________________

1. Cause: placed by a cosmetic specialist as permanent makeup or camouflage

______________________

2. Example: eyeliner ______________________

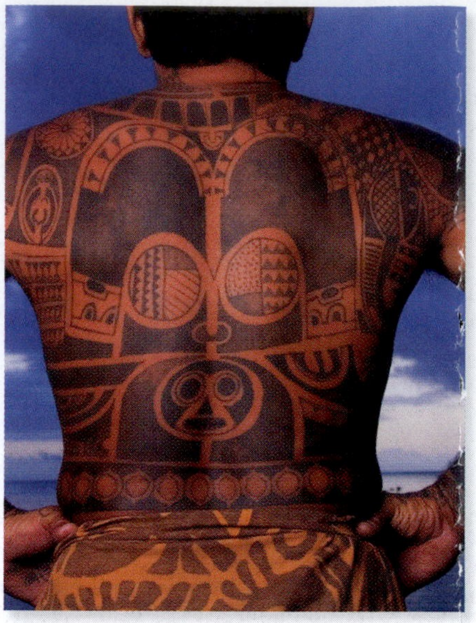

▲ Cultural

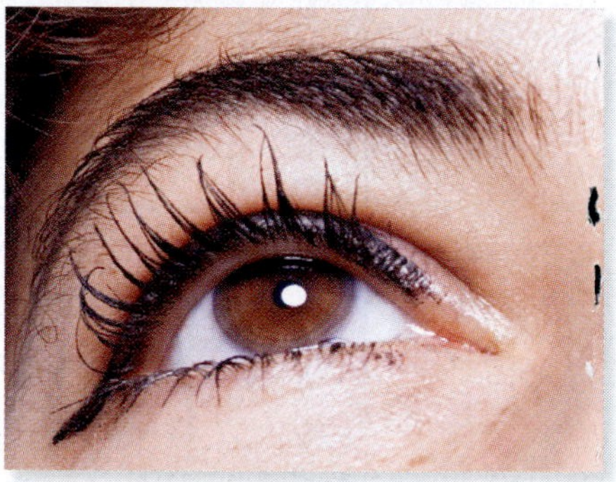

▲ Permanent makeup

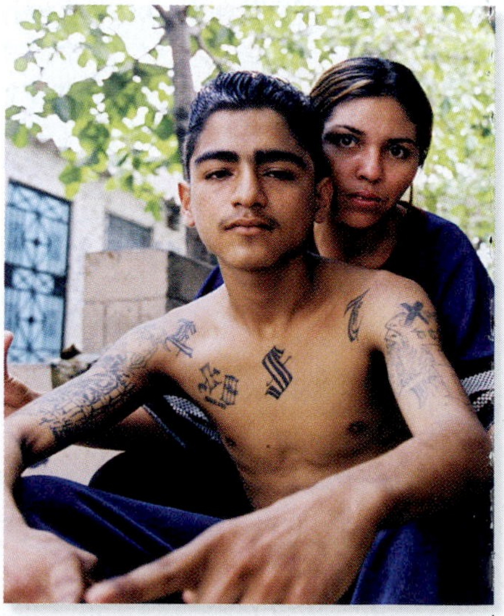

▲ Gang tattoos

◄ Modern

Practice 1

Practice 2

LEVELS OF INFORMATION

Read the paragraph developed from the previous outline. Circle the main idea. Underline the four sentences that state the major supports.

**Four Types of Tattoos**

(1) There are four major types of tattoos: traumatic, amateur, professional, and cosmetic. (2) The first type, traumatic tattoos, is caused by the imbedding of dirt or debris beneath the skin, which leaves an area of pigmentation after healing. (3) For example, this commonly occurs in "road rash" after a motorcycle accident or after a puncture injury from a lead pencil, called a "graphite tattoo." (4) The second type, amateur tattoos, is placed by the person being tattooed or by a friend and often show little artistry or detail. (5) A boyfriend's or girlfriend's name or a gang symbol is tattooed using a pin and India ink, pen ink, charcoal, or ashes as the pigment. (6) The third type, professional tattoos, take two forms: cultural and modern. (7) Cultural tattoos are placed using the time-honored methods of a certain cultural ethnicities. (8) For example, the Samoans use tattoos to display the artistry of their particular heritage. (9) Modern tattoos are performed using a "tattoo gun" and are placed by experienced, paid artists. (10) The fourth type, cosmetic tattoos, is a rapidly growing area of the tattoo industry. (11) Permanent makeup, including eyeliner, lip liner, rouge, and eyebrow pencil, can be placed by a tattoo specialist. (12) Finally, another aspect of cosmetic tattooing is the camouflaging of an undesired tattoo or other physical flaw.

–Adapted from Terrence A. Cronin Jr. *Dermatology Nursing.* Oct 2001 v13 i5 p 380(4).

Practice 3

LEVELS OF INFORMATION IN A PARAGRAPH

Read the following paragraph. Then, fill in the sentence outline with the main idea and missing supporting details.

**Alligators and Rocketships**

(1) Sharing a boundary with Merritt Island's National Wildlife Refuge on the east coast of Florida, John F. Kennedy Space Center serves as a refuge for several endangered species. (2) For example, the endangered manatee flourishes in the shadows of launch platforms. (3) Just south of launch pad 39A, more than 300 manatees graze protected in a sanctuary in the northern end of Banana River. (4) Manatees are so abundant at the Center that they make up around 30 percent of Florida's total manatee population.

(5) Another endangered species at the center is the beloved sea turtle. (6) Between May and September, thousands of endangered sea turtles come ashore on this barrier island in the dark of night to lay their eggs. (7) With its protected shoreline, Kennedy has one of the most dense turtle populations in the northern hemisphere. (8) Bald eagles also find refuge at the space center. (9) At least five active bald eagle nests exist around the Center. (10) Nests can reach more than six feet in diameter and are usually inhabited from September through May. (11) The eagles usually produce one or two chicks per year. (12) No discussion of wildlife at Kennedy is complete without mentioning alligators! (13) While the interactions between man and alligator are few, the biggest problem is during Shuttle landings. (14) Prior to each Kennedy Shuttle landing, it is the task of a special crew to clear the runway of all debris, including any alligators that might be sunning themselves on the runway surface.

▲ **Merritt Island's National Wildlife Refuge**

▲ **Launch platforms**

–Adapted from *"Alligators and Rocketships."* NASA. http://www.nasa.gov/centers/kennedy/shuttleoperations/alligators/kscovrv.html

Practice 3

Main idea (Topic Sentence): ______________________________

______________________________

**A.** Major support: ______________________________

______________________________

**1.** Minor support: Just south of launch pad 39A, more than 300 manatees graze protected in a sanctuary in the northern end of Banana River.

**2.** Minor support: Manatees are so abundant at the Center that they make up around 30 percent of Florida's total manatee population.

**B.** Major support: ______________________________________________

______________________________________________

**1.** Minor support: Between May and September, thousands of endangered sea turtles come ashore on this barrier island in the dark of night to lay their eggs.

**2.** Minor support: ______________________________________________

______________________________________________

**C.** Major support: Bald eagles also find refuge at the space center.

**1.** Minor support: ______________________________________________

**2.** Minor support: ______________________________________________

______________________________________________

**3.** Minor support: The eagles usually produce one or two chicks per year.

**D.** Major support: ______________________________________________

______________________________________________

**1.** Minor support: ______________________________________________

______________________________________________

**2.** Minor support: ______________________________________________

______________________________________________

______________________________________________

More practice with outlines and three levels of information in a paragraph <www.mywritinglab.com>

Practice 3

# Three Parts of a Paragraph

A paragraph is a series of closely related sentences that develop and support the writer's point about a narrowed subject. Often, the paragraph serves as a building block for a longer piece of writing such as an essay, since an essay is composed of two, three, or more paragraphs. In many situations a writer can make a point through one well-developed paragraph. Sometimes, a writer provides a stand-alone paragraph with a title. In addition to a title, a paragraph has three basic parts:

**A Beginning:**
**An introduction of one or more sentences: A topic sentence that states the author's purpose and main point.**

**A Middle:**
**A body of major and minor details that support the topic sentence.**

**An Ending:**
**A conclusion of one or more sentences that reinforces the author's purpose and main point.**

The following graphic describes the function of each part of a paragraph and shows the general format of a paragraph.

**Title:**
Use Key Words or a Phrase to Vividly Describe the Point of Your Paragraph

**The Introduction:**
An introduction is usually one or more sentences that explain the importance of the topic or give necessary background information about the topic.
Your topic sentence states your narrowed subject and your point about the subject.

**The Body:**
The body of a paragraph is made up of a series of sentences that offer major details in support of your topic sentence. If needed, provide minor details that support the major details. Link sentences within the paragraph with clear transitions so your reader can easily follow your thoughts.

**Conclusion:**
The conclusion restates or sums up your paragraph's main idea in one or more sentences.

# Practice 4

The following student essay by Adam Stewart illustrates the use of a title and the three parts of a paragraph. Underline the topic sentence. Circle each of the three parts of the paragraph: Introduction, Body, and Conclusion. Provide a title for the paragraph.

▲ Ambitious

▲ Mediocre worker

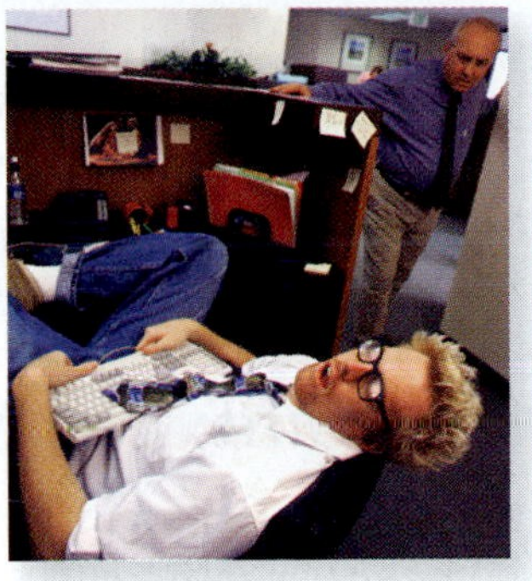

▲ Lazy worker

(1) Although everyone has to work at one point in his or her life and a strong work ethic is looked upon very highly, unfortunately not all workers understand the importance of hard work and a good attitude. (2) Depending upon which category they represent, workers are judged by their coworkers and employers. (3) Three different types of workers make up the workforce, and each type works toward a very different future. (4) First, the ambitious worker comes to work on time, has a good attitude, stays on task, and is always willing to help in any way. (5) Supervisors and coworkers highly value the work ethic of ambitious workers because they always get the job done and do it well beyond expectations. (6) The second type of worker is satisfied with mediocrity. (7) This type of worker comes to work on time, but he or she is not always on the required task. (8) Mediocre workers do what is required and nothing more. (9) Employers and coworkers tolerate mediocre workers because even though they don't always have a good attitude, the job does get done and usually meets expectations. (10) The third type is the lazy worker, also known as the slacker. (11) Everyone hates the slacker. (12) Slackers consistently show up late, rarely accomplish the required task, and continuously try to get the rest of their coworkers off task as well. (13) The slacker, looking for the easy way out, rarely meets expectations. (14) In conclusion, the ambitious workers will be the leaders and high-wage earners; the mediocre workers will likely remain at some dead-end job; and the slackers will probably be fired from job after job, never rethinking their work ethic.

Find more information and practice on each part of the paragraph in the following sections: Introductions—pages 281–283. Topic sentences, major details, and minor details—chapters 4–12. Conclusions—page 294.

More practice with topic sentences and the three parts of the paragraph <www.mywritinglab.com>

# Developing Your Point Using a Paragraph

An effective paragraph is ***focused***, ***detailed***, ***logical***, and ***well expressed***. A writer (1) narrows a topic into a focused main idea; (2) offers only those details that are relevant to the main idea; (3) provides adequate details to support the main idea; (4) organizes these supporting details in a logical flow of information; and (5) uses effective expression through the purposeful choice of words, sentence structure, and grammar.

## The Point: The Main Idea

A focused main idea presents a narrowed subject and the writer's controlling point about the narrowed subject. The controlling point often indicates both the writer's opinion and a pattern of organization. A topic sentence states the focused main idea in a complete sentence.

### Narrow the Topic

Use the following suggestions to guide your thinking as you focus a general topic into a narrowed subject or topic.

- Narrow the topic based on your **opinion**. An opinion is expressed by using words such as *amazing, alarming, beautiful, best, likely, should*, or any other word that states personal values, judgments, or interpretations. Use questions, freewriting, mapping, listing, or another brainstorming technique to discover your opinion about a topic.

| Example: | General Topic | Narrowed Subject |
|---|---|---|
| | Seatbelts | Seatbelts can be dangerous |
| | | Seatbelts save lives |

- Narrow the topic based on a **pattern of organization**. A writer may use a pattern of organization to narrow a subject and generate details. Patterns of organization are also used to develop, organize, and express a main idea, major details, and minor details in a logical order. The following list provides a few examples of patterns of organization and signal words for each one.

| Pattern of Organization | Signal Words |
|---|---|
| Space Order | *Above, below, next to, underneath, scene* |
| Time Order | *First, now, then, before, after, process, use* |
| Example | *For example, exemplify, includes, such as* |
| Classification | *Types, kinds, levels* |
| Compare/Contrast | *Similar, likewise, just as / however, in contrast* |
| Cause/Effect | *Source, origin / results, impact* |

| Example: | General Topic | Narrowed Subject |
|---|---|---|
| | Graffiti | The effects of graffiti |
| | | The types of graffiti |

- Combine topic, opinion, and pattern of organization to generate a narrowed subject.

| Example: | General Topic | Narrowed Subject |
|---|---|---|
| | Seatbelts | Three reasons seatbelts can be dangerous |
| | | Proper use of seatbelts saves lives |
| | Graffiti | The negative effects of graffiti |
| | | Graffiti: A type of artistic expression |

For more information on each of the patterns of organization, see chapters 4–12. <www.mywritinglab.com>

Practice 5

**FOCUS A TOPIC INTO A NARROWED SUBJECT**

Combine the topic with an opinion and pattern of organization signal words to narrow the topic.

1. GENERAL TOPIC: *Health Issue: Weightlifting*

   OPINION: *positive* SIGNAL WORD: *effects*

   NARROWED SUBJECT: ______________________

2. GENERAL TOPIC: *A Public Figure: Tyra Banks*

   OPINION: *admirable* SIGNAL WORD: *traits*

   NARROWED SUBJECT: ______________________

3. GENERAL TOPIC: *Historical Place: Gettysburg*

   OPINION: *most decisive battle in history* SIGNAL WORD: *scene*

   NARROWED SUBJECT: ______________________

4. GENERAL TOPIC: *Business: Saving Money*

   OPINION: *smart* SIGNAL WORD: *steps to*

   NARROWED SUBJECT: ______________________

## Write the Topic Sentence

Once you have focused a topic into a narrowed subject with your opinion and a pattern of organization, you are ready to write a complete sentence to state the main idea. Each of the following topic sentences offers a subject and a controlling point: a **topic** narrowed by the writer's **opinion** and a suggested **pattern of organization**.

TOPIC — WRITER'S OPINION — PATTERN OF ORGANIZATION

Seatbelts can be dangerous for three reasons.

(Seatbelts = TOPIC; can be dangerous = WRITER'S OPINION; three reasons = PATTERN OF ORGANIZATION)

Proper use of seatbelts saves lives.

(Proper = WRITER'S OPINION; use = PATTERN OF ORGANIZATION; seatbelts = TOPIC; saves = WRITER'S OPINION; lives = TOPIC)

Graffiti leads to several negative effects.

(Graffiti = TOPIC; leads to several = PATTERN OF ORGANIZATION; negative = WRITER'S OPINION; effects = PATTERN OF ORGANIZATION)

Graffiti is a type of artistic expression.

(Graffiti = TOPIC; type = PATTERN OF ORGANIZATION; artistic = WRITER'S OPINION; expression = TOPIC)

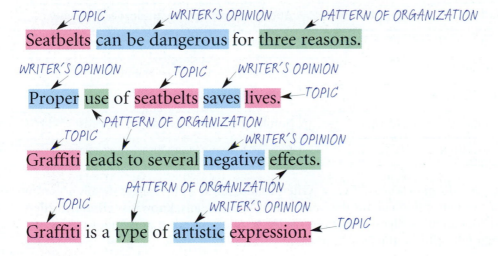

Practice 6

WRITE A TOPIC SENTENCE

Write topic sentences for each of the following narrowed subjects.

1. Narrowed Subject: Benefits of aerobic exercise

TOPIC SENTENCE: ______________________________

______________________________

2. Narrowed Subject: The admirable traits of Tyra Banks

TOPIC SENTENCE: ______________________________

______________________________

3. Narrowed Subject: Gettysburg: Scene of the Most Decisive Battle in the Civil War

TOPIC SENTENCE: ______________________________

______________________________

4. Narrowed Subject: Smart Steps to Save Money

TOPIC SENTENCE: ______________________________

______________________________

More practice with narrowing a subject and writing a topic sentence <www.mywritinglab.com>

## Logical Order

Use a writing plan to establish a logical order for details and a clear flow of ideas. A writing plan includes one or more of the following elements:

***A Pattern of Organization*** As discussed on page 58, a writer uses a pattern of organization to arrange major details and minor details in a logical order. The following chart provides a few examples of patterns of organization and signal words for each one (see Chapters 4–12 for in-depth instruction about patterns of organization and signal words):

| Patterns of Organization | Signal Words |
|---|---|
| Description (Space order) | Above, below, next to, underneath, scene |
| Narrative/Process (Time order) | First, now, then, before, after, next, stage |
| Example | For example, exemplify, includes, such as |
| Classification | Types, kinds, levels |
| Compare/Contrast | Similar, likewise/however, in contrast |
| Cause/Effect | Source, origin/results, impact, reasons |

***Order of Importance*** Often, a writer decides upon and arranges details according to his or her opinion about the importance of the details, known as **climatic order.** Usually, climatic order moves from the least important point and builds to the paragraph's climax, the most important point.

***Order of Topic Sentence*** Often the controlling point of the topic sentence divides the subject into chunks of information. The order of the ideas in the topic sentence often reflects a pattern of organization or an order of importance for details.

## Practice 7

LOGICAL ORDER

The following paragraph from a college textbook demonstrates a writing plan based on the logical order of a topic sentence and pattern of organization. Underline the topic sentence. Circle the pattern of organization's signal words.

> (1) Interpersonal communication is a continuous series of processes that blend into one another. (2) For convenience of discussion we can separate them into five stages. (3) During the first stage, we sense, we pick up some kind of stimulation. (4) Next, we organize the stimuli in some way. (5) Third, we interpret and evaluate what we perceive. (6) Then, we store it in memory, and finally, in stage five, we retrieve it when needed.
>
> –Adapted from DeVito, *The Interpersonal Communication Book*, 10th Ed., p. 91.

## Practice 8

LOGICAL ORDER

Study the following list of ideas. Label each major support in each group A, B, and C to achieve the most logical order. Discuss the reasons for your choices with a small group of peers.

1. Writing for Everyday Life

Dear Koshanda, we enjoyed our recent visit with you in the great state of Texas.

............ the fun day trips you planned and the great food you cooked

............ the surprise send-off party the night before we left

............ the warm welcome your family provided upon our arrival

2. Writing for Working Life

To Whom It May Concern: I am writing to register a complaint about the quality of your product, the price of your product, and the attitude of your employees.

............ attitude of your employees

............ price of your product

............ quality of your product

3. Writing for College Life

Political power in the United States, shared equally among three branches of government, actually rests in the hands of relatively few people.

............ Presidential power: One powerful person

............ Legislative power: 535 powerful people

............ Judicial power: 9 powerful people

## Relevant and Adequate Details

Relevant and adequate details support and develop the main idea. As you narrow a topic, usually you generate many ideas before you decide on one main point. You must evaluate each detail based on its relationship to the point you want to make.

***Relevant details*** explain and support only the writer's point. Once you narrow a subject into a focused main idea, you then include only those details that relate to your opinion and pattern of organization. Relevant details explain and support only your point as a writer.

### Check for Relevant Details

Apply the following questions to each detail to see if it is relevant to a main idea. If the answers are "no" to these questions, then the detail is most likely irrelevant and should not be included as a support.

- Does the detail reinforce the writer's opinion?
- Does the detail carry out the pattern of organization?
- Does the detail support the main idea?
- Does the detail support a major detail?

Practice 9

RELEVANT DETAILS

The following prewrite list includes a focused main idea and a set of details. Use the "Check for Relevant Details" questions given above to identify the irrelevant detail, and cross it out.

Main Idea: Aerobic exercise leads to several benefits.

| First Benefit | Second Benefit | Third Benefit |
|---|---|---|
| stronger bones | stronger muscles | better health |
| builds bone mass | tones muscles | improved looks |
| reduces brittleness | increases range of motion | reduces body fat |

***Adequate details*** offer in-depth explanations and supports for the writer's opinion and pattern of organization. In-depth support of a main idea often requires both major and minor details. Major details directly support the main idea. Minor details support and explain the major details (review the chart on page 51 of this chapter).

### Check for Adequate Details

Apply the following questions to see if you have adequate details to support your main idea. If the answer is "yes" to these questions, then additional details are most likely needed to fully support the main idea.

- Is more information needed to explain the writer's opinion?
- Is more information needed to carry out the pattern of organization?
- Does a major detail need a minor detail of support or explanation?

## Practice 10

ADEQUATE DETAILS

The following list includes a main idea statement, three major supporting details, and minor details that support each major detail. Circle the major detail that needs more support. Add another minor detail of support for the idea you circled.

Main Idea: Follow three smart steps to save money.

| | | | |
|---|---|---|---|
| Major Details: | Step one, avoid debt. | Step two, shop with a plan. | Step three, cut costs. |
| | ↓ | ↓ | ↓ |
| Minor Details: | Pay credit cards off.<br>________<br>________ | Use a list for groceries.<br>Avoid impulse buys.<br>Compare prices. | Consume fewer soft drinks.<br>Bring lunch to work. |

Many writers use concept maps and other brainstorming techniques to generate enough relevant details to convincingly support a point. Chapters 4 to 12 offer detailed instruction and practice with concept maps and other prewriting activities.

## Practice 11

RELEVANT AND ADEQUATE DETAILS

Read the following rough draft of a paragraph. Cross out the irrelevant detail. Underline the point that needs more information to adequately support the main idea.

### A Winter Wonder or Winter Haven Vacation?

(1) Many families take advantage of the winter break in school calendars across the country to enjoy a vacation together. (2) A winter-time vacation actually offers distinct choices in activities, food, and clothing. (3) On the one hand, a family may choose to enjoy the wonder of winter. (4) Fresh snow offers plenty of opportunities for winter sports such as skiing, sledding, snowmobiling, snowboarding, or ice skating. (5) Plus, nothing beats the warmth of a fire and a cup of hot soup after a hard day of play in the cold, fresh air. (6) Of course, the family will need to plan on packing additional special

More practice with relevant and adequate details <www.mywritinglab.com>

Practice 11

clothing. (7) On the other hand, a family may prefer to visit a winter haven in a tropical climate. (8) Balmy beaches offer plenty of fun options such as sunbathing, snorkeling, surfing, and swimming. (9) Then, after a day drenched in sun and sand, nothing satisfies more than an air-conditioned restaurant serving fresh fish and cold drinks. (10) And the family can travel light. (11) In the tropics, all they really need are their swimsuits and a few causal clothes such as shorts, t-shirts, and sandals. (12) Of course, many people just stay home.

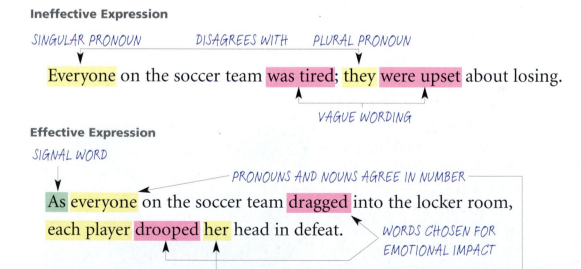

## Effective Expression

Effective expression enhances the writer's purpose through the precise choice and use of words, sentence structure, and grammar.

### Word Choice

Precise word choice communicates exact meaning. Writers choose words that effectively communicate tone, purpose, and order. For example, strong transitions and signal words clue the audience into the logical order of the writer's thoughts. Another example of effective expression is the clear and consistent use of pronouns. In addition, words chosen for their emotional or visual impact create strong mental images in the reader's mind and carry out the writer's purpose.

**Ineffective Expression**

SINGULAR PRONOUN — DISAGREES WITH — PLURAL PRONOUN

Everyone on the soccer team was tired; they were upset about losing.

VAGUE WORDING

**Effective Expression**

SIGNAL WORD

PRONOUNS AND NOUNS AGREE IN NUMBER

As everyone on the soccer team dragged into the locker room, each player drooped her head in defeat.

WORDS CHOSEN FOR EMOTIONAL IMPACT

### Sentence Structure

Four types of sentences serve as the basis for all sentences in the English language: simple sentence, complex sentence, compound sentence, compound-complex sentence. Effective expression uses a variety of sentence types to express ideas in clear and interesting statements. (You will learn more about sentence structure in Chapters 16–17.)

**Simple sentences:**

Michaella had been out of school for years. She was insecure about her abilities.

**Complex sentence:**

Michaella, who had been out of school for years, didn't want to fail.

**Compound sentence:**

She studied for two hours every day; as a result, she earned a 4.0 GPA.

**Compound-Complex sentence:**

Michaella studied for two hours every day because she didn't want to fail; as a result, she earned a 4.0 GPA.

## Grammar

Grammar is a tool of effective expression. Writers use grammar to clarify and polish ideas. Grammar includes a wide variety of language rules such as the following: tense, agreement, and punctuation. (You will learn more about grammar throughout your studies in this text.) During the revision process, many writers focus on one element of expression at a time.

EFFECTIVE EXPRESSION

Practice 12

Revise the following paragraph for effective expression through word choice. In a small group of your peers, revise the underlined parts of the following paragraph for effective expression. Use the following word(s) in your revision. Discuss how the revision improves the effectiveness of the paragraph.

suddenly swerved into

landed

Justine's brand new Maxima

**A Frightful Moment**

(1) Justine was driving her friend Jeremy to his house after a concert last Tuesday evening. (2) An oncoming car is in her lane. (3) Justine jerked her steering wheel to avoid a head on collision. (4) Her car spun 360° off the road. (5) The car lands in the middle of a stand of trees. (6) Thankfully, Justine and Jeremy walked away without injury; unfortunately, their car was totaled.

More practice with evaluating the effectiveness of a paragraph <www.mywritinglab.com>

PORTFOLIO

Workshop



# Analyzing the Effectiveness of a Paragraph

Many student writers benefit from the study of a scoring guide. A scoring guide identifies and describes levels of writing effectiveness. The following scoring guide describes the traits of an effective paragraph as discussed in this chapter: A score of "5" indicates a highly effective paragraph. In a small group of your peers, discuss the differences between a "5" paragraph and a "3" level paragraph.

## Scoring Guide for a Paragraph

**5** A focused main idea presents the narrowed subject and the writer's point, and suggests a pattern of organization. Relevant and in-depth details convincingly support and develop the main idea. Strong transitions indicate careful ordering of details based on a logical pattern of organization. Effective expression enhances the writer's purpose through the precise choice and use of words, sentence structure, and grammar.

**4** A focused main idea presents the narrowed subject and the writer's opinion, and suggests a pattern of organization. Relevant and adequate details support and develop the main idea. Clear transitions indicate an order of details based on a logical pattern of organization. Effective expression carries out the writer's purpose through the competent use and choice of words, sentence structure, and grammar.

**3** A focused main idea presents the narrowed subject and the writer's opinion or a pattern of organization. Relevant details offer enough support to develop the main idea. Occasional transitions indicate the use of a pattern of organization, but details are not always logically ordered. Expression does not interfere with the writer's purpose, even though occasional errors in use and choice of words, sentence structure, and grammar occur.

**2** The main idea presents a general subject or a broad opinion. Details are generalized statements or lists that do not offer enough information to support the main idea. Weak or misused transitions and confused order of details indicate little use of a pattern of organization. Weak expression interferes with the writer's purpose through frequent errors in use and choice of words, sentence structure, and grammar.

**1** The main idea presents a vague, weakly worded opinion about a general subject. Details are missing, superficial, or rambling. Lack of transitions and illogical order of details indicate no use of a pattern of organization. Confused expression interferes with the writer's purpose through pervasive errors in choice and use of words, sentence structure, and grammar.

## EVALUATE THE EFFECTIVENESS OF A PARAGRAPH

# Practice 13

Use the scoring guide to assign a score to each of the following paragraphs written by students about the following topic: *An Important Lesson Everyone Should Learn*. Be prepared to discuss your reasons for each score.

........ Life is full of changes and drama. Never know what is going to happened next step. With ups and downs I had learn lot of things. At this point of our life you cannot trust anyone. You learn more about life everyday. Experience make us learn something new and give us a lesson what we should expect next. My life was full of thrill but it's good to have something like that in your life. How life has teach me a good lesson and how you can learn something from my experience. I want to tell others that never give up in your life, never think that life is ending when u loose something out of your life, because it's always a hope that bring your confidence back. Never depend on others not even your close family. Trust yourself and you will make it. Success never comes easy it's always tuff ways to find it. Unless you don't give up life goes on.

........ A friendly attitude can bring us more reward than a frown any day. We all need to learn the importance of a smile. Before I learned this lesson, I didn't know how to react at work to a disgruntled person or a grumpy coworker. In fact, most of the time I would simply call on a supervisor for help. Unfortunately, this move made me seem incapable of handling a problem on my own. Then one day, someone smiled at me for no reason. A friendly face in the crowd made me feel good. If one person with a smile on her face could make me feel lighter, then a smile might be a powerful way to change how other people felt. Over the next few months, I smiled at every person who looked in my direction, even the nastiest of patrons. As a result, most people were friendlier towards me, and I even felt better about myself. I also became easily able to handle those pesky daily problems. I wish more of us could learn that we have the opportunity to change the world within in us and outside of us, when we smile.

........ Everyone should learn an important lesson in life. Some lessons about being honest. Everyone should learn honesty. Parents teach honesty. Don't shoplift. Don't cheat on tests. Don't lie to friends, even white lies. Everyone should learn kindness. Parents and friends teach kindness. Peers are not kind to them. Too many school yard bullies hurt people. If everyone learned important lessons in life, they would be better off.

........ My mom taught how to deal with stress. As a young child, I was diagnosed with attention deficit disorder. This condition makes many every day situations very stressful. So mom taught me three things that have helped me reduce stress. First, she taught me to think ahead. For example every evening, I lay out my clothes for the next day. Planning what I want to wear the night before saves me time and gives me one less thing to worry about in the morning rush to get out the door. Second, she taught me to be organized. Not only do I plan what I am going to wear, but I make a daily list of assignments and appointments so I know exactly what I need to do and where I need to be. I also keep a backpack filled with supplies such as bottled water, healthy snacks, pen, paper, or any other item I might need. Finally, mother taught me to ask questions and take notes. Asking questions and taking notes keep me focused on a task and keeps my mind from wandering in a million different directions. I am grateful that my mom taught me how to reduce stress. I bet everyone would be better off if they could learn what my mom taught me about coping with stress.

........ Steeling is wrong! Unfortunately not everyone knows this. If every one respected others' property as they do there own we would have less chaos. If everyone that was caught steeling had a good beating put on them I am sure they would second guess doing it again, I am not saying that is how this problem should be resolved but I think it would work. Whether you are a child or a full grown adult I believe this concept should be stressed, let alone it is against the law. The world would be a better place if no one stole, and we would all have more respect for each other and there property.

More practice with effective expression <www.mywritinglab.com>

# 4 The Descriptive Paragraph

**Chapter Preview:**



## A description is an account that creates a vivid mental image.

The ability to describe people, places, or objects accurately is a useful life skill. Whether you are talking with a stylist about the exact hairstyle you want, sharing a funny or startling scene from your day with a friend in an email, or reporting on the structure of a plant cell for a biology class, you will use description to make your point.

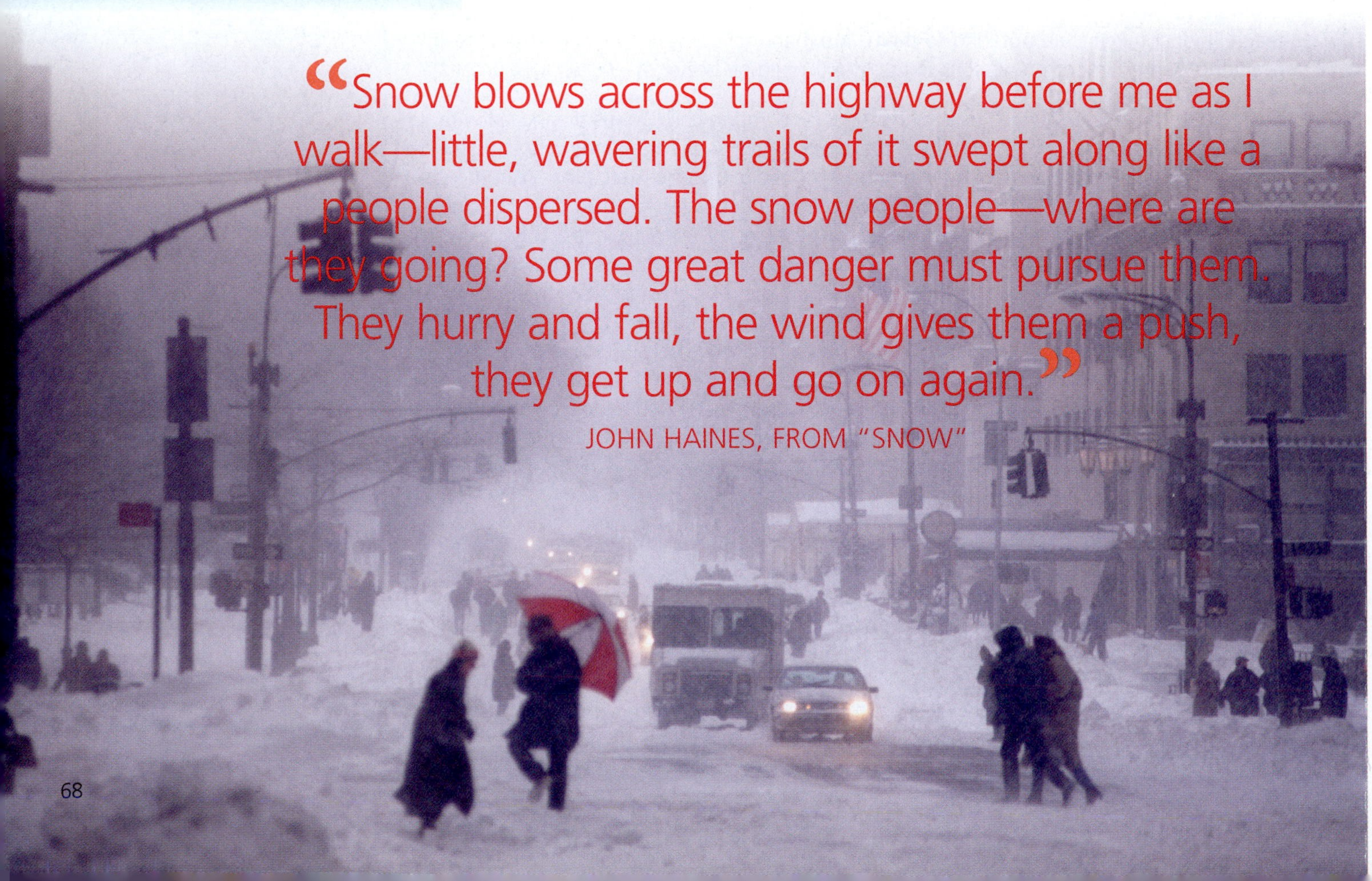

"Snow blows across the highway before me as I walk—little, wavering trails of it swept along like a people dispersed. The snow people—where are they going? Some great danger must pursue them. They hurry and fall, the wind gives them a push, they get up and go on again."

JOHN HAINES, FROM "SNOW"

# What's the Point of Description?

In a descriptive paragraph, the writer uses sensory details such as sights, sounds, smells, tastes, feelings, and textures to create vivid images in the reader's mind. An experienced writer relies on sense memories of a specific experience to call to mind these details. In addition, the writer often uses spatial order to create a clear visual image of a person, place, object, or scene: the location or arrangement in space from top to bottom, bottom to top, right to left, left to right, near to far, far to near, inside to outside, or outside to inside.

Every day, we experience rich sensory details from television, movies, music DVDs, and daily life. Think of a scene that grabbed your attention recently. What is your main impression of the scene? What are several details that make this impression so vivid or memorable?

Description also may include or suggest time order because a person, place, or object usually appears in a situation, or an incident usually occurs or suggests a scene.

Descriptive transition words signal that the details follow a logical order based on one or more of the following elements:

1. The arrangement in space of a person, place, object, or scene
2. The starting point from which the writer chooses to begin the description
3. The time frame as relevant to the description (see Chapter 5 for information about time order)

Getting a mental picture of the person, place, object, scene, or situation helps a writer discover his or her point about the subject being described. Study the following photograph of a popular destination for travelers: the Riverwalk in San Antonio, Texas. Use your sense memory of this or similar scenes to call up sensory details. Fill in the graphic with captions that capture the particular details of specific locations on the Riverwalk. Then answer the question with a one-sentence statement of the overall main idea: "What's the point or impression you are trying to make?"

WRITING FROM LIFE

Practice 1

PHOTOGRAPHIC ORGANIZER: DESCRIPTION

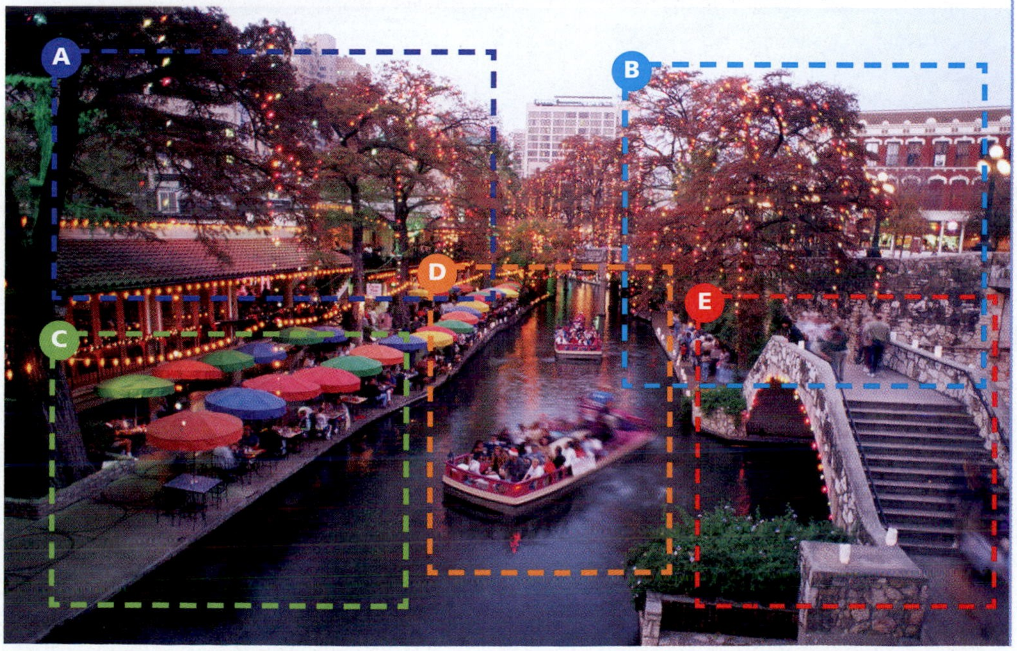

**A** Where is this detail in the scene?

What are the sensory details?

SIGHT: colorful lights in the trees and on the roofs

SOUND: music, people talking, birds, water moving, singing, screaming, laughing

SMELL: restaurant food, other stores food

TASTE:

TOUCH: damp air, windy

**B** Where is this detail in the scene?

What are the sensory details?

SIGHT:

SOUND:

SMELL:

TASTE:

TOUCH:

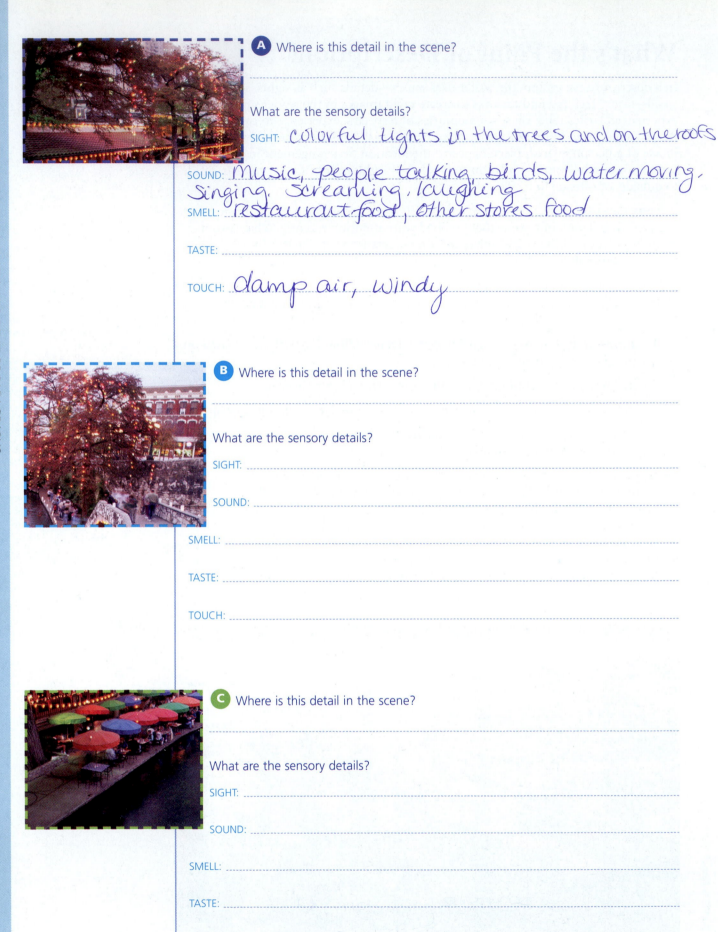

**C** Where is this detail in the scene?

What are the sensory details?

SIGHT:

SOUND:

SMELL:

TASTE:

TOUCH:

**D** Where is this detail in the scene?

What are the sensory details?

SIGHT:

SOUND:

SMELL:

TASTE:

TOUCH:

**E** Where is this detail in the scene?

What are the sensory details?

SIGHT:

SOUND:

SMELL:

TASTE:

TOUCH:

**What's the point?**

Practice 1

## My First Thoughts: A Prewriting Activity

PREWRITING

Brainstorm about the images you just studied. Set a time limit, such as five minutes, and write in your notebook about the images you just studied and the details you generated. Write as quickly as you can without stopping.

# Making a Point Using Description: One Student Writer's Response

The following descriptive paragraph, written as an online review for tourists, offers one writer's point about the Riverwalk in San Antonio. Read this description and the explanations; complete the activities. Then, read the writer's journal entry about her experience writing the paragraph.

**Main Idea:** The main idea is the point the author is making. The topic is "Paseo Del Rio, the San Antonio Riverwalk." **Underline the author's point.**

**Relevant Details:** Relevant details describe elements of the scene to support the point "shimmers with color and light." **Underline additional details that support this point.**

**Effective Expression:** Sensory details such as "cool, damp evenings," "spicy fajitas," "salty margaritas," "lights" and "sunset glimmer" create a vivid mental picture. **Underline 3 more sensory details.**

**Spatial Order:** The phrase "left bank" establishes spatial order. **Circle four more words or phrases that indicate spatial order.**

Paseo Del Rio: A Festival of Color and Light

(1) The Texas spirit of fun and hospitality lights up Paseo Del Rio, the San Antonio Riverwalk. (2) This festive and popular travel destination shimmers with color and light. (3) Along the left bank, two lines of brightly colored café umbrellas—tropical red, Cancun blue, emerald green, lemon yellow—shelter outdoor diners and adorn the cobblestone walk. (4) Above the rainbow rows of umbrellas, white lights strung between oak trees along the walking path glimmer softly in the dusk. (5) Miniature white lights rim the eaves and roofs of the buildings behind the diners and illuminate the graceful drape of the oak branches bending over them. (6) Diners can stay warm on cool, damp evenings with spicy fajitas and salty margaritas as they watch the lights of the Riverwalk and the sunset glimmer upon the water. (7) As they watch, a steady flow of purple trimmed boats putter to midstream from under the bridge on the right side of the river. (8) On this side of the river, the rock walls and the footbridge showcase the rough beauty of the area's natural elements and earth tones. (9) Colorful lights trace the arch under the footbridge. (10) Luminaries sit atop both sides of the bridge's stone-grey railings. (11) At the far side of the bridge, more luminaries light the path along the water's edge. (12) People fill the path with laughter and conversation as they stroll beneath trees shimmering with countless tiny lights. (13) All along the river, this canopy of lights buffers the Riverwalk from the buildings rising in the distance. (14) The lights, the good food, the water, the spectacle of color, the festive atmosphere provide a luscious retreat—Texas style!

Topic sentence
- subject
- attitude or the impression of the writer
- pattern of organization

→ concluding sentence
- wrap up restating the main points.

## THE WRITER'S JOURNAL

The student writer of "Paseo Del Rio: A Festival of Color and Light" completed the following reflection to record her thinking through the writing process. Read her writer's journal that describes a few key choices she made as she wrote.

MAIN IDEA: I spent a good deal of time studying this picture before I began writing, and I still needed several revisions to get the effect I wanted. My first thoughts were about the vivid colors and lights and how much fun the Riverwalk looks—like a festival. The place just seems like a carefully created retreat away from the hectic world that lies just a few blocks away. I found a graphic organizer very helpful during prewriting. Since I have visited the Riverwalk, I used sense memory to recall details, and the graphic organizer helped me focus my point and map out the order of details without having to worry about wording, sentence structure, or punctuation.

RELEVANT DETAILS: During one revision, I discovered that my sentence about the boats wasn't relevant to my point. I had included the boats because they were in the picture, not because they supported the point I wanted to make. So I revised that sentence to include the color of the boats, which does add to the festive atmosphere of the Riverwalk and directly supports my point.

LOGICAL ORDER: I devoted one revision to the words that signal spatial order; I wanted to guide the reader's attention from the left bank to the right bank of the river. I had to really think about how to word these signals so the mind's eye could create a picture and follow my point. So my mental eye went from the lower left bank of umbrellas, to above the umbrellas, and then behind them. Next, I directed the reader's attention to the river in the middle of the picture by focusing on what the diners would be watching—the boat tours. To describe the right side of the river, I moved from "near" to "far" based on the location of the bridge.

EFFECTIVE EXPRESSION: During my last revision, I focused on my word choice. By referring to my thesaurus, I was able to use a variety of verbs and nouns for "light." I wanted to emphasize the beautiful effect of the lights throughout the paragraph.

For a blank version of this form for your own reflections about your writing: <www.mywritinglab.com>

For more information on time order, Chapter 5, "Narration."

# Developing Your Point Using Description

Writers use descriptive paragraphs to make a point through the vivid details they observe and share about a person, place, object, scene, or situation. To make a point by describing details, a writer often relies on spatial order transitions and sensory details. At times, a writer also uses time order to describe an experience.

## The Point: The Main Idea

When you write a description, you limit your topic to concrete details based on sight, sound, smell, taste, and touch. Your opinion or attitude about the subject you are describing is your point or main idea. In a description, your main idea may also include logical order signal words; other times, the logical order is implied without including the signal words.

For example, the first of the following two topic sentences includes (1) the topic, (2) the writer's opinion about the topic, and (3) spatial order signal words. The second topic sentence only includes (1) the topic and (2) the writer's attitude about the topic.

PATTERN OF ORGANIZATION: SPATIAL ORDER — THE TOPIC

From head to toe, Latoya dressed to appear professional and confident.

THE WRITER'S OPINION

Miguel's office reveals his careful attention to organization.

THE TOPIC — THE WRITER'S OPINION

Practice 2

TOPIC SENTENCES

Practice creating topic sentences. The first two items below present a topic, an opinion, and logical order signal word(s). Combine the ideas in each group to create a topic sentence for a descriptive paragraph. Then, complete the practice by composing your own topic sentences.

1. TOPIC: (a favorite place) Grandmother's kitchen

OPINION: offered a haven of old-fashioned country warmth

LOGICAL ORDER SIGNAL WORDS: A small room at the rear of the house

TOPIC SENTENCE: ______________________________

______________________________

______________________________

More practice with creating topic sentences: <www.mywritinglab.com>

**2.** TOPIC: (a treasured possession) The handmade well-pump lamp

OPINION: is an eye-catching and whimsical family treasure

LOGICAL ORDER SIGNAL WORDS: implied: such as in top to bottom

TOPIC SENTENCE: ______

______

**3.** TOPIC: (a useful product) ______

OPINION: sleek, lightweight, flexible, easy to use

LOGICAL ORDER SIGNAL WORDS (as needed): ______

______

TOPIC SENTENCE: ______

______

**4.** TOPIC: (a person of character) My mother (or father, brother, sister, friend, etc.)

OPINION: kindness

LOGICAL ORDER SIGNAL WORDS (as needed): ______

______

TOPIC SENTENCE: ______

**5.** TOPIC: ______

OPINION: ______

LOGICAL ORDER SIGNAL WORDS (as needed): ______

______

TOPIC SENTENCE: ______

______

______

Practice 2

Practice 2

**6.** TOPIC: ______________________________

OPINION: ______________________________

LOGICAL ORDER SIGNAL WORDS (as needed): ______________________________

______________________________

TOPIC SENTENCE: ______________________________

______________________________

**7.** TOPIC: ______________________________

OPINION: ______________________________

LOGICAL ORDER SIGNAL WORDS (as needed): ______________________________

______________________________

TOPIC SENTENCE: ______________________________

______________________________

______________________________

### Transition Words Used to Signal Visual Description

| | | | | | |
|---|---|---|---|---|---|
| above | at the top | beyond | farther | left | right |
| across | back | by | front | middle | there |
| adjacent | behind | center | here | nearby | under |
| around | below | close to | in | next to | underneath |
| at the bottom | beneath | down | inside | outside | within |
| at the side | beside | far away | | | |

## Logical Order

Once you have chosen a topic and focused on a main idea, you are ready to generate and organize details. To organize visual details, spatial order transition words are helpful during the prewriting phase as well as during the drafting part of the writing process. During prewriting, spatial signal words such as *top*, *middle*, or *bottom* can be used as headings to list details. During the drafting stage, explicitly stating spatial transition words creates a mental picture in your reader's mind of how your subject is arranged in space. Strong transition words establish coherence—a clear and easy-to-follow flow of ideas.

Practice 3

**SPATIAL ORDER DETAILS**

Determine the logical order of the following details taken from Maya Angelou's autobiography *I Know Why the Caged Bird Sings*. Rewrite the paragraph, organizing the details by spatial order. *Hint:* Underline the words that signal spatial order. Complete the exercise by answering the question "What's the point?"

............ And when they put their hands on their hips in a show of jauntiness, the palms slipped the thighs as if the pants were waxed.

............ When they tried to smile to carry off their tiredness as if it was nothing, the body did nothing to help the mind's attempt at disguise.

............ In the store the men's faces were the most painful to watch, but I seemed to have no choice.

............ Their shoulders drooped even as they laughed.

What's the point Maya Angelou makes with her use of spatial details?

More practice with spatial order details: <www.mywritinglab.com>

## Relevant Details

A writer narrows a topic into a focused main idea by generating descriptive details that answer questions such as *who, what,* and *where.* As a writer brainstorms, the thinking process brings to mind many sensory as well as spatial details. A writer evaluates the relevancy of each detail and uses only those that illustrate the main idea. Some relevant details describe the appearance of a person, object, place, or scene; other relevant details explain the author's opinion about the topic. Many descriptive details appeal to sight, sound, smell, taste, and touch. A **concept map**, or **graphic organizer**, helps in several ways. First, the graphic can prompt your thinking, memory, and creativity. In addition, the graphic helps to order ideas as they occur to you. A graphic organizer also allows you to visualize the details and see if you have enough details to make your point. Irrelevant details do not explain, support, or illustrate the focused point of the paragraph. In addition to the graphic organizer, writers use the revision process to double check details for relevancy and to eliminate irrelevant details.

**Concept Chart: Description**

TOPIC: *Latoya and professional attire for a job interview*

| WHERE | SIGHT | SMELL | SOUND | TASTE | TOUCH |
|---|---|---|---|---|---|
| Top: Hair | *hair gathered and smoothed into a neat and stylish twist* | | | | |
| Face | *light touch of blush and lip gloss; small gold earrings* | | *calm, assured tone of voice* | | |
| Middle: Blouse and Jacket | *white dress cotton button-up collared shirt; dark blue jacket with a rich pin stripe* | | | | *firm handshake* |
| Skirt | *below the knee; dark blue, A-line* | | | | |
| Bottom: Shoes | *dark blue, polished, low heels, attractive* | | | | |

During the prewriting phase of writing, a writer naturally generates irrelevant details. In fact, an effective writer evaluates the details and uses only the details that support the main idea. All descriptive details should work together to create a strong, unified impression, a mental image of the author's main point.

## Practice 4

RELEVANT CONCRETE DETAILS

The following paragraph develops the ideas recorded in the graphic organizer about Latoya and her professional attire. Circle the main idea. Underline the spatial signal words and the sensory details. Cross out the two details that are not relevant to the main idea.

**Dressed to Impress**

(1) Latoya Bond had been job hunting for months; finally, she landed an interview with a company that she was eager to join. (2) Latoya felt confident that she was well qualified for the position. (3) After all, she was one of the three final candidates chosen from over 100 applications, yet she also knew the importance of making a good impression. (4) From head to toe, Latoya dressed to appear professional and confident. (5) Latoya gathered her hard-to-manage curls into a neat and stylish twist. (6) To complement her no-nonsense hairstyle, Latoya used makeup sparingly but effectively. (7) A little black mascara on her lashes, a touch of blush across her cheeks, and bit of tinted lip balm brought attention to her interested eyes and her earnest smile. (8) She would also be sure to speak with a calm and assured voice. (9) The neatly pressed collar of a white cotton shirt contrasted nicely with her tailored blue pinstriped jacket. (10) Her dark blue A-line skirt reached to just below her knees. (11) Latoya finished her outfit with a flattering pair of blue low-heeled pumps that matched her briefcase and purse. (12) She would offer her prospective employer a firm handshake. (13) Latoya looked as professional and confident as she felt.

More practice with relevant, concrete details in descriptive paragraphs: <www.mywritinglab.com>

## Effective Expression: Concrete Word Choice

Precise word choice communicates exact meaning. Words chosen for a specific emotional or visual impact create strong mental images in the reader's mind and carry out the writer's purpose. As you move through the writing process, think about the impact you want to have on your reader. For the greatest impact, choose concrete and precise words and phrases instead of general or vague expressions. Choose words that *show* instead of *tell*. Consider the following examples:

**General or vague words that tell:**

This property has curb appeal.

**Concrete words that show:**

This beachfront cottage charms potential buyers with its colorful garden, wrap-around porch, and ocean view.

Practice 5

CONCRETE WORD CHOICE

Each item below presents a general sentence using vague words. The phrase in parentheses before each sentence—"(A customer to a mechanic)" in item 1, for example—describes the speaker of the sentence and the person hearing it. Revise each sentence to eliminate vague wording. Consider the point of the writing situation; express ideas with words that have concrete and precise meanings for a specific impact. Discuss your revisions with your class or with a small group of peers.

**1.** (A customer to a mechanic): My car makes a funny sound sometimes.

---

**2.** (A student commenting to his or her companion): The restaurant was disappointing.

---

---

**3.** (A weather reporter to a commuter): The weather is nice (or horrible).

---

**4.** (A staff assistant to Technology Support): The printer is broken.

---

---

---

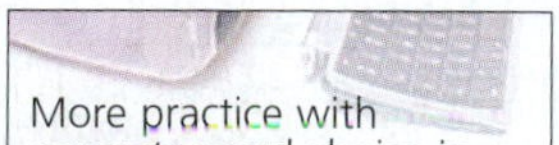

More practice with concrete word choice in descriptive paragraphs: <www.mywritinglab.com>

# Using Description in Your Academic Courses

Many college courses such as literature, composition, history, psychology, ecology, and biology use description. As you study these courses, you will read descriptions of historical places, influential people, natural elements, and scientific experiments. In addition, you will write descriptions to learn or demonstrate what you have learned.

## Practice 6

USING DESCRIPTION IN A HISTORY ASSIGNMENT

Student writer Jean Powell composed the following descriptive paragraph of an important historical site for a report in her American History course. Complete the following activities: (1) Insert appropriate transition words in the blanks. (2) Underline the words or phrases used to create sensory details. (3) Discuss the point of her report with a small group of peers or with your class.

The Vietnam Memorial is made up of two black granite walls joined in a wide-angled V shape. A study of just one of the walls reveals the significance of the memorial. A polished black granite slab stretches hundreds of feet long. At its highest tip, it stands 10 feet tall and then tapers to a height of 8 inches at its end point. Its low tip points .......... the Lincoln Memorial. .......... its polished face are the carved names of service men and women who gave their lives during the Vietnam War. Starting at the highest point on the first panel, thousands of names are listed in chronological order. The high polish of the black granite reflects the image of the world .......... the wall. The reflection of earth, sky, and visitors are seen along with the inscribed names. On the wall, the present and the past mingle. A path runs .......... the base of the wall so visitors can walk the path to read the names. Many create pencil rubbings or leave tokens such as flowers, flags, and personal notes. To the side of the path, a wide grassy park adds to the sense of serenity. The memorial is a quiet place where one can come to terms with loss and grief. Its tranquility is a fitting memorial to a controversial war that cost so many their lives.

More practice with writing descriptive paragraphs: <www.mywritinglab.com>

# Workshop: Writing a Description Paragraph Step by Step

WRITING A DESCRIPTION PARAGRAPH STEP BY STEP

Workshop

PORTFOLIO

PREWRITING

## Prewrite Your Paragraph

The various activities below will walk you through the steps of the prewriting stage of the writing process: choosing a topic; focusing your point; and generating and organizing relevant details.

### Choose Your Topic

The following activities are designed to help you choose a topic.

1. Create a bank of topics. Use the following headings and brainstorm or list as many topics as you possibly can. Don't analyze your thoughts; just jot down topics as quickly as they occur to you. Compare your bank of topics with those of your classmates.
   - The Scene of an Accident
   - A Nature Scene
   - A Pop Icon
   - An Advertisement
   - Emotions (such as fear)
2. Reread the freewrite you composed based on the photograph of the San Antonio Riverwalk. Underline ideas that could be used for a descriptive paragraph. Map out the logical order of details.
3. Select a photograph of a special place. Write captions, brainstorm sensory details, and freewrite about the photograph. Remember to ask "What are the sensory details and how are the details arranged in space?" and "What's the point?" as you generate ideas.

### Focus Your Point

Think about a prewrite you have generated for a descriptive topic. Underline or generate words that suggest your values, opinions, or attitudes about what you described. Think about what strikes you as important about your subject. Consider your audience. Who would be interested in this information and why? Choose a purpose. Write a list of adjectives and sensory details that describe the essence of what you are describing. Use a thesaurus and choose several vivid words to express your thoughts. State in one sentence the point of your description:

AUDIENCE: ______________________________

PURPOSE: ______________________________

WHAT'S THE POINT? ______________________________

______________________________

## Generate and Organize Relevant Details

Using the ideas you have already recorded and the concept chart for a description, generate and organize sensory and spatial details that support your point. (*Hint*: Fill in the "Where" column with spatial signal words such as *left*, *right*, *near*, *far*, *above.*)

-Outsiders point of view
see · laughing
smiling
crying
hugging

**Concept Chart: Description**

TOPIC: Describe a person in your life who makes a difference and how.

WHAT'S THE POINT?
- My mom -

| WHERE | SIGHT | SMELL | SOUND | TASTE | TOUCH |
|---|---|---|---|---|---|
| Top: Shes supporting | | Shell make favorite comfort food. | always gives good advice being calm and understanding | | |
| Face | Never judgemental soft and caring sometimes crying | | | | |
| | | | | | |
| | | | | | |
| | | | | | |

DRAFTING

## Write a Draft of Your Paragraph

Using ideas you generated during the prewriting phase, compose a draft of your paragraph. Return to the prewriting process at any time to generate additional details as needed. Use your own paper.

PORTFOLIO

Workshop

REVISING

## Revise Your Draft

Once you have drafted a description, read the draft and answer the questions in the "Questions for Revising a Descriptive Paragraph" box that follows on the next page. Indicate your answers by annotating your paper. If you answer "yes" to a question, underline, check, or circle examples. If you answer "no" to a question, write needed information in the margins and draw lines to indicate placement of additional details. Revise your paragraph as necessary based on your reflection. (*Hint*: Experienced writers create several drafts as they focus on one or two questions per draft.)

## Questions for Revising a Descriptive Paragraph

- [ ] Have I stated or implied a focused main idea? Have I created a strong impression? Can I state my point in one sentence?
- [ ] Is the logical order of the details clear? Have I used strong transitions to indicate spatial order? Time order?
- [ ] Have I created a vivid mental image through the use of sensory details?
- [ ] Have I made my point with adequate details?
- [ ] Do all the details support my point?
- [ ] Have I chosen concrete words to make my point?

PROOFREADING

## Proofread Your Draft

Once you have made any revisions to your paragraph that may be needed, proofread your paper to eliminate unnecessary errors, such as dangling or misplaced modifiers.

### Grammar in Action: Eliminate Dangling or Misplaced Modifiers

Modifiers are words and phrases that describe other words. A **dangling modifier** occurs when a writer uses a modifier without including the word that the modifier describes.

- **Dangling modifier:**

  INCORRECT: Entering the museum of shrunken heads, my stomach lurched with queasiness.

  (The missing word is "I": It was I, not my stomach, that entered the museum.)

- **Revised sentence:**

  CORRECT: As I entered the museum of shrunken heads, my stomach lurched with queasiness.

A **misplaced modifier** occurs when a writer separates the modifier from the word it is describing.

- **Misplaced modifier:**

  INCORRECT: Scattering in a million directions, Tyrone hustled to scoop up the spilled ball bearings.

  (The ball bearings scattered, not Tyrone)

- **Revised sentence:**

  CORRECT: Tyrone hustled to scoop up the spilled ball bearings scattering in a million directions.

For more information on dangling and misplaced modifiers, see Chapter 23.

Workshop

PORTFOLIO

# Practice 7

DANGLING AND MISPLACED MODIFIERS

Edit the following student paragraph to eliminate one dangling modifier and two misplaced modifiers.

The Amazing Ruby Falls

(1) The caves at Ruby Falls are one of the wonders of the world, eerie yet intriguing. (2) Our tour group was a small one of about ten people. (3) We all piled onto an elevator, stuffy from all the bodies and stinking like a dirty sock, to sink 250 feet underground. (4) We exited the elevator, gasping for air because of the lack of oxygen and the dampness of the cave. (5) The cave was dark with barely any light. (6) We wore helmets mounted with lights. (7) I looked like a real spelunker. (8) We saw stalactites hanging from the ceiling and stalagmites growing up from the ground. (9) The columns, drapes, and flow stone were phenomenal. (10) We walked through an onyx jungle flowing with layers of limestone. (11) The massive monuments were smooth and damp. (12) Some were slimy like a snail. (13) Water trickled from the ceiling in my hair and down my face, a kiss from the cave. (14) We squeezed through stone pathways littered with rock shapes resembling everything from bacon, to a dragon foot, to a form that looked like New York City, all natural. (15) We came across a huge formation; that appeared to be lifelike; the ice sickle stalactites looked like they could break free and assault us. (16) A breathtaking formation that appeared to be lifelike. (17)The caves are amazing.

More practice with correcting dangling and misplaced modifiers: <www.mywritinglab.com>

## REVIEW OF WRITING A DESCRIPTIVE PARAGRAPH: DEVELOP YOUR POINT USING THE WRITING PROCESS

Review

Use the following form to record your thinking about writing a descriptive paragraph. Select and focus a topic for your writing situation, audience, and purpose.

Choose a person, place, object, or scene and identify its significance.

PREWRITING DRAFTING What is your point?

TOPIC, PERSON, PLACE, OBJECT, OR SCENE: ______________________

AUDIENCE: ______________________

PURPOSE: ______________________

______________________

______________________

PREWRITING DRAFTING State your main idea in a topic sentence.

TOPIC: ______________________

OPINION: ______________________

______________________

______________________

PREWRITING DRAFTING Generate relevant details:

REPORTER'S QUESTIONS: WHO, WHAT, WHERE, WHEN? ______________________

______________________

______________________

______________________

______________________

______________________

PREWRITING DRAFTING Generate sensory details:

LOCATION (TOP, MIDDLE, BOTTOM, LEFT, RIGHT): ____________

____________

SIGHT: ____________

____________

SMELL: ____________

____________

SOUND: ____________

____________

TASTE: ____________

____________

TOUCH: ____________

____________

PREWRITING DRAFTING REVISING Use logical order. Use transition words to signal organization of details and relationships between ideas.

SPACE ORDER: ____________

TIME ORDER: ____________

REVISING PROOFREADING Use effective expression. Choose words for clear, precise meaning.

CONCRETE WORDS THAT SHOW INSTEAD OF TELL: ____________

____________

CORRECTED DANGLING OR MISPLACED MODIFIERS: ____________

____________

Review

# Writing Assignments

## Considering Audience and Purpose

Study the photographs at the beginning of the chapter. Assume you are a member of the Riverwalk business community, and the community leaders have asked you and other interested parties for needed safety improvements along the Riverwalk. Suggest and describe one or more specific safety improvements.

## Writing for Everyday Life

Assume you are separated from your family or loved ones during a holiday or a special occasion. Write a letter in which you describe a significant element of the event. For example, describe the decorations of the season or event, a bride's dress, a favorite birthday gift, or the spread of food at a party or dinner. Choose words that reflect one of the following: (1) approval and enjoyment or (2) disapproval and disappointment.

## Writing for College Life

Assume you are writing a report in your psychology class about how a person's mood is reflected in the clothes he or she chooses on any given day. Describe an outfit that reflects an individual's mood.

## Writing for Working Life

Assume you have invented a product that will make life much easier; also assume that the Small Business Association finances the production and marketing of useful new inventions. Write a paragraph describing your product to submit your idea to the Small Business Association.

More ideas for writing a descriptive paragraph: <www.mywritinglab.com>

# 5 The Narrative Paragraph

**Chapter Preview:**

- What's the Point of Narration?
- Making a Point Using Narration: One Student Writer's Response
- Developing Your Point Using Narration
- Using Narration in Your Academic Courses
- Workshop: Writing a Narration Paragraph Step by Step

## Narration is an account of events told in chronological order to make a specific point.

All of us love a good story. Think of a good story that you have heard, read, or watched on TV or in a theater.

A good story is about personalities or characters, whether real or imagined. A good story is full of vivid action and details. A good story makes a point.

A writer uses narration to tell a story to make a specific point. Often we tell stories to warn about dangers, to teach important lessons, to record important historical events, or to amuse and entertain each other. Narration is a chain of events. These events unfold in chronological order—the order in which they occur. Thus, details follow a logical order based on time. The writer presents an event and then shows when and how each of the subsequent events flows from the first event. In addition to relaying an event, a writer also uses vivid actions and details to show the point of the story. Vivid details may include specific sights, sounds, smells, tastes, textures, feelings, and actions.

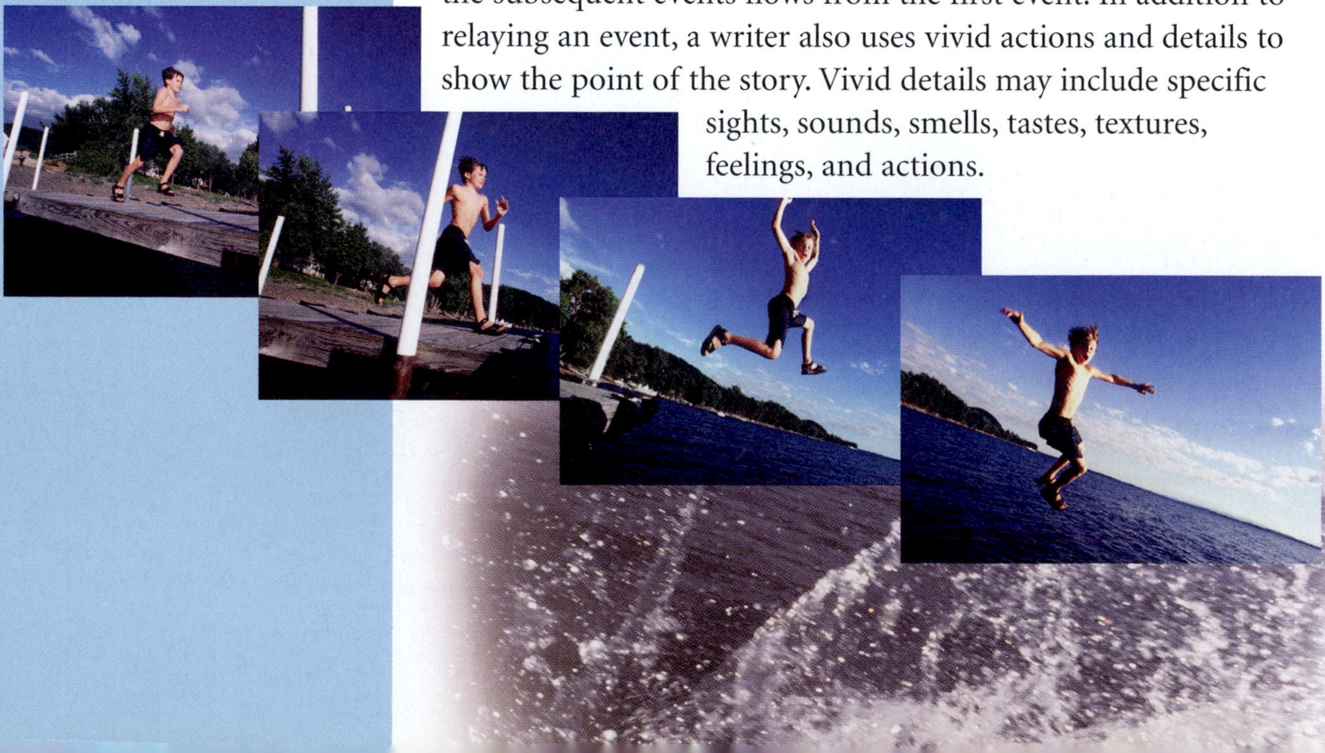

# What's the Point of Narration?

Getting a mental picture of the event helps a writer to discover the point he or she wishes to make. The following sequence of photographs documents a series of events that took place in the life of Jennifer Hudson over the course of three years. Study each photograph in the timeline. Write a caption that states the topic of each picture. Answer the question "What's the point?" with a one-sentence statement of the overall main idea.

WRITING FROM LIFE

Practice 1

PHOTOGRAPHIC ORGANIZER: NARRATION

FIRST EVENT

▲ *American Idol*, April 21, 2004

What happened?

SECOND EVENT

▲ *Dreamgirls*, December 25, 2006

What happened?

THIRD EVENT

◄ *Oscar ceremony*, February 25, 2007

What happened?

**What's the point?**

TOPIC SENTENCE:

## My First Thoughts: A Prewriting Activity

PREWRITING

Set a time limit, such as five minutes, and write in your notebook about the images you just studied. Do not let your pen or pencil stop. Even if you must repeat ideas, keep writing until the time limit is up. Let the ideas flow freely. Getting your first thoughts about a topic on paper is one excellent way to kick-start your writing process.

# Making a Point Using Narration: One Student Writer's Response

The following paragraph offers one writer's narrative inspired by photographs of Jennifer Hudson. Read the narrative paragraph; read the explanations and follow the directions that are given in the annotations of the paragraph. Then, read the writer's journal that describes a few key choices she made as she wrote.

**Chronological Order**
Chronological order is established with the phrase "in the moment."
**Circle four more words or phrases that indicate time order.**

**Main Idea**
The main idea is the point of the narration. Notice the topic is Jennifer Hudson.
**Underline the author's point.**

**Vivid Verbs**
Vivid verbs such as "exploded" creates a mental image and emphasizes action.
**Underline three more vivid verbs.**

**Relevant Details**
Relevant details describe events to support the point about Hudson's success.
**Underline another supporting detail about her success.**

Jennifer Hudson: Achieving a Dream

(1) All of us, at some point in our lives, face the disappointment of failure. (2) And in the moment of disappointment, we are tempted to give up, give in, and settle for less. (3) Fortunately, Jennifer Hudson's story teaches us that success can follow failure. (4) On April 21, 2004, fans booted Hudson off of the third season of *American Idol.* (5) Many critics of the show had expected Hudson, Fantasia Barrino or La Toya London, the other two female African-American power talents, to be the winner. (6) Suddenly, Hudson became the sixth of 12 finalists sent home by the fans. (7) Ultimately, she finished in seventh place. (8) She was a loser. (9) But she didn't give up; she kept on working. (10) For the most part, the general public forgot about Jennifer Hudson, but she did not give in to the pressure. (11) She kept working and looking for the next big break. (12) Then, on December 25, 2006, Hudson exploded back onto the national stage with the release of the smash-hit movie *Dreamgirls*, a film about the struggles of a popular 1960s girl group similar to The Supremes.(13) In the film, Hudson sings a gut-wrenching, show-stopping version of the song "And I Am Telling You I'm Not Going." (14) Her five minute emotional performance pulsed with power. (15) Then, on February 25, 2007, Hudson won the Academy Award for Best Supporting Actress for her role as Effie White in *Dreamgirls*. (16) During her acceptance speech she gushed with gratitude, "thank you all for helping me keep the faith." (17) Jennifer Hudson never gave up, gave in, or settled for less. (18) She offers living proof of success after failure.

## THE WRITER'S JOURNAL

The student writer of "Jennifer Hudson: Achieving a Dream" completed the following reflection to record her thinking through the writing process. Read her writer's journal that describes a few key choices she made as she wrote.

MAIN IDEA: I think that Jennifer Hudson's story shows why American Idol is so popular. It gives ordinary people a shot at becoming rich and famous based on their talent and guts. Yet, for every person who succeeds, hundreds of others fail to achieve their dreams. Hudson seemed to fail on American Idol, yet she came back and showed everybody that "success can follow failure." She is a real inspiration, and that is the main point I wanted to make.

RELEVANT DETAILS: I have watched American Idol from Season One, and I have followed Jennifer Hudson's rise to success because she was on the show. Because I knew so much, I kept putting in details that didn't really relate to my main point. For example, I included this detail in an earlier draft to show how successful Hudson had become: "The film Dreamgirls starred Beyonce Knowles and Eddie Murphy." But it really put more focus on the film, and I wanted to focus on Hudson, during one revision, I decided to delete it.

LOGICAL ORDER: When I read over my first draft, I noticed that the paragraph didn't really flow smoothly. I had used contrast and addition transition words instead of time order words. So I revised to include chronological transitions because this is a narrative. For example, the signal word "suddenly" replaced the contrast signal word "however," and the signal word "ultimately" replaced the addition signal word "and."

EFFECTIVE EXPRESSION (Vivid Verbs): I have a bad habit of using too many verbs like "are," "is," and "was." Our teacher pointed out that too many of these verbs can make a paper boring, and they don't give the reader very much information about the main point. So I revised to replace "to be" verbs with vivid verbs. For example, I revised the verb in sentence 14 from "was powerful" to "pulsed with power." And I revised the verb in sentence 16 from "said" to "gushed with gratitude."

For a blank version of this form for your own reflections about your writing: <www.mywritinglab.com>

During the prewriting phase of writing, a writer naturally generates irrelevant details. In fact, an effective writer often produces far more details than can be used to make a specific point. Irrelevant details do not explain, support, or illustrate the focused point of the paragraph. Often, writers use the revision process to double check details for relevancy and to eliminate irrelevant details.

Practice 5

RELEVANT DETAILS

The following paragraph develops the ideas recorded in the brainstorming list about Aaron Ralston. Circle the main idea. Underline the relevant sensory details. Cross out the two details that are not relevant to the main idea.

The Courage to Survive

(1) Aaron Ralston courageously survived a five-day ordeal. (2) Ralston began his ordeal Saturday morning when he made an attempt to climb over a ten-foot drop between two ledges. (3) Suddenly, an 800-pound rock roared down upon him from above. (4) He quickly scrambled to get out of its path in time. (5) In the next second, the mammoth stone trapped him on the barren rock face. (6) The boulder had smashed and pinned his right hand between it and a sandstone wall. (7) Six-foot-two, lean, and fit, Ralston is an experienced outdoor athlete. (8) He first became interested in climbing in 1996. (9) For five days, Ralston chipped away at the boulder with a pocket knife. (10) Finally, on Tuesday, he ran out of his meager ration of food and water. (11) By Thursday rescue seemed unlikely, so Ralston, parched with thirst, made the gutsy decision to amputate his own hand. (12) Knowing his flimsy pocket knife would not cut through bone, he used the force of the rock to snap his bones just below the elbow. (13) Then after applying a tourniquet, Ralston cut through his own muscles, veins, and arteries. (14) Once he completed the hour long amputation, he rappelled down the mountain. (15) At last, a haggard Ralston hiked out of the canyon.

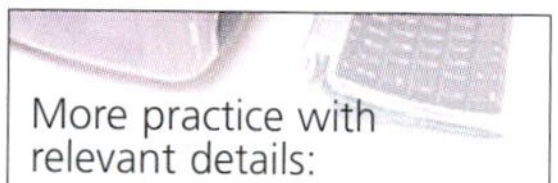

More practice with relevant details: <www.mywritinglab.com>

# Effective Expression: Vivid Verbs

Show; don't tell! Some of the verbs most commonly used by student writers belong to the *to be* family of verbs. However, *to be* verbs such as *am, is, are, was,* and *were* are vague and lifeless. They *tell* instead of *show* action, as in the following sentence: *Ivan was angry*. This sentence tells us about Ivan's emotion, but it doesn't show how he acts when he is angry or how his anger fits into the flow of events.

A writer draws a mental picture for the main idea through the use of vivid verbs.

**Vivid verbs show the action that is taking place:**

Ivan stomped to the trash can and hurled the report into it.

*The verbs "stomped" and "hurled" are biased words. Another witness may have chosen objective language to describe Ivan's actions:*

**Vivid verbs reflect the author's opinion:**

Ivan walked to the trash can and tossed the report into it.

**Vivid verbs express sensory details:**

Ivan snorted with contempt.

Many writers dedicate one full revision to focus on word choices.

## Practice 6

VIVID VERBS

Revise each of the following sentences by replacing *to be* verbs such as *am, is, are, was,* and *were* with vivid verbs.

**1.** The coffee was hot.

---

**2.** Ryanne was injured during the race.

---

**3.** Lance Armstrong was the winner of Tour De France six times.

---

**4.** We were so excited; we were screaming and jumping all around like lunatics.

---

**5.** I am afraid of my next door neighbor's pit bull.

---

Practice 7

VIVID VERBS

Revise the following paragraph by replacing *to be* verbs, such as *are* and *is*, with vivid verbs.

> (1) Robert and his mother, Maxine, are angry at each other again. (2) Seventeen-year-old Robert is sitting silently. (3) His arms are crossed, and he is frowning. (4) His mother is flying around the kitchen; she is slamming the cabinet doors, and pots and pans are rattling. (5) Suddenly, she is yelling at him, and like every other time they fight, Robert leaves.

More practice with vivid verbs: <www.mywritinglab.com>

## Using Narration in Your Academic Courses

Many college courses in subjects such as history, psychology, composition, and literature use narration. As you study these subjects you will read narrations of historical events, case studies, short stories, and novels. In addition, you will write narratives to demonstrate what you have learned. For example, an essay exam may ask you to relate the key events of a major war or the important events in the life of an influential person. Some college writing assignments ask you to draw upon your personal experience and relate it to what you are learning.

# Practice 8

## USING NARRATION IN AN INTERPERSONAL COMMUNICATION ASSIGNMENT

Read the following information from a college communications textbook. On a separate sheet of paper, write a response to the writing assignment, given in the last sentence of the text.

### Ethics in Interpersonal Communication

Because communication has consequences, interpersonal communication involves ethics, a moral aspect of right or wrong. It is believed that there are certain universal ethical principles: you should tell the truth, have respect for another's dignity, and not harm the innocent.

In the U.S. legal system, you have the right to remain silent and to refuse to incriminate yourself. But you don't have the right to refuse to reveal information about the criminal activities of others that you may have witnessed. Psychiatrists and lawyers are often exempt from this general rule. Similarly a wife can't be forced to testify against her husband nor a husband against his wife. In interpersonal situations, however, there aren't any written rules so it's not always clear if or when silence is ethical.

What would you do? While at the supermarket, you witness a mother verbally abusing her three-year-old child. You worry that the mother might psychologically harm the child, and your first impulse is to speak up and tell this woman that verbal abuse can have lasting effects on the child and often leads to physical abuse. At the same time, you don't want to interfere with a mother's right to say what she wants to her child. Nor do you want to aggravate a mother who may later take out her frustration on the child. Write a short narrative that illustrates what you would do in this situation.

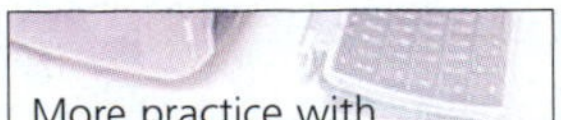

More practice with writing narrative paragraphs: <www.mywritinglab.com>

Workshop

PORTFOLIO

# Workshop: Writing a Narration Paragraph Step by Step

WRITING A NARRATION PARAGRAPH STEP BY STEP

PREWRITING

## Prewriting for Your Paragraph

The various activities that follow will walk you through the steps of the prewriting stage of the writing process: choosing a topic; focusing your point; and generating and organizing relevant details.

### Choose Your Topic

The following activities are designed to help you choose a topic.

1. Create a bank of topics. Use the following headings and either brainstorm or list as many topics as you possibly can. Don't be critical of what you write; just get as many topics written down as quickly as possible. As you think of new topics, add them to the list. Compare your bank of topics with your peers.
   - Heroes
   - Health
   - Pop Culture
   - Memories
2. Generate ideas with a freewrite. Choose one of the topics from your topic bank and think of an event related to the topic. Write about the event for ten minutes without stopping. Include sensory details: sight, sound, smell, taste, and touch.
3. Select a photograph of a special event. Write a caption, brainstorm topics, and freewrite about the photograph. Remember to ask, "What happened?" and "What's the point?" as you generate ideas.

### Focus Your Point

Read a freewrite you have generated for a narrative. Underline words that suggest your values, opinions, or attitudes about the event. Think about what interests you about the event. Use a thesaurus and choose several vivid words to express your thoughts. Identify your audience and purpose. Write a list of vivid verbs that show the actions that occur during the event. State in one sentence the point of the story you are going to tell.

AUDIENCE: ______________________________

______________________________

PURPOSE: ______________________________

______________________________

VIVID VERBS: ______________________________

______________________________

WHAT'S THE POINT? ______________________________

______________________________

## Generate and Organize Relevant Details

Using ideas you have recorded so far and the time line graphic, generate and organize details that support your point.

**What's the point?**

TOPIC SENTENCE: ______________________________

______________________________

______________________________

______________________________

**What happened?**

| |
|---|
| 1 |
| 2 |
| 3 |
| 4 |
| 5 |

DRAFTING

## Write a Draft of Your Paragraph

Using the ideas you generated during the prewriting phase, compose a draft of your paragraph. Return to the prewriting process at any time to generate additional details as needed. Use your own paper.

REVISING

## Revise Your Draft

Once you have created a draft of a narrative, read it and answer the following questions. Indicate your answers by annotating your paper. If you answer "yes" to a question, underline, check, or circle examples. If you answer "no" to a question, write additional details in the margins and draw lines to indicate their placement. Revise your paragraph based on your reflection. (*Hint:* Experienced writers create several drafts as they focus on one or two questions per draft.)

Workshop

PORTFOLIO

## Questions for Revising a Narrative Paragraph:

- ☐ Have I stated or implied a focused main idea? Have I created a strong impression? Can I state my point in one sentence?
- ☐ Is the logical order of the events clear? Have I used strong transitions to indicate time? And space?
- ☐ Have I made my point with adequate details?
- ☐ Do all the details support my point?
- ☐ Have I used vivid verbs to keep my readers interested in what I am saying? Have I used sensory details to make my point?
- ☐ What impact will my paragraph make on my reader?

For more information on correcting unnecessary shifts in verb tense, see Chapter 19.

PROOFREADING

## Proofread Your Draft

Once you have made any revisions to your paragraph that may be needed, proofread your paragraph to eliminate careless errors such as shifts in verb tense.

### Grammar in Action: Unnecessary Shifts in Verb Tense

Verb tense tells your reader when an event occurred. "Sandra laughed" is past tense. "Sandra laughs" is present tense. "Sandra will laugh" is future tense. A shift in tense for no logical reason is confusing to the reader.

- **A Shift in Verb Tense:**

  INCORRECT: Jennifer sighed loudly, rolled her eyes, and stomps off angrily.

- **Consistent Use of Tense:**

  CORRECT: Jennifer sighs loudly, rolls her eyes, and stomps off angrily.

PORTFOLIO

## Workshop Practice 9

TENSE SHIFTS

Edit these sentences for unnecessary shifts in tense.

1. Raul works two jobs and attends a community college. He wanted to become a registered nurse and join the Peace Corps.

TENSE SHIFTS

2. Hurricane Ivan destroyed property along the coast in Pensacola, Florida. The hurricane force winds and waves would batter hotels to pieces and rip roofs off restaurants and homes.

3. Vitali and Carl had fun at the Daytona 500 race. They always pay to sit in the infield. They will grill hamburgers and hot dogs. As they ate, they watched the cars zoom around them.

4. Joe and Jarvonna had a wonderful first date. Joe makes reservations at the Japanese Steak House. After dinner, he surprises her with tickets to watch her favorite team, the Orlando Magic, play the Miami Heat. On the way home, Jarvonna suggested stopping for coffee. Losing track of time, the two talk for hours.

More practice with correcting unnecessary shifts in verb tense: <www.mywritinglab.com>

Practice 9

# Review

## REVIEW OF WRITING A NARRATIVE PARAGRAPH: DEVELOP YOUR POINT USING THE WRITING PROCESS

Use the following form to record your thinking about writing a narrative paragraph. Select and focus a topic for your writing situation, audience, and purpose. Choose a person, place, object, or scene and identify its significance.

PREWRITING DRAFTING What is your point?

TOPIC, SITUATION, OR EVENT: ______________________________

AUDIENCE: ______________________________

PURPOSE: ______________________________

______________________________

PREWRITING DRAFTING State your main idea in a topic sentence.

TOPIC: ______________________________

OPINION: ______________________________

______________________________

PREWRITING DRAFTING Generate relevant details.

REPORTER'S QUESTIONS: WHO, WHAT, WHEN, WHERE, WHY, AND HOW? ______________________________

______________________________

______________________________

SENSORY DETAILS: ______________________________

______________________________

PREWRITING DRAFTING REVISING Use logical order. Use transition words to signal organization of details and relationships between ideas.

SPACE ORDER: ______________________________

TIME ORDER: ______________________________

More ideas for writing a narrative paragraph: <www.mywritinglab.com>

Review

REVISING PROOFREADING Use effective expression. Choose words for clear, precise meaning.

VIVID VERBS: ____________________

CONSISTENT VERB TENSE: ____________________

____________________

# Writing Assignments

## Considering Audience and Purpose

Study the sequence of photographs of Jennifer Hudson at the beginning of the chapter. Assume the pictures are to be used to document her achievements on a website designed to promote her career. Write a narrative that will be recorded as a voice-over and heard as the pictures flash on the screen.

## Writing for Everyday Life

Assume you or someone you know recently took action in an emergency situation. Write a paragraph for a letter to a friend relaying the event as it unfolded. Choose words that reflect one of the following: (1) approval of a courageous act or (2) concern for a foolish act.

## Writing for College Life

Assume you have witnessed an important historical event such as the invention of the wheel, the first flight into space, landing on the moon, the last battle fought in the Civil War, or 9/11. Write a paragraph for a local paper documenting the event as it occurred.

## Writing for Working Life

Assume you are filing for worker's compensation for an injury that occurred on the job. Write a paragraph for a report to your supervisor in which you record the events as they occurred.

# 6 The Process Paragraph

**Chapter Preview**

- What's the Point of Process?
- Making a Point Using Process: One Student Writer's Response
- Developing Your Point Using Process
- Using Process in Your Academic Courses
- Workshop: Writing a Process Paragraph Step by Step

## A process is a series of steps, occurring in chronological order.

Every day we repeat countless processes, from cooking a meal to flossing our teeth. Effective use of processes allows us to perform efficiently in every aspect of our lives. In our personal lives, we follow specific processes to file our taxes or enhance our health. In our professional lives, most of us go through an interview process to secure a job and an evaluation process to get a raise. In our academic lives, we follow set procedures to enroll in classes, learn, and achieve high GPAs.

A process may describe the steps necessary to complete a task such as changing a tire, activating an iPod, or creating a web page. A process may also describe the phases, stages, or cycle of a recurring event such as the phases of the moon, the stages of human development, or the cycle of grief. To write a process paragraph, a writer identifies and explains the logical time order of the individual steps or stages in the task or cycle. An effective process also relies heavily on concrete descriptive details and vivid images so the reader can mentally see the process as it unfolds.

# What's the Point of Process?

Visualizing a process helps a writer discover his or her point about the procedure. The following sequence of photographs documents a series of steps in a set of Pilates exercises called "spine stretch and roll like a ball." Study each photograph in the time line. Write a caption that briefly describes each picture.

WRITING FROM LIFE

Practice 1

**PHOTOGRAPHIC ORGANIZER: PROCESS**

STEP ONE

What is happening?

STEP TWO

What is happening?

STEP THREE

What is happening?

STEP FOUR

What is happening?

**What's the point?**

PREWRITING

## My First Thoughts: A Prewriting Activity

Set a time limit, such as five minutes, and write in your notebook about the images you just studied. Do not let your pen or pencil stop. Even if you must repeat ideas, keep writing until the time limit is up. Let the ideas flow freely. Getting your first thoughts about a topic on paper is one excellent way to overcome writer's block and set your mind to thinking.

# Making a Point Using Process: One Student Writer's Response

The following paragraph offers one writer's point about the set of exercises depicted in the photographs. Read the process and the explanations; answer the questions. Then, read the writer's journal that records decisions made during the writing process. Answer the question "What's the point?"

**Main Idea:** The main idea is the point the author is making about the topic. The topic is "an exercise sequence." **Underline the author's point about this topic.**

**Chronological Order:** The transition "First" signals time order. **Circle four more time order signal words.**

**Effective Expression:** Vivid details such as "sitting tall and straight… as if you were sitting next to a wall" creates a mental picture for the reader. **Draw a box around two more vivid descriptive details.**

**Relevant Details:** Relevant details explain specific steps that build strength and flexibility. Strength is required to curve the spine and pull in the stomach. **Underline a step in the process that builds flexibility.**

Spine Stretch and Roll Like a Ball

(1) "Spine stretch and roll like a ball" is an exercise sequence that builds strength and flexibility in the core area of your body supported by the spine. (2) First, assume the proper starting position. (3) Begin by sitting tall and straight on your mat as if you were sitting next to a wall. (4) Open your legs slightly wider than hip-width apart, placing your heels on the outside edges of the mat. (5) Pull your navel up and in. (6) Extend your arms at shoulder height parallel to your legs and flex your feet, pressing through your heels and pointing your toes toward the ceiling. (7) Next, tighten your buttocks and round your torso up and over. (8) Continually press your lower back behind you and scoop in your abdominals. (9) As you deepen the curve of your spine, press your navel further in as if it could kiss your spine. (10) Imagine your body forming a U-shape. (11) Once you are fully extended, hang your head between your shoulders, and hold the stretch. (12) To roll like a ball from this position, bend your knees and draw both ankles toward the core of your body and balance on your sit bones. (13) Grasp an ankle in each hand; pull your feet close to your buttocks, and place your head snugly between your knees. (14) Imagine your body taking the shape of a small, tight C. (15) Then, inhale and roll back. (16) As you roll, keep your feet close to your body and your head tucked between your knees. (17) Roll until you are balanced on your shoulder blades, but do not roll onto your neck. (18) Throughout the roll, maintain your C-shape and keep your navel pressed into your spine. (19) Finally, exhale as you roll back into your starting position.

## THE WRITER'S JOURNAL

The student of "Spine Stretch and Roll Like a Ball" completed the following reflection to record his thinking through the writing process. Read his writer's journal that describes a few key choices he made as he wrote.

MAIN IDEA: *I loved writing this paragraph about exercising! I decided to assume the role of a coach who was writing an article for a fitness newsletter so I could directly address the reader using the pronoun "you" in an instructional tone.*

RELEVANT DETAILS: *As a prewriting activity, I carefully observed the posture of the woman in each photo sequence and listed concrete descriptive details of how her body was arranged in space in each photograph. I made a separate list for each photograph. By doing so, I found that I needed to explain that each of the four steps is actually made up of several movements. For example, the first step "assume the proper starting position" is made up of three movements. I also drew on my own personal experience of performing similar exercises to generate details suggested by the images. For example, I knew that her flattened stomach was evidence that she had contracted her stomach muscles by pulling her navel in toward her spine.*

LOGICAL ORDER: *I used my first draft to capture the order of steps represented by each photograph. Then, when I revised, I inserted the time order transitions "first" and "next" to indicate the first two major steps of the exercise sequence. As I revised, it occurred to me that the four steps could be divided into two phases. Phase 1 describes the process of the spine stretch, and phase 2 describes the process of rolling like a ball. So, I used the transitional phrase "to roll like a ball from this position" to signal the beginning of the third step of moving from the spine stretch into the roll. I used the transition "then" to signal the fourth step of the exercise. The transition "finally" signals my conclusion.*

EFFECTIVE EXPRESSION: *I was surprised by how much I needed to rely on descriptive words to fully explain the process. I think concrete, vivid expressions such as "kiss your spine," "forming a V-shape," and "a tight, small C" add interest and help the reader understand the process.*

# Developing Your Point Using Process

A process shows how to do something or how something works. To describe a process, a writer uses chronological order (also called time order), relevant concrete descriptive details, and vivid images.

## The Point: The Main Idea

When you write a process paragraph, you limit your topic to a specific set of details based on time order. Most likely, you also have an opinion or point of view about the process, and this opinion or attitude is your point or main idea. A topic sentence states the point or purpose of the steps, directions, or phases.

For example, the following topic sentence contains (1) the topic, (2) the writer's opinion about the topic, and (3) the pattern of organization used to organize details.

The topic is *grief.* The writer's opinion is stated with the phrase *emotional work* and time order is established with the phrases *the six phases* and *in progress.*

| The six phases | of grief | represent an emotional work | in progress. |
|---|---|---|---|
| PATTERN OF ORGANIZATION: TIME ORDER | TOPIC | AUTHOR'S OPINION | PATTERN OF ORGANIZATION: TIME ORDER |

The above chart illustrates the relationship of the topic, the author's opinion, and the pattern of organization in this particular topic sentence. Note that the phrase *the six phases of grief* combines the topic and the pattern of organization.

Practice 2

**TOPIC SENTENCES**

Practice creating topic sentences. The first two items present a topic, an opinion, and time order signal word(s). Combine the ideas in each group to create a topic sentence for a process. Complete the practice by making your own topic sentences.

**1.** TOPIC: Test-taking anxiety

OPINION: can be overcome

TIME ORDER SIGNAL WORDS: in several steps

TOPIC SENTENCE: ______

**2.** TOPIC: Checking the oil and changing the oil in a car

OPINION: easy and quick

TIME ORDER SIGNAL WORDS: process

TOPIC SENTENCE: ______

______

More practice with creating topic sentences: <www.mywritinglab.com>

**3.** TOPIC: Sexual harassment

OPINION: important to report

TIME ORDER SIGNAL WORDS: company procedures

TOPIC SENTENCE: 

**4.** TOPIC: 

OPINION: 

TIME ORDER SIGNAL WORDS: 

TOPIC SENTENCE: 

**5.** TOPIC: 

OPINION: 

TIME ORDER SIGNAL WORDS: 

TOPIC SENTENCE: 

**6.** TOPIC: 

OPINION: 

TIME ORDER SIGNAL WORDS: 

TOPIC SENTENCE: 

**7.** TOPIC: 

OPINION: 

TIME ORDER SIGNAL WORDS: 

TOPIC SENTENCE: 

Practice 2

More practice with creating topic sentences: <www.mywritinglab.com>

## Logical Order

Once you have selected your topic and focused on a main idea, you are ready to generate additional details and organize your ideas into a logical sequence based on time order. A process describes the individual actions that make up each step or phase within the process. Just as time order words in the topic sentence signal a process, time order transition words show the flow of events as the process unfolds. Strong transitions establish coherence, a clear and understandable flow of ideas.

### Transition Words Used to Show Time Order

| | | | | |
|---|---|---|---|---|
| after | during | later | previously | ultimately |
| afterward | eventually | meanwhile | second | until |
| as | finally | next | since | when |
| before | first | now | soon | while |
| currently | last | often | then | |

## Practice 3

TIME ORDER

The following information appears in the safety publication *How to Survive a Submerging Car* sponsored by the Florida Highway Patrol. Determine the logical order of the sentences. Rewrite the paragraph, organizing the details by chronological order. *Hint:* Underline the time order transition words. Complete the exercise by answering the question "What's the point?"

Save Your Life: P.O.G.O. a Sinking Car

........ Although the window should open, do not waste time trying to open the door because the water pressure will keep the doors firmly shut.

........ Then, while the car is still floating, **get out**; crawl through the opened window and swim to shore.

........ The first thing to do in a floating car is to **push** the button to unbuckle your seatbelt.

........ Next, **open** the window; electric windows should still work while the car is floating.

........ When a car plunges into a lake or river, it should float for about three minutes, giving you enough time to safely exit the car before it sinks.

Practice 3

........ P.O.G.O. stands for Push, Open, and Get Out.

........ Once the car sinks, the P.O.G.O. method still works.

........ Wait until the water reaches your neck so that the water pressure inside and outside the car are equal.

........ In a submerged car, first **push** the button that releases your seatbelt.

........ Finally, **get out**; push yourself out of the car and quickly swim to the surface.

........ Then, **open** your car door.

**What's the point?**

.................................................................................................

.................................................................................................

More practice with time order: <www.mywritinglab.com>

## Relevant Details

As a writer narrows a topic into a focused main idea about a process, the thinking process brings to mind many details of time and space. A writer evaluates the relevance of each detail and uses only those that illustrate the main idea. Some relevant details show the action of the process; other details explain the author's opinion about the process. Relevant details also include vivid descriptive and sensory details. These details work together to create a vivid mental image of the author's main point about the process. During the prewriting phase, a time line can help a writer organize ideas as they are generated. Study the following time line used to generate details about the phases of grief.

**The Six Phases of Grief**

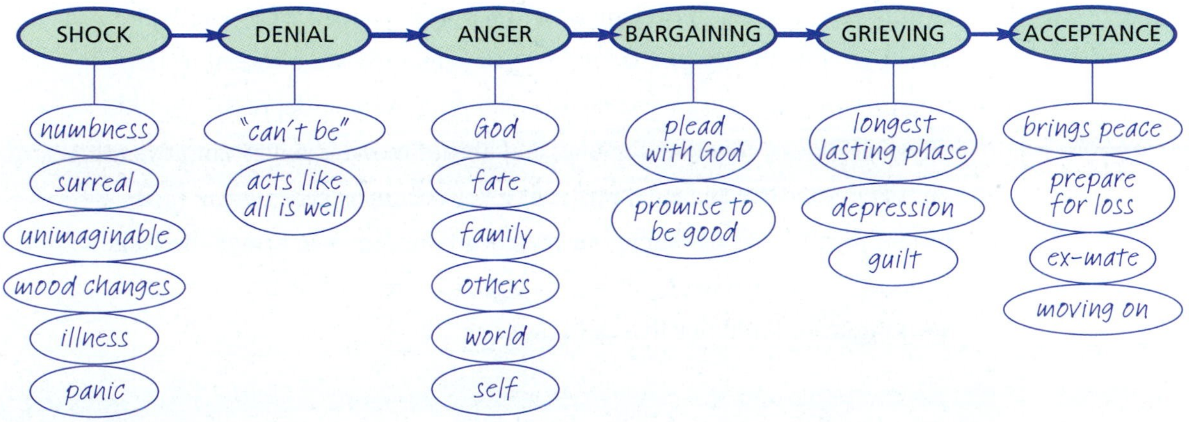


During the prewriting phase of writing, a writer naturally generates irrelevant details. In fact, an effective writer often produces far more details than can be used to make a specific point. Irrelevant details do not explain, support, or illustrate the focused point of the paragraph. A careful writer uses the revision process to double check details for relevancy and to eliminate irrelevant details.

## Practice 4

RELEVANT DETAILS

The following paragraph develops the ideas recorded in the brainstorming list about the six phases of grief. Circle the main idea. Underline at least three concrete details. Cross out the two details that are not relevant to the main idea.

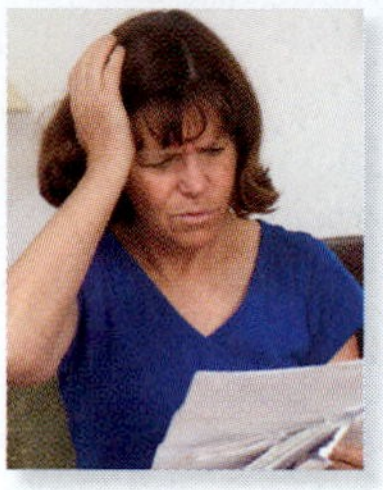

### The Phases of Grief

(1) In her book, *On Death and Dying*, Dr. Elizabeth Kübler-Ross explains the phases of grief we experience when we learn that a loved one is terminally ill. (2) The six phases of grief represent an emotional work in progress. (3) The first phase is shock. (4) During this initial phase, we experience a fog of numbness; life seems surreal as it crumbles around us, and the chore ahead of us seems unimaginable. (5) Throughout the second phase, denial, we work hard to erect the illusion that recovery is possible or that life is still normal. (6) We simply think, "This can't be happening to me." (7) Once we move past denial, we then grapple with the third phase of grief—anger. (8) We aim our anger at God, fate, doctors, family, the world, or even ourselves. (9) Thoughts such as "If only I had…" or "How can others just go on with their lives?" occupy our minds. (10) During traumas such as divorce, we often become angry with our ex-mate. (11) During the fourth phase, known as bargaining, we negotiate with God to cure the problem in exchange for our good behavior. (12) The fifth phase, usually the longest lasting, is grieving. (13) We often labor in mourning for months or years. (14) Chipping away at depression, guilt, physical illness, loneliness, panic, and abrupt mood changes employs all our energies. (15) The final phase of grief occurs as acceptance. (16) Often, for those of us facing our own death, acceptance brings the wage of peace. (17) As survivors of loss, such as divorce, we usually find ourselves working to re-build our lives and move on.

More practice with relevant, concrete details: <www.mywritinglab.com>

## Effective Expression: Vivid Images

Show; don't tell! Create vivid word pictures that deepen your reader's understanding of your point. Two figures of speech create vivid images: simile and metaphor.

A **simile** is an indirect comparison between two different ideas or things that uses *like, as, as if,* or *as though.*

**Example:**

As Robin crossed the finish line, his legs pumped like pistons.

A **metaphor** is a direct comparison between two different ideas or things that does *not* use *like, as, as if,* or *as though.* Often a metaphor uses words such as *is, are,* or *were* to make the direct comparison between the two ideas.

**Example:**

As Robin crossed the finish line, his legs were pumping pistons.

Practice 5

VIVID IMAGES

Revise each of the following sentences to create vivid images by using similes and metaphors suggested by the photos. Discuss your work with your class or in a small group of your peers.

**1.** To ensure a healthful serving size, limit meat portions to 3 ounces.

**2.** Adolescence is a stage of human development made up of great change leading to adulthood.

More practice with vivid images: <www.mywritinglab.com>

3. A successful election campaign is based on a series of strategic decisions.

4. Overcoming addiction requires one to understand and control dangerous inner emotions.

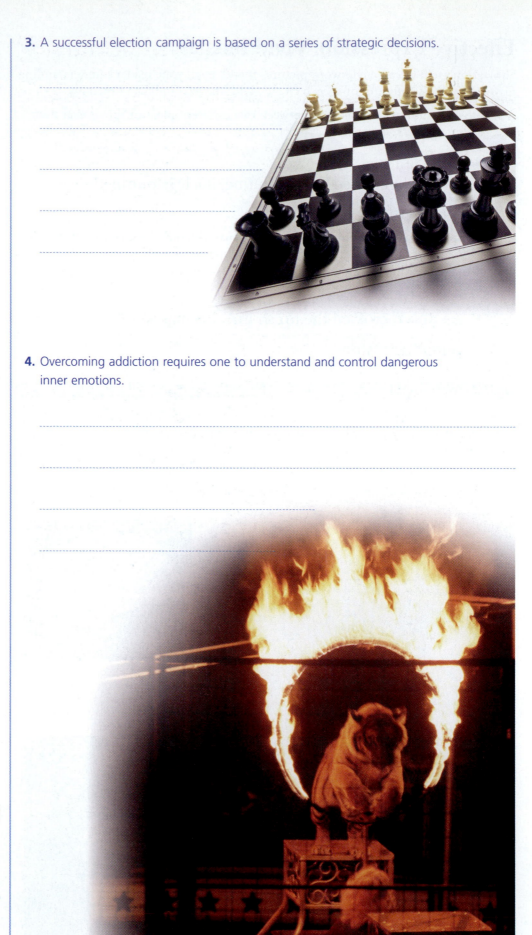

# Using Process in Your Academic Courses

Many college courses such as biology, ecology, history, political science, psychology, and composition use process in their discussions. As you study these courses you will learn about processes involving the physical world, mental health, government, and writing. In addition, you will record processes to learn or demonstrate what you have learned. For example, a science lab may require you to conduct an experiment, record the steps you took, and evaluate the process. Some college writing assignments ask you to reflect upon your personal writing process so you can strengthen your writing skills.

## Practice 6

**USING PROCESS IN A COMPOSITION ASSIGNMENT**

During a composition class, a student wrote the following paragraph in her writer's journal to reflect upon the effectiveness of her writing process. Assume you are her peer editor, and, based on what you have learned in this chapter about writing a process and in Chapter 2 about the writing process, offer advice about her writing process.

*Kristen Elizabeth Spengler*
*Writing 101*
*September 27, 2007*

*My Writer's Journal: My Writing Process*

*(1) I start my writing process by mapping. (2) I make what is like a spider web with one basic idea in the middle of the page and supporting ideas branching off all around it. (3) After brainstorming for a while, I go on the computer and put the ideas I came up with into sentences. (4) Usually, I like to lay it all out on the computer and print it out because it is easier for me to see it while I'm typing my draft. (5) After I type up all the ideas I brainstormed, I write my paragraph, print it out, and turn it in.*

More practice with writing process paragraphs: <www.mywritinglab.com>

PORTFOLIO

Workshop

# Workshop: Writing a Process Paragraph Step by Step

WRITING A PROCESS PARAGRAPH STEP BY STEP

PREWRITING

## Prewrite Your Paragraph

The various activities below will walk you through the steps of the prewriting stage of the writing process: choosing a topic; focusing your point; and generating and organizing relevant details.

### Choose Your Topic

The following activities are designed to help you choose a topic.

**1.** Create a bank of topics. Use the following headings and brainstorm or list as many processes about each topic as you possibly can. Don't criticize your thoughts; just get as many relevant processes written down as quickly as possible. Compare your bank of topics with those of your peers.

- Recycling Trash
- Auditioning
- Studying
- Training an Animal

**2.** Generate ideas with a freewrite. Choose one of the topics from your topic bank and think of the steps necessary to complete the process. Write about the process for ten minutes without stopping.

**3.** Select a photograph or series of photographs that illustrate a process. Write captions; brainstorm steps, directions, or phases; and freewrite about the photograph(s). Remember to ask, "What is happening?" and "What's the point?" as you generate ideas.

### Focus Your Point

Read a freewrite you have generated for a process. Underline words that suggest your values, opinions, or attitudes about the process. Use a thesaurus and choose several vivid words to express your thoughts. Think about why the steps are important. Identify your audience and purpose. Create a list of concrete details and vivid images that show the actions that occur during the process. State in one sentence the point of the process:

AUDIENCE: ..........

PURPOSE: ..........

..........

WHAT'S THE POINT? ..........

..........

..........

## Generate and Organize Relevant Details

Using ideas you have recorded so far and the process flowchart, generate and organize details that support your point.

**What's the point?**

TOPIC SENTENCE: ______________________________

______________________________

______________________________

**What is happening?**

**First Step**

↓

**Second Step**

↓

**Third Step**

↓

**Fourth Step**

## DRAFTING Write a Draft of Your Paragraph

Using the ideas you generated during the prewriting phase, compose a draft of your process paragraph. Return to the prewriting process at any time to generate additional details as needed. Use your own paper.

## REVISING Revise Your Draft

Once you have created a draft of a process, read the draft to answer the following questions. Indicate your answers by annotating your paper. If you answer "yes" to a question, underline, check, or circle examples. If you answer "no" to a question, write needed information in margins and draw lines to indicate placement of additional details. Revise your paragraph as necessary based on your reflection. (*Hint:* Experienced writers create several drafts as they focus on one or two questions per draft.)

Workshop

## Questions for Revising a Process Paragraph

- [ ] Have I stated or implied a focused main idea? Have I created a strong impression? Can I state my point in one sentence?
- [ ] Is the order of the steps, directions, or phases within the process clear? Have I used strong transitions?
- [ ] Have I made my point with adequate details? Have I included only the details that are relevant to my topic sentence?
- [ ] Have I used vivid images to make the process clear to my readers? Have I used concrete details to make my point?

## Proofread Your Draft

Once you have made any revisions to your paragraph that may be needed, proofread your paragraph to eliminate careless errors such as run-on sentences.

### Grammar in Action: Eliminating Run-on Sentences

A **run-on sentence** occurs when two or more independent clauses are punctuated as one sentence. Correct a run-on sentence by applying any of the following four edits: (1) separate independent clauses with a period and capital letter; (2) insert a coordinating conjunction (*and*, *but*, or *nor*, *for*, *so*, or *yet*) and a comma between independent clauses; (3) insert a semicolon between the independent clauses; or (4) insert a semicolon with an appropriate transition between independent clauses.

- **A run-on sentence:**

  Plants take in water through their roots they take in the gas carbon dioxide through their foliage plants use sunlight to turn water and carbon dioxide into food through the process of photosynthesis.

- **Two ways to correct the above run-on sentence:**

**(1)** Plants take in water through their roots, and they take in the gas carbon dioxide through their foliage; plants use sunlight to turn water and carbon dioxide into food through the process of photosynthesis.

ADDED COMMA AND COORDINATING CONJUNCTION "AND" TO SEPARATE INDEPENDENT CLAUSES

ADDED SEMI-COLON TO SEPARATE INDEPENDENT CLAUSES

**(2)** Plants take in water through their roots. In addition, they take in the gas carbon dioxide through their foliage; then, plants use sunlight to turn water and carbon dioxide into food through the process of photosynthesis.

ADDED SEMICOLON AND TRANSITION WORD "THEN" TO SEPARATE INDEPENDENT CLAUSES

ADDED PERIOD TO SEPARATE INDEPENDENT CLAUSES; THE FIRST LETTER OF THE SECOND INDEPENDENT CLAUSE IS NOW CAPITALIZED

For more information on run-ons, see Chapter 21.

## ELIMINATING RUN-ONS

Practice 7

Edit these sentences to eliminate run-ons.

**1.** Using anabolic steroids is a fast way to increase body size some athletes are willing to cheat at a sport they take these steroids to increase body mass beyond what hard work alone could produce.

**2.** Effective questioning occurs in an order that draws out the exact information needed questions should focus on easy-to-answer factual information that puts the person at ease then the interviewer can move to ideas that can't be stated as a fact.

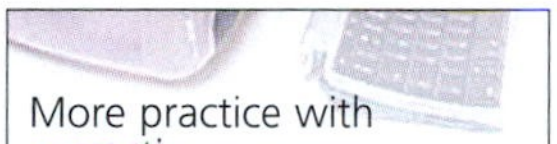

More practice with correcting run-ons: <www.mywritinglab.com>

## REVIEW OF WRITING A PROCESS PARAGRAPH: DEVELOP YOUR POINT USING THE WRITING PROCESS

Review

Use the following form to record your thinking about writing a process paragraph. Select and focus your topic for your writing situation, audience, and purpose. Choose a process made up of several steps or phases and identify its significance.

What is your point?

TOPIC, PROCESS OF STEPS OR PHASES:

AUDIENCE:

PURPOSE:

PREWRITING DRAFTING State your main idea in a topic sentence.

TOPIC: ____________________

____________________

OPINION: ____________________

____________________

____________________

PREWRITING DRAFTING Generate relevant details.

REPORTER'S QUESTIONS: HOW, WHEN, WHAT, WHERE, AND WHO? ____________________

____________________

____________________

DESCRIPTIVE DETAILS: ____________________

____________________

____________________

PREWRITING DRAFTING REVISING Use logical order. Use transition words to signal organization of details and relationship between ideas.

TIME ORDER: ____________________

____________________

SPACE ORDER: ____________________

____________________

____________________

REVISING PROOFREADING Use effective expression. Choose words for clear, precise meaning. Eliminate run-on sentences.

Review

VIVID IMAGES: ........................................

........................................

CORRECTED RUN-ON SENTENCES: ........................................

........................................

........................................





# Writing Assignments

## Considering Audience and Purpose

Study the sequence of photographs about the set of Pilates exercises at the beginning of the chapter. Draft a process paragraph based on one of the following two writing situations:

Assume you are keeping a personal exercise journal. Write a paragraph in which you describe the steps in your exercise sequence. Include the challenges you might face in each phase of the process.

Assume you are an instructor of an exercise class for an elderly group. Think about specific movements in each step of the exercise that might have to be adapted due to poor balance or stiffness of joints. Write a paragraph for the Senior Citizens' Health Club Newsletter that describes the exercises adapted for the elderly.

## Writing for Everyday Life

Assume that a friend or family member has asked you for advice about how to open a bank account; write a paragraph that explains how to do so. Be sure to include information about necessary personal identification and available banking services. Choose words that reflect one of the following: (1) endorsement of the banking services or (2) warning against possible problems.

## Writing for College Life

Assume you are in a college course called Student Success, and you have been assigned to write a brief oral report about how to study. Write a paragraph that records the text for your speech in which you describe the most effective way to take notes during class.

## Writing for Working Life

Assume you are the director of the Human Resources department for a corporation, and you are volunteering your services at a job fair designed to help unemployed citizens secure jobs. You have agreed to teach participants how to handle the interviewing process. Write a paragraph as part of your handout that describes the steps necessary to prepare for an interview.

# 7 The Example Paragraph

**Chapter Preview**

- What's the Point of Examples?
- Making a Point Using Examples: One Student Writer's Response
- Developing Your Point Using Examples
- Using Examples in Your Academic Courses
- Workshop: Writing an Example Paragraph Step by Step

## An example, also called an exemplification, is a specific illustration of a more general idea.

When we communicate – with family members, employers, teachers, or friends – we often use examples to clarify a point we want to make. Think of a situation you were in recently where you used examples to make a point. What makes an example effective?

In everyday life, we illustrate our decorating ideas with paint chips and swatches of fabric. In working life, we offer examples of our hard work and successes when we apply for jobs and promotions. In college life, professors and textbook authors use examples to teach concepts in every discipline.

To write an example paragraph, a writer moves from a general idea to specific examples that support and clarify the main point. Sometimes, as in a science lab report, a writer may present the specific examples first and then come to a general conclusion based on the examples. An effective example paragraph also relies heavily on concrete details, the logical order of importance, and, often, parallel expression.

# What's the Point of Examples?

Generating and organizing examples help a writer to discover his or her point about a particular topic. The following photographs offer three examples of people who have overcome barriers to achieve success. Study each photograph. Write a caption that briefly lists examples of barriers each person might have overcome and examples of the success each has achieved. Then, answer the question, "What's the point?" with a one-sentence statement of the overall main idea.

WRITING FROM LIFE

## Practice 1

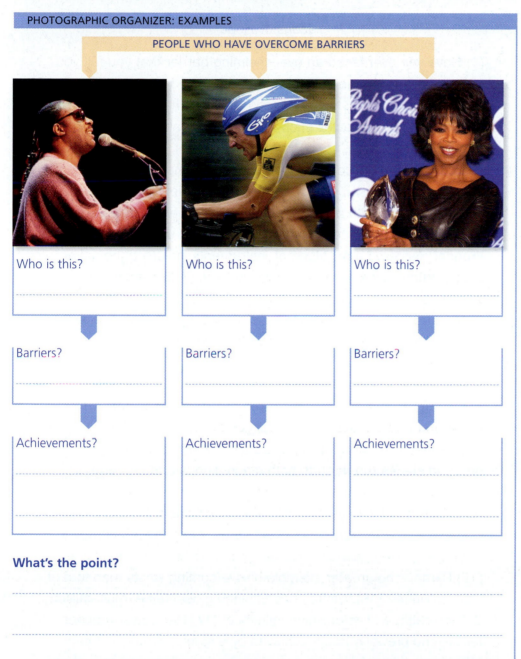

PHOTOGRAPHIC ORGANIZER: EXAMPLES

PEOPLE WHO HAVE OVERCOME BARRIERS

Who is this?

Barriers?

Achievements?

Who is this?

Barriers?

Achievements?

Who is this?

Barriers?

Achievements?

**What's the point?**

PREWRITING

## My First Thoughts: A Prewriting Activity

Set a time limit, perhaps five minutes, and write in your notebook about the images you just studied. Do not let your pen or pencil stop. Even if you must repeat ideas, keep writing until the time limit is up. Let ideas flow freely.

# Making a Point Using Examples: One Student Writer's Response

The following paragraph offers one writer's point about what the people in the photographs exemplify. Read the exemplification. Read the explanations and follow the directions that are given in the annotations of this exemplification paragraph. Then, read the writer's journal entry that records decisions made during the writing process.

**Main Idea:**
The main idea is the point the author is making about the topic. The topic is "those who have overcome." **Underline the author's point about this topic.**

**Listing Order:**
The transitional phrase "for example" signals that the paragraph is developed by examples. **Circle two more transitional phrases that indicate a list of examples.** This paragraph ends with the author's most important example. **Underline the word(s) that suggest the last example is the most important example.**

**Relevant Concrete Details:**
Concrete details list specific examples of each person's successes and barriers. **Draw a box around two more concrete examples of success. Place check marks above an example of a barrier each person faced.**

**Effective Expression:**
Parallelism refers to the way items in a list are worded. To achieve parallelism, a writer uses the same style of wording for a series of items. Using the same form of words in a list makes your ideas easier to follow. **Double underline two more sets of details that are listed in parallel form.**

## Icons of Hope

(1) Have you ever faced an overwhelming barrier that you felt you just couldn't overcome? (2) If so, take heart—you are not alone, and you are not destined to defeat. (3) Others have endured to triumph despite obstacles such as physical disabilities, life-threatening diseases, or poverty and abuse. (4) Those who have overcome serve as icons of hope. (5) For example, singer, songwriter, composer, and instrumentalist Stevie Wonder has inspired millions with albums like *Talking Book* and singles like "Superstition." (6) In addition to his flexible and unique voice, Wonder mastered a multitude of instruments including the guitar, piano, drums, synthesizers, and harmonica. (7) So far he has earned nearly two dozen Grammys and one Academy Award. (8) And he accomplished all this despite being blind since infancy. (9) Another example of hope is professional road bicycle racer Lance Armstrong. (10) Armstrong has won the prestigious Tour de France an historic seven times from 1999 to 2005. (11) According to the official Tour de France website, the three week bike race, consisting of around 20 stages, ranges from 1800 to 2500 miles in total length. (12) Riders complete each stage in the course of one day, and stages run through both mountainous and flat terrain. (13) Though the race itself is a testimony to endurance, Armstrong's achievement offers hope to millions fighting cancer. (14) In 1996, Armstrong underwent surgery and chemotherapy to treat the testicular cancer that had spread to his brain and lungs. (15) Perhaps no greater example of overcoming exists than that of Oprah Winfrey. (16) Winfrey has attained global fame, multi-million dollar wealth, and astonishing influence. (17) Her power reaches far beyond previous levels achieved by a single working woman. (18) Her numerous awards document her excellence as talk show host, actor, producer, editor, and humanitarian. (19) Born to poverty in Mississippi and sexually molested as a young girl, Winfrey emerged into success out of adversity. (20) The next time you feel overwhelmed, remember Stevie, Lance, and Oprah—all icons of success, determination, and hope.

## THE WRITER'S JOURNAL

The student writer of "Icons of Hope" completed the following reflection to record her thinking about the writing process. Read her writer's journal that describes a few key choices she made as she wrote.

MAIN IDEA: *Writing this paragraph took longer than I thought it would. Because I already knew so much about each of these individuals, my brainstorming process produced a lengthy time order list of examples of their challenges and successes. However, when I began my first draft, I kept choosing words that focused on the effects of their barriers and the causes of their successes. So I ditched that draft and began again with my list of examples by my elbow. This draft seemed more like mini-biographies or narratives rather than a paragraph of examples. So I went back to brainstorming. Then, I realized, aha, I didn't have a purpose or audience for the paragraph. I had plenty of details, really more than I could use in one paragraph, but without a purpose and audience, I struggled with the order of ideas and wording. So I decided to assume the role of a an advice columnist for a women's magazine like "Redbook" or "Woman's World." My purpose was to encourage discouraged readers with examples of people who had overcome obstacles—each of us can reach our potential despite any barrier life may present.*

LOGICAL ORDER: *Now that I had a purpose, I could finally break away from time order. So I rearranged the details using order of importance for impact: moving from least important to most important examples. The accomplishments of these people take on a deeper meaning when considered in the light of the barriers they faced, so I began with examples of each one's success and ended with examples of each one's barrier. Deciding whom to list first was tough. Blindness, cancer, poverty and sexual abuse are all important and difficult to overcome. However, because I had chosen women as my main audience, I wanted to end with Oprah, so I created the following outline:*

For a blank version of this form for your own reflections about your writing: <www.mywritinglab.com>

Topic: Icons of Hope

A. Introduction and topic sentence

B. Stevie Wonder (Major Supporting Detail)

1. Examples of accomplishments (Minor Supporting Detail)

2. Example of barrier (Minor Supporting Detail)

C. Lance Armstrong (Major Supporting Detail)

1. Examples of accomplishments (Minor Supporting Detail)

2. Example of barrier (Minor Supporting Detail)

D. Oprah Winfrey (Major Supporting Detail)

1. Examples of accomplishments (Minor Supporting Detail)

2. Example of barriers (Minor Supporting Detail)

RELEVANT DETAILS: Once the organization jelled, I eliminated irrelevant details. For example, I deleted the details about the charity work of these public figures.

EFFECTIVE EXPRESSION: During several revisions, I focused on word choice. I chose the word "icon" as a synonym for "example." I signaled each major detail with listing and example signal words. And I revised to take advantage of the power of parallel language. For example, the last sentence originally stated, "The next time you feel overwhelmed, remember Stevie, Lance, and Oprah—each one examples of hope, people who have reached success through determination."

# Developing Your Point Using Examples

An exemplification illustrates a main point with one or more examples. To exemplify a point, a writer lists the examples, often according to the order of importance; explains each example with relevant concrete details; and often uses parallel expression.

## The Point: The Main Idea

When you write an exemplification, you limit your topic to a set of specific examples, instances, or cases. Most likely, you also have an opinion or point of view about the examples, and this opinion or attitude is your point or main idea. You may reveal your opinion by listing the examples in a particular order of importance. A topic sentence states the point or purpose of the examples.

For example, the following topic sentence contains (1) the topic; (2) the writer's opinion about the topic; and (3) the pattern of organization used to organize details. The topic is *body art.* The pattern of organization is established with the phrase *such as tattooing and piercing* and the verb *exemplifies.* The writer's opinion is stated with the phrase *self-expression.*

TOPIC — PATTERN OF ORGANIZATION: EXEMPLIFICATION

Body art, such as tattooing and piercing, exemplifies self-expression.

WRITER'S OPINION

Sometimes, in an example paragraph, a topic sentence only implies the pattern of organization as in the following version:

Body art offers opportunities for self-expression.

TOPIC — WRITER'S OPINION

When the example pattern of organization is only implied by the topic sentence, then transitions that signal and list examples establish the pattern of organization within the body of the paragraph. Notice in the following example that the two major detail sentences state the topic, pattern of organization, and writer's opinion.

TOPIC SENTENCE

Body art offers opportunities for self-expression.

TOPIC — WRITER'S OPINION

MAJOR DETAIL SENTENCE #1

Tattooing is one example of body art as self-expression.

PATTERN OF ORGANIZATION: EXEMPLIFICATION — TOPIC — WRITER'S OPINION

MAJOR DETAIL SENTENCE #2

Piercing is another example of artistic self-expression.

PATTERN OF ORGANIZATION: EXEMPLIFICATION — TOPIC — WRITER'S OPINION

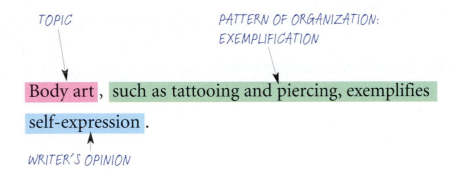

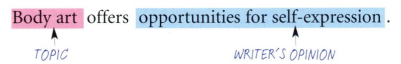

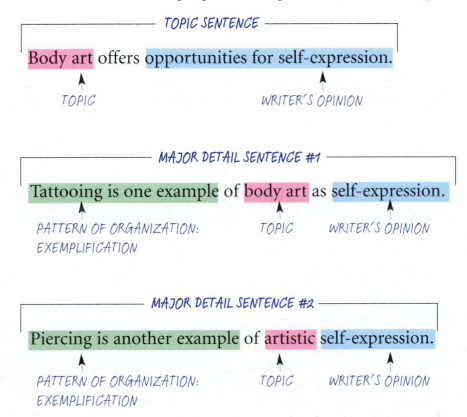

# Practice 2

## TOPIC SENTENCES

The first four items present a topic, an opinion, and example signal word(s). Combine the ideas in each group to create a topic sentence for an example paragraph. Then, complete the practice by making your own topic sentences. (*Hint:* Not all topic sentences for example paragraphs need to include example signal words.)

**1.** TOPIC: Foods OPINION: inflame the condition diverticulitis

EXAMPLE (OR LISTING) SIGNAL WORDS: Certain

TOPIC SENTENCE: ______________________________

______________________________

______________________________

**2.** TOPIC: A friend OPINION: compassion and honesty

EXAMPLE (OR LISTING) SIGNAL WORDS: illustrates

TOPIC SENTENCE: ______________________________

______________________________

______________________________

**3.** TOPIC: Solar energy OPINION: is versatile and cheap

EXAMPLE (OR LISTING) SIGNAL WORDS: not included; only implied

TOPIC SENTENCE: ______________________________

______________________________

______________________________

**4.** TOPIC: SUV drivers OPINION: rugged, aggressive

EXAMPLE (OR LISTING) SIGNAL WORDS: ______________________________

TOPIC SENTENCE: ______________________________

______________________________

______________________________

More practice with creating topic sentences: <www.mywritinglab.com>

**5.** TOPIC: ______________ OPINION: ______________

EXAMPLE (OR LISTING) SIGNAL WORDS: ______________

TOPIC SENTENCE: ______________

______________

**6.** TOPIC: ______________ OPINION: ______________

EXAMPLE (OR LISTING) SIGNAL WORDS: ______________

TOPIC SENTENCE: ______________

______________

**7.** TOPIC: ______________ OPINION: ______________

EXAMPLE (OR LISTING) SIGNAL WORDS: ______________

TOPIC SENTENCE: ______________

______________

Practice 2

## Logical Order

Once you have selected your topic and focused on a main idea, you are ready to generate additional details and list your ideas based on their order of importance. To use examples to illustrate a main point, a writer moves from a general idea to a major support to a minor support. To signal the movement between these levels of ideas, a writer uses transitions to signal or list examples. Strong transitions establish coherence, a clear and understandable flow of ideas.

### Transitions Used to Signal Examples

| | | | |
|---|---|---|---|
| an illustration | for instance | once | to illustrate |
| for example | including | such as | typically |

### Transitions Used to List Examples

| | | | | |
|---|---|---|---|---|
| also | final | for one thing | last of all | second |
| and | finally | furthermore | moreover | third |
| another | first | in addition | next | |
| besides | first of all | last | one | |

Practice 3

LISTING ORDER

The following information was published on a government website for consumer protection. Determine the logical order of the sentences. Complete the exercise by answering the question "What's the point?" Discuss your answers with your class or with a small group of peers.

**Consumer Beware!**

.......... The third and most common example of fraud is phishing.

.......... Phishing is an email message that lures a consumer to a phony website.

.......... The email sender pretends to be from a legitimate government organization, bank, or retailer.

.......... The phishy email stated, "We recently reviewed your account, and we need more information to help us provide you with secure service."

.......... The message also directed the receiver "to visit the Resolution Center and complete the 'Steps to Remove Limitations.'"

.......... A recent instance of phishing came from a phony PayPal site.

.......... A second example of fraud is the phone scam; a caller pretends to represent a trusted organization or company.

.......... In one instance, a caller claims to work for the court and says the listener has been called for jury duty.

.......... The caller then demands personal information such as a social security number, birth date, and credit card numbers.

.......... The first and least common example of fraud is the handyman sting.

.......... The handyman offers to fix the problem, such as replacing a roof or removing a fallen tree, for a cash fee lower than any reputable company could offer.

.......... The handyman shows up on the doorstep of a home in obvious need of repair, usually after severe weather such as a tornado or hurricane.

.......... Most often, the money is paid upfront, and the work is never completed.

**What's the point?**

..............................................................................

..............................................................................

..............................................................................

More practice with listing order: <www.mywritinglab.com>

## Relevant Details

As a writer narrows a topic into a focused main idea, the thinking process brings to mind many details that answer the questions *who, what, when, where, why,* and *how.* A writer evaluates the relevancy of each detail and uses only those that exemplify the main idea. Some relevant details express major examples of the main point; minor details may further illustrate major examples. Some major and minor details may explain the author's opinion about the examples. During the prewriting phase, a list can help a writer organize ideas as they are generated. Study the following list generated about the topic "Examples of State Gun Laws."

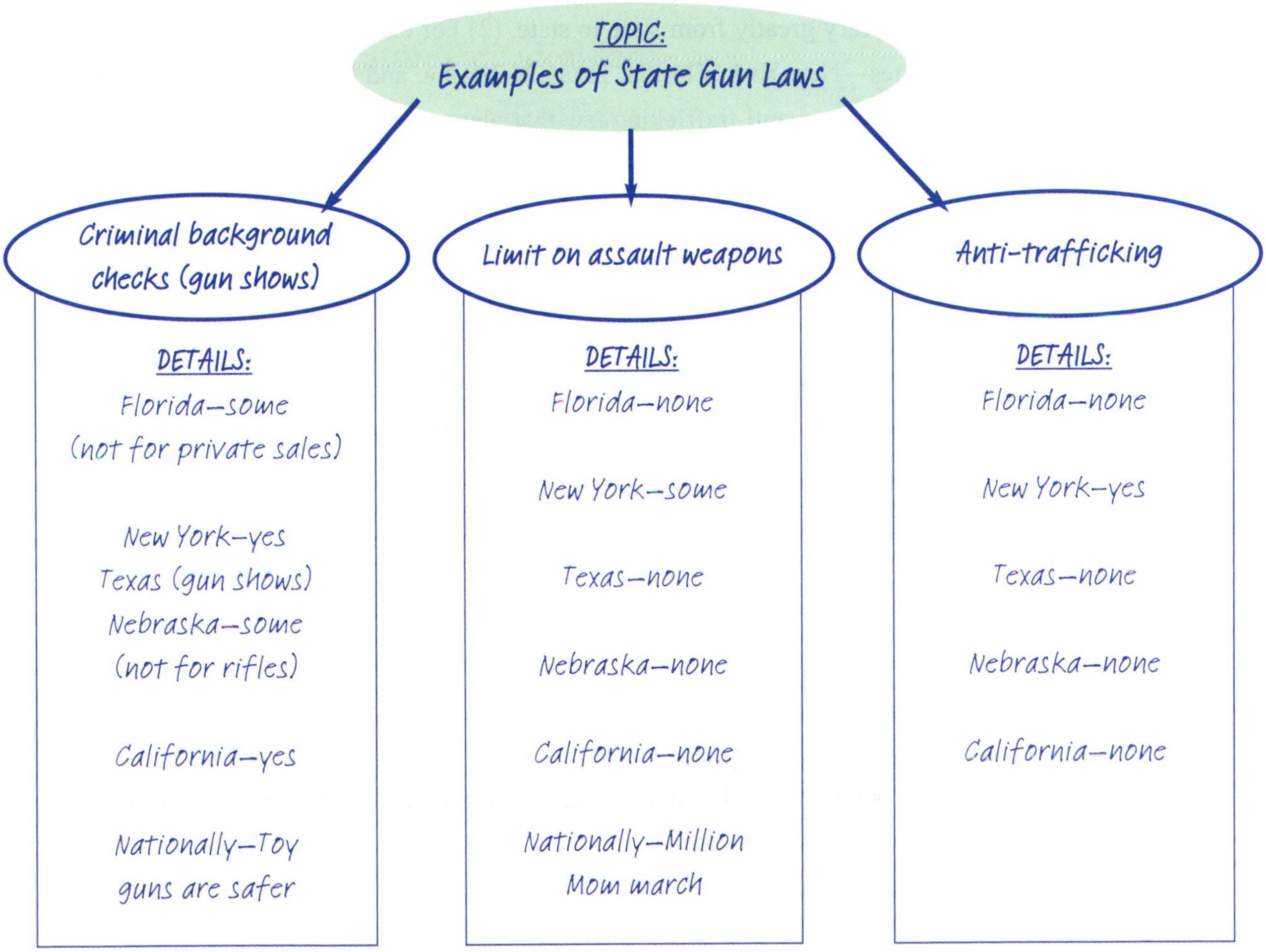


During the prewriting phase of writing, a writer naturally generates irrelevant details. In fact, an effective writer often produces far more details than can be used to make a specific point. Irrelevant details do not exemplify, explain, or support the focused point of the paragraph. A careful writer uses the revision process to double check details for relevancy and to eliminate irrelevant details.

2. A healthy heart lifestyle includes the following: getting plenty of sleep, eating a balanced diet, and regular exercise.

3. In my current position, I am responsible for training new employees, to balance the cash registers, and the work schedules for the week.

4. Tongue piercing is not risk free; for example, a tongue piercing can become infected, cracking a tooth.

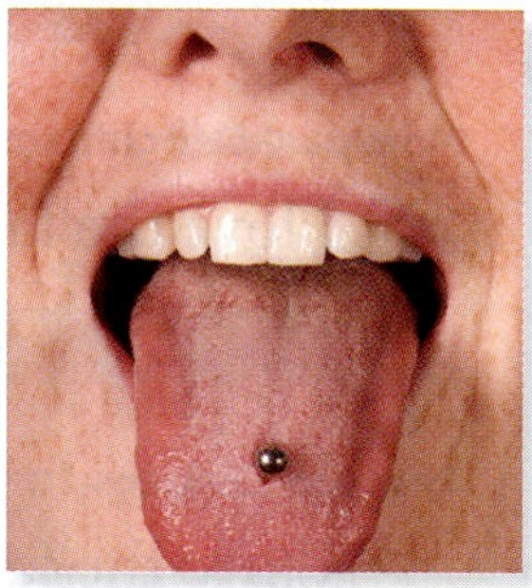

5. The professor gave us a choice between two options for our final exam: a final written exam or giving a ten minute speech with a PowerPoint presentation.

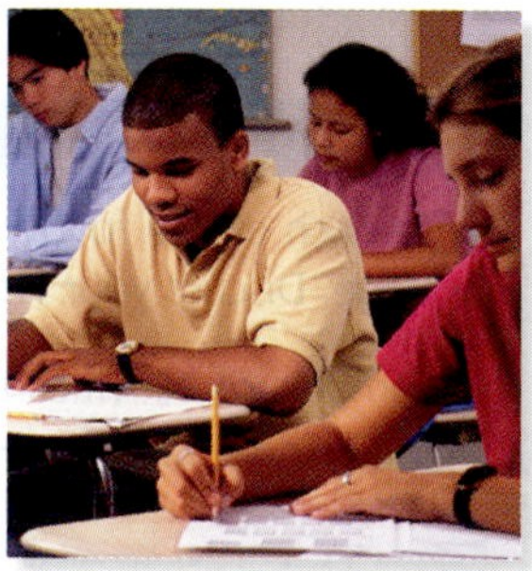

# Using Examples in Your Academic Courses

Every college course uses examples to clarify ideas. As you study these courses, you will study examples of governments, important historical figures, psychological concepts, scientific principles, effective speeches, and so on. In addition, you will prove what you have learned by providing examples of the concepts and skills you have studied.

Practice 6

## USING EXAMPLES IN A SHORT-ANSWER COMMUNICATION ESSAY EXAM

Assume your college professor of communication has given your class a set of practice study questions to help you prepare for an upcoming mid-term exam. A peer in your study group prepared the following answer to one of the study questions. Based on what you have learned about writing an effective example paragraph, offer suggestions to strengthen her paragraph.

**Sample Question:** According to page 115 of your textbook, *The Interpersonal Communication Textbook,* 10th ed., by Joseph A. DeVito, effective listening has several "major purposes and payoffs." In one paragraph, identify three of these purposes and payoffs.

### Listening: The Purposes and Payoffs

(1) According to Joseph A. DeVito, effective listening has several major purposes and payoffs. (2) For example, one major purpose of effective listening is to learn about others, the world, and oneself. (3) By being open to ideas other than one's own, one avoids problems and deepens logical thinking. (4) Another purpose of effective listening is to relate to others. (5) By being kind and helpful and loving, one develops long lasting relationships. (6) A third purpose of effective listening is to influence others. (7) By respecting the opinions of others, one earns the trust and respect of others. (8) One should always remember that hearing is not listening because hearing is merely a passive, physical process.

More practice with writing example paragraphs: <www.mywritinglab.com>

Workshop

# Workshop: Writing an Example Paragraph Step by Step

PORTFOLIO

WRITING AN EXAMPLE PARAGRAPH STEP BY STEP

PREWRITING

## Prewrite Your Paragraph

The various activities that follow will walk you through the steps of the prewriting stage of the writing process: choosing a topic; focusing your point; and generating and organizing relevant details.

### Choose Your Topic

The following activities are designed to help you choose a topic.

**1.** Create a bank of topics. Use the following headings to brainstorm or list as many examples about each topic as you possibly can. Don't criticize your thoughts; just get as many relevant examples written down as quickly as possible. Add more topics and examples as they occur to you. Compare your bank of topics with those of your peers.

- Pollution
- Job Skills
- Effective Teachers
- Alternative Energy Supplies

**2.** Generate ideas with a freewrite. Choose one of the topics from your topic bank and think of the examples that illustrate the topic. Write about the topic and examples for ten minutes without stopping.

**3.** Select a photograph or series of photographs that illustrate a topic. Write a caption, brainstorm examples, freewrite about the photograph(s). Remember to ask, "What does the picture illustrate?" and "What's the point?"

### Focus Your Point

Read a prewrite you have generated for an exemplification. Underline words that suggest your values, opinions, or attitudes about the topic and the examples. Think about why the details are important. Identify your audience and purpose. Write a list of additional concrete examples that illustrate your point. State in one sentence the point of the examples.

AUDIENCE: ______________________________

PURPOSE: ______________________________

______________________________

WHAT'S THE POINT? ______________________________

______________________________

______________________________

## Generate and Organize Relevant Details

Using ideas you have recorded so far and the following idea map, generate and organize details that support your point.

**Example: Illustrations of an Idea**

**What's the point?**

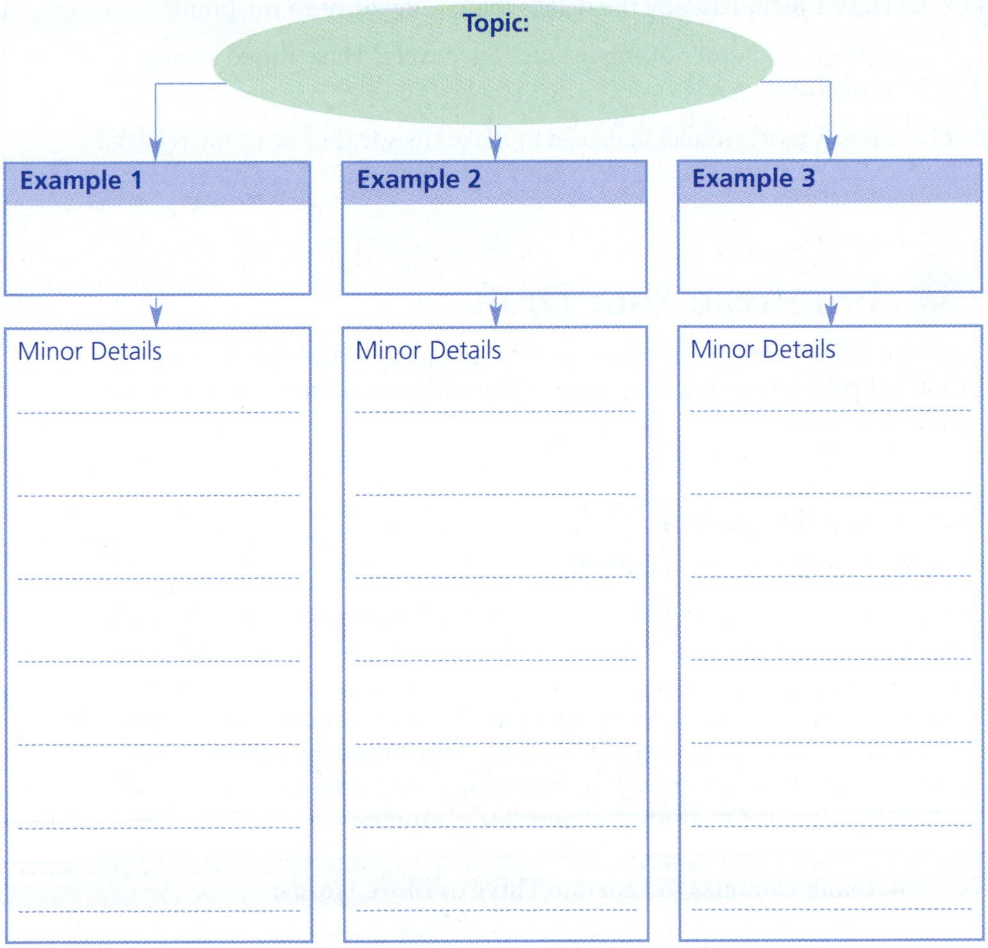


## Write a Draft of Your Paragraph

Using ideas you generated during the prewriting phase, compose a draft of your example paragraph. Return to the prewriting process at any time to generate additional details as needed. Use your own paper.

## Revise Your Draft

Once you have created a draft of an example paragraph, read the draft and answer the questions in the "Questions for Revising an Example Paragraph" box that follows. Indicate your answers by annotating your paper. If you answer "yes" to a question, underline, check, or circle examples. If you answer "no" to a question, write additional details in the margin and draw lines to indicate their placement. Revise your paragraph based on your reflection. (*Hint:* Experienced writers create several drafts as they focus on one or two questions per draft.)

## Questions for Revising an Example Paragraph

- ☐ Have I stated or implied a main idea? Have I made my point? Can I state my point in one sentence?
- ☐ Have I used concrete details to make my point?
- ☐ Have I included only the details that are relevant to my point?
- ☐ Have I used order of importance effectively? Have I used strong transitions?
- ☐ Have I used parallel language to make my ideas clear to my readers?

PROOFREADING

## Proofread Your Draft

Once you have made any revisions to your paragraph that may be needed, proofread your paragraph for proper usage and punctuation, such as using commas in a series.

For more information on using commas in a series, see Chapter 29.

### Grammar in Action: Using Commas in a Series

Use commas to separate three or more words, phrases, or clauses in a series. One of the following conjunctions is used between the last two items of a series: *but*, *or*, *yet*, *so*, *for*, *and*, or *nor*: for example, *sending*, *receiving*, and *forwarding emails*. Some experts state that the comma before the conjunction is optional. However, leaving the last comma of the series out may cause confusion, so many experts advise including it. In writing for college, we suggest you include it. Study the following examples:

- **Using Commas to Separate Three or More Words:**

  David Chappell is candid, creative, and comical.

  Coordinating conjunction

- **Using Commas to Separate Three or More Phrases:**

  Texas offers vacation experiences that are enjoyable and educational: exploring Big Ben National Park, visiting The Alamo, and touring the NASA Space Center.

  Coordinating conjunction

- **Using Commas to Separate Three or More Clauses:**

  Our company is looking for employees who can find solutions, who can work as a team, and who can excel in their roles.

  Coordinating conjunction

PORTFOLIO

Workshop

Practice 7

## USING COMMAS IN A SERIES

Edit these sentences for proper use of commas in a series.

**1.** I only need three pairs of shoes—running shoes low heeled pumps and reef sandals.

**2.** The study of psychology includes units such as the biology of the brain the development of the mind and the social behaviors of a human being.

**3.** Those who snore are those who are more likely to have heart attacks who are more likely to be in an automobile accident and who are more likely to suffer from daytime fatigue.

More practice with using commas in a series: <www.mywritinglab.com>

Review

## REVIEW OF WRITING AN EXAMPLE PARAGRAPH: DEVELOP YOUR POINT USING THE WRITING PROCESS

Use the following form to record your thinking about writing an example paragraph. Select and focus your topic for your writing situation, audience, and purpose.

Choose a topic that is best explained with examples and identify its significance.

PREWRITING DRAFTING

What is your point?

TOPIC, EXAMPLES:

AUDIENCE:

PURPOSE:

PREWRITING DRAFTING State your main idea in a topic sentence.

TOPIC: ______________________________

OPINION: ______________________________

______________________________

______________________________

PREWRITING DRAFTING Generate relevant details.

REPORTER'S QUESTIONS: WHO, WHAT, WHERE, WHEN, WHY, HOW? ______________________________

______________________________

CONCRETE EXAMPLES: ______________________________

______________________________

PREWRITING DRAFTING REVISING Use logical order. Use transition words to signal organization of details and relationship between ideas.

TRANSITIONS TO SIGNAL EXAMPLES: ______________________________

______________________________

TRANSITIONS TO LIST EXAMPLES: ______________________________

______________________________

REVISING PROOFREADING Use effective expression. Use parallel expressions. Correctly use commas in a series.

PARALLEL EXPRESSIONS: ______________________________

CORRECT USE OF COMMAS IN A SERIES: ______________________________

______________________________

Review

# Writing Assignments

## Considering Audience and Purpose

Study the sequence of photographs about the examples of people who have overcome barriers at the beginning of the chapter. Choose one of the following writing situations and compose a paragraph.

Assume you are part of a committee that is creating and burying a time capsule. The committee chose these pictures to place in the time capsule. Write a paragraph that explains how one or all of these individuals exemplify American culture in the early $21^{st}$ century.

Assume you are a fan of one of the individuals depicted in the photographs. Write a one-paragraph letter of appreciation in which you list and explain examples of his or her admirable traits.

## Writing for Everyday Life

Assume that you are keeping a personal journal and you want to capture the essence of your daily life so your children and grandchildren will know about the customs, fashions, or nature of this time in your life and our society. Use examples to make your point. Choose words that reflect one of the following attitudes: (1) realistic, (2) idealistic.

## Writing for College Life

Assume you are a member of the Student Government Association, and you are helping with freshman orientation. Identify two or three aspects of college life about which new students should be aware. Use examples to make your point.

## Writing for Working Life

Assume a peer is applying for a job as a supervisor of a sales team at Best Buy or Radio Shack (or some other job that requires leadership and commitment) and has asked you for a recommendation. Interview the peer; then write a one-paragraph recommendation in which you use examples to support your recommendation.

More ideas for writing an example paragraph: <www.mywritinglab.com>

# 8 The Classification Paragraph

**Chapter Preview**

- What's the Point of Classification?
- Making a Point Using Classification: One Student Writer's Response
- Developing Your Point Using Classification
- Using Classification in Your Academic Courses
- Workshop: Writing a Classification Paragraph Step by Step

## A classification is a division of a topic into one or more subgroups.

Whether we are grocery shopping, studying, job hunting, or searching for that special someone, we often gather and group information based on types. For example, most of us have experienced or observed the social cliques that form in high schools, neighborhoods, and on the job.

A writer uses classification to sort, group, and label items and ideas based on shared traits or types. In everyday life, we fulfill various social roles such as life-partner, parent, sibling, friend, employee, or student. In working life, we promote people to higher levels of responsibility and pay based on particular types of skills and attitudes. In college life, each of us probably prefers certain kinds of courses, likes certain types of teachers, and does better on certain types of tests.

To write a classification paragraph, a writer divides a topic into subgroups based on shared traits or qualities. The writer lists and often labels each subgroup, describes its traits, and offers examples that best represent the group. Because groups and subgroups are listed, transitions are often used to signal logical order and ensure coherence. An effective classification uses details of description and examples, logical order, and (as in any effective paragraph) sentence variety.

# What's the Point of Classification?

Identifying and labeling groups or types helps a writer to discover his or her point about a particular topic. Study the following set of photographs: In the space provided (1) identify the major fashion "look" represented by the three photographs. (2) List the traits of each subgroup. (3) Describe specific examples based on the outfits in the photographs. (4) Answer the question "What's the point?"

WRITING FROM LIFE

Practice 1

**PHOTOGRAPHIC ORGANIZER: CLASSIFICATION**

TOPIC: TYPES OF FASHION

| 1ST TYPE | 2ND TYPE | 3RD TYPE |
|---|---|---|
|  |  |  |

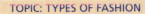

**1.** What is the best label for the fashions shown in each of these images?

**2.** Traits: | Traits: | Traits:

**3.** Examples: | Examples: | Examples:

**What's the point?**

PREWRITING

## My First Thoughts: A Prewriting Activity

Brainstorm about the images you just studied. Set a time limit, such as five minutes, and write in your notebook about the images and the details you generated. Write as quickly as you can without stopping. Let the ideas flow freely. Getting your first thoughts about a topic on paper is one excellent way to kick-start your writing process.

# Making a Point Using Classification: One Student Writer's Response

The following paragraph offers one writer's point about the types of fashions illustrated by the photographs. Read the classification paragraph below and the annotations. Complete the activities in bold type given in the annotation. Some responses may vary. Then, read the writer's journal that records decisions she made during the writing process.

**Main Idea:** The main idea is the point the author is making about the topic. The topic is fashion. **Underline the author's point about this topic.**

**Effective Expression:** Parallelism refers to the way ideas are worded. To achieve parallelism in this sentence, the writer repeated a *who-clause* three times. **Underline two additional sentences that repeat a *who-clause* three times.**

**Listing Order:** The transitional phrase, "another type" signals that the paragraph is developed by listing types of fashion. **Underline one or more transitional words or phrases that signal a list of types, traits, or examples.**

3° of Cool

(1) Fashion offers a wide variety of styles for personal expression. (2) Obviously, designers create fashion collections to appeal to specific styles. (3) Interestingly, styles reflect the values of a culture and a person. (4) In the first part of the 21st century, fashion reveals a mass devotion to cool. (5) Three high-name-recognition designers offer pop-culture cool to the socialite, the urbanite, and the professional. (6) First, Jennifer Lopez appeals to the socialite who seeks the trendy, high-fashion cool in her JLO Collection. (7) The JLO look is for the sociable woman who is comfortable with herself, who doesn't look exactly like everyone else, and who is sexy, fun, and fashionable. (8) One outfit featured in a runway show illustrates JLO's trendy style. (9) The outfit sported mid-thigh brown boots; skin-tight red leggings; black short-shorts; a body-hugging tan sweater top; a wide waist-cinching brown belt; a luxurious fur collar and luxurious fur puffed long-sleeves. (10) Offering another type of pop-culture cool, P. Diddy appeals to the urbanite who seeks sophisticated, laid-back cool in his Sean John Collection. (11) The Sean John look is for the man on the street who exudes confidence, who stands out from the crowd, and who thrives in both urban and suburban settings. (12) One of his casual sportswear outfits epitomizes urban cool. (13) The outfit is simple yet distinctive: loose-fit, dark rinse denims; a large, dark silver buckle on a black belt; a crisp, white cotton tee-shirt; a matching bleached white windbreaker; and sleek dark glasses. (14) Finally, Tommy Hilfiger appeals to the professional

who seeks chic, in-control cool in his H Hilfiger Collection. (15) The Hilfiger look is for the career woman who knows what she wants, who leads by example, and who values quality. (16) Separate pieces combine to create a tailored, elegant outfit: a soft melon-colored, knee-length pencil skirt in a rich no-wrinkle fabric; a starched and fitted berry and white striped shirt; and a tailored blazer in the same soft melon-colored, no-wrinkle fabric as the skirt. (17) Each designer put his or her own spin on the cool look, so the socialite, the urbanite, and the professional can all be cool.

**Relevant Details:**
Relevant details include descriptive details of traits and examples. Descriptive details include sensory details such as "melon" and "starched."
**Circle two more details that appeal to the senses.**

## THE WRITER'S JOURNAL

The student writer of "3° of Cool" completed the following reflection to record her thinking through the writing process. Read her writer's journal that describes a few key choices she made as she wrote.

MAIN IDEA: *I experimented with my writing process with this paragraph. Instead of just beginning to type or freewrite, this time I used a classification photographic organizer to generate several lists of details. Once I generated and labeled my ideas, I still had trouble starting a draft. I needed an introduction, a purpose for writing about these particular looks. Finally, I decided to assume I was writing an assignment for a sociology class, and my purpose was to describe a cultural value reflected in fashion. Finally, I composed a draft. Sometimes, I could quickly write the lists in parallel language; other times, the lists seemed awkwardly worded. Instead of getting stuck on wording, I continued to write out my ideas. Once the first draft was completed, I took a much needed break!*

RELEVANT DETAILS: *First, I filled in the boxes labeled "Traits" with a list of adjectives that described the outfit in each picture. Then, in the boxes labeled "Example," I described a specific detail from the outfit that illustrated the adjective. This approach helped me to create and label the following groups of details:*

| | |
|---|---|
| NAME | JLO |
| TRAITS: | Cool, fun, sexy, trendy, fashionable, youthful |
| EXAMPLE: | Luxurious fur, body-hugging, wide belt, waist-cinching, skin-tight red leggings, mid-thigh high boots |

| | |
|---|---|
| NAME | Sean John |
| TRAITS: | urban wear, casual, sophisticated, sporty |
| EXAMPLE: | crisp, white tee-shirt, loose-fit denims, large silver belt buckle |

| | |
|---|---|
| NAME | Hilfiger |
| TRAITS: | hip, chic, spirited, elegant, youthful, tailored, finished |
| EXAMPLE: | pencil straight/knee-length fitted skirt, no-wrinkle, soft-berry/white stripes melon-colored shirt/blazer |

After brainstorming these details, I put my pencil down, walked around, and thought about what labels best describe each fashion look. Suddenly, it hit me that these were all cool, hip looks that reflect pop culture. The JLO look seemed best suited for a social event like a concert or a club, so I labeled it the socialite look. The Sean John look seemed perfect for hanging in the neighborhood, catching a movie, or going to a comedy club in the city, so I labeled it the urbanite look. The Hilfiger look seemed ideal for the up-and-coming career woman, so I labeled it the professional look.

LOGICAL ORDER: I decided to order my discussion of the styles from trendy to traditional.

EFFECTIVE EXPRESSION: Later when I reread my paragraph, I underlined the sentences I wanted to revise for parallel expression. I decided to

For a blank version of this form for your own reflections about your writing: <www.mywritinglab.com>

describe each fashion group with the same sentence structure: The ____________ look is for the ____________ woman (or man) who ____________, who ____________, and who ____________. I also used parallel expressions to describe each outfit. For example, the sentence that describes Sean John's outfit reads, "The outfit is simple yet distinctive: loose-fit, dark rinse denims; a large, dark silver buckle on a black belt; a crisp, white cotton tee-shirt; a matching bleached white windbreaker; and sleek dark glasses." This sentence uses adjective-noun phrases separated by semicolons. I enjoyed writing this paragraph and had fun creating parallel expressions.

# Developing Your Point Using Classification

A classification makes a main point by grouping or sorting ideas. To support a point through classification, a writer divides a topic into subgroups based on common traits or principles. Writers offer relevant concrete details of descriptions and examples, and (as in every piece of writing) control sentence structure.

## The Point: The Main Idea

When you write a classification, you limit your topic to a set of ideas or groups based on types, shared traits, and common principles. Most likely, you also have an opinion or point of view about the groups, traits, or common principles. This opinion or attitude is your point or main idea. You also reveal your opinion by discussing the groups or traits in a particular order of importance. A topic sentence states the point or purpose of the groups, types, or traits.

For example, the following topic sentence contains (1) the topic; (2) the writer's opinion about the topic; and (3) the pattern of organization used to organize details.

The topic is *friendship*. The pattern of organization is established with the phrase *three types of*. The writer's opinion is stated with the phrase *equally important interpersonal relationships*.

TOPIC — PATTERN OF ORGANIZATION: CLASSIFICATION SIGNAL WORDS — WRITER'S OPINION

Friendships offer three types of equally important interpersonal relationships.

The example above illustrates the relationship between the topic, the writer's opinion, and the pattern of organization in this particular topic sentence.

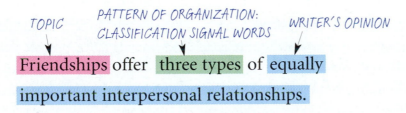

# Practice 2

## TOPIC SENTENCES

Practice creating topic sentences. The first three items present a topic, an opinion, and classification signal word(s). Combine the ideas in each group to create a topic sentence for a classification. Then, complete the practice by writing your own topic sentences.

**1.** TOPIC: leisure activities OPINION: relaxing and inexpensive, strengthen family ties

CLASSIFICATION SIGNAL WORDS: two types of

TOPIC SENTENCE: ______________________________

______________________________

**2.** TOPIC: diet OPINION: healthful

CLASSIFICATION SIGNAL WORDS: several traits

TOPIC SENTENCE: ______________________________

______________________________

**3.** TOPIC: credit OPINION: a wise consumer must understand

CLASSIFICATION SIGNAL WORDS: types of

TOPIC SENTENCE: ______________________________

______________________________

**4.** TOPIC: singer Faith Hill OPINION: ______________

CLASSIFICATION SIGNAL WORDS: ______________________________

TOPIC SENTENCE: ______________________________

______________________________

**5.** TOPIC: ______________ OPINION: ______________

CLASSIFICATION SIGNAL WORDS: ______________________________

TOPIC SENTENCE: ______________________________

______________________________

**6.** TOPIC: ______________ OPINION: ______________

CLASSIFICATION SIGNAL WORDS: ______________

TOPIC SENTENCE: ______________

______________

**7.** TOPIC: ______________ OPINION: ______________

CLASSIFICATION SIGNAL WORDS: ______________

TOPIC SENTENCE: ______________

______________

Practice 2

# Logical Order

Once you have divided a topic into groups, types, or traits and focused on a main idea, you are ready to generate additional details and list your ideas in their order of importance. To make a point using classification, a writer moves from a general idea (the group) to a major support (a particular trait of the group) to a minor support (an example of the trait). To signal the movement between these levels of ideas, a writer uses transitions to signal or list groups, types, or traits. Strong transitions establish coherence, a clear and understandable flow of ideas.

**Words That Are Used to Signal Groups, Types, or Traits**

| | | | | |
|---|---|---|---|---|
| aspect | classify | group | quality | style |
| attribute | classification | ideal | rank | trait |
| brand | collection | kind | section | type |
| branch | division | level | set | typical |
| categories | element | order | sort | variety |
| characteristic | feature | part | status | class |
| form | principle | stratum | | |

**Transitions That Combine with Signal Words to List Groups, Types, or Traits**

| | | | | |
|---|---|---|---|---|
| also | final | for one thing | last of all | second |
| and | finally | furthermore | moreover | third |
| another | first | in addition | next | |
| besides | first of all | last | one | |

Practice 3

LISTING ORDER

The following information appears in a college science textbook. Determine the logical order of the sentences. *Hint:* Underline the transitions that signal or list groups, types, or traits. Complete the exercise by answering the question "What's the point?" Discuss your answers with your class or with a small group of peers.

**Two Types of Tumors**

........ First, benign tumors are not cancerous; they are abnormal masses of essentially normal cells.

........ Another type of tumor is the malignant tumor.

........ Third, benign tumors always remain at their original site in the body.

........ One type of tumor is the benign tumor. Benign tumors have several traits.

........ Malignant tumors have several distinct traits.

........ Second, arising from a single cancer cell, a malignant tumor displaces normal tissue as it grows.

........ First, this tumor is cancerous; it is a mass of cancer cells.

........ Third, cells may also split off from the malignant tumor, invade the circulatory system (lymph vessels and blood vessels), and travel to new locations, where they can form new tumors.

........ Second, benign tumors can cause problems if they grow in certain organs like the brain, but usually they can be removed by surgery.

........ If the tumor is not killed or removed, some of the cancer cells spread into surrounding tissues, enlarging the tumor.

—Adapted from Campbell, Reece, Taylor, and Simon. *Biology: Concepts & Connections,* 5th ed. Benjamin Cummings 2008. p.135.

**What's the point?**

............................................................

## Relevant Details

As a writer narrows a topic into a focused main idea, the thinking process brings to mind many details that answer the questions such as *who, what, when, where, why,* and *how.* A writer evaluates the relevancy of each detail and uses only those that clarify or support the main idea based on classification. Some relevant details identify subgroups, types, or traits of the main point. Minor details may offer examples of subgroups, types, or traits. Some major and minor details may explain the writer's opinion about the topic and how it is being classified. During the prewriting phase, a list can help a writer organize ideas as they are generated. Study the following concept map used to generate ideas about the topic "Two types of comedy that dominate television."

**Concept Map**

| Topic: Two types of comedy that dominate television. | | |
|---|---|---|
| | Type 1: Sketch comedy | Type 2: Situation comedy |
| Traits: | Better for adult audience | Better for family |
| Performer: | Ensemble routine | Ensemble routine |
| Origin: | Evolved from vaudeville | Evolved from radio |
| Length: | Short scenes or sketches (1–10 mins.) | 30 min. story line |
| Material: | Actors improvise/write scripts Avoids violence, uses bad language | Writers create scripts Avoids violence and bad language |
| Focus: | Politics, current events, issues | Social relationships at home and work |
| Examples: | Colgate Comedy Hour, Monty Python's Flying Circus, SNL, Mad TV, Chappelle's, Ed Sullivan (best show of all) | I Love Lucy, Friends, Seinfeld, Everybody Hates Chris |

During the prewriting phase of writing, a writer naturally generates irrelevant details. In fact, an effective writer often produces far more details than can be used to make a specific point. Irrelevant details do not explain or support the focused point of the paragraph. A careful writer uses the revision process to double-check details for relevancy and to eliminate irrelevant details.

## Practice 4

RELEVANT CONCRETE DETAILS

The following paragraph develops the ideas recorded in the brainstorming list about comedy. Circle the main idea. Underline two traits for each group. Cross out the two details that are not relevant to the main point.

### Television Comedy: Sketches and Sitcoms

(1) Two types of comedy have long dominated television. (2) One type is sketch comedy. (3) Sketch comedy is an ensemble routine that evolved from vaudeville into a bit for television on variety shows as the *Colgate Comedy Hour* and the *Ed Sullivan Show*. (4) Sketch comedy is a series of short comedy scenes that typically range from one to ten minutes. (5) Often the actors improvise the sketch, making it up as they go; then they write the script based on their improvisation. (6) This kind of humor avoids violence, often uses offensive language, and focuses on politics, issues, and current events. (7) Well-known examples of sketch comedy include *Monty Python's Flying Circus*, *Saturday Night Live*, *Mad TV*, and *Chappelle's Show*. (8) However, the *Ed Sullivan Show* remains the all time best variety show to have appeared on television. (9) A second type of comedy dominating television is the sitcom or situation comedy, also an ensemble routine. (10) The sitcom evolved from radio shows such as *Amos and Andy*; sitcoms continue to flourish on television. (11) Sitcoms are usually set in a specific location such as a home or office, and they present amusing story lines about a group of characters such as a family, friends, or co-workers in an office. (12) Often episodes are self-contained stories that are resolved in less than 30 minutes; some sitcoms do use ongoing story lines based on developing relationships between characters. (13) This type of humor avoids violence, rarely uses offensive language, and focuses on social relationships. (14) Well-known examples of situation comedy include *I Love Lucy*, *Friends*, *Seinfeld*, and *Everybody Hates Chris*. (15) Overall, sitcoms are more appropriate for family viewing than sketch comedy.

## Effective Expression: Controlled Sentence Structure

Control of sentence structure enhances effective expression. You can express ideas through the use of four sentence types: simple, compound, complex, and compound-complex. Study the following definitions and examples of these four types of sentences:

1. A **simple sentence** contains one independent clause.

INDEPENDENT CLAUSE

Two types of comedy have long dominated television.

2. A **compound sentence** contains two or more independent clauses. These clauses can be joined with:

   a. A comma and a coordinating conjunction (*for, and, nor, but, or, yet, so*: FANBOYS),

   INDEPENDENT CLAUSES

   Sitcoms are usually set in a specific location such as a home or office, and they present amusing story lines about a group of characters such as a family and neighbors or co-workers in an office.

   b. A semicolon,

   The sitcom evolved from radio shows such as *Amos and Andy*; they continue to flourish on television.

   INDEPENDENT CLAUSES

   OR

   c. A semicolon with a conjunctive adverb.

   INDEPENDENT CLAUSE

   Often the ensemble of actors improvises the sketch; then they write the script based on their improvisation.

   INDEPENDENT CLAUSE

3. A **complex sentence** contains one independent clause and one or more dependent clauses. A dependent clause begins with a subordinating conjunction (such as *although, because, when, who, which,* and *that*) placed immediately before a subject and verb. Sometimes, the subordinating conjunction also serves as the subject of the verb in the dependent clause.

INDEPENDENT CLAUSE

Sketch comedy is a series of short comedy scenes that often range between one and ten minutes.

DEPENDENT CLAUSE

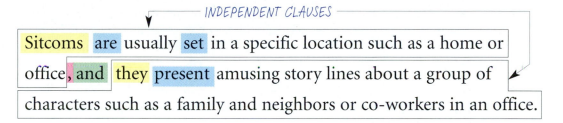

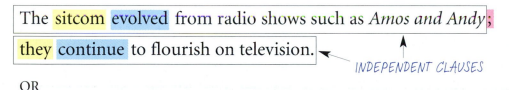

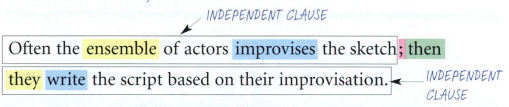

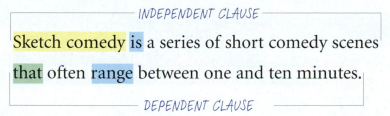

4. A **compound-complex** sentence contains two or more independent clauses and one or more dependent clauses. This sentence type combines the traits of the compound and complex sentences.

INDEPENDENT CLAUSE

Often episodes are self-contained stories
that are resolved in less than 30 minutes;
some sitcoms do use ongoing story lines based
on developing relationships between characters.

DEPENDENT CLAUSE — INDEPENDENT CLAUSE

## Practice 5

SENTENCE VARIETY

Label each of the following sentences as a simple, compound, complex, or compound-complex sentence. Revise each sentence into the new type of sentence indicated. Discuss your work with your class or with a small group of your peers.

______________ **1.** Foods from wheat, rice, oats, cornmeal, barley, or another cereal grain are grain products. Bread, pasta, oatmeal, breakfast cereals, tortillas, and grits are examples of grain products.

REVISE INTO A COMPOUND SENTENCE: ______________________________

______________________________________________

______________________________________________

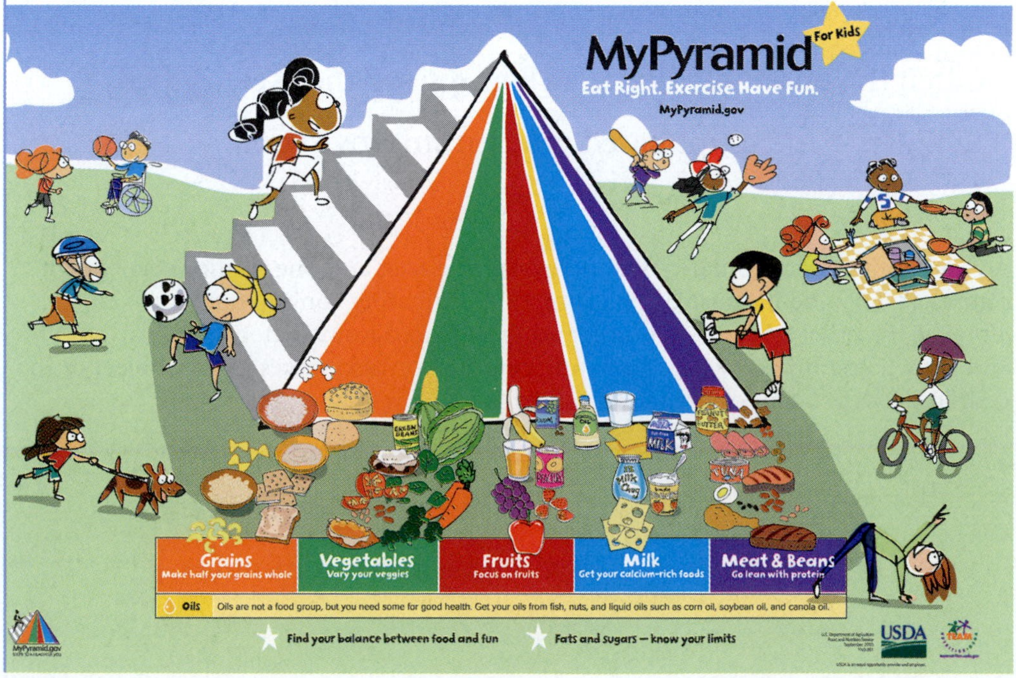

More practice with sentence variety: <www.mywritinglab.com>

Practice 5

______ **2.** Oils are fats that are liquid at room temperature, like canola, olive, and other vegetable oils used in cooking.

REVISE INTO A COMPOUND-COMPLEX SENTENCE: ______

______ **3.** Vegetables are organized into subgroups. These subgroups include dark green vegetables, orange vegetables, dry beans and peas, and starchy vegetables.

REVISE INTO A COMPLEX SENTENCE: ______

______ **4.** The new food pyramid, which includes steps to illustrate the need for physical activity, classifies food into six food groups; these groups include grains, vegetables, fruits, oils, milk, and meats and beans.

REVISE INTO SIMPLE SENTENCES: ______

## Using Classification in Your Academic Courses

Often, writing in college requires research. Research deepens your understanding of a topic in several ways: (1) you locate facts; (2) you consider the opinions of experts; (3) you weed out false facts; and (4) you clarify your own point about a topic based on the information you collect. Classification plays a key role in research because information is organized based on types. Two well-known methods of classifying information are the Dewey Decimal System and the Library of Congress System. Your college library uses one of these two types to arrange books on the shelves by labeling them with a system of letters and numbers. When you are assigned a research topic, you will use classification to find the information you need.

# Practice 6

**USING CLASSIFICATION FOR LIBRARY RESEARCH:**
CLASSIFICATION OF INFORMATION—THE LIBRARY OF CONGRESS SYSTEM

Listed below are the letters and titles of the main classes and one subgroup of the Library of Congress Classification. Study the list and answer the questions.

A – GENERAL WORKS
B – PHILOSOPHY. PSYCHOLOGY. RELIGION
C – AUXILIARY SCIENCES OF HISTORY
D – HISTORY (GENERAL) AND HISTORY OF EUROPE
E – HISTORY: AMERICA
F – HISTORY: AMERICA
G – GEOGRAPHY. ANTHROPOLOGY. RECREATION
H – SOCIAL SCIENCES
- H – Social Sciences (General)
- HA – Statistics
- HB – Economic theory. Demography
- HC – Industries. Land use. Labor
- HE – Transportation and communications
- HF – Commerce
- HG – Finance
- HJ – Public Finance
- HM – Sociology (General)
- HN – Social history and conditions. Social problems. Social reform
- HQ – The family. Marriage. Women
- HS – Societies: secret, benevolent, etc.
- HT – Communities. Classes. Races
- HV – Social pathology. Social and public welfare. Criminology
- HX – Socialism. Communism Anarchism

J – POLITICAL SCIENCE
K – LAW
L – EDUCATION
M – MUSIC AND BOOKS ON MUSIC
N – FINE ARTS
P – LANGUAGE AND LITERATURE
Q – SCIENCE
R – MEDICINE
S – AGRICULTURE
T – TECHNOLOGY
U – MILITARY SCIENCE
V – NAVAL SCIENCE
Z – BIBLIOGRAPHY. LIBRARY SCIENCE. INFORMATION RESOURCES (GENERAL)

—"Library of Congress Classification Outline." *Library of Congress* 5 July 2005. 2 March 2006 http://www.loc.gov/catdir/cpso/lcco/lcco.html

**1.** Write the letter of the group that would contain the following book titles:

............... *Dealing with Relatives (—even if you can't stand them): Bringing Out the Best in Families at Their Worst* by Rick Brinkman and Rick Kirschner.

............... Encyclopedia of Family Health

**2.** Write the letter of the group that you would search for the following information:

............... The principles of Islam

............... The author Toni Morrison, winner of the Nobel Prize for Literature

More practice using classification: <www.mywritinglab.com>

# Workshop: Writing a Classification Paragraph Step by Step

WRITING A CLASSIFICATION PARAGRAPH STEP BY STEP

Workshop

PORTFOLIO

PREWRITING

## Prewrite Your Paragraph

The various activities below will walk you through the steps of the prewriting stage of the writing process: choosing a topic; focusing your point; and generating and organizing relevant details.

### Choose Your Topic

The following activities are designed to help you choose a topic.

**1.** Create a bank of topics. Use the following headings to brainstorm or list as many categories and subgroups about each topic as you possibly can. Don't analyze your thoughts; just get as many relevant categories written down as quickly as possible. Add more topics and categories as they occur to you. Compare your bank of topics with those of your peers.

- Birth Order (traits of oldest, middle, youngest, only child)
- Music
- Technology
- Vehicles
- Life Roles

**2.** Generate ideas with a freewrite. Choose one of the topics from your topic bank and think of the traits that set a group or subgroup apart. Write about the traits of the group and subgroups for ten minutes without stopping.

OR

Select a photograph or series of photographs that illustrate a group or subgroup. Write a caption, brainstorm traits, and freewrite about the photograph(s). Remember to ask, "What is the group or subgroup represented by this picture(s)?" and "What's the point?"

### Focus Your Point

Read a freewrite you have generated for a classification. Underline words that suggest your values, opinions, or attitudes about the topic and its subgroups or categories. Think about why the traits are important. Think about what examples best represent the group, categories, or subgroups. Identify your audience and purpose. Write a list of additional concrete traits and examples that explain your point. State in one sentence the point of the groups, traits, and examples:

AUDIENCE: ______________________

PURPOSE: ______________________

Workshop

## Generate and Organize Relevant Details

Use the graphic organizer below to either organize the ideas you have already created or to generate details to support your point.

**Types (groups) of**

| 1st Type/group | 2nd Type/group | 3rd Type/group |
|---|---|---|
| **Traits:** | **Traits:** | **Traits:** |
| **Examples:** | **Examples:** | **Examples:** |

**What's the point?**

## Write a Draft of Your Paragraph

Using the ideas you generated during the prewriting phase, compose a draft of your classification paragraph. Return to the prewriting process at any time to generate additional details as needed. Use your own paper.

## Revise Your Draft

Once you have created a draft of a classification paragraph, read the draft and answer the following questions. Indicate your answers by annotating your paper. If you answer "yes" to a question, underline, check, or circle examples. If you answer "no" to a question, write additional details in the margins and draw lines to indicate their placement. Revise your paragraph based on your reflection.

### Questions for Revising a Classification Paragraph

- ☐ Have I made my point? Can I state my point in one sentence?
- ☐ Have I divided my topic into types, groups, or categories? Have I clearly labeled each group? Have I discussed the common traits and examples of each group?
- ☐ Have I used strong transitions of classification?
- ☐ Have I used concrete details to make my point?
- ☐ Have I included only the details that are relevant to my topic sentence?
- ☐ Have I used the following to make my ideas clear to my readers: vivid verbs and images, parallel language, controlled sentence structure?

## Proofread Your Draft

Once you have made any revisions to your paragraph that may be needed, proofread your paper to eliminate distracting errors such as comma splices.

For more information on eliminating comma splices, see Chapter 22.

### Grammar in Action: Eliminating Comma Splices

Comma splices and run-on sentences have been categorized as two of the most common errors in student writing. Both the comma splice and the run-on occur when writers join ideas without the proper punctuation.

A **comma splice** occurs when a writer uses *only a comma* to join two or more independent clauses.

Americans enjoy many vacation options, some choose family bonding activities such as trips to family reunions or theme parks, others choose special interest activities such as Bike Week in Daytona Beach or spring break in Cancun.

Workshop

A **comma splice** can be corrected in three different ways.

**Three Rules for Properly Joining Two or More Independent Clauses**

A writer can properly join two or more independent clauses in several ways:

1. Use a comma AND a coordinating conjunction (*for, and, nor, but, or, yet, so,*: FANBOYS).
2. Use a semicolon.
3. Use a semicolon with a transition (*for example, in addition, however, therefore, thus,* etc.).

Study the following examples:

1. Americans enjoy many vacation options; some choose family bonding activities such as trips to family reunions or theme parks, but others choose special interest activities such as Bike Week in Daytona Beach or spring break in Cancun.
2. Some choose family bonding activities such as trips to family reunions or theme parks; others choose special interest activities such as Black College Reunion (BCR) in Daytona Beach or spring break in Cancun.
3. Americans enjoy many vacation options; for example, some choose family bonding activities such as trips to family reunions or theme parks.

# Workshop Practice 7

PORTFOLIO

## ELIMINATING COMMA SPLICES

Edit these sentences to eliminate comma splices. *Hint:* Underline subjects once and verbs twice to identify independent clauses.

1. My car matches my personality, we are both dependable and conservative.

2. Both of us are dependable, for example, I have perfect attendance, put in long hours, and meet my goals.

3. I have perfect attendance, put in long study hours, and maintain a high GPA, my Toyota Camry has a perfect maintenance record, gets great gas mileage, and lives up to its reputation.

More practice with eliminating comma splices: <www.mywritinglab.com>

## REVIEW OF WRITING A CLASSIFICATION PARAGRAPH: DEVELOP YOUR POINT USING THE WRITING PROCESS

Review

Use the following form to record your thinking about writing a classification paragraph. Select and focus your topic for your writing situation, audience, and purpose. Choose a topic that is best explained through classification and identify its significance.

PREWRITING DRAFTING What is your point?

TOPIC, GROUPS, TYPES, TRAITS: ________________________________

________________________________

AUDIENCE: ________________________________

PURPOSE: ________________________________

________________________________

PREWRITING DRAFTING State your main idea in a topic sentence.

TOPIC: ________________________________

OPINION: ________________________________

________________________________

PREWRITING DRAFTING Generate relevant details.

REPORTER'S QUESTIONS: WHO, WHAT, WHERE, WHEN, WHY, HOW? ________________________________

________________________________

SUBGROUPS (Use vivid labels for each group): ________________________________

________________________________

TYPES: ________________________________

________________________________

TRAITS: ________________________________

________________________________

# 9 The Comparison and Contrast Paragraph

**Chapter Preview**

- What's the Point of Comparison and Contrast?
- Making a Point Using Comparison and Contrast: One Student Writer's Response
- Developing Your Point Using Comparison and Contrast
- Using Comparison and Contrast in Your Academic Courses
- Workshop: Writing a Comparison and Contrast Paragraph Step by Step

## A comparison examines how two or more things are similar. A contrast looks at how two or more things are different.

Comparing and contrasting ideas is an essential part of critical thinking. When we choose between Subway and McDonald's or Apple and Dell computers, we are weighing the similarities or differences of products and services and making a choice by comparison shopping. What are some basic comparable points for any consumer to consider when shopping? What are some other situations in which we use comparable points as the basis of our thinking or actions?

In everyday life, we compare or contrast the neighborhoods and prices of homes we want to buy, or the honesty and policies of political candidates as we decide for whom we will vote. In working life, we compare or contrast the salaries, benefits, and working conditions among several career opportunities. In college life, we compare and contrast leaders, governments, cultures, literature, technology, writers, or philosophies in a wide range of courses.

To write a comparison or a contrast paragraph, identify the comparable points between two (or more) topics. Once you identify the points of comparison, brainstorm a list of similarities and differences for each one. Then, list and explain examples of each similarity or difference.

▲ *Hurricane Katrina*

▲ *Hurricane Rita*

# What's the Point of Comparison and Contrast?

Often ideas become clearer when they are analyzed based on how they relate to one another. The comparison and contrast patterns of organization allow a writer to explore the ways in which ideas are related. The following set of photographs document some similarities and differences between Hurricane Katrina and Hurricane Rita. These two hurricanes both hit the Gulf Coast in the summer of 2005. Study the sets of images. Answer the following questions about each comparable point.

WRITING FROM LIFE

Practice 1

PHOTOGRAPHIC ORGANIZER: COMPARE AND CONTRAST: POINTS OF SIMILARITIES AND DIFFERENCES

Comparable Topics: ____________________ ____________________

Similar to or different from

What is the 1st comparable point? ____________________

____________________ ____________________

____________________ ____________________

Similar to or different from

What is the 2nd comparable point? ____________________

____________________ ____________________

____________________ ____________________

Similar to or different from

What is the 3rd comparable trait? ____________________

____________________ ____________________

____________________ ____________________

**What's the point?** ____________________

____________________

PREWRITING

## My First Thoughts

Brainstorm about the images you just studied. Set a time limit, such as five minutes, and write in your notebook about the images and the details you generated. Write as quickly as you can without stopping. Let the ideas flow freely. Getting your first thoughts about a topic on paper is one excellent way to kick-start your writing process.

# Making a Point Using Comparison and Contrast: One Student Writer's Response

The following paragraph offers one writer's point about the similarities and differences between hurricanes Katrina and Rita as illustrated by the photographs. Read the comparison and contrast paragraph below and the annotations. Complete the activities in bold type given in the annotation. Then, read the writer's journal that records decisions made during the writing process.

**MAIN IDEA:**
The main idea is the point the author is making about the topic.
**Circle the two topics being compared and contrasted and underline the author's point about the two topics.**

**LOGICAL ORDER:**
Words of comparison or contrast signal similarities or differences.
**Underline three more transitions of comparison or contrast.**

**RELEVANT DETAILS:**
Relevant details include descriptive details about similarities or differences between comparable points.
**Underline two more details of similarities or differences.**

**EFFECTIVE EXPRESSION:**
This sentence gives equal weight to the hurricanes by joining two sentences with a semicolon.
**Underline another sentence that expresses balanced ideas with the use of a semicolon.**

### Their Eyes Were Watching Storms

(1) The 2005 hurricane season produced over two dozen named storms. (2) Although two of those storms—Hurricane Katrina and Hurricane Rita—revealed the devastating power of Gulf Coast hurricanes, they prompted very different evacuation experiences. (3) Both hurricanes became major category 5 storms with well-formed eyes and wide spirals of wind and rain, and both hurricanes weakened before hitting landfall. (4) For example, Hurricane Katrina produced sustained winds between 125 and 175 mph, storm surges between 13 and 30 feet, and affected the entire Gulf Coast region. (5) Likewise, Hurricane Rita produced sustained winds of 175 mph, storm surges of 15–20 feet, and also affected major portions of the Gulf Coast region. (6) Another similarity occurred in the aftermath of both storms: massive flooding. (7) Hurricane Katrina's storm surges gushed into communities like New Orleans and destroyed homes, businesses, and entire neighborhoods; similarly, Hurricane Rita's storm surge leveled the entire coastal community of Holly Beach. (8) Even though both storms left a swath of destruction, a degree of difference in the destruction is visible. (9) Katrina left New Orleans completely submerged with no land in sight; Rita left patches and ribbons of dry ground along the coast. (10) Despite the similar dangers posed by these two storms, the evacuation response differed greatly. (11) Thousands of people did not evacuate before Katrina hit land. (12) As a result, they were trapped and stranded for days at the Superdome, in hospitals, and in their homes. (13) In contrast, people did decide to evacuate before Hurricane Rita hit land. (14) As a result, thousands of people were trapped for hours in their cars on the Interstate as they tried to flee the storm. (15) The shared fury of storms and differences between the evacuation responses serve as warnings about the need for uniform evacuation plans.

## THE WRITER'S JOURNAL

The student writer of "Their Eyes Were Watching Storms" completed the following reflection to record her thinking through the writing process. Read her writer's journal that describes a few key choices she made as she wrote.

MAIN IDEA: *Before writing anything, I really studied the details of each set of pictures. The power of the images and the importance of the event forced me to stop and think. Although I feel deeply about the topic, I did not want my emotions to limit my understanding of the similarities and differences between the two storms. So I assumed the role of a researcher reporting on the situation in a detached tone. To help me generate details, I used the graphic organizer in the chapter opening.*

RELEVANT DETAILS: *The pictures jolted my memory about the horror of these storms, and I wanted to use what I lived through and saw on the news to make my point. To help me organize details and figure out how to present my ideas, I created two types of outlines: comparable point by point and topic block by topic block.*

| POINT BY POINT | TOPIC BLOCK BY TOPIC BLOCK |
|---|---|
| **A. Size and Scope** | **A. Katrina** |
| 1. Katrina | 1. Size and scope |
| 2. Rita | 2. Evacuation |
| **B. Evacuation** | 3. Aftermath |
| 1. Katrina | **B. Rita** |
| 2. Rita | 1. Size and scope |
| **C. Aftermath** | 2. Evacuation |
| 1. Katrina | 3. Aftermath |
| 2. Rita | |

LOGICAL ORDER: *I used the point-by-point outline. I revised several times to improve my word choice and get better control of my flow of ideas. I also carefully controlled sentences to give equal weight to comparable points. In one revision, I changed the order of points. Instead of listing the comparable points based on time order, I listed them in order of importance. I began with the two points of similarities to establish the significance of the storms. For emphasis, I ended with a major difference between the two experiences.*

For a blank version of this form for your own reflections about your writing: <www.mywritinglab.com>

EFFECTIVE EXPRESSION: On my last draft, I changed the adjective for "evacuation plans" in the last sentence from "effective" to "uniform." To give the two ideas equal weight, I revised the following sentence from "While Katrina left parts of New Orleans completely submerged with no land in sight, Rita left patches and ribbons of dry land all along the coastal city it destroyed" to "Katrina left parts of New Orleans completely submerged with no land in sight; Rita left patches and ribbons of dry land all along the coastal city it destroyed." I really like my title. It's a play on the word "eye," and it's a literary reference in honor of author Zora Neale Hurston and her novel Their Eyes Were Watching God.

# Developing Your Point Using Comparison and Contrast

A **comparison** makes a point by discussing the *similarities* between two or more topics. A **contrast** makes a point by discussing the *differences* between two or more topics. To support a point through comparison or contrast, a writer identifies the comparable points of the topic, offers relevant and concrete descriptions and examples for each comparable point, and effectively uses coordination and subordination of ideas.

## The Point: The Main Idea

When you write a comparison or a contrast piece, you limit your thoughts to a set of topics based on their relationship to each other. Most likely you have an opinion or belief about the two topics and their comparable points. Your opinion is your point or main idea. In a comparison or contrast paragraph, you also reveal your opinion by discussing the topics and their points of similarities or differences in the order of your own choosing. A topic sentence states the overall point of the comparison or the contrast between the two topics.

For example, the following topic sentence contains (1) the comparable topics, (2) the writer's opinion about the topic, and (3) the pattern of organization used to organize the details.

The comparable topics are *Giada De Laurentiis* and *Rachael Ray, celebrity chefs.* The pattern of organization is established with words *even though* and *differ.* The writer's opinion is stated with the clause *styles differ greatly.*

PATTERN OF ORGANIZATION: TRANSITION WORDS THAT SIGNAL CONTRAST

TOPIC

Even though Giada De Laurentiis and Rachael Ray are both celebrity chefs, their styles differ greatly.

WRITER'S OPINION

Practice 2

## TOPIC SENTENCES

Practice creating topic sentences. The first two items present a topic, an opinion, and comparison and contrast signal word(s). Combine the ideas in each group to create a topic sentence for a comparison or a contrast. Then, complete the practice by making your own topic sentences.

**1.** TOPIC: The communication styles of men and women

OPINION: significant

COMPARISON OR CONTRAST SIGNAL WORDS: differ three ways

TOPIC SENTENCE: ______

**2.** TOPIC: Two 2008 hybrid cars the Toyota Prius and the Honda Civic

OPINION: equal value

COMPARISON OR CONTRAST SIGNAL WORDS: similar ratings for safety and fuel economy

TOPIC SENTENCE: ______

**3.** TOPIC: Private diary; blog

OPINION: fulfill purposes

COMPARISON OR CONTRAST SIGNAL WORDS: Although share similar traits, differences

TOPIC SENTENCE: ______

**4.** TOPIC: Nonverbal gestures; spoken language

OPINION: believable

COMPARISON OR CONTRAST SIGNAL WORDS: more, than

TOPIC SENTENCE: ______

More practice with creating topic sentences: <www.mywritinglab.com>

Practice 2

**5.** TOPIC: Surfing; skateboarding

OPINION: ______

COMPARISON OR CONTRAST SIGNAL WORDS: ______

TOPIC SENTENCE: ______

______

**6.** TOPIC: ______

OPINION: ______

COMPARISON OR CONTRAST SIGNAL WORDS: ______

TOPIC SENTENCE: ______

______

## Logical Order

Once you have identified the comparable points between your topics and have focused on a main idea, you are ready to generate and organize additional details. To make a point using comparison or contrast, a writer moves from a general idea (the comparison or contrast of two or more topics) to a major support (a comparable point about the topics) to minor supports (details or examples of the comparable point about the topics). To signal the movement among these levels of ideas, a writer uses transitions to signal similarities or differences and examples. Strong transitions establish coherence, a clear and understandable flow of ideas.

### Words That Signal Comparison

| | | | | |
|---|---|---|---|---|
| alike | in a similar fashion | just as | resemble | similarly |
| as | in a similar way | just like | same | |
| as well as | in like manner | like | similar | |
| equally | in the same way | likewise | similarity | |

### Words That Signal Contrast

| | | | | |
|---|---|---|---|---|
| although | conversely | differently | nevertheless | to the contrary |
| as opposed to | despite | even though | on the contrary | unlike |
| at the same time | difference | in contrast | on the one hand | yet |
| but | different | in spite of | on the other hand | |
| by contrast | different from | instead | still | |

## Practice 3

ORDER OF SIMILARITIES OR DIFFERENCES

The following information appears as a paragraph in a college literature textbook. Determine the logical order of the sentences. Complete the exercise by answering the question "What's the point?"

### The Fable and the Parable

.......... The fable and the parable are age-old literary forms of fiction that grew out of the oral tradition of story-telling.

.......... Although these two types of stories may seem similar, they differ in several important ways.

.......... This universal truth is the basis of a moral lesson that is clearly stated at the end of the story.

.......... First, the fable is a short story that illustrates a universal truth.

.......... In addition, to make its point, a fable uses fantastical plots and mythical creatures, talking animals, animate objects, and people as characters.

.......... For example, in Aesop's fable "The Tortoise and the Hare," the main characters are a talking turtle and rabbit in an absurd race against each other, and the point or lesson is that "steady progress brings success while arrogance leads to loss."

.......... Like a fable, the parable is a short story designed to teach a lesson or convey a moral based on a universal truth.

.......... In another contrast to a fable, a parable uses human beings as characters and realistic situations for the plot.

.......... However, while a fable clearly states its moral as a fitting end to its story, a parable implies its lesson and leaves room for various interpretations.

.......... For example, the parables Jesus used in his teachings have at least two levels of meaning.

.......... In "The Parable of the Prodigal Son," Jesus told a story about a realistic, everyday situation that anyone in the audience could easily understand, and he told the story in a way that also had a symbolic meaning for his disciples or followers.

.......... Ultimately, both the fable and the parable are told to create a vivid and unforgettable word-picture.

**What's the Point?**

----------------------------------------

----------------------------------------

More practice with logical order: <www.mywritinglab.com>

## Relevant Details

As a writer narrows a topic into a focused main idea, the thinking process brings to mind many details that answer the questions *who*, *what*, *when*, *where*, *why*, and *how*. A writer evaluates the relevancy of each detail and uses only those that clarify or support the main idea. In a comparison or contrast paragraph, some relevant major details include those that identify comparable topics or points. Relevant minor details offer examples and explanations of the similarities or differences between comparable points. Relevant details include descriptions, explanations, and examples of similarities or differences between two or more topics. Details are logically ordered to best support the point.

**Comparable Topics in a Venn Diagram**

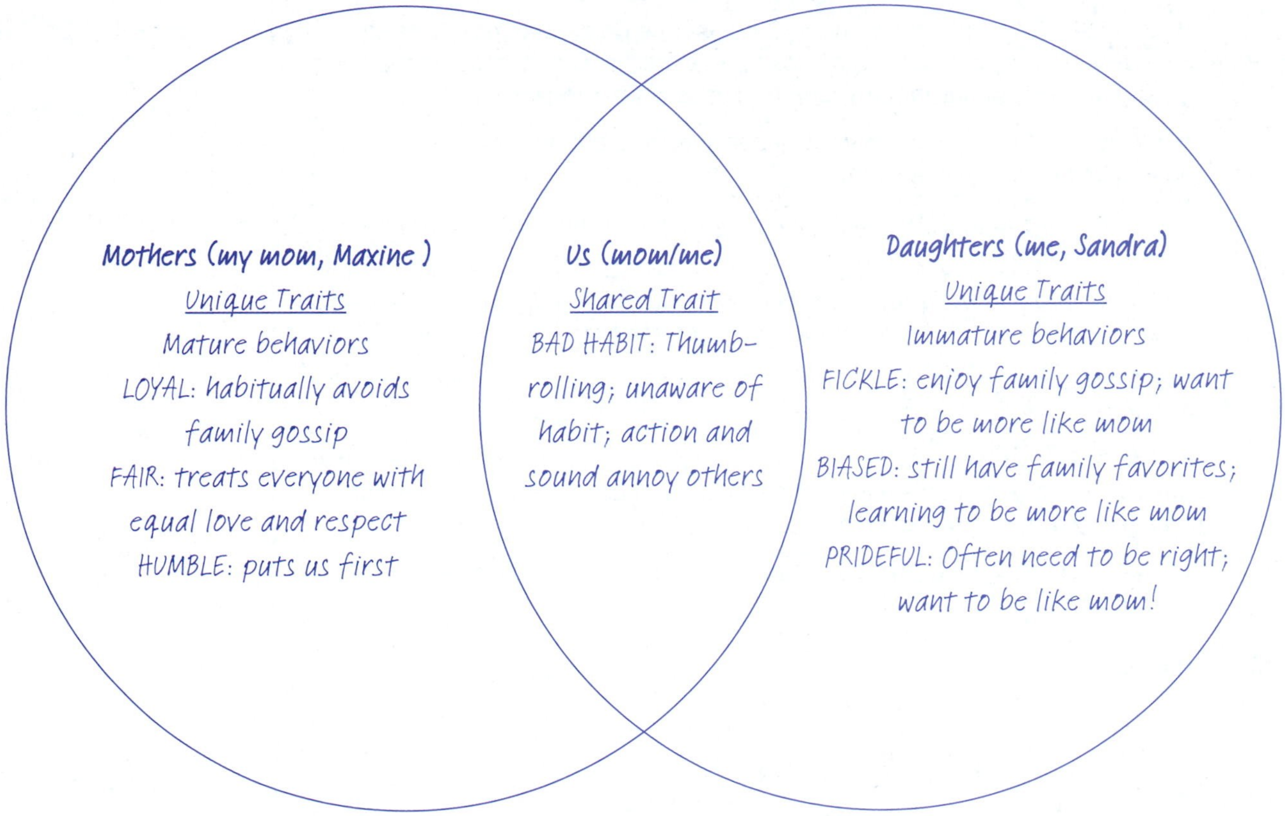


During the prewriting phase of writing, a writer naturally generates irrelevant details. In fact, an effective writer often produces far more details than can be used to make a specific point. Irrelevant details do not explain or support the focused point of the paragraph. A careful writer uses the revision process to double check details for relevancy and to eliminate irrelevant details.

RELEVANT CONCRETE DETAILS

Practice 4

The following paragraph explains and illustrates the ideas generated using the Venn diagram. Circle the main idea. Underline the words that signal similarities or differences and three supporting points of similarities discussed in the paragraph. Cross out two details that are not relevant to the main point.

**Bonds of Habits Tie Us Together**

(1) I never realized how similar parents and their children can be. (2) My mother, Maxine, has a habit of rolling her thumbs. (3) She sits with her hands clasped, fingers laced, and thumbs rolling. (4) The action creates a soft rhythmic swish as the pad of one thumb brushes the top of her other thumb. (5) I don't know why, but the sight and sound of mother's thumb-rolling drives me to distraction. (6) Sometimes, I can hardly concentrate on my thoughts. (7) She remains completely unaware of the habit or how much it bothers me. (8) The one time I mentioned the behavior, she was embarrassed, and she tried for a while to break herself of the habit. (9) Although I vowed never to develop any such quirk, I recently caught myself in the middle of my own mother-like thumb roll. (10) As my husband described his golf swing, his eyes kept darting to my hands in the same way my own eyes react to Mom's thumb roll. (11) Suddenly he fell silent mid-sentence. (12) We heard a sound just like the one made by mother's thumb roll. (13) Just like my mother, I sat with my hands clasped, fingers-laced, and thumbs rolling. (14) My husband asked, "Maxine," (he called me by mother's name instead of my name!) "Maxine, are you aware that you are a thumb-roller? (15) And that, for some reason, it gets on my nerves?" (16) My habit of leaving lids loose on containers also drives my husband nuts. (17) Now I know just how maddeningly similar parents and their children can be.

More practice with relevant details: <www.mywritinglab.com>

## Effective Expression: Use of Coordination and Subordination

Effective expression reflects a writer's thoughtful match of ideas to words and structure. Two types of sentence structures enable effective expression of comparison or contrast: coordination and subordination.

**Coordination** expresses an **equal** relationship between **similarities** with words such as: *and, likewise, similarly, also.* Coordination expresses an **equal** relationship between **differences** with words such as *but, yet, or, however, in contrast.*

A **compound sentence** is an example of **coordination.**

**Example**

An athlete trains the body for competitions; *likewise*, a student trains the mind for final exams.

**Subordination** expresses an **unequal** relationship between **similarities** with words such as: *as, just as, just like, like.* **Subordination** expresses an **unequal** relationship between **differences** with words such as *although, even though, while.*

A **complex sentence** is an example of **subordination.**

**Example**

*Just as* an athlete trains the body for competitions, a student trains the mind for final exams.

For more information on coordination and subordination, see Chapters 17 and 21.

### Practice 5

USING COORDINATION AND SUBORDINATION

Label each of the following sentences as a compound or a complex sentence. Identify the pattern of organization expressed by each sentence as comparison, contrast, or both. Revise sentence 5 from a compound sentence into a complex sentence. Discuss your work with your peers.

**1.** Although the pessimist and the optimist face many of the same challenges in life, they differ greatly in their actions, words, and thoughts.

SENTENCE TYPE: ______________________________

PATTERN OF ORGANIZATION: ______________________________

**2.** Just as the pessimist faces rejection and disappointments, the optimist endures those same hardships common to all humans.

SENTENCE TYPE: ______________________________

PATTERN OF ORGANIZATION: ______________________________

**3.** The pessimist focuses on problems and remains passive; in contrast, the optimist focuses on solutions and takes action.

SENTENCE TYPE: ______________________________

PATTERN OF ORGANIZATION: ______________________________

______________________________

4. The pessimist speaks words of condemnation and complaints, yet the optimist speaks words of affirmation and thanksgiving.

SENTENCE TYPE: ______________________________

PATTERN OF ORGANIZATION: ______________________________

5. The pessimist assumes the worst outcome as a given; the optimist expects a positive result as a probability.

REVISED INTO COMPLEX SENTENCE: ______________________________

______________________________

Practice 5

More practice with relevant details: <www.mywritinglab.com>

# Using Comparison and Contrast in Your Academic Courses

College writing assignments are often based on information gathered through class lectures, textbook reading assignments, and research. For example, essay exams often test students on material given in class or assigned in readings. Note-taking is an excellent pretest and prewriting activity. When you take or revise notes, set up a graphic organizer into which you can plug information from your class notes or reading assignments. A popular note-taking graphic divides an 11-inch by 8.5-inch page into three sections: a 8-inch by 3-inch left margin for key words; a 8-inch by 5-inch right margin for notes; and a 3-inch by 8.5-inch wide bottom margin for a summary. This format allows you to write, reflect, and write for understanding as you study.

## USING COMPARISON AND CONTRAST IN AN ART APPRECIATION COURSE: TAKING NOTES

Practice 6

Study the following set of notes taken during a lecture in a college art appreciation class. In the bottom margin (on the next page), write a short paragraph that states and supports the main idea of the notes.

| | |
|---|---|
| **Tragic hero** | Virtuous, admirable, rich, powerful, and male, but flawed; inner conflict and guilt; accepts responsibility for suffering; loses all. |
| Example | 5th Century BCE: In Oedipus the King, Oedipus loses power, wealth, family, and independence due to his limited wisdom and great pride. |
| **Melodramatic hero** | A symbol of good, male or female, a stereotype of courage and honesty, etc. No flaws; no inner conflict or guilt; fights against and defeats evil; all ends well. |
| Example | Pauline, the heroine of Perils of Pauline, is a "damsel in distress" who escapes many life-threatening, thrilling perils (dangers) due to her courage and ingenuity. |

More practice using comparison and contrast: <www.mywritinglab.com>

Practice 6

**Summary** What are the differences between a tragic hero and a melodramatic hero?

Workshop

# Workshop: Writing a Comparison and Contrast Paragraph Step by Step

WRITING A COMPARISON AND CONTRAST PARAGRAPH STEP BY STEP

PORTFOLIO

PREWRITING

## Choose Your Topic

The following activities are designed to help you choose a topic.

**1.** Create a bank of topics. Use the headings given below to brainstorm, or list as many similarities or differences about sets of topics as you possibly can. Don't criticize your thoughts. Add more topics, similarities, or differences as they occur to you. Revisit topic banks created during your study of previous chapters and identify comparable topics. Compare your bank of topics with those of your peers.

- Family Members
- Natural Disasters
- Neighborhoods
- Movies

**2.** Generate ideas with a freewrite. Choose one of the topics from your topic bank and think about the points of similarities or differences. Write about the similarities or differences for ten minutes without stopping.

OR

Select a set of photographs that illustrate the similarities or differences between two topics. Write a caption, brainstorm comparable points, and freewrite about the photograph(s). Remember to ask, "What are the similarities or differences represented by these images?" and "What's the point?"

## Focus Your Point

Read a prewrite you have generated for a comparison or contrast paragraph. Identify your audience and purpose. Annotate the text: underline or insert words that suggest your values, opinions, or attitudes about the topics and their points of similarity or difference. State in a sentence or two the importance of each similarity or difference between the comparable topics. Generate one or more concrete examples for each comparable point. Finally, state the point of comparison or contrast in one sentence.

AUDIENCE:

PURPOSE:

## Generate and Organize Relevant Details

Using ideas you have recorded so far and the concept chart below, generate and organize details that support your point.

| Concept Chart: Comparison/Contrast | | | |
|---|---|---|---|
| COMPARABLE TOPICS: | TOPIC A | LIKE OR UNLIKE | TOPIC B |
| 1st attribute, point, basis of comparison | | Like or unlike | |
| 2nd attribute, point, basis of comparison | | Like or unlike | |
| 3rd attribute, point, basis of comparison | | Like or unlike | |

**What's the point?**

DRAFTING

## Write a Draft of Your Paragraph

Using the ideas you generated during the prewriting phase, compose a draft of your comparison or contrast paragraph. Return to the prewriting process at any time to generate additional details as needed. Use your own paper.

REVISING

## Revise Your Draft

Once you have created a draft of your comparison or contrast paragraph, read the draft and answer the following questions. Indicate your answers by annotating your paper. If you answer "yes" to a question, underline, check, or circle examples. If you answer "no" to a question, write additional details in the margins and draw lines to indicate their placement. Revise your paragraph based on your reflection.

Workshop

## Questions for Revising a Comparison and Contrast Paragraph

- ☐ Have I chosen appropriately comparable topics? Have I clearly labeled each comparable point as a similarity or a difference?
- ☐ Have I made my point? Can I state my point in one sentence?
- ☐ Are my ideas logically and clearly ordered? Have I used strong transitions of comparison or contrast?
- ☐ Have I used concrete details to make my point?
- ☐ Have I included only the details that are relevant to my topic sentence?
- ☐ Have I used the following to make my ideas clear and interesting to my readers: vivid verbs and images, parallel language, controlled sentence structure, coordination, or subordination?

PROOFREADING

## Proofread Your Draft

Once you have revised your paragraph, proofread to ensure precise usage and grammar, such as editing for proper use of a comma after introductory elements.

### Grammar in Action: Commas after Introductory Elements

Commas are used after introductory elements: a word, phrase, or dependent clause that comes before an independent clause.

A dependent clause—an incomplete thought containing a subject and a verb—is signaled by a subordinating conjunction *(although, because, while...)* or a relative pronoun *(who, which, that...).*

An independent clause is a complete thought containing a subject and a verb.

- **Introductory word used with independent clause**

  Similarly, Sandra twiddles her thumbs.

- **Introductory phrase used with independent clause**

  In contrast, comedy's main purpose is to entertain.

- **Introductory dependent clause used with independent clause**

  Although Bob and Tom are both baby boomers, they differ greatly in values and lifestyles.

For more information on using commas after introductory elements, see Chapter 29.

Workshop

Practice 7

## COMMAS AND INTRODUCTORY ELEMENTS

Edit the following sentences for proper use of a comma after an introductory element. Identify the type of introductory element used in each sentence.
*Hint:* To identify a dependent clause, look for subordinating conjunctions and relative pronouns immediately in front of a subject and verb. To identify an independent clause, underline subjects once and verbs twice; then check to be sure a subordinating conjunction or relative pronoun does not come first.

__________ 1. Unlike those who are habitually late Consuelo has received three merit raises for prompt, efficient work.

__________ 2. Like a fire hydrant opened full force Deborah poured out her grief.

__________ 3. However the traveling nurse program offers better pay and greater mobility.

__________ 4. The oldest child enjoyed the full attention of her parents; in contrast the youngest child always had to share her parent's attention with her siblings.

More ideas for writing a comparison and contrast paragraph: <www.mywritinglab.com>

Review

## REVIEW OF WRITING A COMPARISON OR CONTRAST PARAGRAPH: DEVELOP YOUR POINT USING THE WRITING PROCESS

Use the following form to record your thinking about writing a comparison or contrast paragraph.

PREWRITING DRAFTING Select and focus your topic for your writing situation, audience, and purpose. Choose a topic that is best explained through comparison or contrast and identify its significance. What is your point?

TWO (OR MORE) COMPARABLE TOPICS: ______________________________

______________________________

AUDIENCE: ______________________________

PURPOSE: ______________________________

______________________________

PREWRITING DRAFTING State your main idea in a topic sentence.

TWO (OR MORE) COMPARABLE TOPICS: ______________________________

OPINION: ______________________________

______________________________

PREWRITING DRAFTING Generate relevant details.

REPORTER'S QUESTIONS: WHO, WHAT, WHERE, WHEN, WHY, HOW? ______________________________

______________________________

POINTS OF SIMILARITIES: ______________________________

______________________________

POINTS OF DIFFERENCE: ______________________________

______________________________

PREWRITING DRAFTING REVISING Use logical order. Use transition words to signal organization of details and relationship between ideas.

TRANSITIONS OF COMPARISON: ______________________________

______________________________

TRANSITIONS OF CONTRAST: ______________________________

______________________________

REVISING PROOFREADING Use coordination and subordination. Use commas to set off introductory elements.

USE OF COORDINATION AND SUBORDINATION: ______________________________

COMMAS WITH INTRODUCTORY ELEMENTS: ______________________________

______________________________

INTRODUCTORY WORDS: ______________________________

INTRODUCTORY PHRASES: ______________________________

______________________________

INTRODUCTORY DEPENDENT CLAUSES: ______________________________

______________________________

Review

# Writing Assignments

## Considering Audience and Purpose

Study the set of photographs about hurricanes Katrina and Rita at the beginning of the chapter. Write a letter to the editor of your local newspaper. Contrast what happened with both, what should have happened, and what must happen in the future. Answer the question, "What can we do better?" Call for action! Use a reasonable tone and avoid name calling.

## Writing for Everyday Life

Assume that you have just experienced a life-altering event, such as a near-death experience, a graduation, a marriage, the birth of a child, a severe loss, or the breaking of a bad habit. You have been asked to talk about "Change" to a specific audience such as the Rotary Club, a civic group. Identify your audience and write a short speech in which you discuss three before-and-after comparable points. Allow your tone through word choice to reflect either sadness and regret or pride and encouragement.

## Writing for College Life

Assume you are in a biology class and you read the following textbook question on the study guide for the final exam: "In what ways did the human skeleton change as upright posture and bipedalism evolved? Describe the changes by comparing the human skeleton and the skeleton of a quadruped such as a baboon." – Campbell, Mitchell, and Reece. *Biology: Concepts and Connections*, 5th ed. 2005 Longman. p. 620.

Test what you already know about the subject by writing a paragraph. Identify the comparable points of similarities and/or differences between the two topics. Look up words in your dictionary as needed.

## Writing for Working Life

Assume that you are applying for a management position at a local business or mid-sized company. You had the following positions and experiences, which are listed on your résumé: Treasurer, Student Government Association; Certified in various computer programs and software; Member of Toastmasters, a public-speaking organization. Write a paragraph in which you compare the skills you've developed with the skills needed at the job for which you are applying.

# 10 The Definition Paragraph

## Chapter Preview



## A definition explains what a word or concept means.

We are all familiar with the word *definition*. In fact, we apply or create definitions in every aspect of life. Call to mind what you already know about a definition. Answer the following questions: How would you define "a good life"? What are the traits and examples of "a good life"? What information should be included in a definition?

The definition pattern of organization is helpful in all areas of life. In personal life, you rely upon a doctor's definition of your symptoms when you seek medical treatment. In working life, you define your job duties to ensure your best performance. In college life, you will define the specialized meanings and examples of words in each content area.

To write a definition, the writer names a concept, explains its traits, describes the concept using similar terms, and offers examples of the concept. Often a contrast clarifies meaning; thus, a writer may also include an example and explanation of what the term or concept is *not*.

# What's the Point of a Definition?

The following definition-concept chart shows three visual examples of a concept and one visual example of what the concept is not. Study the chart and the visual examples. Then, write answers to the questions asked in the chart. Consider these questions as you write your answers: What is the concept being defined? What are some examples? What traits does each example represent? Then, answer the question, "What's the point?" with a one-sentence statement of the overall main idea.

WRITING FROM LIFE

Practice 1

PHOTOGRAPHIC ORGANIZER: DEFINITION-CONCEPT CHART

What does the concept represent?

What are some examples?

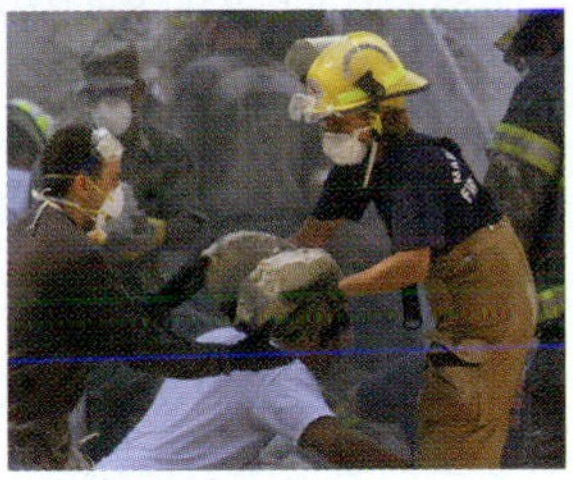

What is it NOT?

Concept?

What is this concept? Synonyms? Traits?

**What the point?**

*Concept map adapted from following sources:*

Frayer, D., Frederick, W. C., and Klausmeier, H. J. (1969). *A Schema for Testing the Level of Cognitive Mastery.* Madison, WI: Wisconsin Center for Education Research.

Schwartz, R., & Raphael, T. (1985). "Concept of definition: A Key to Improving Student's Vocabulary." *The Reading Teacher*, 39, 198-205.

PREWRITING

## My First Thoughts: A Prewriting Activity

Brainstorm about the images you just studied. Set a time limit, such as five minutes, and write in your notebook about the images and the details you generated. Write as quickly as you can without stopping. Let the ideas flow freely. Getting your first thoughts about a topic on paper is one excellent way to kick-start your writing process.

# Making a Point Using Definition: One Student Writer's Response

The following paragraph offers one writer's point about the concept depicted in the photographs. Read the definition and the paragraph's annotations. Complete the activities in bold type given in the annotations. Then read the writer's journal entry that records decisions made during the writing process.

**MAIN IDEA:**
The main idea states the author's point about a concept. The concept being defined is "hero."
**Underline the writer's point about the concept.**

**RELEVANT DETAILS:**
Relevant details include descriptive details about traits and examples.
**Circle three additional traits of a hero.**

**LISTING ORDER:**
The transition "third" indicates that at least three traits are listed.
**Underline the two transitions that introduce supporting details.**

**EFFECTIVE EXPRESSION:**
Figurative language paints a vivid image for your reader. "Bravery bobbling on a bungee" gives a human trait to the concept "Bravery."
**Circle one other phrase that uses figurative language.**

An Everyday Hero

(1) An everyday hero is one who dies to self to live for others. (2) We need more everyday heroes. (3) First, we need compassionate, brave, hard-working men and women to feed the poor, tend to the sick, or confront a crisis. (4) Second, we need people of humility who value the needs of others above their own, and we need people of valor who risk all to meet those needs. (5) Third, we need people of dedication who toil no matter how hard and how daunting the labor may be. (6) We do not need mere thrill-seekers, people who contrive a risk for fun, who fly high on adrenaline, and who find bravery bobbling on a bungee. (7) Indeed, we need heroes like Mother Teresa. (8) This humble servant chose to live among the poorest of the poor in Calcutta, India, so she could care for "the unwanted, the unloved, the uncared for." (9) Certainly, we need more heroes like the rescue workers of 9/11. (10) Heroic responders from all parts of the country rushed to the fallen towers of the World Trade Center, and with diligence and reverence, they moved our mountain of grief. (11) Without doubt, we need more heroes like the unpaid workers of the Red Cross. (12) Selfless volunteers from all walks of life risk their own lives to give aid to the sick and dying in the muddy, ransacked villages of the world. (13) These few examples represent thousands and thousands of unnamed heroes across the globe. (14) Even so, most assuredly, we need more everyday heroes.

## THE WRITER'S JOURNAL

The student writer of "An Everyday Hero" completed the following reflection to record her thinking through the writing process. Read her writer's journal that describes a few key choices she made as she wrote.

MAIN IDEA: This paragraph is the result of careful planning and many revisions. The definition chart helped me identify the traits and descriptive details of the examples of heroes during my prewriting session. Interestingly, by filling in the map, I discovered my own views about what makes a person a hero. The images made me feel sad for the victims, yet inspired by the volunteers. My purpose is to call the reader to become an everyday hero in everyday life.

RELEVANT DETAILS: The map enabled me to think about my feelings and record some descriptive synonyms such as "compassionate, brave, and hard-working."

LOGICAL ORDER: As I read my first draft, I noticed that I had not used strong transitions. Instead, I had relied upon repeating key phrases such as "we need..." to unite the ideas. Although I liked the effect of the repeated phrases, I decided to experiment by adding listing transitions for the traits in the first several sentences. Then, I chose to use emphatic signal words to introduce the examples: "indeed, certainly, without doubt, most assuredly." During this revision, I also moved the topic sentence; originally, I thought I would end the paragraph with the actual definition of "everyday hero." I wanted to build up to the definition at the end, but it seemed to sound better when I placed it as the first sentence.

EFFECTIVE EXPRESSION: In my final revision, I focused on effective expression. Since the topic "heroes" seems like a lofty ideal to me, I wanted to use figurative language. So I used "moved our mountain of grief" to describe the rubble of the towers and suggest the emotional significance of the event and the 9/11 heroes. The bungee jumper is a great example of what a hero is not, so I used the phrase "bravery bobbling on a bungee" to depict the selfish risk bungee jumping seems to be (in my opinion, anyway!). I wanted the alliteration of the "b" sound to create a silly contrast to the serious images of heroes. At the last minute, I wanted to change every instance of the word "everyday hero" to "hero." I wonder which version would best reach a general audience? I need feedback! Due date looming—this draft is a go!

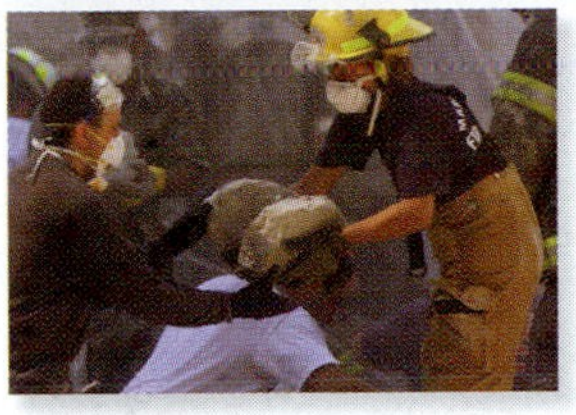

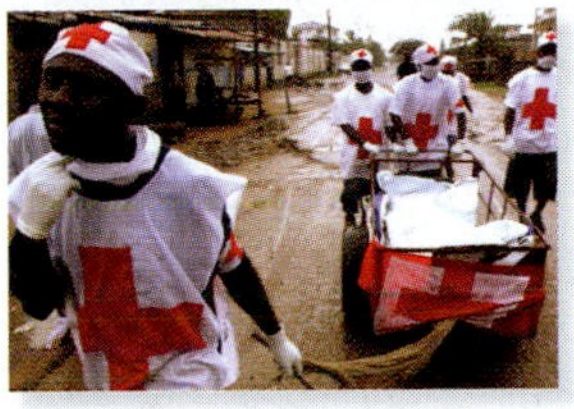

For a blank version of this form for your own reflections about your writing: <www.mywritinglab.com>

# Developing Your Point Using Definition

A definition clarifies the meaning of a concept. A definition makes a point by classifying a concept, describing its traits, describing what it is *like*, describing what it is *not like*, and illustrating it with examples. To support a point by definition, a writer classifies a concept, offers relevant and concrete descriptions and examples of what it is and what it is not, and may also use figurative language.

## The Point: The Main Idea

When you write a definition paragraph, you limit your thoughts to a set of details that clarify the meaning of a concept. Most likely, you have an opinion or belief about the concept, characteristics, or examples. Your opinion is your point or main idea. A topic sentence states the overall point of the definition. Often a definition topic sentence emphasizes one aspect of the definition: its class, its traits, what it is like, or what it is not like.

For example, each of the following three topic sentences contains (1) a concept, (2) the writer's attitude about the concept, and (3) the pattern of organization.

**Definition by Classification: Group or Traits**

TOPIC — PATTERN OF ORGANIZATION: DEFINITION SIGNAL WORDS — WRITER'S OPINION

A classical hero is a male character who suffers tragic loss due to his pride and ignorance.

**Definition by Comparison: Synonyms or Analogies**

TOPIC — PATTERN OF ORGANIZATION: DEFINITION SIGNAL WORDS — WRITER'S OPINION

Faith is like the sap of a tree or the fountainhead of a flowing well.

**Definition by Contrast: Negation or What It Is Not**

TOPIC — PATTERN OF ORGANIZATION: DEFINITION SIGNAL WORDS — WRITER'S OPINION

A compassionate intervention is not an accusing, condemning, or violent action.

Practice 2

## TOPIC SENTENCES

The first three items present a topic, an opinion, and definition signal words. Combine the ideas in each group to create a topic sentence for a definition. Then, complete the practice by making your own topic sentences.

**1.** TOPIC: Depression

OPINION: treatable illness that affects the body and mind

DEFINITION SIGNAL WORDS: is a

TOPIC SENTENCE: 

**2.** TOPIC: A hypocrite

OPINION: a spy or traitor

DEFINITION SIGNAL WORDS: is

TOPIC SENTENCE: 

**3.** TOPIC: Forgiveness

OPINION: denial of the wrong, but rather acceptance of the apology

DEFINITION SIGNAL WORDS: does not mean

TOPIC SENTENCE: 

**4.** TOPIC: sociology

OPINION: Neutral

DEFINITION SIGNAL WORDS: is

TOPIC SENTENCE: 

More practice with creating topic sentences: <www.mywritinglab.com>

Practice 2

**5.** TOPIC: ______________________

OPINION: ______________________

DEFINITION SIGNAL WORDS: ______________________

TOPIC SENTENCE: ______________________

**6.** TOPIC: ______________________

OPINION: ______________________

DEFINITION SIGNAL WORDS: ______________________

TOPIC SENTENCE: ______________________

**7.** TOPIC: ______________________

OPINION: ______________________

COMPARISON OR CONTRAST SIGNAL WORDS: ______________________

TOPIC SENTENCE: ______________________

______________________

## Logical Order

Once you have narrowed your topic into a focused subject, you are ready to generate and organize additional details. To make a point using definition, a writer moves from a general idea (the concept to be defined) to major and minor supporting details. These include traits and examples of *what it is, what it is like,* or *what it is not like.* To signal the relationship between these levels of ideas, a writer often uses the following pattern of wording: "A concept is…"; "A term means…"; "for example." Strong signal words establish coherence, a clear and understandable flow of ideas.

### Key Words and Transition Words That Signal Definition

| | | | | |
|---|---|---|---|---|
| **Key words:** | are | constitutes | indicates | means |
| | connotes | defined as | is | suggests |
| | consists of | denotes | is not | |
| **Transition words:** | also | in addition | one trait | |
| | another trait | in particular | specifically | |
| | for example | like | such as | |

Practice 3

RELATIONSHIP OF DETAILS

The following ideas were published on a government Website. Determine the logical order of the following sentences.

**Sexual Harassment**

.......... Sexual harassment is a form of sex discrimination that violates the Civil Rights Act of 1964.

.......... Furthermore, unwelcome sexual advances, requests for sexual favors, and other verbal or physical conduct of a sexual nature constitutes sexual harassment when submission to or rejection of this conduct explicitly or implicitly affects an individual's employment, unreasonably interferes with an individual's work performance or creates an intimidating, hostile or offensive work environment.

.......... Fourth, unlawful sexual harassment may occur without economic injury to or discharge of the victim.

.......... In addition, sexual harassment can occur in a variety of circumstances, including but not limited to the following:

.......... The following two examples of sexual harassment illustrate a demand for sexual favor and the creation of a hostile working envoirnment:

.......... First, the victim as well as the harasser may be a woman or a man; the victim does not have to be of the opposite sex.

.......... Second, the harasser can be the victim's supervisor, an agent of the employer, a supervisor in another area, a co-worker, or a non-employee.

.......... Third, the victim does not have to be the person harassed, but could be anyone affected by the offensive conduct.

.......... Fifth, the harasser's conduct must be unwelcome.

.......... After weeks of this, the supervisor makes it known to the employee that the only way the employee will get the promotion he or she is seeking is to date the supervisor.

.......... In one example, an employee feels threatened by his or her supervisor because of the persistent teasing and sex-related hints that occur.

.......... In another example, a co-worker constantly tells sexually explicit jokes and makes demeaning comments about male coworkers and clients.

—Adapted from United States Equal Employment Opportunity Commission. *"Facts about Sexual Harassment."* 13 March 2006

More practice with logical order: <www.mywritinglab.com>

## Relevant Details

As a writer narrows a topic into a focused main idea, the thinking process brings to mind many details that answer questions such as *who, what, when, where, why,* and *how.* A writer evaluates the relevancy of each detail and uses only those that clarify or support the main idea. In a definition paragraph, some relevant major details include those that classify and describe the traits of a term or concept. Relevant minor details offer examples and illustrations of the term or concept as defined. Some major and minor details may explain the writer's opinion about the concept. Relevant details include types, traits, descriptions, and examples of the concept being defined.

During the prewriting phase, a concept chart can help a writer organize ideas. Study the following Definition Concept Chart about the topic "graffiti."

**Definition Concept Chart**

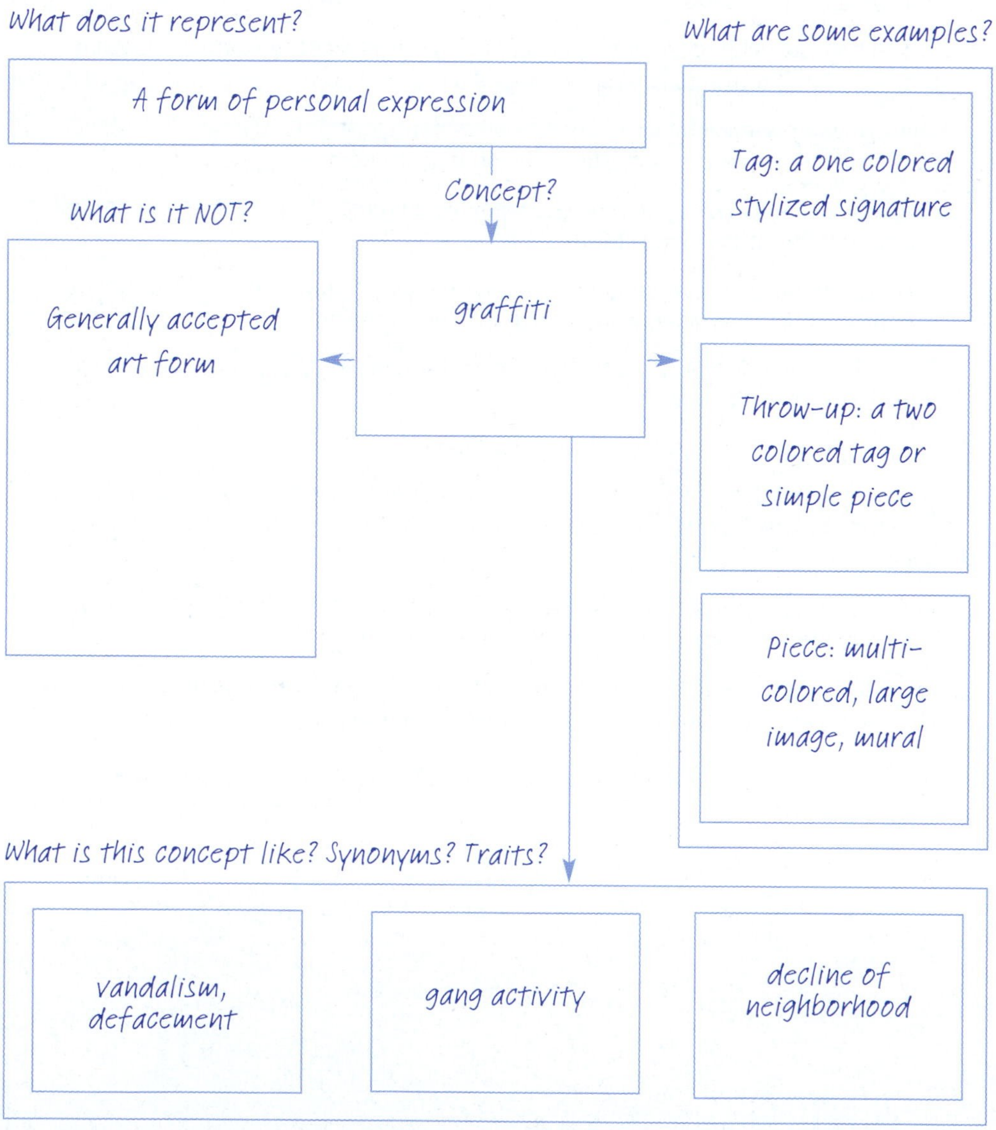


During prewriting, a writer naturally generates irrelevant details. In fact, an effective writer often produces far more details than can be used to make a specific point. Irrelevant details do not explain or support the focused point of the paragraph. A careful writer uses the revision process to double-check details for relevancy and to eliminate irrelevant details.

## Practice 4

RELEVANT DETAILS

The following paragraph develops the ideas generated about graffiti during the brainstorming and prewriting phase. Circle the main idea. Underline the three major details. Cross out two details that are not relevant to the main point.

**Graffiti**

(1) Although graffiti is a common sight, many do not understand its true nature: vandalism. (2) Graffiti, a form of personal expression, is the unlawful markings of an individual or group on private and public surfaces. (3) One type of graffiti is known as a tag, a stylized signature of a tagger or writer. (4) A tag is quickly created with one color that starkly contrasts with the background upon which it is written. (5) Tags can be written with spray paint, fat-tipped markers, etching tools, or pre-tagged stickers. (6) Another kind of graffiti is the throw-up, a two-dimensional image made with large bubble letters that are outlined in black or white and filled in with another color. (7) A writer often uses throw-ups to bomb an area in a short amount of time. (8) A third type of graffiti, similar to a mural, is the piece, short for masterpiece. (9) Time-consuming to create, a piece is a large, colorful, and complex image that usually reflects a political or social issue. (10) Piecing demonstrates a high level of aerosol paint control. (11) Unlike more widely accepted forms of art, graffiti is not generally regarded as aesthetically pleasing, nor is it thought of as a means to explore or enhance the appreciation of beauty. (12) Graffiti is much more likely to be labeled as vandalism and defacement, and seen as evidence of a gang or a neighborhood in decline. (13) Instances of graffiti are evident in both urban and suburban public areas such as parks, restrooms, buildings, and trains. (14) Graffiti can be removed by scraping, power washing, chemically treating, or painting the affected surface. (15) Many communities fight graffiti by offering legal walls as concrete canvases for graffiti writers.

More practice with relevant details: <www.mywritinglab.com>

## Effective Expression: Sound Structure and Vivid Images

Effective expression reflects a writer's thoughtful match of ideas to words and structure. Writers rely heavily on the various forms of the *to be* verb (such as *is*) to write a definition. Often the use of *is* leads to nonstandard phrasing or bland expressions. To add interest and maintain clarity, consider the following hints:

**Hint 1:** Avoid *is when* and *is where* to construct your definition. One way to revise to eliminate *is when* and *is where* is to follow the verb with a synonym that renames the subject of the sentence.

**Nonstandard**

Addiction is when a person has a compulsive need for a habit-forming substance such as alcohol, nicotine, or heroin.

**Revised**

Addiction is a compulsive need for a habit-forming substance such as alcohol, nicotine, or heroin.

**Nonstandard**

Utopia is where a person can find perfect laws and social conditions.

**Revised**

Utopia is an ideal society made up of perfect laws and social conditions.

**Hint 2:** Use *is* to create a vivid image. A vivid image often allows the writer to express a point about the concept being defined.

Addiction is a self-made prison of compulsive need.

Utopia is a paradise made up of perfect laws and social conditions.

**Hint 3:** Replace *is* with an action verb. An action verb often allows the writer to express a point about the concept being defined.

Addiction imprisons a person in the compulsive need for habit-forming substances such as alcohol, nicotine, and heroin.

Utopia promises an ideal society made up of perfect laws and social conditions.

Practice 5

## SOUND STRUCTURE AND VIVID IMAGES

Revise the following sentences to avoid nonstandard phrasing or bland expressions. Discuss your work with your class or with a small group of your peers.

**1.** An input device is where a machine feeds data into a computer, such as a keyboard.

REVISED: ______________________________

______________________________

**2.** A character is when any symbol requires a byte of memory or storage in computer software.

REVISED: ______________________________

______________________________

**3.** A cursor is where a special symbol such as a blinking underline character signifies where the next character will be displayed on the screen; to type in different areas of the screen, you must move the cursor.

REVISED: ______________________________

______________________________

______________________________

**4.** Located at the top of a computer's keyboard and labeled F1 through F12, function keys are where you can find shortcuts to certain tasks in the Windows operating system; for example, on some keyboards, F1 is the "help" shortcut key.

REVISED: ______________________________

______________________________

______________________________

**5.** A computer virus is when a program or code (written computer instructions) is loaded onto a computer without the consent of the user; a computer virus can quickly use up all of the computer's memory and bring the system to a halt.

REVISED: ______________________________

______________________________

______________________________

______________________________

More practice with sound sentence structure and vivid images.
<www.mywritinglab.com>

# Using Definition in Your Academic Courses

The definition paragraph serves as an excellent way to write for understanding. By defining key concepts and specialized vocabulary in your content courses, you will deepen your learning.

Practice 6

**USING DEFINITION IN A COMMUNICATIONS ASSIGNMENT: DEFINING SPECIALIZED VOCABULARY**

The following definition concept chart is based on information taken from a college communications textbook. Demonstrate your understanding of the concept and the relationship among the details in the definition. Using your own words, write a definition of the concept in the space below.

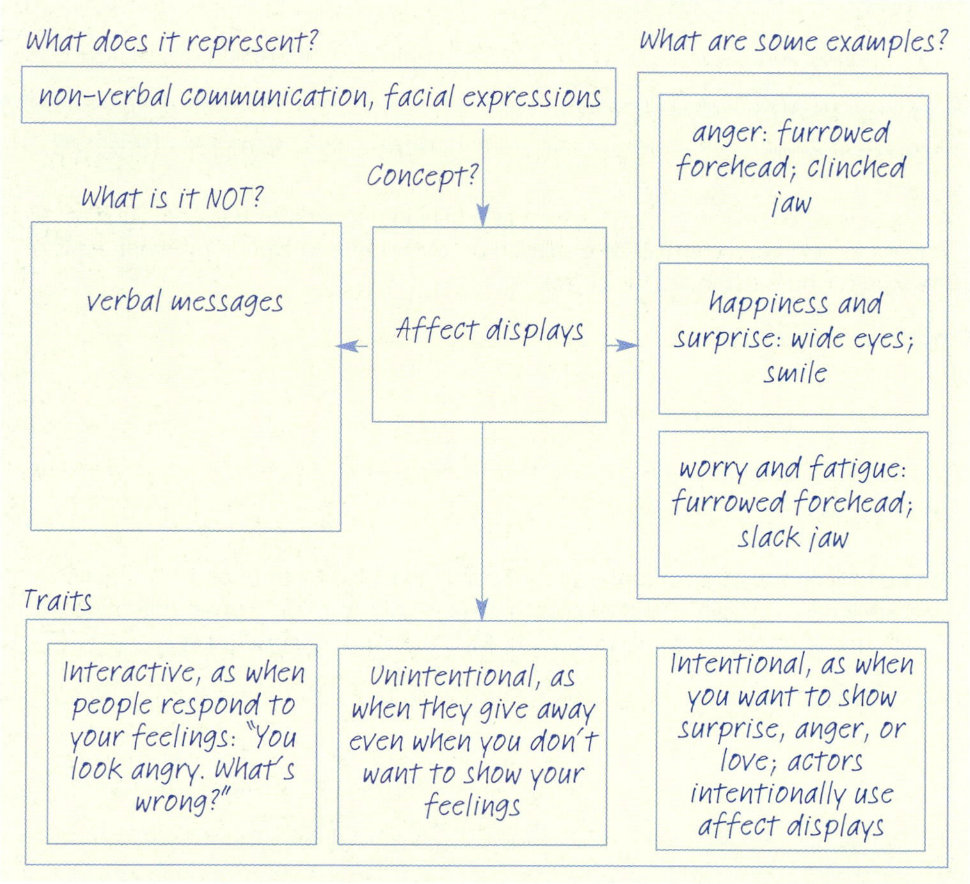


—DeVito, Joseph A. *The Interpersonal Communication Book, 10th ed.* Allyn & Bacon, 2004, p. 182.

More practice with writing definition paragraphs: <www.mywritinglab.com>

# Workshop: Writing a Definition Paragraph Step by Step



WRITING A DEFINITION PARAGRAPH STEP BY STEP

Workshop

PORTFOLIO

PREWRITING

## Choose Your Topic

The following activities are designed to help you choose a topic.

1. Create a bank of topics. Use the headings below to brainstorm or list as many concepts to be defined as you possibly can. Don't analyze your thoughts; just get as many topics written down as quickly as possible. Add more topics as they occur to you. Revisit topic banks created during your study of previous chapters for terms or concepts you could define. Compare your bank of topics with those of your peers.
   - Hip Hop Music
   - Role Models
   - Pollution
   - Success
2. Generate ideas with a freewrite. Choose one of the topics from your topic bank and think about the following: To what group does the concept belong? What are the characteristics of the concept? What are some examples of the concept?

   OR

   Select a set of photographs that illustrates the essence of a concept. For each photo: brainstorm types, traits, synonyms, contrasts, and examples. Freewrite about the photograph(s). Remember to ask, "What's the point?"

## Focus Your Point

Read a freewrite you have generated for a definition. Underline words that suggest your values, opinions, or attitudes about the concept and its traits. Think about why the concept is important. Think about what examples best represent each trait and a situation that best illustrates the concept. Identify your audience and purpose. Write a list of additional concrete examples that explain your point. State in one sentence the point of the definition:

AUDIENCE: ..........

PURPOSE: ..........

..........

..........

..........

..........

..........

## Generate and Organize Relevant Details

Using ideas you have recorded so far and the following definition concept chart, generate and organize details that support your point.

**Definition Concept Chart**

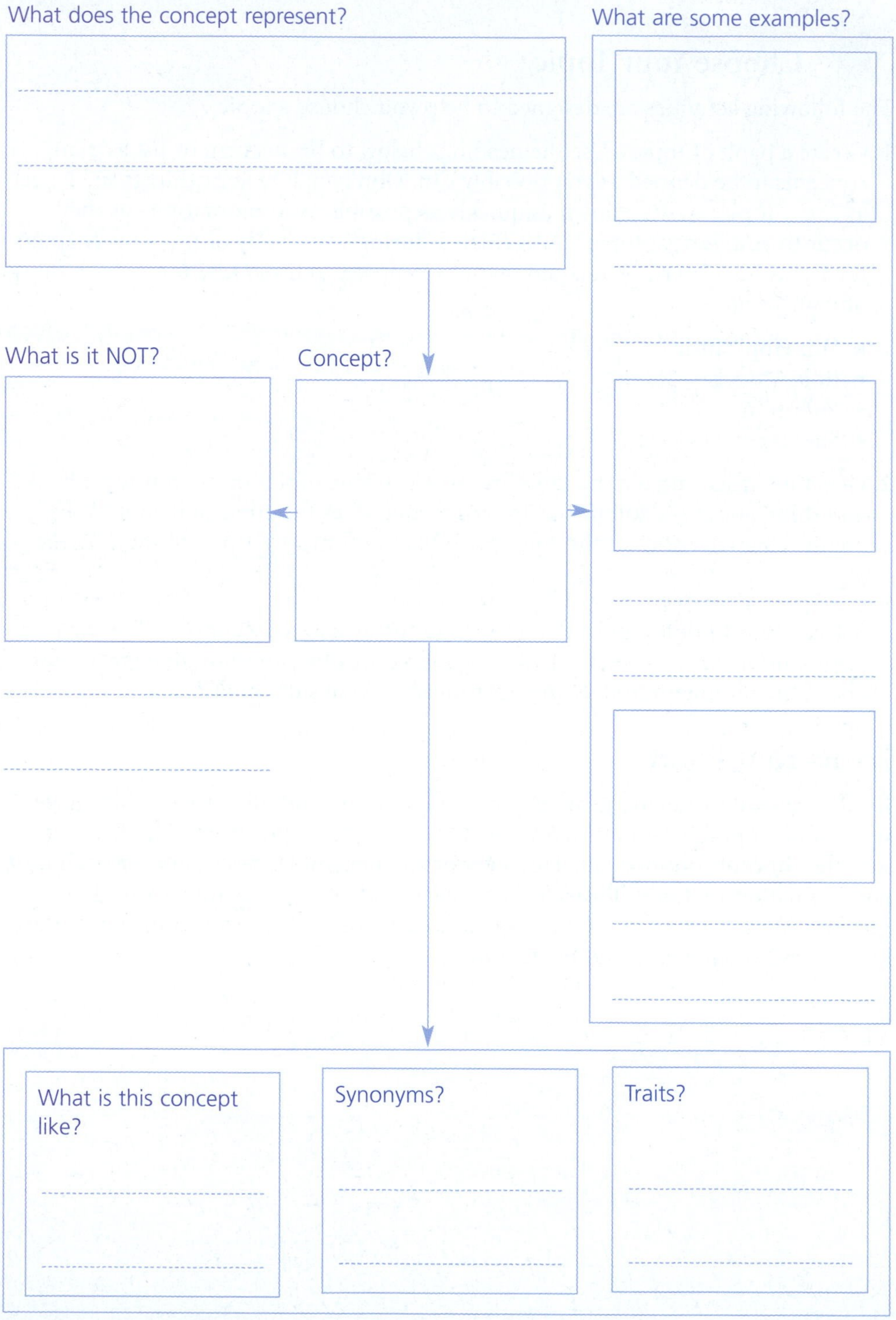


WHAT'S THE POINT? ______________________________

DRAFTING

## Write a Draft of Your Paragraph

Using the ideas you generated during the prewriting phase, compose a draft of your definition paragraph. Return to the prewriting process at any time to generate additional details as needed. Use your own paper.

REVISING

## Revise Your Draft

Once you have created a draft of a definition paragraph, read the draft and answer the following questions. Indicate your answers by annotating your paper. If you answer "yes" to a question, underline, check, or circle examples. If you answer "no" to a question, write additional details in the margins and draw lines to indicate their placement. Revise your paragraph based on your reflection.

## Questions for Revising a Definition Paragraph

- ☐ Have I chosen an important concept to define? Have I clearly classified and illustrated the concept?
- ☐ Have I stated or implied a focused main idea? Can I state my point in one sentence? Have I created a strong impression?
- ☐ Have I effectively used order of importance? Have I used strong transitions of definition?
- ☐ Have I made my point with adequate details? Have I used concrete details to make my point?
- ☐ Have I included only the details that are relevant to my topic sentence?
- ☐ Have I used the following to make my ideas clear and interesting to my readers: vivid verbs and images, parallel language, controlled sentence structure, coordination, or subordination?

PROOFREADING

## Proofread Your Draft

Once you have made any revisions to your paragraph that may be needed, proofread your paragraph for proper usage and punctuation, such as using commas to set off nonessential information.

Workshop

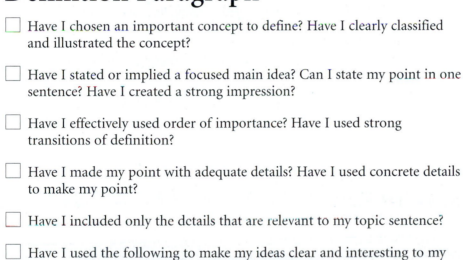

For more information on using commas with nonessential information, see Chapter 29.

Workshop

## Grammar in Action: Proper Use of Commas with Nonessential Information

In a sentence, some information that describes or modifies a word is nonessential. Nonessential information doesn't restrict the meaning of the word being described or modified. Nonessential information can be words, phrases, or clauses. If you can leave the information out of the sentence without changing the meaning of the sentence, then the information is nonessential. Use **commas before** and **after** nonessential words, phrases, and clauses. Use commas after nonessential words, phrases, and clauses that introduce a sentence.

- **Nonessential Word:**

  Regular physical activity, moreover, promotes health, psychological well-being, and a healthy body weight.

  My husband, Bob, runs six miles every other day.

- **Nonessential Phrase:**

  For example, a healthful diet includes a variety of fruits and vegetables each day.

  Janine, eating a healthful diet and exercising, has lost 25 pounds.

- **Nonessential Clause:**

  My great-grandmother, who is nearly 90 years old, goes bowling every week.

  Sandra's diet, which is laden with high-fat, high-calorie foods, must change to ensure her good health.

Practice 7

### PROPER COMMA USE WITH NONESSENTIAL INFORMATION

Edit these sentences for proper use of commas before and after nonessential words, phrases, or clauses. Underline the nonessential information and insert the commas as needed.

1. Patience however is not tolerance of harmful wrongdoing.
2. Jerome who has been my friend since childhood does not tolerate gossip.
3. Jerome wanting to stand on his principles broke up with a girl who was a gossip.
4. Patience is on the other hand acceptance based on forgiveness.
5. Once Iva who was a gossip until Jerome broke up with her changed her ways, Jerome asked her out again.

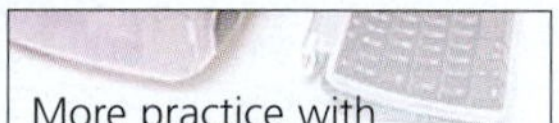

More practice with using commas with nonessential information: <www.mywritinglab.com>

Review

**REVIEW OF WRITING A DEFINITION PARAGRAPH:** DEVELOP YOUR POINT USING THE WRITING PROCESS

Use the following form to record your thinking about writing a definition paragraph. Select and focus your topic for your writing situation, audience, and purpose. Choose a topic that is best developed through definition and identify its significance.

PREWRITING DRAFTING What is your point?

CONCEPT TO BE DEFINED: ______________________

AUDIENCE: ______________________

PURPOSE: ______________________

______________________

______________________

PREWRITING DRAFTING State your main idea in a topic sentence.

CONCEPT TO BE DEFINED: ______________________

OPINION: ______________________

______________________

______________________

PREWRITING DRAFTING Generate relevant details.

REPORTER'S QUESTIONS: WHO, WHAT, WHERE, WHEN, WHY, HOW? ______________________

______________________

TRAITS OF THE CONCEPT: ______________________

DESCRIPTION OF THE CONCEPT (what is the concept *like*: synonyms): ______________________

______________________

WHAT THE CONCEPT IS NOT: ______________________

EXAMPLES OF THE CONCEPT: ______________________

Review

PREWRITING DRAFTING REVISING

Use logical order. Use transition words to signal organization of details and relationship between ideas.

TRANSITIONS THAT SIGNAL DEFINITION: ____________________

TRANSITIONS THAT LIST DETAILS: ____________________

____________________

REVISING PROOFREADING

Use effective expression. Use standard sentence structure and vivid images. Correctly use commas with nonessential information..

STANDARD SENTENCE STRUCTURE AND VIVID IMAGES: ____________________

____________________

PROPER USE OF COMMAS WITH NONESSENTIAL INFORMATION: ____________________

____________________

# Writing Assignments

## Considering Audience and Purpose

Study the set of photographs about the people and situations at the beginning of the chapter. Assume you have benefited personally from the efforts of one of the people depicted in the images. Brainstorm a list of attributes of this person. Write a one-paragraph thank-you letter to this person in which you define what he or she means to you.

## Writing for Everyday Life

Assume that you have agreed to seek counseling to improve a relationship with a family member or co-worker. The counselor has asked you to define your role in the relationship. Identify the type of relationship you have with your family member or co-worker, the major traits of the relationship, and examples or incidents that illustrate the nature of your relationship. Allow your tone—through your word choice—to reflect one of the following: (1) concern or (2) resentment.

## Writing for College Life

Assume you are a first-semester college student who is enrolled in a study skills class, and you have been assigned to write a paragraph that defines student success. Based on your experience and observations, write a definition of student success that addresses attitudes, behaviors, and skills.

## Writing for Working Life

Assume that you work in a retail store that sells clothes, electronics, or some other specialized merchandise. Also assume that sales and morale are down. Write a one-paragraph memo to your supervisor in which you define the morale problem.

More ideas for writing a definition paragraph: <www.mywritinglab.com>

# 11 The Cause and Effect Paragraph

**Chapter Preview**

- What's the Point of Cause and Effect?
- Making a Point Using Cause and Effect: One Student Writer's Response
- Developing Your Point Using Cause and Effect
- Using Cause and Effect in Your Academic Courses
- Workshop: Writing a Cause and Effect Paragraph Step by Step

## A cause is the reason an event took place. An effect is the result of an event. Cause leads to effect.

Understanding the relationship between cause and effect is a vital critical thinking skill used in all aspects of life. For example, when an illness strikes us, we must correctly identify the cause of our symptoms in order to treat it. In addition, we must take into account the side effects of any medication we take to treat the illness. What are some other instances in which we consider causes and effects?

Thinking about cause and effect points out the relationship between events based on reasons and results. For example, in your personal life, you may have identified that stress causes you to eat for comfort. In working life, you may have identified the need to master certain software programs to be competitive in the job market. In college life, you may have identified how logical causes and effects play a role in the study of history, science, or economics. To write a cause and effect paragraph, identify a set of related events, objects, or factors. Then, label each event, object, or factor within the group as either a cause or an effect. Be sure to test each event as a true cause. Events that occur at or near the same time may be coincidental and unrelated. Then, present your details in a logical order that explains why each cause leads to a specific effect.

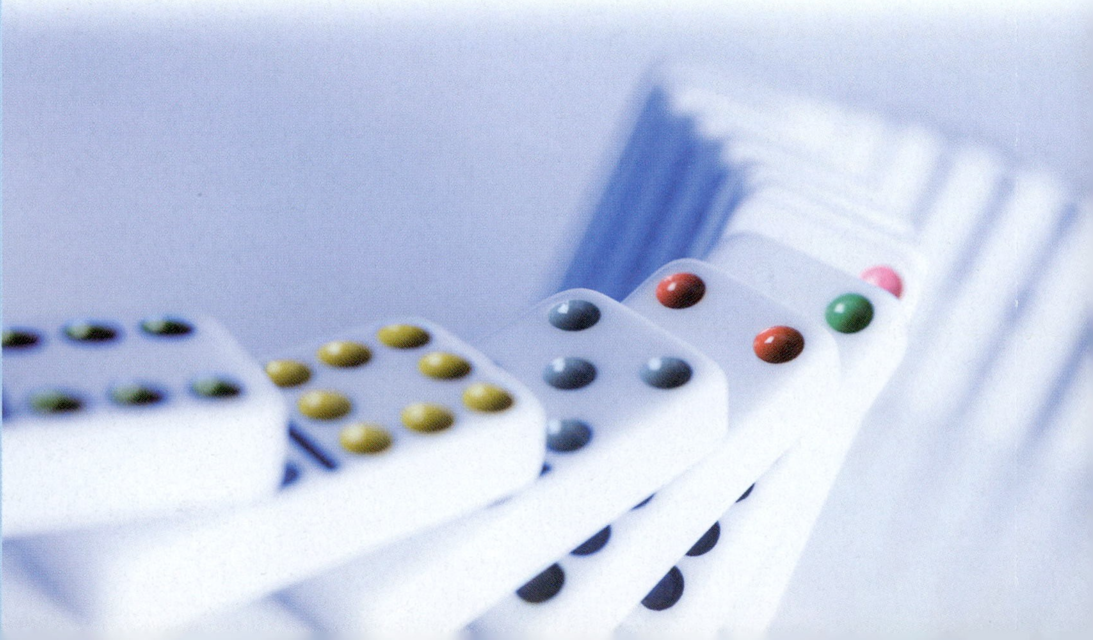

# What's the Point of Cause and Effect?

Often ideas become clearer when they are analyzed based on how they relate to one another. The cause and effect pattern of organization allows a writer to explore the ways in which ideas are related based on reasons and results. The following set of photographs documents a set of causes and effects. Study the images and write captions that identify the appropriate causes and effects illustrated. Answer the following questions: What is this? Why did this happen? What is the further effect? Answer the question "What's the point?" with a one-sentence statement of the overall main idea.

WRITING FROM LIFE

Practice 1

PHOTOGRAPHIC ORGANIZER: CAUSE AND EFFECT

What is this?

Why did it happen?

What is this further effect?

Why did it happen?

Habitat for Humanity®

▲ A volunteer organization

▲ Volunteers building homes

What is this?

Why did it happen?

What is this?

Why did it happen?

What's the point?

PREWRITING

## My First Thoughts: A Prewriting Activity

Brainstorm about the images you just studied. Set a time limit, such as five minutes, and write in your notebook about the images and the details you generated. Write as quickly as you can without stopping. Let the ideas flow freely. Getting your first thoughts about a topic on paper is one excellent way to kick-start your writing process.

# Making a Point Using Cause and Effect: One Student Writer's Response

The following paragraph offers one writer's point about the causes and effects illustrated by the photographs. Read the cause and effect paragraph; complete the activities. Then read the writer's journal that records decisions made during the writing process.

**EFFECTIVE EXPRESSION:** Precise word choice makes your point credible. Writers often confuse the word "affect," a verb that means to influence with "effect," a noun which means result. **Circle a verb that can be replaced with "affects." Circle two nouns that can be replaced with "effect."**

**STRONG TRANSITIONS:** The transitional word "because" signals that "natural disasters and poverty" occur as causes before "Habitat for Humanity calls for volunteers." **Underline three more transitional words or phrases that signal cause or effect.**

**RELEVANT DETAILS:** Relevant details include descriptive details that describe the qualities of a cause or effect. "Quality and affordable" are important traits of the homes built by Habitat for Humanity. These traits become the effect or goals. **Circle three more relevant details that describe a cause or effect.**

**MAIN IDEA:** The main idea is the point the author is making about the topic. The topic is Habitat for Humanity. **Underline the author's point about this topic.**

A Noble Response: A Joyous Result

(1) Volunteer work is a noble response to human need, and one basic human need is safe and comfortable shelter. (2) Habitat for Humanity affects this basic need. (3) Because of the impact of natural disasters and poverty on housing, Habitat for Humanity calls for volunteers to build quality and affordable houses that results in home ownership for those in need. (4) In recent years, natural disasters such as earthquakes, mudslides, hurricanes, and tsunamis have caused countless homes to be reduced to rubble or obliterated. (5) As a result, hundreds of thousands of people are left homeless and without resources to rebuild. (6) Currently, poverty influences many around the world by causing families to live in shoddy structures with little hope of improving their living conditions. (7) Habitat for Humanity was established to meet these very needs. (8) Consequently, strangers voluntarily come together to accomplish one goal: to build a house for a family. (9) The end results are obvious. (10) First, the family, who also helped build their home, owns their home. (11) In addition, and just as importantly, along with home ownership comes the joy and pride of an improved quality of life. (12) Habitat for Humanity is a noble response to human need with joyous results.

## THE WRITER'S JOURNAL

The student writer of "A Noble Response: A Joyous Result" completed the following reflection to record his thinking through the writing process. Read his writer's journal that describes a few key choices he made as he wrote.

MAIN IDEA: At first, I had a hard time focusing my topic. I couldn't decide if I wanted to write about the cause and effects of volunteering in general, or the reasons and results of volunteering for Habitat for Humanity. Since I had a week to write my paragraph, I took a couple of days just thinking about how to focus the topic. As I drove to school, worked on my car, or cooked supper, I found myself thinking about which way to go. Finally, I figured out that the topic of volunteering was too broad for one paragraph, and I decided to explore the causes and effects of HH.

RELEVANT DETAILS: Once I decided on my focus, the graphic organizer really helped me generate ideas, and, as a result, I composed the first draft fairly quickly. I divided my discussion into two groups: (1) two reasons Habitat for Humanity was established and (2) a few of the impacts of HH.

LOGICAL ORDER: While the body of the paragraph came quickly and easily, I spent a great deal of time thinking about how to start and end the paragraph. Finally, I decided to use some of the ideas that came to me as I thought about volunteering in general—meeting human needs. And then it occurred to me how noble HH is, and what joy HH brings to people's lives—perfect ideas with which to begin and end a paragraph about HH. These ideas helped me with my title, too!

EFFECTIVE EXPRESSION: I revised several times for effective word choice. For example, in the sentence about natural disasters, I changed the wording from "homes to be destroyed" to "homes reduced to rubble or obliterated." The revised wording seemed to best describe the details in the photographs. For the same reasons, I also revised the sentence about poverty to change the wording from "substandard houses" to "shoddy structures."

Habitat for Humanity®

For a blank version of this form for your own reflections about your writing: <www.mywritinglab.com>

# Developing Your Point Using Cause and Effect

A cause and effect paragraph makes a point by discussing the reasons and results among a set of events, objects, or factors. To support a point through cause and effect, a writer identifies a set of events, objects, or factors. A writer then identifies the specific details of cause and effect between each of the events, objects, or factors. The writer tests each reason and result to weed out true causes and effects from coincidence. The writer discusses the specific details in the order that reflects the logical relationship among causes and effects. In addition, the writer uses precise word choice for effective expression.

## The Point: The Main Idea

When you write a cause and effect paragraph, you limit your thoughts to a set of topics based on their relationship to each other. Most likely you have an opinion or belief about the topics and their causes and effects; your opinion is your point or main idea. A topic sentence states the overall point of the causes and effects.

For example, the following topic sentence contains (1) the topic, (2) the writer's opinion about the topic, and (3) the pattern of organization used to organize the details.

TOPIC — PATTERN OF ORGANIZATION: SIGNAL WORDS — WRITER'S OPINION

Addiction to television has led to several negative effects on American students.

The topic is the *addiction to television of American students.* The pattern of organization is established with the signal words *led to several effects.* The writer's opinion is stated with the modifier *negative.*

Practice 2

**TOPIC SENTENCES**

The first four items present a topic, an opinion, and cause or effect signal word(s). Combine the ideas in each group to create a topic sentence for a cause and effect. Then, complete the practice by making your own topic sentences.

**1.** TOPIC: smoking cigarettes

OPINION: adverse

CAUSE OR EFFECT SIGNAL WORDS: leads to physical effects

TOPIC SENTENCE:

2. TOPIC: bullying

OPINION: low

CAUSE OR EFFECT SIGNAL WORDS: stems from low self-esteem and anger

TOPIC SENTENCE:

3. TOPIC: violence and sex in television programming

OPINION: popular demand by the audience

CAUSE OR EFFECT SIGNAL WORDS: is due to

TOPIC SENTENCE:

4. TOPIC: alternative sources of energy

OPINION: must be developed

CAUSE OR EFFECT SIGNAL WORDS: for several reasons

TOPIC SENTENCE:

5. TOPIC: the war in Iraq

OPINION:

CAUSE OR EFFECT SIGNAL WORDS:

TOPIC SENTENCE:

6. TOPIC:

OPINION:

CAUSE OR EFFECT SIGNAL WORDS:

TOPIC SENTENCE:

Practice 2

More practice with creating topic sentences: <www.mywritinglab.com>

## Logical Order

Once you have identified a topic, a set of factors, their relationships based on cause and effect, and have focused on a main idea, you are ready to generate and organize additional details. To make a point using cause or effect, a writer moves from a general idea (the overall causal relationship) to a major support (a specific cause or effect of the topic) to minor supports (details or examples of a specific cause or effect). To signal the movement among these levels of ideas, a writer uses transitions to signal causes, effects, and examples. Strong transitions establish coherence, a clear and understandable flow of ideas.

### Transitions That Signal Cause and Effect

| | | | | |
|---|---|---|---|---|
| accordingly | consequently | hence | on account of | so |
| as a result | due to | if...then | results in | therefore |
| because of | for that reason | leads to | since | thus |

### Verbs That Signal Cause and Effect (sample list)

| | | | | | |
|---|---|---|---|---|---|
| affect | constitute | create | force | institute | restrain |
| cause | construct | determine | induce | preclude | stop |
| compose | contribute | facilitate | initiate | prevent | |

### Nouns That Signal Cause and Effect (sample list)

| | | | | |
|---|---|---|---|---|
| actor | consequence | end | influence | product |
| agent | creation | event | issue | result |
| author | creator | grounds | outcome | source |
| condition | effect | impact | outgrowth | |

Practice 3

ORDER OF CAUSES AND EFFECTS

The following ideas appeared in an article published by the *National Women's Health Information Center.* Number the sentences by logical order. Complete the exercise by answering the question: "What's the point?"

**How Is A Stroke Prevented?**

.......... Along with taking needed medications, eating a healthful diet lowers your risk for a stroke.

.......... The more stroke risk factors you have, the greater the chance that you will have a stroke.

.......... A stroke is the result of cerebrovascular disease, which is a disease of the blood vessels in the brain.

.......... You can't control some risk factors, such as aging, family health history, race and gender.

.......... However, you do control habits that may affect the likelihood of having a stroke.

.......... If you have any of these conditions, then take your medication as prescribed by your health care provider.

.......... Therefore, eat a diet low in saturated fat and rich in fruits, vegetables, and whole grains.

.......... For example, habits that lead to health conditions such as heart disease, high blood pressure, high cholesterol, and diabetes can contribute to a stroke.

.......... For example, eating too many animal foods and whole milk dairy products can result in high cholesterol which raises your risk for a stroke.

.......... Finally, aspirin therapy may reduce the risk of strokes due to blood clots, but check with your health care provider before starting to take aspirin on a daily basis.

.......... In addition to watching what foods you eat, you can also reduce your stroke risks by exercising for at least 30 minutes a day on most days of the week.

.......... In addition, smoking is a significant risk factor leading to strokes; so, if you smoke, stop!

.......... If it is hard to quit on your own, then nicotine patches, support groups, and programs are available to help you stop smoking.

.......... Regular exercise reduces cholesterol and the build up of fatty plaque that causes the blood clots that lead to strokes.

—Adapted from United States Department of Health and Human Services. "*Stroke.*" *Women's Health.gov* The National Women's Health Information Center. 26 March 2006. http://www.4woman.gov/faq/stroke.htm#4

What's the Point?

..................................................................................................

..................................................................................................

..................................................................................................

..................................................................................................

More practice with logical order: <www.mywritinglab.com>

Practice 3

## Relevant Details

As a writer narrows a topic into a focused main idea, the thinking process brings to mind many details that answer the questions such as *who*, *what*, *when*, *where*, *why*, and *how*. A writer evaluates the relevancy of each detail and uses only those that clarify or support the main idea. In a cause and effect paragraph, some relevant major details include those that identify a specific cause or effect. Relevant minor details offer examples and explanations of the cause or effect. Relevant details include descriptions, examples, and explanations of the causal relationship between a set of events, situations, objects, or factors.

One writer generated these ideas while brainstorming using a fishbone cause and effect concept map.

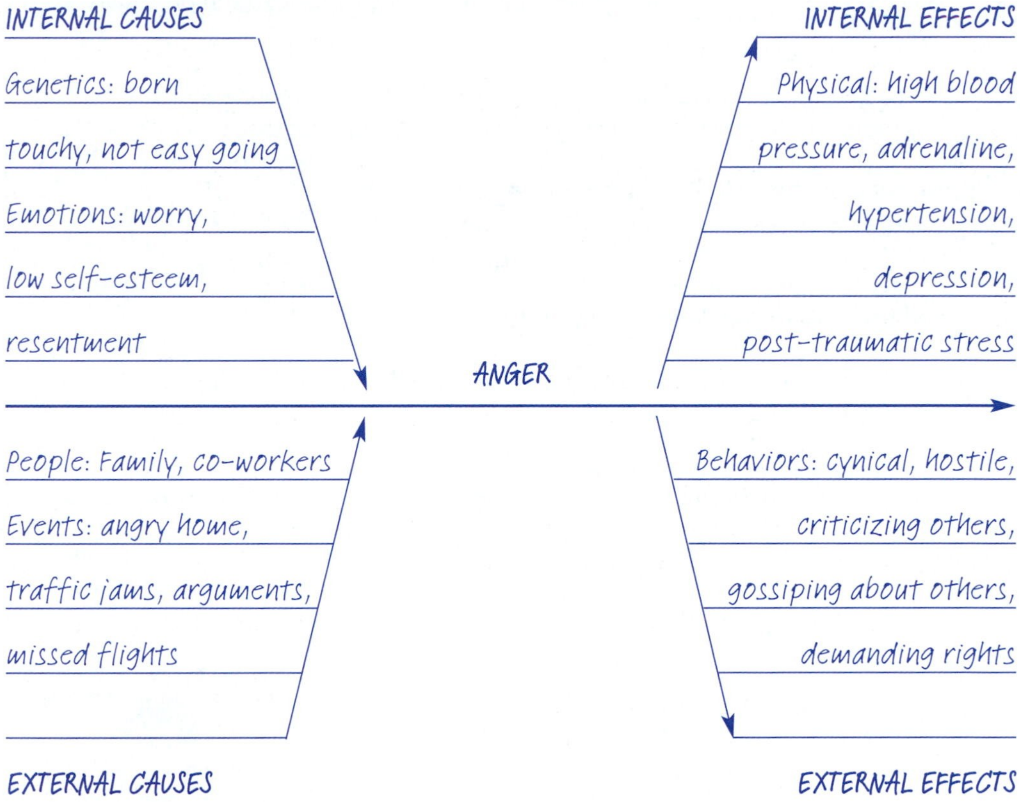


During the prewriting phase of writing, a writer naturally generates irrelevant details. In fact, an effective writer often produces far more details than can be used to make a specific point. Irrelevant details do not explain or support the focused point of the paragraph. A careful writer uses the revision process to double-check details for relevancy and to eliminate irrelevant details.

RELEVANT DETAILS

# Practice 4

The following paragraph develops the ideas generated about anger during the brainstorming phase using the fishbone cause and effect concept map shown on page 212. Circle the main idea. Underline two causes and two effects. Cross out two details that are not relevant to the main point.

**Anger Inside and Out**

(1) Anger can be a normal, healthy emotion, yet anger can also spiral out of our control and lead to problems that affect our work, our families, and our lives. (2) To control anger, we need to understand its causes and effects. (3) Basically, anger is the result of both internal and external forces. (4) Genetics and emotions are two internal forces that give rise to anger. (5) According to experts, some people are born innately touchy and easily angered. (6) Others of us are born with mild, easy-going tendencies. (7) Another internal force is the complex mixture of our emotions. (8) Worry, low self-esteem, anxiety, or resentment can cause anger to flare. (9) In addition, external forces such as people and events can trigger anger. (10) For example, if we have been raised in an environment of anger without learning how to cope with negative feelings, we are much more likely to be easily angered. (11) As a result, a disagreement with a family member or co-worker, a traffic jam, or a cancelled airline flight ignites angry feelings. (12) Not only does our anger arise from internal and external forces, but also our anger has internal and external effects. (13) Anger has immediate physical effects: it causes our heart rate, blood pressure, and adrenaline to rise. (14) Ultimately, chronic anger can lead to hypertension or depression. (15) Post-traumatic stress syndrome also leads to depression. (16) Chronic anger also may result in cynical and hostile behavior towards others. (17) When we feel angry, we may act out our hostility by criticizing others, gossiping about them, or rudely demanding our rights. (18) Ultimately, uncontrolled anger damages our relationships with others and diminishes our quality of life. (19) We need to understand the reasons and results of our anger before we can hope to control this volatile emotion.

More practice with relevant details: <www.mywritinglab.com>

## Effective Expression: Correct Use of Words

Effective expression reflects a writer's thoughtful choice of words for impact on the reader. Some words, such as *affect* and *effect,* seem closely related because they are similar in their sounds and spellings. These similarities often cause confusion and lead to the misuse of the words. However, their meanings are clearly distinct, so thoughtful writers use the correct word for effective expression.

***Affect*** is a verb that means **to influence.**

**Example**

Video games **affect** learning by improving concentration and visual skills.

***Effect*** is a noun that means **result.**

**Example**

Video games have a positive **effect** on learning by improving concentration and visual skills.

***Effect*** is a verb that means **to bring about.**

**Example**

The new law will **effect** a change in the sentencing of sex offenders.

### Practice 5

**CORRECT USE OF AFFECT AND EFFECT**

Complete the following sentences with the correct use of the words *affect* and *effect.* (*Hint:* Substitute the words *influence* or *result* as a test for exact meaning in the context of the sentence.)

1. The lack of bright light during winter months produces an ____________ known as Seasonal Affective Disorder (SAD), a form of depression.
2. The long, dark hours of winter ____________ as much as 6 percent of the population.
3. The ____________ of SAD include loss of energy, social withdrawal, overeating, weight gain, and difficulty concentrating.
4. Researchers believe that reduced sunlight ____________ the biological rhythms that control the body's internal clock.
5. Researchers also believe that heredity, age, and the body's chemical balance ____________ the onset of SAD.
6. Exposure to sun and sun lamps for one to three hours a day ____________ a positive change in the mood of one who suffers from SAD.

More practice with commonly confused words: <www.mywritinglab.com>

# Using Cause and Effect in Your Academic Courses

Often college writing assignments require that you combine information you learn from your textbooks with your observations about how that information applies to real-world situations. Textbooks may provide graphic organizers to emphasize key concepts and make them easy to understand. Use these graphic organizers to learn and apply the concept. A good way to review your textbook notes is to add examples you have observed in life to the concept you are studying.

## Practice 6

### USING CAUSE AND EFFECT IN A SOCIOLOGY ASSIGNMENT

Study the following graphic taken from a college sociology textbook. In a small group or with a peer, add examples of each concept that you and your peer(s) have observed. Then, write a paragraph in answer to the question at the end of the practice. Use a dictionary as necessary.

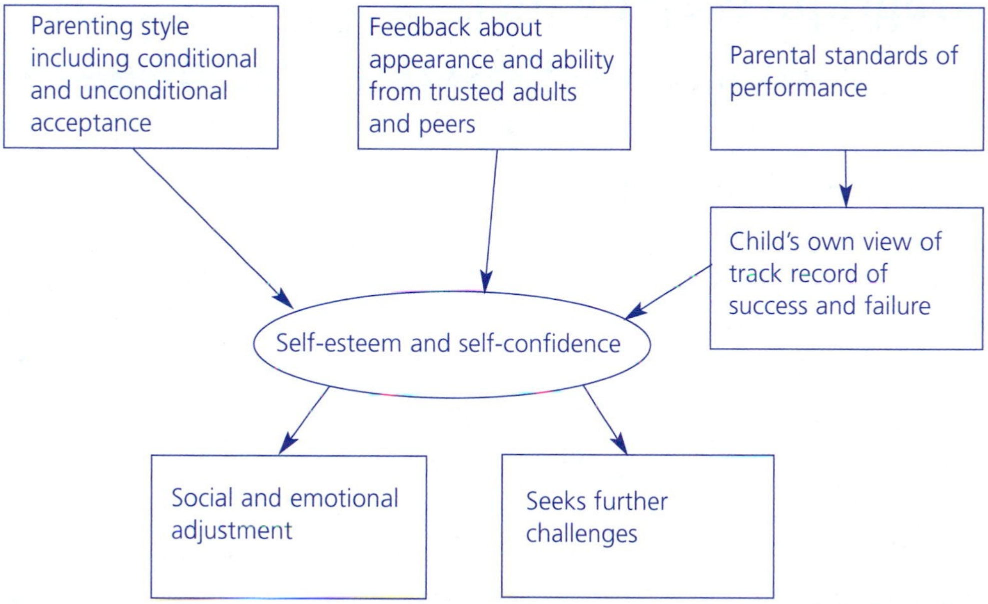


—Jaffe, Michael L. *Understanding Parenting, 2nd Ed.* Allyn & Bacon. 1997 p. 241.

EXAMPLE OF PARENTAL STANDARD: ______

______

EXAMPLE OF CHILD'S VIEW OF SUCCESS AND FAILURE: ______

______

EXAMPLE OF FEEDBACK: ______

______

EXAMPLE OF PARENTING STYLE: ______

______

More practice with writing cause and effect paragraphs: <www.mywritinglab.com>

Practice 6

EXAMPLE OF FURTHER CHALLENGE: ____________________

____________________

EXAMPLE OF ADJUSTMENT: ____________________

____________________

On a separate sheet of paper, answer the following question:
What factors influence children's self-esteem and self-confidence?

Workshop

# Workshop: Writing a Cause and Effect Paragraph Step by Step

WRITING A CAUSE AND EFFECT PARAGRAPH STEP BY STEP

PREWRITING

## Choose Your Topic

The following activities are designed to help you choose a topic.

1. Create a bank of topics: Use the following headings to brainstorm or list as many causes and effects as you possibly can. Don't criticize your thoughts; just get as many relevant causes and effects written down as quickly as possible. Add more topics, causes, or effects as they occur to you. Revisit topic banks created during your study of previous chapters; identify causes and effects. Compare your bank of topics with those of your peers.
   - You Tube
   - Friendship
   - Fuel-efficient Cars
   - Romance
2. Reread a freewrite you created (such as the one based on the photographs of the people in the chapter opening or the one generated in Practice 3). Underline ideas that you could use for a cause and effect paragraph. Number the points you recorded to indicate a logical order. Add major or minor details of explanation and examples as needed.

   OR

   Select a set of photographs that illustrate a set of related events, situations, objects, or factors. Generate a list that identifies the details of each event, situation, object, or factor as either a cause (reason) or an effect (result). Freewrite about the photograph(s). Remember to ask, "What's the point?"

## Clarify Your Point

Read a prewrite you have generated for a cause and effect. Underline words that suggest your values, opinions, or attitudes about the events. Think about why the information is important. Think about what examples best represent each cause or effect. Think about a situation that best illustrates the concept. Identify your audience and purpose. Write a list of additional concrete examples that explain your point. In one sentence, state the point of the cause and effect.

AUDIENCE: ..............................................................

PURPOSE: ..............................................................

WHAT'S THE POINT? ..............................................................

..............................................................

## Generate and Organize Relevant Details

Use the graphic organizer below to either organize the ideas you have already created or to generate details to support your point.

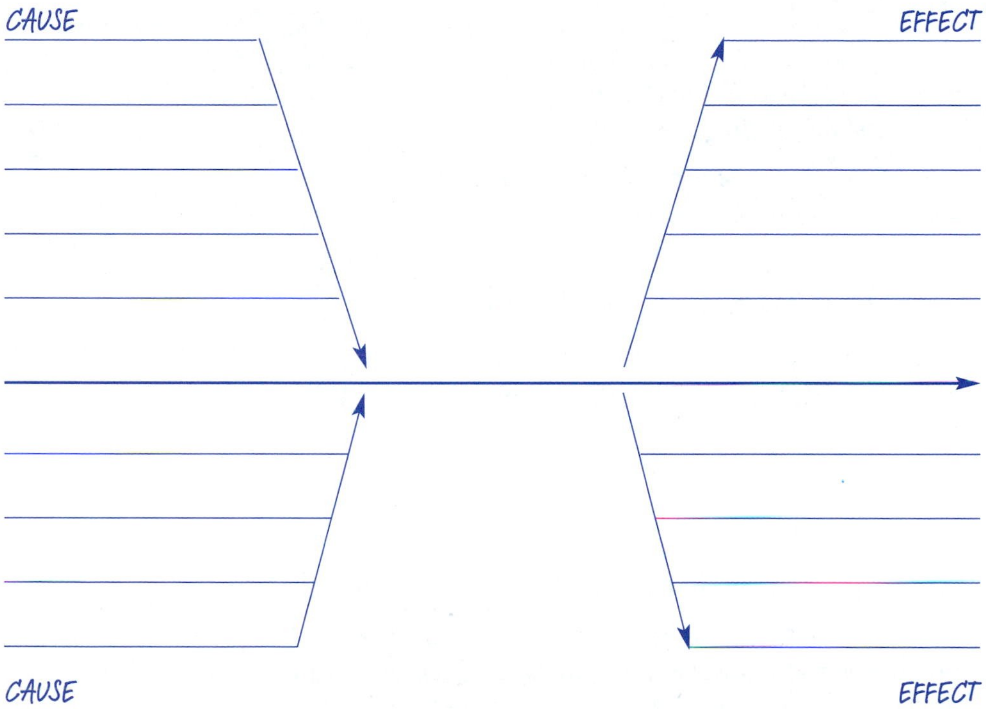


WHAT'S THE POINT?: ..............................................................

..............................................................

..............................................................

DRAFTING

## Write a Draft of Your Paragraph

Using the ideas you generated during the prewriting phase, compose a draft of your cause and effect paragraph. Return to the prewriting process at any time to generate additional details as needed. Use your own paper.

REVISING

## Revise Your Draft

Once you have created a draft of your cause and effect paragraph, read the draft and answer the following questions. Indicate your answers by annotating your paper. If you answer "yes" to a question, underline, check, or circle examples. If you answer "no" to a question, write additional details in the margins and draw lines to indicate their placement. Revise your paragraph based on your reflection.

Workshop

# Questions for Revising a Cause and Effect Paragraph

- ☐ Have I chosen an important set of related events, situations, objects, or factors?
- ☐ Have I made my point? Can I state my point in one sentence?
- ☐ Have I effectively used a logical order based on short-term, long-term, most important, least important, obvious, or subtle causes and effects? Have I used strong transitions of cause and effect?
- ☐ Have I included only the details that are relevant to my topic sentence?
- ☐ Have I used the following to make my ideas clear and interesting to my readers: vivid verbs and images, parallel language, controlled sentence structure, coordination, subordination, precise use of words such as *affect* and *effect?*
- ☐ Have I used concrete details to make my point?

PROOFREADING

## Proofread Your Draft

Once you have made any revisions to your paragraph that may be needed, proofread your paper to eliminate unnecessary errors, such as editing for commonly confused words.

### Grammar in Action: Commonly Confused Words

As you learned earlier in this chapter, some words, such as *affect* and *effect,* seem closely related because they are similar in their sounds and spellings. These similarities often cause these words to be confused with one another and lead to their misuse. However, their meanings are clearly distinct, so thoughtful writers choose the precise word for effective expression. The following list presents a group of words that are commonly confused. Memorize this list of words and their meanings so you can use each one precisely in your writing.

| | |
|---|---|
| **its, it's** | **its** (possessive form of it); **it's** (contraction of *it is* or *it has*) |
| **their, they're, there** | **their** (possessive of they); **they're** (contraction of *they are*); **there** (points to a place) |
| **to, two, too** | **to** (suggests movement or direction); **two** (a number); **too** (also) |
| **whose, who's** | **whose** (possessive form of *who*); **who's** (contraction of *who is* or *who has*) |
| **your, you're** | **your** (possessive form of *you*); **you're** (contraction of *you are*) |

Workshop

## Practice 7

### PRECISE USE OF COMMONLY CONFUSED WORDS

Edit these sentences by crossing out the word used incorrectly and inserting the correct word. (*Hint:* Some words are used correctly.)

1. Who's purse is over their on the counter by the refrigerator?
2. You too are two young to see an R rated movie.
3. Michealle and Koshanda have cut and donated their hair to Locks of Love, a non-profit organization that makes wigs for cancer patients.
4. Devon, who's brother is an NFL linebacker, has to tickets too the playoffs.
5. The supervisors said that your going to leave you're car at the airport while your traveling because there willing to pay for the parking charges.

More practice with commonly confused words: <www.mywritinglab.com>

## Review

### REVIEW OF WRITING A CAUSE AND EFFECT PARAGRAPH: DEVELOP YOUR POINT USING THE WRITING PROCESS

Use the following form to record your thinking about writing a cause and effect paragraph. Select and focus your topic for your writing situation, audience, and purpose. Choose a topic that is best developed through cause and effect and identify its significance.

PREWRITING DRAFTING What is your point?

CAUSES (REASONS FOR AN EVENT, OBJECT, OR FACTOR): ____________________

____________________

EFFECTS (RESULTS OF AN EVENT, OBJECT, OR FACTOR): ____________________

____________________

CAUSES LEADING TO EFFECTS: ____________________

AUDIENCE: ____________________

PURPOSE: ____________________

PREWRITING DRAFTING State your main idea in a topic sentence.

TOPIC: ____________________

OPINION: ____________________

PREWRITING DRAFTING Generate relevant details.

REPORTER'S QUESTIONS: WHO, WHAT, WHERE, WHEN, WHY, HOW? ______________________

______________________

CAUSES, DESCRIPTIONS, EXAMPLES, EXPLANATIONS: ______________________

______________________

EFFECTS, DESCRIPTIONS, EXAMPLES, EXPLANATIONS: ______________________

______________________

PREWRITING DRAFTING REVISING Use logical order. Use transition words to signal organization of details and relationship between ideas.

TRANSITIONS THAT SIGNAL CAUSES: ______________________

______________________

TRANSITIONS THAT SIGNAL EFFECTS: ______________________

______________________

REVISING PROOFREADING Use effective expression. Use words precisely. Avoid misuse of commonly confused words.

AFFECT: ______________________

EFFECT: ______________________

ITS, IT'S: ______________________

THEIR, THEY'RE, THERE: ______________________

TO, TWO, TOO: ______________________

WHOSE, WHO'S: ______________________

YOUR, YOU'RE: ______________________

______________________

Review

# Writing Assignments

## Considering Audience and Purpose

Study the set of photographs at the beginning of the chapter. Assume you are the one who now owns the home built by Habitat for Humanity. Assume that as you worked beside the volunteers to build your home, you became friendly with the project director, Wilma Weindmyer. Write a one-paragraph thank-you letter to Ms. Weindmyer that explains the impact of building and owning your own home.

## Writing for Everyday Life

Assume that you are the mentor of a young person who is a member of your family or community. Assume the young person is making some choices that can have lasting negative consequences. Perhaps the youth is hanging out with the wrong crowd, or skipping school, or experimenting with drugs. Write a one-paragraph letter that explains the dangers of the wrong choices or the benefits of mature choices. Choose your words to reflect one of the following: (1) stern warning or (2) warm encouragement.

## Writing for College Life

Assume you are applying for a scholarship set up to aid a person currently enrolled as a full-time college student with at least a 3.0 GPA. Assume you must compete with other students to win the scholarship by writing a one-paragraph essay on the topic "Education Matters." Write a paragraph that explains one or both of the following: (1) the impact the education has had and will have on you; (2) the impact you hope to have as an educated member of society.

## Writing for Working Life

Assume that you are applying for a job with a company or organization. Perhaps you are applying for a job as a health care provider, teacher, office manager, or computer programmer. Write a one-paragraph cover letter that explains the impact you can have on the job due to your skills, work ethic, and character.

More ideas for writing a cause and effect paragraph: <www.mywritinglab.com>

# 12 The Persuasive Paragraph

## Chapter Preview

- What's the Point of Persuasion?
- Making a Point Using Persuasion: One Student Writer's Response
- Developing Your Point Using Persuasion
- Using Persuasion in Your Academic Courses
- Workshop: Writing a Persuasion Paragraph Step by Step

## A persuasive claim is a strong stand on a debatable topic supported by facts, examples, and opinions.

In almost every area of our lives, we engage in some form of persuasion. Whether convincing a friend to see a particular movie or proving we are the right candidate for a particular job, we use reasons, logic, and emotion to get others to agree with our views. What are some other situations that use persuasion to influence our beliefs and behaviors? Why are certain arguments or points of view so persuasive?

To be persuasive, a writer asserts a strong stand on one side of a debatable issue. Then the writer supports that stand by offering convincing evidence such as reasons, facts, examples, and expert opinions. In everyday life, our court system is based on proving claims of guilt or innocence. In working life, we use reasons to resolve workplace disputes. In college life, we encounter debatable claims in every discipline. In addition to asserting a claim and supporting it with evidence, a persuasive writer acknowledges and rebuts (disproves, challenges) the opposition.

# What's the Point of Persuasion?

The purpose of persuasion is to convince the reader to agree with a particular claim about a debatable topic. Persuasion is a call to action or a call to a change of mind. The following posters are designed to persuade young women about smoking cigarettes. Study the photographs. In the space provided, identify the claim, reasons, and an opposing point of view about smoking. Answer the question "What's the point?" with a one-sentence statement of the overall main idea.

WRITING FROM LIFE

Practice 1

**PHOTOGRAPHIC ORGANIZER: PERSUASION**

What is this idea?

_______________

_______________

_______________

What is this reason?

_______________

_______________

_______________

What is this reason?

_______________

_______________

_______________

What is this opposing point? _______________

_______________

_______________

**What's the point?**

_______________

_______________

_______________

PREWRITING

## My First Thoughts: A Prewriting Activity

Brainstorm about the images you just studied. Set a time limit, such as five minutes, and write in your notebook about the images and the details you generated. Write as quickly as you can without stopping. Let the ideas flow freely. Getting your first thoughts about a topic on paper is one excellent way to kick-start your writing process.

# Making a Point Using Persuasion: One Student Writer's Response

The following paragraph offers one writer's point about the argument against smoking as illustrated by the photographs. Read the persuasive paragraph below and the annotations. Complete the activities in bold type given in the annotations. Then, read the writer's journal that records decisions made during the writing process.

**EFFECTIVE EXPRESSION:** To persuade a reader, an author uses subjective words that qualify ideas and express opinions and value judgments. The word "always" qualifies the action of tobacco companies as absolute and unwavering. **Circle three more subjective words.**

**RELEVANT DETAILS:** In persuasion, relevant details include facts, consequences, and information from experts or authorities on the topic. **This detail does all three. Underline another factual detail.**

**STRONG TRANSITION:** The transition phrase "in truth" signals that the author is offering a reason in support of the claim. **Circle three more transitional words or phrases that signal a reason of support.**

**MAIN IDEA:** The main idea is the point or claim the author is making about the topic. The topic is "smoking." **Underline the writer's point about this subject.**

### Calling All Girls: Tell Tobacco Companies to Butt Out

(1) Tobacco companies spend millions of dollars each year to convince young women to smoke. (2) Their aim is to lure teenage girls into a lifetime of addiction that will generate billions of dollars in profit. (3) In 1999, nearly 165,000 American women died prematurely from smoking-related diseases such as lung cancer and heart disease ("Women and Smoking"). (4) Advertisements always depict women who smoke as icons of "In." (5) For example, a particular Newport poster depicts a beautiful, thin young woman with a wide smile holding a cigarette while dancing with a guy as good looking and wide-smiling as she. (6) They seem cool, popular, and sexy. (7) "Fire it up" with "Newport pleasure" is a call to fire up life with fun. (8) In truth, this image is deceiving. (9) Just as the poster states (by law), smoking has many harmful effects. (10) In fact, according to "Women and Smoking: A Report of the Surgeon General—2001," women who smoke two or more packs of cigarettes a day face a risk for cancer 20 times higher than for women who do not smoke. (11) In truth, nonsmokers do not increase their risk of lung cancer or heart disease. (12) Nonsmokers, when they do become pregnant, do not put the health of their unborn babies at risk. (13) Furthermore, nonsmokers are fashionable. (14) Nonsmokers are creative. (15) Nonsmokers are and do have fun. (16) In fact, nonsmokers have more money than smokers to spend on pleasure such as fashion, video games, music, or special interests like art. (17) Therefore, teenage girls should tell tobacco companies to "butt out" because smoking is out. (18) Not smoking is the real cool, the real in.

### Works Cited

Centers for Disease Control and Prevention. "Women and Smoking: A Report of the Surgeon General—2001." 31 Jan. 2004. 3 Apr. 2006. Path: A-Z Index; Smoking; Smoking and Women; At a Glance; Health Consequences of Tobacco Use Among Women.

## THE WRITER'S JOURNAL

The student writer of "Calling All Girls: Tell Tobacco Companies to Butt Out" completed the following reflection to record her thinking through the writing process. Read her writer's journal that describes a few key choices she made as she wrote.

MAIN IDEA: I really enjoyed writing this paragraph because I started smoking as a teenager, and thankfully, was able to quit when I became pregnant with my first child. The only reason I could kick the habit was because the smell and taste of smoke made me sick once I became pregnant. As I studied the photographs and filled out the graphic organizer, the details made it clear to me how important fitting in and being cool is to girls. It seemed apparent to me that the Newport poster would probably be far more appealing and persuasive to most young women, so I wanted to counter that image immediately in my paragraph.

RELEVANT DETAILS: I also wanted to include some compelling facts from a reliable source, so I searched the Centers for Disease Control for information on women and smoking. My works cited entry documents the path that I took to locate relevant information in the site.

LOGICAL ORDER: I decided to order my reasons by countering the opposition. So I began each of my major supports with a discussion about the false image of the Newport poster, and then concluded with the positive ideas illustrated about the "In/Out" poster. It was during my revisions, however, that I included the transition word therefore. I like the way this word gave power to the conclusion.

EFFECTIVE EXPRESSION: During a revision, I noted that I had used a series of three short, parallel sentences about the traits of nonsmokers beginning with "In truth, nonsmokers are…" I played around with a few versions of these ideas. At first, I combined them into one sentence with compound verbs: "Nonsmokers are fashionable, creative, and fun." But I liked the emphasis that the three short, parallel sentences gave to these details. After all, these sentences state important reasons that support my claim. I also revised to use subjective words. Words such as lure, almost, and deceiving depict negative views of the tobacco advertisers. I also edited for proper use of point of view. I was tempted to shift into the use of you to call the reader to action. But I decided that I wanted to appeal to the family and friends of young women as well. So I stuck with the third person point of view and used girls, woman, she, smokers, nonsmokers, and they.

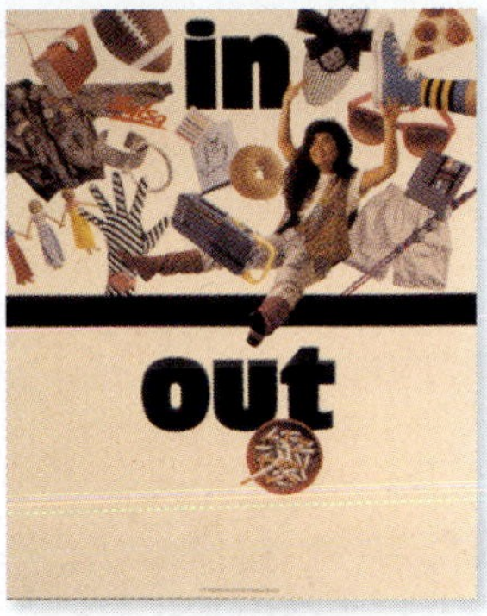

For a blank version of this form for your own reflections about your writing: <www.mywritinglab.com>

# Developing Your Point Using Persuasion

A persuasive paragraph makes a point by supporting one side of a debatable topic and refuting the opposing side. The details that support and refute the point include reasons based on facts, examples, effects, and expert opinions on the topic. In addition, a writer uses effective expression to qualify ideas and control the point of view.

## The Point: The Main Idea

When you write a persuasive paragraph, you limit your thoughts to the reasons that support one side and refute the opposing side of a debatable topic or issue. A persuasive paragraph gives your opinion or stand on the issue. A topic sentence states the debatable topic, the writer's persuasive opinion, and, possibly, a pattern of organization. Because persuasion is a purpose, the writer may choose any particular pattern of organization to support a claim. Often, the pattern of organization is only suggested rather than stated. In addition, the writer's persuasive opinion is frequently signaled by the following types of subjective words or phrases: *all, always, only, must, must not, should, should not,* or *too.* These subjective words qualify an idea as debatable.

For example, the following topic sentence contains (1) the debatable topic, (2) the writer's persuasive opinion, and (3) a pattern of organization.

DEBATABLE TOPIC — WRITER'S OPINION — DEBATABLE TOPIC

Colleges and universities should provide substance free housing for students for several reasons.

PATTERN OF ORGANIZATION

The debatable topic or issue is *substance free housing for students at colleges and universities*. The writer's opinion is expressed with the verb phrase *should provide.* Note that the verb *provide* calls for action, and the helping verb *should* qualifies the action. The phrase *for several reasons* signals a list that will most likely contain facts, examples, effects, expert opinion, and reasons against the opposing view.

### Practice 2

**TOPIC SENTENCES**

The first four items present a debatable topic, the writer's opinion, and a pattern of organization. Combine the ideas in each group to create a topic sentence for a persuasive paragraph. Then, complete the practice by making your own topic sentences.

**1.** TOPIC: education about crystal meth

OPINION: horrific, is our best hope to end this plague

PATTERN OF ORGANIZATION: the consequences of

TOPIC SENTENCE: 

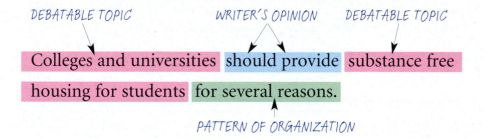

**2.** TOPIC: consumers, hybrid vehicles

OPINION: should demand

PATTERN OF ORGANIZATION: due to their economic and environmental benefits

TOPIC SENTENCE:

**3.** TOPIC: procrastination by students, academic

OPINION: is the leading, failure

PATTERN OF ORGANIZATION: cause of

TOPIC SENTENCE:

**4.** TOPIC: breakfast

OPINION: is important

PATTERN OF ORGANIZATION: more than any other meal of the day.

TOPIC SENTENCE:

**5.** TOPIC: graffiti

OPINION:

PATTERN OF ORGANIZATION:

TOPIC SENTENCE:

Practice 2

More practice with creating topic sentences: <www.mywritinglab.com>

Practice 2

**6.** TOPIC: ____________________

OPINION: ____________________

PATTERN OF ORGANIZATION: ____________________

TOPIC SENTENCE: ____________________

____________________

____________________

**7.** TOPIC: ____________________

OPINION: ____________________

PATTERN OF ORGANIZATION: ____________________

TOPIC SENTENCE: ____________________

____________________

____________________

## Logical Order

Once you have identified a debatable topic, you are ready to generate and organize the details. To make a persuasive point, a writer moves from a general idea (the claim) to a major support (a reason, fact, example, expert opinion, or reason against the opposing view) to a minor support (also a reason, fact, example, expert opinion, or reason against the opposing view). Transitions and signal words indicate the importance and movement among details. Strong transitions and signal words establish coherence, a clear and understandable flow of ideas.

### Transitions That Signal Persuasion

| | | | | |
|---|---|---|---|---|
| accordingly | finally | in conclusion | obviously | thus |
| admittedly | first (second, third, etc.) | indeed | of course | to be sure |
| although | for | in fact, in truth | on the one hand | truly |
| because | furthermore | in summary | on the other hand | undoubtedly |
| but | granted | last | since | |
| certainly | hence | meanwhile | some believe | |
| consequently | however | nevertheless | some may say | |
| despite | | nonetheless | therefore | |
| even so | | | | |

## Signal Words That Qualify an Idea as Persuasive (sample list)

| | | | | | |
|---|---|---|---|---|---|
| all | every | might | only | seem | too |
| always | has/have to | must | ought to | should | usually |
| believe | it is believed | never | possibly, possible | sometimes | |
| could | may | often | probably, probable | think | |

More practice with logical order: <www.mywritinglab.com>



Practice 3

ORDER OF SUPPORTS FOR A CLAIM

Number each sentence according to the logical order of the ideas. Complete the exercise by answering the question "What's the point?"

**For the Sake of the Children**

........... Obviously, in addition to risk of injury from explosions during the cooking process, a drug made from such materials has devastating health effects.

........... A few of these risks include fire hazards, chemical explosions, physical and sexual abuse, and medical neglect.

........... According to John W. Gillis, the director of the Office for Victims of Crime, "children who live at or visit home-based meth labs face acute health and safety risks."

........... Crude home labs make crystal meth from common household products such as paint thinner, rubbing alcohol, battery acid, lye-based cleaning products, gasoline, kerosene, fertilizer, and chlorine bleach.

........... As these chemicals are cooked with a heat source, they become volatile and explosive.

........... In addition, because of the natural hand-to-mouth behavior of young children, they are likely to absorb or ingest toxic chemicals used to make the drug.

........... Of course, removal of a child from his or her home is a traumatic experience; however, the dangers posed by the "meth" lifestyle far outweigh the risks posed by removing the child from these chaotic homes.

........... For example, many of these chemicals damage vital organs, cause cancer, and lead to other severe health problems.

........... In that same year, 26 were injured and two died as a direct result of meth-lab activities in the home.

........... According to the El Paso Intelligence Center, in 2001, over 2,000 children lived in meth homes.

—Swetlow, Karen. *"Children at Clandestine Methamphetamine Labs: Helping Meth's Youngest Victims."* OVC Bulletin. Office for Victims of Crime. U.S. Department of Justice. June 2003. 3 April 2006. <http://www.ojp.usdoj.gov/ovc/publications/bulletins/children/197590.pdf>.

**What's the point?**

..........................................................................

..........................................................................

..........................................................................

## Relevant Details

As you narrow a topic into a focused main idea, you generate supporting details that answer the questions such as *who*, *what*, *when*, *where*, *why*, and *how*. Evaluate the relevancy of each detail and use only those that clarify or support the main idea. The supports of a persuasive claim are reasons, facts, examples, effects, expert opinions, and details that refute the opposing view.

Compare the following chart of Persuasive Supporting Details with the ideas in the persuasive thinking map about metal detectors in public schools.

| **Persuasive Supporting Details** | |
|---|---|
| REASON | A cause of an event or action. An explanation. A basis or foundation of an idea. |
| FACT | A specific detail that is true based on objective proof. Objective proof can be physical evidence, an eyewitness account, or the result of accepted scientific investigation. |
| EXAMPLE | An illustration or instance of a general idea. |
| EFFECT | A result or consequence of an event or action. Consider positive effects of claim and negative effects of opposing views. |
| EXPERT OPINION | A view based on much training and extensive knowledge in a given field. Be sure to stay with opinions of experts in the field of the topic that is being debated. For example, a physician, an expert in medicine, is not an expert in criminal justice. |
| SUPPORTS THAT REFUTE | To refute is to disprove or counter an opposing point; supports include reasons, facts, effects, examples, and expert opinions. |

**Persuasive Thinking Map**

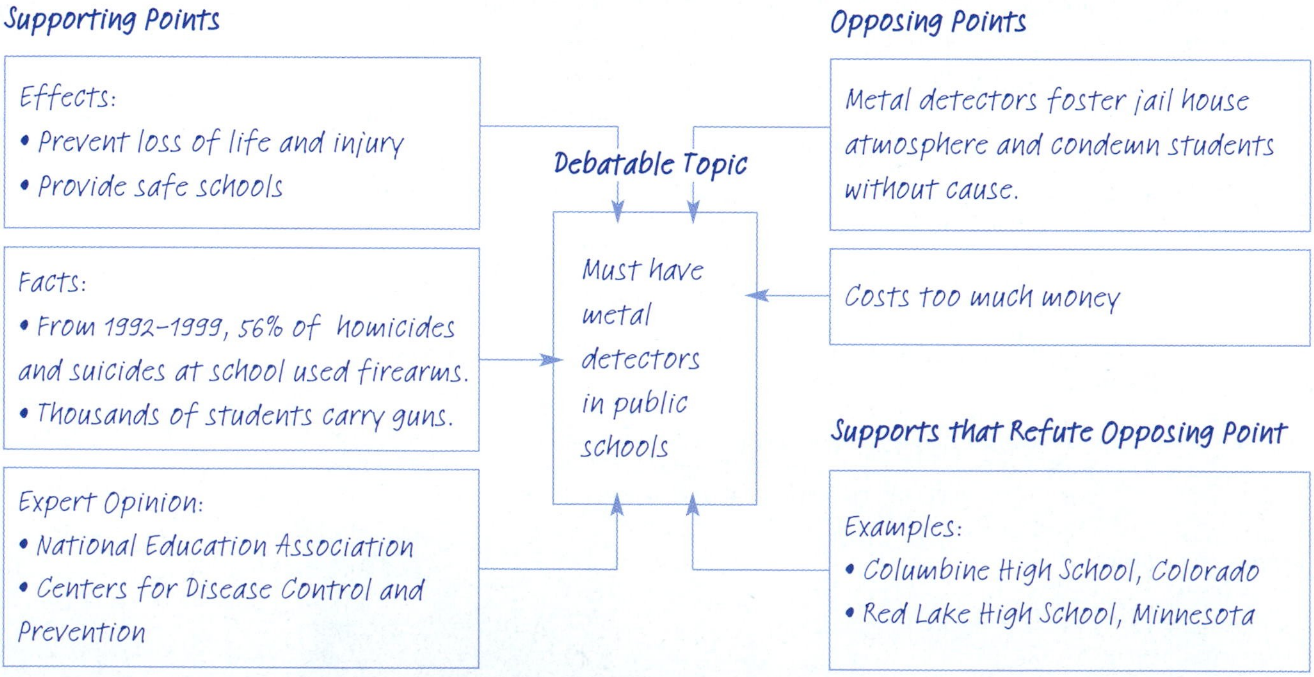

Supporting Points
Effects:
• Prevent loss of life and injury
• Provide safe schools
Facts:
• From 1992–1999, 56% of homicides and suicides at school used firearms.
• Thousands of students carry guns.
Expert Opinion:
• National Education Association
• Centers for Disease Control and Prevention
Debatable Topic
Must have metal detectors in public schools
Opposing Points
Metal detectors foster jail house atmosphere and condemn students without cause.
Costs too much money
Supports that Refute Opposing Point
Examples:
• Columbine High School, Colorado
• Red Lake High School, Minnesota


More practice with relevant details: <www.mywritinglab.com>

During the prewriting phase of writing, a writer naturally generates irrelevant details. In fact, an effective writer often produces far more details than can be used to make a specific point. Irrelevant details do not explain or support the focused point of the paragraph. A careful writer uses the revision process to double-check details for relevancy and to eliminate irrelevant details.

RELEVANT CONCRETE DETAILS

Practice 4

The following paragraph develops the ideas about metal detectors in public schools generated using a persuasive thinking map. Circle the main idea. Underline one example of each of the following: fact, example, effect, and a support that refutes the opposing view. Cross out the detail that is not relevant to the main point.

**Pay the Price: Stop the Shootings**

(1) Public school officials should use metal detectors to screen students for possession of firearms in order to reduce the numbers of injuries and deaths. (2) The use of metal detectors signals students that safety measures are in place and that violence will not be tolerated. (3) Some oppose the use of metal detectors as a step that fosters a jail house atmosphere and condemns students as guilty without cause. (4) These opponents to metal detectors also decry the economic cost of screening students for possession of firearms. (5) Unfortunately, evidence indicates that the need to provide a safe school and the right to a safe school far outweigh these concerns. (6) According to the Centers for Disease Control and Prevention, from 1992 to 1999, 56% of homicides and suicides occurring at school involved firearms. (7) In addition, the National Education Association estimates that "on a daily basis, 100,000 students carry guns to school, 160,000 miss classes due to fear of physical harm, and 40 are injured or killed by firearms." (8) Tragic school shootings have already occurred and signal that the danger is clear and present. (9) For example, in 1999 at Columbine High School, in Colorado, two students massacred 12 fellow students and a teacher, injured 24 other people, and then committed suicide. (10) As recently as 2005, at Red Lake High School in Minnesota, a student killed five students and injured seven others after he had killed his grandfather and his grandfather's girlfriend at home. (11) He also shot himself. (12) All of these shooters obviously suffered mental health problems. (13) Though these incidents are extreme, they are not isolated. (14) These incidents show that public schools must screen students for weapons. (15) The cost of not doing so is too high!

**Works Cited**

Centers for Disease Control and Prevention. "Source of Firearms Used by Students in School-Associated Violent Deaths—United States, 1992–1999." Morbidity and Mortality Weekly Report. 7 March 2003. 52(09); 169-72. <http://www.cdc.gov/mmwr/mmwr/preview/mmwrhtml//mm5209a1.htm>.

"School Violence." National Education Association. Washington, D. C. 1993.

## Effective Expression: Use of Subjective Words to Persuade

Effective expression is the result of a writer's thoughtful choice of words for impact on the reader. Subjective words reflect a strong stand because they express opinions, emotions, value judgments, and interpretations. Because subjective words express personal opinions, they can bring meanings and stir reactions in the reader not intended by the writer. Therefore, a thoughtful writer carefully chooses subjective words for effective expression. Note the differences between the neutral words and the subjective words in the following list:

| Neutral Words | Subjective Words |
|---|---|
| injury | wound, gash |
| perpetrator | criminal, delinquent, achiever |
| shelter | haven, hut |

Practice 5

**EFFECTIVE EXPRESSION: USE OF SUBJECTIVE WORDS TO PERSUADE**

Use your dictionary and thesaurus to find an effective biased word to fill in the blank in each sentence. In the spaces after each sentence, describe the impact you intend to have on your reader through your choice of words. Discuss your work with your class or small group.

**1.** Spanking is a ______________________________

______________________________

**2.** Laws that require cyclists to wear helmets are ______________________________

______________________________

**3.** Completion of a college education requires ______________________________

______________________________

**4.** Burning the United States flag is an act of ______________________________

______________________________

**5.** President George W. Bush is ______________________________

______________________________

More practice with using subjective words: <www.mywritinglab.com>

# Using Persuasion in Your Academic Courses

Often college textbooks present graphics to help you think critically and come to your own conclusions about a debatable topic. An excellent study technique is to write a paragraph in response to the information and questions. Many professors of these courses will also ask you to write an essay in which you explain your understanding of a controversial issue. You may find that you can use the information from the textbook as a resource for your writing assignment.

Practice 6

**USING PERSUASION IN AN AMERICAN GOVERNMENT ASSIGNMENT:** RESPONDING TO A CONTROVERSIAL ISSUE

Study the following information and graphic taken from an American Government college textbook about the campaign for the Senate, 2002. You may want to discuss your interpretation of the information with your class or small group. On a separate sheet of paper, write a paragraph that answers the questions and supports a claim about the given information.

Take a few moments to study the breakdown of a sample budget for a typical senate campaign, shown below, and then answer the following critical thinking questions: Where does the majority of campaign funding come from? What constitutes the single largest expense for the typical campaign? About what proportion of campaign funds comes from PACs? (A PAC is a Political Action Committee, which is a special interest group such as a labor union, tobacco company, or gun association.) Is this proportion smaller or larger than you thought?

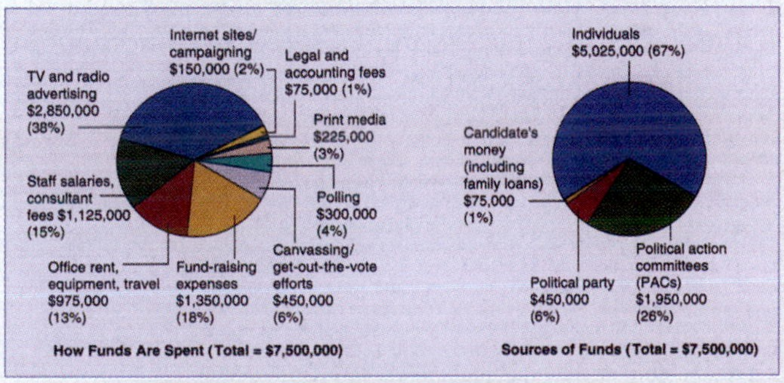


—From Sabato O'Connor and Keith Haag, *American Government: Continuity and Change*, 2004, Texas Edition, Pearson 2004, p.558.

More practice with writing persuasion paragraphs: <www.mywritinglab.com>

PORTFOLIO

Workshop

# Workshop: Writing a Persuasive Paragraph Step by Step

WRITING A PERSUASIVE PARAGRAPH STEP BY STEP

PREWRITING

## Choose Your Topic

The following activities are designed to help you choose a topic.

1. Create a bank of topics: Use the following debatable topics to brainstorm or list as many facts, effects, and examples as you possibly can. Don't analyze your thoughts; just get as many ideas written down as quickly as possible. Add more debatable topics and examples as they occur to you. Revisit topic banks created during your study of previous chapters. Compare your bank of topics with those of your peers.
   - Violence in Cartoons
   - Sex Education
   - Teenage Drivers
   - Conserving Energy
2. Choose a list of topics from activity 1. Brainstorm possible points the opposition could use to challenge your ideas. Identify relevant expert opinions you will need to include. Determine where you could locate those opinions. For example, can you interview an expert? Locate an expert opinion on the Internet? Read a newspaper or magazine article?

   OR

   Select a set of photographs that illustrate a debatable topic. Generate a list that includes facts, effects, examples, and opposing points. Search for expert opinions to include. Freewrite about the photograph(s). Remember to ask, "What's the point?"

## Focus Your Point

Read a prewrite you have generated for a persuasive paragraph. Underline words that suggest your values, opinions, or attitudes about the events, situations, objects, or factors. Why is the subject important? Think about the reasons, facts, effects, and examples that best represent your claim. Identify your audience. Think about what specific reaction you want from your audience. Do you want to change your audience's mind about an issue, raise your audience's awareness about an issue, or call your audience to take a specific action? In one sentence, state the claim of your persuasion.

AUDIENCE: ______________________________

PURPOSE—AUDIENCE REACTION: ______________________________

______________________________

### Generate and Organize Relevant Details

Use the persuasive thinking map below to either organize the ideas you have already created or to generate details that support your point.

**Persuasive Thinking Map**

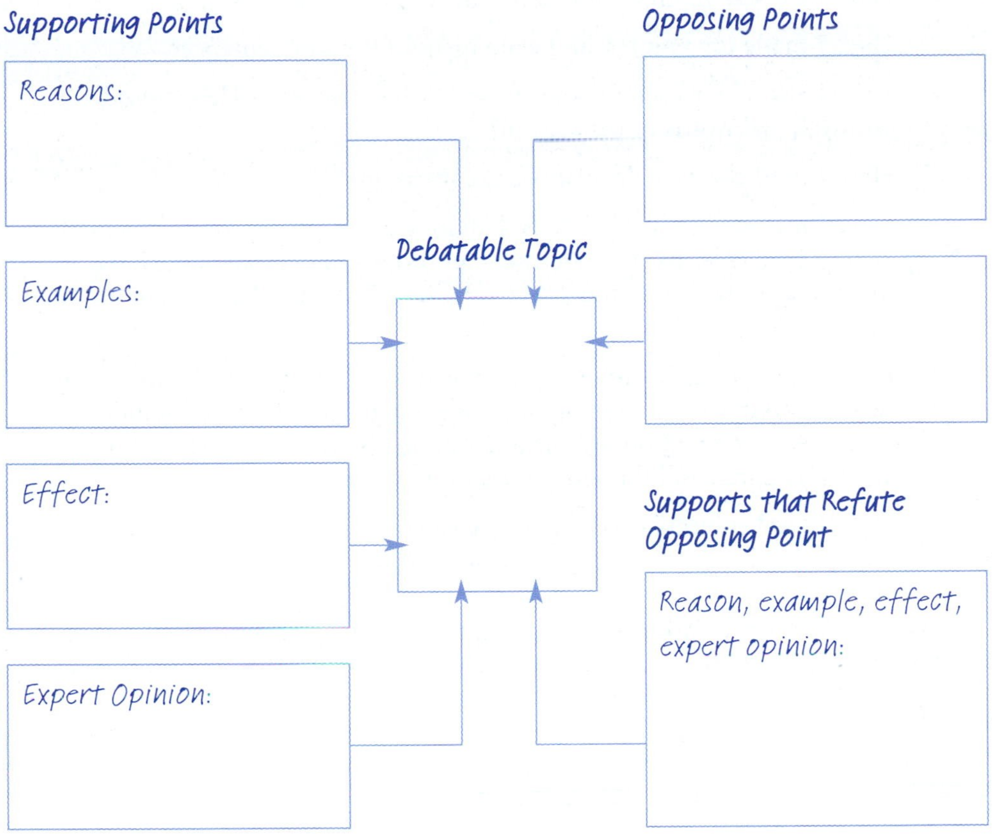


**What's the point**?

---

---

## Write a Draft of Your Paragraph

Using the ideas you generated during the prewriting phase, compose a draft of your persuasion paragraph. Return to the prewriting process at any time to generate additional details as needed. Use your own paper.

## Revise Your Draft

Once you have created a draft of a persuasion paragraph, read the draft and answer the following questions. Indicate your answers by annotating your paper. If you answer "yes" to a question, underline, check, or circle examples. If you answer "no" to a question, write additional details in the margins and draw lines to indicate their placement. Revise your paragraph based on your reflection.

Workshop

PORTFOLIO

Workshop

## Questions for Revising a Persuasive Paragraph

- [ ] Have I chosen an important debatable topic?
- [ ] Have I made my point? Can I state my point in one sentence?
- [ ] Have I effectively used reasons, facts, effects, examples? Have I used strong signal words of persuasion?
- [ ] Have I used concrete details to make my point?
- [ ] Have I included only the details that are relevant to my topic sentence? Have I used effective and relevant expert opinions? Have I addressed important opposing points effectively? Have I documented my sources properly?
- [ ] Have I used the following to make my ideas clear and interesting to my readers: vivid verbs and images, parallel language, controlled sentence structure, coordination, subordination, precise use of words such as *affect* and *effect,* and thoughtful use of biased words?
- [ ] Have I used subjective words to persuade my reader?

Make any revisions to your paragraph that may be needed. Once that's done, turn your attention to the matter of editing for consistent use of point of view.

PROOFREADING

## Proofread Your Draft

Once you have made any revisions to your paragraph that may be needed, proofread you paper to ensure appropriate usage and grammar, such as the consistent use of point of view.

PORTFOLIO

### Grammar in Action: Consistent Use of Point of View

Point of view is established with the use of personal pronouns. Personal pronouns identify three points of view: first person, second person, and third person.

**Personal Pronouns and Points of View**

- **First Person** (informal tone)
  I, me, mine, myself, my,
  we, us, ours, our, ourselves
- **Second Person** (informal tone)
  you, your, yours, yourselves
- **Third Person** (formal tone)
  he, him, his, himself,
  she, her, hers, herself,
  it, its, itself
  they, them, their, theirs, themselves

Common sense tells us that we cannot shift between several individuals' points of view. However, often, we shift point of view carelessly, as in the following sentence:

> Television addiction contributes to our obesity. When you choose to sit in front of a television from the minute you get home until you go to bed, you leave no time for exercise.

Consistent use of point of view strengthens coherence or the clear flow of ideas. Therefore, we should carefully edit our writing to ensure consistent use of point of view, as in the following edited version of the sentence above.

> Television addiction contributes to our obesity. When we choose to sit in front of a television from the minute we get home until we go to bed, we leave no time for exercise.

Workshop

PORTFOLIO

## Practice 7

### CONSISTENT USE OF POINT OF VIEW

Edit these sentences for consistent use of point of view. Cross out the pronoun that causes a shift in point of view and insert a noun or pronoun that establishes consistent use of point of view. Discuss your answers with a small group of peers or with your class.

1. A parent must monitor children's access to the Internet because you are vulnerable to predators in chat rooms and virtual communities like MySpace.com.
2. Some people believe that abstinence is the only way you can prevent unwanted pregnancies and the spread of sexually transmitted diseases.
3. People should not talk on the cell phone and drive at the same time. I was run off the road by a man who was obviously having an intense cell phone conversation while he was driving.
4. Getting enough sleep is crucial to a person's long-term health. When you deprive yourself of sleep, you deprive the body of its ability to repair itself through rest.
5. Women should limit their intake of alcohol to one serving of red wine per day; keep in mind that one serving is five ounces.

More practice with point of view consistency: <www.mywritinglab.com>

Review

## REVIEW OF WRITING A PERSUASIVE PARAGRAPH: DEVELOP YOUR POINT USING THE WRITING PROCESS

Use the following form to record your thinking about writing a persuasive paragraph. Select and focus your topic for your writing situation, audience, and purpose. Choose a topic that can be stated as a debatable claim and identify its significance.

PREWRITING DRAFTING What is your point?

DEBATABLE CLAIM: ______________________________

AUDIENCE: ______________________________

PURPOSE: ______________________________

PREWRITING DRAFTING State you main idea in a topic sentence.

TOPIC: ______________________________

OPINION, DEBATABLE CLAIM: ______________________________

PREWRITING DRAFTING Generate relevant details.

REPORTER'S QUESTIONS: WHO, WHAT, WHERE, WHEN, WHY, HOW? ______________________________

______________________________

PERSUASIVE SUPPORTING DETAILS: ______________________________

REASONS: ______________________________

FACTS: ______________________________

EXAMPLES: ______________________________

EFFECTS: ______________________________

EXPERT OPINIONS: ______________________________

OPPOSING POINTS: ______

SUPPORTS THAT REFUTE OPPOSING POINTS: ______

______

PREWRITING DRAFTING REVISING Use logical order. Use transition words to signal the relationship among supporting details and to qualify ideas.

TRANSITIONS THAT SIGNAL PERSUASION: ______

SIGNAL WORDS THAT QUALIFY IDEAS: ______

REVISING PROOFREADING Use effective expression. Use subjective words for a thoughtful effect. Use a consistent point of view.

SUBJECTIVE WORDS: ______

POINT OF VIEW: ______

FIRST PERSON: ______

SECOND PERSON: ______

THIRD PERSON: ______

Review

# Writing Assignments

## Considering Audience and Purpose

Study the set of photographs at the beginning of the chapter. Assume you are an advertiser, and you have been asked to write a brochure to go along with one of the posters. Choose which side of the topic you wish to represent (the tobacco company or the anti-smoking public health announcement). Write a one-paragraph argument in support of the side of the issue you represent.

## Writing for Everyday Life

Assume that you and your family, or you and a group of your friends, have decided to take a vacation together. Each of you has a different destination and activity in mind. Write a one-paragraph email to your family or group of friends in which you convince them to travel to your choice of destinations. Be sure to include facts, effects, examples, expert opinions, and reasons that counter any opposition to your choice. Allow your word choice and tone to reflect your enthusiasm.

## Writing for College Life

Assume that you disagree with a grade you have received for a course or an assignment. Write a one-paragraph letter to your professor in which you argue for the grade you believe you have earned. Be sure to include facts that prove what you have learned, examples of what you have learned, and the benefits of what you have learned. As part of your proof, include ideas and concepts you have learned from your professor (as an expert in the field). Allow your word choice and tone to reflect both respect for the professor and self-confidence in your abilities.

## Writing for Working Life

Assume that you are a supervisor of a shift of workers at a fast food restaurant or at a department store. Assume that you are short of staff, and the busy season is approaching: you need more workers. Write a one-paragraph memo to your district manager, Derwood Kuntz, persuading him to authorize you to hire three additional workers. Be sure to include reasons, facts, examples, effects, and points that will counter any opposition he may pose.

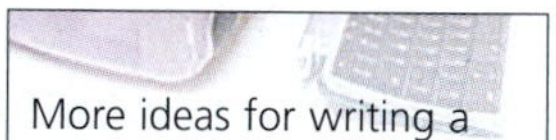

More ideas for writing a persuasive paragraph: <www.mywritinglab.com>

PART 3

# Writing an Essay

# 13

# Understanding the Essay

## Chapter Preview

- What's the Point of an Essay?
- Making a Point Using an Essay: One Writer's Response
- Developing Your Point: Writing an Essay
- The Traits of an Effective Essay
- Workshop: Writing an Essay Step by Step

## An essay is a series of closely related ideas.

All of us of have had some experience studying, writing, or reading essays. What do you already know about essays? Where do you see essays? What are the traits of an essay?

Perhaps the most common and flexible form of writing, an essay allows powerful personal expression. The essay is used for academic papers, business reports, business letters, newspaper and magazine articles, Web articles, and personal letters, as well as letters to the editor of a paper or journal. By mastering the task of writing an essay, you empower your ability to think, to reason, and to communicate.

# What's the Point of an Essay?

Like a paragraph, an **essay** is a series of closely related ideas that develop and support the writer's point about a topic. In fact, the paragraph serves as a building block for an essay since an essay is composed of two, three, or more paragraphs. Therefore, the skills you developed to write a paragraph will also help you write an effective essay.

## The Four Parts of an Essay

An essay has four basic parts: a **title**; a beginning, made up of an **introductory paragraph**; a middle, made up of **body paragraphs**; and an ending, often made up of a **concluding paragraph**. The following chart shows the general format of an essay.

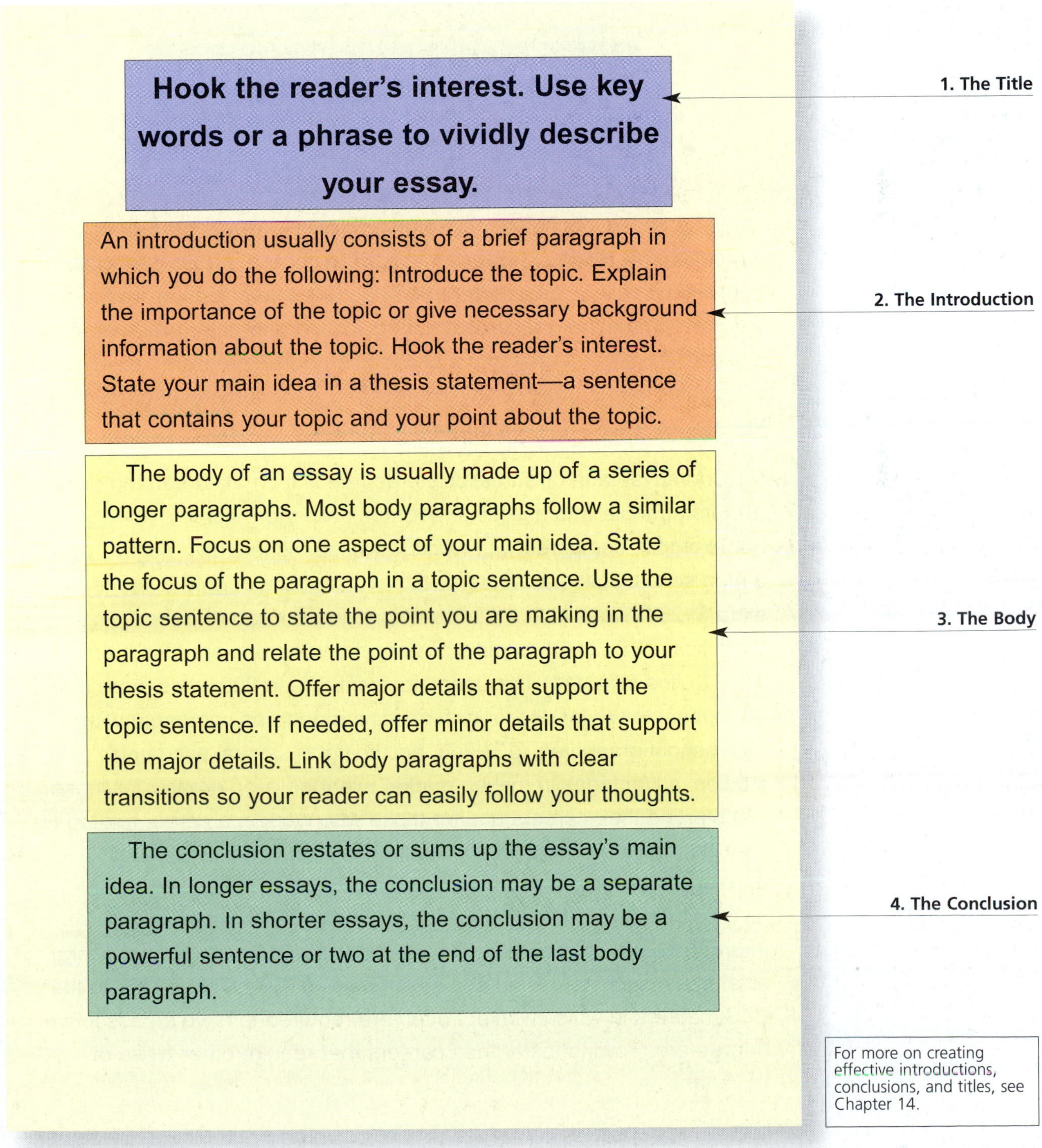
Hook the reader's interest. Use key words or a phrase to vividly describe your essay.
1. The Title
An introduction usually consists of a brief paragraph in which you do the following: Introduce the topic. Explain the importance of the topic or give necessary background information about the topic. Hook the reader's interest. State your main idea in a thesis statement—a sentence that contains your topic and your point about the topic.
2. The Introduction
The body of an essay is usually made up of a series of longer paragraphs. Most body paragraphs follow a similar pattern. Focus on one aspect of your main idea. State the focus of the paragraph in a topic sentence. Use the topic sentence to state the point you are making in the paragraph and relate the point of the paragraph to your thesis statement. Offer major details that support the topic sentence. If needed, offer minor details that support the major details. Link body paragraphs with clear transitions so your reader can easily follow your thoughts.
3. The Body
The conclusion restates or sums up the essay's main idea. In longer essays, the conclusion may be a separate paragraph. In shorter essays, the conclusion may be a powerful sentence or two at the end of the last body paragraph.
4. The Conclusion

For more on creating effective introductions, conclusions, and titles, see Chapter 14.

# Making a Point Using an Essay: One Writer's Response

Read the following essay from the U.S. Bureau of Labor Statistics' Web site. Study the annotations and complete the activities suggested in the annotations.

**The Introduction:** The writer begins with a bold statement designed to hook the reader's interest. The next several sentences offer important background information about an associate degree. The introduction ends with the thesis statement. Notice that the thesis statement states the topic, "associate degree," and the writer's focus, "many advantages" and "many resources."

**The Title:** The writer used a phrase to appeal to the reader's desire to get a "jump start" on the future. The title introduces the topic "Associate Degree" and sums up the point of her essay in just a few words.

**The Body:** The body of this essay is made up of several paragraphs. This topic sentence states a primary support for the thesis–one advantage of an associate degree: "increased earning power." By repeating the key term "advantage," the writer ties this body paragraph to the thesis statement.

**This detail** supports the topic sentence and is introduced with the transition "First."

This sentence is a minor detail that supports a major detail.
**Underline the phrase that introduces this detail.**

**Second major detail** that supports the topic sentence. Note the transition word "also."

**Third major detail** that supports the topic sentence is introduced with the transition "However."

## Associate Degree: Two Years to a Career or a Jump Start to a Bachelor's Degree

by Olivia Crosby

(1) In two years, you can increase your earnings, train for some of the fastest growing jobs in the economy, and pave the way for further education. (2) How? (3) Earn an associate degree. (4) An associate degree is a college degree awarded after the completion of about 20 classes. (5) It either prepares students for a career after graduation, or it allows them to transfer into a bachelor's degree program. (6) An associate degree offers many advantages, and many resources exist to help you decide upon a specific degree and college.

(7) One advantage of an associate degree is increased earning power. (8) First, people with associate degrees earn more money. (9) For example, compared with workers whose highest held degree was a high school diploma, workers with an associate degree averaged an extra $128 a week in 2001, according to the Bureau of Labor Statistics (BLS). (10) People with associate degrees are also more likely to find jobs. (11) The unemployment rate in 2001 was more than 30 percent lower for people with associate degrees compared with high school graduates. (12) And, according to several academic studies, advantages in the job market might be even greater for those just starting their careers and for those who work in a career related to their degree. (13) However, for most people, the best part about earning an associate degree is the opportunity to enter interesting professions. (14) Training is available for those with nearly any interest, from technical fields like electronics and health care to liberal arts areas, such as design and social work. (15) And according to the BLS, careers in which workers often are required to have an associate degree are growing faster than careers that require other types of training.

(16) Another advantage of an associate degree is that it is widely available, offering a variety of experiences. (17) Degrees are available from public community colleges, private two-year colleges, for-profit technical institutes, and many four-year colleges and universities. (18) Taking classes from home is more common in associate degree programs than in any other type of educational program. (19) More than 9 percent of associate degree students used distance learning in 1998, according to the U.S. Department of Education. (20) Other students have a more traditional college experience. (21) These students choose schools that offer on-campus housing and meals. (22) And nearly all schools offer extracurricular activities—such as sports, clubs, and volunteer groups—as well as academics.

**This topic sentence** states another primary support for the thesis–"another advantage" of an associate degree. This phrase links this paragraph to the previous paragraph with the transition "another," and the word "advantage" ties this body paragraph to the thesis statement. **Underline the words in the topic sentence that state the author's point in this paragraph.**

(23) In addition to the many advantages of an associate degree, many resources exist to help you make the best decisions about your career and how to train for it. (24) First, most libraries and career centers have the Encyclopedia of Associations and the *Occupational Outlook Handbook.* (25) These books offer information about work-related associations. (26) The *Handbook* also describes hundreds of careers and how to train for them. (27) Second, counselors at colleges and career centers have information about local associate degree programs, labor markets, and financial aid. (28) Third, the easiest way to learn about specific degree programs is to request information from the schools that offer them. (29) Nearly every school provides free publications, and many maintain Web sites describing programs and facilities. (30) For more details, consider calling, writing, or visiting prospective teachers. (31) Faculty and counselors are usually happy to speak with would-be students about courses and careers.

**This topic sentence** offers another primary support for the thesis. The sentence begins with a transitional phrase "In addition to the many advantages of an associate degree." This phrase links this paragraph to the previous paragraphs and the thesis statement. **Circle the words that state the author's focus in this paragraph. Underline the three major supporting details in this paragraph. Remember to look for transition words.**

(32) An associate degree increases your chance for financial power and personal fulfillment—in just two years. (33) And with the many resources to help you decide on a degree and school along with the flexible paths to access, a bright future awaits you. (34) So don't delay; begin today!

—Adapted from Olivia Crosby, "Associate Degree: Two Years to a Career or a Jump Start to a Bachelor's Degree," US Department of Labor.

**The Conclusion:**
This essay ends by restating the writer's main idea and calling the reader to action. **Underline the words that restate the essay's main point.**

WRITING FROM LIFE

Practice 1

WRITING FOR COLLEGE LIFE

Test your understanding of the essay's structure. Read the student essay below straight through once. Complete the activities beneath the essay as you read the essay a second time. After reading, complete the outline with information from the essay.

Lacey Durrance

Professor Ragan

ENC 1101: Section 47

October 10, 2007

Traits of a Successful College Student

(1) First-time college students don't realize the reality shock they will receive when they get to college. (2) High school and college atmospheres are extremely different in many ways. (3) College campuses and classes are often larger, college teachers have different expectations, and college students face many new challenges. (4) College is a big part of growing up, and with growing up comes certain traits needed to make it in college. (5) To get through college successfully, all first-time college students must be dedicated, responsible, and independent. (6) Many won't realize this until it is too late, and without these traits, they won't succeed.

(7) Dedication is a primary part of being successful in college. (8) Students must want a good grade and know what they need to do to achieve it. (9) Students must work hard and take action to learn at a college level. (10) Assignments can't be left until the last minute like they might have been in high school. (11) College students must be willing to speak up in class and ask questions when they don't understand, even if they are afraid they will look foolish. (12) Dedication means setting priorities for success; dedication means putting off going out with friends; dedication means caring about producing the best work possible. (13) Dedicated students will do their work and do it well, spending hours reading textbooks, reviewing notes, and revising essays. (14) College is very different in the sense that much is expected from students, and they won't be walked through anything.

(15) For many, being responsible during high school wasn't really necessary. (16) Students could forget to do their homework and "blame it on the dog," yet the teacher most likely would extend the deadline. (17) In contrast, college students must be responsible for their actions and accept the consequences. (18) Paying attention to what's due and when assignments should be turned in is a prime example. (19) Most college teachers stick to their deadlines and expect students to do so also. (20) Being on time to class is another example of being responsible. (21) Unlike high school, there are no bells or signals that start college classes. (22) Students must manage their time to get themselves to class on time. (23) Responsibility plays a key role in a successful college career.

(24) However, having dedication and being responsible aren't the only traits college students need to survive. (25) College students must also be independent in everything they do. (26) Teachers expect students to take notes without assigning them to do so. (27) In high school, teachers often gave out notes to study from or told students where and when to take them. (28) This isn't the story in college. (29) College students must do their work without being reminded everyday. (30) However, teachers are there to help their students understand the class material. (31) They will guide their students yet not help complete their work. (32) Being independent is a skill to acquire for college success, as well as life-long success.

(33) College is hard work, and students must have these traits to be successful. (34) Most first-time college students will struggle with the new experience, yet by being dedicated, responsible, and independent, they will thrive in the college world.

**1.** Based on the title of the essay, what is the writer's topic and main point?

**2.** In the introduction, how does the writer "hook" the reader's interest?

Practice 1

3. Underline the thesis statement. Rewrite the thesis statement using your own words here.

---

---

4. What ideas did the writer restate in her conclusion?

---

---

5. The writer used a brief outline to plan and organize her ideas before she wrote her essay. Recreate her plan by completing the following outline. Fill in the blanks with her thesis statement and topic sentences.

I. INTRODUCTION

THESIS STATEMENT: ______

---

---

II. FIRST BODY PARAGRAPH TOPIC SENTENCE: ______

---

---

III. SECOND BODY PARAGRAPH TOPIC SENTENCE: ______

---

---

IV. THIRD BODY PARAGRAPH TOPIC SENTENCE: ______

---

---

V. CONCLUSION TOPIC SENTENCE: ______

---

---

# Developing Your Point: Writing an Essay

## The Four Levels of Information in an Essay

### Types of Details

Two types of details are often needed to thoroughly explain a main idea: primary and secondary details. **Primary details** directly explain or support the thesis statement. **Secondary details** indirectly support the thesis statement. In an essay, topic sentences of the body paragraphs are the primary supports for the thesis statement. The examples, reasons, and facts within the body of a paragraph support the topic sentence. They serve as secondary details that support the thesis statement.

### Levels of Details

Secondary supports can also be divided into two levels: major details and minor details. A **major detail** supports a topic sentence. A **minor detail** supports a major detail. Thus, a topic sentence supports the thesis statement, and secondary supports explain a topic sentence. The following flow chart illustrates these levels of information in an essay. This chart represents a basic three-paragraph essay. This format is often expanded to include two or more body paragraphs.

For more on outlining, see Chapter 2.

**Levels of Information in an Essay**

**Introduction:** Offers important background information about the topic
Offers the reader a reason to read about the topic. Hooks the reader's interest

↓

**Thesis Statement:**
- States the main idea of the essay in a complete sentence
- Uses specific, effective wording
- Covers all the details in the essay

**Introductory Paragraph**

↓

**Topic Sentence**
- Offers one primary support for the thesis statement
- States the author's main idea of the paragraph
- Covers all the details in the paragraph

↓

**Major Detail**
- Explains or supports the topic sentence
- Is a secondary support for the thesis statement
- Is more general than a minor detail

↓

**Minor Detail**
- Explains or supports a major detail
- Is a secondary support for the thesis
- Is one of the most specific ideas in the paragraph

**Body Paragraph:**
Most essays have two or more body paragraphs. The ideas in a body paragraph often move from general to specific: from topic sentence to major support to minor support. This pattern is often repeated in each body paragraph.

↓

**Conclusion:** Refers to the main idea of the essay: Sums up the primary supports of the essay
Reinforces the writer's overall point

**The Conclusion:**
A short essay may require just a sentence or two at the end of the final body paragraph. Longer essays often need a separate short paragraph to summarize the major points of the essay.

Practice 2

IDENTIFYING THE LEVELS OF DETAIL IN AN ESSAY

An outline can help you see the levels of information in your essay. Read the following three-paragraph essay. Underline the thesis statement. Next, underline the three major details in the body paragraph. Then, complete the outline with information from the essay.

Street Luging for the Extreme Thrill

(1) Extreme sports take athletic competition to new levels of danger and excitement. (2) They often offer a combination of speed, height, danger, and mind-blowing stunts. (3) Street luging illustrates the allure of extreme sports.

(4) Street luging, like many extreme sports, involves high levels of speed, danger, and adrenaline. (5) First, street luging is all about speed. (6) A pilot lies on his or her back on a luge (a type of skateboard, eight and a half feet long) and flies through a street course at speeds of around 70 miles per hour. (7) As a result, the urethane wheels of the luge may actually flame fire and melt during a run due to the high speeds. (8) Second, street luging courses are known for their rough, hazardous road surfaces and obstacles. (9) For example, very dangerous courses are known as *bacon* while less dangerous ones are labeled *scrambled eggs*. (10) And frequently, luges snag or hook together, wobble, wipe out, or slam into barriers that mark the course. (11) Finally, the dangers of street luging are related to another important attraction of extreme sports—the thrilling rush of an adrenaline high. (12) The adrenaline rush is due to high levels of dopamine, endorphins, and serotonin produced by the body in response to the danger. (13) Adrenaline floods the body with additional surges of energy, power, and well-being so that a person can either fight or flee the danger. (14) Many extreme sports participants are called adrenaline junkies. (15) Luge pilots refer to this feeling as being "amped."

(16) Extreme sports include a wide variety of thrill-seeking sports such as wave surfing, wind surfing, BASE jumping (jumping from buildings, antennas or towers, spans or bridges, or cliffs), parachuting, and drag racing. (17) Overall, street luging offers athletes all the dangers and thrills that all extreme sports enthusiasts find so attractive.

**I.** (Introduction) Extreme sports take athletic competition to new levels of danger and excitement. They often offer a combination of speed, height, danger, and mind-blowing stunts.

Thesis Statement: Street luging illustrates the allure of extreme sports.

**II.** (Body) Street luging, like many extreme sports, involves high levels of speed, danger, and adrenaline.

**A.** ____________________

**1.** A pilot lies on his or her back on a luge (a type of skateboard, eight and a half feet long) and flies through a street course at speeds of around 70 miles per hour.

**2.** As a result, the urethane wheels of the luge may actually flame fire and melt during a run due to the high speeds.

**B.** ____________________

____________________

**1.** Very dangerous courses are known as *bacon* while less dangerous ones are labeled *scrambled eggs.*

**2.** Frequently, luges snag or hook together, wobble, wipe out, or slam into barriers that mark the course.

**C.** ____________________

____________________

**1.** ____________________

____________________

____________________

**2.** Adrenaline floods the body with additional surges of energy, power, and well-being so that a person can either fight or flee the danger.

**3.** Many extreme sports participants are called adrenaline junkies.

**4.** ____________________

____________________

**III.** (Conclusion) Extreme sports include a wide variety of thrill-seeking sports such as wave surfing, wind surfing, BASE jumping (jumping from buildings, antennas or towers, spans or bridges, or cliffs), parachuting, and drag racing. Overall, street luging offers athletes all the dangers and thrills that all extreme sports enthusiasts find so attractive.

Practice 2

# The Traits of an Effective Essay

The word essay means attempt, to make an effort to accomplish an end. An essay is a writer's attempt to share his or her unique and specific point about a specific subject to a specific audience for a specific purpose. An effective essay supports a **main idea** with **relevant details** in **logical order,** using **effective expression.**

## The Point: Main Idea

What's the point of a focused main idea? To make a clear and powerful point to your reader! An effective essay makes a clear point by focusing on a main idea. A focused main idea is the result of several thinking steps: selecting and narrowing a topic and writing a thesis statement.

### Select and Narrow a Topic

For more on using prewriting techniques and selecting a topic, see Chapter 2.

Many writers break this step into two parts. First, a writer often generates a list of topics. This list serves as a bank of ideas that can be applied to a wide variety of writing situations. Second, a writer considers the writing situation.

Understanding the writing situation helps the writer narrow the topic. For example, the length of an essay often depends on your audience and purpose. A paper for an academic audience such as a history professor may have a required length of 1,000 words. In contrast, a local newspaper may limit the length of letters to the editor to 500 words. The scope of the topic needs to match the required length. For example, the 500-word letter to the editor cannot cover all the reasons one should volunteer at the local soup kitchen for the poor. Instead, you would need to narrow the topic to just two or three reasons. And you would choose only those details that are of interest to your specific audience.

For more on the writing situation, and topic, purpose, and audience, see Chapter 2.

Practice 3

THE WRITING SITUATION

The following pictures present specific writing situations. Each picture represents an audience, and each caption states the purpose for writing to that audience. First, match the audience and purpose to its appropriate topic. Then, write the letter of the topic in the appropriate space. Finally, discuss your answers with your class or in a small group.

Topics:
a. The importance of a specific lesson
b. Wisdom gained from an education
c. The proper way to discipline a child
d. Why voting is important

.......... Writing Situation 1: To Inform – to share, explain or demonstrate information

.......... Writing Situation 2: To Persuade – to change this audience's opinion or call them to action

.......... Writing Situation 3: To Express – to share personal opinions, feelings or reactions

.......... Writing Situation 4: To Reflect – to record your understandings about what you have experienced or learned

Your purpose for writing is another important part of the writing situation. Most likely you write for three general purposes: to inform, to entertain, or to persuade. A specific writing situation may call for a more specific purpose such as to express a personal opinion or to reflect upon the significance of an event.

## Practice 4

### TOPIC, PURPOSE, AND AUDIENCE

Generate a list of topics appropriate for each of the following writing situations. Discuss your answers with your class or in a small group.

Situation **1:**

PURPOSE: To inform

AUDIENCE: Speech class teacher and peers

TOPICS: ______________________________

______________________________

______________________________

______________________________

Situation **2:**

PURPOSE: To express displeasure or satisfaction

AUDIENCE: A manager or supervisor

TOPICS: ______________________________

______________________________

______________________________

______________________________

Situation **3:**

PURPOSE: To persuade

AUDIENCE: The general public

TOPICS: ______________________________

______________________________

______________________________

______________________________

Practice 6

THESIS STATEMENT:

3. TOPIC: Major depressive disorder

WRITER'S POINT: a common type of mood disorder with several long-term effects

THESIS STATEMENT:

4. TOPIC: Use of chat rooms and online discussion boards

WRITER'S POINT: Five tips for effectiveness

THESIS STATEMENT:

5. TOPIC: Weight training machines and free weights

WRITER'S POINT: similarities and differences

THESIS STATEMENT:

6. Cell phones cause a lot of problems.

REVISED THESIS STATEMENT:

7. Smoking is a bad habit.

REVISED THESIS STATEMENT:

**8.** The football team the Houston Texans are a bunch of losers.

REVISED THESIS STATEMENT: ______________________________

______________________________

______________________________

**9.** My job at Cypress Gardens in Winter Haven, Florida, was very interesting.

REVISED THESIS STATEMENT: ______________________________

______________________________

______________________________

**10.** I am going to talk about the dangers of compulsive gambling on the gambler and his family.

REVISED THESIS STATEMENT: ______________________________

______________________________

______________________________

Practice 6

## Relevant Details

In an effective essay, the writer provides enough relevant details to adequately or thoroughly support the essay's main idea.

### Generate Details with a Writing Plan

Most writers generate details during the prewriting stage by listing or freewriting. Once you have generated an adequate amount of details, you need to organize them into a writing plan. Many writers use clustering or outlining to help them create a plan for the essay. Clustering and outlining are excellent ways to see if you have enough details to support the point of your essay.

For more on listing and freewriting, see Chapter 2.

Some writers begin the writing process by generating details, then drafting a thesis statement, while other writers draft a working thesis statement first and then generate details. The following two practices offer you an opportunity to work with both approaches. In your own writing, you should experiment to see which approach works best for you.

For concept maps of specific patterns of organization, such as narration, classification, and definition, see Chapters 4-12.

# Practice 7

## DRAFTING A THESIS, GENERATING DETAILS, AND CREATING A WRITING PLAN

Read the thesis statement. Note that the thesis statement suggests three body paragraphs with the controlling idea "three simple steps." First, study the following set of details created during a brainstorming session. Then, group the details into chunks of information by completing the outline with details from the list. Finally, state the main idea of each paragraph in a topic sentence.

THESIS STATEMENT: *Three simple steps can lead to a long, healthy life.*

DETAILS: *eating healthy* *being active* *managing stress*

*need thirty minutes of moderate exercise nearly every day*

*managing stress reduces cardiovascular disease, chronic fatigue,*

*and psychological disorders*

*eat five or more servings of fruit or vegetables daily*

*healthful diet reduces the risk of cancer/other chronic diseases*

*exercise reduces obesity, diabetes, high blood pressure, heart disease,*

*and stroke*

*start slow, build up gradually*

*balance obligations*

*get plenty of rest*

*make time for recreation and fun*

*control portions*

*drink plenty of water*

*stay committed*

*dance, garden, swim, walk, jog, lift weights, etc.*

*talk over problems/challenges with a friend or counselor*

I. INTRODUCTION

THESIS STATEMENT: Three simple steps can lead to a long, healthy life.

II. TOPIC SENTENCE: The first step to a long, healthy life is a healthful, balanced diet.

A. SUPPORTING DETAIL: Healthful diet reduces the risk of cancer and other chronic diseases.

B. SUPPORTING DETAIL: 

C. SUPPORTING DETAIL: 

D. SUPPORTING DETAIL: 

III. TOPIC SENTENCE: The second step to long-term health is being active.

A. SUPPORTING DETAIL: 

B. SUPPORTING DETAIL: 

C. SUPPORTING DETAIL: 

D. SUPPORTING DETAIL: 

E. SUPPORTING DETAIL: 

IV. TOPIC SENTENCE: 

A. SUPPORTING DETAIL: 

B. SUPPORTING DETAIL: 

C. SUPPORTING DETAIL: 

D. SUPPORTING DETAIL: 

E. SUPPORTING DETAIL: 

5. CONCLUSION

Practice 7

For more on creating and using concept maps, see Chapter 2.

Often, a writer uses a prewriting technique, such as a concept map, to generate primary and secondary details. Then, the writer drafts a working thesis statement to summarize the point of the details generated with the concept map.

## Practice 8

### GENERATE DETAILS, DRAFT A THESIS, CREATE A WRITING PLAN

Study the following list of details. Create a writing plan by filling in the concept map with groups of details from the list. Then, write a one-sentence summary (a thesis statement) of the main point that they support. Next, write topic sentences to state the main idea of each group of details. Finally, fill in the outline based on the concept map. Use complete sentences.

| | | |
|---|---|---|
| respects others | builds consensus | seeks solutions |
| stays on point | fosters team work | remains professional |
| avoids gossip | diffuses confrontations | sticks with facts, not feelings |
| functions of effective communication on the job | gets to the point quickly | encourages input from others |
| | states clear expectations | |

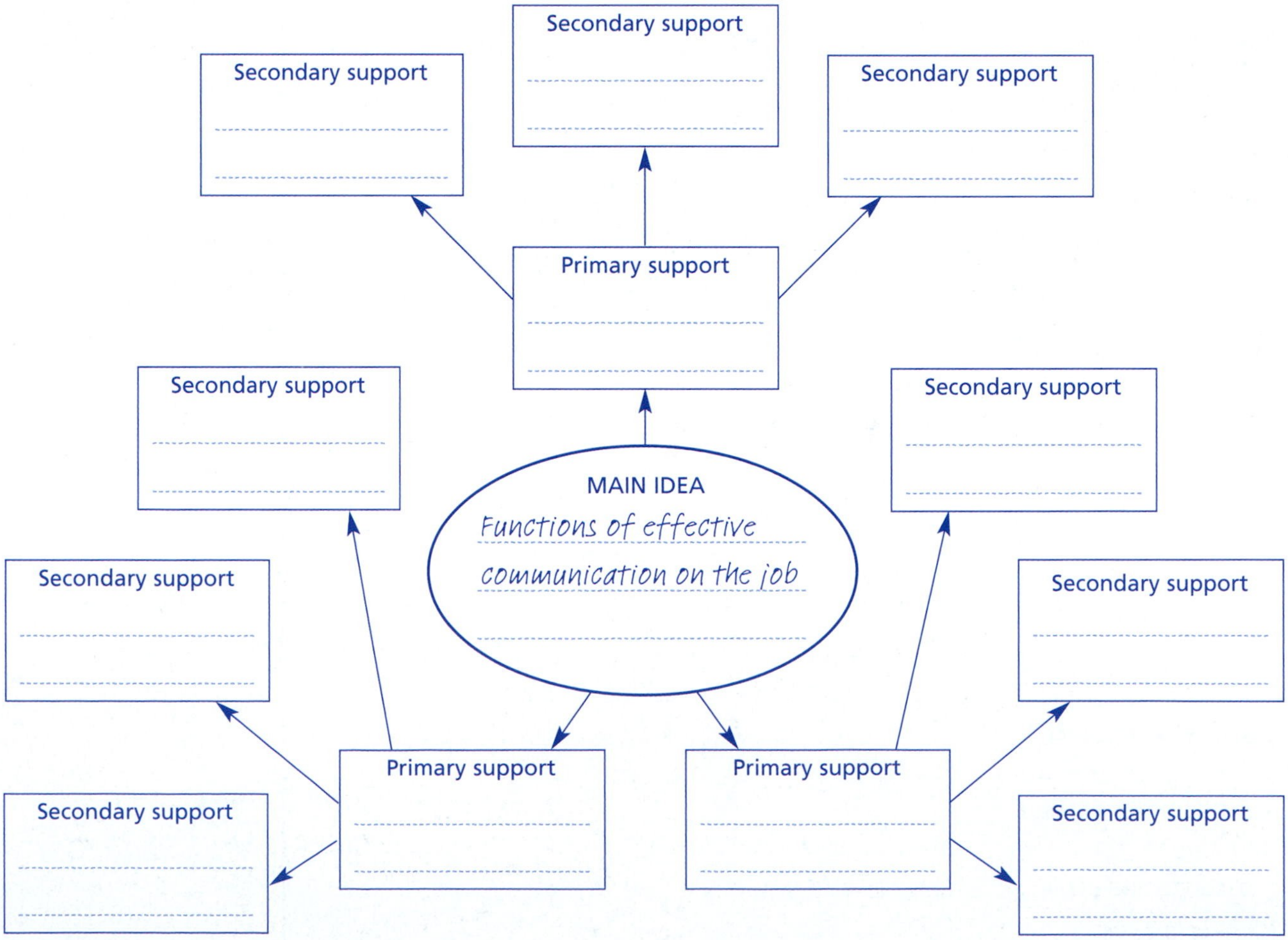


One-sentence summary of primary supports:

I. INTRODUCTION

THESIS STATEMENT: To succeed on the job, you need effective communication skills.

II. ______________________________

A. ______________________________

______________________________

B. ______________________________

______________________________

C. ______________________________

III. ______________________________

A. ______________________________

B. ______________________________

______________________________

C. ______________________________

______________________________

IV. ______________________________

A. ______________________________

______________________________

B. ______________________________

C. ______________________________

______________________________

V. CONCLUSION

Practice 8

## Evaluate Details

In an effective essay, every detail supports the thesis statement. *All* the details work together as a unit to explain and support the writer's point. During the prewriting process, a writer brainstorms many details, some of which may not be related to the focus of the main idea. Therefore, as you create your writing plan, you should test the details to be sure that each one is relevant to the thesis statement. Drop those details that do not support either the thesis statement or the thesis statement's primary supports. You also may want to check details for relevance once more during the revision stage of the writing process.

### Practice 9

TESTING DETAILS FOR RELEVANCE

Study the following writing plan. Cross out details that are not relevant to the thesis statement. The following questions will help you test details for unity. Share your work with your class or in a small group of peers.

- What is the topic and controlling idea of the thesis statement? Circle the topic. Underline the controlling idea.
- Which details are the primary supporting details (the ones that will be used as topic sentences for body paragraphs)? Number the three primary supports A, B, and C.
- What are the secondary details? Number each secondary detail to correspond to a primary point: A1, A2, and so on; B1, B2, and so on; and C1, C2, and so on.

THESIS STATEMENT: Due to the nature of lightning, you must follow lightning safety guidelines to reduce risk of injury or death.

_________ Lightning is a complex event.

_________ A spark of lightning can reach over five miles in length, soar to temperatures of approximately 50,000 degrees Fahrenheit, and contain 100 million electrical volts.

.......... Lightning is described as having two components: leaders and strokes.

.......... The leader is the probing feeler sent from the cloud.

.......... The return streaks of light are a series of strokes that produce the actual lightning bolt or flash that we see.

.......... Fires are usually started by unusually long-lasting hot lightning bolts.

.......... Lightning is also common, unpredictable, and dangerous.

.......... At any given moment, there are 1,800 thunderstorms in progress somewhere on the earth. This amounts to 16 million storms each year.

.......... An average of 25 million flashes of lightning from the cloud to ground occur every year.

.......... Lightning has been seen in volcanic eruptions, extremely intense forest fires, surface nuclear detonations, heavy snowstorms, and in large hurricanes.

.......... No one can predict the location or time of the next stroke of lightning.

.......... Lightning has been the second largest storm killer in the U.S. for the last 40 years, exceeded only by floods.

.......... Lightning strikes can cause paralysis, brain damage, and cardiac arrest.

.......... Following proven lightning safety guidelines can reduce your risk of injury or death.

.......... Seek safe shelter when you first hear thunder or see dark threatening clouds developing overhead or lightning.

.......... Count the seconds between the time you see lightning and the time you hear the thunder.

.......... You should already be in a safe location if that time is less than 30 seconds.

.......... The safest location during lightning activity is an enclosed building.

.......... Stay inside until 30 minutes after you last hear thunder.

.......... Rain will not kill you.

Practice 9

## Logical Order

In an effective essay, body paragraphs are arranged in a clear, logical order for a coherent flow of ideas. Likewise, effective writers link each paragraph to the next so that readers can follow their chain of thought.

You can achieve a coherent flow of ideas in several logical ways.

1. *Follow the order of ideas as presented in the thesis statement.* Often the controlling idea of the thesis statement divides the topic into chunks of information.

2. *Follow space order.* At times, a writer describes how something is arranged in space to develop a main idea. Description moves from top to bottom, side to side, front to back, or the reverse of these.

3. *Follow time order.* A writer may record an event or a process as it unfolds in time.

4. *Present ideas in order of importance.* Often, a writer decides upon and arranges details according to his or her opinion about the importance of the details, known as **climactic order**. Usually, climactic order moves from least important point in the first body paragraph and builds to the essay's climax, the most important point in the final body paragraph.

# Practice 10

## COHERENCE TECHNIQUES: THESIS-STATEMENT, SPACE, TIME, AND CLIMACTIC ORDER

Complete the exercises, and share your responses with your class or in a small group.

1. **Follow the order of ideas as presented in the thesis statement.** Underline the three chunked parts of the controlling idea. Then, write and arrange in coherent order three topic sentences (primary supports) suggested by the thesis statement.

**I.** Introduction

THESIS STATEMENT: ______________________________

______________________________

______________________________

**II.** ______________________________

**III.** ______________________________

**IV.** ______________________________

______________________________

**V.** Conclusion

**2. Follow space order**. Write and arrange in space order three topic sentences (primary supports) suggested by the following thesis statement. Use the photographs to generate your primary supports.

**I.** Introduction

THESIS STATEMENT: *Although Goth fashion varies widely, the look makes a bold, nontraditional fashion statement.*

**II.** ______________________

**III.** ______________________

**IV.** ______________________

**V.** Conclusion

**3. Follow time order.** Write and arrange in time order three topic sentences (primary supports) suggested by the following thesis statement. Use the photographs to generate your primary supports.

**I.** Introduction

THESIS STATEMENT: *Technology plays a key role in the restoration of Sand Key Beach, Florida.*

▲ Before restoration

**II.** ______________________

______________________

▲ During restoration

**III.** ______________________

**IV.** ______________________

**V.** ______________________

______________________

______________________

▲ After restoration

**VI.** Conclusion

**4. Present ideas in order of importance.** Write and arrange in climactic order three topic sentences (primary supports) suggested by the following thesis statement.

**I.** Introduction

THESIS STATEMENT: *Stress challenges us in almost every aspect of our lives.*

**II.** 

**III.** 

**IV.** 

**V.** Conclusion

Practice 10

## ORDERING PARAGRAPHS

Study the following writing plans. In the space provided next to each primary support (topic sentence) number the statements in each group II, III, or IV to show the most coherent order. Then, indicate which coherence technique you used in the numbered spaces:

TSO = Thesis Statement Order;
TO = Time Order; SO = Space Order;
CO = Climactic Order.

.......... **1.** I. Introduction

THESIS STATEMENT: *The sunrise blazed in a belt of fire.*

.......... Below the smoldering belt, the sea flared in reflected waves of orange, yellow, and red.

.......... The entire canopy of the earth glowed like the underside of a red hot ember.

.......... Where sky met earth, the sun paused, a perfect, brilliant ball of flame upon a belt of smoky purple.

V. Conclusion

.......... **2.** I. Introduction

THESIS STATEMENT: *iPods are an excellent investment because they are equipped with the ability to store and play large libraries of music, store and play movies, and store personal information through calendars, address books, and personal notes.*

.......... iPods are able to store and play large libraries of music.

.......... iPods can store and play movies.

.......... iPods organize personal information through calendars, address books, and personal notes.

V. Conclusion

.......... **3.** I. Introduction

THESIS STATEMENT: *Ballroom dancing is popular for several reasons.*

.......... Most importantly, according to many people, ballroom dancing provides them with a life-long hobby.

.......... A significant reason that many people begin ballroom dancing is the rigorous exercise required to accomplish the moves.

.......... Many people take up ballroom dancing just to meet new friends and have a good time.

V. Conclusion

.......... **4.** I. Introduction

THESIS STATEMENT: *Real learning occurs before, during, and after each class.*

.......... After class, review class notes, compare class notes to your reading notes, and summarize what you learned in your own words.

.......... During class, listen actively, take notes, and ask questions.

.......... Before class, read the assigned material, take notes, and think of questions to ask during class.

V. Conclusion

## Connecting Paragraphs

In addition to ordering paragraphs coherently, writers clearly connect each paragraph to the next so that readers can follow their chain of thought. You can use several options to connect paragraphs to each other. The following chart lists and illustrates each option.

| Connecting Paragraphs | |
|---|---|
| **Echo or repeat important words or phrases from the thesis statement in body paragraphs.** | |
| I. Thesis statement: | We can *ease* the *pain* that occurs from illness or injury in several different ways. |
| II. Topic sentence: | *Pain* can be *eased* by deep breathing. |
| III. Topic sentence: | Visualization and imagery *ease pain.* |
| **Refer to the main idea of the previous paragraph in the topic sentence of the present paragraph.** | |
| I. Thesis statement: | Applying the principles of computer ergonomics reduces the chances of injury and fatigue. |
| II. Topic sentence: | The *computer screen* should be *placed properly* to avoid painful injuries to the neck. |
| III. Topic sentence: | *Proper placement* of the *monitor* not only *reduces* the possibility of *neck injury* but also eases eye fatigue. |
| **Use transitional words, phrases, or sentences.** | |
| I. Thesis statement: | Sleep disorders can deprive sufferers of much needed rest and complicate their lives. |
| II. Topic sentence: | *One type* of sleep disorder is known as night terrors. |
| III. Topic sentence: | *Another type* of sleep disorder, nightmares, torments many people. |
| IV. Transition sentence and topic sentence: | *At least the previous two disorders occur in the privacy of one's home.* Narcolepsy, a *third kind* of sleep disorder, can occur suddenly anywhere, and at any time without warning. |
| **Tie the last idea in one paragraph to the opening of the next paragraph.** | |
| I. Thesis statement: | Hurricane activity is on the rise, is likely to increase, and calls for new methods of preparation. |
| II. Topic sentence and ending idea of paragraph: | Hurricane activity is on the rise because of higher ocean temperatures and lower vertical wind shear. Therefore, these *climate changes* are likely to continue for as many as 10 to 40 years. |
| III. Topic sentence: | *These shifts in climate* call for new methods of hurricane preparation. |

Practice 12

CONNECTING PARAGRAPHS

Read the following essay. Underline the connections between paragraphs. Circle the key ideas that are repeated throughout the essay. Discuss with your class or in a small group the different types of connections the writer used and evaluate their effectiveness.

A Song of Humility

(1) The neighborhood of my youth hummed with the songs of our carefree play. (2) The beat of hammers building forts and the zings of the over-ripe ammunition of our orange wars in Winter Haven, Florida, blended beautifully with the music of the times. (3) The Beatles, and all the other really far-out groups, deafened us to any world but our very own. (4) No one was more deaf than I.

(5) At that time, I was particularly deaf to the family that lived two streets over and halfway down a dusty clay side road. (6) This out of sync family lived poorer than we did. (7) They grew their own food, raised chickens, and loved loud country music. (8) Every time I passed their house, I felt sorry for them, in a smug sort of way. (9) One afternoon the mama of that family labored up the hill to our house. (10) Her son had cut a record, and she "would be obliged if we was to listen to it" and tell her what we thought. (11) I was too busy marveling at her stained clothes and dusty feet to hear how respectfully my mother responded.

(12) Mother treated everyone with respect and tried to teach her children to do so as well. (13) She insisted that the whole family listen to the twangy tune about love and shirttails, but only I took great joy in mocking it. (14) Mother told me to return the record and say she thought it "a fine tune." (15) When I objected, she said, "Consider this an avoidable duty!" (16) I stood a long time studying the rusty door of that family's dust-covered house, wondering why I hadn't the courage to do my duty.

(17) Finally, my good friend Florence appeared at the end of the alley. (18) "Florence," I cried in great relief, "come here quick." (19) I ran to meet her, and we stood a few feet away with our backs turned from the door I so dreaded. (20) In the loud, exuberant tones of an inconsiderate child, I belted out the details of my dilemma. (21) "You ought to hear this … stupid … only hicks … and I have to … Hey, wait for me," I said to her retreating back. (22) I had hoped to push my obligation into her hands. (23) "Naw," she said without looking back, "I'm already late."

Practice 12

(24) So, I turned to do my hated duty. (25) Then I saw the son, the singer, dart from the door into the shadows of the house. (26) I wheeled about and cried, "Florence, come back." (27) I ran to her, begging, "He heard me. (28) What should I do? (29) He heard everything I said." (30) Florence shrugged and turned away. (31) I pivoted and marched to the steps. (32) The son stepped out to meet me. (33) My words resonated in the silence that loomed between us, and I cursed the supper time desertion of the dusky streets. (34) "Young lady," he said gently. (35) I looked at him. (36) "Thank ya for bringing back my demo."

(37) To this day, the timbre of his voice shames me. (38) I had mocked him, yet he sought to soothe my soul. (39) And, now, when I feel the deafness of prejudice threaten me, I remember the song of humility I learned that day from a fine young singer.

## Effective Expression: Using a Thesaurus

One aspect of effective expression is choosing the precise word to convey your point with power and clarity. Effective writers often refer to a thesaurus to avoid repetition and to find the exact words needed to make their point. A thesaurus is a collection of words, their synonyms (words of similar meaning), and their antonyms (words of opposite meaning). Some thesauruses list words alphabetically: A–Z. Other thesauruses list words by types or groups of related words. You can find both kinds on the Internet. For example, *Roget's II: The New Thesaurus* 3rd ed. online at Bartleby.com offers both versions. You can find words by looking at the headwords as in the following two illustrations:

| **Alphabetical Index:** | | | **Categorical Index:** |
|---|---|---|---|
| A-1 | to | all right | like, dislike |
| all-round | to | atrocity | restraint, unrestraint |
| atrophy | to | big | explosion, collapse |

Features vary from thesaurus to thesaurus, so be sure to read the instructions on how to use a specific one. Some features include a main entry, parts of speech, a definition, a list of synonyms, a list of antonyms, field or usage labels (such as Law or slang), and a *see also* cross reference.

Practice 13

EFFECTIVE EXPRESSION: USING A THESAURUS

Study the two entries from *Roget's II: The New Thesaurus* 3rd ed.* Then, answer the questions.

**spew**

VERB: To send forth (confined matter) violently: belch, disgorge, eject, eruct, erupt, expel. Geology : extravasate. See EXPLOSION.

**extravasate**

VERB: Geology. To send forth (confined matter) violently: belch, disgorge, eject, eruct, erupt, expel, spew. See EXPLOSION.

1. What part of speech are these two words? ______________________________

2. Is the word "Geology" a synonym, an antonym, or a field label? ______________

3. Is the word "Explosion" in both entries a field label, a cross reference,

   or a synonym? ______________________________________________

4. Insert a word from the entries that best completes the point of the following statement:
   Jeremiah's parents ______________ their breath in relief as he safely completes his parachute jump.

**All* examples from *Roget's II: The New Thesaurus* 3rd ed. Boston: Houghton Mifflin, 1995.

# Workshop: Writing an Essay Step by Step

Workshop

PORTFOLIO

WRITING AN ESSAY STEP BY STEP

To create an effective essay, use the complete writing process. Begin by prewriting; then, move on to drafting, revising, and editing. Writing rarely develops in a neat and orderly process. Some writers need to generate details before they can compose a working thesis statement. Others have to know exactly what their main point is before they can generate details. The following series of workshops encourages you to follow the prewriting steps in a certain order. Feel free to move between steps or to return to any step in the process as needed.

Workshop

## Prewriting

During the prewriting stage, you figure out what you want to say, why you want to say it, and to whom you want to say it.

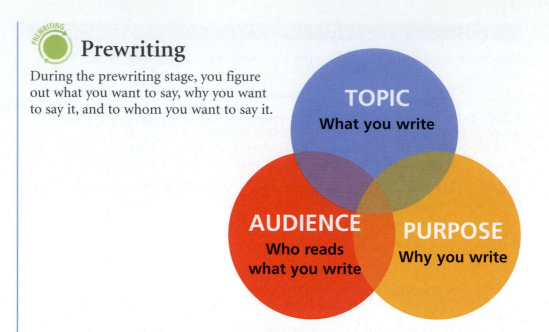

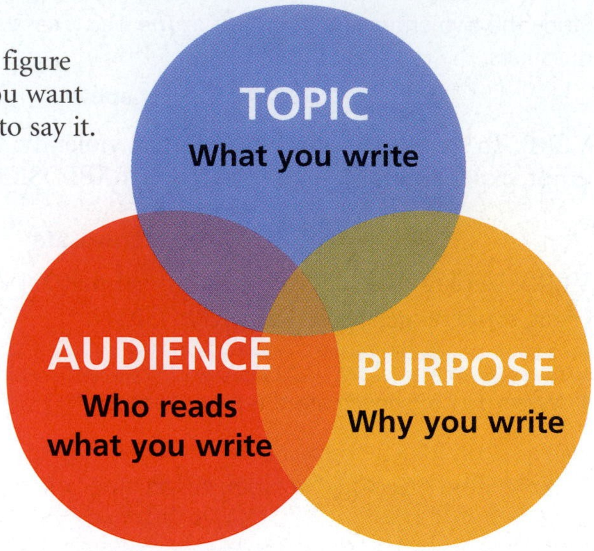


For an overview of the writing process, see Chapter 2.

For more on the prewriting stage of the writing process, see Chapter 2.

### Select and Narrow Your Topic

Select a topic on your own, pick a topic from a previous practice or workshop, or choose one of the following topics. Identify your audience and purpose.

- Movie heroes (or villains)
- Violence in sports
- Technology everyone should own
- A great achievement
- A fun activity
- Common fears

### Create a Tentative Thesis

Then, draft a tentative thesis statement.

TOPIC: ______________________

AUDIENCE: ______________________

PURPOSE: ______________________

______________________

THESIS STATEMENT: ______________________

______________________

______________________

______________________

## Generate Supporting Details

Generate primary and secondary supporting details by listing or using the concept map. Use the reporter's questions *who? what? when? where? how?* and *why?* to produce details.

For more information on patterns of organization, see Chapters 4-12 and Chapter 15.

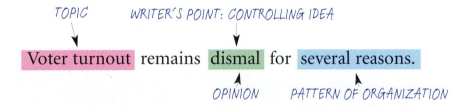

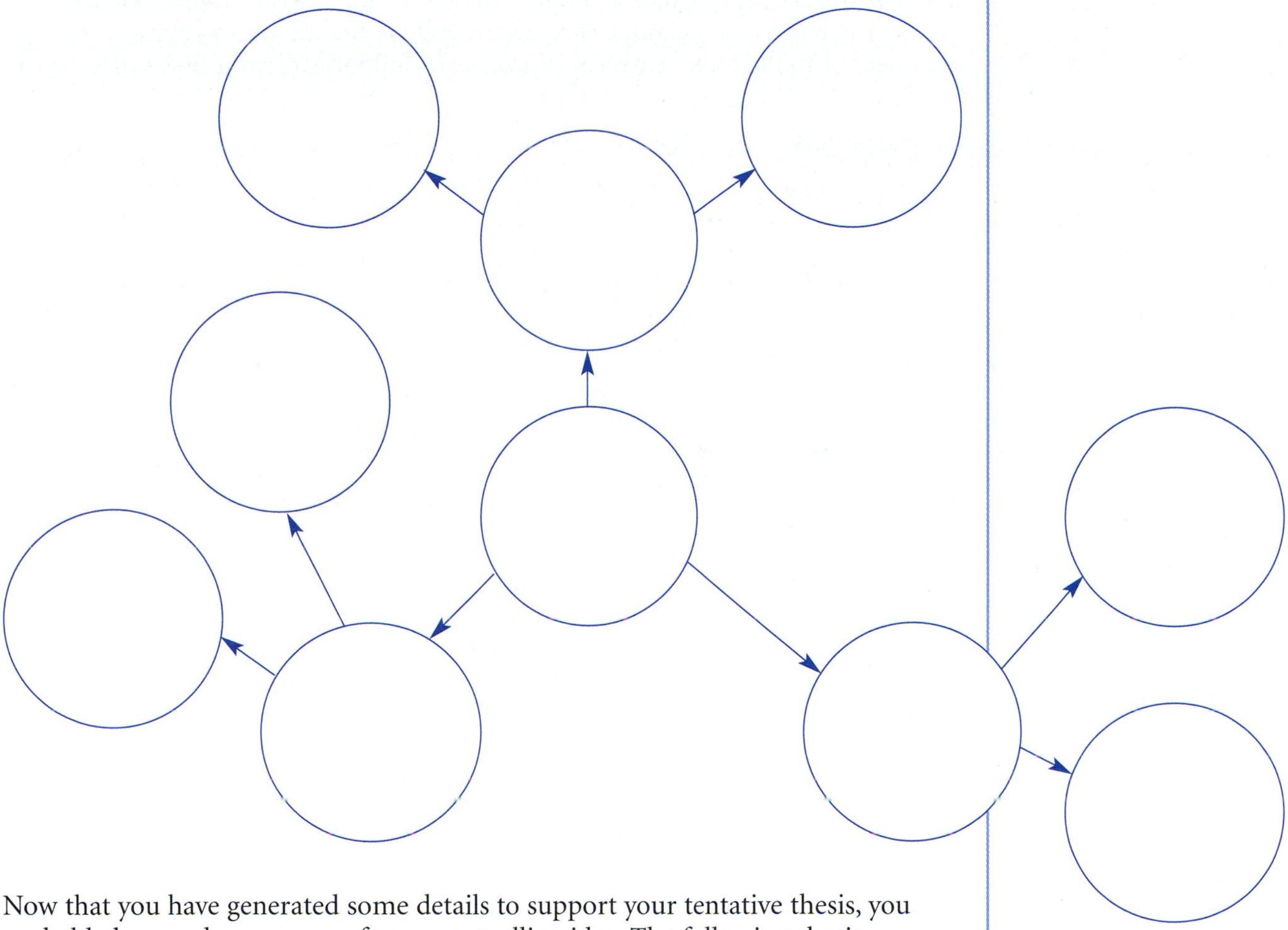

Now that you have generated some details to support your tentative thesis, you probably have a clearer sense of your controlling idea. The following thesis statement has been revised to focus the topic by including the writer's opinion and a pattern of organization.

TOPIC → Voter turnout

WRITER'S POINT: CONTROLLING IDEA → dismal

Voter turnout remains dismal for several reasons.

OPINION → dismal

PATTERN OF ORGANIZATION → several reasons.

Workshop

## Revise Your Thesis Statement

Revise your thesis so that it includes the topic, your point about the topic, and, if appropriate, a pattern of organization.

REVISED THESIS STATEMENT:

## Evaluate Your Details

Use a writing plan to test your details. Complete the following outline with your revised thesis statement and details from your list or concept map. Make sure you have an adequate amount of details to convince your reader of your point. If you do not have the necessary major and minor details to support each topic sentence, brainstorm additional details. Delete details that are not related to your thesis statement or to the topic sentences (the primary supports for your thesis statement).

**I.** INTRODUCTION

THESIS STATEMENT: ______________________________

______________________________

______________________________

______________________________

______________________________

______________________________

**II.** ______________________________

______________________________

**A.** ______________________________

**B.** ______________________________

**III.** ______________________________

______________________________

**A.** ______________________________

**B.** ______________________________

**IV.** ______________________________

______________________________

**A.** ______________________________

**B.** ______________________________

**V.** CONCLUSION

PORTFOLIO Workshop

## Write a Draft of Your Essay

Often, a writer pauses during the drafting stage of the writing process to scan what has been written so far, particularly when using a computer to write. Sometimes, while scanning, a writer may begin to make small revisions. Scanning may help a writer stay focused and can help with expression. However, you should resist the urge to spend very much time revising at this point. Your main purpose is to get a rough draft written. You can make effective revisions once you have a working draft.

For more on the drafting stage of the writing process, see Chapter 2.

Using your writing plan, write a rough draft of the body of your essay. Don't worry about the introduction and conclusion for now. Have a dictionary and thesaurus nearby just in case you get stuck trying to think of a word.

## Revise Your Essay Draft

Revision is much more than simply recopying the essay so that it is neater. A good revision requires time. So, put your essay aside for an hour or two, or even better, a day or two. You want to look at your essay with fresh eyes. Then, set aside enough time to revise your essay more than once—that way, you do not have to think of everything in one sitting. During the revising stage of your writing, think about your essay on two different levels: logic and style. The following chart offers you some helpful questions to guide you through your revision.

For more on the revising stage of the writing process, see Chapter 2.

### Questions for Revising an Essay

- ☐ Does the essay have a clearly stated thesis statement?
- ☐ Are my topic sentences clearly stated?
- ☐ Have I provided relevant support?
- ☐ Is each body paragraph fully developed with major and minor details as needed?
- ☐ Which ideas need more support?
- ☐ Is each topic sentence directly related to my thesis statement?
- ☐ Is each detail in each body paragraph related to its topic sentence?
- ☐ Have I used logical order?
- ☐ Have I provided clear connections between paragraphs?
- ☐ Have I provided clear connections between sentences within paragraphs?
- ☐ Have I used effective expression?
- ☐ Do my sentences vary in type and length?

For more information about sentence variety, see Chapter 18.

Workshop

Reread your essay, and as you revise, mark up your rough draft with the changes you intend to make: (1) cross out irrelevant details and vague, weak, or trite expressions, and write stronger words directly above or near them; (2) draw arrows to show where you want to move information; (3) add more details in the margin and draw a line to indicate where you will put them.

## One Student Writer's Revision Process

At the beginning of this chapter, you read the essay Lacey Durrance composed for her English class. Take a moment to reread her final draft on page 246–247. Then, study her revisions of one draft of the essay's first two paragraphs. How does this draft differ from her final draft?

Traits of a Successful College Student

(1) First-time college students don't realize the reality shock they will receive when they get to college. (2) High school and college atmospheres are extremely different in many ways. (3) Schools are larger; there are different teachers with different expectations, and different experiences. (4) College is a big part of growing up, and with growing up comes certain traits that you need to have to make it in college. (5) All first-time college students must have dedication, be responsible, and be independent, to get through college successfully. (6) Many won't realize this until it is too late and without these traits, they won't succeed.

(7) Dedication is the biggest part of being successful in college. (8) Students must want a good grade, and know what they need to do to achieve it. (9) Among my own personal experiences of being a first time college student, dedication has played a major part of being successful. (10) I had to change my learning process to adapt to college and so have former students. (11) Students must be hard working and take action to learn at a college level. (12) Things can't be left until the last minute like they might have been in high school. (13) College students can't only want a good grade, but must do the work to get that grade. (14) Dedication will get their work done and do it well. (15) College is very different in the sense that a lot is expected from students, and they won't be walked through anything.

## Proofreading Your Essay

Once you have revised your essay to your satisfaction, take time to carefully proofread your work. Check for the mistakes that you commonly make such as spelling errors, misplaced or missing commas, shifts in verb tense, or shifts in point of view. Publishing a clean, error-free draft proves you are committed to excellence and that you take pride in your work.

Proofread to correct spelling and grammar errors. Mark the corrections you need to make directly on the most recent draft of your essay. Create a neat, error-free draft of your essay.

For more on the proofreading stage of the writing process, see Chapter 2.

PORTFOLIO

# Workshop Review

**REVIEW:** UNDERSTANDING THE ESSAY

**1.** What are the four parts of an essay?

a. ______

b. ______

c. ______

d. ______

**2.** What are the four levels of information in an essay?

a. ______

b. ______

c. ______

d. ______

**3.** What are two types of details in an essay?

a. ______

b. ______

**4.** What are the two levels of secondary supports?

a. ______

b. ______

**5.** An effective essay supports a ______ idea with ______ details in ______ order and ______ expression.

**6.** What are the four phases of the writing process for composing an essay?

a. ______

b. ______

c. ______

d. ______

# 14

# Effective Introductions, Conclusions, and Titles

## Introductions, conclusions, and titles work together to emphasize the writer's point.

**Chapter Preview**

- What's the Point of Effective Introductions, Conclusions, and Titles?
- Making a Point Using Effective Introductions, Conclusions, and Titles: One Student Writer's Response
- Developing Your Point Using Effective Introductions, Conclusions, and Titles

The importance of effective introductions, conclusions, and titles is obvious in the composition of a movie. Think of a good movie you have seen lately. How did its title hook your interest? How did the title relate to the point of the movie? How effective was the opening of the film? How was the conclusion of the movie related to its beginning?

Just as in a successfully constructed movie, an essay with an effective introduction, conclusion, and title is more likely to impact an audience with a well made point.

# What's the Point of Effective Introductions, Conclusions, and Titles?

Effective introductions, conclusions, and titles work together to emphasize the writer's point in an essay.

WRITING FROM LIFE

Practice 1

**PHOTOGRAPHIC ORGANIZER: INTRODUCTIONS, CONCLUSIONS, AND TITLES**

Study the following series of pictures of Mount St. Helens before, during, and after an eruption. First, answer the questions below for each of the photographs to identify the major details that could be used in an essay about the event. Then, write captions that provide a title, an introduction, and a conclusion for the point made by the images.

Title: ______________________________

Introduction: ______________________________

______________________________

FIRST EVENT

What is this?

______________________________

______________________________

SECOND EVENT

What's happening?

______________________________

______________________________

THIRD EVENT

What is this?

______________________________

______________________________

What the point?

______________________________

______________________________

Conclusion:

______________________________

______________________________

PREWRITING

## My First Thought Box: A Prewriting Activity

Set a time limit, such as five minutes, and write in your notebook about the images you just studied. Do not let your pen or pencil stop. Even if you must repeat ideas, keep writing until the time limit is up. Let the ideas flow freely. Getting your first thoughts about a topic on paper is a great way to start the writing process.

# Making a Point Using Effective Introductions, Conclusions, and Titles: One Student Writer's Response

The following paragraph offers one writer's response to the call to write a title, introduction, and conclusion based on the images of Mount St. Helens' eruption. Read the text below and the annotations. Complete the activities in bold type given in the annotations. Then, read the writer's journal that records decisions she made during the writing process.

**Title:**
An effective title can be a word or phrase that helps the reader understand the writer's point by stating the topic and suggesting the writer's opinion about the topic.
**Underline the topic and circle the writer's opinion.**

Nature's Fierce Power Humbles Humanity

**Introduction:**
An effective introduction stirs the reader's interest, establishes the relevance of the topic, and often suggests or states the main idea.
**Underline the sentence that states the main idea.**

An ancient Chinese proverb states, "Human will can conquer nature." However, the 1980 eruption of Mount St. Helens in Washington makes a mockery of such a thought. The 1980 eruption of Mount St. Helens demonstrates the devastating power of nature and the powerlessness of humanity.

**Conclusion:**
An effective conclusion restates the main idea to reinforce the writer's point in the reader's memory.
**Underline the words that restate the topic and the writer's opinion.**

As Maya Angelou stated, "Nature has no mercy at all."

### THE WRITER'S JOURNAL

The student who wrote "Nature's Fierce Power Humbles Humanity" wrote the following journal entry to record her thoughts about using an introduction, conclusion, and title. Read her writer's journal that describes a few key choices she made as she wrote. Underline any strategies that you might be able to use in your own writing.

*When I first saw the images of the 1980 eruption of Mount St. Helens, I was blown away by the devastating power of nature. I guess being so coddled by technology, I never really thought about how little control we have over nature. Of course, since then, Hurricane Katrina has made it quite clear to me just how vulnerable we are. Yet, just as we did before Katrina struck, many have forgotten this terrible truth. I had an idea about the point I wanted to make, but I waited until after I composed* the body of my essay before I worked on my introduction, conclusion, and title. It's really hard for me to introduce a point until I know exactly what that point is, and I like to tie my conclusion to my introduction so that my essay creates an unbroken circle of thought. Hey, I just noticed that my title, introduction, thesis statement, and conclusion create a summary of my essay. I am going to use this strategy when I read information for my academic courses. What a great way to take notes!

# Developing Your Point Using Effective Introductions, Conclusions, and Titles

Thoughtful introductions, conclusions, and titles enhance the effectiveness of an essay. Often these three aspects of the essay are written after the thesis statement and body paragraphs have been drafted. Although titles are the first part of the essay that catches the reader's attention, many writers create them after the introduction and conclusion.

For more on the parts of an essay, see Chapter 13.

## Effective Introductions

An effective introduction serves the following purposes:

- It introduces the essay topic.
- It explains the importance of the essay topic and/or gives necessary background information about the topic.
- It hooks the reader's interest.
- It presents the essay's main idea in a thesis statement.

For more on thesis statements, see Chapter 13.

Many writers choose to end the introductory paragraph with the thesis statement.

The following chart describes and illustrates several types of introductions you can use to effectively begin your essay. The thesis statement in each introduction is underlined.

For more on using narration to tell an anecdote, see Chapter 5 and Chapter 15.

| **Types of Introductions** | |
|---|---|
| **An interesting illustration or anecdote** | EXAMPLE: The Wooten family makes a point of sharing the evening meal as special family time. Every evening, just as the family begins to dine and enjoy each other's company, the phone begins its non-stop ringing with unwanted harassment from telemarketers. Thankfully, the family can now put a stop to the harassment. <u>The National Do Not Call Registry is open for business, putting consumers in charge of the telemarketing calls they get at home.</u> |

| Types of Introductions ...*continued* | |
|---|---|
| **A surprising fact or statement** | **EXAMPLE:** Nearly one in seven Americans has key clinical data missing from their medical files, according to a report in *The Journal of the American Medical Association* (JAMA). And in 44 percent of cases the absent information would have impacted a doctor's diagnosis, potentially putting patients' health at risk. You can take a few simple steps to maintain accurate and accessible personal-health records and safeguard your well-being.<br><br>– Adapted from "Read This Before Your Next Doctor's Appointment," First Magazine |
| **A direct quotation** | **EXAMPLE:** In 1961 a copy writer named Shirley Polykoff was working for the Foote, Cone & Belding advertising agency on the Clairol hair-dye account when she came up with the line: "If I've only one life to live, let me live it as a blond!" In a single slogan she had summed up what might be described as the secular side of the Me Decade. "If I've only one life to live, let me live it as ______!" (You have only to fill in the blank.)<br><br>– Tom Wolfe, "The Me Decade and the Third Great Awakening" |
| **A definition** | **EXAMPLE:** Hope is belief that the impossible is possible. Hope is the future counted in the present. Hope is a light, a map, and a compass. Hope gave me the will to fight and survive cancer. |
| **A contradiction or opposing view** | **EXAMPLE:** Many wanna-be runners don't even try because they believe they don't have the right physique. Their legs are too short. Their stomach is too big. Their shoulders are too broad. Their body weight is too much. These people are wrong. The body is unimportant. The mind is everything. Running is not a physical sport. It's mental.<br><br>– "Mind Over Body," Running Fit Prevention Guide |
| **A vivid description** | **EXAMPLE:** Two gas stations. A car repair shop barely visible through the rusty open hoods of dismantled race cars. A man clad in overalls selling roasted peanuts from the back of his truck. These are a few sights at the unpretentious intersection that is the small town of Barberville in Northwest Volusia. To some, the settlement along the corner of U.S. 17 and State Road 40 represents one of the area's last strongholds of unspoiled country life.<br><br>– Maria Herrera, "Rural Residents Wary of Road Project" |
| **A general or historical background** | **EXAMPLE:** Charles Darwin was born in 1809 the same day as Abraham Lincoln. Even as a boy, Darwin's consuming interest in nature was evident. When he was not reading nature books, he was in the fields and forests fishing, hunting, and collecting insects. His father, an eminent physician, could see no future for a naturalist and sent |

For more on using definition, see Chapter 10 and Chapter 15.

For more on using description, see Chapter 4 and Chapter 15.

| | |
|---|---|
| | Charles to the University of Edinburgh to study medicine. But Charles, only 16 years old at the time, found medical school boring and distasteful. He left Edinburgh without a degree and then enrolled at Christ College at Cambridge University, intending to become a minister. At Cambridge, Darwin became the protégé of the Reverend John Henslow, a professor of Botany. Soon after Darwin received his B.A. degree in 1831, Henslow recommended the young graduate to Captain Robert Fitzroy, who was preparing the survey ship *Beagle* for a voyage around the world. It was a tour that would have a profound effect on Darwin's thinking and eventually on the thinking of the whole world.<br><br>– Neil Campbell and Jane Reece, *Essential Biology* |

## Practice 2

### INTRODUCTIONS

Read the following four introductory paragraphs. Underline the thesis statement and identify the type of introduction used in each one. Discuss your answers with your class or in a small group of peers.

**a.** An interesting illustration or anecdote
**b.** A surprising statement or fact
**c.** A direct quotation
**d.** A definition
**e.** A contradiction or opposing view
**f.** A vivid description
**g.** General or historical background

............ **1.** Heat kills! In fact, excessive heat is the number one weather-related killer, causing more fatalities per year than floods, lightning, tornadoes, hurricanes, winter storms, and extreme cold, according to the National Weather Service's storm data from 1994 to 2003. Therefore, when you exercise in warm, humid temperature, protect yourself by taking a few sensible safety measures.

............ **2.** To Frederick Douglass is credited the plea that, "the Negro be not judged by the heights to which he has risen, but by the depths from which he has climbed." Judged on that basis, the Negro woman embodies one of the modern miracles of the modern World.

*– Mary McLeod Bethune, "A Century of Progress of Negro Women"*

............ **3.** The roll of honor read at the 9/11 ceremonies was a tapestry of America, of native-born Americans of all ethnic origins and more recent immigrants. Of course, we know too well that some of the assassins and others plotting against America were immigrants who betrayed our ideas, so it is natural that many people feel we should now close the door altogether, beginning with immigrants from Muslim countries. Natural, and wrong. What is long overdue, however, is a sustained national dialogue on immigration.

*– Mortimer B. Zuckerman, "Our Rainbow Underclass"*

............ **4.** When we first saw Henry, we knew he had to be ours. He had only been recently rescued from a cruel breeder who supplied greyhounds to local race tracks. We were told that the breeder caged Henry in a metal crate with shredded newspaper for bedding for 18-22 hours each day. He feed Henry cheap 4-D meat for Greyhounds. The 'D' stands for dying, diseased, disabled and dead livestock. Henry had barely survived the E. coli poisoning from this feed. At one time, almost every detail of Henry's skeleton could be seen beneath his thin skin. The fact is that these kinds of abuses are more common than not. Greyhound racing should be outlawed.

# Effective Conclusions

An **effective conclusion** fulfills the following purposes:

- It brings the essay to an end.
- It restates the essay's main idea and sums up the major points in the essay.

In longer essays, the conclusion may be a separate paragraph. In shorter essays, the conclusion may be a powerful sentence or two at the end of the last body paragraph. Just remember that a conclusion must stay on point, so don't introduce new information.

The following chart describes and illustrates several types of conclusions you can use to effectively and powerfully end your essay.

For more on using description, see Chapter 4 and Chapter 15.

| Types of Conclusion | |
|---|---|
| **A question** | EXAMPLE: Don't you want to experience the well-being that results from a healthful diet and regular exercise? |
| **A quotation** | EXAMPLE: Just as renowned coach of the Green Bay Packers Vince Lombardi said, "The difference between a successful person and others is not a lack of strength, not a lack of knowledge, but rather in a lack of will." |
| **A call to action** | EXAMPLE: This is not a time for indecision or hesitation. This is a time for commitment and action. Tell your federal, state, and local governments that you demand a coordinated response plan for natural disasters. |
| **A suggestion** | EXAMPLE: Your best friend is the one who will tell you a hard truth for your own good. |
| **A warning about consequences** | EXAMPLE: If instruments used for ear and body piercing are not properly cleaned and sterilized between clients, then you could contract HIV, hepatitis B, or hepatitis C. |
| **A vivid image** | EXAMPLE: And when this happens, when we allow freedom to ring, when we let it ring, when we let it ring from every village and every hamlet, from every state and every city, we will be able to speed up that day when all God's children, black men and white men, Jews and Gentiles, Protestants and Catholics, will be able to join hands and sing in the word of the Old Negro Spiritual – Free at last! Free at last! Thank God Almighty, we are free at last! <br><br>–Martin Luther King, "I Have a Dream" |
| **A summary** | EXAMPLE: Therefore, it is especially important to wash your hands before, during, and after you prepare food, before you eat, after you use the bathroom, after handling animals or animal waste, when your hands are dirty, and more frequently when someone in your home is sick. <br><br>–National Center for Infectious Diseases, "Wash Your Hands Often" |

Practice 3

CONCLUSIONS

Read the following four conclusions. Identify the type of conclusion for each selection. Discuss your answers with your class or in a small group of peers.

**a.** A question
**b.** A quotation
**c.** A call to action
**d.** A suggestion
**e.** A warning about consequences
**f.** A vivid image
**g.** A summary

............ **1.** Fellow citizens, we will meet violence with patient justice—assured of the rightness of our cause and confident of the victories to come.
*–President George W. Bush, "Address to a Joint Session of Congress and the American People, 2001."*

............ **2.** The crew of the space shuttle Challenger honored us by the manner in which they lived their lives. We will never forget them, nor the last time we saw them, this morning, as they prepared for their journey and waved goodbye and "slipped the surly bonds of earth" to "touch the face of God."
*—President Ronald Reagan, Eulogy for the Challenger Astronauts, 1986.*

............ **3.** The measure of a student's achievement is not in the grade from a teacher, too often these days a symbol of high inflation and low value, but in the wisdom gained from learning. Daniel Pederson stated it best in *Newsweek*, March 3, 1997: "When *A* stands for average, do grades mean anything at all?"

............ **4.** Our life on earth has already reaped many benefits from past and current space exploration. The establishment of a human colony on the moon would further enhance the quality of life on this planet. Products designed for independent life on the moon will someday become part of everyday life on Earth, advancing research in robotics, communications, medicine, computer technologies, food and nutrition, clothing, environmental and architectural design, rocketry, fuel and energy, building materials, and agriculture. We should shoot for the moon!

## Effective Titles

An **effective title** fulfills the following purposes:

- It hooks the reader's interest.
- It vividly describes the topic of your essay.

You should write your essay, reread your essay for its overall impact, and then create your title. Your title should be brief, and you should not use italics, quotations, or underlining for emphasis. Instead, center the title on the page about an inch above the introductory paragraph. Capitalize the first word and other key words of the title, except for prepositions such as *in, on, for, at* and articles such as *a, an,* and *the.* The following chart describes and illustrates several types of effective titles.

| Types of Titles | | |
|---|---|---|
| **The question title:** States the main point as a question. | **EXAMPLES:** | Is Cloning Moral?<br>Why Clone? |
| **The descriptive title:** Uses key words to form the thesis statement. | **EXAMPLES:** | The Arrogance of Cloning<br>Cloning Offers Hope |

For more on using description, see Chapter 4 and Chapter 15.

For more on using patterns of organization to develop paragraphs and essays, see Chapters 4-12 and Chapter 15.

| | | |
|---|---|---|
| **The recommendation title:** Calls for action. | EXAMPLES: | Cloning Must Be Banned<br>Clone On! |
| **The general-specific title:** States the general topic, followed by a controlling point. | EXAMPLES: | Cloning: An Unethical Procedure<br>Cloning: The Scientific Method<br>Working for Progress |
| **The pattern(s) of organization title:** Uses the words that establish the essay's central pattern(s) of organization. | **DESCRIPTION** EXAMPLES: | The Town of My Birth<br>The Beauty of the Beach |
| | **NARRATION** EXAMPLES: | Sojourner Truth's Journey<br>An Unforgettable Memory |
| | **PROCESS** EXAMPLES: | How to Deal with Cranky Customers<br>Starting Your Own Business |
| | **EXAMPLE/ ILLUSTRATION** EXAMPLES: | Winning Isn't Easy<br>Pets Are People Too |
| | **CLASSIFICATION** EXAMPLES: | Types of Sexual Harassment<br>Kinds of Camps for Kids |
| | **COMPARISON/ CONTRAST** EXAMPLES: | The Differences between Male Talk and Female Talk |
| | **DEFINITION** EXAMPLES: | The Forgiving Heart<br>The Meaning of Bravery<br>What It Means to Be Compulsive |
| | **CAUSE/EFFECT** EXAMPLES: | Why Parents Send Their Kids to Camp<br>The Reasons Students Cheat<br>The Effects of Hurricane Katrina |
| | **PERSUASION** EXAMPLES: | The Need for Smaller Classes in Public Schools<br>We All Have the Right to Die<br>Commit to Life to the Very End |

## Practice 4

TITLES

Read the following three-paragraph business memo and supply a title in the blank labeled RE (for the topic of the memo).

Memo

To: Sales Associates

From: Shanika Thomas, Store Manager

Date: 3 November 2007

RE: ..................................................

Do you want to win the $200 bonus promised to each employee of the store which best represents our company's ideals: professional, friendly, fast service? Corporate representatives will be popping in unannounced sometime over the next few weeks to rate us as individuals and as a team.

To ensure our win, keep the following tips in mind. Reflect professionalism in your personal attire, the store's appearance (keep shelves stocked and orderly), and in your work ethic. Reflect friendliness in your attitudes to supervisors, coworkers, and, most importantly, to our customers. Finally, be quick to help each other and the customer. Greet the customer promptly and politely. The moment a customer walks in through our door, make that person feel as if he or she is the most important person on earth.

If each and every one of you continues to do the fine job that has put our store in the finals of this competition, we will all be winners!

# Practice 4 Review

**REVIEW:** EFFECTIVE INTRODUCTIONS, CONCLUSIONS, AND TITLES

Complete the chart by filling in the blanks with information from the chapter:

**Types of Introductions**

- An interesting illustration or anecdote
- A surprising fact or statement
- A direct quotation
- A definition
- A contradiction or opposing view
- ______________________
- ______________________

**Types of Conclusions**

- A question
- ______________________
- ______________________
- A suggestion
- A warning about consequences
- A vivid image
- A summary

**Types of Titles**

- The Question Title
- The Descriptive Title
- ______________________
- The General-Specific Title

**The Patterns of Organization Title:**

______________________

- Description
- Narration
- Process
- Example/Illustration
- Classification
- Comparison/Contrast
- Definition
- Cause/Effect
- Persuasion

# 15 Using Patterns of Organization to Develop Essays

**Chapter Preview**



## Patterns of organization help arrange, present, and develop ideas into an essay.

We use patterns of organization to clearly arrange and present thoughts and ideas as we engage in academic, business, and everyday life. Students who go to RateMyProfessor.com are looking for certain traits in and ratings about a teacher and may compare these qualities with those of another teacher. Factory owners must think about the effects of commonly used chemicals in the manufacturing process and train their employees on safety procedures. To make a particular dish or dessert, cooks must closely follow a recipe's steps and instructions and do those steps in order. Similarly, many writers use patterns of organization to develop their ideas into an essay.

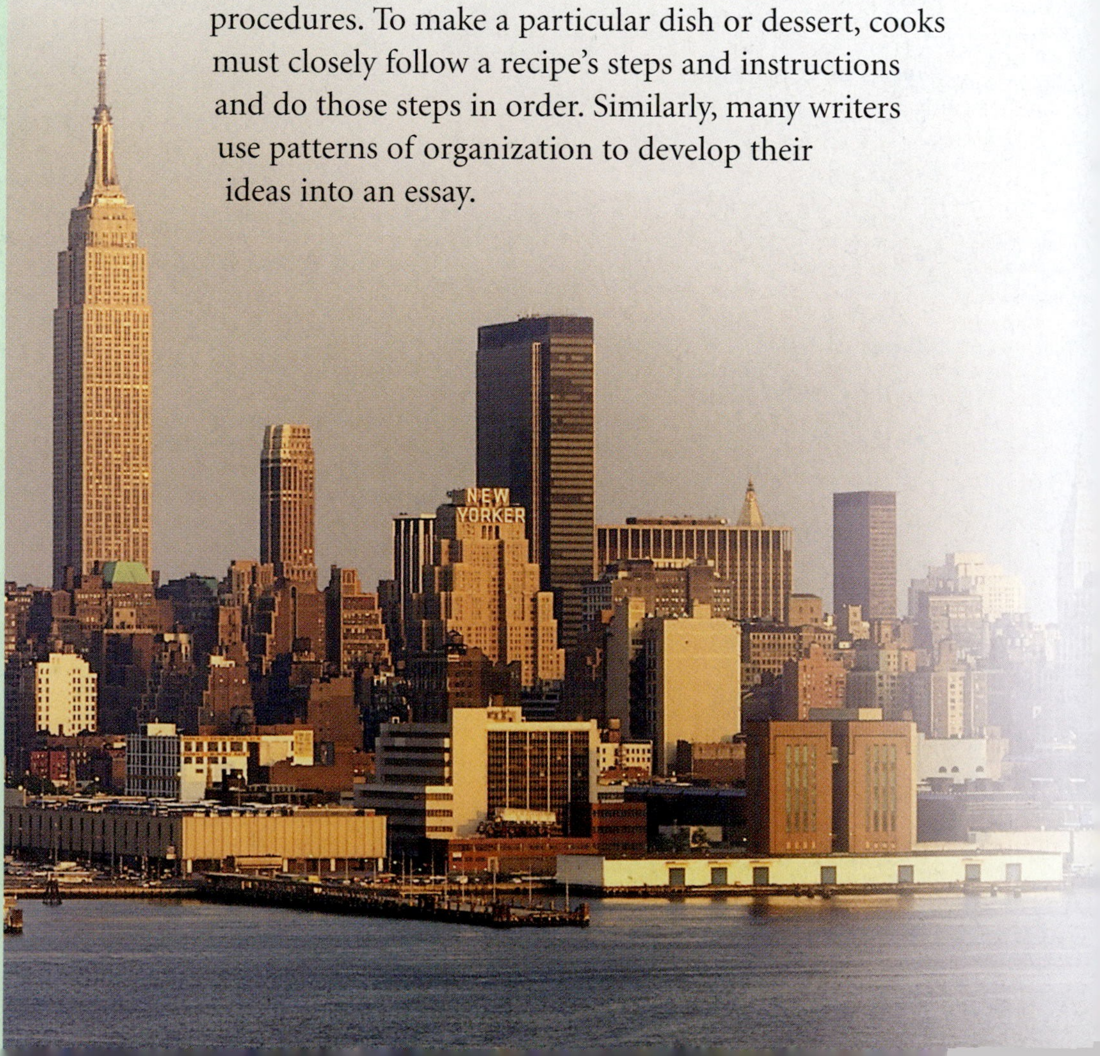

# What's the Point of Using Patterns of Organization to Develop Essays?

WRITING FROM LIFE

Practice 1

**PHOTOGRAPHIC ORGANIZER: USING PATTERNS OF ORGANIZATION IN ESSAYS**

Study the following series of pictures. First, answer the questions below each of the photographs to identify the major details that could be used in an essay about the event. Then, write captions that provide a title, an introduction, and a conclusion for the point made by the images.

NARRATION: A Chain of Events TOPIC: My New York Experience

FIRST EVENT — SECOND EVENT — THIRD EVENT

What happened?

---

---

What happened?

---

---

What happened?

---

---

What's the point of the narration?

---

Now that you have used a pattern of organization to brainstorm about a topic, think about how patterns of organization can help you write an essay. Answer the question:

What's the point of learning about using patterns of organization to write an essay?

---

---

## My First Thoughts: A Prewriting Activity

PREWRITING

Set a time limit, such as five minutes, and jot down in your notebook your thoughts about using patterns of organization. In addition to the examples mentioned above, what are some other situations that require thinking about time sequences, comparisons, contrasts, definitions, or persuasive ideas?

# Making a Point Using Patterns of Organization: One Student Writer's Response

THE WRITER'S JOURNAL

Read the following student journal entry that records the writer's thoughts about using patterns of organization to develop an essay.

*Earlier in the semester, I learned about using patterns of organization to develop paragraphs, so I see how useful they will be during the writing of essays. Based on the timeline for "My New York Experience," I can see that an essay uses several paragraphs to discuss a topic. The graphic also shows that each paragraph discusses just one part of the topic. It also occurred to me that the topic is "New York" and the pattern of organization is time order (based on "experience"). So all the details in the essay have to be details of time, but I also think some description is also going to be needed. Patterns of organization can help me limit a topic and think up details of support. Patterns of organization can help me keep on topic and put my ideas in the order that makes the most sense.*

# Developing Your Point in a Descriptive Essay

The ability to describe people, places, or things accurately is a useful life skill.

In your personal life, you may need to file a police report or insurance claim about the damage, loss, or theft of your property. You must be able to describe the damaged, lost, or stolen goods.

In your college life, you will rely upon description in many content courses. For example, you may need to describe a natural environment for a science class or a piece of artwork for a humanities class.

In your working life, you may need to describe the physical specifications of office equipment.

To write a **descriptive essay**, a writer describes a person, place, or object based on its location or the way it is arranged in space. Spatial order describes an arrangement of details from top to bottom, from bottom to top, from right to left, from near to far, far to near, from inside out, or outside to inside. The writer also relies upon sensory details such as sight, sound, smell, taste, and touch to create vivid mental images so that the reader can see what is being described. **Descriptive transition words** signal that the details follow a logical order based on two elements:

For information on writing a descriptive paragraph, see Chapter 4.

1. How the person, place, or object is arranged in space.
2. The starting point from which the writer chooses to begin the description.

### Transition Words Used to Signal Description

| | | | | | | |
|---|---|---|---|---|---|---|
| above | at the side | beneath | close to | here | nearby | there |
| across | at the top | beside | down | in | next to | under |
| adjacent | back | beyond | far away | inside | outside | underneath |
| around | behind | by | farther | left | right | within |
| at the bottom | below | center | front | middle | | |

## A Descriptive Essay: One Student Writer's Response

Read the following descriptive essay written by student Allyson Melton for an English class. Read the essay a second time, then, complete the activities and answer the questions that follow.

The Brilliance of Nature

1 (1) Too often, the brilliance of nature goes unnoticed. (2) This became very apparent to me, early one morning, on my way to work. (3) As I merged with the flock of procrastinating people, late as usual, I sped along, aware of the neon yellow dashes on the road flashing by as I sped along. (4) The flock of us grudgingly slowed to a stop as we approached a red light. (5) While waiting impatiently for the signal to go green, I diverted my eyes from the glare of the traffic light. (6) The sights and sounds around me revealed a vision of color and movement.

2 (7) The view to my left filled my vision with color and movement. (8) The road was lined with trees, each one proudly standing tall. (9) Dressed in their brightly colored costumes of jade, olive, emerald, and lime, they stood against the heavens as a magnificent tribute to the earth. (10) Their brown trunks, solid and strong-willed, stood unwaveringly in the face of time.

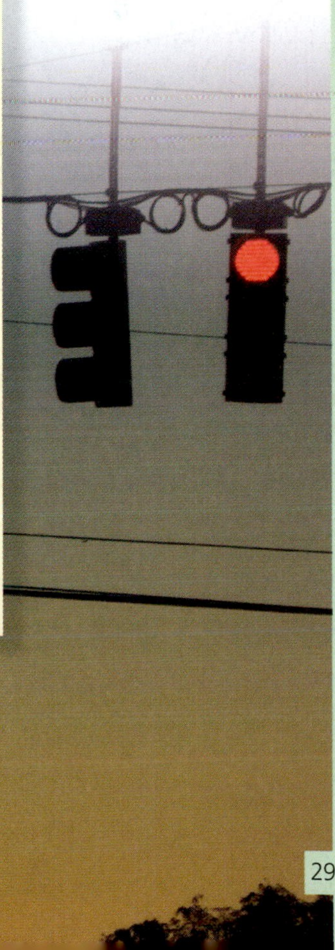

(11) A skirt of green grass encircled the weathered tree roots. (12) To my right, a gleaming shopping center towered above the people who milled around its base. (13) Shoppers constantly lined in and out of the mall doors; they reminded me of ants carrying grains of sand or tiny crumbs to and from their anthill. (14) The light gray sidewalk provided a path mostly for bicyclists, spinning their wheels in an effort to gain ground, and joggers, bobbing along with the iPod ear buds plugged in like drooping antennae.

3 (15) The view ahead wavered in a vapor of exhaust fumes and noise. (16) The road, packed with cars of all colors and shapes, stretched before me. (17) Everything from the small, bright red sports car to the gigantic, black Hummer had come to a stop on this stretch of asphalt. (18) I rolled my window down to feel the cool morning air only to be greeted by honking horns and obnoxious music from nearby cars. (19) The bass from the music of the car beside me was so loud I could feel the boom, boom, boom move through my frame and land at the top of my head with an extra "boom" for emphasis. (20) Before quickly rolling my window up again, I caught a whiff of the sharp smell of exhaust fumes.

4 (21) The red light still burned brightly, so I ventured a quick look up at the sky and couldn't look away. (22) It contained every hue imaginable, moving from pink to purple, blue to gray, and orange to yellow. (23) The newly risen sun, so yellow it was nearly white, shimmered in the mist of the new day. (24) Golden sun rays sprayed a flock of birds with a splendid display of light and shadow. (25) Their wings had hypnotic powers in their rhythmic beatings. (26) Hundreds, even thousands formed a fluid ribbon of birds, winding through the topaz sky in a graceful stream, never fraying from its curve. (27) Though I couldn't see even one bird up close, I could imagine their feathers blowing in the cool morning air as they swept through the sky. (28) As I watched, the stream continued to speed across the sky without hesitation, as if they all knew exactly where they were going. (29) When I finally broke my gaze, I looked around again.

5 (30) The people in their cars around me were still staring fixatedly forward at that commanding red light while the glory of nature flew over their heads. (31) As the birds continued to flow across the heavens, the light switched to green. (32) As much as I wanted to linger and watch them, I had to move forward again.

Practice 2

## READING AND EVALUATING THE ESSAY

Complete the activities below after you have read the essay a second time.

**1.** What kind of title does the writer use? ______

**2.** What type of introduction does the writer use? ______

______

**3.** Underline the thesis statement.

**4.** For each of the body paragraphs, underline the topic sentence. Circle the descriptive transition words. List two major details for each paragraph below.

Major Details (Paragraph 2): ______

______

Major Details (Paragraph 3): ______

______

Major Details (Paragraph 4): ______

______

**5.** What type of conclusion does the writer use? ______

**6.** What is the purpose of the essay? Explain your answer. ______

______

**7.** Who is the audience for the essay? Explain your answer. ______

______

**8.** What did you like best about the essay? Why? ______

______

______

**9.** What about the essay could be improved? ______

______

For more on types of titles, introductions, and conclusions, see Chapter 14.

For more on thesis statements, see Chapter 13.

For more on topic sentences, see Chapter 3 and Chapter 13.

For more on purpose and audience, see Chapter 2.

## Writing Assignments for a Descriptive Essay

Plan and illustrate your essay with one or more photographs of your own choosing. Write caption(s) for the photograph(s) that reflect your point(s).

### Considering Audience and Purpose

Assume you are a witness or victim of an ATM robbery, and authorities have asked you to write a description of the two thieves and the getaway car. Your description will be included in the official police report, will be used by a sketch artist to create a picture of the thieves and their car, and may be distributed to the media to alert the public.

### Writing for Everyday Life

Most of us have a favorite spot or place to which we return or that we reminisce about with fondness. Describe your favorite place or the favorite spot of someone you know. Write an essay that describes the site's special qualities for the regional newspaper of this favorite location.

### Writing for College Life

Assume you are writing an essay for a sociology class about popular culture. Describe a person or object that represents an aspect of pop culture: a film actor; the costume or instrument of a singing artist; a cartoon character.

### Writing for Working Life

Assume you work for a travel agency, and your clients—parents with three children ranging in ages from 3 to 15—ask you for advice about where to go for a one-week vacation. The family has expressed an interest in going someplace that offers natural beauty and outdoor activities. Write a letter to the parents describing the destination you recommend for their vacation.

### Additional Descriptive Topics

A scene that provokes strong emotions

A vandalized or dilapidated neighborhood

Ideal gifts for a loved one

A person of interest

An exotic animal and its habitat

The scene after violent weather

## Developing Your Point in a Narrative Essay

Narration is a fundamental part of everyday life.

- In your personal life, you may wish to share an important moment or event you experienced with a friend or family member in a letter or email.
- In your college life, you will study biographies and write essays about important figures in subjects such as history, science, and the arts. You will also study and narrate significant events that have occurred in various fields of study, such as wars in history or case studies in psychology.

For information on writing a narrative paragraph, see Chapter 5.

- In your working life, you may need to narrate an individual or departmental accomplishment in a report, memo, or letter.

In a **narrative essay,** a writer shows a series of events or actions that occur during a specific period of time. The writer presents an event and then shows when each of the additional events occurred in relation to it. Thus, narrative details follow a logical order based on time or chronological order. The following transition words establish the flow of ideas or coherence of a narration essay by signaling when actions or events occurred and in what order.

### Transition Words Used to Signal Narration

| | | | | |
|---|---|---|---|---|
| after | during | later | previously | ultimately |
| afterward | eventually | meanwhile | second | until |
| as | finally | next | since | when |
| before | first | now | soon | while |
| currently | last | often | then | |

## A Narrative Essay: One Writer's Response

Read the following narrative essay. Read the essay a second time, then, complete the activities and answer the questions that follow.

The Meanest Fish

1 (1) The Gar is the ugliest of any fresh water fish—olive brown with black spots and a yellow-white belly. (2) These fish have a long crooked snout filled with irregularly spaced and very sharp teeth. (3) They also are the meanest of all fish, a fact which I discovered three days after my eleventh birthday during a fishing trip on the Tomoka River in East Central Florida.

2 (4) Like many rivers in Florida, the Tomoka is a narrow, sluggish, tea colored river that snakes its way through dense hammocks of palms, live oak, and palmettos. (5) Canoes are about the only mode of transportation that can make it through some of the long, almost impenetrable stretches of the river. (6) On weekends, we would launch off from the dock at Sanchez Park and often paddle for hours up and down the river, dropping a fishing line every now and then, and most of the time losing our bait to the catfish living along the banks. (7) This particular trip was a special one. (8) I had just received a new fishing pole for my birthday and was anxious to try it out. (9) I perched on the front seat of the canoe; my brother sat on the bottom in the middle, and my Dad took the back seat, providing most of the momentum and all of the steering. (10) My paddling was enthusiastic, but not very efficient because, whenever possible, I would pull my paddle out of the water to knock down the banana spider webs strung between the low branches of the overhanging trees. (11) I would tell

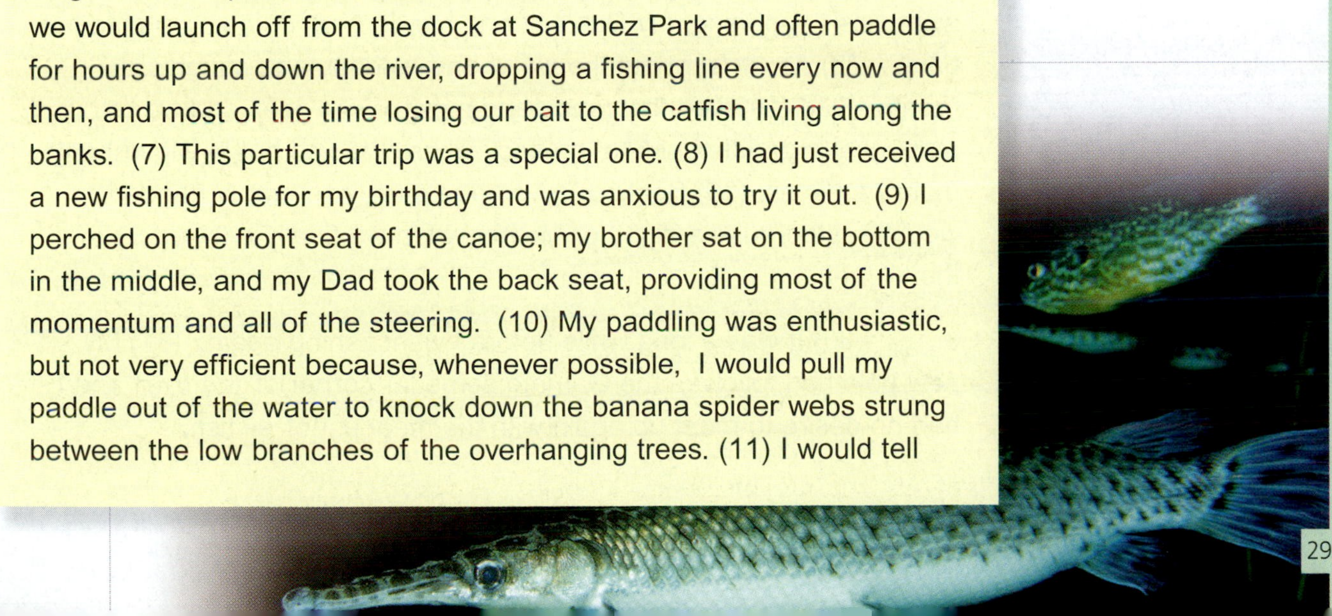

my brother that the spider was going to fall on his head. (12) He would yell and start jumping around, and then Dad would yell at him to sit still and me to stop teasing him. (13) It was all great fun!

3 (14) Eventually, we pulled around a bend in the river to a favorite fishing hole, known to be home to some extra large catfish. (15) Catfish are great because they always put up a good fight, even the small ones. (16) We decided to eat our baloney sandwiches and drink our root beer before it got too hot. (17) Of course, eager to try out my new fishing gear, I had no desire to eat and was soon threading a hunk of my baloney onto my hook. (18) Catfish will bite at just about anything, but baloney seems to be one of their favorite snacks.

4 (19) I dropped my hook in the water and was just getting ready to settle down when something hit the bait hard. (20) Suddenly, my pole was bent almost double, and I was yelling at the top of my lungs. (21) Since we were in such shallow water, I only had about six feet of line out, and when I yanked back in surprise, a huge Gar fish popped out of the water, back over my head, and into my brother's lap! (22) He started screaming at the large slimy fish, and his sandwich and root beer went sailing over his head and right into Dad's lap.

(23) "Gar! Gar! Gar!" my brother was screaming.

(24) "Gar! Gar! Gar!" I was screaming.

(25) "Sit still or you'll…" was what Dad was screaming, but he didn't get to finish.

5 (26) My brother and I had sort of leapt in opposite directions so for a frozen moment the canoe was counterbalanced, but then, inevitably, time resumed, and over the canoe tipped, taking us, our lunch, our gear, and the Gar along with it. (27) Fortunately, the river was so shallow that our feet hit the mushy bottom, and before we knew what was happening, my Dad's strong hands drug us both up onto the bank. (28) As we spat out the water and baloney and caught our breath, Dad retrieved the canoe and most of our gear, and we managed to paddle back to the dock where we had put in without any more problems. (29) Soaked, covered in mud, and empty handed, we presented quite a sight for Mother when we finally showed up in the kitchen.

6 (30) It was a long while before I went fishing again. (31) My new pole had followed the Gar into some far corner of the river, and I had no desire to meet up again with the meanest of all fish.

# Practice 3

## READING AND EVALUATING THE ESSAY

Complete the activities below after you have read the essay a second time.

1. What kind of title does the writer use? ____________

2. What type of introduction does the writer use? ____________

____________

3. Underline the thesis statement.

4. For each of the body paragraphs, underline the topic sentence. Circle the narrative transition words. List two major details for each paragraph below.

Major Details (Paragraph 2): ____________

____________

Major Details (Paragraph 3): ____________

____________

Major Details (Paragraph 4): ____________

____________

5. What type of conclusion does the writer use? ____________

6. What is the purpose of the essay? Explain your answer. ____________

____________

7. Who is the audience for the essay? Explain your answer. ____________

____________

8. What did you like best about the essay? Why? ____________

____________

____________

9. What about the essay could be improved? ____________

____________

For more on types of titles, introductions, and conclusions, see Chapter 14.

For more on thesis statements, see Chapter 13.

For more on topic sentences, see Chapter 3 and Chapter 13.

For more on purpose and audience, see Chapter 2.

# Writing Assignments for a Narrative Essay

Plan and illustrate your essay with one or more photographs of your own choosing. Write caption(s) for the photograph(s) that reflect your point(s).

## Considering Audience and Purpose

Assume you have been asked to speak to a group of teenagers about peer influences on their development. You have decided to use a personal childhood experience to develop your ideas. Your purpose is to explain how one childhood experience with a peer influenced you.

## Writing for Everyday Life

Most of us, like the writer of "The Meanest Fish," have a vivid memory from childhood that shows the strength of our family, the joy of being young and carefree, or a challenge we have overcome. What does a vivid memory from childhood reveal about you, your family, or someone you know? Recount a vivid memory in an essay that will be published in a newsletter for family members and friends who live far away.

## Writing for College Life

Narrate an important event such as the terrorist attack on 9/11, the swearing in of the President of the United States, the launching of a space shuttle, the civil rights march on Washington and Dr. Martin Luther King's "I Have a Dream Speech," as though you had witnessed it. Write a report for your college history class about the event as you saw it unfold.

## Writing for Working Life

Assume you are applying for a management job with a retail store such as Wal-Mart, Target, or J.C.Penney. What life and work experiences can you relate that show your ability to listen, solve problems, manage merchandise, and motivate others? Write an essay sharing an incident or series of events that show you are the best candidate for the job.

## Additional Narrative Topics

A clash with authority

An important lesson learned

A life-changing experience

An ideal day or a horrible day

The story behind a celebrity's rise to fame

The time you met someone important to you

# Developing Your Point in a Process Essay

The ability to clearly communicate the steps in a process is a basic skill for success in all areas of life.

- In your personal life, you may want to share advice with a friend or relative about how to reduce stress or how to handle a job interview.
- In your college life, many academic disciplines, such as biology, sociology, and psychology, rely on process. For example, you may be required to record the process you used in a science lab activity, or you may choose to write a research paper on the stages of grief for a psychology class.
- In your working life, you may need to write a marketing plan, an action plan, or a company procedure.

For information on writing a process paragraph, see Chapter 6.

A **process essay** shows actions that can be repeated at any time, with similar results. Like narration, a process essay is organized by time order (also called chronological order). A writer uses the process pattern of organization for three reasons:

1. To give steps, directions, or procedures for completing a task.
2. To analyze or study the steps, cycles, or phases of a process.
3. To explain how to complete a task and to analyze the process.

The following transition words establish the flow of ideas or coherence of a process essay.

## Transition Words Used to Signal a Process

| | | | | |
|---|---|---|---|---|
| after | during | later | previously | ultimately |
| afterward | eventually | meanwhile | second | until |
| as | finally | next | since | when |
| before | first | now | soon | while |
| currently | last | often | then | |

# A Process Essay: One Writer's Response

Read the following process essay. Read the essay a second time, then, complete the activities and answer the questions that follow.

How to Find Your Keys

1 (1) In order to find your keys, you must first understand the important role keys play in your life. (2) Fortunately, this important role becomes abundantly clear when you are standing in the hallway ready to dash out the door for work or school and you realize your keys are missing. (3) You cannot lock your door. (4) You cannot start your car. (5) You have nothing to jangle impatiently while waiting in line at Dunkin Donuts for coffee. (6) You are going to be late. (7) Keys are indeed important. (8) However, there is no need

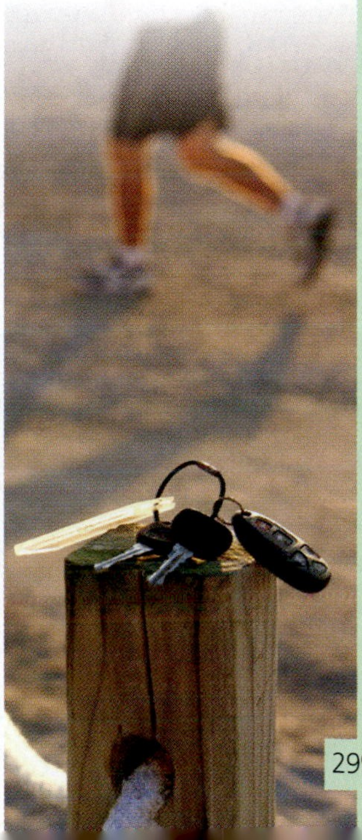

to panic, even though you may lose your job if you are late one more time or fail the midterm or not have time to stop at Dunkin Donuts. (9) OK, perhaps a little panic is warranted. (10) The important thing to remember is that if you approach the search for your keys calmly and logically, none of these catastrophes need occur.

2 (11) The first step is to check your person. (12) Start with your hands. (13) You would not be the first person to scour the house or apartment for something you are already holding. (14) This is very similar to the "glasses perched on top of head" phenomenon. (15) Check your pockets. (16) Better yet, empty your pockets so you don't have to guess what all that stuff in your pockets actually is just by touch. (17) Check your coat pockets. (18) Now check your other coat's pockets even though they couldn't possibly be there because you hate that coat and you never wear it. (19) If you have a purse, see appendix A, "Major Excavations." (20) These procedures will establish that you are not, in fact, in physical contact with your keys.

3 (21) Next you will undertake the process of "retracing your steps" which is essentially a form of backward time travel. (22) You may have to travel back several hours so you must be patient. (23) Sometimes it helps if you actually walk backwards, undress, climb back into bed, etc. (24) But be careful! (25) All this backward motion requires a degree of physical coordination and you haven't had your coffee yet. (26) At some point, you will probably have to venture into the dirty clothes hamper. (27) No one said finding lost keys did not require courage and fortitude. (28) If you travel all the way back to the moment when you walked in the door the previous evening and have still not located your keys, you may have to adopt a more creative strategy. (29) But first you will have to travel forward in time to get back to the present. (30) I will wait.

4 (31) As a last resort, think creatively. (32) If you have pets, remember that they always know more than they let on and should always be suspected. (33) Carefully inspect pet bedding, food bowls, and under the sofa. (34) Even if you have caged birds or fish, check the seed cup and the little castle that bubbles in the aquarium. (35) You never know. (36) If all else fails, you can resort to the SDSM or Slow Desperate Spin Maneuver. (37) This is where you stand in the middle of your apartment and slowly spin around, trying to look on every surface simultaneously, hoping for a glimpse of your keys, sparkling like a gold nugget at the bottom of a mountain stream. (38) This of course never works, but sometimes the dizziness created

by this move will jog your memory and you will remember you left your keys on the kitchen counter next to the empty peanut butter jar.

5 (39) As you can see, by following this careful and thoughtful process, you will never again be separated from your keys for very long. (40) And keys in hand, you will stride purposefully into a bright and meaningful future or at least until you get to the donut shop.

## READING AND EVALUATING THE ESSAY

Practice 4

Complete the activities below after you have read the essay a second time.

**1.** What kind of title does the writer use? ______

**2.** What type of introduction does the writer use? ______

**3.** Underline the thesis statement.

**4.** For each of the body paragraphs, underline the topic sentence. Circle the process transition words. List two major details for each paragraph below.

Major Details (Paragraph 2): ______

Major Details (Paragraph 3): ______

Major Details (Paragraph 4): ______

**5.** What type of conclusion does the writer use? ______

**6.** What is the purpose of the essay? Explain your answer. ______

______

**7.** Who is the audience for the essay? Explain your answer. ______

______

**8.** What did you like best about the essay? Why? ______

______

**9.** What about the essay could be improved? ______

______

For more on types of titles, introductions, and conclusions, see Chapter 14.

For more on thesis statements, see Chapter 13.

For more on topic sentences, see Chapter 3 and Chapter 13.

For more on purpose and audience, see Chapter 2.

# Writing Assignments for a Process Essay

Plan and illustrate your essay with one or more photographs of your own choosing. Write caption(s) for the photograph(s) that reflect your point(s).

## Considering Audience and Purpose

Assume you are a student-worker in the admissions and registration office at your college. You have been asked to create a brochure for students that illustrates and explains the registration process from a student's point of view. Write several paragraphs that take students through the registration process. Consider creating a brochure based on what you write.

## Writing for Everyday Life

At some point in our lives, all of us suffer the loss of a loved one or a valued object. Tell how you or someone you know coped with such a loss. Write a letter to a friend in which you share the steps you or someone you know took to overcome the grief of loss.

## Writing for College Life

Assume you are enrolled in the college class Introduction to Psychology, and your professor has assigned a chapter about stress. Your professor wants to know what you already know about stress before you read the chapter. Write an essay that explains several steps one can take to reduce stress.

## Writing for Working Life

Assume that you are on a committee at work that is looking into ways in which employees can better manage their time and increase productivity. What recommendations would you make for employees whose tasks include phone calling, emailing, writing reports, filing paperwork, and attending meetings? Interview a staff assistant (such as in the English, science, or some other department at your college) for timesaving tips on the job. Write a report in which you outline several timesaving steps. Insert the appropriate information into the following MLA citation format to document your source:

```
Last Name of Person Interviewed, First Name of Person
    Interviewed. Personal Interview. Day Month Year.
```

## Additional Process Topics

How to win an argument

How to get a promotion or recommendation

How to develop a friendship

How to save money or shop smart

How to make a piece of art, such as a print, woodcut, or an etching

How to set up a program or piece of technology (such as a cell phone, email, website, or blog)

# Developing Your Point in an Illustration Essay

Illustration may be the pattern of organization that you will use most often.

- In your personal life, think about how you often rely on examples and illustrations to make your point, such as when you recommend a restaurant or movie to a friend.
- In your college life, illustrations and examples effectively clarify a main point in all areas of study. For example, for a history class, you may choose to explain the contributions Frederick Douglass made to the civil rights of African Americans by offering several examples or illustrations.
- In your working life, examples and illustrations help prove that you or an employee under your supervision deserve a raise.

For information on writing an example paragraph, see Chapter 7.

In the illustration essay, a writer offers a focused main idea about a particular topic and then offers a series of examples or illustrations to clarify or support the main idea. Example words signal that a writer is giving an instance of a general idea.

## Transition Words Used to Signal Examples and Illustration

| | | | |
|---|---|---|---|
| an illustration | for instance | once | to illustrate |
| for example | including | such as | typically |

# An Illustration Essay: One Student Writer's Response

Read the following example and illustration essay written by student Beth Zivistski for an English class. Read the essay a second time, then, complete the activities and answer the questions that follow.

Fads: POG-Mania

1 (1) In all areas of life, our society is constantly swept up in the latest craze, and with the rise of every new fad comes the depressing downfall of the former fad. (2) Fads make their way into the world as fast as they are shut out. (3) A fad arises out of a particular culture, becomes intensely popular for a brief time, and then loses popularity suddenly and dramatically. (4) Ironically, fad-mania blindly leads to the retirement of great ideas, such as the fabulous milk cap game now known as POGs.

2 (5) Milk cap games were an excellent example of a fad that arose out of a particular culture. (6) Milk cap games originated when milk and juice were sold in glass bottles rather than the current disposable containers. (7) This fad-game first got its name from a brand of a tropical fruit drink made up of passion fruit, orange, and

guava juice called POG. (8) Kids collected the round wax coated cardboard disks that sealed the bottles and invented simple games that everyone could play. (9) Nearly every household, rich or poor, had access to milk caps, which made the game very inclusive. (10) Children enjoyed this popular form of entertainment until the establishment of screw-on lids and disposable containers virtually put an end to milk caps and these engaging games.

3 (11) Most fads, such as milk games, began as a simple, fun idea. (12) For example, the standard rules for POG playing were simple. (13) Two or more players placed an equal number of POGs into a common stack. (14) The milk caps would be piled artwork side up on a level surface. (15) To determine who would go first, players flipped a POG or played Ro-Sham-Bo (Paper, Scissors, Rock). (16) The first player threw his or her "kini" or slammer, an object used to hit the stack of POGs. (17) Usually a slammer was bigger, thicker, and heavier than a POG, often made of plastic or different types of metal. (18) All of the milk caps that landed face down went to that player. (19) The milk caps left over were restacked for the next player's turn. (20) The players exchanged turns until every milk cap had been won, and the player with the most milk caps was the winner. (21) Like all fads, the POG craze started simply, in this instance, with children using the milk caps for inexpensive fun.

4 (22) POGs were also an illustration of the intense popularity to which a fad could rise. (23) As the fad grew in popularity, companies flooded the market with POG products. (24) In the early 1990s, a number of companies started their own series of game pieces to compete in the new craze. (25) For example, the company Tilt, Poison, and Kapz offered POGs decorated with skulls, crossbones, and eight balls. (26) Even fast food restaurants illustrated POG mania as they latched onto the new fad and included POGs in their kid's meals. (27) POGs were not just a source of entertainment through game play. (28) They became available in sets of original artwork, sports and team logos, or even pictures of the latest Saturday morning cartoons. (29) Purchasing POGs became an obsession. (30) For example, people began collecting POGs, and some felt the need to own every single POG in a series. (31) These factors made POGs collectable as well as tradable. (32) The popularity of POGs was also evident in its international following, as illustrated by the World Pog Federation (WPF), created by players who loved POGs so much that they wanted an official body to direct the craze. (33) The WPF created its own official brand that was printed with the POG logo on the back. (34) The

front artwork carried a variety of designs including cartoons, POG history, and POG incentives.

5 (35) POGs also illustrated the criticism and blame most fads face for fostering undesirable consequences and behaviors. (36) For example, many criticized POGs for fostering overspending. (37) When so many companies offered such a wide range of POG series available for purchase, expenses for a POG devotee quickly mounted up. (38) Children used their allowances to buy POGs; adults spent exorbitant amounts of money ensuring they had complete sets of brand name POGs for sports teams, athletes, or other popular cultural icons. (39) Another example of the criticism against POGs was the belief that the game was a form of gambling. (40) People would play for keeps in the hopes of enlarging their POG holdings. (41) Oftentimes, players would lose their own POGs in the process; then they would have to purchase more. (42) Many critics opposed POGs as an illustration of the antisocial behaviors that a fad can generate. (43) For example, fights sometimes broke out over POGs. (44) This game, for some children, was much more than entertainment; therefore, if these children lost a certain favored POG, they would react as children often do with tears, insults or even fists. (45) POGs, and especially slammers, were often stolen. (46) In addition, many educators complained that POG playing served as a distraction to school work. (47) Eventually, these negative aspects led to the banning of POGs by many public schools in North America.

6 (48) Like all fads, POGs decreased suddenly and dramatically in popularity. (49) Today, instead of lining the shelves in major retail markets, POGs may possibly be found on eBay or in specialty game and card shops. (50) Like fads, POG playing rose out of its culture, began as a way to have fun, reached intense heights of popularity, garnered criticism, and then faded away as just another one of those crazy trends that swept across the nation and over international borders. (51) Even so, POG playing is still fondly remembered by those who still love them to this day. (52) POGs illustrate the irony of fad-mania: the short lived devotion to a really good idea.

# Practice 5

For more on types of titles, introductions, and conclusions, see Chapter 14.

For more on thesis statements, see Chapter 13.

For more on topic sentences, see Chapter 3 and Chapter 13.

For more on purpose and audience, see Chapter 2.

## READING AND EVALUATING THE ESSAY

Complete the activities below after you have read the essay a second time.

1. What kind of title does the writer use? ______

2. What type of introduction does the writer use? ______

3. Underline the thesis statement.

4. For each of the body paragraphs, underline the topic sentence. Circle the example or illustration transition words. List two major details for each paragraph below.

Major Details (Paragraph 2): ______

______

Major Details (Paragraph 3): ______

______

Major Details (Paragraph 4): ______

Major Details (Paragraph 5): ______

______

5. What type of conclusion does the writer use? ______

6. What is the purpose of the essay? Explain your answer. ______

______

7. Who is the audience for the essay? Explain your answer. ______

______

8. What did you like best about the essay? Why? ______

______

______

9. What about the essay could be improved? ______

______

# Writing Assignments for an Illustration Essay

Plan and illustrate your essay with one or more photographs of your own choosing. Write caption(s) for the photograph(s) that reflect your point(s).

## Considering Audience and Purpose

Assume you serve as a member of the Parent-Student-Teacher Association (PSTA), and you have been asked to write a report to be submitted to the principal. The purpose of the report is to explain the improvements your group wants to be funded. Identify and illustrate the need for three improvements at the school.

## Writing for Everyday Life

Think about the creativity and cleverness of the human mind as seen through various inventions. Which invention best represents human achievement in our generation? Write an essay for your local newspaper that illustrates the most helpful invention of our time.

## Writing for College Life

Think about the importance of integrity, reliability, or candor in our culture. What three people in the news illustrate these concepts? Write an essay for a college course in ethics that gives three illustrations of people who epitomize integrity, reliability, or candor.

## Writing for Working Life

Assume that you are a local businessperson and you have been asked to share with a youth group your thoughts on the value of an education. What examples or illustrations would you choose to convince students to make education a top priority? What knowledge or skills did you gain through your education that helped you succeed in your business? Write a speech to be given to the youth and their parents in which you illustrate the importance of an education.

## Additional Illustration Topics

- Lack of morality on television
- The best or worst commercials
- Annoying or dangerous driving behaviors
- A healthful diet or an outlandish diet
- Good gifts that don't cost much money
- Acts of kindness

# Developing Your Point in a Classification Essay

Classification allows you to order or group your thoughts based on traits of a category.

- In your personal life, you may want to warn a young person in your family or social group about types of peer pressure or dangerous behaviors to avoid.
- In your college life, you will use classification in the sciences to write about classes of species or habitats; in the humanities, to write about styles of artists, artistic movements, modes of architecture, literature, and branches of philosophies; in business and history classes, to write about the kinds of economic systems and governments.
- In your working life, you may need to write reports that identify types of markets for your products, job descriptions based on the nature of the position you need to fill, or a cover letter that describes the set of skills you bring to the workplace.

For information on writing a classification paragraph, see Chapter 8.

Writers use the **classification essay** to sort or divide ideas into smaller groups and then describe the common traits of each subgroup. The writer lists each subgroup, describes its characteristics, and offers examples that represent the group. Because groups and subgroups are listed, transitions that suggest additional categories are often used to ensure coherence.

## Transitions Used to Signal Classification

| | |
|---|---|
| another (group, kind, type) | first (group, categories, kind, type, order) |
| characteristics | second (group, class, kind, type, traits) |

# A Classification Essay: One Student Writer's Response

Read the following classification essay written by Josiah Cobb for a music appreciation class. Read the essay a second time, then, complete the activities and answer the questions that follow.

### Types of Guitars

1 (1) When people think of guitars, they most likely think of an oldies band such as the Beatles and their guitars, or an iconic performer like B.B. King and his guitar "Lucille" or, more currently, Mark Tremonti and his signature Paul Reed Smith guitar. (2) However, most people are unaware of the differences among guitars. (3) Not all guitars are alike. (4) True, guitars share fundamental traits: they are stringed instruments with a neck, a flat back, incurving sides, and a flat peg disc with rear tuning pegs. (5) However, apart from these shared traits, a range of guitars from acoustic to electric have evolved that enable musicians to create an array of distinct sounds.

(6) Currently, four types of guitars allow musicians to produce a variety of sounds in today's music.

2 (7) The acoustic guitar is a favored instrument used in most types of current music. (8) Bands today rely on the bright sound of the acoustic guitar to fill in the gaps with the guitar's unique, deep, full sound. (9) The acoustic guitar is simply a hollow body that has a neck and a set of thick bronze strings which together produce a bigger sound than the other types of guitars. (10) Because most acoustic guitars are not amplified by an external device, their sound is not loud and often cannot compete with other instruments in a band or orchestra. (11) However, one of the secrets to a good sounding acoustic guitar is the pick-up, which detects the mechanical reverberations of the strings and acts as a microphone. (12) A pick-up is mounted on the body of the guitar close to the strings. (13) The Simon & Garfunkel folk song "Fifty-Ninth Street Bridge" offers an excellent example of the rhythmic, strumming sound created with the acoustic guitar.

3 (14) The classical or nylon guitar is a kind of acoustic guitar designed especially for finger picking, which is the art of plucking the string with the fingers instead of using a pick to strum over the strings. (15) The classical guitar has nylon strings instead of bronze strings, and the body of the classical guitar is larger than the other types of guitars. (16) This design produces a reverberation as if it were in a large room. (17) In addition, the neck of the guitar is broader than the ones on steel string guitars, allowing for more complex finger work. (18) Classical guitars do have acoustic pick-ups in them most of the time. (19) One of the most popular examples of the classical guitar's crisp, nimble tones can be heard in "Classical Gas" by Mason Williams.

4 (20) A third kind of guitar is the electric guitar. (21) The unique design of the electric guitar makes it a versatile instrument. (22) The body of the electric guitar is solid, small, and can be any shape. (23) Most electric guitars today have two pick-ups. (24) The modern day pick-ups are usually small rectangular pieces of plastic with six small magnets. (25) These pick-ups use the magnets to feel the vibrating string and then transfer the sound through an amplifier so the player can hear the pitch of the strings. (26) Many guitarists love the electric guitar because they can get any sound out of it they want. (27) For instance, by using the neck pick-up, the guitarist can get the really low end sound of a hardcore band, or by using the bridge pick-up, he

or she can get the bright high end sound of ska music. (28) The electric guitar also lets the musician mimic the sounds of other types of guitars such as the acoustic, Dobro, or the classical. (29) One illustration of a well-known song performed on the electric guitar is U2's blazing, bone-rattling song "Vertigo."

5 (30) A fourth type of guitar is the Dobro. (31) Though not many people know about the Dobro or think of it as a guitar, it is one of the hardest forms of guitar to learn. (32) The Dobro is an instrument that is very small and is placed on a table so the strings are parallel to the ground. (33) The player then takes a guitar pick and plucks the strings as if finger picking but with a pick. (34) In addition, instead of using fingers to produce certain pitches from the guitar, the player uses a slide. (35) A slide is usually either a small piece of wood with metal, or a glass tube into which a finger is inserted. (36) The Dobro uses an electric guitar pick-up, which gives it a country guitar sound. (37) A prime example of the Dobro twang can be heard in the classic country song "An Old Cowboy's Dream" by Don Edwards.

6 (38) Although guitars come in various shapes and styles and produce a wide range of sounds, each one has the same basic idea: a set of strings pulled to a certain tension to combine different pitches and create something that everyone enjoys—music.

## Practice 6

### READING AND EVALUATING THE ESSAY

Complete the activities below after you have read the essay a second time.

**1.** What kind of title does the writer use? ______________________

**2.** What type of introduction does the writer use? ______________________

**3.** Underline the thesis statement.

**4.** For each of the body paragraphs, underline the topic sentence. Circle the classification transition words. List two major details for each paragraph below.

Major Details (Paragraph 2): ______________________

______________________

______________________

______________________

For more on types of titles, introductions, and conclusions, see Chapter 14.

For more on thesis statements, see Chapter 13.

For more on topic sentences, see Chapter 3 and Chapter 13.

Major Details (Paragraph 3): ____________________

____________________

____________________

____________________

Major Details (Paragraph 4): ____________________

____________________

____________________

____________________

Major Details (Paragraph 5): ____________________

____________________

____________________

**5.** What type of conclusion does the writer use? ____________________

For more on purpose and audience, see Chapter 2.

**6.** What is the purpose of the essay? Explain your answer. ____________________

____________________

**7.** Who is the audience for the essay? Explain your answer. ____________________

____________________

**8.** What did you like best about the essay? Why? ____________________

____________________

____________________

**9.** What about the essay could be improved? ____________________

____________________

____________________

Practice 6

# Writing Assignments for a Classification Essay

Plan and illustrate your essay with one or more photographs of your own choosing. Write caption(s) for the photograph(s) that reflect your point(s).

## Considering Audience and Purpose

Assume you are a member of Students Against Destructive Decisions (SADD). The original mission of this group focused on preventing drunk driving. However, SADD has expanded its role to include several types of destructive decisions such as underage drinking, other drug use, violence, depression, and suicide. Many people do not know about this expanded focus. To get the word out about SADD, your local chairperson has asked you to write an essay to accompany short video clips (acted out by other local members) that will be posted on YouTube.com. Your purpose is to describe the different types of destructive decisions for which SADD offers help.

## Writing for Everyday Life

Many of us have an ideal in mind when we think about a person who fulfills a particular role in our lives: a mate, a job, a teacher, a friend, and so on. What are the traits of any one of these ideals? Write a tribute to a boss, company, friend, teacher, or family member in which you describe the ideal traits of a boss, job, friend, mate, or child.

## Writing for College Life

Assume that you are a student in a college music appreciation course, and your class is discussing how types of music reveal cultural values. What types of music best reflect American culture? Write an essay for this class that identifies three or four types of American music. (Feel free to change the term "American" to reflect any culture of your choice.)

## Writing for Working Life

Assume you are an employee at a grocery store that has been receiving a record number of complaints such as the following examples: empty shelves, rude or slow cashiers, sticky floors, no one to answer questions, and so on. Write a letter for the employee suggestion box in which you classify typical customer complaints and discuss types of employee attitudes that could reduce complaints.

## Additional Classification Topics

Kinds of vacations people take

Types of technology that record or play music

The basic food groups in a balanced diet

The market for a particular product, celebrity, or experience: *Harry Potter* novels, Halle Berry, or white water rafting

Styles of personal expression: fashion, clothing, or interior design

Categories of movies, television shows, or books

# Developing Your Point in a Comparison and Contrast Essay

Many ideas become clearer when you evaluate them in relation to one another.

- In your personal life, comparing and contrasting products before a purchase makes you a wise shopper.
- In your college life, you will be asked to compare and contrast leaders, governments, cultures, literature, writers, and philosophies in a wide range of courses such as history, humanities, English, science, and economics classes.
- In your working life, you may compare and contrast bids on a job, phone or Internet services for your office, or prospective employees during an interview process.

For information on writing a comparison and contrast paragraph, see Chapter 9.

The **comparison and contrast essay** shows the similarities and differences between or among topics based on comparable points. The following transition words signal comparison and contrast.

## Transition Words That Signal Comparison

| | | | | |
|---|---|---|---|---|
| alike | in a similar fashion | just as | resemble | similarly |
| as | in a similar way | just like | same | |
| as well as | in like manner | like | similar | |
| equally | in the same way | likewise | similarity | |

## Transition Words That Signal Contrast

| | | | |
|---|---|---|---|
| although | conversely | differently | nevertheless |
| as opposed to | despite | even though | on the contrary |
| at the same time | difference | in contrast | on the one hand |
| but | different | in spite of | on the other hand |
| by contrast | different from | instead | still |

# A Comparison and Contrast Essay: One Student Writer's Response

Read the following student comparison and contrast essay written by student J. R. Hill for an English class. Then, complete the activities and answer the questions that follow.

### Reading the Waves

1 (1) Along the edges of Florida's East coast lie miles and miles of inviting blue-green ocean water and alluring sun-bleached beaches to which thousands of bronzed surfers flock on any given day. (2) Each of these beaches varies in its sand composition, reef formations, and surfing conditions. (3) Although the East coast of Florida is made mainly of soft, sandy beaches and a hard ocean

bottom, for every mile traveled from Miami to Jacksonville, no beach along the Atlantic coast remains the same as the specific conditions change that cause waves to form and break. (4) Two main surf spots, the Ponce Inlet Jetty and the Sun Glow Pier, only a few miles apart, represent the distinctly different surfing experiences available on Florida's East coast.

2 (5) The first difference between the Ponce Inlet Jetty and the Sun Glow Pier is the shape of the beaches. (6) Many expert surfers looking for a challenge choose the Ponce Inlet Jetty because of its rocky beach formation off which waves form. (7) The Inlet has a long stretch of rocks jutting up from the beach and reaching hundreds of feet out into the ocean, creating a cove. (8) In contrast, the Sun Glow Pier does not have a rock formation hemming in an inlet off which the waves can form. (9) Instead this coast stretches out as an unbroken, barrier-free contour of beach, ideal for beginner surfers.

3 (10) The floor of the ocean and thus the depth of the water just off the coast of the Ponce Inlet Jetty and the Sun Glow Pier also differ significantly. (11) On the one hand, because of the protective jetty at Ponce Inlet, the sand on the ocean floor there does not dramatically shift so the depth of the ocean floor near the jetty remains fairly consistent and uniform. (12) On the other hand, since Sun Glow Pier does not have a rock jetty, the sand there constantly shifts and redistributes the depth of the ocean floor near the coast. (13) The few Pier pilings add to the unevenness of the water's depth. (14) Sand gathers around the pilings and leaves holes where sand is swept away between pilings.

4 (15) Not only do the beaches, ocean floor, and water depth differ, but also the formation of waves at the two locations varies greatly. (16) At the Ponce Inlet Jetty, the waves form off the rock jetty and shape into a solid, organized wave. (17) When a wave comes to shore, the jetty pushes it into an A shape, also called an A-frame wave or peak. (18) The A-frame gains size in a matter of seconds to form a clean, structured, and powerful wave. (19) The wave then breaks on

▼ *Sun Glow Pier* beach

the fairly flat or uniform ocean bottom on top of two or three feet of water. (20) Unlike the well-formed, powerful waves of Ponce Inlet, the waves at Sun Glow have no solid objects (such as the rock jetty and the even ocean floor) off which to push. (21) Without solid objects and consistent water depth to help form it, the wave remains in its natural form. (22) In its natural form, the wave breaks in unorganized sections because the uneven depth of the ocean floor does not push the wave to break evenly. (23) The wave may look as if it is crumbling from the top to the bottom.

5 (24) The variations in the waves at these two beaches offer two very different surfing experiences. (25) The duration and flexibility of the surfer's ride differ at each location. (26) The consistent depth of water at the Ponce Inlet Jetty makes the wave break harder and faster, which enables the surfer to gain fast speeds. (27) At these fast speeds, the surfer is able to execute a great number of technical maneuvers. (28) After completing one maneuver, the surfer still has enough wave power to push through into the next maneuver. (29) Many surfers enjoy this long ride with clean conditions, making the Ponce Inlet Jetty a popular surf spot for expert surfers, as well as those who are learning to master more intricate moves. (30) In contrast, due to the uneven bottom and the unorganized, quickly crumbling waves, the waves at the Sun Glow Pier lose a great amount of power. (31) Unlike the longer ride at the Ponce Inlet Jetty, this weaker wave at the Sun Glow Pier leaves the surfer a short amount of time to complete maneuvers. (32) Generally, a surfer can only complete one or two maneuvers, and once a maneuver is completed, the surfer is left to fight for speed to continue on the wave to shore. (33) The wave at the Sun Glow Pier is great for the beginner surfer who needs to learn the basics and understand waves.

6 (34) The Ponce Inlet Jetty and the Sun Glow Pier, though only a few short miles apart, are two entirely different beaches. (35) These two spots are prime examples of the different surfing experiences available to surfers along Florida's East coast. (36) So before surfers grab their boards, they should carefully read their wave!

▼ *Ponce Inlet Jetty*

Practice 7

READING AND EVALUATING THE ESSAY

Complete the activities below after you have read the essay a second time.

**1.** What kind of title does the writer use? ____________

**2.** What type of introduction does the writer use? ____________

**3.** Underline the thesis statement.

**4.** For each of the body paragraphs, underline the topic sentence. Circle the comparison and contrast transition words. List two major details for each paragraph below.

Major Details (Paragraph 2): ____________

____________

Major Details (Paragraph 3): ____________

____________

Major Details (Paragraph 4): ____________

____________

Major Details (Paragraph 5): ____________

____________

**5.** What type of conclusion does the writer use? ____________

**6.** What is the purpose of the essay? Explain your answer. ____________

____________

**7.** Who is the audience for the essay? Explain your answer. ____________

____________

**8.** What did you like best about the essay? Why? ____________

____________

**9.** What about the essay could be improved? ____________

____________

For more on types of titles, introductions, and conclusions, see Chapter 14.

For more on thesis statements, see Chapter 13.

For more on topic sentences, see Chapter 3 and Chapter 13.

For more on purpose and audience, see Chapter 2.

# Writing Assignments for a Comparison and Contrast Essay

Plan and illustrate your essay with one or more photographs of your own choosing. Write caption(s) for the photograph(s) that reflect your point(s).

## Considering Audience and Purpose

Assume you have just moved from a large city to a small town, and other members of your family or friends are considering making the same move. Write a letter that discusses the differences (or similarities) between living in a particular large city (such as Chicago, New York, or Atlanta) and living in a small town of your choice.

## Writing for Everyday Life

Assume you have an account on a social networking Web site, such as Facebook or MySpace, and you compose and post your thoughts on a regular basis. Recently, you have noticed that many of us see a tremendous change in our circumstances, attitudes, or beliefs. This week you are writing about the specific ways that you or someone you know has changed over time or due to a specific event. Contrast what someone you know or you were like earlier in life to what that person or you are like currently.

## Writing for College Life

Assume you have been working with two of your peers on a required group project and the two students differed greatly in their performance. What were the differences in their attitudes, work habits, and products? Use the goals stated on a course syllabus as the context your evaluation of their performances. Write the required report to your teacher in which you contrast your peers' performance.

## Writing for Working Life

Assume you are a realtor, and a client of yours is moving into the area from across the country. Your client has asked you to identify a couple of homes in a specific price range. You have found two homes in which your client may be interested. How do the two homes compare in terms of location, price, square footage, and special features? Write a letter to your client that compares and contrasts the two homes.

## Additional Comparison and Contrast Topics

Two pieces of music, art, or books

A scene before and after a terrible storm

Comparable products: Palm Pilots and other personal digital assistants

Communication habits of men and women

Dating customs of different cultures or generations

Disciplining children as opposed to punishing them

An original and a remade movie, or a book and a movie based on it

# Developing Your Point in a Definition Essay

You may encounter definitions most often in academic settings. However, the definition pattern of organization is also helpful in all areas of life.

- In your personal life, knowing the definition of "whole grains" and being able to identify examples that fit the definition will protect you against false advertising and enable you to make healthful choices.
- In your college life, you will be expected to know the specialized meanings and examples of many terms in each content area.
- In your working life, you need to understand the terms of your company's insurance policy and examples of what is covered so you can make a claim when needed or offer reasonable coverage to your employees.

For information on writing a definition paragraph, see Chapter 10.

In the **definition essay,** the writer explains the meaning of a new, difficult, or special term. A definition may include traits, comparisons, causes, or effects. In addition, a writer may include an explanation of what the term or concept is *not.* Examples are used to illustrate the various components or elements of the term being defined. The following key words and transition words signal the definition pattern of organization.

## Key Words and Transition Words That Signal Definition

| | | | | |
|---|---|---|---|---|
| **Key Words:** | are | denotes | is | means |
| | connotes | indicates | is not | suggests |
| **Transition Words:** | also | in addition | one trait | |
| | another trait | in particular | specifically | |
| | for example | like | such as | |

## A Definition Essay: One Writer's Response

Read the following definition essay. Read the essay a second time, then, complete the activities and answer the questions that follow.

Just What Is a Blog?

1 (1) What exactly is a blog? (2) Is it a movie creature from outer space that eats clueless teenagers? (3) Is it a Scandinavian Desert? (4) Is it some special type of lumber? (5) Actually, the term *blog* is a shortening of the phrase "web log." (6) It is essentially an online journal, diary, or collection of articles, which is arranged in reverse chronological order, with the latest articles or "postings" appearing first. (7) "Bloggers" are those individuals or groups who create blogs, and the blogs they write cover a wide range of topics, including personal observations, politics, hobbies, and even official corporate news. (8) In the past few years, the "blogosphere," as the blog community is sometimes known, has exploded in popularity.

(9) A form of online communication, a blog serves as an important alternative source for news, opinion, and information outside the mainstream media.

2 (10) It is important to note that a blog is not a forum of hard news full of carefully verified facts. (11) Thus, a blog is not necessarily a reliable source of information, and any information gained from a blog should be checked against a known to be reliable source. (12) A blog is not private; information posted on a blog is communicated to the World Wide Web. (13) Nor does a blog necessarily offer a true portrait of a blogger. (14) Information on a blog could be erroneous, or even fictitious. (15) Understanding what a blog is not enables full and safe enjoyment of what a blog offers.

3 (16) Blogs appeal to people because of their spontaneity, informality, and passion; they reflect the fact that most of us gather and absorb information in an unstructured way. (17) First, blogs resemble informal conversations with friends, as opposed to the sanitized and filtered content of most types of media. (18) Most blogs are personal, as the following blog excerpt demonstrates: "It's funny how nothing changes between friends. (19) When Matt and Anson arrived, it was as if we had never missed a day. (20) Things just fell into place." (21) Second, blog postings are often spontaneous expressions, like views shared around the water coolers at work; some bloggers have even been fired for their off-the-cuff postings. (22) For example, Amy Nora Burch was fired for posting unflattering comments about her job at Harvard University in 2004. (23) "Most of it is total heat of the moment stuff," Burch said, according to an article published in *The Harvard Crimson.* (24) Of course not all spontaneous postings lead to such serious outcomes. (25) Third, blog postings are often fueled by controversies. (26) As blogs have grown in popularity and influence, political consultants, news services, and corporations have begun using them as tools to communicate and in some instances, manipulate. (27) When a controversial issue hits the blogs, it sometimes causes what is called a "blogstorm" or "blog swarm." (28) Such a blogstorm occurred the moment CBS national news anchor Dan Rather claimed proof that President George W. Bush received preferential treatment during his National Guard duty.

4 (29) Blogs are easy to set up and offer a rich array of options. (30) Many easy to use software packages, such as Moveable Type and Blogjet, are available for creating blogs, and the many hosting sites available for blogs such as Blogger and LiveJournal are also simple to use and free. (31) For example, the instructions to set up a blog at Blogger, (www.blogger.com), read "Create a blog in three easy steps: create an account; name your blog; choose a template." (32) In addition to being easy to set up, blogs offer a rich communication environment. (33) Because blogs are web-based, many of them take advantage of the power of hyperlinking, which allows them to link their content to other sites or other blogs dealing with similar themes or more in-depth information. (34) "Blogrolls" are lists of other blogs linked to a particular article. (35) Feedback comment systems allow blog readers to respond to postings in a blog and create a discussion thread similar to those found on online discussion boards. (36) Some blogs also incorporate audio and video content into their postings. (37) Automation tools have even been developed that allow blogs to talk to each other and keep their content updated!

5 (38) Blogs are a good example of the unexpected effects of new technologies. (39) Because of blogs, friends and family members can enjoy instant and ongoing communication. (40) Pictures of a new baby can be instantly and simultaneously shared with family members who live in various parts of the country or world. (41) Because of blogs, people who would never meet in person are able to connect online. (42) Star Wars junkies, skateboarders, vegans, dog lovers—anyone with any special interest can develop a blog and instantly connect with others who share their passion. (43) Because of blogs, information is easier to access. (44) For example, blogs provided evacuees from hurricane Katrina with coveted information about the neighborhoods and homes they had to leave behind and to which they longed to return. (45) One such blogger, Brian Oberkirch (http://slidell.weblogswork.com), offered information about and photographs of Slidell, Louisiana. (46) Blogs like this one respond to the need of the moment and offer a surprising depth of vital information, as in this case, to homeowners, employers, and employees so they could make reasonable, informed decisions about their futures.

6 (47) If you've never seen a blog before, a good place to start is Google's Blog Search. (48) There you can search blogs by keywords such as "pets" or "movies." (49) And if you have some thoughts you would like to share with the world, you might want to give blogging a try!

## Practice 8

### READING AND EVALUATING THE ESSAY

Complete the activities below after you have read the essay a second time.

1. What kind of title does the writer use? ______

2. What type of introduction does the writer use? ______

3. Underline the thesis statement.

4. For each of the body paragraphs, underline the topic sentence. Circle the definition signal words. List two major details for each paragraph below.

Major Details (Paragraph 2): ______

______

Major Details (Paragraph 3): ______

______

Major Details (Paragraph 4): ______

______

Major Details (Paragraph 5): ______

______

5. What type of conclusion does the writer use? ______

6. What is the purpose of the essay? Explain your answer. ______

______

7. Who is the audience for the essay? Explain your answer. ______

______

8. What did you like best about the essay? Why? ______

______

9. What about the essay could be improved? ______

______

For more on types of titles, introductions, and conclusions, see Chapter 14.

For more on thesis statements, see in Chapter 13.

For more on topic sentences, see Chapter 3 and Chapter 13.

For more on purpose and audience, see Chapter 2.

# Writing Assignments for a Definition Essay

Plan and illustrate your essay with one or more photographs of your own choosing. Write caption(s) for the photograph(s) that reflect your point(s).

## Considering Audience and Purpose

Assume you are in need of financial aid to continue your education, and you have found several available scholarships from a particular organization such as the following: The Hispanic Scholarship Fund, The United Negro Scholarship Fund, The Organization of Chinese Americans, or the Truman Scholarship. All of these scholarships require essays. Most of these essays ask candidates to define some aspect of themselves. Adapt one of the following topics to the organization of your choice, and write an essay to compete for a scholarship:

1. Define your heritage based on its significance.
2. Define yourself as a leader.
3. Define the kind of contribution you hope to make.

## Writing for Everyday Life

Assume a couple in your family or the family of someone you know is going to celebrate their 50th anniversary and their union has served as a model of a strong and loving relationship. What would you say has made their partnership so successful? Write the text for a speech you will deliver at their anniversary celebration in which you define *partnership* and honor their life together.

## Writing for College Life

Assume that in a college health class you have been studying about the connection between the mind and body and how important self-understanding is to a healthful lifestyle. How well do you know yourself? What brings you joy? What is your idea of a fulfilling, purposeful life? What is your mission? How do you want to be remembered? Write an essay that expresses a mission statement for your life in which you define your ideals and goals.

## Writing for Working Life

Assume you are starting a small business, such as a restaurant, a fitness club, a toy store, or some kind of specialty shop. To receive financial backing from investors, you have been asked to write a mission statement for your business. Write an essay that defines your small business. What service or commodity are you selling? Who are your potential customers? Why is this service or commodity needed? Where is the best location for your business? How will your product or service be superior to other similar products or services?

## Additional Definition Topics

A computer term such as a computer virus, spam, or search engine

A disorder such as insomnia, anorexia, Type 2 Diabetes, or Seasonal Affective Disorder

A natural phenomenon such as a sinkhole, tropical depression, fault line, or coral reef

# Developing Your Point in a Cause and Effect Essay

Understanding the relationship between cause and effect is a vital critical thinking skill that enhances all areas of life.

- In your personal life, understanding the cause of a misunderstanding, or recognizing the effect of an over-the-counter or prescription drug can protect your relationships and your health.
- In your college life, you will be asked to analyze the causes and effects of wars, inventions, discoveries, natural disasters, economic recessions, or mental and physical diseases. An analysis of causes and effects deepens your understanding of information in every content area.
- In your working life, to ensure success you need to understand why a product sells, reasons for poor performance, or the effects of decisions on employee morale or the company's budget.

For information on writing a cause and effect paragraph, see Chapter 11.

A writer uses the **cause and effect essay** to explore why something happened or what results came from an event. A cause explores the reason something happens, and an effect examines the result or outcome. The following transition words signal cause and effect.

## Transitions That Signal Cause and Effect

| | | | | | |
|---|---|---|---|---|---|
| accordingly | because of | due to | leads to | since | therefore |
| as a result | consequently | if…then | results in | so | thus |

## A Cause and Effect Essay: One Writer's Response

Read the following cause and effect essay from the National Institute on Alcohol Abuse and Alcoholism. Read the essay a second time, then, complete the activities and answer the questions that follow.

**Alcoholism: Getting the Facts**

1 (1) For most people who drink, alcohol is a pleasant accompaniment to social activities. (2) Moderate alcohol use—up to two drinks per day for men and one drink per day for women and older people—is not harmful for most adults. (3) (A standard drink is one 12-ounce bottle or can of either beer or wine cooler, one 5-ounce glass of wine, or 1.5 ounces of 80-proof distilled spirits.) (4) Nonetheless, a large number of people get into serious trouble because of their drinking. (5) Currently, nearly 17.6 million adult Americans abuse alcohol or are alcoholic. (6) Several million more adults engage in risky drinking that could lead to alcohol problems. (7) These patterns include binge drinking and heavy drinking on a regular basis. (8) In addition, 53 percent of men and women in the United States report that one or more of their close relatives has a drinking problem. (9) Due to the scope of this problem, it

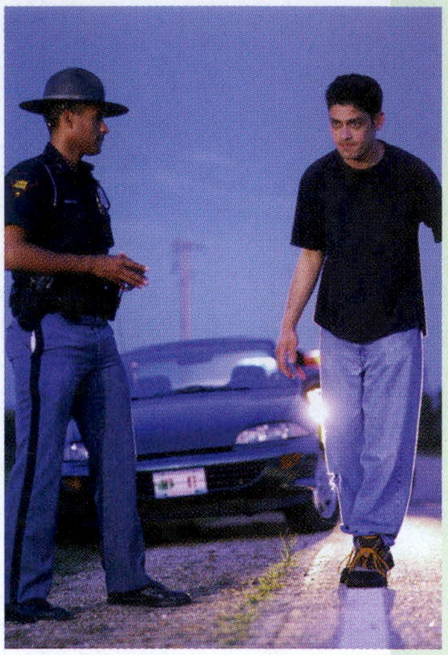

is important to understand the effects of alcoholism and alcohol abuse, as well as identify their causes.

**2** (10) Alcoholism, also known as "alcohol dependence," is a disease with at least four recognizable effects or symptoms. (11) One impact of alcoholic dependence is a strong craving for alcohol. (12) An alcoholic feels a strong need, or compulsion, to drink. (13) Another impact is a loss of control: alcoholics cannot limit their drinking on any given occasion. (14) People who are not alcoholic sometimes do not understand why an alcoholic can't just "use a little willpower" to stop drinking. (15) However, alcoholism has little to do with willpower. (16) Alcoholics are in the grip of a powerful craving that can be as strong as the need for food or water. (17) Third, alcohol dependence eventually results in physical dependence: withdrawal symptoms, such as nausea, sweating, shakiness, and anxiety, occur when an alcoholic stops drinking. (18) Finally, a tolerance for alcohol develops. (19) Thus the need to drink greater amounts of alcohol in order to "get high" occurs.

**3** (20) Alcohol abuse differs from alcoholism in that it does not result in an extremely strong craving for alcohol, loss of control over drinking, or physical dependence. (21) Alcohol abuse, a pattern of drinking, leads to one or more of the following four situations within a 12-month period. (22) Alcohol abuse often leads to failure to fulfill major work, school, or home responsibilities. (23) Drinking occurs in situations that are physically dangerous, such as while driving a car or operating machinery. (24) Alcohol-related legal problems are recurring, such as being arrested for driving under the influence of alcohol or for physically hurting someone while drunk. (25) Finally, drinking continues despite ongoing relationship problems that are caused or worsened by the drinking. (26) Although alcohol abuse is basically different from alcoholism, many effects of alcohol abuse are also experienced by alcoholics.

**4** (27) The long-term consequences of alcohol misuse are serious —in many cases, life threatening. (28) Heavy drinking can increase the risk for certain cancers, especially those of the liver, esophagus, throat, and larynx (voice box). (29) Heavy drinking can also cause liver cirrhosis, immune system problems, brain damage, and harm to the fetus during pregnancy. (30) In addition, drinking increases the risk of death from automobile crashes as well as recreational and on-the-job injuries. (31) Furthermore, both homicides and suicides are more likely to be committed by persons who have been drinking. (32) In purely economic terms, alcohol-related problems cost society approximately $185 billion per year. (33) In human terms, the costs cannot be calculated.

**5** (34) Many people wonder why some individuals can use alcohol without problems but others cannot. (35) Alcohol misuse occurs for several reasons. (36) One important reason has to do with genetics. (37) Scientists have found that having an alcoholic family member makes it more likely that if a person chooses to drink he or she too may develop alcoholism. (38) Genes, however, are not the whole story. (39) In fact, scientists now believe that certain factors in a person's environment influence whether a person with a genetic risk for alcoholism ever develops the disease. (40) A person's risk for developing alcoholism can increase based on the person's environment, including where and how he or she lives; family, friends, and culture; peer pressure; and even how easy it is to get alcohol.

**6** (41) Those who choose to ignore these facts about alcoholism and alcohol abuse may be the very ones who will suffer the devastating effects associated with drinking-related problems.

—Adapted from "Getting the Facts," National Institute on Alcohol Abuse and Alcoholism (2001)

# Practice 9

## READING AND EVALUATING THE ESSAY

Complete the activities below after you have read the essay a second time.

1. What kind of title does the writer use? ______

2. What type of introduction does the writer use? ______

______

3. Underline the thesis statement.

4. For each of the body paragraphs, underline the topic sentence. Circle the cause and effect transition words. List two major details for each paragraph below.

Major Details (Paragraph 2): ______

______

Major Details (Paragraph 3): ______

______

Major Details (Paragraph 4): ______

______

Major Details (Paragraph 5): ______

5. What type of conclusion does the writer use? ______

6. What is the purpose of the essay? Explain your answer. ______

______

7. Who is the audience for the essay? Explain your answer. ______

______

8. What did you like best about the essay? Why? ______

______

9. What about the essay could be improved? ______

______

For more on types of titles, introductions, and conclusions, see Chapter 14.

For more on thesis statements, see Chapter 13.

For more on topic sentences, see Chapter 3 and Chapter 13.

For more on purpose and audience, see Chapter 2.

# Writing Assignments for a Cause and Effect Essay

Plan and illustrate your essay with one or more photographs of your own choosing. Write caption(s) for the photograph(s) that reflect your point(s).

## Considering Audience and Purpose

Assume you are a volunteer with an organization such as Meals on Wheels, Habitat for Humanity, or Scouts, or that you volunteer at a particular place such as a school, hospital, or animal shelter. You have been asked to give a speech to an audience of college students to raise awareness about volunteering. Write a speech that discusses the need for and benefits of volunteering.

## Writing for Everyday Life

Many of us have rebelled against our parents (or another authority figure) or know someone who has. What are some of the things against which youth rebel? Why? Is most youthful rebellion harmless or are serious long-term effects more likely? Why? Write an encouraging letter to a young person who is in conflict with authority that explains some of the causes and possible effects of youthful rebellion.

## Writing for College Life

Assume you are enrolled in a sociology class discussing the ways in which technology has changed society during your lifetime or over the lifetime of your grandparents. What are some of the intended benefits or unexpected outcomes of having televisions, automobiles, dishwashers, digital recorders, cell phones, iPods, or other pieces of technology? Write an essay for this class explaining the effects of a specific piece of technology on modern culture.

## Writing for Working Life

Assume your company has asked you to speak about the "elements of success" during an employee training day. Think of highly successful people such as Oprah Winfrey, Bill Gates, Rita Rossi Colwell, Michael Jordan, Hillary Rodham Clinton, Reverend Billy Graham, or Soraya. What motivates or drives people to such high levels of success? Write a speech to motivate a group of work colleagues by explaining the reasons for success.

## Additional Cause and Effect Topics

Excessive mood swings or compulsive behavior

Low or high self-esteem

Benefits of a particular exercise: walking, jogging, so on

Benefits of humor

A natural disaster such as a hurricane, tornado, or tsunami

Benefits of team sports

Addiction to or withdrawal from a drug such as nicotine or caffeine

# Developing Your Point in a Persuasive Essay

Persuasion is used in every aspect of life.

- In your personal life, you come across attempts to persuade you in magazine, radio, and television advertisements. As a parent, you may persuade your children to eat healthful foods and get lots of exercise. Or you may persuade your partner to go on a much needed vacation.
- In your college life, you will be asked to take stands on issues in all the areas you study. For example, in a social science class, you may want to argue for or against gun control or in a science class, you may take a stand for or against cloning.
- In your working life, you use persuasion when you try to convince a prospective employer that you are the best candidate for the job. Or you may need to write your own advertisement to get people to come to your store or restaurant.

For information on writing a persuasive paragraph, see Chapter 12.

In a **persuasive essay,** a writer takes a strong stand on a debatable issue and offers thoughtful, convincing reasons in its support. To create a credible argument, a writer uses facts and examples, offers expert and informed opinions, considers consequences, and answers the opposition. The following transitions signal persuasion.

### Transition Words Used to Signal Persuasion

| | | | | |
|---|---|---|---|---|
| accordingly | even so | in conclusion | nonetheless | therefore |
| admittedly | finally | indeed | obviously | thus |
| although | first (second, third, etc.) | | of course | to be sure |
| because | for | in fact | on the one hand | truly |
| but | furthermore | in summary | on the other hand | undoubtedly |
| certainly | granted | last | since | |
| consequently | hence | meanwhile | some believe | |
| despite | however | nevertheless | some may say | |

## A Persuasion Essay: One Writer's Response

Read the following persuasion essay. Read the essay a second time, then, complete the activities and answer the questions that follow.

### Ban Cell Phones: Save Lives

1 (1) No one understands the dangers of using a cell phone while driving better than Rob and Patti Pena. (2) On November 3, 1999, their 2-year-old daughter Morgan Lee died as a result of injuries sustained in a car crash the previous day. (3) As she sat securely strapped into her car seat in the back seat of her mother's car, a driver who ran a stop sign while using his cellular phone broadsided their car. (4) The only legal penalty the driver faced was a $50 fine and two traffic tickets.

(5) Regrettably, the tragic loss of Morgan Lee is not an isolated case. (6) According to a study by the Harvard Center for Risk Analysis, researchers estimated that the use of cell phones by drivers caused approximately 2,600 deaths. (7) Cell phone use while driving should be banned.

2 (8) Of course, not everyone agrees that talking on a cell phone while driving should be outlawed. (9) In fact, many believe that this behavior is no more dangerous than the many other tasks drivers perform while driving. (10) Obviously, drivers constantly multitask as they eat, fiddle with the radio or air conditioner, light a cigarette, apply makeup, read a map, and converse with their passengers. (11) Obviously, common sense dictates that these tasks should be kept to a minimum. (12) Certainly, any activity that absorbs a driver's attention has the potential to adversely affect the driver's control of the vehicle and reaction to hazards and traffic signals. (13) However, to suggest that one set of careless behaviors excuses another reckless behavior defies common sense. (14) Common sense also suggests that the dangers posed by these distractions do not compare to the dangers posed by using a cell phone while driving.

3 (15) Human Factors experts study the relationship between human limitations and the design of technology. (16) These experts note that drivers face visual, auditory, mechanical, and cognitive distractions. (17) Using a cell phone while driving incorporates every one of these distractions. (18) Darla Burton offers an excellent example of how using a cell phone while driving combines all four.

4 (19) The cell phone in Darla's purse rings as she speeds down the Interstate. (20) Immediately, she becomes visually distracted as she takes her eyes off the road and leans across the front seat to grab her purse. (21) The insistent ringing serves as an auditory alarm that urges her to hurry her movements. (22) As she rummages for the phone in her purse and fumbles with the mechanics of opening and answering the flip phone, she swerves out of her lane. (23) A passing motorist blares his car's horn in warning; Darla jerks her car back into her own lane. (24) The caller is her boyfriend, and with an angry voice, he continues an argument that began days ago. (25) Darla, distracted cognitively as she argues with her boyfriend, becomes lost in the conversation and unaware of her bearings. (26) Suddenly, she notices that her exit is looming quickly. (27) Without thinking or looking in her rear view and side mirrors, she veers across three lanes to make the exit. (28) Luckily, she narrowly avoids sideswiping another vehicle.

(29) Darla's behavior is typical of many people who use a cell phone while driving.

5 (30) Those who oppose banning cell phone use while driving argue that hands-free cell phones reduce these risks, and they do, but not enough. (31) Hands-free cell phones may limit visual and mechanical distractions, but auditory and cognitive distractions are still issues of concern. (32) Some believe that these distractions are no different than the distraction of talking with a passenger in the car. (33) However, talking on a cell phone is significantly different than talking with a passenger in a car. (34) First, a passenger in a vehicle often contributes to the safety of the driving situation by providing an additional set of eyes and ears to warn against road hazards. (35) When a driving situation demands the focused attention of the driver, a passenger in the car helps control the flow of conversation so that the driver can safely attend to the task of driving. (36) In addition, most people are conditioned to immediately respond to a ringing phone. (37) This need to answer often overrides convenience or safety issues and drags attention away from the challenges of the road.

6 (38) The sheer number of cell phone users also adds to the seriousness of the problem. (39) There are currently 190 million cell phone users in this country alone. (40) A record 24 million new cell phone subscribers signed up between June 2004 and June 2005. (41) According to a 1995 *Prevention Magazine* survey, 85% of cell phone owners drive while using their cell phones. (42) If that trend has continued, then about 162 million drivers currently talk on their phones while driving, at least some of time. (43) In addition, current in-car communication services allow users to check e-mail and calendars, surf the web, and even send faxes while driving. (44) The wireless industry plans to offer an even wider range of mobile options such as digital streaming, which have the potential to further distract drivers.

7 (45) Remember Morgan Lee Pena and the thousands of other possible victims of someone's need to stay plugged in. (46) Join the fight to ban cell phone use while driving. (47) Write to your politicians, and tell them to support cellular phone legislation. (48) Urge them to ban cell phone use while driving and to enact strong penalties against violators. (49) Write to your cellular provider and ask the company to support laws that restrict cellular phone use while driving. (50) Finally, if you take a cell phone with you in your car, set a good example; pull over and stop before you make or take a call. (51) Tell your friends and family to do the same for their safety and the safety of others. (52) Stay safe! (53) Save lives! (54) Don't talk; just drive!

## Practice 10

**READING AND EVALUATING THE ESSAY**

Complete the activities below after you have read the essay a second time.

**1.** What kind of title does the writer use? ______________________

**2.** What type of introduction does the writer use? ______________________

**3.** Underline the thesis statement.

**4.** For each of the body paragraphs, underline the topic sentence. Circle the persuasion signal words. List two major details for each paragraph below.

Major Details (Paragraph 2): ______________________

______________________

Major Details (Paragraph 3): ______________________

Major Details (Paragraph 4): ______________________

Major Details (Paragraph 5): ______________________

______________________

Major Details (Paragraph 6): ______________________

______________________

______________________

**5.** What type of conclusion does the writer use? ______________________

**6.** What is the purpose of the essay? Explain your answer. ______________________

______________________

______________________

**7.** Who is the audience for the essay? Explain your answer. ______________________

______________________

**8.** What did you like best about the essay? Why? ______________________

**9.** What about the essay could be improved? ______________________

For more on types of titles, introductions, and conclusions, see Chapter 14.

For more on thesis statements, see Chapter 13.

For more on topic sentences, see Chapter 3 and Chapter 13.

For more on purpose and audience, see Chapter 2.

# Writing Assignments for a Persuasive Essay

Plan and illustrate your essay with one or more photographs of your own choosing. Write caption(s) for the photograph(s) that reflect your point(s).

## Considering Audience and Purpose

Assume you are a reporter for your college's newspaper. Identify a problem that affects many people on your campus, such as poor lighting in the parking lot, inadequate parking, or poor food service. Write a column calling for administrative action to correct the problem. Your purpose is to offer compelling evidence that action must be taken.

## Writing for Everyday Life

Think about the amount of graphic violence and sexual content on television shows and the numbers of hours people spend watching these images. Should sponsors such as Kellogg, Nike, McDonald's, and Wal-Mart support shows that contain graphic violent and sexual content? Write a letter to a company that sponsors a particularly graphic television show to persuade the company to withdraw its sponsorship.

## Writing for College Life

Assume you are taking a sociology course, and you have been studying about the impact of clothes (or fashion) on human behavior. Your professor directs your attention to Northwest High School, where school uniforms will soon be required. What are some of the reasons administrators and parents might have for supporting school uniforms, and what are some of the reasons students may oppose them? Write a letter to the principal of the school taking a strong stand for or against school uniforms for students attending Northwest High School.

## Writing for Working Life

Assume you are the manager of a retail store in a local mall, and one of your employees has consistently performed at a high level. Write a letter to your supervisor in which you recommend a promotion and raise for your employee.

## Additional Persuasive Topics

Animal testing for cosmetic or medical research

Manned space flights

Abstinence-only sex education courses

Stricter gun laws

Surveillance cameras installed in all public places

Decriminalization of marijuana

# Developing Your Point in a Layered-Plan Essay

Often, writers find that the most effective way to express their view about a particular topic is to layer several patterns of organization into one essay.

- In your personal life, you may find it necessary to write an apology for a misunderstanding with a family member or friend. In your letter, you may find it helpful to discuss the *types* of stresses you have been facing, the *effects* such stresses have had upon you, and the *reasons* you value your friend or family member.
- In your college life, you will combine patterns of organization as you study topics in greater depth. For example, in humanities you may choose to write about the *origin*, *types*, and *impact* of art or artifacts produced by a particular culture.
- In your working life, you may need to write a report that *defines* a problem, *compares* several solutions, and *recommends* a course of action.

In an **essay that layers patterns of organization**, a writer divides the topic into subsections based on a series of patterns of organization best suited for each paragraph that develops the main point. For example, "alcoholism," discussed in an earlier essay by using causes and effects, could also be discussed by layering several patterns of organization. As a disease, alcoholism has recognizable stages or cycles that could be discussed using process. In addition, several types of treatment are available and could be discussed using classification. Or perhaps sharing personal testimonies or case histories of recovering alcoholics in the form of narratives could convince someone to seek help. Many other topics also can be developed in greater depth by layering plans.

Transition words used within each paragraph signal the type of pattern of organization used to develop that particular paragraph. Therefore, draw from the lists of transitions given throughout this chapter for each of the specific patterns of organization as needed.

## A Layered-Plan Essay: One Student Writer's Response

Study the following layered-plan essay written by student Doug Frazier. Read the essay a second time, then, complete the activities and answer the questions that follow.

The Games People Play

1 (1) Games have always been a part of human culture. (2) Archeologists have uncovered the use of board games as far back as 4000 B.C. in ancient Babylonia. (3) While board games apparently appeared as the first type of game, other forms such as card games and tiled games evolved as people began to understand, enjoy, and develop the concept of games. (4) The variety and enjoyment of games expanded as technology advanced through the millennia.

(5) Most recently, over the past 30 years, the newest and perhaps most radical change to games has occurred with the invention of the computer video game. (6) The advent of computer video games enabled a significant jump in gaming evolution. (7) While video games share many of the same traits as traditional games, the distinct qualities of computer games intensify both the dangers and the pleasures of gaming.

2 (8) To appreciate the impact of video games on the gaming experience, a general understanding of a few types and features of traditional games is necessary. (9) Overall, traditional games often reflect three types of intense, real-life experiences: physical combat or skill, intellectual strategy, and chance. (10) The group of games based on physical skills is made up of a wide range of activities such as races, archery, and darts; the outcome of these games relies upon the physical abilities of the players. (11) Another group of games are based on strategy, such as chess, and rely upon the player's ability to make rational decisions. (12) Many games combine the first two types of games so that players need both physical skill and strategy to win such as in organized sports like soccer, baseball, and football. (13) The third type of game utilizes chance and often uses dice or some kind of random number selection that dictates the outcome; examples of these games include bingo and lotteries. (14) Often games of chance also combine with strategy, so that knowledge or skill helps determine the outcome. (15) For example, through a series of plays, Monopoly and poker combine chance and strategy to determine a winner.

3 (16) All of these traditional games share a few basic traits. (17) First, games usually offer an avatar or icon that represents the player; in Monopoly the original avatars were metal tokens based on objects found in households across America (the flat iron, purse, lantern, car, thimble, shoe, top hat, and the rocking horse); in sports the avatars are the team's name and mascot like the Eagle for the Philadelphia Eagles in the National Football League. (18) Traditional games, also, present an environment that challenges the players or allows the players to challenge each other, and traditional games keep track of the player's success or scores. (19) In addition, traditional games foster social interaction; part of the fun of playing is experiencing the game with someone else.

4 (20) A comparison of traditional games to video games finds many similarities. (21) Just like traditional games, video games offer avatars. (22) For example, in the video game *King Kong* based on director Peter Jackson's version of the classic story, players can choose the adventurer Jack Driscoll as the avatar, or choose Kong, thus playing the game through the eyes of the ape. (23) Both traditional and video games present environments in which challenges are posed by the game player and opponent; in addition, both traditional and video games keep track of a player's success or score and reward the players when they overcome challenges or challengers. (24) Moreover, video games actually combine physical skill, strategy, and chance. (25) Physical skill is needed to rapidly figure out and adapt to the immense amount of visual information provided on the video screen. (26) In addition, the player must make rational decisions based on this information and make moves in a logical sequence. (27) Thus video games, like many traditional games, require strategy. (28) Finally, many video games are programmed to allow apparently random events to occur, so they are similar to games of chance as well.

5 (29) Although traditional and video games are similar, they do indeed differ in drastic ways. (30) Traditional games are much more unpredictable than video games. (31) Traditional board and card games require other players to enrich the environment and to create the uncertainty which generates the fun. (32) Video games, on the other hand, are a form of artificial intelligence (A.I.) programmed into the computer. (33) While A.I. is impressive, it is ultimately limited and lacks the unpredictable flexibility of human thought; therefore, the outcomes of the challenges are ultimately much more predictable. (34) Traditional games and video games differ in the social experiences they offer. (35) A.I. fosters an antisocial experience. (36) Often, video players do not need other players. (37) Traditionally, games have been seen as such an enjoyable activity partly because of the time spent making and enjoying friends. (38) During this time, players learn how to win and lose with dignity and to respect the integrity of others. (39) In contrast, many video games absorb individual players in countless hours of isolated play. (40) The great majority of these games also demand that players engage in simulated antisocial acts of murder and mayhem. (41) For example, "Carmageddon" is described on the package as "The racing game for the chemically imbalanced." (42) The goal of this gory video game is to "waste contestants, pedestrians, and farmyard animals for points and credit."

(43) Some critics of video games consider these differences from traditional games alarming and dangerous.

6 (44) Experts warn that violent video games can have a negative impact. (45) These types of video games may increase aggressive thoughts, feelings, and behaviors; arouse hostility; and decrease helping behaviors. (46) Because video game players must make active decisions to choose violent strategies to win, players may learn that violence is fun and rewarding. (47) Another negative effect may be that players become numbed or blunted emotionally to violence and come to accept violence as a normal part of life. (48) Because players view violence as inevitable, they may not develop the skills needed to make nonviolent choices when they are faced with real life challenges.

7 (49) The ways in which video games differ from traditional games may present some reasons for caution; still the distinctive nature of video games offers some positive pleasures. (50) A video game player often learns how to play the game through trial and error by playing. (51) So video games are fun to explore. (52) As the player explores the world of the video game, he or she must rethink choices and come up with strategies based on new information. (53) In addition, to achieve ultimate victory, a player must think about the short-term and long-term effects of each decision or move in the game. (54) Finally, many players enjoy figuring out the limits of the game. (55) The fun lies in figuring how the game's program works and if there are any flaws in the program. (56) Thus, video games make critical thinking enjoyable.

8 (57) Traditional and computer games share many traits. (58) Both require physical skill, chance, and strategy to win. (59) However, video games offer a different kind of gaming experience. (60) Video games are often violent and antisocial by nature, yet they make problem solving a fun activity. (61) Some critics consider video games far more dangerous than traditional games.

Practice 11

## READING AND EVALUATING THE ESSAY

Complete the activities below after you have read the essay a second time.

**1.** What kind of title does the writer use? ______

**2.** What type of introduction does the writer use? ______

**3.** Underline the thesis statement.

**4.** For each of the body paragraphs, underline the topic sentence. Circle the layered-plan signal words. List two major details for each paragraph below.

Major Details (Paragraph 2): ______

______

Major Details (Paragraph 3): ______

______

Major Details (Paragraph 4): ______

______

Major Details (Paragraph 5): ______

______

Major Details (Paragraph 6): ______

Major Details (Paragraph 7): ______

______

**5.** What type of conclusion does the writer use? ______

**6.** What is the purpose of the essay? Explain your answer. ______

______

**7.** Who is the audience for the essay? Explain your answer. ______

______

**8.** What did you like best about the essay? Why? ______

**9.** What about the essay could be improved? ______

For more on types of titles, introductions, and conclusions, see Chapter 14.

For more on thesis statements, see Chapter 13.

For more on topic sentences, see Chapter 3 and Chapter 13.

For more on purpose and audience, see Chapter 2.

# Writing Assignments for a Layered-Plan Essay

Plan and illustrate your essay with one or more photographs of your own choosing. Write caption(s) for the photograph(s) that reflect your point(s).

## Considering Audience and Purpose

Assume you are a dissatisfied customer with several complaint issues, and you are writing a formal complaint to the manager. Identify the types of complaints you have; discuss the causes of your dissatisfaction, and list the steps you expect the manager to take to rectify the situation.

## Writing for Everyday Life

Technological advances are rapidly accelerating. How important is it to stay abreast of the new technologies? Why? What are the types of new technologies, such as podcasting or multimedia cell phones? Which ones are most accessible, easy to use, affordable, or important? Why? Write a consumer report for an online posting in which you analyze the importance of keeping up with technology.

## Writing for College Life

Assume you are taking a college humanities course, and you have been studying the concept of cultural traditions. Many of us have favorite traditions or rituals that have been handed down to us by our families or cultures. How does a tradition or ritual reflect a particular family, culture, heritage, or value? Write an essay in which you analyze the significance of a particular ritual or tradition.

## Writing for Working Life

Assume you work in an environment full of conflict, and you have learned effective conflict resolution skills. Identify some typical conflicts that occur on a particular job: Between a team supervisor and a team member at a car dealership? Between a waiter and a diner? Between colleagues at a walk-in health clinic? What causes these conflicts? What are the steps to effective conflict resolution? Write a report for a supervisor that documents a conflict, evaluates the causes of the conflict, and recommends steps to resolve the conflict.

## Additional Layered-Plan Topics

Minimum wage
National identity cards
A living will
Inspiring or effective teachers
A popular public figure
Internet fraud

Review

## REVIEW: MAKING YOUR POINT USING PATTERNS OF ORGANIZATION

Complete the chart by filling in the blanks with information from the chapter:

**A descriptive essay** describes a person, place, or object based on its location or the way it is arranged in ........................ ; relies upon ........................ details such as sight, sound, smell, taste, and touch to create vivid mental images so that the reader can see what is being described.

**A narrative essay** shows a series of ........................ or actions that occur during a specific period of ........................

**A process essay** shows actions in time order (also called chronological order) that can be repeated at any time, with similar results for three reasons:

**1.** To give steps, ........................, or procedures for completing a task.

**2.** To analyze or study the steps, ........................, or phases of a process.

**3.** To explain how to complete a task and to analyze the process.

**An illustration essay** offers a focused main idea about a particular topic and then offers a series of ........................ or ........................ to clarify or support the main idea.

**A classification essay** sorts or divides ideas into smaller groups and then describes the common ........................ of each subgroup. The writer lists each ........................, describes its characteristics, and offers examples that represent the group. Because groups and subgroups are listed, transitions that suggest additional categories are often used to ensure coherence.

**A comparison and contrast essay** shows the ........................ and ........................ between or among two topics based on comparable points.

**A definition essay** explains the meaning of a new, difficult, or special ......................... A definition may include traits, comparisons, causes, or effects. In addition, a writer may include an explanation of what the term or concept is ......................... Examples are used to illustrate the various components or elements of the term being defined.

**A cause and effect essay** discusses why something happened or what results came from an event. A cause explores the ........................ something happens, and an effect examines the ........................ or outcome.

**A persuasive essay** takes a strong stand on a debatable issue and offers thoughtful, convincing reasons in its support. To create a credible argument, a writer uses ........................ and ........................, offers expert and informed ........................, considers consequences, and answers the .........................

**A layered-plan essay** divides the topic into subsections based on a ........................ of ........................ of organization best suited for each paragraph that develops the main point.

REVISING

PART 4

# The Basic Sentence

# 16 Subjects, Verbs, and Simple Sentences

**Chapter Preview**

- What's the Point of Subjects, Verbs, and Simple Sentences?
- Understanding the Point of Subjects, Verbs, and Simple Sentences: One Student Writer's Response
- Applying the Point: Subjects, Verbs, and Simple Sentences

Homework pg 342-354 read and do exercise Do practices * w/exception of 1+le

* Notes
• a simple sentence is also called an independent clause

* A simple sentence, also called an *independent clause*, includes a subject and verb and expresses a complete thought. *

Communicating about a real-life situation helps us to understand the purpose of subjects, verbs, and simple sentences. The photograph on the facing page illustrates one immediate effect of strenuous exercise. Read the statements given in Practice 1 about the effect of strenuous exercise, and answer the question "What's the point of subjects, verbs, and simple sentences?"

# What's the Point of Subjects, Verbs, and Simple Sentences?

Practice 1

WRITING FROM LIFE

PHOTOGRAPHIC ORGANIZER: SUBJECTS, VERBS, AND SIMPLE SENTENCES

Read the following set of statements. Circle the one that makes the most sense. Discuss why the statement you chose makes sense and why the other two do not.

Swigs a bottle of water in one long gulp.

Danielle, hot and flushed.

Danielle, hot and flushed, swigs a bottle of water in one long gulp.

**What's the point of subjects, verbs, and simple sentences?**

## Understanding the Point of Subjects, Verbs, and Simple Sentences: One Student Writer's Response

The following paragraph offers one writer's reaction to the statements about Danielle and the importance of subjects, verbs, and simple sentences.

> *The first statement "swigs a bottle of water in one long gulp" doesn't make any sense by itself. Who's doing this? "Danielle, hot and flushed" doesn't make any sense by itself either. I need more information! The ideas do make sense when they are put together. Danielle takes a drink because she's hot. It's hard to figure out what someone is saying when a subject or a verb is missing. I think both must be needed to say something.*

## Applying the Point: Subjects, Verbs, and Simple Sentences

A subject and verb unite to state a focused and complete thought in a sentence. You already have a great deal of experience using subjects, verbs, and simple sentences. As we think silently, we use subjects and verbs to frame most of our thoughts. Most often, we converse with each other by using subjects and verbs, and much of what we read in newspapers, magazines, books, and on the Internet is expressed by using subjects and verbs.

### Subjects

A **subject** is the person, place, object, or topic about which a writer expresses a focused thought or makes an assertion. To identify a subject, ask: Who or what did this? Alternatively, ask: Who or what is this?

#### Types of Subjects

A subject is expressed in a variety of ways based on the focus of the writer's thought or point. Three common types of subjects include the **simple subject**, the **action/being subject**, and the **compound subject**.

**Simple Subjects: Three Types**

- **Simple Subject, Type 1:** A single person, place, object, or topic is the focus of thought.

SUBJECT

Wilma Mankiller served as the first female chief of the Cherokee Nation from 1985–1995.

- **Simple Subject, Type 2:** A group of words expresses the focus of thought.

SUBJECT

What the government knows about the assassination of President Kennedy is still a matter of debate.

- **Simple Subject, Type 3:** A suggestion, command, or order is the focus of thought.

Make a difference by voting.

"YOU" IS UNDERSTOOD, BUT NOT STATED, AS THE SUBJECT OF THE SENTENCE, WHICH IS A COMMAND.

**Action/Being Subject: Two Types**

- **Action/Being Subject, Type 1:** An action word ending with *-ing* is the point of a focused thought.

Laughing reduces stress.

ACTION/SUBJECT

- **Action/Being Subject, Type 2:** A state of being word ending with *-ing* is the point of a focused thought.

ACTION/SUBJECT

For many Mexican immigrants, living in the United States during the 21st century increases economic opportunities.

**Compound Subject**

- **Compond Subject:** Two or more people, places, objects, or topics are the subjects of a focused thought.

COMPOUND SUBJECTS

Florida, Texas, and California lead the national growth of online banking.

COMPOUND SUBJECTS ARE OFTEN JOINED BY THE COORDINATING CONJUNCTION "AND."

# Practice 2

*

SUBJECTS

Underline the subject once in each of the following sentences. Then, identify each subject by its type, writing *simple, compound*, or *action/being* in the blanks. (*Hint:* Compound subjects can combine action/being subjects.) Share and discuss your responses in a small group or with your class.

Simple **1.** Nurses use their training to perform five basic tasks.

~~Action/being~~ Compound action/being **2.** Assessing the patient and aiding in the diagnosis of the illness are two tasks of nurses.

~~Compound~~ Simple **3.** The remaining three tasks include participating in the planning of a patient's care, carrying out the plan, and evaluating the effectiveness of the treatment.

Simple **4.** What nurses observe in the daily care of their patients affects the treatment plan and the effectiveness of the treatment.

Action/being **5.** Nursing offers flexible work schedules in 4, 8, 10, or 12 hour shifts.

Compound Subject **6.** Home care, private practice, hospitals, clinics, and hospices are just a few areas of practice for nurses.

~~Action/being~~ Simple **7.** Consider entering the rewarding profession of nursing.

you is the subject (simple understanding subject)

**8.** Write a sentence using a simple subject. Suggested topic: An Ideal Job.

Chase Smith was the first and youngest boy to be a cook at his first job.

More practice with subjects: <www.mywritinglab.com>

## Verbs

A **verb** makes an assertion about a subject. A verb states an occurrence (*occur, happen*), a state of being (*is, seems*), or an action (*run, talk*) of the subject. Various verb forms express different kinds of information about the subject of a sentence. Three basic types of verbs include **linking verbs, action verbs,** and **helping verbs.** (See Chapters 25–26 for more information about verbs.)

## Linking Verbs

A **linking verb** connects the subject to a word that renames, describes, or defines the subject. Linking verbs often describe a state of being. The following chart lists common linking verbs and a few examples of their uses in sentences.

## Commonly Used Linking Verbs

- ***am, is, are, was, were, am being, has been...***

SUBJECT — LINKING VERB

The ice cream is cold and sweet.

- ***appear, become, look, seem, turn***

SUBJECT — LINKING VERB

The cheese turned moldy.

- ***feel, smell, sound, taste***

SUBJECT — LINKING VERB

The burrito tasted spicy.

Practice 3

*

**LINKING VERBS**

Fill in each blank with a linking verb that best completes the meaning of the sentence. Discuss your responses in a small group or with your class.

**1.** With an excess of water or mud on normally dry land, a flood ~~appeared~~ becomes a serious danger.

**2.** Flash floods ~~were~~ are the result of large volumes of rainfall within a short time.

**3.** Flooding is the most common of all natural disasters.

**4.** A tsunami flood looks like a dangerous, sky-high wall of water carrying rocks, mud, and other debris.

**5.** Write a sentence using a linking verb. Suggested topic: Flood Damage to a Home.

With all the flooding, much of the wood in the house appears to be rotted.

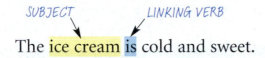

More practice with verbs: <www.mywritinglab.com>

## Action Verbs

An **action verb** shows the behavior of the subject.

SUBJECT → ACTION VERB

Justin and Mia prepared their house for the upcoming storm.

SUBJECT → ACTION VERB

Before the flood, Justin and Mia raised the furnace, water heater, washer, dryer, and furniture off the floors in their home.

Practice 4

**ACTION VERBS**

Underline the action verb twice in each of the following sentences.

1. Justin installed check valves in sewer traps to prevent floodwater from backing up into the drains of their home.
2. To stop floodwater from entering their home, Justin and Mia constructed barriers of sandbags around all of their doors.
3. They also sealed the walls in their basement with a waterproofing compound to avoid seepage.
4. Just as importantly, Justin and Mia bought flood insurance.
5. Write a sentence using an action verb. Suggested topic: A Severe Storm.

While Justin was busy Mia packed up anything that was on high shelves.

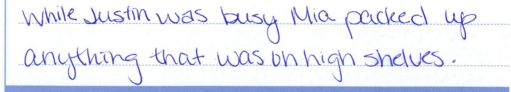

More practice with verbs: <www.mywritinglab.com>

### Helping Verbs

A **helping verb** is used with a main verb to create a verb phrase. Helping verbs are also used to form questions. The verbs *be, do,* and *have* can be used alone or as helping verbs.

VERB PHRASE

HELPING VERB — MAIN VERB

Jermaine **has** **prepared** a supply kit in case of an emergency.

VERB PHRASE

HELPING VERB — MAIN VERB

**Has** Jermaine **prepared** a supply kit?

VERB PHRASE

HELPING VERB — MAIN VERB

Jermaine **has** not **bought** all the supplies.

THE WORD "NOT" IS AN ADVERB THAT NEGATES THE VERB, SO "NOT" IS NEVER PART OF THE VERB PHRASE.

| Common Helping Verbs | | | | | | |
|---|---|---|---|---|---|---|
| be<br>being<br>been<br>am<br>are<br>is<br>was<br>were | do<br>does<br>did | have<br>had<br>has | may<br>might<br>must | should<br>could<br>would | can<br>will<br>shall | have to<br>have got to<br>ought to<br>supposed to<br>used to |

## Practice 5

HELPING VERBS

Underline the verb phrase twice in each of the following sentences.

1. Hurricanes, ice storms, and tornadoes can be devastating natural disasters.
2. Due to lack of road access, emergency services may be delayed for up to 72 hours after a major disaster.
3. Food items should include canned or powdered drinks, ready-to-eat canned meat, fruits, vegetables, and cereals.
4. One gallon of water per person per day for three days is recommended for drinking, cooking, and washing.
5. Write a sentence using a helping verb. Suggested topic: Contents of an Emergency Kit.

you can find a flash light in an emergency kit.

* homework

For more practice with verbs: <www.mywritinglab.com>.

For more information on correcting fragments, see Chapter 22.

# The Simple Sentence

A **simple sentence** is a group of related words that includes a subject and verb and expresses a complete thought. A simple sentence is also known as an **independent clause**. An idea that is missing a subject or verb is a fragment or incomplete thought.

## Distinguishing between a Fragment and the Simple Sentence

**Fragment with missing subject:**

VERB

Uses her status as a superstar to bring media attention to refugees around the world.

**Fragment with missing verb:**

SUBJECT

Angelina Jolie using her status as a superstar to bring media attention to refugees around the world.

**Simple Sentence:**

SUBJECT VERB

Angelina Jolie uses her status as a superstar to bring media attention to refugees around the world.

Practice 6

SIMPLE SENTENCES

Create a simple sentence from each of the following fragments. From the box below, fill in the blank with a subject or verb that best completes each thought.

| Verbs | Subjects |
|---|---|
| is | Volunteers |
| do | Government programs |
| provide | |

1. Volunteering the act of serving others without reward.

   Volunteering ........ the act of serving others without reward.

2. May not be the most effective solutions to serious social problems.

   ........................................ may not be the most effective solutions to serious social problems.

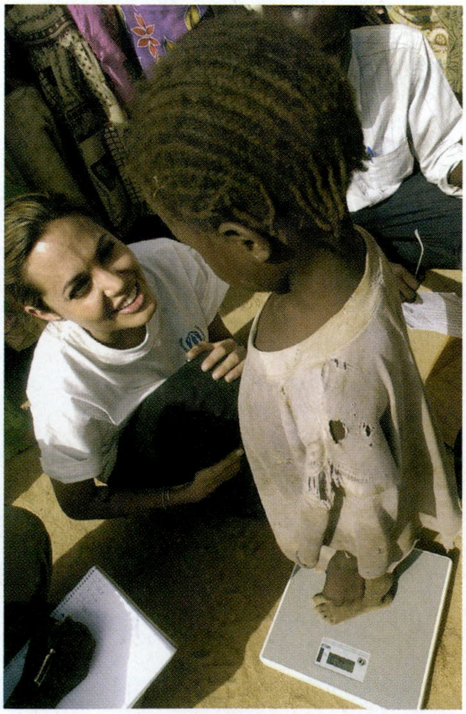

More practice with simple sentences: <www.mywritinglab.com>

**3.** Often, volunteers the best solutions to society's most pressing problems.

Often, volunteers .................. the best solutions to society's most pressing problems.

**4.** Have had a positive impact on violence, poverty, and substance abuse.

.......................... have had a positive impact on violence, poverty, and substance abuse.

**5.** American adult volunteers the work of over 9 million full-time employees.

American adult volunteers ....... the work of over 9 million full-time employees.

Adapted from "Calculating the Economic Impact of Volunteers," Points of Light Foundation & Volunteer Center National Network

Practice 6

# Locating Subjects and Verbs to Identify Complete Thoughts

To avoid fragments and to state ideas as complete thoughts, proofread to identify the subjects and verbs of each sentence. Identifying prepositional phrases as you proofread will help you locate the subject of the sentence.

## Understand the Prepositional Phrase

A **preposition** is a word that has a noun or pronoun as its object and states a relationship between its object and another word. A prepositional phrase begins with a preposition and ends with the object of the preposition.

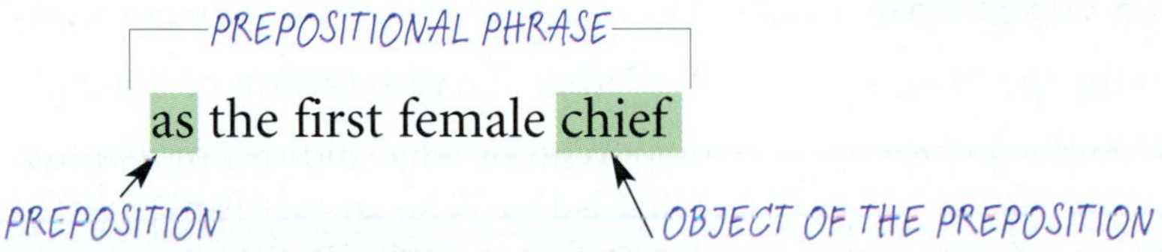


The following chart lists a few common prepositions and examples of their objects.

| Common Prepositions with Possible Objects | | | |
|---|---|---|---|
| **Preposition** | **Object** | **Preposition** | **Object** |
| about | the house | in | my wallet |
| along | the street | for | Texas |
| after | the movie | from | the past |
| as | the parent | of | the boys |
| below | the surface | on | the chair |
| by | evening | to | the college |
| during | the storm | with | patience |

## Find the Prepositional Phrases

The object of the preposition can never be the subject or verb of a sentence. Since subjects and verbs are often surrounded by prepositional phrases, you need to identify these phrases. Identifying prepositional phrases keeps you from confusing them with the subject of the sentence. And often, once these phrases are identified, the subject and verb—or lack of either—becomes easier to recognize.

**Practice 7**

**IDENTIFYING PREPOSITIONAL PHRASES**

Place parentheses around all (prepositional phrases) in the following simple sentences.

1. Wilma Pearl Mankiller served from 1985 through 1995 as the first female Chief of the Cherokee Nation.
2. Former Chief Mankiller lives in Oklahoma on the land allotted to her paternal grandfather, John Mankiller, in 1907.
3. Her family name "Mankiller" appears to be an old military title for the person in charge of protecting the village.
4. As Principal Chief of the Cherokee people, she represented the second largest tribe in the United States.
5. As part of the government's Indian relocation policy, Mankiller, along with her family, was forcibly removed from her father's land in Oklahoma to California during her early childhood.

## The FIL Process

To identify subjects and verbs, follow these three simple steps:

1. **F**ind Prepositional Phrases: Place parentheses around (prepositional phrases).
2. **I**dentify the Verb: Underline the verb (action or linking) twice.
3. **L**ocate the Subject: Ask: Who or what did this or who or what is this? The answer is the subject. Underline the subject once.

More practice with subjects, verbs, and simple sentences: <www.mywritinglab.com>

VERB — SUBJECT — PREPOSITIONAL PHRASE — PREPOSITIONAL PHRASE

Applicants (for firefighting jobs) generally must pass a written exam (along with tests) (of strength, physical stamina, coordination, and agility).

PREPOSITIONAL PHRASE

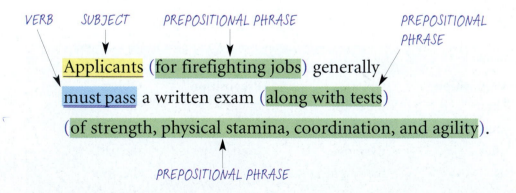

## Practice 8

### IDENTIFYING SUBJECTS AND VERBS

Identify the subjects and verbs in the following simple sentences. Annotate each sentence: Place (prepositional phrases) in parentheses, underline the verb twice, underline the subject once.

1. At one time, in the city of San Diego, the firefighters of Fire Engine 22 were all women.
2. The crew of Melissa Cleary, Robyn Benincasa, Joi Evan, and April Lallo did not intend to create an all female unit; for as a matter of fact, women account for only 8 percent of the San Diego firefighting force.
3. A firefighter, like each of these women, must bid for a position and wait for seniority to win a spot.
4. The women of Engine 22 are required to perform the same tasks as men.
5. Who of us are like these women; who dares to believe in self?

Adapted from "Girls Only: San Diego's All-Female Firefighting Crew," *Good Morning America.* ABC News. Jan. 24, 2006

More practice with subjects, verbs, and simple sentences: <www.mywritinglab.com>

## Practice 9

### SUBJECTS, VERBS, AND SIMPLE SENTENCES REVIEW

Read the following paragraph written by a student. In each sentence, underline the subject once, underline the verb twice, and place parentheses around the (prepositional phrase). *Hint:* Some sentences use the understood subject *you*. Then, write three simple sentences of your own.

(1) Who stands to gain the most from doing a good job? (2) You do! (3) Through hard work, you will make your manager's job a little easier. (4) However, more importantly, your best efforts work best for you. (5) You can be known as a hard worker, a problem solver, and a risk taker. (6) You, as a hard worker, are building up a list of positive references. (7) You, as a problem solver, are polishing your people skills. (8) You, as a risk taker, are learning how to be a great boss by being a great employee. (9) Ninety percent of all development occurs on the job. (10) Doing your best right now is the best preparation for the future. (11) Every job is a stepping stone to your future. (12) So do your best right now. (13) The seed for your future is sown today.

Write three simple sentences. Suggested topic: The Ideal Job.

1. ______________________________

______________________________

2. ______________________________

______________________________

3. ______________________________

______________________________

More practice with subjects, verbs, and simple sentences: <www.mywritinglab.com>

# Writing Assignments

## Writing for Everyday Life

Read the following thank-you note for a surprise birthday party. In each sentence, underline the subject once, underline the verb twice, and place parentheses around the (prepositional phrase). Use your own paper.

Dear Dave and Jennifer:

Please accept my thanks for such a wonderful surprise birthday party. I really was surprised. I was able to visit with so many people. I haven't seen most of them in a long time! Everyone loved the spicy food and cold drinks. The theme of "Mexican Nights" was perfect. Thanks, too, for the great gift. Bob, along with the children, also sends you a big thank you. We owe you one!

Thanks, again,

Beverly

## Writing for College Life

Read the following paragraph written for a psychology class. In each sentence, underline the subject once, underline the verb twice, and place parentheses around the (prepositional phrase). Use your own paper.

Natural disasters such as tsunamis and hurricanes are stressors. These stressors can affect the mental well-being of victims. Survivors of a disaster often deal with shock, fear, grief, anger, resentment, guilt, shame, helplessness, and hopelessness. They may feel emotionally numb, lose interest in daily activities, have trouble concentrating, and experience memory loss. In addition, physical symptoms such as tension, fatigue, sleeplessness, and bodily aches or pain are common. Victims may also suffer with nightmares or images from the disaster. These reactions are normal and expected.

## Writing for Working Life

Read the following email exchanged between professionals at a bank. Identify subjects, verbs, and prepositional phrases. Insert missing subjects or verbs as needed. *Hint:* Some sentences use the understood subject *you*. Use your own paper.

TO: Dwayne <Dwayne@ITsolutions.com>
FROM: Kendis Moore Kendis@ITsolutions.com
SUBJECT: Promotion

Dear Dwayne,
Please accept my congratulations for your promotion to Manager of Information Systems. You and your team will handle activities like installation and upgrading of hardware and software. In addition, you will manage programming and systems design, development of computer networks, and implementation of Internet and intranet sites. By the end of the month, please analyze the computer needs of the organization. Once again, congratulations, and feel free to call on me for assistance.

Best regards,

Kendis Moore

Supervisor of Technology

# Academic Learning Log

PORTFOLIO

### WHAT HAVE I LEARNED?

To test and track your understanding, complete the following sentences. Use several sentences as needed for each response.

**1.** A subject is ________________________________

________________________________

**2.** The three types of subjects are ________________________________

________________________________

**3.** A verb ________________________________

The three basic types of verbs are ________________________________

**4.** A simple sentence is ________________________________

________________________________

**5. How will I use what I have learned?**
In your notebook, discuss how you will apply to your own writing what you have learned about subjects and verbs.

**6. What do I still need to study about subjects and verbs?**
In your notebook, describe your ongoing study needs by describing what, when, and how you will continue studying subjects and verbs.

# 17 Compound and Complex Sentences

**Chapter Preview**

- What's the Point of Compound and Complex Sentences?
- Understanding the Point of Compound and Complex Sentences: One Student Writer's Response
- Applying the Point: Compound and Complex Sentences

A compound sentence joins together two or more independent clauses. A complex sentence combines one independent or main clause and one or more dependent clauses.

Communicating about a real-life situation helps us to understand the purpose of compound and complex sentences. The photograph on the facing page illustrates the anonymous aspects of electronic communication. Read the statements given in Practice 1, complete the activities, and answer the question "What's the point of compound and complex sentences?"

# What's the Point of Compound and Complex Sentences?



Writing from Life

Practice 1

PHOTOGRAPHIC ORGANIZER: COMPOUND AND COMPLEX SENTENCES

The following ideas are stated using four types of sentences: (1) simple, (2) compound, (3) complex, and (4) compound-complex. Discuss with a small group of peers in what ways these sentences differ from each other.

1. Cyber-bullying is the use of electronic communication to harass a person or group.
2. Social networking sites like MySpace and Bebo are booming in popularity, and incidents of cyber-bullying are on the rise.
3. Cyber-bullying, which includes sending cruel or threatening messages or images, is a willful and harmful act.
4. Cyber-bullies are often boldly aggressive and persistent because they can remain anonymous and engage in private, unsupervised messaging; therefore, they are difficult to catch and can inflict much psychological harm.

**What's the point of compound and complex sentences?**

# Understanding the Point of Compound and Complex Sentences: One Student Writer's Response

The following paragraph offers one writer's thoughts about the differences among sentence types.

> *To study the list of sentences, I underlined the subjects and verbs in each one. As I did, I noticed that the first sentence was the only one that focused on one topic. It had only one subject and verb. The rest of the sentences had two or more ideas. I also noticed that some sentences joined ideas with words like "and," "which," and "therefore." Another way the sentences differed was the use of punctuation. Some used commas, and one used a semicolon. I always struggle with commas and semicolons. I need to learn how to use them. Overall, I would say using different types of sentences will give me more ways to say what I want to say.*

For more on simple sentences, see Chapter 16.

# Applying the Point: Compound and Complex Sentences

A **clause** is a group of related words that includes a subject and a verb. Two types of clauses provide the basis of all sentences: the (1) **independent clause** and the (2) **dependent clause**.

### 1. The Independent Clause

A focused and complete thought expressed with a subject and a verb; also known as a *main clause* or **simple sentence**.

INDEPENDENT CLAUSE (COMPLETE THOUGHT)

Severe dehydration may result in shock and death.

SUBJECT VERB

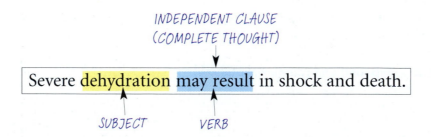

**2. The Dependent Clause**

(1) An incomplete thought expressed with a subject and verb marked by a subordinating conjunction such as *after*, *before*, or *when*.

DEPENDENT CLAUSE (INCOMPLETE THOUGHT)

before Jasmine began the triathlon

SUBORDINATING CONJUNCTION — SUBJECT — VERB

(2) An incomplete thought marked by a relative pronoun, such as *who* or *which*, acting as the subject of the verb.

RELATIVE PRONOUN (ACTING AS SUBJECT) — VERB — DEPENDENT CLAUSE (INCOMPLETE THOUGHT)

which included a three-mile run, a one-half-mile swim, and a 16-mile bike ride

Practice 2

TYPES OF CLAUSES

Identify each of the following clauses as **I** for independent or **D** for dependent. *Hint:* Circle subordinating conjunctions and relative pronouns.

........ **1.** The human body is two-thirds water.

........ **2.** When too much body fluid is lost.

........ **3.** A person who takes in too little fluid.

........ **4.** Excessive sweating, as well as vomiting and diarrhea, which can cause dehydration.

........ **5.** Sports safety requires drinking plenty of fluids before, during, and after exercising to prevent dehydration.

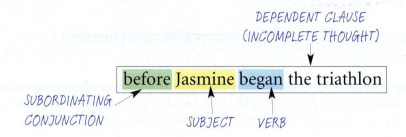

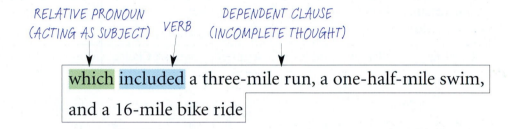

More practice with compound and complex sentences: <www.mywritinglab.com>

# A Compound Sentence

A compound sentence is made up of two or more independent clauses. A **compound sentence** links two or more independent clauses together as **equally important** ideas through one of three methods.

## Three Ways to Combine Independent Clauses into a Compound Sentence

1. **A comma and a coordinating conjunction**: The coordinating conjunction serves as a transition that shows the relationship of ideas within the sentence. Use the acronym FANBOYS to help you remember the seven coordinating conjunctions—*for*, *and*, *nor*, *but*, *or*, *yet*, or *so*

*[Independent clause,] and [independent clause.]*

| Coordinating Conjunctions (FANBOYS) and Meanings | | | | | | | |
|---|---|---|---|---|---|---|---|
| **Coordinating Conjunction** | For | And | Nor | But | Or | Yet | So |
| **Meaning** | Result | Addition | Negation | Contrast | Choice | Contrast | Result |

SUBJECT — VERB — INDEPENDENT CLAUSE — COMMA ENDS FIRST CLAUSE

Many customers pay for their gas at the pump, so
fewer customers go into the gas station's store.

SUBJECT — VERB — INDEPENDENT CLAUSE — COORDINATING CONJUNCTION COMBINES INDEPENDENT CLAUSES

2. **A semicolon, conjunctive adverb, and a comma:** The conjunction shows the relationship of ideas within the sentence. In addition, the conjunctive adverb introduces the next clause. A comma follows the conjunctive adverb since it is an introductory element of the next clause:

*[Independent clause;] therefore, [independent clause.]*

| Common Conjunctive Adverbs and the Relationships They Express | | | | | |
|---|---|---|---|---|---|
| **Addition** | **Cause or Effect** | **Comparison or Contrast** | **Example** | **Emphasis** | **Time** |
| also | accordingly | however | for example | certainly | finally |
| besides | as a result | in comparison | for instance | indeed | meanwhile |
| further | consequently | in contrast | | in fact | next |
| furthermore | hence | instead | | still | then |
| in addition | therefore | likewise | | undoubtedly | thereafter |
| incidentally | thus | nevertheless | | | |
| moreover | | nonetheless | | | |
| | | otherwise | | | |
| | | similarly | | | |

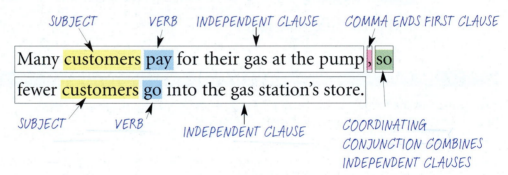

SUBJECT — VERB — INDEPENDENT CLAUSE — SEMICOLON ENDS FIRST CLAUSE

Gas Station TV embeds 20-inch HD monitors in the gas pump;
therefore, customers see news and advertisements at the gas pump.

CONJUNCTIVE ADVERB — COMMA SIGNALS INTRODUCTORY ELEMENT FOR NEXT CLAUSE — SUBJECT — VERB — INDEPENDENT CLAUSE

**3. A semicolon:** A semicolon joins two closely related independent clauses.

*[Independent clause;] [independent clause.]*

SUBJECT — INDEPENDENT CLAUSE — VERB — SEMICOLON ENDS FIRST CLAUSE

The consumer at the pump is a captive audience;
Gas Station TV shows ads of products for sale inside the gas station's convenience store.

SUBJECT — VERB — INDEPENDENT CLAUSE

## Practice 3

**COMPOUND SENTENCES**

Insert the proper punctuation in each of the following compound sentences. **Hint:** Identify the subjects and verbs. Place parentheses around (prepositional phrases); underline the subject once; underline the verb twice.

1. We need to conserve energy hence we should improve our gas mileage.
2. An idling car gets zero miles per gallon and an idling car (with a large engine) wastes a lot of gas.
3. Driving (at a constant speed) improves gas mileage therefore using cruise control saves gas.
4. (In an overdrive gear) the speed (of the car's engine) slows down the use (of the overdrive gears) saves gas and reduces engine wear.
5. Write a compound sentence. Suggested topic: Ways to Conserve Energy.

---

---

---

For more information on how to identify subjects, verbs, and prepositional phrases, see Chapter 16.

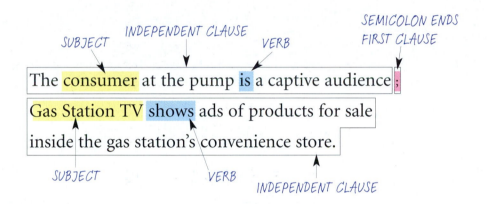

## Practice 4

**COMPOUND SENTENCES**

Create compound sentences by combining the following sets of simple sentences. Vary the ways in which you join ideas. Use appropriate conjunctions and punctuation to show the relationship between ideas within each new sentence.

**1.** Both men and women value the handiness of the Internet. They use the Internet for different purposes.

---

---

**2.** Women are more likely to go online for information about personal issues. They get maps, use email, and access information about health and religion.

---

---

**3.** Men are more likely to go online to listen to music, take a class, and use a Webcam. They check the weather and get information about news, sports, politics, jobs, and finances.

---

---

**4.** Men and women equally use the Internet for online banking and shopping. Men are more likely to pay bills, trade stocks, and bid in auctions.

---

---

**5.** Write a compound sentence. Suggested topic: Advantages of the Internet.

---

---

Adapted from Jennifer LeClaire, "Study: Men and Women Use Internet Differently." TechNewsWorld. Dec. 29, 2005.

More practice with compound and complex sentences: <www.mywritinglab.com>

# A Complex Sentence

A **complex sentence** contains one independent or main clause and one or more dependent clauses. A **dependent clause** expresses a **subordinate** or minor detail about an idea in the independent clause. A complex sentence joins independent and dependent clauses by placing a subordinating conjunction at the beginning of the dependent clause. **Subordinating conjunctions** state the relationship between the main clause and the subordinate clause.

| Subordinating Conjunctions and the Relationships They Express | | | | |
|---|---|---|---|---|
| **Cause** | **Contrast** | **Time** | **Place** | **Condition** |
| as | although | after | where | even if |
| because | as if | as | wherever | if |
| in order that | even though | as long as | | only if |
| now that | though | before | | unless |
| since | whereas | once | | when |
| so | while | since | | whether or not |
| | | until | | |
| | | when | | |
| | | whenever | | |
| | | while | | |

A subordinating conjunction always signals the beginning of a dependent clause. However, many subordinating conjunctions can also be other parts of speech.

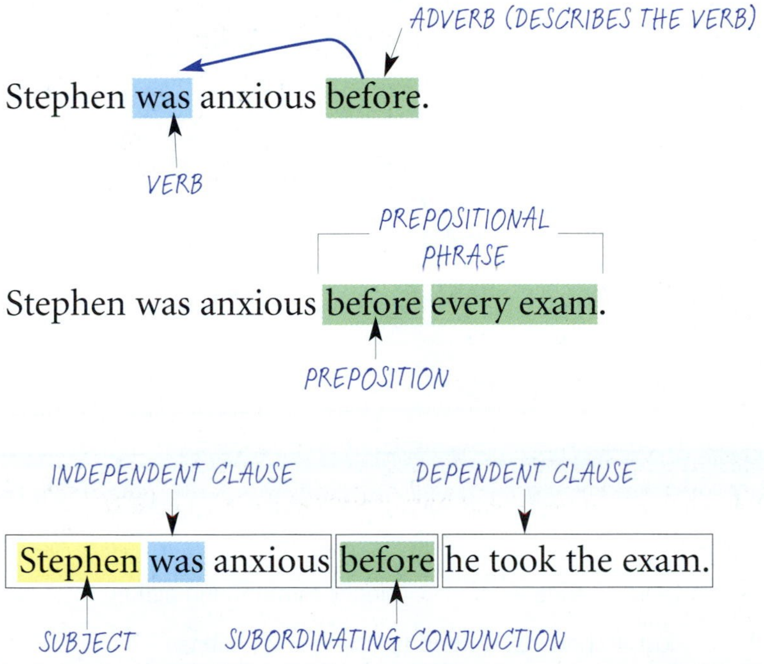


Practice 5

COMPLEX SENTENCES

Underline the dependent clauses in each sentence. In the blank after each sentence, state the relationship between the dependent clause and the main clause.

**1.** When a person wants to lose weight, he decides to exercise regularly and stick to a low-calorie diet. ____________

**2.** Jordan feels much better because he is exercising regularly and eating healthfully. ____________

**3.** Now that he has lost 25 pounds, he has more energy. ____________

## Practice 5

**4.** He now eats sensibly wherever he goes. ..................

**5.** Write a complex sentence using a subordinating conjunction. State the relationship between your dependent and main clauses. Suggested topic: Your Favorite Food.

..................................................................................................

..................................................................................................

A special kind of subordinating conjunction is the relative pronoun. A **relative pronoun** connects the dependent clause to a noun in the main clause. The choice of a relative pronoun indicates whether the dependent clause is describing a person or thing.

| Relative Pronouns and What They Indicate | | |
|---|---|---|
| **People** | **Things** | **People or Things** |
| who<br>whom<br>whose | which | that |

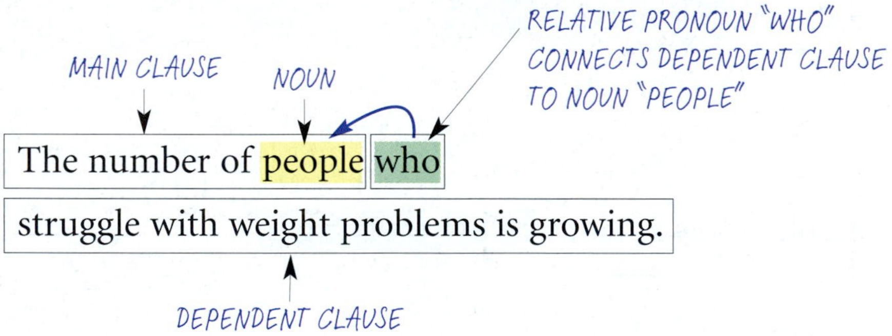


## Practice 6

COMPLEX SENTENCES

Insert the relative pronoun that best completes each sentence. Circle the nouns described by the relative pronoun.

**1.** Mindfulness refers to an attitude .................. blends thought and action.

**2.** Connor, .................. lost 40 pounds, wanted to change bad habits.

**3.** Therefore, he gave up eating hamburgers, French fries, and Coca-Cola, .................. were his favorite foods.

**4.** Instead, he ate a wide variety of foods .................. were high in vitamins and low in calories.

**5.** Write a complex sentence using a relative pronoun. Suggested topic: An Important Decision.

..................................................................................................

..................................................................................................

More practice with compound and complex sentences: <www.mywritinglab.com>

## Placement and Punctuation of a Dependent Clause within a Complex Sentence

**1. Before the main clause:** A dependent clause at the beginning of a sentence acts as an introductory element and must be set off with a comma.

*Subordinating conjunction dependent clause*, **main clause**.

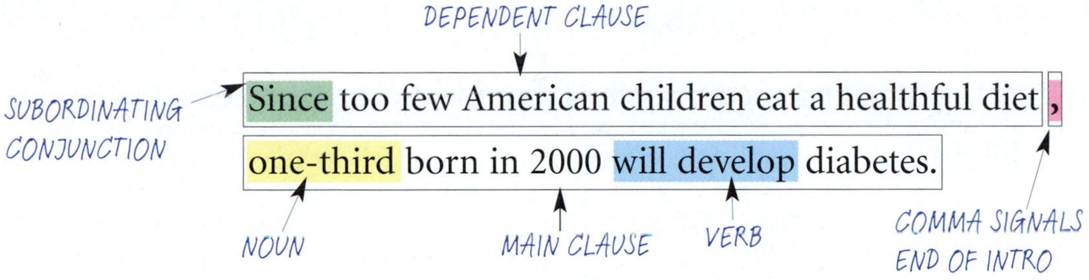


**2. In the middle of the main clause**: The context of the clause controls the use of commas. Many dependent clauses in the middle of a sentence are **relative clauses.** Relative clauses are either essential or nonessential.

(a) If the dependent clause adds information **essential** to the meaning of sentence, no commas are needed. Most often essential information limits or restricts the meaning of a common noun such as *man* or *woman*.

**Main** *relative pronoun dependent clause* **clause**.

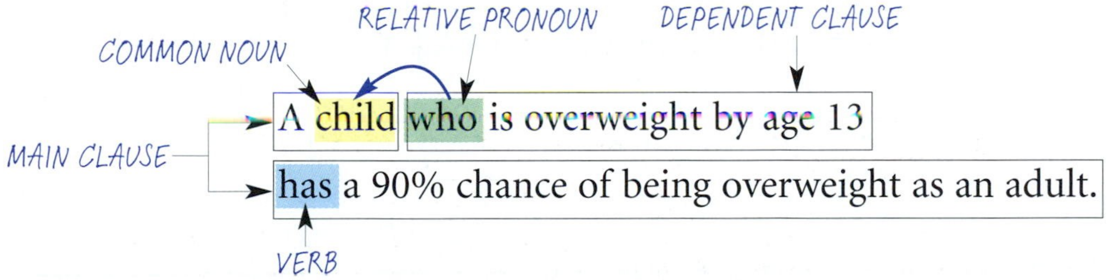


(b) If the dependent clause adds information that is **nonessential** to the meaning of the main clause, insert commas before and after the dependent clause. Usually a nonessential clause describes a proper noun.

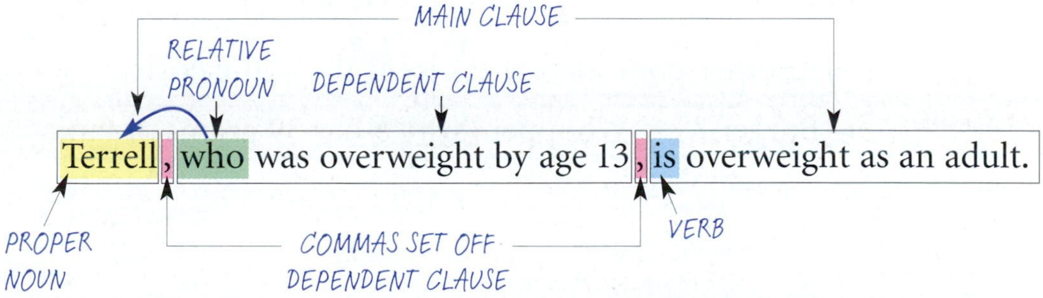

**3. After the main clause:** The context of the clause controls the use of commas in these instances:

(a) If the dependent clause begins with a **subordinating conjunction**, no comma is needed.

**Main clause** *subordinating conjunction dependent clause.*

MAIN CLAUSE · SUBJECT · VERB

A Big Mac and medium fries are poor dietary choices
because they amount to 940 calories and 50 grams of fat.

SUBORDINATING CONJUNCTION · DEPENDENT CLAUSE

(b) If the dependent clause begins with a relative pronoun, determine if the information is essential or nonessential. An **essential** dependent clause does not need a comma:

**Main clause** *dependent clause.*

MAIN CLAUSE · SUBJECT · VERB · RELATIVE PRONOUN

Taco Bell's Nachos BellGrande is a dish that has 708 calories,
44 grams of fat, and 1,300 milligrams of sodium.

ESSENTIAL DEPENDENT CLAUSE

(c) Insert a comma before a dependent clause that is **nonessential**:

**Main clause,** *relative pronoun dependent clause.*

SUBJECT · VERB

MAIN CLAUSE

Another poor dietary choice is the 690-calorie
Burger King Whopper, which has 39 grams of fat.

COMMA INTRODUCES NONESSENTIAL DEPENDENT CLAUSE · RELATIVE PRONOUN · DEPENDENT CLAUSE

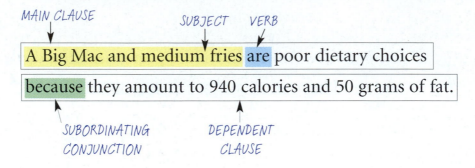

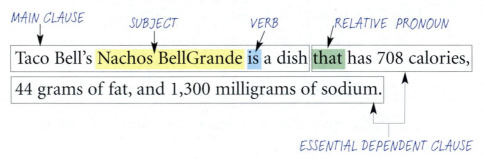

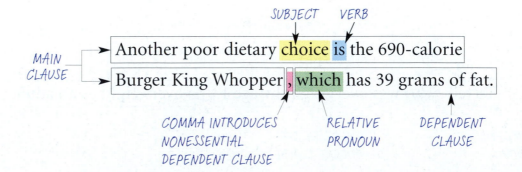

## Practice 7

COMPLEX SENTENCES

Edit each of the following complex sentences for proper punctuation. *Hint:* One sentence is already correctly punctuated.

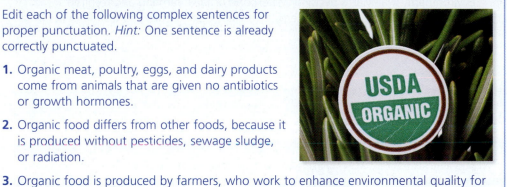

1. Organic meat, poultry, eggs, and dairy products come from animals that are given no antibiotics or growth hormones.
2. Organic food differs from other foods, because it is produced without pesticides, sewage sludge, or radiation.
3. Organic food is produced by farmers, who work to enhance environmental quality for future generations.
4. Before a product can be labeled organic, the farmer must meet USDA organic standards.
5. Write a complex sentence. Suggested topic: A Reason to Eat Organic Food.

Adapted from U.S. Department of Agriculture. "Organic Food Standards and Labels: The Facts." April 2002.

## Practice 8

COMPLEX SENTENCES

Create five complex sentences by combining the following sets of simple sentences. Use appropriate subordinating conjunctions, relative pronouns, and punctuation to show the relationship between ideas within each new sentence.

1. Wal-Mart is the nation's largest grocer. Wal-Mart offers USDA certified organic food in its nearly 4,000 stores.

2. Wal-Mart promises to offer organic food at a reasonable price. Foods like Organic Cocoa Puffs and Oreos will cost only 10 percent more than the regular kind.

3. Wal-Mart will force down the price of organic food for consumers. Many live on a tight budget and can't afford to pay the higher prices for organic foods.

4. Wal-Mart campaigns to sell organic foods. The company will educate millions of consumers about the differences between organic and conventional foods.

More practice with compound and complex sentences: <www.mywritinglab.com>

Practice 8

**5.** Wal-Mart's decision to offer organic food will have a tremendous impact on the environment. Wal-Mart's decision will expand organic farming and result in substantially less pesticide and chemical fertilizer being applied to vast amounts of land.

Adapted from Mark Pollen, "Mass Natural," *New York Times Magazine,* June 4, 2006.

## A Compound-Complex Sentence

A **compound-complex sentence** is two or more independent clauses and one or more dependent clauses. A compound-complex sentence joins coordinate and subordinate ideas into a single sentence. All the punctuation rules for both compound and complex sentences apply to the compound-complex sentence.

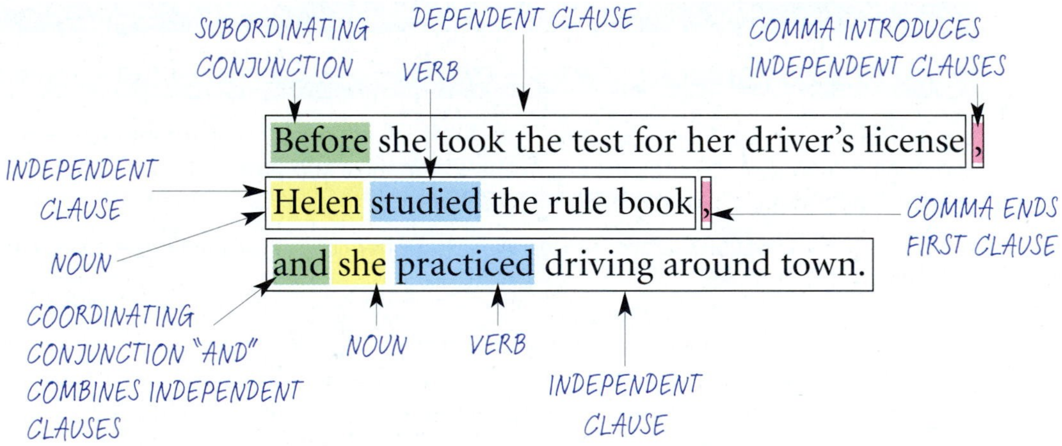


Practice 9

COMPOUND-COMPLEX SENTENCES

Create and properly punctuate four compound-complex sentences by combining the following simple sentences. Discuss your work with a classmate or with a small group of peers.

**1.** Shelly is a defensive driver. She keeps her eyes moving. She avoids a fixed stare.

**2.** Shelly was first learning to drive. Another driver ran a stop sign. Shelly's car was wrecked beyond repair.

**3.** Shelly didn't cause the accident. The accident left her with three broken ribs. She might have been able to avoid the collision.

---

---

**4.** Shelly wasn't watching the road. She was thinking about her upcoming graduation. She never saw the other car coming.

---

---

**5.** Write a compound-complex sentence. Suggested topic: Dangerous Driving Habits.

---

---

More practice with compound and complex sentences: <www.mywritinglab.com>

## Practice 10

### FOUR SENTENCE TYPES REVIEW

Write and properly punctuate four different types of sentences. Suggested topic: A Favorite Holiday.

**1.** Simple ______

---

**2.** Compound ______

---

**3.** Complex ______

---

**4.** Compound-Complex ______

---

More practice with compound and complex sentences: <www.mywritinglab.com>

# Writing Assignments

## Writing for Everyday Life

The following journal entry is from the personal diary of a person who wants to lose weight and get healthy. Edit the paragraph for correct punctuation of sentence types. Use your own paper.

Dear Diary:
Today, I am starting a new lifestyle that will include a healthful diet and regular exercise so I need to identify my current exercising and eating habits. The first is easy because I don't exercise. I will drive around a parking lot for 30 minutes looking for a close parking space and I spend way too much time in front of the television. I watch TV every night from 4:00 p.m. until bedtime which is usually 11:00 p.m. My diet consists mostly of diet sodas and fast food! I sure do have my work cut out for me.

## Writing for College Life

Read the following paragraph, written for a humanities course, about the impact of art on the viewer. The assignment asked students to react to a piece of art of their own choosing, such as a sculpture, photograph, or painting. Edit the paragraph for correct punctuation of sentence types. Use your own paper.

The powerful impact of art on a person is evident in my own response to Michelangelo's statue of David. Although I have seen only photographs of this remarkable sculpture, its beauty and balance are striking. Michelangelo who is perhaps the most gifted artists of all times captured the physical strength and grace of this Jewish hero from the Old Testament. Muscles of perfect proportion reveal David's strength a stance of action reveals his agility and a steady gaze reveals his confidence. Michelangelo's David looks like the hero who could kill a lion with his bare hands, fell a giant with one well placed stone from his sling, and establish a kingdom. I appreciate this piece of art because it captures the essence of the beauty of humanity; David seems strong yet gentle.

## Writing for Working Life

Read the following memo written from an employee to a supervisor. Edit the paragraph for correct punctuation of sentence types. Use your own paper.

To: April Gulleme, Manager
From: Ricardo Menendez
RE: Customer Complaints

As you requested, I am submitting a report that includes customer complaints and recommendations gathered from the suggestion box. Some customers complained about slow service in contrast others complained about being interrupted too often by servers while a few servers received rave reviews. Some customers complained during the week about the noisy atmosphere yet others complimented the lively entertainment on the weekends.

I recommend two actions. First, the servers who are efficient and appreciated by customers can mentor the other servers these server-trainers will be paid for their efforts. Second, we can offer and advertise different types of entertainment on different days of the week; for example, on weekends we can offer lively entertainment; on weeknights we can offer toned-down, easy-listening music.

# Academic Learning Log

PORTFOLIO

## WHAT HAVE I LEARNED?

To test and track your understanding, answer the following questions.

**1.** What is a clause, and what are the two types of clauses? ______________________

______________________________________________

______________________________________________

**2.** What is a simple sentence? ______________________

**3.** What is a compound sentence? ______________________

**4.** What is a complex sentence? ______________________

______________________________________________

**5.** What is a complex-compound sentence? ______________________

______________________________________________

**6. How will I use what I have learned?**
In your notebook, discuss how you will apply to your own writing what you have learned about sentence types. When will you apply this knowledge during the writing process?

**7. What do I still need to study about sentence types?**
In your notebook, describe your ongoing study needs by describing what, when, and how you will continue studying sentence types.

REVISING

PART 5

# Writing Clear Sentences

# 18

# Sentence Variety

## Sentence variety is the use of sentences of different lengths, types, and purposes.

### Chapter Preview



Communicating about a real-life situation helps us to understand the purpose of sentence variety. The photograph on the facing page illustrates a woman who deals with stress on a daily basis. Read the accompanying short paragraph about the woman in Practice 1, complete the activities, and answer the question "What's the point of sentence variety?"

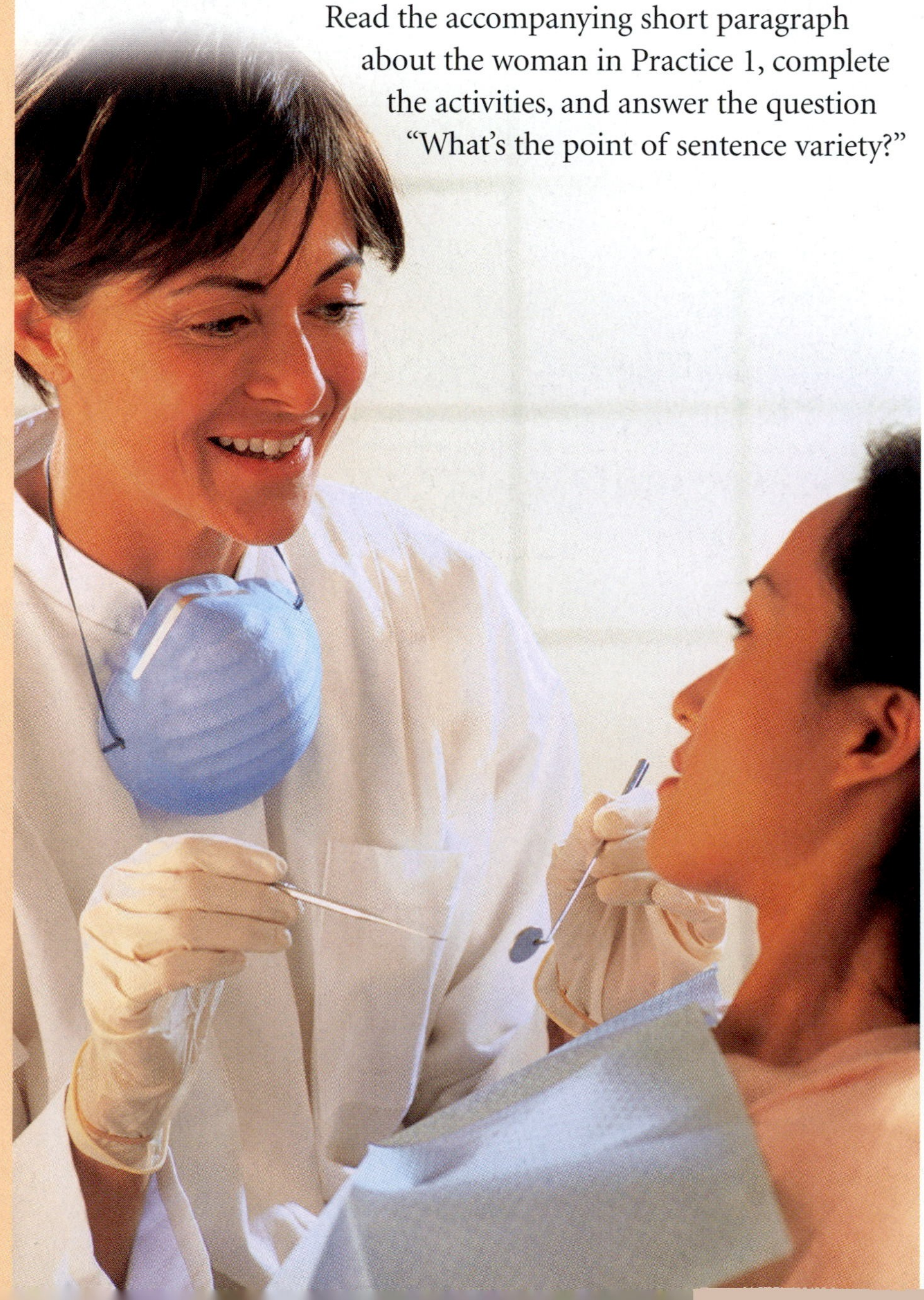

# What's the Point of Sentence Variety?

**PHOTOGRAPHIC ORGANIZER: SENTENCE VARIETY**

WRITING FROM LIFE

Practice 1

Read the following short paragraph. What do all the sentences have in common? Describe the overall effect of the paragraph.

Marla has a high-stress lifestyle. She is a single mother of a preschool child. She works as a receptionist for a dentist's office. She is going to school full time. She is training to be a dental hygienist. She is always on the go. She is learning to cope with stress.

**What is the point of sentence variety?**

---

---

---

---

---

---

## Understanding the Point of Sentence Variety: One Student Writer's Response

The following paragraph records one writer's thoughts about the point of sentence variety in the paragraph about Marla in Practice 1.

*In the paragraph about Marla and her stress, every sentence begins the same way, with her name or the pronoun "she," and four of the seven sentences use the verb "is." In addition, the sentences are all about the same length, using six to nine words, and they are all simple sentences. The paragraph seems boring and bland.*

# Applying the Point: Sentence Variety

**Sentence variety** adds interest and power to your writing. You can achieve sentence variety by varying the purposes, types, and openings of your sentences.

## Vary Sentence Purpose

Every sentence expresses a purpose.

### Four Purposes for Sentences

1. **Declarative sentences** make a statement to share information and are punctuated with a period. Declarative sentences are often used to state a main idea and supporting details.

   Carjacking has become one of the most prevalent crimes in many parts of the world.

2. **Interrogative sentences** ask a question and are punctuated with a question mark. Usually, the writer also provides an answer to the question. An interrogative sentence may be used to introduce a topic and lead into a topic sentence.

   How can you protect yourself from becoming a victim of a carjacking?

3. **Imperative sentences** give a command that demands an action and are punctuated with a period. Imperative sentences are often used to give directions to complete a process or persuade a reader to take action.

   Avoid becoming a victim of a carjacking. Follow these three steps.

4. **Exclamatory sentences** express a strong emotion and are punctuated with an exclamation point. Exclamatory sentences emphasize a significant point.

   Your life is more important than your car!

Most often, you will rely upon the declarative sentence to share information with your reader. However, thoughtful use of a question, command, or exclamation gives your writing variety and adds interest to your ideas.

Practice 2

VARY SENTENCE PURPOSE

Read the following paragraph, adapted from "Carjacking: Don't Be a Victim," an August 2003 article on the U.S. Department of State Website. Identify the purpose of each sentence.

**Don't Be a Victim**

(1) Did you know that carjackers actually devise attack plans to control a victim and steal a car? (2) Two common attack plans include the bump and the Good Samaritan. (3) In the bump, the attacker bumps the victim's vehicle from behind. (4) When the victim gets out to assess the damage and exchange information, the attacker steals the victim's vehicle. (5) In the Good Samaritan attack plan, the carjacker stages what appears to be an accident. (6) The attacker may even pretend to be injured! (7) The victim stops to assist, and the vehicle is taken. (8) If you are bumped from behind or if someone tries to alert you to a problem about your vehicle, pull over only when you reach a safe public area. (9) Don't confront the carjacker. (10) The objective is not to thwart the criminal but to survive!

Sentence 1. ____________ Sentence 6. ____________

Sentence 2. ____________ Sentence 7. ____________

Sentence 3. ____________ Sentence 8. ____________

Sentence 4. ____________ Sentence 9. ____________

Sentence 5. ____________ Sentence 10. ____________

More practice with sentence variety: <www.mywritinglab.com>

## Vary Sentence Types

You learned in Chapters 16 and 17 about the four types of sentences: simple, compound, complex, and compound-complex. When we rely on one type of sentence more than the others, our writing becomes dull and flat, like a speaker delivering a speech in a monotone. As writers combine sentences, they must decide if the combined ideas are equal in importance, or if one idea is more important than another.

**Coordinating ideas** makes each idea equal in importance. To combine coordinate ideas, use a comma and a coordinating conjunction (FANBOYS: *for, and, nor, but, or, yet,* or *so*).

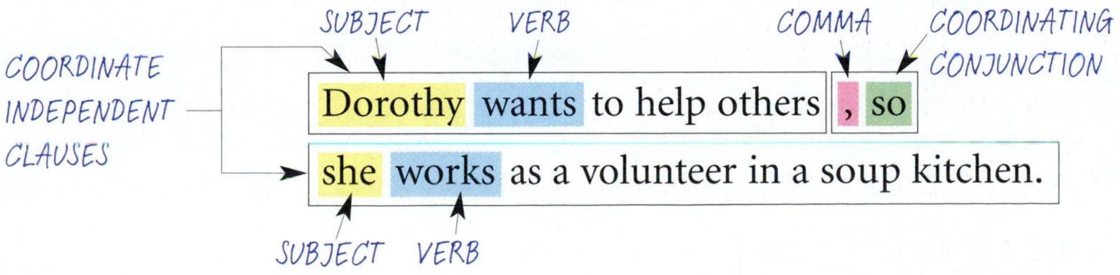

**Subordinating ideas** makes one idea dependent on (and less important than) another idea. To make an idea subordinate, use a subordinating conjunction (*although, after, as, because, before, since, unless,* etc.). If the new subordinate clause begins the sentence as an introductory element, include a comma at the end of the subordinate clause to set it off from the main independent clause.

SUBORDINATE CLAUSE
SUBORDINATING CONJUNCTION · SUBJECT · VERB · COMMA

Because Dorothy wants to help others, she works as a volunteer in a soup kitchen.

SUBJECT · VERB · INDEPENDENT CLAUSE

As you study methods of combining sentences, you will learn how to coordinate or subordinate ideas. To add interest and emphasis to your writing, vary the type of your sentences. Many writers use the revision process to combine sentences to achieve variety and interest.

## Combine Two or More Simple Sentences into One Simple Sentence

A series of short simple sentences often creates a choppy flow of ideas. Combining closely related short simple sentences into one simple sentence creates a smooth flow of ideas. Short simple sentences can be combined in several ways.

### COMBINE SENTENCES WITH A COMPOUND SUBJECT

When two separate simple sentences possess the same verb, they can become one sentence with a compound subject; a **compound subject** is two or more nouns or pronouns joined by the coordinating conjunction **and.** Note that the verb form of a compound subject must be plural. This method of coordinating ideas places equal emphasis on each subject.

For more about subject-verb agreement, see Chapter 24.

**Original Sentences:**

SUBJECT · VERB · SUBJECT · REPEATED VERB

Strength is one of three major components of fitness. Flexibility is another of three major components of fitness. Endurance is also one of the three major components of fitness.

SUBJECT · REPEATED VERB

**Sentences Combined With A Compound Subject:**

COMPOUND SUBJECTS · PLURAL VERB

Strength, flexibility, and endurance are three major components of fitness.

COMMAS IN A SERIES · COORDINATING CONJUNCTION

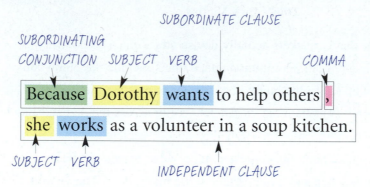

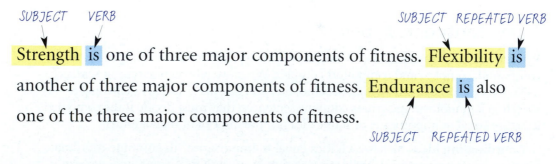

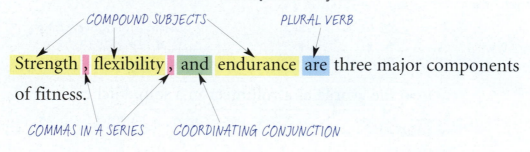

VARY SENTENCE TYPES

Practice 3

Combine the following simple sentences into a new simple sentence using compound subjects. *Hint:* Delete words or reword ideas as needed to create a smooth flow of ideas.

**1.** Isokinetic exercise contributes to strength development. In addition, isotonic exercise contributes to a person's development of strength.

**2.** Aerobic activities use oxygen, carbohydrates, and fats to produce energy. These activities also rely on proteins to produce energy.

**3.** One influence on aerobic capacity is a person's genetic makeup. Other influences are gender and body size.

**4.** Exercise intensity refers to the difficulty of the exercise session. Exercise duration refers to the length of the exercise session. Exercise frequency refers to the regularity of exercise sessions.

**5.** Write a simple sentence with a compound subject. Suggested topic: Benefits of Exercise.

More practice with sentence variety: <www.mywritinglab.com>

## COMBINE SENTENCES WITH A COMPOUND VERB

When two separate simple sentences possess the same subject, they can become one sentence with a **compound verb**, two or more verbs joined by a coordinating conjunction of addition or contrast: *and, or, but,* or *yet*. When only two verbs are joined, no comma is needed before the conjunction. This method of coordinating ideas places equal emphasis on each verb.

**Original Sentences:**

SUBJECT VERB

Face-recognition software programs take images of human faces.

The programs analyze the facial images to identify them.

REPEATED SUBJECT VERB

**Sentences Combined With A Compound Verb:**

SUBJECT COMPOUND VERBS

Face-recognition software programs take and analyze images of human faces to identify them.

COORDINATING CONJUNCTION

Practice 4

**VARY SENTENCE TYPES**

Combine the following simple sentences into a new simple sentence using compound verbs.

**1.** A face-recognition program takes a facial image from a public video camera or a database. The program measures characteristics of the face such as the distance between the eyes, the length of the nose, and the angle of the jaw.

---

---

---

---

**2.** The program creates a unique file called a *template*. The software then compares the template with a database of other images to find a match.

---

---

---

**3.** Facial recognition can be used to protect your private information. It can also be used to invade your privacy.

---

---

---

**4.** Face-recognition technology can protect your computer and cell phone files. It can verify your ATM access. It can capture your image during everyday activities without your permission.

---

---

---

---

**5.** Write a simple sentence with a compound verb. Suggested topic: The Benefits of an ATM Card.

---

---

---

More practice with sentence variety: <www.mywritinglab.com>

Practice 4

## COMBINE SENTENCES WITH A PARTICIPLE PHRASE

**Participle phrases** are used as adjectives to describe a noun or pronoun. A participle phrase is placed directly in front of the noun or pronoun it describes and is set off with a comma. This sentence combination subordinates an idea; it places less emphasis on the idea in the participle phrase.

For more about participles, see Chapter 26.

The **present participle** is the *-ing* form of a verb, such as *causing* or *biting.*

A **present participle phrase** begins with a present participle; ends with an object, a noun, or a pronoun; and indicates two actions occurring at the same time.

**Original Sentences:**

West Nile Virus [SUBJECT] can cause [VERB] severe or fatal illness. The virus [SUBJECT] spreads [VERB] through mosquito bites.

**Sentences Combined With A Present Participle Phrase:**

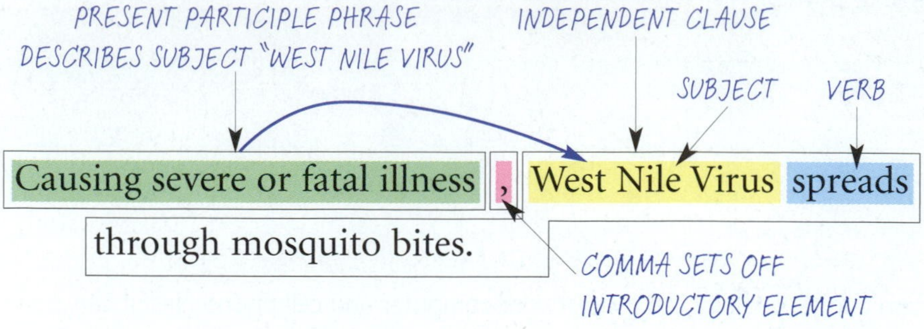


A **past participle** is the *-ed* or *-en* form of a verb, such as *talked* or *bitten*.

A **past participle phrase** begins with a past participle; ends with an object, a noun, or a pronoun; and is often created by revising a sentence with a *to be* verb and a past participle into a past participle phrase.

**Original Sentences:**

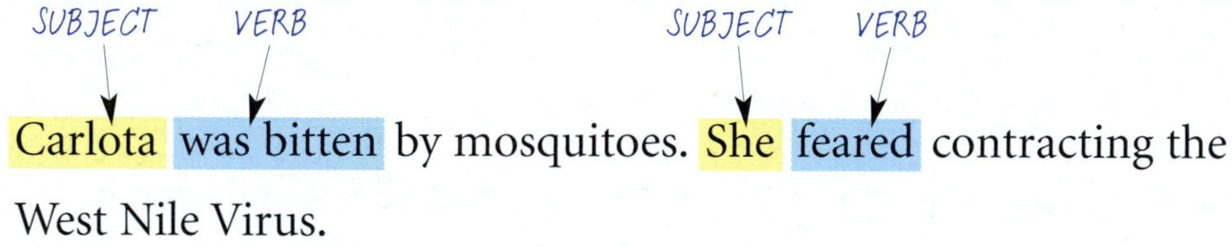

SUBJECT
VERB
SUBJECT
VERB
Carlota was bitten by mosquitoes. She feared contracting the West Nile Virus.


**Sentences Combined With A Past Participle Phrase:**

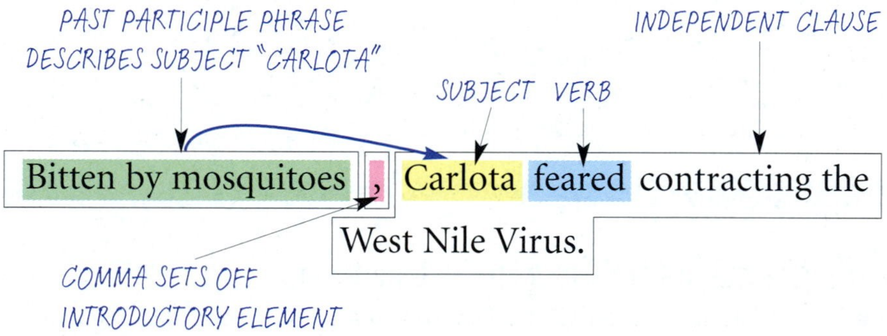


Practice 5

VARY SENTENCE TYPES

In each of the items below, combine the two given sentences into one new sentence using a present participle phrase as an introductory element. Use appropriate punctuation.

1. The West Nile Virus is a seasonal epidemic in North America. It flares up in the summer and continues into the fall.

2. West Nile fever causes symptoms such as fever, body aches, headache, and sometimes swollen lymph glands and rash. West Nile fever generally lasts only a few days.

3. West Nile Virus can develop into a serious form of the disease. West Nile encephalitis includes symptoms such as headache, high fever, neck stiffness, stupor, coma, and convulsions.

4. Kadeem wore long-sleeves, long pants, and socks when outdoors. Kadeem attempted to reduce the risk of contracting West Nile Virus.

5. Write a sentence using the present participle phrase as an introductory element. Suggested topic: Flu Medicines.

More practice with sentence variety: <www.mywritinglab.com>



Practice 5 Practice 6

VARY SENTENCE TYPES

In each of the items below, combine the two given sentences into one new sentence using a past participle phrase as an introductory element. Use appropriate punctuation.

1. DEET is intended to be applied to the skin or to clothing. It is primarily used to protect against insect bites.

2. DEET was developed by the United States Army. DEET was developed in response to the Army's experience of jungle warfare during World War II. DEET protects against tick and mosquito bites.

3. Laboratory rats were exposed to frequent and long-term use of DEET. The rats experienced serious brain cell death and behavior changes.

Practice 6

**4.** Harm to human health from DEET has not proven to be significant. DEET is the most common active ingredient in insect repellents.

---

---

**5.** Write a sentence using a past participle phrase. Suggested topic: Annoying or Dangerous Insects.

---

---

More practice with sentence variety: <www.mywritinglab.com>

### COMBINE SENTENCES WITH AN APPOSITIVE

An **appositive phrase** renames or restates a noun or pronoun. This sentence combination subordinates an idea; it places less emphasis on the idea expressed by an appositive. An appositive can appear at the beginning, middle, or end of a sentence since it appears next to the noun or pronoun it renames. The use of commas depends upon where the appositive appears.

#### Placement of Appositives and Commas

**Beginning of sentence:** An appositive at the beginning of a sentence is an introductory element. Use a comma to set off an appositive at the beginning of the sentence.

**Original Sentences:**

SUBJECT VERB

Mercedes is an executive for a consulting firm in Ohio.

Mercedes conducts background checks on applicants for a job.

REPEATED SUBJECT VERB

**Sentences Combined With An Appositive:**

APPOSITIVE PHRASE DESCRIBES SUBJECT "MERCEDES"

INDEPENDENT CLAUSE

SUBJECT VERB

An executive for a consulting firm in Ohio, Mercedes conducts background checks on applicants for a job.

COMMA SETS OFF INTRODUCTORY ELEMENT

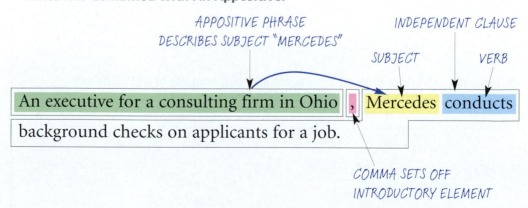

**Middle of sentence:** Use a pair of commas to set off an appositive phrase that interrupts an independent clause.

**Original Sentences:**

SUBJECT · VERB

Business managers use Google and Yahoo to conduct background checks on job applicants. Google and Yahoo are powerful search engines for the Web.

COMPOUND SUBJECT · VERB

**Sentences Combined With An Appositive:**

SUBJECT · VERB · OBJECT (COMPOUND NOUNS) · COMMAS SET OFF APPOSITIVE PHRASE

INDEPENDENT CLAUSE (INTERRUPTED BY APPOSITIVE PHRASE)

Business managers use Google and Yahoo, powerful search engines for the Web, to conduct background checks on job applicants.

APPOSITIVE PHRASE DESCRIBES OBJECT "GOOGLE AND YAHOO"

**End of sentence:** Use a comma to set off an appositive phrase at the end of a sentence.

**Original Sentences:**

SUBJECT · VERB

Students should be wary of posting personal information on Facebook. Facebook is a popular social networking site.

SUBJECT · VERB

**Sentences Combined With An Appositive:**

INDEPENDENT CLAUSE

SUBJECT · VERB

Students should be wary of posting personal information on Facebook, a popular social networking site for college students.

OBJECT (NOUN) · COMMA SETS OFF APPOSITIVE PHRASE · APPOSITIVE PHRASE DESCRIBES OBJECT "FACEBOOK"

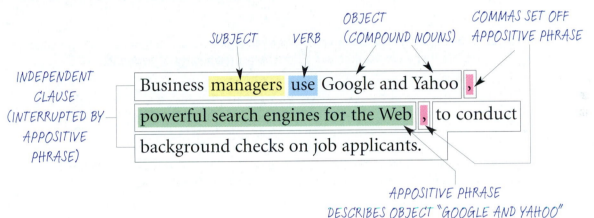

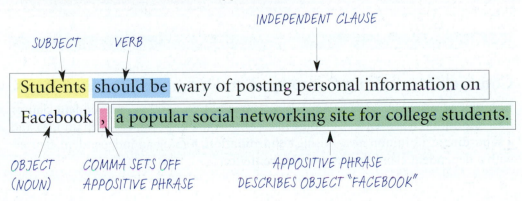

Practice 7

VARY SIMPLE SENTENCES

In each of the items below, combine the given simple sentences into one new sentence using an appositive phrase. In your answers, follow the appositive placement suggested in parentheses at the end of each item. Use appropriate punctuation.

**1.** Many students post risqué images and shocking experiences with drinking, drug use, and sexual behavior on social networking sites. Many students are foolish to risk their public reputations by posting risqué and shocking images and statements. *(beginning of sentence)*

**2.** Some students experiment with a wide range of personal behaviors. They are eager to explore their new freedom away from home. *(beginning of sentence)*

**3.** Personal behavior is a reflection of a person's judgment. The personal behavior of an employee may concern an employer. *(middle of sentence)*

**4.** An employer should not have the legal right to consider personal behavior. Personal behavior is a matter covered by the right to privacy. *(end of sentence)*

**5.** Write a sentence with an appositive phrase. Suggested topic: A Social Networking Site Such as MySpace or Facebook.

More practice with sentence variety: <www.mywritinglab.com>

## Combine Ideas Using Compound and Complex Sentence Types

For information on how to create compound and complex sentences, see Chapter 17.

Combine ideas of equal importance using **coordination**, joining independent clauses into a **compound sentence.** Combine ideas of unequal importance—a main idea and a subordinate, or minor, idea—using **subordination**, joining an independent clause with a dependent clause into a **complex sentence.**

Practice 8

VARY SIMPLE SENTENCES

Use subordination and coordination to logically combine the ideas in the ten sentences below into five sentences. Punctuate properly. (*Note:* For more help on how to create compound and complex sentences and punctuate them correctly, see Chapter 17.)

(1) As a departing employee, keep in mind you may want to return to the organization. (2) You should strive to be remembered as professional. (3) To leave a good impression, emphasize the positive experiences. (4) Don't criticize colleagues or supervisors. (5) Leaving a poor impression can lead to a poor recommendation and a series of shut doors. (6) Leaving a positive impression can result in an excellent recommendation and open options for the future. (7) Resist the urge to leave a nasty note to a boss or coworker. (8) Act as professionally on the last day as on the first. (9) For example, Randall left the firm with an excellent last impression. (10) His boss and coworkers have agreed to act as references for future jobs.

More practice with sentence variety: <www.mywritinglab.com>

## Vary Sentence Openings

Most often, we begin our sentences with the subject followed by the verb. To add interest and to shift the emphasis of an idea, you can vary the ways in which you begin a sentence. You have already worked with several types of sentence openings: participle phrases, appositives, and dependent clauses. Two additional ways to begin a sentence include using adverbs and prepositional phrases. As introductory elements in a sentence, both an adverb and a prepositional phrase are set off with a comma.

### ADVERB

- Describes or modifies another adverb, a verb, or an adjective
- Answers the questions: *How? How often? How much? When? Where?* and *Why?*
- Usually ends in *-ly: angrily, beautifully, frequently*

ADVERB — COMMA SETS OFF INTRODUCTORY ELEMENT

Patiently , Liza listened to the speaker.

**PREPOSITIONAL PHRASE**

- Begins with a preposition and ends with a noun or pronoun, the object of the preposition
- Object of the preposition describes or modifies another word in the sentence
- Common prepositions and objects: *about the yard, at the store, by the door, in the house, on the way, to the corner, with you*

PREPOSITIONAL PHRASE — COMMA SETS OFF INTRODUCTORY ELEMENT

After the lecture , Liza recopied her notes.

## Practice 9

**VARY SENTENCE OPENINGS**

Revise the openings of the sentences to vary emphasis and expression. Move the position of the adverb or prepositional phrase to the beginning of a sentence as appropriate.

**1.** Some speakers cleverly use disclaimers to deflect a negative image based on the message.

______________________________

______________________________

**2.** You may fear, for example, your audience's ridicule or rejection.

______________________________

______________________________

**3.** You may use a disclaimer in these cases to separate you from your message.

______________________________

______________________________

**4.** President Nixon defiantly left the White House with the disclaimer, "I am not a crook."

______________________________

______________________________

______________________________

______________________________

More practice with sentence variety: <www.mywritinglab.com>

Practice 9

**5.** Write a sentence that begins with an adverb or prepositional phrase. Suggested topic: A Public Person.

Adapted from Joseph A. DeVito, *Messages: Building Interpersonal Communication Skills,* 4th Ed.

## Vary Sentence Length

To add interest to your writing, vary the length of your sentences. When a writer relies too heavily on one length of sentence, the writing seems dull, flat, or uninteresting. Too many long sentences make a piece boring or confusing. Too many short sentences can seem choppy and immature. The sentence-combining techniques you have learned throughout this chapter will also help you create sentences of varying lengths.

Practice 10

VARY SENTENCE LENGTH

Revise the following paragraph written for a college humanities course. Vary the length of the sentences below by combining those thirteen sentences into six new sentences.

(1) Conversation is a five-step process. (2) The first step is the greeting. (3) The greeting can be either verbal or nonverbal. (4) The second step is feedforward. (5) Feedforward gives the other person a general idea about the topic of conversation. (6) The third step is business. (7) Business is the conversation's focus and details. (8) The fourth step is feedback. (9) Feedback is verbal and nonverbal responses from the other person. (10) Step five is the closing. (11) The closing is the goodbye. (12) The closing ends the conversation. (13) The closing can be verbal and nonverbal signals.

Adapted from Joseph A. DeVito, *Messages: Building Interpersonal Communication Skills,* 4th Ed.

# Practice 11

## SENTENCE VARIETY REVIEW

Assume you are acting as a peer editor for a classmate who wrote the following paragraph in response to a question on an exam study guide. Revise the paragraph for sentence variety by varying sentence purposes, types, openings, and lengths.

(1) There are different kinds of dietary fat. (2) Saturated fats are found in animal products such as meat, eggs, milk, and dairy products, and palm oil and coconut oil are saturated fats from plants. (3) Polyunsaturated fats are corn oil, soybean oil, and cottonseed oil, and some fish are sources of polyunsaturated fats. (4) Monounsaturated fats are found in peanut oil, olive oil, and canola oil. (5) Cholesterol is a fat-like substance. (6) The liver manufactures cholesterol, and cholesterol circulates in the bloodstream. (7) Saturated fats raise cholesterol levels, but polyunsaturated fats lower cholesterol. (8) Saturated fats are the most dangerous of the three.

Adapted from B. E. Pruitt and Jan J. Stein, *HealthStyles*, 2nd Ed.

More practice with sentence variety: <www.mywritinglab.com>

# Writing Assignments

## Writing for Everyday Life

The following letter to the editor of a local newspaper was written in protest to a city's decision to install video cameras and a face-recognition program to reduce crime. Revise the letter to create a variety of purposes, types, patterns, openings, and length of sentences. Use your own paper.

Dear Editor:

A serious violation of our rights has come to my attention. Our city has installed a face-recognition program. They say the program is to reduce crime. The cameras are an invasion of our privacy. These cameras are installed at every major intersection. The government has no right to do this. This will record our actions without our knowledge or consent. I wonder how many rights we will lose in the fight against crime and terror. City and county commissioners voted for this program. We must vote them out of office.

–Julie Q. Public

## Writing for College Life

Assume your humanities teacher has assigned a short response paper about the significance of landmarks such as Carnegie Hall. Assume you have composed the following piece of writing. Revise the draft to create a variety of purposes, types, patterns, openings, and length of sentences. Use your own paper.

*The Golden Gate Bridge stands as a symbol of human ingenuity. It was completed in 1937. It cost $35 million. The bridge spans the The Golden Gate. The Golden Gate is the strait connecting the San Francisco Bay to the Pacific Ocean. The bridge was once the longest suspension bridge in the world. It is now the second longest one. The bridge is 1.7 miles long. It is 90 feet wide. It has six lanes. The bridge is known for its beauty. Its color is an orange vermilion called International orange. The color was chosen for two reasons. It blends well with the natural environment. It is visible in fog. Lighting outlines the bridge's cables and towers. The lighting enhances the beauty of the bridge. The lights attract many visitors. This bridge is a remarkable engineering feat.*

## Writing Assignments CONTINUED

### Writing for Working Life

Jerome Offiah, a recent graduate looking for employment, knows that many employers surf the Web for information about potential employees. Jerome Offiah maintains a blog on a social networking service such as MySpace and has drafted the following posting to make a positive impression on potential employers. Revise his draft to create a variety of purposes, types, patterns, openings, and length of sentences. Use your own paper.

> I wonder if you are looking for a solid, reliable employee. I am your man. I am a recent college graduate. I majored in business and graduated with a 3.5 GPA. I can identify problems and research solutions. I collaborate with others. I bring these abilities to the workforce. I value hard work. I value being on time. I appreciate constructive criticism. I have several goals. I want to work with a large corporation. I hope to advance into management. I look forward to the opportunity to travel. I am a hard worker and a quick learner. You can count on me.

PORTFOLIO

Academic Learning Log

**WHAT HAVE I LEARNED ABOUT USING SENTENCE VARIETY?**

To test and track your understanding of sentence variety, answer the following questions.

**1.** What are the four purposes for sentences?

(a) ______________________________

(b) ______________________________

(c) ______________________________

(d) ______________________________

**2.** What are the six ways to combine simple sentences?

(a) ______________________________

(b) ______________________________

(c) ______________________________

(d) ______________________________

(e) ______________________________

(f) ______

**3.** What are five ways to vary sentence openings?

(a) ______

(b) ______

(c) ______

(d) ______

(e) ______

**4.** Why is it important to vary sentence length?

______

**5. How will I use what I have learned?**

In your notebook, discuss how you will apply to your own writing what you have learned about sentence variety. When will you apply this knowledge during the writing process?

**6. What do I still need to study about sentence types?**

In your notebook, describe your ongoing study needs by describing what, when, and how you will continue studying and using sentence variety.

Academic Learning Log

PORTFOLIO

# 19 Sentence Clarity: Point of View, Number, and Tense

**Chapter Preview**

- What's the Point of Sentence Clarity?
- Understanding the Point of Sentence Clarity: One Student Writer's Response
- Applying the Point: Sentence Clarity

Sentence clarity creates a logical flow of ideas through consistency in person, point of view, number, and tense.

Communicating about a real-life situation helps us to understand the purpose of sentence clarity. The photograph on the facing page illustrates a particular situation. Read the accompanying original and revised sentences about the situation in Practice 1, complete the activities, and answer the question "What's the point of sentence clarity?"

# What's the Point of Sentence Clarity?

Practice 1

WRITING FROM LIFE

PHOTOGRAPHIC ORGANIZER: SENTENCE CLARITY

What do you think the following sentence means? How could the sentence seem confusing to some readers?

**Original Sentence:** Jonathan and his son often walked on the beach and talk about his ups and downs in everyday life.

Is the above sentence describing a current or past event? Whose everyday life is being discussed—Jonathan's or his son's, or do they share about both their lives?

Read the revised sentence below for clarity. How is the revised sentence different from the original? Which revised words clarify the meaning of the sentence?

**Revised Sentence:** Jonathan and his son often walk on the beach and talk about the ups and downs of their everyday lives.

**What is the point of sentence clarity?**

## Understanding the Point of Sentence Clarity: One Student Writer's Response

The following paragraph offers one writer's reaction to the clarity of the sentence about the walk on the beach.

> *The first sentence doesn't make much sense because of the way the verbs and pronouns are used. The verb "talk" is in the present tense, yet the verb "walked" is in the past tense. An event can't take place in the present and past at the same time. Also, the use of the pronoun "his" is very confusing. Do they only talk about one person? Then which one? In the revised sentence, the verbs match in time, and the pronoun "their" refers to both people. The revised sentence also changed "life" to "lives" to match "their."*

# Applying the Point: Sentence Clarity

**Sentence clarity** is the precise choice of the form and arrangement of words and groups of words within a sentence. A clearly stated sentence is consistent in person, point of view, number, and tense. As a result, sentence clarity creates a coherent flow of ideas within and among sentences. Often, sentence and paragraph clarity emerge during the revision process. As you study the sentence clarity techniques in this chapter, revise pieces of your own writing and peer edit for a classmate. Apply and track what you are learning as you go.

## Use Consistent Person and Point of View

The term **person** refers to the use of pronouns to identify the difference between the writer or speaker, the one being written or spoken to, and the one being written about or spoken of. **Point of view** is the position from which something is considered, evaluated, or discussed; point of view is identified as first person, second person, or third person. Person and point of view also communicate tone.

### Three Points of View

| Person | Traits | Pronouns |
|---|---|---|
| **First Person** | The writer or speaker; informal, conversational tone | singular: *I, me*<br>plural: *we, our* |
| **Second Person** | The one being written or spoken to; can remain unstated; informal, conversational tone | singular: *you*<br>plural: *you* |
| **Third Person** | The one being written about or spoken of; formal, academic tone | singular: *he, she, it, one*<br>plural: *they* |

## Illogical Shift in Person

For more information about subject-verb agreement, see Chapter 24.

An abrupt or **unnecessary shift in person or point of view** causes a break in the logical flow of ideas. The key is to use the same phrasing throughout a paragraph. When you revise for consistency, remember that the number of the verb may need to change as well. (More information on correcting illogical shifts in number appears on page 399 in this chapter.)

**Illogical Shift In Person:**

THIRD PERSON

Everyone wants to improve gas mileage no matter what type of vehicle you drive.

SECOND PERSON

**Revisions:**

THIRD PERSON

Everyone wants to improve gas mileage no matter what type of vehicle he or she drives.

PRONOUN AND VERB AGREE IN NUMBER

PRONOUN AND VERB AGREE IN NUMBER

You want to improve gas mileage no matter what type of vehicle you drive.

SECOND PERSON

"–S" IN VERB DELETED

### CONSISTENT PERSON AND POINT OF VIEW

Practice 2

Edit the following statements to ensure consistent use of person in each sentence. Change verbs as necessary to agree with their subjects.

**1.** Garlic may be just what a person needs to reduce your risk of developing a cold, the flu, or cancer.

**2.** Thinking one is adding a healthy ingredient, you may choose to peel, chop, mash, ground, and cook garlic in your recipe.

**3.** People benefit most from eating one to five fresh cloves as a regular part of our daily diets.

**4.** If one is prone to high blood pressure, blood clots, and high cholesterol, you might include fresh garlic in your diet.

**5.** When you eat that much fresh garlic, one may develop both bad breath and body odor.

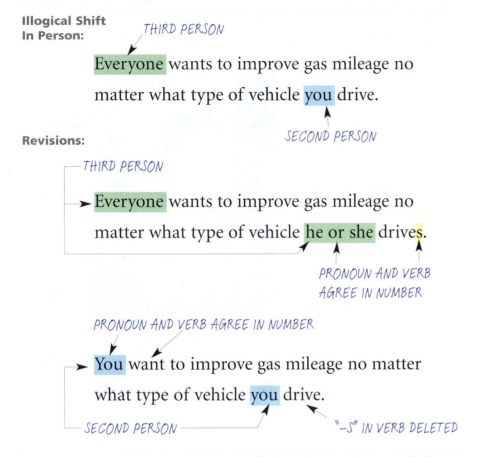

# Practice 5

## CONSISTENT NUMBER

Revise the following paragraph to change the point of view from first person to second person. Change nouns, pronouns, and verbs as needed for consistency in point of view and number.

### Recycling for the Greater Good

(1) Every day, each one of us, as American consumers, contributes 4.4 pounds of garbage to our landfills. (2) I follow three simple steps to reduce solid waste. (3) First, I reduce the amount of garbage I will generate. (4) I buy the largest practical size package possible. (5) By doing so, I get more product with less packaging. (6) Second, I reuse products and packaging whenever possible. (7) For example, I reuse boxes, bags, tins, jars, and plastic containers. (8) I also donate unwanted clothing, appliances, and furniture to charities, and I use canvas bags to tote my groceries home from the store. (9) Finally, I recycle aluminum cans, newspapers, magazines, phone books, cereal boxes, paper towels, egg cartons, carpeting, motor oil, trash bags, and plastic containers. (10) Every day, I make a choice to make a difference.

More practice with sentence clarity: <www.mywritinglab.com>

## Use Consistent Tense

**Consistent tense** expresses the logical sequence of events or existence. Verb *tense* expresses the time or duration of an action or state of being. Primary tenses include three timeframes: The **past** *was*; the **present** *is*; the **future** *will be.* The following chart outlines several hints to achieve sentence clarity through consistent tense.

| For Consistent Tense |
|---|
| **1. Use the same verb tense for each action or state occurring within the same timeframe.**<br>**Past Tense**: Monica graduated from college and began searching for a job.<br>**Present Tense**: Monica graduates from college and begins searching for a job.<br>**Future Tense**: Monica will graduate from college and begin searching for a job. |
| **2. Change tense to indicate a logical movement in timeframe from one action or state to another.**<br>**Past to Present Tense**: Stephen, who changed careers, currently works as an insurance adjuster for Allstate.<br>**Present to Future Tense**: Although Stephen currently holds an entry level position, he will advance into a management position. |
| **3. Choose and remain in one primary tense to express your points.**<br>**Past tense expresses completed action**:<br>Monica sat attentively, made direct eye contact, and spoke with confidence. She understood the importance of making a good first impression, so she listened carefully to each question and offered thoughtful responses.<br>**Present tense expresses the immediacy of a current event**:<br>Monica sits attentively, makes direct eye contact, and speaks with confidence. She understands the importance of making a good first impression. So she listens carefully to each question and offers thoughtful responses. |

### Illogical Shift in Tense

Abruptly changing from one verb tense to another without a logical reason, also called an **illogical shift in tense**, breaks the logical flow of ideas and causes confusion.

**Illogical Shift In Tense:**

PRESENT TENSE

Monica does not rely solely on the classifieds to find a job; she followed other leads.

PAST TENSE

**Revisions:**

PRESENT TENSE

Monica does not rely solely on the classifieds to find a job; she follows other leads.

PRESENT TENSE

PAST TENSE

Monica did not rely solely on the classifieds to find a job; she followed other leads.

PAST TENSE

## Practice 6

CONSISTENT TENSE

Edit the following essay to ensure consistency in tense.

### The Winning Interview

(1) The best jobs go to the candidates with the best interviewing skills. (2) Preparing for a job interview is essential to a successful interview. (3) If you were facing a job interview, consider the following tips. (4) Before the interview, study yourself and the job. (5) First, study your own strengths and weaknesses; be prepared to address both. (6) Second, study the job description and list five reasons you were best qualified for the job. (7) Third, study the company, its products, and its services. (8) During the interview, look and act like you were interested. (9) First, dress professionally. (10) Second, be positive so you showed enthusiasm for the job. (11) Finally, at the end of the interview, ask questions focused on the job and its responsibilities.

## Practice 7

CONSISTENT TENSE

Many pieces of writing move logically and effectively from past to present tense. Edit the following essay to ensure consistency in tense based on the logical movement of time.

### One Successful Man!

(1) Bill Gates is considered by many to be one of the most successful and generous businessmen alive. (2) Married to Melinda Gates, father to three children, and co-founder of Microsoft, this billionaire sees the widening gap between the rich and the poor as a moral challenge, so he and his wife were dedicating their lives and fortune to helping others.

(3) Currently, Microsoft employs over 60,000 workers in 102 countries and regions around the world. (4) Bill Gates' generosity equaled his business success. (5) In 2000, Gates and his wife Melinda establishes the Bill & Melinda Gates Foundation. (6) Their foundation is dedicated to "reducing poverty inequities in the United States and around the world," according to the foundation's website. (7) Thus, the foundation's $30.6 billion assets were used to improve the quality of technology, education, and health across the globe. (8) Their generosity found a kindred spirit in billionaire investor Warren Buffett. (9) In 2006, Buffett donated an additional $31 billion to the Gates Foundation. (10) In that same year, Gates announce his decision to resign from Microsoft and work full time with the foundation. (11) Bill Gates was indeed a most successful and generous man.

Practice 7 Practice 8

CONSISTENT TENSE

Revise the following paragraph from past tense to consistent use of present tense.

An Occupational Therapist

(1) After she passed a national certification exam, Jamie entered the health care field as an occupational therapist with a bachelor's degree. (2) She wanted to help people improve their abilities to perform tasks in their daily living and working environments. (3) She worked with individuals who had conditions that were mentally, physically, developmentally, or emotionally disabling. (4) She also helped them to develop, recover, or maintain daily living and work skills. (5) Her clients included a wide variety of people: school age children with Attention Deficit Disorder, injured workers, and the elderly. (6) She developed treatment plans, directed activity programs, supervised assistants, and documented the progress of treatments. (7) She earned around $54,000 annually.

Practice 8

Practice 9

CONSISTENT TENSE

Revise the following paragraph from present tense to consistent use of past tense.

### A Court Reporter

(1) Many members of an upscale Northeastern community are scammed by a thief running a Ponzi scheme. (2) This scheme takes money from new investors to pay returns to existing investors. (3) In preparation for trial, investigators set up a series of meetings with the victims. (4) Alfonzo Diaz, a court reporter, creates a verbatim transcript of the meetings. (5) The exact spoken words are crucial to the case. (6) As the court reporter, Diaz establishes a complete, accurate, and secure legal record, using the voice-writing method. (7) He speaks directly into a voice silencer—a hand-held mask containing a microphone. (8) He records everything that is said, including gestures and emotional reactions. (9) In addition, Diaz, like many other court reporters, also provides closed-captioning services to the one deaf victim. (10) Diaz earns $42,000 per year.

More practice with sentence clarity: <www.mywritinglab.com>.

Practice 9 Practice 10

SENTENCE CLARITY REVIEW

Revise the following student paragraph for consistent use of point of view, number, and tense.

(1) It is 5:00 p.m. on a Friday, and the commuters in town are in his car driving home from work. (2) As always, someone is driving carelessly, taking risks they know they are not suppose to take, such as speeding or cutting sharply in front of other drivers. (3) Careless drivers rarely think about why he or she drives so recklessly. (4) One major cause of careless driving is the driver's emotions. (5) Any kind of emotion can take your mind off the road. (6) For example, last Saturday, a teenage boy is so excited and happy about winning a football game that he raced home at high speeds, nearly sideswiping another car on the way. (7) Another emotion that causes careless driving is anger. (8) When people have heated arguments while driving, for example, sometimes you release the adrenaline running through your body by driving aggressively. (9) You rode the bumpers of other cars and swerved in and out of lanes to pass slower drivers. (10) Emotion, whether positive or negative, is a major cause of careless driving.

# Writing Assignments

## Writing for Everyday Life

Revise the following short article, written for a neighborhood newsletter, for sentence clarity. Use your own paper.

**Attention All Residents:** We are going green!
As a community, we have taken several steps to help the environment. First, last week, the neighborhood begins a recycling program. Everyone receives three blue plastic storage bins for their plastic, aluminum, and glass garbage. On Tuesday of each week, put your recycling bins at their curbs for the 9:00 a.m. pick up. Second, watering restrictions will begin next week. Residents can water your yards or wash their cars only on Tuesday, Thursday, and Sunday after 5:00 p.m. or before 8:00 a.m. Finally, to save gas car pooling for around town errands are available every morning between 9:00 a.m. and noon. Everyone can make a difference! Go green!

## Writing for College Life

Edit the following paragraphs, written in response to a short essay question on a history exam, for sentence clarity. Use your own paper.

**Test Question:** What were the differences between Native American and European combat styles?

**Student Answer:** Indians conducted warfare very differently from Europeans. Your weapons included bows and arrows, knives, tomahawks, spears, and clubs. War parties do not attack in battle formations but use the forest as their cover and ambushed enemies in guerrilla-like raids. Thus, you did not stand and fight in a "civilized" fashion. Rather "they were always running and traversing from one place to another," complained de Soto. The tactic made it impossible to shoot you. In addition, a skilled Indian archer easily fires off "three or four arrows" with great accuracy by the time musketeers prepared his awkward weapon for firing. The bowmanship of the Native Americans made combat with him very dangerous because, as de Soto stated, an Indian bowman "seldom misses what he shoots at."

In contrast, Europeans were trained to fight on open fields, during fair weather, and in the daylight hours. Strictly disciplined, European soldiers marched in step and fight in formation. Officers march at the head of the column. At first they used matchlock muskets, which proved to be awkward, inaccurate, and unreliable. So Europeans resorted to "total war." For example in one battle, you encircled the village, set fire to the wigwams, and shoot all escaping Indians. Eventually, the lighter and more accurate flintlock rifle replaced your muskets, yet the total war tactic continued.

# Writing Assignments CONTINUED

## Writing for Working Life

Edit the following cover letter for a job to ensure sentence clarity. Use your own paper.

Pete Kramer
200 North Gravel Lane
Murphyville, Georgia 32345
204-573-2345
pkramer@aol.com

March 30, 2007

Ms. Sara Livermore
Director of Human Resources
Livermore Construction
43231 Hightower Road, Suite 300
Jacksonville, Florida 54323

Dear Ms. Livermore:

My teacher, Mr. Connors, told me that you were looking for an electrician's apprentice at your firm, Livermore Construction. I have just finished an intensive 16-week training program. I learn all the parts of the electrician's trade and also pass the test for the Electrical Workers Union Apprentice Certificate. I'm very interested in working for an innovative company that support young people by partnering with the Smokey Mountain Job Corps Center.

I noticed in your advertisements that you includes CAT 5 wiring in all the houses you builds. During the last five weeks of my training, I help install CAT 5 wiring in a local school. My teachers say that I learn new techniques quickly and that I am very responsible and reliable. Once you begin working, you should keep up with training, so once I begin working, I plan on continuing my education at the Jacksonville Community College. I know you are looking for employees who learn quickly, work independently, and constantly improve their skills.

I will be attending a vocational competition in Jacksonville with my teacher Mr. Connors from April 15 to April 19. If it was convenient I would like to visit Livermore Construction and talks with you about the possibility of employment. I will call you next week to schedule a time. My resume is enclosed. If you have any questions regarding my qualifications or my schedule, please call me.

With confidence,
Pete Kramer
enc.

—Adapted from the Job Corps Wheel of Career Opportunity Website at <JCStudent.org>, U.S. Department of Labor

PORTFOLIO

# Academic Learning Log

**WHAT HAVE I LEARNED ABOUT SENTENCE CLARITY?**

To test and track your understanding of sentence clarity, answer the following questions. Use several sentences as needed for each response.

1. What is sentence clarity? ..............................

..............................

2. What are three techniques used to achieve sentence clarity?

   (a) .............................. ,

   (b) .............................. , and

   (c) .............................. .

3. **How will I use what I have learned?** In your notebook, discuss how you will apply to your own writing what you have learned about sentence clarity. When will you apply this knowledge during the writing process?

4. **What do I still need to study about sentence types?** In your notebook, describe your ongoing study needs by describing what, when, and how you will continue studying and using sentence clarity.

REVISING

# 20

## Chapter Preview

- What's the Point of Parallelism?
- Understanding the Point of Parallelism: One Student Writer's Response
- Applying the Point: Parallelism

# Parallelism

Parallelism is the expression of equal ideas—similar words, phrases, or clauses—in a sentence in the same, matching grammatical form.

Memorable quotations can help us to understand the purpose of parallelism. The photographs on the next page represent well-known public figures who made powerful statements. Read the quotations, complete the activities, and answer the question "What's the point of parallelism?"

"We shall fight on the beaches, we shall fight on the landing grounds, we shall fight in the fields and in the streets, we shall fight in the hills; we shall never surrender."

—WINSTON CHURCHILL

# What's the Point of Parallelism?

Practice 1

WRITING FROM LIFE

PHOTOGRAPHIC ORGANIZER: PARALLELISM

Each of the following well-known quotations uses parallelism to make an idea memorable and powerful. What do these statements have in common?

"I came; I saw; I conquered."

–JULIUS CAESAR

"We have nothing to fear but fear itself."

—FRANKLIN D. ROOSEVELT

"Scratch a lover; find a foe."

—DOROTHY PARKER

**What is the point of parallelism?**

# Understanding the Point of Parallelism: One Student Writer's Response

The following paragraph records one writer's definition of parallelism based on the traits of the example quotations.

> The sentences have a few things in common. Each one repeats words or similar types of words. For example, the quote "I came; I saw; I conquered" uses three short simple sentences; they repeat the subject "I" and use the same kind of verb. This quote shows a chain of actions. "Scratch a lover; find a foe" has two short sentences, and both begin with a verb. "Nothing to fear but fear" repeats a word. So I think parallelism repeats the same kind of words, phrases, and sentences. Parallelism is kind of musical. It's got rhythm.

# Applying the Point: Parallelism

**Parallelism** refers to the balance of equal ideas expressed in the same grammatical form. Parallel expressions bring clarity, interest, and power to a piece of writing. You can achieve parallelism by emphasizing equal ideas using similar structures and patterns of words, phrases, or clauses. You can also use certain types of conjunctions and punctuation to signal parallel structures.

## Parallel Words

Parallel structure uses a pair or series of closely related compound words to emphasize a point. Parallel words often, but not always, use similar **suffixes** (word endings).

- Parallel Words

**Nonparallel:**

NOUN — predators; ADJECTIVE — wandering

Prehistoric Paleo-Indians were predators and wandering.

**Revised for Parallelism:**

PARALLEL NOUNS — predators, wanderers

Prehistoric Paleo-Indians were predators and wanderers.

**Nonparallel:**

ADVERB — skillfully; PREPOSITIONAL PHRASE — with diligence

Paleo-Indians skillfully hunted game and with diligence gathered berries.

**Revised for Parallelism:**

PARALLEL ADVERBS — skillfully, diligently

Paleo-Indians skillfully hunted game and diligently gathered berries.

**Nonparallel:**

NONPARALLEL VERBS

They flaked and crafting flint into spears.

**Revised for Parallelism:**

PARALLEL VERBS

They flaked and crafted flint into spears.

Practice 2

PARALLEL WORDS

Revise the following sentences to achieve emphasis through parallel words.

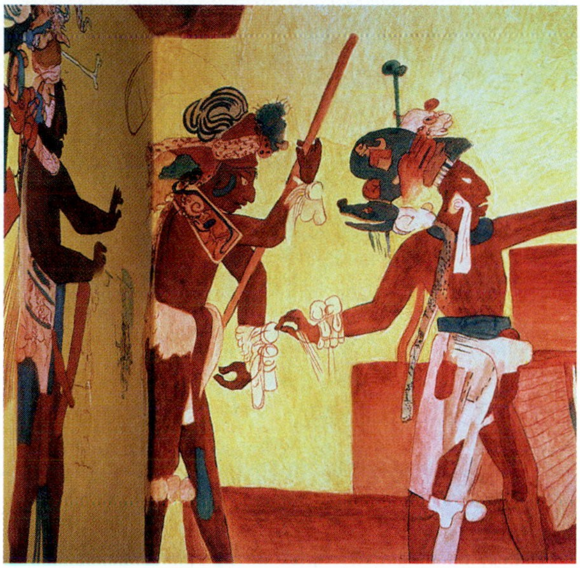

1. The Mayas of Mexico civilization produced abundant crops, building elaborate cities and temples, and crafted jewelry out of precious metals.

2. Powerfully nobles and priests ruled over ordinary inhabitants in the strict Maya social order.

3. The Mayas lacked a central government and thus suffering a civil war that allowed invaders to conquer them.

4. Write a sentence that uses parallel words. Suggested topic: An Interesting Historical Fact.

## Parallel Phrases

Parallel structure uses a pair or series of closely related compound phrases to emphasize a point. Parallel phrases repeat similar word patterns or groups.

- **Parallel Phrases**

**Nonparallel:**

INFINITIVE PHRASE — GERUND PHRASE

The Mayas learned to build cities, jewelry crafting, and to develop trade, around A.D. 300.

INFINITIVE PHRASE

**Revised for Parallelism:**

PARALLEL INFINITIVE PHRASES

The Mayas learned to build cities, to craft jewelry, and to develop trade, around A.D. 300.

**Nonparallel:**

PRESENT PARTICIPLE PHRASE — PAST PARTICIPLE PHRASES

Planting the seeds, weeded the crops, and reaped the harvest, Maya women worked hard.

**Revised for Parallelism:**

PARALLEL PRESENT PARTICIPLE PHRASES

Planting the seeds, weeding the crops, and reaping the harvest, Maya women worked hard.

**Nonparallel:**

WORD (NOUN) — PHRASE (NOUN)

Architecture and building a system of roads were two major accomplishments of the Incas.

**Revised for Parallelism:**

PARALLEL NOUN PHRASES

Developing a style of architecture and building a system of roads were two major accomplishments of the Incas.

Practice 3

PARALLEL PHRASES

Revise the following sentences to achieve emphasis through parallel phrases.

1. Between 1200 and 1535 A.D., the Inca population lived in the part of South America extending from the Equator and ended at Chile's Pacific coast.

2. To see their enemies and in self defense, they built enormous fortresses on top of steep mountains, such as the famous Sacasahuman, located in Cuzco, the Inca Empire capital.

3. Incas erected temples made of stone blocks, each weighing several tons and fitted precisely and tightly together.

4. Write a sentence that uses parallel phrases. Suggested topic: An Amazing Achievement.

Adapted from "Inca," EMuseum@Minnesota State University, Mankato, 2003

More practice with parallelism: <www.mywritinglab.com>

## Parallel Clauses

Parallel structure uses a set of closely related clauses to emphasize a point. Parallel structure begins with a clause and continues with clauses to create a balanced, logical statement. Parallel structure establishes a pattern of similarly structured clauses to express closely related ideas. Use parallel words and phrases within clauses.

For more information on sentence types and sentence elements, see Chapter 16, "Subjects, Verbs, and Simple Sentences," and Chapter 17, "Compound and Complex Sentences."

- **Parallel Clauses**

**Nonparallel:**

INDEPENDENT CLAUSE

Only a few million people inhabited the Americas by 1490, yet roughly 75 million people who were living in Europe.

DEPENDENT CLAUSE (ILLOGICAL MIXED STRUCTURE)

**Revised for Parallelism:**

PARALLEL INDEPENDENT CLAUSES

Only a few million people inhabited the Americas by 1490, yet roughly 75 million people inhabited Europe.

**Nonparallel:**

DEPENDENT CLAUSE

Myth teaches that Europeans discovered an uninhabited America; in history, Native peoples inhabited a cultivated, civilized America.

INDEPENDENT CLAUSE

**Revised for Parallelism:**

PARALLEL INDEPENDENT CLAUSES

Myth teaches that Europeans discovered an uninhabited America; history teaches that Native peoples inhabited a cultivated, civilized America.

PARALLEL DEPENDENT CLAUSES

## Practice 4

### PARALLEL CLAUSES

Revise the following sentences to achieve emphasis through parallel clauses.

1. Over several centuries, Native Americans developed as many as 2200 different languages, in addition, establishing small groups in which family formed into clans and clans into tribes.

2. Native Americans sought to manage and preserve natural resources in contrast to Europeans who sought to civilize and control a wild land.

3. When Native Americans planted their crops, they planted around trees, stumps, and rocks; Europeans completely cleared the land so it could be plowed.

4. Write a sentence that uses parallel clauses. Suggested topic: Native American Indians.

More practice with parallelism: <www.mywritinglab.com>

Native American Snake Mound ▼

## Punctuation for Parallelism

The comma and the semicolon (sometimes along with coordinating conjunctions), and numbered, lettered, or bulleted items in a list signal ideas of equal importance. Ideas marked by these pieces of punctuation are best expressed with parallelism.

> **Coordinating conjunctions** always signal an equal relationship among words, phrases, and clauses. Use commas between parallel items in a series. Use a comma with a coordinating conjunction to join independent clauses.

**Examples**

COMMAS

To build a relationship, do not criticize, condemn, or complain.

PARALLEL WORDS (VERBS)

COORDINATING CONJUNCTION

PARALLEL GERUND PHRASES (NOUNS: SUBJECTS)

Reacting calmly, listening carefully, and speaking thoughtfully can defuse disagreements.

COMMAS COORDINATING CONJUNCTION

PARALLEL INDEPENDENT CLAUSES

Criticism makes others resentful, yet praise makes others joyful.

COMMA COORDINATING CONJUNCTION

**Semicolons** signal two or more closely related independent clauses.

SEMICOLON

Immediacy is the union between people; it is the creation of oneness; it is the communication of interest.

PARALLEL INDEPENDENT CLAUSES SEMICOLON

**Numbers, letters, or bullets** signal items in a list. Lists are often used in résumés, business letters, and presentations. Note that colons can introduce a list, and semicolons can separate items.

NUMBERS SIGNALING LIST ITEMS COLON

SEMICOLON

Training session suggestions include the following: (1) expressing interest in the customers; (2) using the names of customers; and (3) meeting the needs of the customer.

PARALLEL ITEMS IN A LIST

SEMICOLON

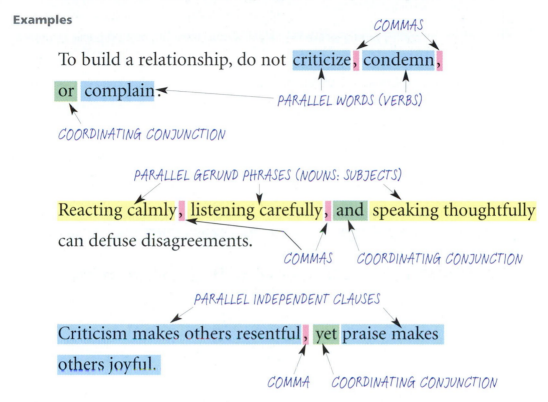

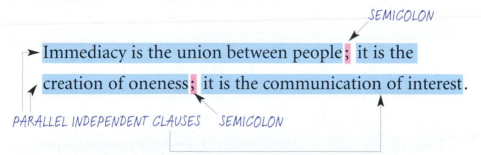

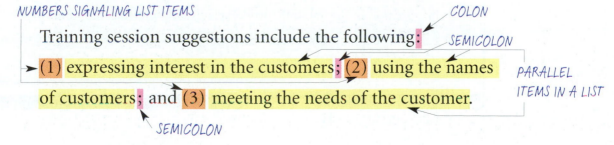

## Practice 5

### PARALLELISM

Edit the following sentences for proper use of punctuation for parallel expression.

1. Space is an important factor in communication; for example three types of distances include personal social and public distances.
2. Personal distance ranges from 18 inches to about 4 feet social distance ranges from 4 to 12 feet public distance ranges from 12 to more than 25 feet.
3. People interact in three types of territories: (1) primary territories like a bedroom or office; secondary territories like the cafeteria or a classroom seat (3) public territories like a restaurant or shopping mall.
4. Write a sentence using parallelism. Suggested topic: The Media and Personal Space.

---

---

---

Adapted from Joseph A. DeVito, *Messages: Building Interpersonal Communication Skills,* 4th Ed.

More practice with parallelism: <www.mywritinglab.com>

## Practice 6

### PARALLELISM REVIEW

Edit and revise the following paragraph for parallel expression and proper punctuation of parallel expressions..

**Interpersonal Silence**

(1) In the U.S. legal system, you have the right to remain silent and refusing to incriminate yourself. (2) But you don't have the right to refuse revealing information about the criminal activities of others; you must reveal details of a crime you have witnessed. (3) Rightly or wrong, psychiatrists and lawyers are often exempt from this general rule. (4) A wife can refuse to testify against her husband a husband can refuse to testify against his wife. (5) In interpersonal situations, however, there aren't any written rules; therefore, it's not always clear whether silence is ethical or improper withholding information. (6) For example, most people would agree that you have the right to withhold information that has no bearing on the matter at hand. (7) Private information irrelevant to the workplace usually includes the following: personal relationships sexual orientation or religion.

# Writing Assignments

## Writing for Everyday Life

Assume you are putting together a cookbook of your grandmother's favorite recipes to reproduce and give as gifts to family members. Edit the following recipe for parallel expression. Use your own paper.

Chocolate Fudge Square Cake

Cake Batter for Cake:
1 stick of margarine
2 Tbsp. of cocoa
3/4 cup of flour
1 cup of chopped nuts
Mini marshmallows
2 eggs

Cake Icing:
2 Tbsp. of cocoa
2 Tbsp. of melted margarine
2 cups of confectioner sugar
mixed with 2 Tbsp. or more milk

Beat margarine and cocoa. Adding unbeaten eggs one at a time. Add sugar, flour, and salt. Stir in nuts. Poured into greased 7 x 11 inch pan. Bake at 350° for 25 to 30 minutes. Removing from oven. Cover with scant layer of marshmallows and returning to oven until marshmallows are puffy and soft. Remove from oven. Poured and spread icing over marshmallows for marbled effect.

## Writing for College Life

Assume you are giving a PowerPoint presentation in your Communication class. Edit the following outline of your PowerPoint slides so that each element is parallel. Use your own paper.

**Title Slide:**

The Self in Interpersonal Communication

**Slide One:**

Dimensions of the Self
Self-Concept
Being Aware of Self
Self-Esteem

**Slide Two:**

Self-Disclosure
Influences on Self-Disclosure
Rewarding Self-Disclosure
Dangers of Self-Disclosure

**Slide Three:**

Communication Apprehension
The Nature of Communication Apprehension
Theories of Communication
Apprehension Management

—From Joseph A. DeVito, *The Interpersonal Communication Book*, 10th ed., Longman 2004, p. viii.

## Writing Assignments CONTINUED

### Writing for Working Life

Edit the following portion of a résumé to ensure parallel expression.

CAREER OBJECTIVE

- To secure a Management position
- I want to contribute to the success of the organization.

SUMMARY OF QUALIFICATIONS

- Experienced in retail management.
- I am skilled in the following areas: analytical thinking, client orientation, creative thinking, decision-making, problem solving, time management, leading others, interpersonal skills, oral communication, written communication, and computer skills.

WORK EXPERIENCE

- Target, sales associate
  From: 11/6/98 – 6/23/01
- State Farm Insurance, worked as secretary to Team Supervisor of Claims Unit
  From: 7/1/01 – To: Present

PORTFOLIO

## Academic Learning Log

WHAT HAVE I LEARNED ABOUT PARALLELISM?

To test and track your understanding, answer the following questions. Use several sentences as needed for each response.

**1.** What is parallelism? ________________________________

________________________________

**2.** Parallel ____________ often, but not always, use similar suffixes (word endings).

**3.** Parallel phrases repeat similar ________________________________

**4.** Repeat parallel patterns of ____________ to pace ideas through the thoughtful arrangement and sequence of sentence types.

**5.** What types of punctuation signal parallelism? (a) ____________ ;

(b) ____________ ; and (c) ____________ .

**6. How will I use what I have learned?** In your notebook, discuss how you will apply to your own writing what you have learned about parallelism. When will you apply this knowledge during the writing process?

**7. What do I still need to study about sentence types?** In your notebook, describe your ongoing study needs by describing what, when, and how you will continue studying and using parallelism.

PART 6

# Recognizing and Avoiding Errors

* Homework - Do practices 1-7

* run-ons + comma splices powerpoint on blackboard!

# Comma Splices and Run-ons

A comma splice is an error that occurs when a comma is used by itself to join two sentences. A run-on is an error that occurs when two sentences are joined without any punctuation.

According to research, comma splices and run-ons are two of the most common errors made by student writers. The photograph on the next page shows a natural phenomenon that stirs human emotions and imagination. Read about this special place and then answer the question "What's the point of learning about correcting comma splices and run-ons?"

# What's the Point of Correcting Comma Splices and Run-ons?

**PHOTOGRAPHIC ORGANIZER: COMMA SPLICES AND RUN-ONS**

WRITING FROM LIFE

Practice 1

*1-4 practices

Read the following short description of Niagara Falls, adapted from a 1913 essay written by Rupert Brooke for the *Westminster Gazette*. This version contains one comma splice and two run-ons. How do these errors affect the reading of the passage?

**Niagara Falls**

Half a mile or so above the Falls, on either side, the water of the great stream begins to run more swiftly in confusion it descends with ever-growing speed it begins chattering and leaping, breaking into a thousand ripples, throwing up joyful fingers of spray, sometimes it is divided by islands and rocks sometimes the eye can see nothing but a waste of laughing, springing, foamy waves.

Adapted from "Niagara Falls," Rupert Brooke

**What's the point of learning about correcting comma splices and run-ons?**

# Understanding the Point of Correcting Comma Splices and Run-ons: One Student Writer's Response

The following paragraph offers one writer's response to the opening paragraph about Niagara Falls.

*I had to read the paragraph several times to figure out what the author was saying. I couldn't tell when one sentence ended and another one started. I guess a comma splice or run-on occurs because a writer joins sentences without the proper punctuation. Without proper punctuation that signals the end of one thought and the beginning of another, ideas become confusing as they run on. Proper punctuation signals the beginning or end of each sentence. Proper punctuation makes ideas clear and easy to follow.*

# Applying the Point: Correcting Comma Splices and Run-ons

Comma splices and run-on sentences are punctuation errors that occur where independent clauses are improperly joined to form a compound sentence. To properly combine clauses into a compound sentence, the end of each independent clause must be signaled by appropriate punctuation, such as a semicolon, a comma followed by a coordinating conjunction, or a period at the end of the sentence.

## Comma Splice

A **comma splice** occurs when a comma is used by itself (without a coordinating conjunction) to join two independent clauses.

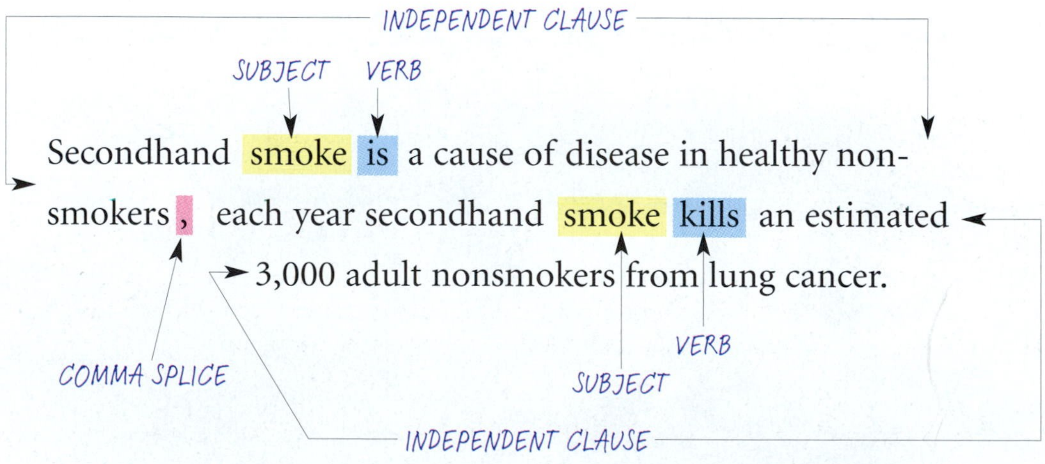

## Run-on

A **run-on** sentence occurs when two independent clauses are joined without any punctuation.

INDEPENDENT CLAUSE — RUN-ON (MISSING PUNCTUATION)

SUBJECT — VERB — SUBJECT

Secondhand smoke causes respiratory problems it also causes reddening, itching, and watering of the eyes.

VERB

INDEPENDENT CLAUSE

**Practice 2**

IDENTIFYING COMMA SPLICES AND RUN-ONS

Test your ability to identify comma splices, run-on sentences, and properly combined clauses. In each blank, write **CS** for comma splice, **RO** for run-on, or **C** for correctly punctuated.

CS (FANBOY needed) **1.** More than 126 million nonsmoking Americans are exposed to secondhand smoke in homes, vehicles, workplaces, and public places, almost 60 percent of U.S. children between the ages of 3 and 11—or almost 22 million children—are exposed to secondhand smoke.

RO **2.** There is no risk-free level of secondhand smoke exposure even brief exposure can be dangerous.

C **3.** Secondhand smoke, also known as environmental tobacco smoke, is a complex mixture of gases and particles including smoke from the burning cigarette, cigar, or pipe tip and exhaled smoke.

CS **4.** Two types of secondhand smoke exist, sidestream smoke is the smoke released from the burning end of a cigarette, exhaled mainstream smoke is the smoke exhaled by the smoker.

RO **5.** Secondhand smoke is a known human carcinogen (cancer-causing agent) more than 50 compounds in secondhand smoke have been identified as known or reasonably anticipated human carcinogens secondhand smoke contains at least 250 chemicals that are known to be toxic or carcinogenic.

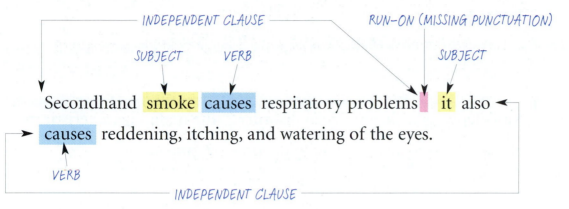

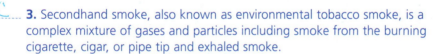

More practice with correcting comma splices and run-ons: <www.mywritinglab.com>

## Five Ways to Correct Comma Splices and Run-ons

As a writer, you have the choice of several ways to correct or avoid comma splices and run-ons. Each method creates a specific effect. Most experts recommend using a variety of these methods, rather than always relying on the same one.

### 1. Separate sentences using a period and capital letter

Punctuating the independent clauses as separate sentences is a method often used to correct comma splices and run-ons.

**Incorrect:**

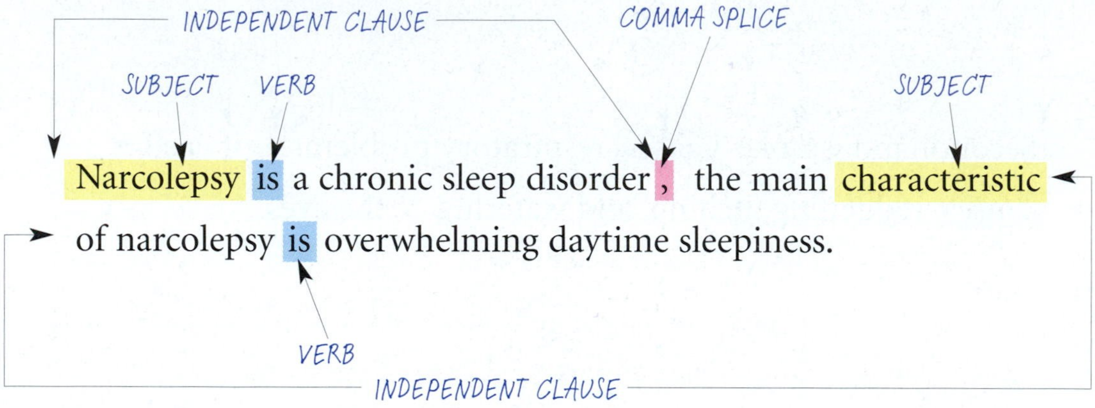


**Incorrect:**

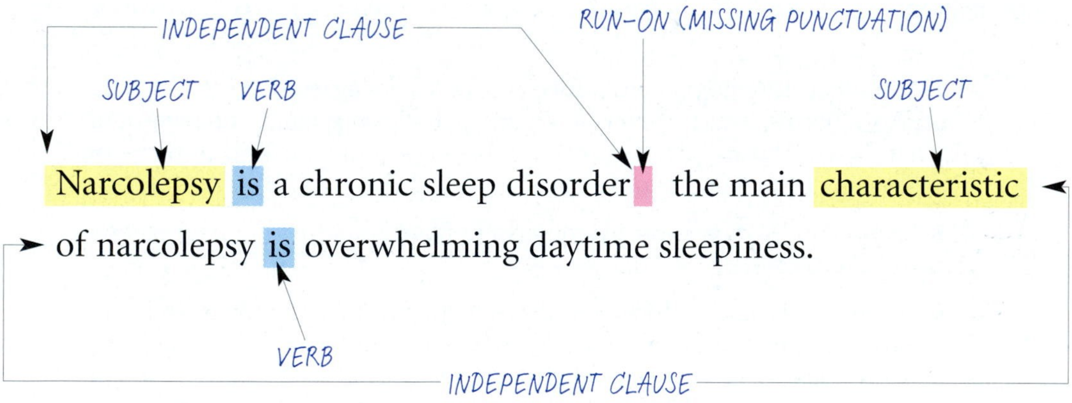


**Revised (Correct):**

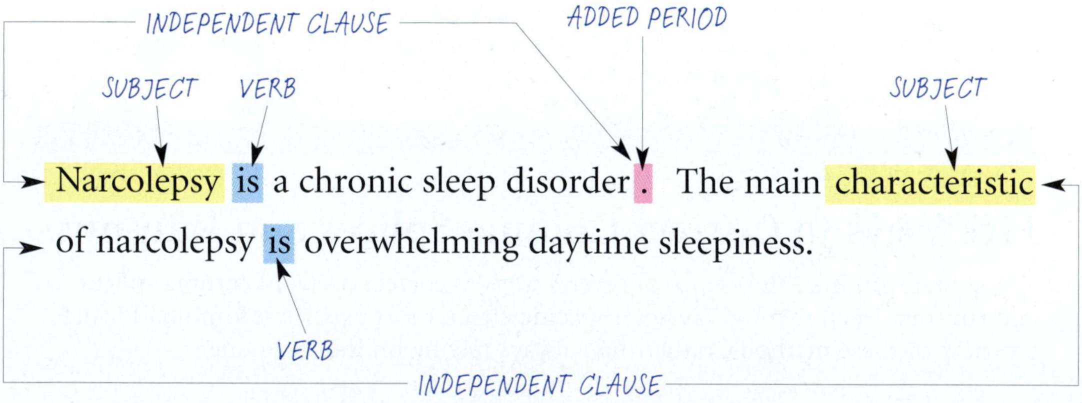

## Practice 3

COMMA SPLICES AND RUN-ONS

Edit the following sentences to eliminate comma splices and run-ons. Separate clauses by inserting a period and capital letter as needed.

1. A person with narcolepsy is likely to become drowsy or to fall asleep, often at inappropriate times and places, daytime sleep attacks may occur with or without warning and may be irresistible.
2. Drowsiness may persist for prolonged periods of time nighttime sleep may be fragmented with frequent awakenings.
3. There is strong evidence that narcolepsy may run in families, eight to twelve percent of people with narcolepsy have a close relative with the disease.
4. Narcolepsy can occur in both men and women at any age, its symptoms are usually first noticed in teenagers or young adults.
5. Write a compound sentence. Suggested topic: Sleep Problems.

---

---

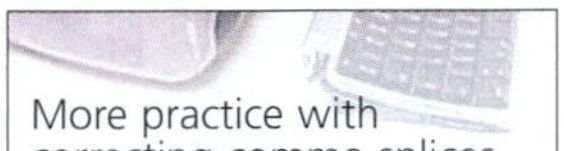

More practice with correcting comma splices and run-ons: <www.mywritinglab.com>

## 2. Join sentences with a comma followed by a coordinating conjunction

Sentences can be properly joined by inserting a comma followed by a coordinating conjunction between the independent clauses. The acronym FANBOYS stands for each of the coordinating conjunctions: *for, and, nor, but, or, yet, so*. This method of combining sentences states the relationship between ideas of equal importance.

**Incorrect:**

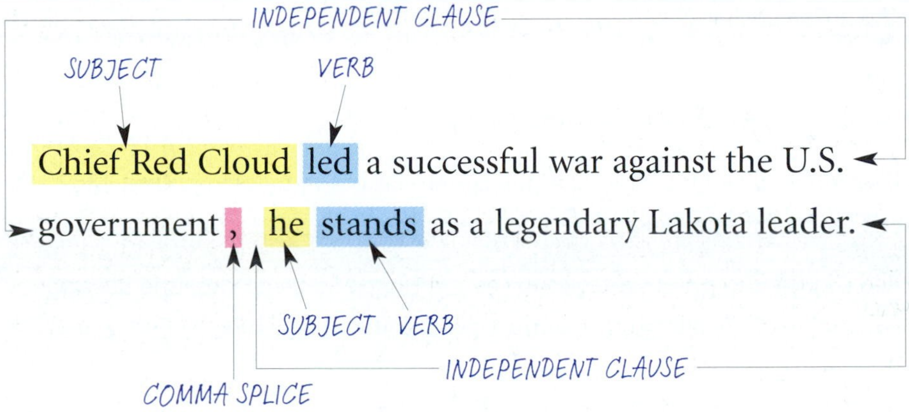

**Incorrect:**

INDEPENDENT CLAUSE

SUBJECT — VERB

Chief Red Cloud led a successful war against the U.S. government he stands as a legendary Lakota leader.

SUBJECT — VERB

INDEPENDENT CLAUSE

RUN-ON (MISSING PUNCTUATION)

**Revised (Correct):**

INDEPENDENT CLAUSE

SUBJECT — VERB

Chief Red Cloud led a successful war against the U.S. government, so he stands as a legendary Lakota leader.

ADDED COMMA — SUBJECT — VERB

INDEPENDENT CLAUSE

ADDED COORDINATING CONJUNCTION SIGNALS A STATED EFFECT

More practice with correcting comma splices and run-ons: <www.mywritinglab.com>

## Practice 4

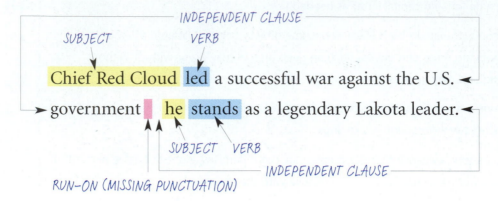

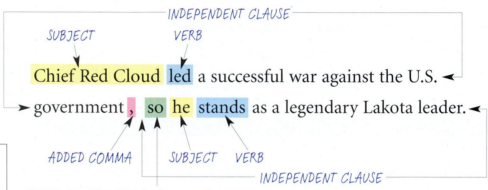

### COMMA SPLICES AND RUN-ONS

Edit the following sentences to eliminate comma splices and run-ons. Join independent clauses with a comma and a coordinating conjunction.

1. Chief Red Cloud waged war against the United States the army had constructed forts along the Bozeman Trail.
2. Bozeman Trail served as a route to the Montana gold fields for miners and settlers, the trail cut through the heart of Indian Territory.
3. Red Cloud remembered the removal of the Eastern Lakota from Minnesota in 1862 and 1863, he launched a series of assaults on the forts.
4. Chief Red Cloud's successful strategies forced the United States to close the Bozeman Trail he negotiated a treaty resulting in the United States abandoning its forts along the trail.
5. Write a compound sentence using a comma and a coordinating conjunction. Suggested topic: A Heroic Action.

## 3. Join sentences with a semicolon

Use the semicolon to join independent clauses when no conjunction is present. A semicolon indicates that the two sentences of equal importance are so closely related that they can be stated as one sentence; however, a semicolon alone does not state the relationship between the two clauses. The relationship between clauses may be one of the following: *time, space, order of importance, general to specific, addition, cause, effect, comparison,* or *contrast.*

**Incorrect:**

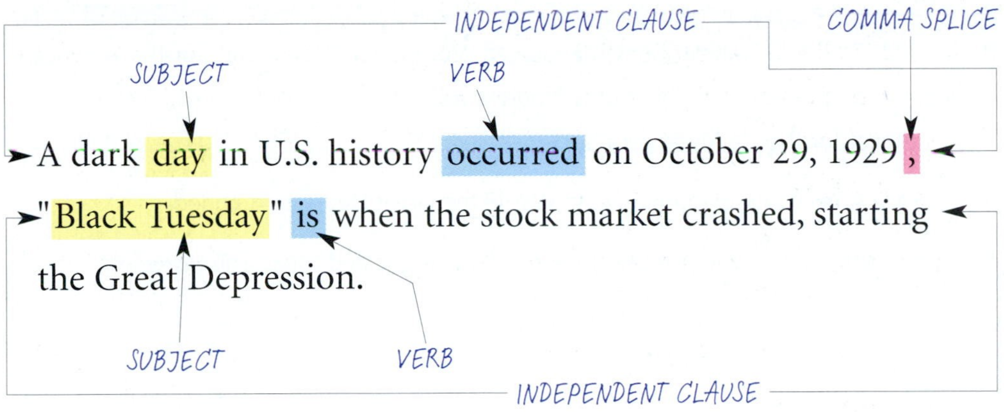


**Incorrect:**

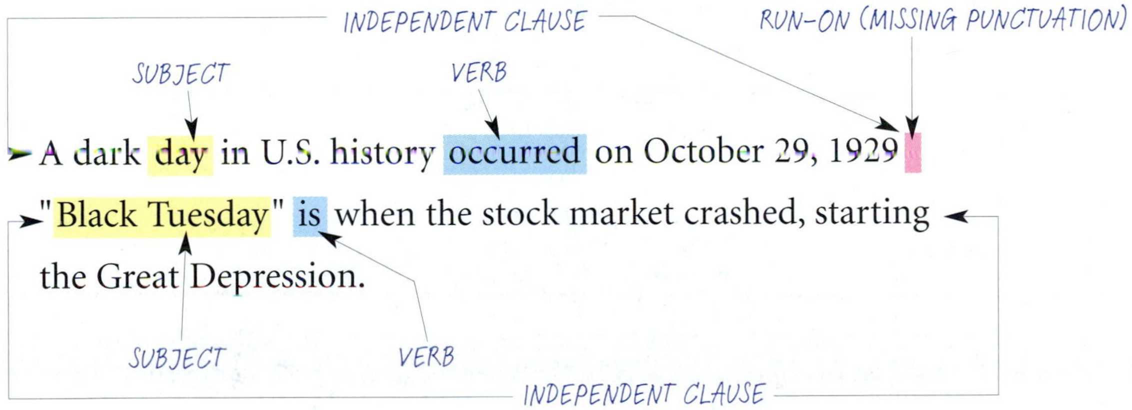


**Revised (Correct):**

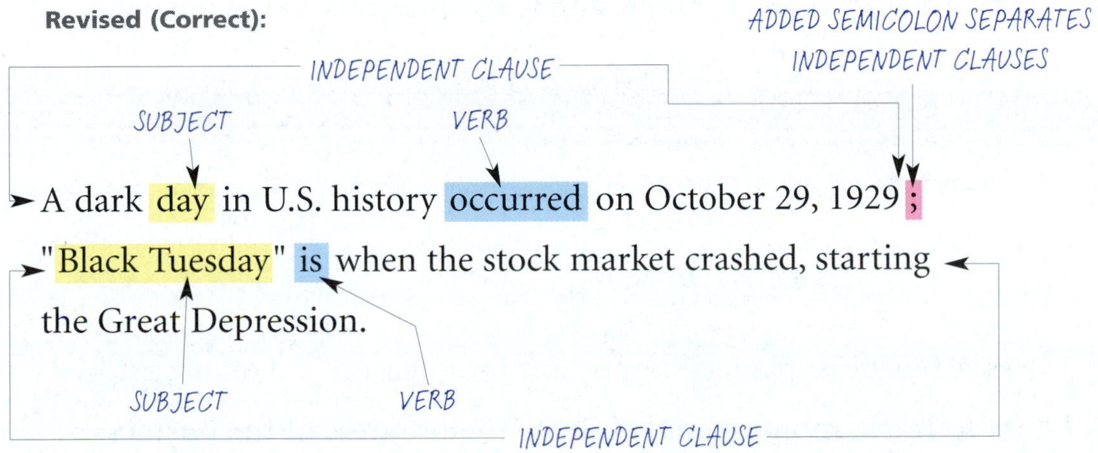


The first clause makes a general statement; the second clause provides a specific detail.

## Practice 5

**COMMA SPLICES AND RUN-ONS**

Edit the following sentences by inserting semicolons as needed to correct comma splices and run-ons.

1. Unemployment skyrocketed a quarter of the workforce was without jobs by 1933, and many people became homeless.
2. President Herbert Hoover attempted to handle the crisis, he was unable to improve the situation.
3. In 1932, President Franklin Delano Roosevelt promised a "New Deal" for the American people Congress created The Works Progress Administration (WPA), which offered work relief for thousands of people.
4. In 1941, America entered into World War II, the Great Depression ended.
5. Write a compound sentence using a semicolon. Suggested topic: The Homeless.

More practice with correcting comma splices and run-ons: <www.mywritinglab.com>

### 4. Join sentences with a semicolon followed by a conjunctive adverb

For more information about joining ideas of equal importance, see Chapter 17 "Compound and Complex Sentences."

Use the semicolon with a conjunctive adverb to join independent clauses. Conjunctive adverbs are transition words that state the relationships between ideas of equal importance. A few common examples include *also, for example, however, then, therefore,* and *thus.*

**Incorrect:**

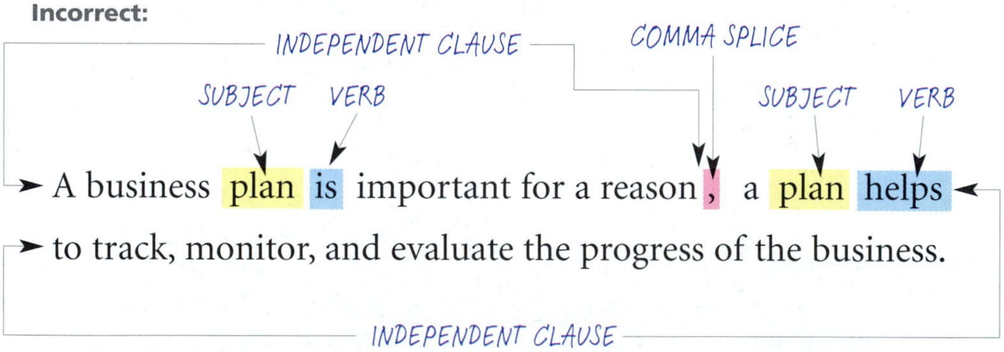
INDEPENDENT CLAUSE
COMMA SPLICE
SUBJECT
VERB
SUBJECT
VERB
A business plan is important for a reason, a plan helps
to track, monitor, and evaluate the progress of the business.
INDEPENDENT CLAUSE

**Incorrect:**

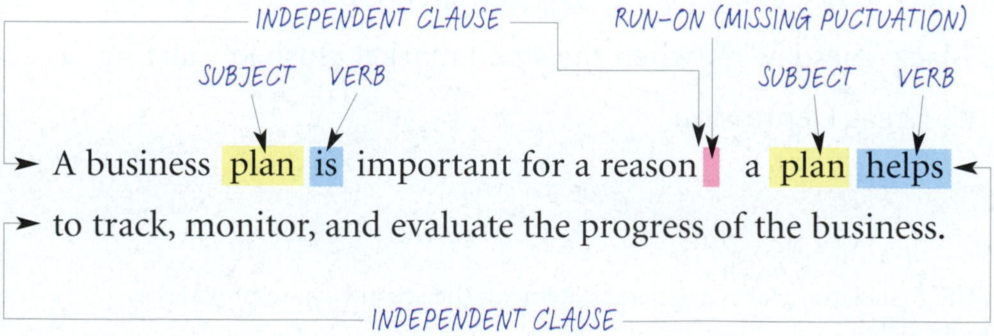
INDEPENDENT CLAUSE
RUN-ON (MISSING PUCTUATION)
SUBJECT
VERB
SUBJECT
VERB
A business plan is important for a reason a plan helps
to track, monitor, and evaluate the progress of the business.
INDEPENDENT CLAUSE

**Revised (Correct):**

INDEPENDENT CLAUSE — ADDED SEMICOLON SEPARATES INDEPENDENT CLAUSES

SUBJECT VERB — ADDED CONJUNCTIVE ADVERB — SUBJECT

A business plan is important for a reason ; for example , a plan helps to track, monitor, and evaluate the progress of the business.

VERB — ADDED COMMA WITH INTRODUCTORY ELEMENT

INDEPENDENT CLAUSE

Not only do these transitions state the relationship between ideas, but they also introduce an independent clause and must be set off with a comma.

## Practice 6

COMMA SPLICES AND RUN-ONS

Edit and revise the following sentences, adapted from the article "Writing a Business Plan" on the U.S. Small Business Administration website, <www.Business.gov>, to correct comma splices and run-ons. Join independent clauses with a semicolon and one of the following transitions: *consequently, for example, furthermore, in addition,* or *therefore.*

1. Fit-for-Business Health Club will provide helpful services to corporations and businesses in the area, it will offer affordable wellness programs to improve the health of the members of a company's workforce.

2. Healthy employees are more productive than chronically ill employees, to prevent injuries or illnesses costs less than to treat them after they occur.

3. Fit-for-Business will help employees change their behavior patterns and choose more healthy lifestyles, Fit-for-Business will lower companies' health care costs and raise worker productivity.

4. Founded by three owners, the company began in San Francisco, it is a privately held corporation.

5. Write a compound sentence using a semicolon and conjunctive adverb. Suggested topic: Going to the Gym.

---

---

More practice with correcting comma splices and run-ons: <www.mywritinglab.com>

## 5. Join sentences using subordinate ideas

For more information on complex sentences, see Chapter 17, "Compound and Complex Sentences."

Not all ideas are of equal importance. Frequently, writers choose to join ideas in a complex sentence made up of an independent clause and one or more dependent clauses. A subordinating conjunction signals the beginning of a dependent clause and states its subordinate relationship to the independent clause. Some examples of subordinating conjunctions include *although, as, because, if,* and *when.* Relative pronouns also connect a dependent clause to an independent clause. Examples of relative pronouns include *that, which,* and *who.*

**Incorrect:**

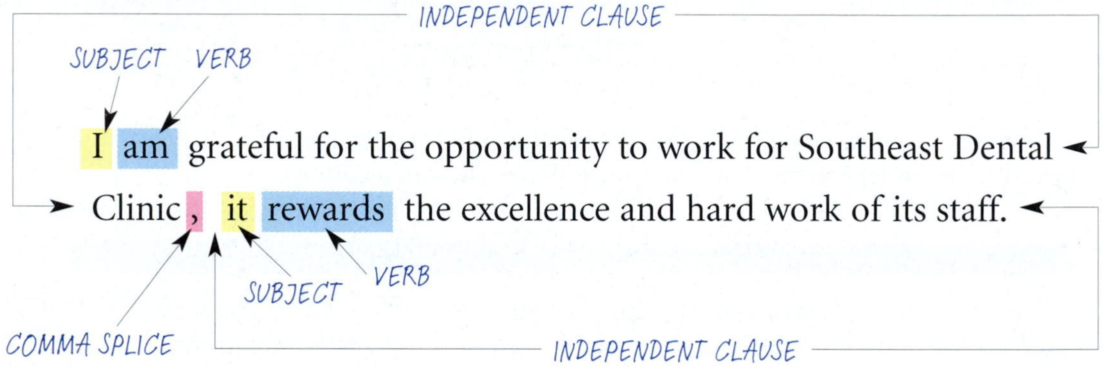

INDEPENDENT CLAUSE
SUBJECT
VERB
I am grateful for the opportunity to work for Southeast Dental Clinic, it rewards the excellence and hard work of its staff.
SUBJECT
VERB
COMMA SPLICE
INDEPENDENT CLAUSE


**Incorrect:**

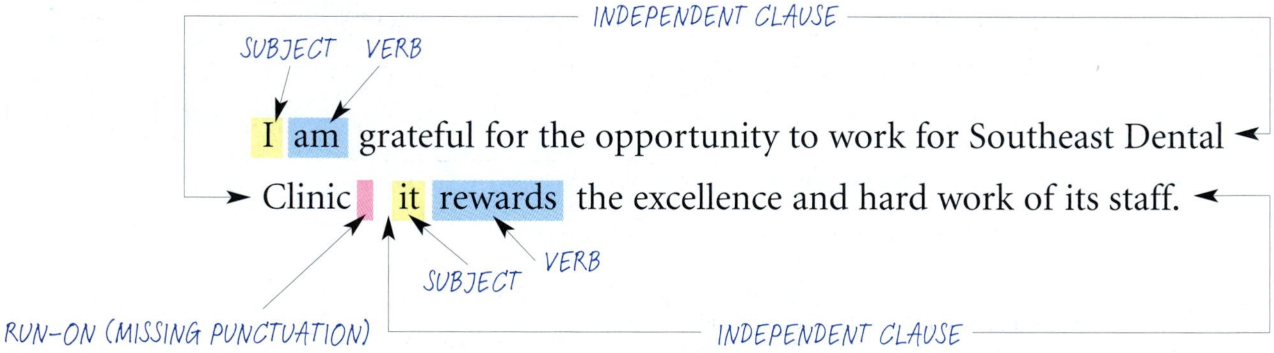


**Revised #1 (Correct):**

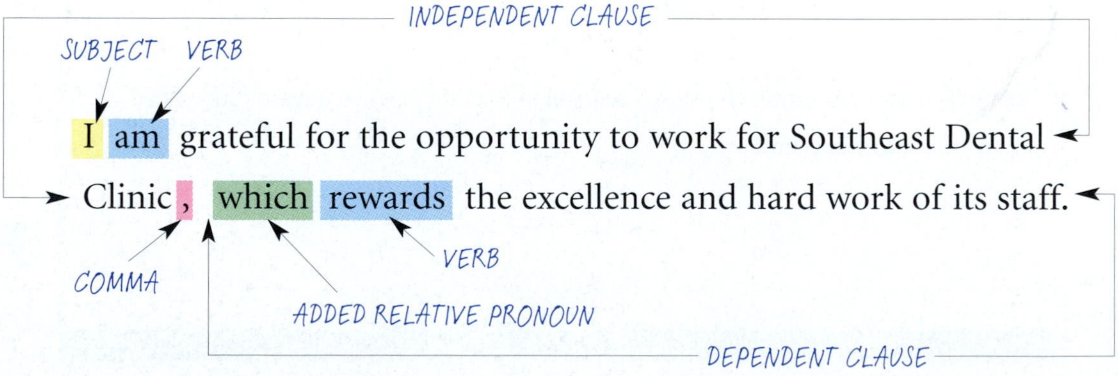

**Revised #2 (Correct):**

DEPENDENT CLAUSE

ADDED SUBORDINATING CONJUNCTION

Because Southeast Dental Clinic rewards the excellence and hard work of its staff, I am grateful for the opportunity to work for the clinc.

COMMA SETS OFF INTRODUCTORY ELEMENT — SUBJECT — VERB

INDEPENDENT CLAUSE

# Practice 7

## RUN-ONS AND COMMA SPLICES

Revise the following compound sentences into complex sentences to correct comma splices and run-ons. Use the following subordinating conjunctions: *as, because, even though, that, who.*

**1.** I've become an integral member of your team and accomplished a great deal, however, I'm still working for the initial salary on which we agreed two years ago.

Even though I've become an integral member of your team and accomplished a great deal, I'm still working for the initial salary on which we agreed two years ago

*All including* #5

**2.** My contract states ~~the terms of our agreement~~ we agreed to renegotiate my salary in two years based on my accomplishments.

As my contract states, we agreed to renegotiate my salary in two years based on my accomplishments.

**3.** I have a record of accomplishments and high performance reviews, I'm respectfully requesting an immediate pay raise of six percent.

Because I have a record of accomplishments and high performance review, I'm respectfully requesting an immediate pay raise of six percent.

**4.** Mr. Jamal Rinker is my immediate supervisor he supports my request for a raise.

Mr. Jamal Rinker, who is my immediate supervisor, supports my request for a raise.

**5.** I feel strongly about this. I've earned an immediate pay raise.

I feel strongly about this, I've earned an immediate pay raise.

More practice with correcting comma splices and run-ons: <www.mywritinglab.com>

# Practice 8

## COMMA SPLICES AND RUN-ONS

Edit and revise the following sentences to correct run-ons and comma splices.

**1.** One of the most common symptoms of depression is a constant and overwhelming feeling of sadness another symptom is an empty, apathetic feeling.

**2.** Anxiety often accompanies depression, it may be intense, as though one is in great danger.

**3.** Depression affects the appetite in one way or another, one often loses interest in eating because the food has no taste.

**4.** Anxiety is high, an individual may not be able to eat.

**5.** Some who are depressed may not be able to eat other people will overeat out of frustration or misery.

More practice with correcting comma splices and run-ons: <www.mywritinglab.com>

RUN-ONS AND COMMA SPLICES REVIEW

Practice 9

PORTFOLIO

Edit and revise the paragraph below, adapted from the article "Why Sleep Is Important," from the National Institute of Health website, to correct run-ons and comma splices. Use your own paper.

**Sleep Is a Basic Human Need**

Sleep is a natural part of everybody's life but many people know very little about how important it is, and some even try to get by with little sleep. Sleep is something our bodies need to do it is not optional. Even though the exact reasons for sleep remain a mystery, we do know that during sleep many of the body's major organ and regulatory systems continue to work actively. Some parts of the brain actually increase their activity dramatically, the body produces more of certain hormones. Sleep, like diet and exercise, is important for our minds and bodies to function normally. In fact, sleep appears to be required for survival. Rats deprived of sleep die within two to three weeks, a time frame similar to death due to starvation. An internal biological clock regulates the timing for sleep. It programs each person to feel sleepy during the nighttime hours and to be active during the daylight hours. Light is the cue that synchronizes the biological clock to the 24-hour cycle of day and night. Sleepiness due to chronic lack of adequate sleep is a big problem in the United States it affects many children as well as adults. Children and even adolescents need at least 9 hours of sleep each night to do their best most adults need approximately 8 hours of sleep each night.

# Writing Assignments

## Writing for Everyday Life

Read the following letter of protest written to a county council. Edit to correct comma splices and run-ons. Use your own paper.

Dear Roberta Clancy, Chairperson of the County Council:

Recent news articles published the council's intention to allow WC Homes, Inc. to cut down a pair of century-old oak trees on the Marsh Loop these trees evidently stand in the way of progress. WC Homes, Inc. plans to develop a neighborhood of 1,000 single homes and the trees will block access to the entrance of the neighborhood. Marsh Loop has long been known for its unique beauty and importance as a wildlife refuge. Developers are rapidly changing this rare and important natural environment into an over-built urban area. Many voters agree with me you cut down these trees you will be out of office.

Sincerely,

Jane Watts

More practice with correcting comma splices and run-ons: <www.mywritinglab.com>

# Writing Assignments CONTINUED

## Writing for College Life

The following paragraph was written during an essay exam for a health class. The exam question asked the student to explain the need for proper technique in weight training. Edit to correct comma splices and run-ons. Use your own paper.

Weight training is an excellent exercise you can improve your strength, increase muscle tone, lose fat, gain muscle mass, and improve bone density. You use a sloppy technique, you stand a good chance of doing more harm than good. Common injuries can occur during weight training these include sprains, strains, tendonitis, fractures, and dislocations. The Mayo Clinic offers several suggestions on proper technique. First, remember to breathe holding your breath during weightlifting can increase your blood pressure to dangerous levels. Second, don't overdo it. The amount of weight you lift should make your muscles feel tired after 10 to 15 repetitions. A weight that causes fatigue at 12 repetitions creates muscle strength and toning. Finally, don't rush. And don't jerk the weights up, lift and lower the weights in a slow, fluid movement.

## Writing for Working Life

Read the following letter written as a follow-up to a job interview. Edit to correct comma splices and run-ons. Use your own paper.

Dear Ms. Tucker:

Thank you very much for taking time to talk with me about the position of department manager. I enjoyed meeting you and the members of the department and I am excited about the chance to work with such a dynamic team. I, too, am a self-starter yet a team player. I like to encourage individuals to take ownership of projects, but still involve team-member support. Based on our meeting, I believe this is the job for me my qualifications are an excellent fit, particularly my training in technology and communication. The position is exactly what I'm looking for I'm confident that I can be a significant contributor to the success of the graphics department. I sincerely hope you agree. Thank you, again, for giving so much of your time I look forward to hearing from you.

Sincerely,

Justin M. Agler

PORTFOLIO

# Academic Learning Log

## WHAT HAVE I LEARNED ABOUT CORRECTING COMMA SPLICES AND RUN-ONS?

To test and track your understanding, complete the following ideas. Use several sentences as needed for each response.

**1.** A comma splice is ____________________

____________________

____________________

____________________

**2.** A run-on sentence is ____________________

____________________

____________________

____________________

**3.** What are the five ways to eliminate comma splices and run-ons?

____________________

____________________

____________________

____________________

____________________

**4. How will I use what I have learned about correcting comma splices and run-ons?** In your notebook, discuss how you will apply to your own writing what you have learned about comma splices and run-ons.

**5. What do I still need to study about correcting comma splices and run-ons?** In your notebook, describe your ongoing study needs by describing what, when, and how you will continue studying comma splices and run-ons.

# 22

**Chapter Preview:**

- What's the Point of Correcting Fragments?
- Understanding the Point of Correcting Fragments: One Student Writer's Response
- Applying the Point: Correcting Fragments

# Fragments

## A fragment is an incomplete thought.

Thinking about a real-life situation helps us to understand the impact of fragments on our ability to communicate. The following photo illustrates a couple in search of a place to live. Read about the situation below and answer the question "What's the point of learning about fragments?"

# What's the Point of Correcting Fragments?

WRITING FROM LIFE

Practice 1

PHOTOGRAPHIC ORGANIZER: FRAGMENTS

Suppose you are looking for a new apartment. You ask two landlords the same questions. Below are the two replies:

**Landlord A:**
"If it's a little messy, well... sometimes partial refunds... for damages... not leaving behind personal belongings..."

**Landlord B:**
"You will get your security deposit back if you leave the apartment in the same or better condition than it is in right now, if you don't leave any of your belongings behind, and if you pay your last month's rent. We can go around the apartment right now and make a list of the condition of each room so we'll have a reference point when you're ready to move out."

With which landlord will you be able to communicate easily and clearly if you move in?

---

**What's the point of learning about fragments?**

---

---

---

---

---

---

# Understanding the Point of Correcting Fragments: One Student Writer's Response

The following paragraph offers one writer's reaction to the statements about the security deposit given by the landlords.

> Landlord A never finishes a thought, so I have no idea what he means. His answers are vague, and he doesn't seem to care about being understood. Maybe he thinks I should just know what he means. In contrast, Landlord B spoke clearly using complete sentences. I know exactly what is expected.
>
> Landlord B is going to be easier to talk to and understand. The difference between the two responses makes me realize how important it is to use complete sentences if you want to be understood. When others can understand your thoughts, you can connect with them and even change how they think about things or how they act. That's real power.

# Applying the Point: Correcting Fragments

The ability to write ideas in complete thoughts or sentences is an important tool in building coherent paragraphs and essays. A sentence has two traits.

**SENTENCE: Complete Thought-Complete Information**

**TRAIT ONE:** A sentence states a complete and independent thought.

**TRAIT TWO:** A sentence contains a subject and a verb.

COMPLETE THOUGHT

You should visit your doctor.

SUBJECT (You) VERB (should visit)

A **sentence** contains all the information needed to clearly express a complete thought. In contrast, a fragment is often recognized by what is missing from the thought. A **fragment** is an incomplete thought.

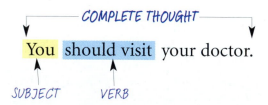

### FRAGMENT: Incomplete Thought-Missing Information

A **fragment** is missing one of the following: a subject, a verb, or both subject and verb.

| | |
|---|---|
| Missing Subject: | Does not disqualify you from exercising. |
| Missing Verb: | Edward taking a physical exam. |
| Missing Subject and Verb: | To safely participate and to reduce risk of injury. |

Even when a group of words includes both a subject and a verb, it still can be a fragment. A subordinating conjunction signals a fragment that has both a subject and a verb. These types of fragments are missing an independent clause:

**Fragment (Missing an Independent Clause):**

INCOMPLETE THOUGHT

Because youth are less active than in the past.

SUBORDINATING CONJUNCTION SUBJECT VERB

To identify a fragment, ask the following questions:

- Does the idea have a verb?
- What is the subject of the verb?
- Does the idea express a complete thought?

Practice 2

#### IDENTIFYING FRAGMENTS

Identify fragments and sentences. Write **F** for *fragment* next to the incomplete thoughts. Write **S** for *sentence* next to the complete thoughts.

........ **1.** Regular physical activity, fitness, and exercise are critically important.

........ **2.** For the health and well being of people of all ages.

........ **3.** Research has proven that all individuals can benefit from regular physical activity.

........ **4.** Whether they engage in vigorous exercise or some type of moderate physical activity.

........ **5.** Those who do not exercise on a regular basis.

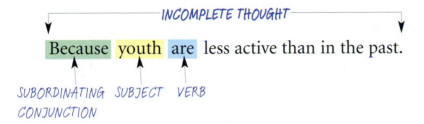

More practice identifying fragments: <www.mywritinglab.com>

# Types of Fragments

This section discusses seven common types of fragments ([1] prepositional phrase, [2] appositive phrase, [3] infinitive phrase, [4] gerund phrase, [5] participle phrase, [6] dependent clause, [7] relative clause) and techniques you can use to revise fragments into sentences. Fragments are either phrases or dependent clauses punctuated as if they are sentences. A writer may use two techniques to revise fragments into sentences:

- Combine existing ideas.
- Add missing ideas

## Phrase Fragments

A **phrase** is a group of words that acts as a single unit. A phrase is a fragment because it does not contain both a subject and a verb. To create a sentence, add information (such as a subject, a verb, or both) to the phrase, or join the phrase to an existing sentence.

### 1. PREPOSITIONAL PHRASE

A **prepositional phrase** begins with a preposition (such as *at*, *or*, *in*, *to*, *toward*, *for*, *since*, and *of*) and ends with the object of the preposition. A prepositional phrase adds information about direction, manner, space, and time such as *in the house* or *after the game*.

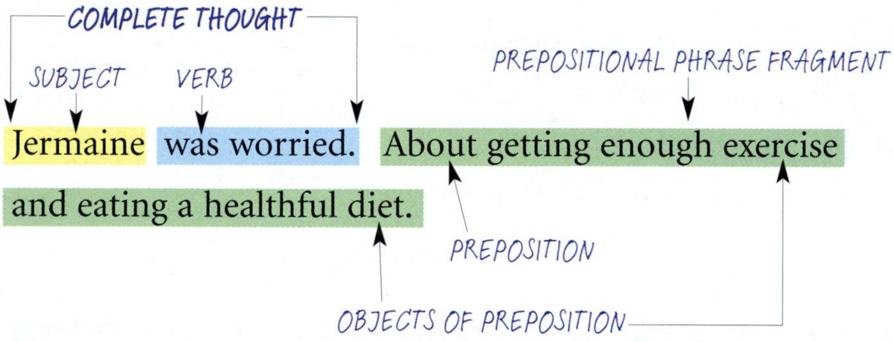


**Revised to Combine Ideas:**

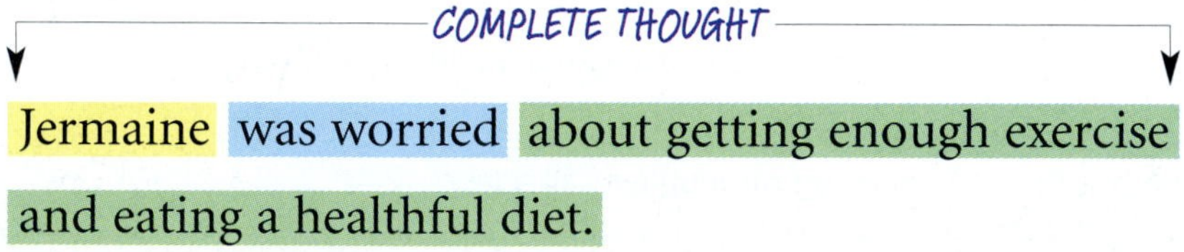


**Revised to Add Ideas:**

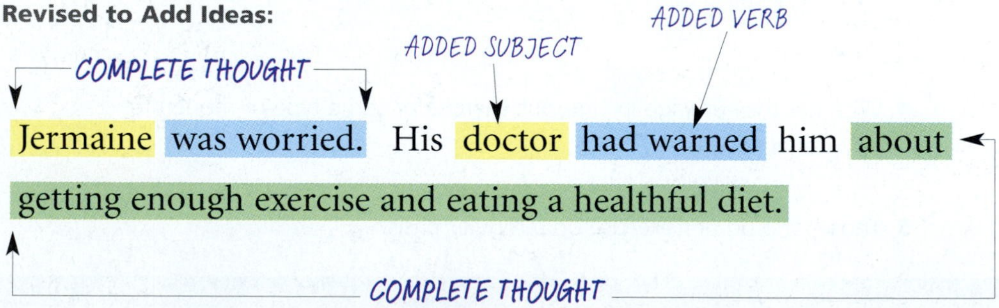

**PREPOSITIONAL PHRASE FRAGMENTS**

Practice 3

Build two new sentences using the prepositional phrase. First, combine the existing sentence with the prepositional phrase to create a new sentence. Then, create another new sentence by adding missing information to the prepositional phrase.

**prepositional phrase:**

for your health and weight management

**sentence:**

Body composition is important to consider.

**1.** COMBINE IDEAS: ..............................

..............................

**2.** ADD IDEAS: ..............................

..............................

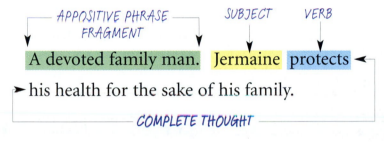

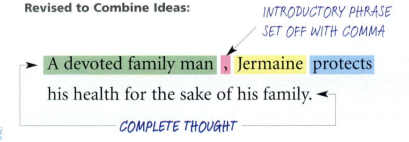

More practice correcting prepositional phrase fragments: <www.mywritinglab.com>

## 2. APPOSITIVE PHRASE

An **appositive phrase** contains a noun that renames or describes another noun in the same sentence. An appositive phrase combines with an complete thought to add detail. Place an appositive phrase next to the noun it renames.

APPOSITIVE PHRASE FRAGMENT — SUBJECT — VERB

A devoted family man. Jermaine protects his health for the sake of his family.

COMPLETE THOUGHT

**Revised to Combine Ideas:**

INTRODUCTORY PHRASE SET OFF WITH COMMA

A devoted family man, Jermaine protects his health for the sake of his family.

COMPLETE THOUGHT

**Revised to Add Ideas:**

COMPLETE THOUGHT — ADDED VERB — COMPLETE THOUGHT — ADDED SUBJECT

Jermaine is a devoted family man. Therefore, he protects his health for the sake of his family.

## Practice 4

**APPOSITIVE PHRASE FRAGMENTS**

Build two new sentences using the appositive phrase. First, combine the existing sentence with the appositive phrase to create a new sentence. Then, create another new sentence by adding missing information to the appositive phrase.

**Appositive phrase:**

the range of motion around a joint

**Sentence:**

Flexibility can help prevent injuries through all stages of life.

**1.** COMBINE IDEAS: ______________________________

______________________________

**2.** ADD IDEAS: ______________________________

______________________________

______________________________

______________________________

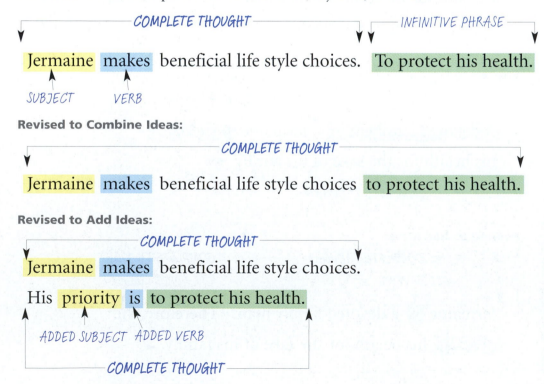

More practice correcting appositive phrase fragments: <www.mywritinglab.com>

### 3. INFINITIVE PHRASE

An infinitive is a form of a verb, but it is not a verb. Combining *to* with a verb forms an **infinitive** as in the following: *to go, to talk,* and *to think*. An **infinitive phrase** is made up of an infinitive and the object of the infinitive such as *to quit smoking* or *to run a mile*. An infinitive phrase can act as a noun, adjective, or adverb.

COMPLETE THOUGHT — INFINITIVE PHRASE

Jermaine [SUBJECT] makes [VERB] beneficial life style choices. To protect his health.

**Revised to Combine Ideas:**

COMPLETE THOUGHT

Jermaine makes beneficial life style choices to protect his health.

**Revised to Add Ideas:**

COMPLETE THOUGHT

Jermaine makes beneficial life style choices.

His priority [ADDED SUBJECT] is [ADDED VERB] to protect his health.

COMPLETE THOUGHT

**INFINITIVE PHRASE FRAGMENTS**

Practice 5

Build two new sentences using the infinitive phrase. First, combine the existing sentence with the infinitive phrase to create a new sentence. Then, create another new sentence by adding missing information to the infinitive phrase.

**Infinitive phrase:**

to improve your flexibility

**Sentence:**

Swim or stretch to lengthen your muscles.

**1.** COMBINE IDEAS: ______________________________

**2.** ADD IDEAS: ______________________________

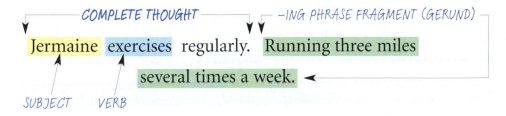

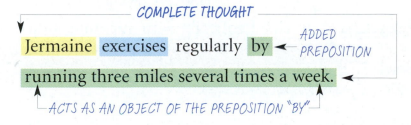

More practice correcting infinitive phrase fragments: <www.mywritinglab.com>

## *-ING* PHRASES: GERUNDS AND PARTICIPLES

An *-ing* phrase can function as either a noun or an adjective. An *-ing* phrase used as a noun is called a **gerund**. An *-ing* phrase used as an adjective is called a **participle**.

### 4. Gerund Phrase

A gerund is a form of a verb, but it is not a verb. A gerund is a noun that ends in *-ing*, such as *going, talking,* and *thinking.* A **gerund phrase** is made up of a gerund and the object of the gerund such as *quitting smoking* or *running three miles.* A gerund phrase functions as a noun. For example, a gerund phrase can be the subject of a sentence or an object of a verb or preposition.

COMPLETE THOUGHT — -ING PHRASE FRAGMENT (GERUND)

Jermaine exercises regularly. Running three miles several times a week.

SUBJECT — VERB

**Revised to Combine Ideas:**

COMPLETE THOUGHT

Jermaine exercises regularly by running three miles several times a week.

ADDED PREPOSITION

ACTS AS AN OBJECT OF THE PREPOSITION "BY"

**Revised to Add Ideas:**

COMPLETE THOUGHT

ADDED VERB

He enjoys running three miles several times a week.

ADDED SUBJECT — ACTS AS AN OBJECT OF THE VERB "ENJOYS"; ACTS AS A NOUN

## Practice 6

*-ING* FRAGMENTS

Build two new sentences using the gerund phrase. First, combine the existing sentence with the *-ing* phrase to create a new sentence. Then, create another new sentence by adding missing information to the gerund phrase.

***-ing* phrase:**

stretching 30 minutes every day

**Sentence:**

Jogging three times a week keeps Alex in shape.

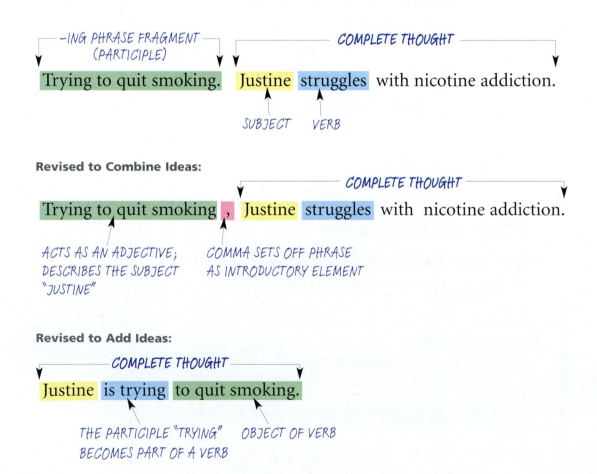

**1.** COMBINE IDEAS: ______________________________

______________________________

**2.** ADD IDEAS: ______________________________

______________________________

**5.** Participle Phrase

A participle is a form of a verb, but it is not a verb. A **participle** is an adjective that ends in *-ing,* such as *going, talking,* and *thinking.* A **participle phrase** is made up of a participle and the object of the participle such as *quitting smoking,* or *running a mile.* A participle phrase functions as an adjective; it describes nouns and other adjectives.

-ING PHRASE FRAGMENT (PARTICIPLE) — COMPLETE THOUGHT

Trying to quit smoking. Justine struggles with nicotine addiction.

SUBJECT (Justine) — VERB (struggles)

**Revised to Combine Ideas:**

COMPLETE THOUGHT

Trying to quit smoking, Justine struggles with nicotine addiction.

ACTS AS AN ADJECTIVE; DESCRIBES THE SUBJECT "JUSTINE"

COMMA SETS OFF PHRASE AS INTRODUCTORY ELEMENT

**Revised to Add Ideas:**

COMPLETE THOUGHT

Justine is trying to quit smoking.

THE PARTICIPLE "TRYING" BECOMES PART OF A VERB

OBJECT OF VERB

## Practice 7

### –*ING* FRAGMENTS

Build two new sentences using the participle phrase. First, combine the existing sentence with the participle phrase to create a new sentence. Then, create another new sentence by adding missing information to the participle phrase.

**Participle phrase:**

listening to her body

**Sentence:**

Tisha monitors her heart rate, physical discomfort, and level of fatigue.

**1.** COMBINE IDEAS: ________________________________________

________________________________________

**2.** ADD IDEAS: ________________________________________

________________________________________

More practice correcting *-ing* fragments: <www.mywritinglab.com>

## Practice 8

### PHRASE FRAGMENTS

Read the following sets of ideas. Identify the type of phrase fragment. Then, revise the ideas to eliminate fragments by combining or adding ideas.

**1.** Bones play many roles in the body. Providing structure, protecting organs, anchoring muscles, and storing calcium.

TYPE OF FRAGMENT: ________________________________________

REVISED SENTENCE: ________________________________________

________________________________________

________________________________________

________________________________________

**2.** Adequate calcium consumption and weight-bearing physical activity are necessary. To build strong bones and optimize bone mass.

TYPE OF FRAGMENT: ________________________________________

REVISED SENTENCE: ________________________________________

________________________________________

________________________________________

More practice correcting phrase fragments: <www.mywritinglab.com>

**3.** The body cannot produce calcium. A mineral needed to produce bone.

TYPE OF FRAGMENT: ____________________

REVISED SENTENCE: ____________________

**4.** By the age of 20. The average woman has acquired most of her skeletal mass.

TYPE OF FRAGMENT: ____________________

REVISED SENTENCE: ____________________

**5.** Eating foods and drinking beverages that contain lots of calcium during childhood.

TYPE OF FRAGMENT: ____________________

REVISED SENTENCE: ____________________

**6.** Rap star Nelly got milk. To build his bones.

TYPE OF FRAGMENT: ____________________

REVISED SENTENCE: ____________________

Practice 8

## Clause Fragments

For more on dependent and subordinate clauses, see Chapters 16 and 17.

A **clause** is a set of words that contains a subject and a verb. An **independent clause** states a complete thought in a sentence that begins with a capital letter and ends with punctuation such as a period or a semicolon. In contrast, a **dependent clause** expresses an incomplete thought or fragment.

### 6. DEPENDENT CLAUSE

A **dependent clause**, also known as a **subordinate clause**, does not make sense on its own. A dependent clause is formed by placing a subordinating conjunction in front of a subject and a verb:

INCOMPLETE THOUGHT

After Dylan scored the winning home run.

SUBORDINATING CONJUNCTION SIGNALS INCOMPLETE THOUGHT (After)
SUBJECT (Dylan)
VERB (scored)

A **subordinating conjunction** states the relationship between two clauses:

COMPLETE THOUGHT

DEPENDENT CLAUSE

After Dylan scored, the team celebrated.

SUBORDINATING CONJUNCTION INDICATES THE ORDER OF EVENTS (After)
SUBJECT (Dylan)
VERB (scored)
COMMA SETS OFF INTRODUCTORY CLAUSE (,)
INDEPENDENT CLAUSE EXPLAINS WHAT HAPPENED (the team celebrated.)

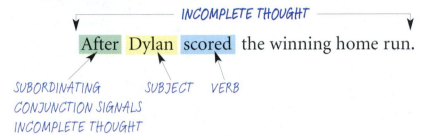

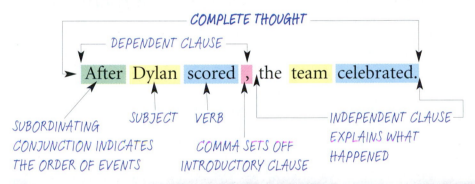

The following chart lists common subordinating conjunctions based on the relationships they express.

| Subordinating Conjunctions and the Relationships They Express | | | | |
|---|---|---|---|---|
| **Cause** | **Contrast** | **Time** | **Place** | **Condition** |
| as | as if | after | where | even if |
| because | although | as | wherever | if |
| in order that | even though | as long as | | only if |
| now that | though | before | | unless |
| since | whereas | once | | when |
| so | while | since | | whether or not |
| | | until | | |
| | | when | | |
| | | whenever | | |
| | | while | | |

To create a sentence, combine a dependent clause with an independent clause. Or revise the dependent clause into an independent clause by dropping the subordinating conjunction.

DEPENDENT CLAUSE FRAGMENT

SUBORDINATING CONJUNCTION

Because healthy employees are more productive. Some corporations provide health club benefits for their employees.

SUBJECT VERB

COMPLETE THOUGHT

**Revised to Combine Ideas:**

DEPENDENT CLAUSE

COMMA SETS OFF INTRODUCTORY CLAUSE

Because healthy employees are more productive, some corporations provide health club benefits for their employees.

COMPLETE THOUGHT

**Revised to Add Ideas:**

INDEPENDENT CLAUSE FORMED BY DROPPING "BECAUSE"

SEMICOLON JOINS TWO INDEPENDENT CLAUSES

Healthy employees are more productive; therefore, some corporations provide health club benefits for their employees.

COMPLETE THOUGHT

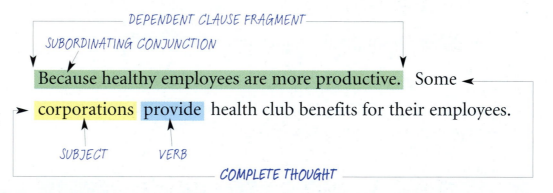

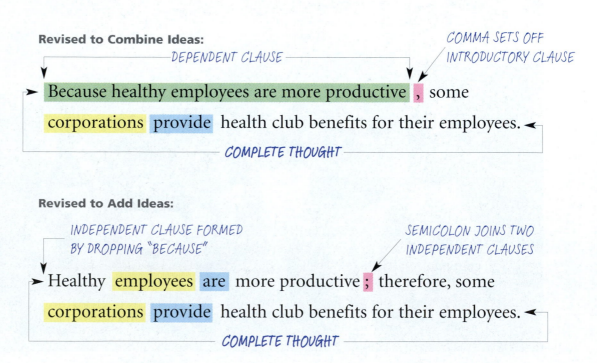

Practice 9

DEPENDENT CLAUSE FRAGMENTS

Build two new sentences using the following sets of ideas. First, combine the existing sentence with the dependent clause to create a new sentence. Then, create another new sentence by revising the dependent clause into an independent clause.

**Dependent clause:**

because young children grow rapidly and have increased iron requirements

**Sentence:**

Young children are at risk of iron deficiency.

**1.** COMBINE IDEAS: ______________________________

______________________________

**2.** ADD IDEAS: ______________________________

______________________________

More practice correcting dependent clause fragments: <www.mywritinglab.com>

## 7 RELATIVE CLAUSE

One type of dependent clause is the relative clause, such as *who scored the winning home run.* A **relative clause** describes a noun or pronoun in an independent clause. A **relative pronoun** introduces the relative clause and relates it to the noun or pronoun it describes.

| Relative Pronouns | | | | |
|---|---|---|---|---|
| who | whom | whose | which | that |

Join the relative clause to the independent clause that contains the word it describes. Or revise the relative clause into an independent clause by replacing the relative pronoun with a noun.

COMPLETE THOUGHT — RELATIVE CLAUSE FRAGMENT

Many people suffer from iron deficiency. Which can cause anemia.

SUBJECT (people) — VERB (suffer) — RELATIVE PRONOUN; SUBJECT OF INCOMPLETE THOUGHT (Which)

**Revised to Combine Ideas:**

COMPLETE THOUGHT

COMMA INTRODUCES RELATIVE CLAUSE

Many people suffer from iron deficiency, which can cause anemia.

ADDS NONESSENTIAL INFORMATION ABOUT "IRON DEFICIENCY"

**Revised to Combine Ideas:**

COMPLETE THOUGHT

For many people, iron deficiency can cause anemia.

NOUN REPLACES "WHICH" AS SUBJECT OF "CAN CAUSE" — VERB

## Practice 10

### RELATIVE CLAUSE FRAGMENTS

Build two new sentences using the relative clause. First, combine the existing sentence with the relative clause to create a new sentence. Then, create another new sentence by revising the relative clause into an independent clause.

**Relative clause:**

which impairs mental and physical development in infants and children

**Sentence:**

The most common cause of anemia is iron deficiency.

**1.** COMBINE IDEAS: ______________________________

______________________________

**2.** ADD IDEAS: ______________________________

______________________________

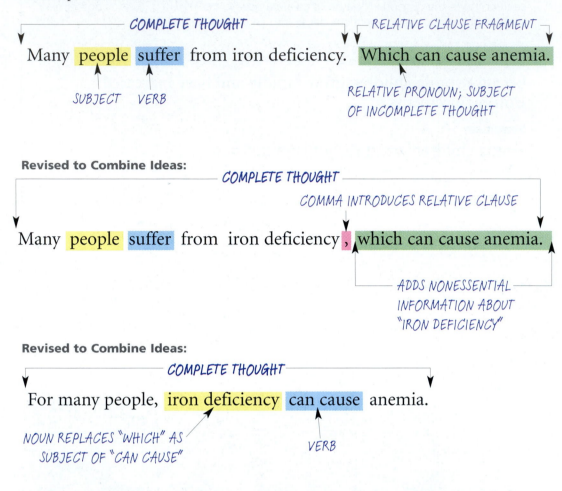

More practice correcting relative clause fragments: <www.mywritinglab.com>

# Practice 11

## CLAUSE FRAGMENTS

Revise the ideas to eliminate clause fragments.

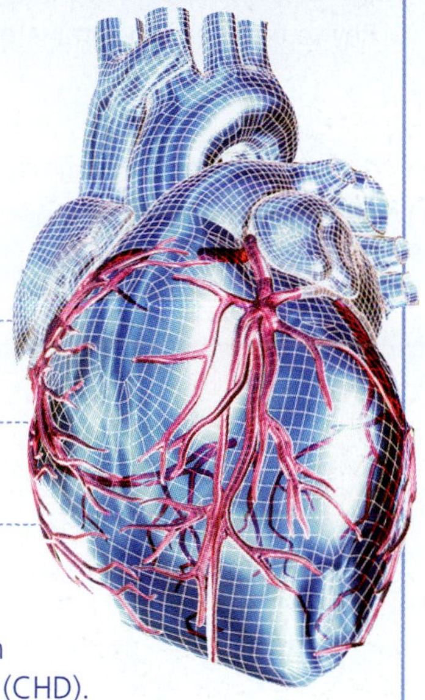

**1.** The heart needs a constant supply of oxygen and nutrients. Which are carried to it by the blood in the coronary arteries.

**2.** When the coronary arteries become narrowed or clogged by cholesterol and fat deposits. They cannot supply enough blood to the heart, and the result is coronary heart disease (CHD).

**3.** Cholesterol is a waxy, fat-like substance. That occurs naturally in all parts of the body. That your body needs to function normally.

**4.** Unlike age, high cholesterol can be controlled. Which is a factor beyond our control.

**5.** You are at higher risk of having coronary heart disease. If you smoke, are overweight, and eat a high-fat diet.

More practice correcting clause fragments: <www.mywritinglab.com>

# Practice 12

## FRAGMENTS

Revise the ideas to eliminate fragments by combining or adding ideas.

**1.** Sleep apnea is a common disorder. That can be very serious.

**2.** Sleep apnea can occur 20 to 30 times or more an hour. A pause that typically lasts 10–20 seconds or more.

**3.** Moving out of deep sleep and into light sleep several times during the night, resulting in poor sleep quality.

**4.** During sleep, enough air cannot flow into your lungs through your mouth and nose even though you try. To grasp a breath.

**5.** Your breathing may become hard and noisy and may even stop. For short periods of time (apneas).

## Practice 13

Proofread the following paragraph for fragments. Revise to eliminate fragments by combining or adding ideas.

### How to Maintain Your Weight

(1) In order to stay at the same body weight, people must balance the amount of calories in the foods and drinks they consume. (2) With the amount of calories the body uses. (3) Physical activity is one important way to use food energy. (4) Most Americans spend much of their working day in activities that require little energy. (5) In addition, many Americans of all ages now spend a lot of leisure time each day being inactive. (6) For example, watching television or working at a computer. (7) To burn calories, devote less time to sedentary activities like sitting. (8) Spend more time in activities like walking to the store or around the block. (9) Use stairs rather than elevators. (10) Less sedentary activity and more vigorous activity may help you reduce body fat and disease risk. (11) Try to do 30 minutes or more of moderate physical activity on most—preferably all—days of the week. (12) The kinds and amounts of food people eat affect their ability to maintain weight. (13) High-fat foods contain more calories per serving than other foods. (14) Which may increase the likelihood of weight gain. (15) However, even when people eat less high-fat food. (16) They still can gain weight from eating too many foods high in starch, sugars, or protein. (17) Eat a variety of foods. (18) Emphasizing pasta, rice, bread, and other whole-grain foods as well as fruits and vegetables. (19) These foods are filling, but lower in calories than foods rich in fats or oils. (20) The pattern of eating may also be important. (21) Snacks provide a large percentage of daily calories for many Americans. (22) Unless nutritious snacks are part of the daily meal plan. (23) Snacking may lead to weight gain. (24) A pattern of frequent binge eating, with or without alternating periods of food restriction, may also contribute to weight problems.

—Adapted from "Balance the Food You Eat With Physical Activity—Maintain or Improve Your Weight." Nutrition and Your Health: Dietary Guidelines for Americans. U. S. Department of Agriculture. Dec. 1995.

More practice correcting fragments: <www.mywritinglab.com>

# Writing Assignments

## Writing for Everyday Life

Read the following letter to a doctor requesting information. Edit to eliminate fragments. Use your own paper.

Dear Dr. Alito:

Please send my records to the office of Dr. Alice Godbey. Who is currently treating me for a stress fracture in my right shin. Because your office ordered the x-rays of the injury. You must approve their release. Since you are my primary physician, Dr. Godbey's office will return the x-rays to your office. After my surgery.

Sincerely,

Sandra Acuri

## Writing for College Life

Read the following paragraph written for a history class. Edit to eliminate fragments. Use your own paper.

Sojourner Truth who was first known as Isabella Baumfree. Born a slave somewhere around 1797. While in slavery. She had five children with the man she married, Thomas Jeffery Harvey. Fleeing slavery around 1827. She left the country and lived in Canada. Isabella returned to New York. When the state abolished slavery in 1829. She worked with Elijah Pierson preaching on street corners for more than a decade. Later, she became a well-known speaker against slavery and for women's rights. She is still noted today. For her famous speech, "Ain't I a Woman."

## Writing for Working Life

Read the following request for supplies in a department of a retail business. Edit to eliminate fragments. Use your own paper.

To: Office Supply Department
From: Customer Service Department
Re: Order # 3214

According to our records. Our order for three computer desks, three computer chairs, and three filing cabinets was placed three weeks ago. At that time, you assured us that you would deliver this order promptly. Since our need was urgent. To meet the needs of our customers. We have added three new employees. Employees who began reporting to work two weeks ago. If these items are not delivered by the end of the week, I will refer this matter to your supervisor.

Academic Learning Log

WHAT HAVE I LEARNED ABOUT CORRECTING FRAGMENTS?

To test and track your understanding of correcting fragments, complete the following ideas. Use several sentences as needed for each response.

1. What are the two traits of a sentence?

---

---

2. A fragment is ________

---

3. A phrase is ________

---

4. A clause is ________

---

5. Two types of clauses are ________ and ________ clauses.

6. The five types of phrases discussed in this chapter include the ________, ________, ________, ________, and ________

7. Two ways to eliminate fragments include ________ ideas or ________ ideas.

8. **How will I use what I have learned?** In your notebook, discuss how you will apply to your own writing what you have learned about correcting fragments.

9. **What do I still need to study about fragments?** In your notebook, describe your ongoing study needs by describing what, when, and how you will continue studying fragments.

# 23 Misplaced and Dangling Modifiers

**Chapter Preview**

- What's the Point of Correcting Misplaced and Dangling Modifiers?
- Understanding the Point of Correcting Misplaced and Dangling Modifiers: One Student Writer's Response
- Applying the Point: Correcting Misplaced and Dangling Modifiers

## A modifier is a word or phrase that describes, clarifies, or gives more information about another word in a sentence.

A misplaced modifier is a word or phrase illogically separated from the word it describes.

Modifiers are words that describe, restrict, or limit other words in a sentence. For example, modifiers help us communicate what we see or how we feel. The photo on the next page illustrates a person experiencing intense feelings.

# What's the Point of Correcting Misplaced and Dangling Modifiers?

Practice 1

WRITING FROM LIFE

**PHOTOGRAPHIC ORGANIZER: MISPLACED AND DANGLING MODIFIERS**

Read the sentence below that describes the marathon runner and answer the question.

> Running the marathon, her legs cried out in pain.

**What is the point of correcting misplaced and dangling modifiers?**

# Understanding the Point of Correcting Misplaced and Dangling Modifiers: One Student Writer's Response

*When I first read the sentence, I kind of laughed because it created such a funny image in my mind of "legs crying." I know the author didn't mean to be funny. But the way the idea is worded takes away from the serious nature of the situation. And as a reader, I don't know who ran the marathon. Information is either jumbled or missing from this sentence. I suggested the following revision: "While running the marathon, Lynda cried out in pain from leg cramps."*

# Applying the Point: Correcting Misplaced and Dangling Modifiers

Sentence clarity can be achieved through appropriately placed and clearly expressed modifiers. A **modifier** is a word or phrase that describes, clarifies, or gives more information about another word in a sentence. Confusion in meaning occurs when a modifier is misplaced in the sentence or when the word being modified is not stated in the sentence. To avoid confusion, place modifiers next to the word that is being described.

## Misplaced Modifiers

A **misplaced modifier** is a word or phrase illogically separated from the word it describes. The following chart offers a few examples and revisions of common types of misplaced modifiers.

### Misplaced Modifiers

**MISPLACED WORDS** A misplaced word is separated from the word it limits or restricts.

WORD "ONLY" DESCRIBES ?

? ?

Belle Glade, Florida only has been flooded twice by hurricanes.

**Revision #1**

WORD "ONLY" DESCRIBES "TWICE"

Belle Glade, Florida has been flooded only **twice** by hurricanes.

**Revision #2**

Only Belle Glade, Florida has been flooded twice by hurricanes.

WORD "ONLY" DESCRIBES "BELLE GLADE"

**MISPLACED PHRASE** A phrase that describes a noun is placed next to the wrong noun and separated from the noun it describes.

PHRASE "WITHOUT HER GLASSES" DESCRIBES ?

? ?

She couldn't tell what kind of animal it was without her glasses.

**Revision**

PHRASE "WITHOUT HER GLASSES" DESCRIBES "SHE"

Without her glasses, she couldn't tell what kind of animal it was.

ADDED COMMA SETS OFF INTRODUCTORY PHRASE

**Example**

? ?

Jammed into his backpack, Sean hunted through the papers.

PHRASE "JAMMED INTO HIS BACKPACK" DESCRIBES ?

ADDED COMMA SETS OFF INTRODUCTORY PHRASE

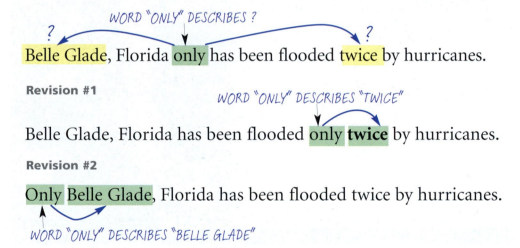

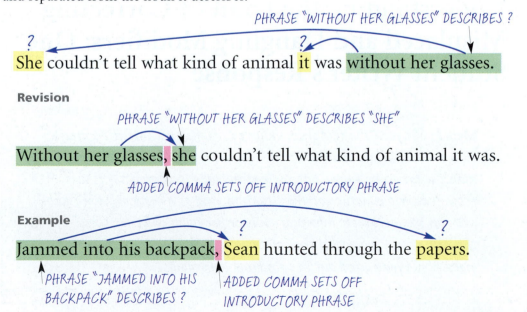

**Revision**

Sean hunted through the papers jammed into his backpack.

PHRASE "JAMMED INTO HIS BACKPACK" DESCRIBES PAPERS

**MISPLACED CLAUSE** A dependent clause that describes a particular word is placed next to the wrong word and is separated from the word the clause describes.

**Example**

CLAUSE "WHO GAVE BIRTH TO TWINS" DESCRIBES ?

The 60-year-old woman was hounded by the reporter who gave birth to twins.

**Revision**

CLAUSE "WHO GAVE BIRTH TO TWINS" DESCRIBES "WOMAN"

The 60-year-old woman who gave birth to twins was hounded by the reporter.

## Practice 2

**CORRECTING MISPLACED MODIFIERS**

Revise the following student sentences to correct misplaced modifiers.

**1.** The groom dropped the wedding ring, trembling with nervousness.

The groom, trembling with nervousness, dropped the wedding ring.

**2.** Topped with onions and mushrooms, the guests enjoyed filet mignon.

The guests enjoyed the filet mignon, topped with onions and mushrooms.

**3.** Only Margarita drinks wine on the weekends.

**4.** Tired and sweaty, the sun beat down on the runners.

**5.** Kirstie Alley had joined Jenny Craig, who claims to have lost 65 pounds.

## Dangling Modifiers

A **dangling modifier** is a word, phrase, or clause that modifies a word not stated in the sentence. Therefore, the dangling modifier seems to describe the nearest word, yet it doesn't make sense. To revise dangling modifiers, you may need to add or rephrase ideas.

### Dangling Modifiers: Two Revision Tips

A **dangling modifier** is a phrase that describes a word not stated in the sentence.

**EXAMPLES What or whom do these phrases describe in each sentence below?**

**Sentence #1**

While cleaning the house, a fifty dollar bill turned up.

**Sentence #2**

Observing the wildlife, the canoe glided through the waters.

**Sentence #3**

Running in second place, the finish line came into view.

**REVISION TIP #1** Change the dangling modifier into a logical clause with a subject and a verb.

**Revised Sentence #1**

ADDED SUBJECT AND VERB TO CREATE DEPENDENT CLAUSE

While I was cleaning the house, a fifty dollar bill turned up.

**Revised Sentence #2**

ADDED SUBORDINATING CONJUNCTION, SUBJECT, AND VERB TO CREATE DEPENDENT CLAUSE

As we were observing the wildlife, the canoe glided through the waters.

**Revised Sentence #3**

ADDED SUBJECT AND VERB TO CREATE INDEPENDENT CLAUSE

I was running in second place; the finish line came into view.

ADDED SEMICOLON JOINS TWO INDEPENDENT CLAUSES

**REVISION TIP #2** Revise the main clause to include the word being modified.

More practice with misplaced and dangling modifiers: <www.mywritinglab.com>

**Revised Sentence #1**

PHRASE "WHILE CLEANING THE HOUSE" DESCRIBES ADDED SUBJECT

While cleaning the house, I found a fifty dollar bill.

ADDED SUBJECT AND VERB

**Revised Sentence #2**

PHRASE "OBSERVING THE WILDLIFE" DESCRIBES ADDED SUBJECT

Observing the wildlife, we glided the canoe through the waters.

ADDED SUBJECT

**Revised Sentence #3**

PHRASE "RUNNING IN SECOND PLACE" DESCRIBES ADDED SUBJECT

Running in second place, I saw the finish line come into view.

ADDED SUBJECT AND VERB

## Practice 3

CORRECTING DANGLING MODIFIERS

Revise the following student sentences to eliminate dangling modifiers.

**1.** Driving across country, hotels advertised "Kids stay for free."

Driving across country, I saw hotels advertised "Kids stay for free."

**2.** Popping up to stand on a surf board, abdominal muscles must be strong.

Popping up to stand on a surf board, surfers abdominal muscles must be strong.

**3.** Getting on the rollercoaster, my stomach felt queasy.

**4.** My essay was finally finished after thinking and writing for several hours.

**5.** Broken in three places, Marla needed surgery and a cast.

More practice with misplaced and dangling modifiers: <www.mywritinglab.com>

## Practice 4

**CORRECTING MISPLACED AND DANGLING MODIFIERS**

Revise to correct misplaced and dangling modifiers. Move or add ideas as needed.

**1.** As a kid, my parents had pretty strict rules. ____________________

**2.** Marianne Pearl is the widow of Danny Pearl, played by Angelina Jolie in *A Mighty Heart*.

____________________

**3.** Joanna gave a dog to her daughter named Spot. ____________________

**4.** Jamal was referred to a specialist suffering from a rare infection. ____________________

**5.** After broiling for 10 minutes, I turned off the oven. ____________________

More practice with misplaced and dangling modifiers: <www.mywritinglab.com>

## Practice 5

**MISPLACED AND DANGLING MODIFIERS REVIEW**

In the space provided on the next page, revise the following paragraph to eliminate misplaced and dangling modifiers.

Cubicles roll off the assembly line that are parts of homes at a Toyota plant in Japan. Cubicles, also called units, come equipped with stairways, closets, and bathtubs. Kasugai Housing Works, run by Toyota Motor Corp., a plant for prefabricated housing, applies technology acquired from years of making cars to homebuilding. For example, a smart key opens and closes the front door similar to the remote car key. Car painting skills and techniques provide scratch-resistant coatings to walls. In addition, Toyota's homes are mass produced like cars. About 85 percent of the work on the metal frame cubicles is finished at the plant. Made to order, a huge crane stacks the prefabricated cubicles and tops them with a roof in just six hours. Varying in size up to 20 feet long, an average Japanese home is made of 12 units or cubicles. Visiting housing parks, floor plans, interiors, and materials are mixed and matched.

More practice with misplaced and dangling modifiers: <www.mywritinglab.com>

Practice 5

# Writing Assignments

## Writing for Everyday Life

Edit the following posting for a blog on a social networking site such as MySpace.com. Eliminate misplaced or dangling modifiers. Use your own paper.

Thursday, January 26, 2006

We had the best weekend ever! Only our friends come to visit a couple of times a year. We decided to swim with the dolphins eager to have fun. Surprised by their sleek and smooth skin, our hands gently caressed the dolphins. The dolphins loved swimming with us. They actually made eye contact with us. It was an awesome experience.

# Writing Assignments CONTINUED

## Writing for College Life

Edit the following part of a report, written for a psychology class. Eliminate misplaced or dangling modifiers. The student was asked to illustrate a personal trait. Use your own paper.

I go to unfamiliar places by myself. Swimming in shark-infested waters, my parents worry about me. I walk alone through dark areas to get to my car without pepper spray. I make friends with weird people, making poor choices about what is safe and what is threatening. I am too trusting.

As a very young child, my parents had to keep an extra close eye on me. As the story goes, I had a tendency to wander off in search of new companions. At the age of four, my parents, brother, and sister lost track of me on a day trip to Wet N' Wild. Unconcerned, I skipped through the masses, tugging on the shorts of giants, asking "Do you know my Dad? Have you seen my Mom?" Eventually, I spotted a woman who must have been a lifeguard in a red bathing suit. She wasn't, but when I asked her for help to find my family, she obliged, returning me to my panic-stricken mother and father.

## Writing for Working Life

Edit the following performance evaluation of an employee. Eliminate misplaced or dangling modifiers. Use your own paper.

To: Human Resources
From: Anna Shrimali, Manager
RE: Evaluation of Joanna Santiago

Joanna Santiago has been employed for three months. As an employee, her work is completed to a level above and beyond expectations. She is well able to deal with any type customer prone to listen carefully and act quickly. In addition, her efforts have saved our diligent company several thousands dollars. Only Ms. Santiago thinks of the good of the team, accepting the hardest assignments without complaint. I fully recommend Ms. Santiago for both a promotion and a raise.

## WHAT HAVE I LEARNED ABOUT MISPLACED AND DANGLING MODIFIERS?

To test and track your understanding, answer the following questions.

**1.** What is a misplaced modifier? ______________________________

______________________________________________

**2.** How is a misplaced modifier corrected? ______________________________

______________________________________________

**3.** What is a dangling modifier? ______________________________

______________________________________________

**4.** What are two ways to correct a dangling modifier? ______________________________

______________________________________________

______________________________________________

**5. How will I use what I have learned about misplaced and dangling modifiers?**
In your notebook, discuss how you will apply to your own writing what you have learned about misplaced and dangling modifiers. When during the writing process will you apply this knowledge?

**6. What do I still need to study about misplaced and dangling modifiers?**
In your notebook, describe your ongoing study needs by describing what, when, and how you will continue to study about misplaced and dangling modifiers.

Academic Learning Log

Agreement?

- Understanding the Point of Subject-Verb Agreement: One Student Writer's Response
- Applying the Point: Subject-Verb Agreement

Homework page 468-485 all practice problems!

# Subject-Verb Agreement: Present Tense

## In the present tense, subjects and verbs must agree in number. Singular subjects must take singular verbs; plural subjects must take plural verbs.

Subject-verb agreement in the present tense ranks as one of the most common errors in written and spoken English. For many people, subject-verb agreement reflects regional speech or dialect. For example, many Southerners use the expression "you was" instead of "you were." Understanding the difference between regional speech and standard English is an important step in the educational process.

# What's the Point of Subject-Verb Agreement?

WRITING FROM LIFE

Practice 1

## PHOTOGRAPHIC ORGANIZER: SUBJECT-VERB AGREEMENT

Complete the following activity and answer the question "What's the point of subject-verb agreement?"

Assume you are a manager, and you are interviewing possible candidates for a job opening in your department. A question you asked drew nearly identical responses from two separate candidates. Which one sounds more professional? Why?

**Manager's question:**
What is a current example of your greatest strength as an employee?

**Candidate 1:**
My greatest strengths is listening, following directions, and problem solving. For example, I listens carefully to the procedures that comes to us from the home office. As a result, I is now sharing the steps of a new procedure about receiving goods with fellow workers to prevent confusion before it happen.

**Candidate 2:**
My greatest strengths are problem solving, listening, and following directions and procedures. For example, I carefully listen to solve problems and understand the procedures that come to us from the home office. As a result, I am now training fellow employees in the steps of a new process for receiving goods to avoid a problem before it happens.

Subjects - who/what?

Verb - action linking

**What's the point of subject-verb agreement?**

Candidate two sounds much more professional because everything flows and fits together. The point of subject-verb agreement is so that things fit together and take the right form.

## Understanding the Point of Subject-Verb Agreement: One Student Writer's Response

The following paragraph records one writer's thoughts about the point of subject-verb agreement in the job interview example.

*Candidate 2 sounded much more polished and educated. Candidate 1 mixed singular subjects with plural verbs or plural subjects with singular verbs. In contrast, Candidate 2 used singular subjects with singular verbs and plural subjects with plural verbs. In fact, in our group discussion of the example, we made a chart to show the contrast between the two responses:*

*Candidate 1:*

| Subject | Verb |
|---|---|
| strengths | is |
| I | listens |
| procedures | that comes |
| I | is |
| it | happen |

*Candidate 2:*

| Subject | Verb |
|---|---|
| strengths | are |
| I | listen |
| procedures | that come |
| I | am |
| it | happens |

*As our group talked about singular and plural subjects and verbs, I got really confused because of how the letter "s" is used to make a word plural. My group explained to me that the "s" is used to make subjects plural, but the "s" is also used to make some verbs singular.*

## Applying the Point: Subject-Verb Agreement

In the present tense, subjects and verbs must agree in number. A singular subject must have a singular verb; a plural subject must have a plural verb. The following chart uses the sample verb "think" to illustrate present tense agreement in number.

| Present Tense Agreement | | | | |
|---|---|---|---|---|
| | Singular **Subject** and | **Verb** | Plural **Subject** and | **Verb** |
| First Person | I | think | We | think |
| Second Person | You | think | You | think |
| Third Person | He<br>She<br>It | thinks | They | think |

For standard verbs, only the third person singular verb is formed by adding *-s* or *-es*.

| Third person singular subject | → | present tense verb ends with *-s* or *-es* |
|---|---|---|
| He<br>She<br>It | →<br>→<br>→ | apologizes<br>accepts<br>catches |

# Practice 2

## SUBJECT-VERB AGREEMENT

Fill in the following charts with the correct form of each subject and verb. A few blanks are completed as examples.

| **1. To Listen** | **Subject** | **Verb** |
|---|---|---|
| First Person (singular) | I | listen |
| Second Person | ~~She~~ you | listen~~s~~ |
| Third Person (singular) | They | listen |

| **2. To Hear** | **Subject** | **Verb** |
|---|---|---|
| First Person (plural) | I | hear |
| Second Person | ~~She~~ you | hear~~s~~ |
| Third Person (plural) | They | hear |

| **3. To Watch** | **Subject** | **Verb** |
|---|---|---|
| First Person (singular) | I | watch |
| Second Person | ~~She~~ you | watch |
| Third Person (singular) | They | watch |

| **4. To Hope** | **Subject** | **Verb** |
|---|---|---|
| Second Person (singular) | I | hope |
| Second Person | ~~She~~ you | hope~~s~~ |
| Third Person (singular) | They | hope |

| **5. To Fax** | **Subject** | **Verb** |
|---|---|---|
| First Person (plural) | I | faxed |
| Second Person | you | faxed |
| Third Person (singular) | He | faxes |

Practice 3

SUBJECT-VERB AGREEMENT

Circle the verb form that agrees with the subject of each of the following sentences.

1. Drugs (is are) a factor in careless driving because a drug (affects affect) a driver both mentally and physically.
2. For example, Samuel (takes take) a new headache medicine, and the side effects (includes include) drowsiness.
3. Then, he (decides decide) to drive even though he (has have) taken this new medicine.
4. The medication (makes make) him drowsy, and it (becomes become) difficult to stay alert.
5. Due to the medication, Samuel's reflexes (is are) also much slower so that they (causes cause) a delay in his reactions to driving conditions.

More practice with subject-verb agreement: <www.mywritinglab.com>

# Key Verbs in the Present Tense: *To Have, To Do, To Be*

Three key verbs are used both as main verbs and as helping verbs to express a wide variety of meanings: *to have, to do,* and *to be*. Memorize their present tense singular and plural forms to ensure subject-verb agreement.

| *To Have:* Present Tense | | | | |
|---|---|---|---|---|
| | Singular **Subject** | and **Verb** | Plural **Subject** | and **Verb** |
| **First Person** | I | have | We | have |
| **Second Person** | You | have | You | have |
| **Third Person** | He<br>She<br>It | has | They | have |

Practice 4

SUBJECT-VERB AGREEMENT: *TO HAVE*

Write the form of the verb *to have* that agrees with the subject in each of the following sentences.

1. Patty Blair has a disability known as Fragile X syndrome.
2. Fragile X syndrome has an effect on speech and motor skills as well as mental abilities.
3. Despite Patty's disability, she has a full-time job.
4. Several companies have discovered the rewards of employing mentally disabled workers.
5. Write a sentence using *has* or *have* as a verb. Suggested topic: Overcoming a Physical Disability.

---

---

| *To Do:* Present Tense | | |
|---|---|---|
| | Singular **Subject** and **Verb** | Plural **Subject** and **Verb** |
| **First Person** | I do | We do |
| **Second Person** | You do | You do |
| **Third Person** | He / She / It — does | They do |

More practice with subject-verb agreement: <www.mywritinglab.com>

Practice 5

SUBJECT-VERB AGREEMENT: *TO DO*

Write the form of the verb *to do* that agrees with the subject in each of the following sentences.

1. Mentally disabled people do well in certain jobs.
2. A person with Down's Syndrome, David Welch, does well working in a systematic way as a mail clerk.
3. He does his best work when he follows a routine system of steps.
4. David works with a highly educated and professional team; they do seem to enjoy his positive attitude and dependable work habits.
5. Write a sentence using *do* or *does* as the verb. Suggested topic: Doing One's Best.

.................................................................................................

.................................................................................................

The verb **to do** is often used with the adverb "not" to express a negative thought. Frequently this negative is stated in the form of the contractions *doesn't* and *don't* that combine the verb and the adverb into shorter words. The verb part of the contraction must still agree with its subject.

More practice with subject-verb agreement: <www.mywritinglab.com>

| *To Do* and *Not:* Contraction Form | | |
|---|---|---|
| | Singular **Subject** and **Verb** | Plural **Subject** and **Verb** |
| **First Person** | I don't agree | We don't agree |
| **Second Person** | You don't seem well | You don't seem well |
| **Third Person** | He / She / It — doesn't care | They don't care |

## Practice 6

### SUBJECT-VERB AGREEMENT: *TO DO* AND *NOT*

Fill in the blank with the form of the verb *to do* that agrees with the subject of each of the following sentences. Use the contractions *doesn't* and *don't* as needed.

1. He ....does.... not have to study to earn high grades, but I ....do.... not pass unless I study for hours.
2. It ....does.... hurt your reputation to admit that you are wrong.
3. Even when we ask politely, they ....don't.... turn down the music.
4. You ....do.... understand why I am so angry.
5. Write a sentence using *do, does, doesn't,* or *don't*. Suggested topic: A Helpful Piece of Advice.

..............................................................................................................

..............................................................................................................

More practice with subject-verb agreement: <www.mywritinglab.com>

The ***to be*** verb is unusual because it uses three forms in the present tense: *am*, *is*, and *are*.

| ***To Be:* Present Tense** | | | | |
|---|---|---|---|---|
| | Singular **Subject** | and **Verb** | Plural **Subject** | and **Verb** |
| **First Person** | I | am | We | are |
| **Second Person** | You | are | You | are |
| **Third Person** | He<br>She<br>It | is | They | are |

## Practice 7

### SUBJECT-VERB AGREEMENT: *TO BE*

Write the form of the verb *to be* that agrees with the subject of each of the following sentences.

1. A cell phone ....is.... a multi-purpose device.
2. Cell phones ....are.... able to take pictures, download music, and access the Internet.
3. We ....are.... delighted with the innovations in cell phones.
4. Made by Digit Wireless, the Fastap keyboard ....is.... a full typewriter keyboard for a cell phone.
5. Write a sentence using a form of the verb *to be*. Suggested topic: A Useful Tool.

..............................................................................................................

..............................................................................................................

More practice with subject-verb agreement <www.mywritinglab.com>

## Subjects Separated from Verbs

The standard order of ideas in a sentence places the subject first, immediately followed by the verb. However, subjects are often separated from their verbs by **prepositional phrases.**

A **preposition** is a word that has a noun or pronoun as its object and states a relationship between its object and another word. A prepositional phrase begins with a preposition and ends with the object of the preposition. The object of the preposition can never be the subject of a sentence. Identifying prepositional phrases keeps you from confusing them with the subject of the sentence. The verb of a sentence agrees with the subject, not the object of the preposition.

**Example**

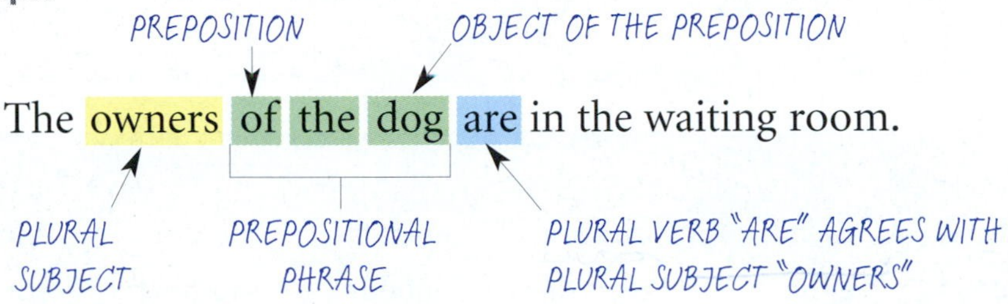


The following chart of prepositional phrases lists a few common prepositions and sample objects.

| Common Prepositional Phrases | | | |
|---|---|---|---|
| **Preposition** | **Object** | **Preposition** | **Object** |
| at | work | of | concern |
| from | home | on | the desk |
| in | the office | with | experience |

For more information on prepositions, see Chapter 16

Practice 8

SUBJECT-VERB AGREEMENT

Choose the verb form that agrees with the subject of each of the following sentences. Cross out prepositional phrases. Underline the subject. Circle the appropriate verb.

1. A résumé of many short-term jobs (is are) not desirable.
2. An employer at most companies (does do) want committed, goal-oriented employees.
3. Prospective employees with a résumé of a long-held job (has have) proof of their commitment and perseverance.
4. A history of frequently changing jobs (raises raise) concerns with prospective employers.
5. Most hiring managers, in a recent interview, (states state) length of time in previous employment as a very important factor in hiring.

## Singular or Plural Subjects

To establish subject-verb agreement, first identify a subject as plural or singular. Some subjects may seem singular or plural when actually they are not. The following section identifies and discusses several of these types of subjects and the rules of their agreement with verbs.

## Indefinite Pronouns

Indefinite pronouns do not refer to specific nouns. Most indefinite pronouns are singular; a few are plural, and some can be either singular or plural. Consider the context of the indefinite pronoun to achieve subject-verb agreement.

- **Singular indefinite pronouns agree with singular verbs.**

**Example**

Everyone has a phone.

SINGULAR INDEFINITE PRONOUN

SINGULAR VERB "HAS" AGREES WITH SINGULAR INDEFINITE PRONOUN "EVERYONE"

| Singular Indefinite Pronouns | | | | | |
|---|---|---|---|---|---|
| anybody | each | everyone | neither | no one | somebody |
| anyone | either | everything | nobody | nothing | someone |
| anything | everybody | much | none | one | something |

- **Plural indefinite pronouns agree with plural verbs.**

**Example**

Few have their phones.

PLURAL INDEFINITE PRONOUN

PLURAL VERB "HAVE" AGREES WITH PLURAL INDEFINITE PRONOUN "FEW"

| Plural Indefinite Pronouns | | | |
|---|---|---|---|
| both | few | many | several |

- **Some indefinite pronouns are singular or plural based on context and meaning. The context determines agreement with singular or plural verbs.**

**Example of Indefinite Pronoun That Is Singular Based on Context**

All has stopped.

INDEFINITE PRONOUN IS SINGULAR BASED ON CONTEXT

SINGULAR VERB "HAS" AGREES WITH SINGULAR INDEFINITE PRONOUN "ALL"

**Example of Indefinite Pronoun That Is Plural Based on Context**

All have their chances.

INDEFINITE PRONOUN IS PLURAL BASED ON CONTEXT

PLURAL VERB "HAVE" AGREES WITH PLURAL INDEFINITE PRONOUN "ALL"

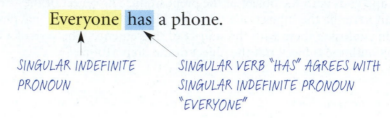

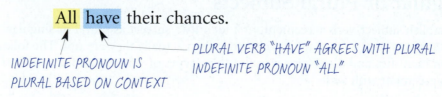

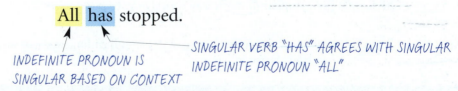

| Singular or Plural Indefinite Pronouns Based on Context | | | | |
|---|---|---|---|---|
| all | any | more | most | some |

**SUBJECT-VERB AGREEMENT: INDEFINITE PRONOUNS**

Practice 9

Choose the verb form that agrees with the subject of each of the following sentences. Cross out prepositional phrases. Underline the subject. Circle the appropriate verb.

1. Most ~~of us~~ (has have) a person ~~in our lives~~ who acts as an admirable role model.
2. Some ~~of our role models~~ (is are) our family members.
3. However, sometimes, one ~~of these role models~~ (is are) a friend.
4. For example, a few of my role models (is are) my mom, my best friend, and my pastor.
5. Write a sentence using a plural indefinite pronoun. A suggested topic: A Problem in Society.

## Collective Nouns

Collective nouns are singular forms of names of groups. They name a collection of people, animals, or items as a unit. The agreement between a collective noun and a verb depends on the context of the sentence.

- **When a collective noun acts as one unit, a singular verb is needed to achieve agreement.**

  **Example**

  The flock of birds is about to take flight.

  COLLECTIVE NOUN "FLOCK" REFERS TO ONE GROUP (OF BIRDS)

  SINGULAR VERB "IS" AGREES WITH SINGULAR MEANING OF "FLOCK"

- **When a collective noun represents the individuals in a group, a plural verb is needed to achieve agreement.**

  **Example**

  The jury have differing views about the evidence.

  COLLECTIVE NOUN "JURY" REFERS TO THE INDIVIDUALS ON THE JURY

  PLURAL VERB "HAVE" AGREES WITH PLURAL MEANING OF "JURY"

| Common Collective Nouns | | | | |
|---|---|---|---|---|
| assembly | class | crowd | gang | staff |
| audience | clergy | enemy | group | team |
| band | committee | faculty | herd | tribe |
| cast | company | family | jury | troop |
| choir | crew | flock | pride | unit |

Practice 10

**SUBJECT-VERB AGREEMENT: COLLECTIVE NOUNS**

Choose the verb form that agrees with the subject of each of the following sentences. Cross out prepositional phrases. Underline the subject. Circle the appropriate verb.

**1.** Every July 7th, a herd of bulls (runs run) in the streets of San Fermíín in Pamplona.

**2.** The herd (is are) conforming their individual behaviors to the behaviors of the majority as they are driven from their pen to the bullfighting ring.

**3.** A crowd ~~of mostly men~~ (runs run) in front of the bulls.

**4.** The crowd (is are) supposed to know how to run in front of a bull so that they do not endanger other participants.

**5.** Write a sentence using a collective noun. Suggested topic: Going to a Concert.

-------------------------------------------

-------------------------------------------

## Either-or/Neither-Nor

***Either or neither*** often signal a singular subject that requires a singular verb.

- **To ensure subject-verb agreement, identify and cross out prepositional phrases.**

"EITHER" REFERS TO ONE OF "THE MEN" AND THUS IS A SINGULAR SUBJECT

SINGULAR VERB "IS" AGREES WITH SINGULAR SUBJECT "EITHER"

Either ~~of the men~~ is eligible for employment.

PREPOSITIONAL PHRASE

***Either-or/neither-nor*** joins parts of a subject; the verb agrees with the nearer part of the subject.

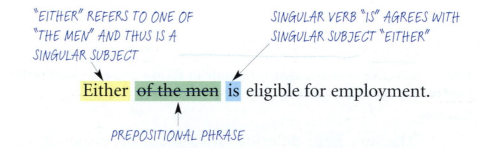

- **When all parts of the subject are singular, the verb is singular.**

"EITHER"/"OR" JOINS SINGULAR SUBJECTS "MIGUEL" AND "TANYA"

SINGULAR VERB "HAS" AGREES WITH SINGULAR SUBJECTS "MIGUEL" AND "TANYA"

Either Miguel or Tanya has the key to the house.

SINGULAR SUBJECTS

- **When all parts of the subject are plural, the verb is plural.**

"NEITHER"/"NOR" JOINS PLURAL SUBJECTS "TREES" AND "BUSHES"

PLURAL VERB "WERE" AGREES WITH PLURAL SUBJECTS "TREES" AND "BUSHES"

Neither the trees nor the bushes were damaged in the storm.

PLURAL SUBJECTS

- **When one part of the subject is singular and the other part is plural, the verb agrees with the nearer part.** For smooth expression, place the plural part of the subject closer to the verb.

"EITHER"/"OR" JOINS SUBJECTS "TRUCK" AND "CARS"

PLURAL VERB "NEED" AGREES WITH NEARER (PLURAL) SUBJECT "CARS"

Either the truck or the cars in the driveway need to be moved.

SINGULAR SUBJECT PLURAL SUBJECT

Practice 11

**SUBJECT-VERB AGREEMENT:** *EITHER-OR/NEITHER-NOR*

Choose the verb form that agrees with the subject of each of the following sentences. Cross out prepositional phrases. Underline the subject. Circle the appropriate verb.

1. Neither of the men (has have) applied for a student loan.
2. For many students, either student loans or scholarships (is are) necessary to pay for higher education.
3. Either the counselors or your faculty advisor (has have) information about financial aid.
4. Neither the President of the Student Government Association nor the campus representatives (does do) the will of the student body.
5. Write a sentence using *neither* or *either*. Suggested topic: Paying for School.

---

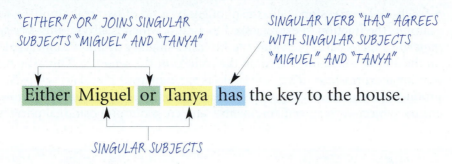

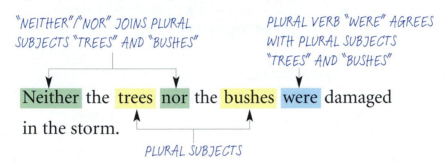

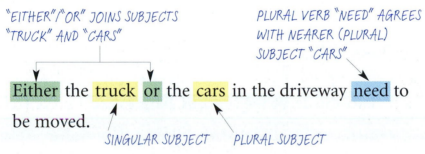

## Fractions, Titles, and Words

A **fractional expression** states the quotient or ratio of two real numbers; for example, the fraction ¾ expresses a 3 to 4 ratio, which is also *seventy-five percent* or a *majority*. Fractional expressions can be either singular or plural subjects, depending on the author's meaning based on the context of the sentence. Thus, the verbs in fractional expressions match the subjects as singular or plural accordingly. Sums and products of mathematical processes are singular and require singular verbs. To ensure subject-verb agreement, identify and cross out prepositional phrases.

PLURAL SUBJECT (BASED ON CONTEXT)

PLURAL VERB "EXPRESS" AGREES WITH PLURAL SUBJECT "MAJORITY"

A majority ~~of voters~~ express their displeasure at the polls.

PREPOSITIONAL PHRASE

SINGULAR SUBJECT (BASED ON CONTEXT)

SINGULAR VERB "WAS DESTROYED" AGREES WITH SINGULAR SUBJECT "FIFTY PERCENT"

Fifty percent ~~of the house~~ was destroyed in the fire.

PREPOSITIONAL PHRASE

PLURAL SUBJECT (BASED ON CONTEXT)

PLURAL VERB "HAVE ROTTED" AGREES WITH PLURAL SUBJECT "TWO-THIRDS"

Two-thirds ~~of the oranges~~ have rotted on the trees.

PREPOSITIONAL PHRASE

SINGULAR SUBJECT

SINGULAR VERB "IS" AGREES WITH SINGULAR SUBJECT "TWO AND FOUR"

Two and four is six.

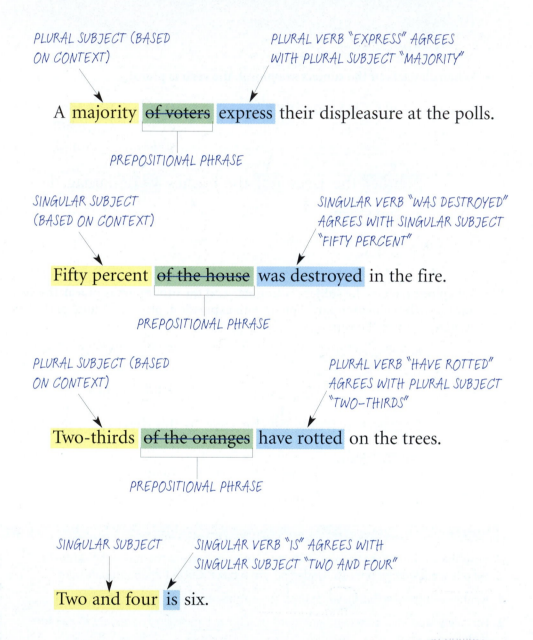

- **Titles** are singular subjects and require a singular verb.

SINGULAR SUBJECT — PREPOSITIONAL PHRASE

*War of the Worlds* ~~with Tom Cruise~~ was a disappointing movie.

SINGULAR VERB "WAS" AGREES WITH SINGULAR SUBJECT "WAR OF THE WORLDS"

PREPOSITIONAL PHRASE — SINGULAR SUBJECT

"Irreplaceable" ~~by Beyoncé~~ was recorded for the album *B-Day*.

SINGULAR VERB "WAS RECORDED" AGREES WITH SINGULAR SUBJECT "'IRREPLACEABLE'"

Some **words that end in -*s*** seem to refer to a single idea or item, but are plural and require a plural verb.

Our thanks are given the voters who went to the polls.

PLURAL SUBJECT — PLURAL VERB "ARE GIVEN" AGREES WITH PLURAL SUBJECT "THANKS"

My assets have increased over the past ten years.

PLURAL SUBJECT — PLURAL VERB "HAVE INCREASED" AGREES WITH PLURAL SUBJECT "ASSETS"

## Practice 12

### SUBJECT-VERB AGREEMENT: FRACTIONS, TITLES, AND WORDS

Choose the verb form that agrees with the subject in each of the following sentences. Cross out prepositional phrases. Underline the subject. Circle the appropriate verb.

1. My glasses (is are) broken.
2. Thirty percent of my life earnings (is are) paid in taxes.
3. Eighty percent of students (turns turn) their work in on time.
4. "Waiting on the World to Change" (is are) the first single release from John Mayer's studio album *Continuum*.
5. Write a sentence using a fraction, title, or plural word that seems singular. Suggested topic: A Favorite DVD.

---

---

More practice with subject-verb agreement: <www.mywriting lab.com>

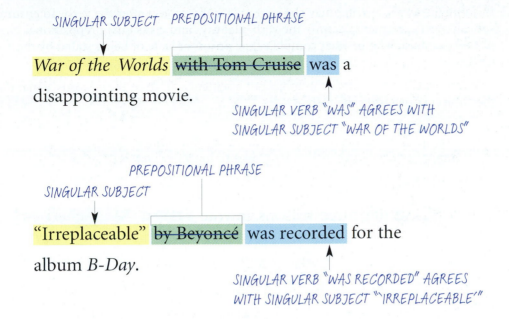

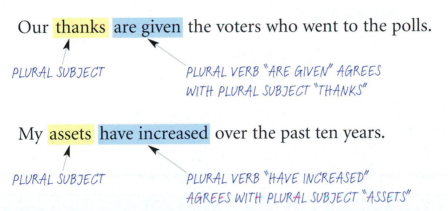

## Subjects after Verbs

In some instances, a writer may choose to place the subject after the verb. To ensure subject-verb agreement, identify the verb, identify (and cross out) prepositional phrases, and ask who or what completes the action or state of being stated by the verb.

***There*** **and** ***Here*** are never the subject of a sentence. Both of these words signal that the subject comes after the verb.

SIGNALS THAT SUBJECT APPEARS AFTER VERB

PLURAL VERB "ARE" AGREES WITH THE PLURAL SUBJECT "REASONS"

There are three reasons to vote ~~against the amendment~~.

PLURAL SUBJECT

PREPOSITIONAL PHRASE

SIGNALS THAT SUBJECT APPEARS AFTER VERB

SINGULAR VERB "IS" AGREES WITH THE SINGULAR SUBJECT "PAYCHECK"

Here is your paycheck.

SINGULAR SUBJECT

**Agreement in Questions** relies on understanding that the subject comes after the verb or between parts of the verb.

SINGULAR VERB

SINGULAR SUBJECT

Where is the closest fast-food restaurant?

PLURAL VERB "DO HARM" AGREES WITH THE PLURAL SUBJECT "LIGHTS"

How do the lights ~~from the boardwalk~~ harm the turtles' nesting season?

PLURAL SUBJECT

PREPOSITIONAL PHRASE

Writers having difficulty determining the subject in a question can identify it by reversing the word order into a statement: in the examples above, "The lights do harm…" and "The closest fast-food restaurant is…"

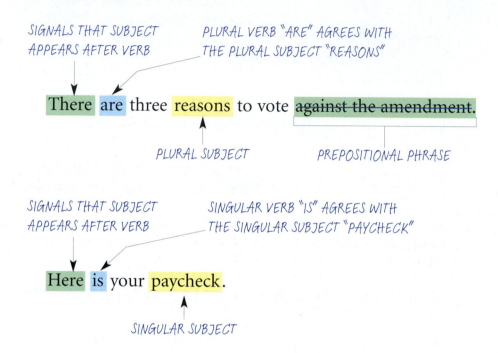

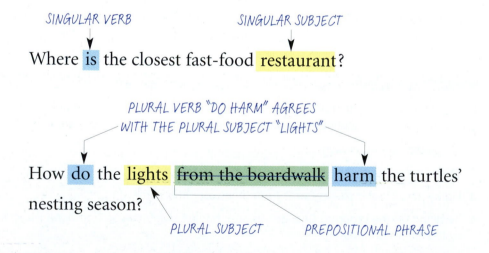

Practice 13

SUBJECT-VERB AGREEMENT: SUBJECTS AFTER VERBS

Choose the verb form that agrees with the subject of each of the following sentences. Cross out prepositional phrases. Underline the subject. Circle the appropriate verb.

1. There (is, are) four reports due by the end of the month.
2. Here (is, are) the pliers, hammer, and screwdriver that have been missing.
3. (Do, Does) the chicken in the refrigerator need to be cooked tonight?
4. Where (is, are) the first aid station?
5. Write a question. Suggested topic: How to Get to a Specific Location.

................................................................................

................................................................................

## Agreement with Relative Pronouns

Agreement with relative pronouns relies on identifying the relationship among a **relative pronoun** (a pronoun such as *that, which, who,* and *whom* that introduces a dependent clause), its **antecedent** (the word the pronoun refers to), and its verb. When a relative pronoun refers to a plural antecedent, it requires a plural verb. When a relative pronoun refers to a singular antecedent, it requires a singular verb. Note that relative pronouns signal a dependent clause. The antecedent for the relative pronoun is often found in the independent clause.

INDEPENDENT CLAUSE | DEPENDENT CLAUSE

She is one of the workers who are eligible for a raise.

SINGULAR SUBJECT — SINGULAR VERB — RELATIVE PRONOUN "WHO" REFERS TO PLURAL ANTECEDENT "WORKERS" — PLURAL VERB "ARE" AGREES WITH PLURAL ANTECEDENT "WORKERS"

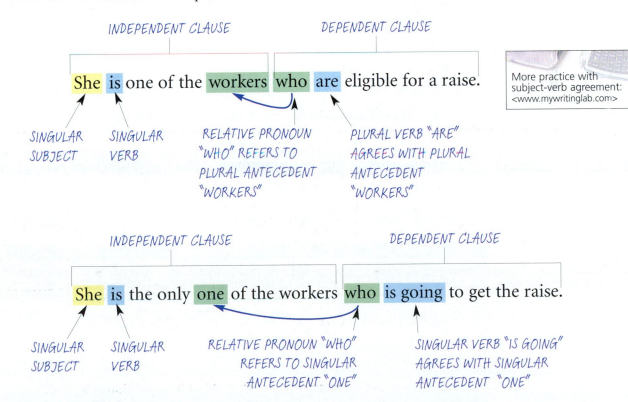

More practice with subject-verb agreement: <www.mywritinglab.com>

INDEPENDENT CLAUSE | DEPENDENT CLAUSE

She is the only one of the workers who is going to get the raise.

SINGULAR SUBJECT — SINGULAR VERB — RELATIVE PRONOUN "WHO" REFERS TO SINGULAR ANTECEDENT "ONE" — SINGULAR VERB "IS GOING" AGREES WITH SINGULAR ANTECEDENT "ONE"

| Relative Pronouns | | | |
|---|---|---|---|
| who | which | that | whoever |

## Practice 14

### SUBJECT-VERB AGREEMENT: RELATIVE PRONOUNS

Choose the verb form that agrees with the subject of each of the following sentences. Cross out prepositional phrases as needed. Underline the antecedent of the relative pronoun once. Underline the relative pronoun twice. Circle the appropriate verb.

**1.** Robert, who (has have) an impressive résumé, will apply for the management position.

**2.** The three sandwiches, which (is are) in the brown paper bag, belong to me.

**3.** One of the dogs that (is are) in the kennel needs to be fed and walked.

**4.** The computer virus that (has have) affected everyone's computer also caused my system to crash.

**5.** Write a sentence using a relative pronoun. Suggested topic: A Necessary Item.

------------------------------------------------------------

------------------------------------------------------------

More practice with subject-verb agreement: <www.mywritinglab.com>

## Practice 15

### SUBJECT-VERB AGREEMENT REVIEW

Read the following short paragraph. Edit to ensure subject-verb agreement in the present tense.

We is about to walk through the security scanner at the airport when we is asked by the airport personnel to step aside into a special area. They asks us to sit quietly and wait for the security supervisor. My mother becomes impatient and begin demanding an explanation. She wants to know why we is being stopped from boarding our plane. She worry that we will miss our flight. My sister and her husband is having their first baby, so we wants to be sure we get there in time for the birth. My mother whisper under her breath to me, "This is a situation that are meant to test one's patience!"

# Writing Assignments

## Writing for Everyday Life

Read the following testimonial written as an endorsement by a member of a local gym. Edit the paragraph to ensure subject-verb agreement. Use your own paper.

If you is looking to make a dramatic change in how you looks and feels, then you need to hire **Ryan Belcher** with **Gold's Gym** as your personal trainer.

My progress is the result of his training. He creates routines that is based on your specific needs. For example, my friend and I has been out of shape and overweight for years. Every training session, Ryan do his best to push us to work harder than we believes we can. We lift weights for strength; we does aerobics for endurance, and we stretch for flexibility. **"I now has more lean muscle than fat."**

One hundred percent of Ryan's clients reaches their goals.

## Writing for College Life

The following paragraph was written by a student to earn five points on a math exam. The student had to explain the steps he took to correctly solve the math problem. Edit to ensure subject-verb agreement. Use your own paper.

I has repaired my answer to the question I missed on this week's quiz. To correctly solve this equation, I use the distributive law. The test question is "What is the value of x in the problem: $2(x + 3) + 4(x - 5) = 10$?" These is my steps to solve this problem.

Step 1: I multiplies each of the terms in the first expression in parentheses by two. 2 times x are 2x, and 2 times 3 are 6. The equation now is $2x + 6 + 4(x - 5) = 10$.

Step 2: I multiply each of the terms in the second expression in parentheses by four. 4 times x equal 4x, and 4 times −5 equal $-20 = 10$. The equation is now $2x + 6 + 4x - 20 = 10$.

Step 3: Now I add and subtracts like terms, so the equation is now $6x - 14 = 10$.

Step 4: I add 14 to both sides of the equation: $6x = 24$.

Step 5: Finally I divides each side by six. Six go into six one times, and six go into 24 four times. $x = 24 \div 6$. x is 4.

# Writing Assignments CONTINUED

## Writing for Working Life

Read the following flyer written by an entrepreneur who is starting up a landscaping and lawn maintenance business. Edit to ensure subject-verb agreement. Use your own paper.

> **Does your garden beds need weeding or replanting?**
> **Does your grass need mowing?**
> **Are you one of those people who needs help selecting the right plant for the right location?**
> **Lush Lawns** are the company to meet your needs. **Lush Lawns** employ experts who knows how to create and maintain beautiful landscapes. **Lush Lawns** plant, weed, mulch, edge, and mow for a low monthly price. It don't pay to wait.
> **Call now and begin enjoying a lush lawn of your own.**

## Academic Learning Log

PORTFOLIO

WHAT HAVE I LEARNED ABOUT SUBJECT-VERB AGREEMENT?

To test and track your understanding, answer the following questions.

**1.** What is the rule for subject-verb agreement? ______________________

______________________________________________

**2.** How is the third person singular verb formed?
The third person singular is formed ______________________

**3.** What are the three forms of the present tense of the verb *to be*? ______________

**4.** ______________________ separate subjects from their verbs.

**5.** Indefinite and collective pronouns are singular or plural based on the ______________ of the sentence.

**6.** When *either-or* joins part of a subject, the verb agrees with the ______________ part of the subject.

**7.** Sums and products of mathematical expressions require ______________ verbs.

**8.** ______________ and ______________ are never the subject of a sentence.

**9.** In a ............................ , the subject comes after the verb or between parts of the verb.

**10.** Agreement with relative pronouns relies on identifying the relationship among a relative pronoun, its ....................................., and its verb.

**11. How will I use what I have learned about subject-verb agreement?**
In your notebook, discuss how you will apply to your own writing what you have learned about subject-verb agreement.

**12. What do I still need to study about subject-verb agreement?**
In your notebook, describe your ongoing study needs by describing what, when, and how you will continue studying subject-verb agreement.

# 25

**Chapter Preview**

- What's the Point of the Past Tense of Verbs?
- Understanding the Point of the Past Tense of Verbs: One Student Writer's Response
- Applying the Point: The Past Tense of Verbs

# The Past Tense of Verbs

## The past tense of verbs describes actions or events that have already occurred.

The past tense is one of the most commonly used verb tenses in English. Thinking about a real-life situation helps us to understand the need for the past tense as we communicate. The following photograph illustrates the challenges of mountain climbing. Study the picture, complete the activity, and answer the question "What's the point of the past tense of verbs?"

# What's the Point of the Past Tense of Verbs?

PHOTOGRAPHIC ORGANIZER: THE PAST TENSE OF VERBS

Writing From Life

Practice 1

Assume your friend has survived a dangerous situation and has been asked to share his experience with others. He asks you to read what he has written so far. What do you notice about his use of the past tense? How does his use of verb tense affect his message?

Surviving a Fall Off the Mountain

Our 7,400-foot climb up the winter slopes of Mt. Hood challenges and exhilarated us. Thankfully, we decide to take Mountain Locator Units, small beacons that could send out radio signals to rescuers. When a storm moved in, we start our descent in blowing snow. We had no visual reference around us, so we couldn't know if we were going up or down. Then the three of us who were roped together with Champion, a black Labrador mix, disappear over an icy ledge. Champion provided warmth for us as we huddled under sleeping bags and a tarp. She takes turns lying on each one of us during the night. The activation of an emergency radio beacon bringed rescuers to us. We survived because we were prepared, we didn't panic, and Champion keeps us warm.

**What's the point of the past tense of verbs?**

# Understanding the Point of the Past Tense of Verbs: One Student Writer's Response

The following paragraph offers one writer's reaction to the paragraph "Surviving a Fall Off the Mountain."

> *When I first read this paragraph, I noticed that the writer kept shifting between the present and past tenses for no real reason. The shifts were so noticeable that I really couldn't focus on his story because the verb errors jumped out so much. So my advice is to edit each of the following verbs from the present tense to the past tense: "challenges" becomes "challenged"; "decide" becomes "decided"; "start" becomes "started"; "disappear" becomes "disappeared"; "takes" becomes "took"; and "keeps" becomes "kept." The misspelling of the verb "bringed" also caught my attention. The proper spelling is "brought." By the way, I had to look some of these verbs up in the dictionary to make sure of their spelling. Once the writer makes these edits, his message will be much stronger.*

# Applying the Point: The Past Tense of Verbs

The **simple past tense** is used to describe a completed action or event. The action or event might have taken place long ago or it might have happened recently, but either way, the past tense is used to indicate that it has already occurred. The simple past tense is also often used to tell a story. Frequently, the use of the past tense is signaled by particular expressions of time: *yesterday, last night, last week, last year, three years ago,* and so on. The following time line illustrates the sequence of tenses.

The past tense takes on different forms for regular and irregular verbs.

## Regular Verbs in the Past Tense

The following chart states the general rule for forming the past tense of regular verbs, the spelling rules for exceptions, and examples of each rule.

**Rules for Forming Past Tense of Regular Verbs**

| | Base Form | Past Tense |
|---|---|---|
| **General Rule:** Regular verbs form the past tense by adding ***-ed*** to the base form of the verb. | walk → | walk***ed*** |
| **Spelling Exceptions:** There are several exceptions to the way in which regular verbs form the past tense: | | |
| 1. When the base form of the verb ends in ***-e***, only add ***-d***. | live<br>save → | live***d***<br>save***d*** |
| 2. When the base form of the verb ends with a consonant and ***-y***, delete the ***-y*** and add ***-ied*** in its place. | cry<br>try → | cr***ied***<br>tr***ied*** |
| 3. When the base form of the verb ends with ***-p*** or ***-it***, double the last letter before adding the ***-ed***. | stop<br>permit → | sto***pped***<br>permi***tted*** |

**Practice 2**

REGULAR VERBS IN PAST TENSE

Fill in each blank with the past tense form of the regular verb in parentheses.

**1.** Chimpanzees possibly .............................. (use) "hammers" as long as 4,300 years ago.

**2.** Researchers .............................. (discover) the hammers in the West African country, Ivory Coast.

**3.** The chimpanzees .............................. (crack) nuts with the hammers.

**4.** A "chimpanzee stone age" .............................. (start) in ancient times.

**5.** Write a sentence with a regular verb in the past tense. Suggested topic: An Important Invention.

..............................................................................................................................

..............................................................................................................................

..............................................................................................................................

## Irregular Verbs in the Past Tense

Unlike regular verbs, irregular verbs do not use *-ed* to form the past tense. Nor does the past tense of irregular verbs conform to uniform spelling rules with clear exceptions. The English language utilizes many irregular verbs that have unpredictable spellings. In fact, some of the most commonly used verbs are irregular, and most writers commit these words to memory so their proper use is automatic. The chart below lists the base form and past tense form of some commonly used irregular verbs. It is not a comprehensive list, however. When in doubt about the correct form of a verb, careful writers consult a dictionary to find the form and spelling of the past tense of an irregular verb.

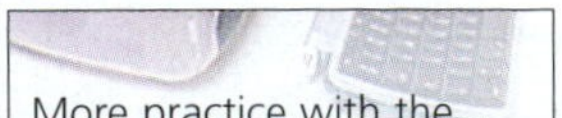

More practice with the past tense of verbs: <www.mywritinglab.com>

**Some Common Irregular Verbs in the Past Tense**

| Base Form | Past Tense | Base Form | Past Tense |
|---|---|---|---|
| be | was, were | light | lit |
| become | became | lose | lost |
| break | broke | make | made |
| bring | brought | mean | meant |
| buy | bought | meet | met |
| choose | chose | pay | paid |
| come | came | put | put |
| cut | cut | quit | quit |
| deal | dealt | read | read |
| dig | dug | ride | rode |
| drink | drank | ring | rang |
| drive | drove | rise | rose |
| eat | ate | run | ran |
| fall | fell | say | said |
| feed | fed | see | saw |
| feel | felt | sell | sold |
| fly | flew | send | sent |
| forget | forgot | shake | shook |
| forgive | forgave | shine | shone (shined) |
| freeze | froze | sing | sang |
| get | got | sit | sat |
| go | went | sleep | slept |
| grow | grew | speak | spoke |
| hang | hung | spend | spent |
| hang (execute) | hanged | swim | swam |
| have | had | take | took |
| hear | heard | teach | taught |
| hide | hid | tear | tore |
| hold | held | tell | told |
| hurt | hurt | think | thought |
| keep | kept | throw | threw |
| know | knew | understand | understood |
| lay (to place) | laid | wake | woke (waked) |
| lead | led | wear | wore |
| leave | left | win | won |
| let | let | write | wrote |
| lie (to recline) | lay | | |

**IRREGULAR VERBS IN PAST TENSE**

**Practice 3**

Fill in the blanks with the past tense form of the irregular verbs in the parentheses.

1. A slave named James Armistead made (make) history as the most important Revolutionary War spy.
2. Armistead took (take) on the role of an escaped slave to enter the camp of the traitor Benedict Arnold.
3. As an orderly and a guide, Armistead went (go) North with Arnold to learn about British war plans without being detected.
4. As a double agent, he also gave (give) incorrect information to the British troops.
5. Write a sentence using the past tense of an irregular verb. Suggested topic: The Civil War.

................................................................

................................................................

................................................................

More practice with the past tense of verbs: <www.mywritinglab.com>

## Key Verbs in the Past Tense: *To Have, To Do, To Be*

Three key verbs are used both as main verbs and as helping verbs to express a wide variety of meanings: *to have, to do,* and *to be.* These three verbs are irregular verbs, so it's essential to memorize their correct forms in the past tense.

| To Have | To Do | To Be |
|---|---|---|
| had | did | was (singular) |
| | | were (plural) |

**IRREGULAR VERBS IN PAST TENSE**

**Practice 4**

Fill in the blanks with the past tense form of the verbs *to have, to do,* or *to be.*

1. Researchers recently ................ a large study that shows how midday napping reduces one's chance of coronary mortality by more than a third.
2. The most effective naps ................ those that occurred at least three times per week for an average of at least 30 minutes.
3. These men and women ................ a 37 percent lower coronary mortality risk than those who took no naps.
4. The protective effect of napping ................ especially strong among working men.
5. Write a sentence using the past tense of *to have, to do,* or *to be.* Suggested topic: Sleep Problems.

................................................................

................................................................

................................................................

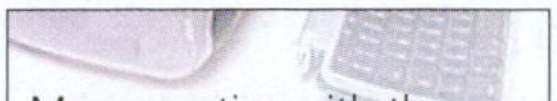

More practice with the past tense of verbs: <www.mywritinglab.com>

## *Can/Could/Would*

**Helping verbs** are auxiliary verbs that team up with main verbs for precise expression of an action or state of being. Three helping verbs are often confused in usage: *can, could,* and *would.* These auxiliary verbs help express the meaning of ability, opportunity, possibility, permission, and intention. The following provides definitions and examples for each of these three helping verbs.

### Three Commonly Confused Helping Verbs: *Can, Could, Would*

- ***Can* expresses physical or mental ability in the present tense.**

"CAN" EXPRESSES A PHYSICAL ABILITY

I can run a marathon.

"CAN" EXPRESSES A MENTAL ABILITY

I can solve mathematical equations.

- ***Could* expresses physical or mental ability, opportunity, possibility, or permission in the past tense.**

"COULD" EXPRESSES A PHYSICAL OR MENTAL ABILITY

She could run a marathon.

"COULD" EXPRESSES A LOST OPPORTUNITY

You could have tried harder than you did.

"COULD" EXPRESSES POSSIBILITY

He could have been the culprit.

"COULD" EXPRESSES PERMISSION

He said that we could begin the driving test.

- ***Would* expresses past routine or intention in the past tense.**

"WOULD" EXPRESSES PAST ROUTINE

He would win every race.

He would have won every race, but he lost the last one.

"WOULD" EXPRESSES PAST INTENTION

She said she would do the dishes.

More practice with the past tense of verbs: <www.mywritinglab.com>

## Practice 5

**USING *CAN, COULD,* AND *WOULD***

Complete each sentence with the helping verb that best completes the idea: *can, could,* or *would.*

1. On social-networking sites like MySpace and Facebook, Internet users ______________ create elaborate profiles that include photographs, music, and videos.

2. Social-networking sites ______________ serve a variety of purposes depending on the needs of the user.

3. For example, Eduardo ______________ stay in contact with his college friends after they graduated and moved to different parts of the country.

4. The friends ______________ post updates on a weekly basis that documented their personal and professional lives.

5. Write a sentence using *can, could,* or *would* as helping verbs. Suggested topic: A Social Network Such as MySpace.

______________________________________________

______________________________________________

______________________________________________

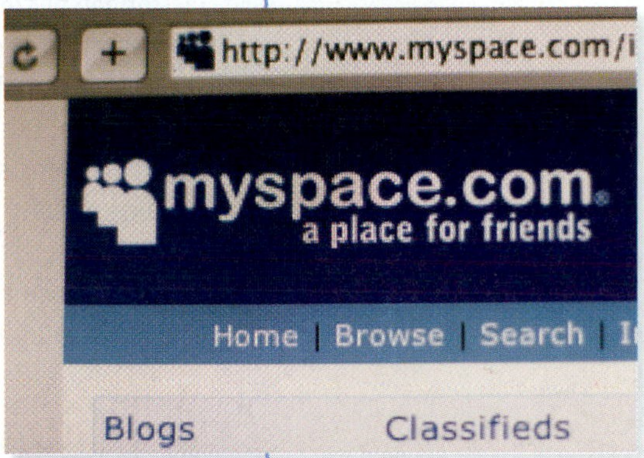


## Practice 6

**PAST TENSE REVIEW**

Read the following passage. Edit to ensure proper use of the past tense.

Oprah Winfrey spend five years and $40 million dollars building her dream school in Africa: The Oprah Winfrey Leadership Academy. She place the all-girls school on 22 lush acres and builded over 28 buildings. The complex was maked to feature large rooms decorated with colorful African art. In addition, Winfrey supply the facility with luxuries such as 200-thread-count sheets, a yoga studio, and a beauty salon, as well as indoor and outdoor theaters. She want to provide her girls with the very best so they know how much she cared for them. Some criticized Oprah for helping children in Africa instead of children in America. However, Oprah point out that American children could benefit from a public school system. African children should not.

# Writing Assignments

## Writing for Everyday Life

Read the following letter to the editor about a local issue. Edit the paragraph to ensure proper usage of the past tense. Use the chart on page 492 of this chapter or a dictionary to confirm the spellings of irregular verbs. Use your own paper.

Just recently, two major insurance companies announced that they will no longer write insurance policies in Mississippi. The next day, the Insurance commissioner says he hopes these companies will have changed their stance. What he would have said was "good riddance." After Hurricane Katrina, fair-weather insurance companies cause added grief and expense by denying valid claims. These insurance companies was eager to write policies as long as we policy holders have no losses. Once they see the extent of our loss, they bailed on us. Even as Hurricane Katrina striked, I just know I would lose everything. So I say what the Commissioner should have said, "Good riddance, fair-weather insurance companies!"

## Writing for College Life

The following paragraph was written by a student for a psychology class to define and illustrate the concept of *gunnysacking*. Edit to ensure proper usage of the past tense. Use the chart on page 492 of this chapter or a dictionary to confirm the spellings of irregular verbs. Use your own paper.

A gunnysack is a large burlap bag, and gunnysacking is a conflict strategy that stores up grievances for later use. Early in their relationship, Chris and Pat frequently resort to gunnysacking. For example, when they first begin living together, Chris could come home late every night, and every night, Pat can recount a long list of past wrongs that he had committed. "You forget my birthday," she says, "and you leave my car on empty last Thursday. You are so inconsiderate." Of course, gunnysacking leads to gunnysacking, so Chris always threw his own accusations. To save their relationship, Chris and Pat learn to focus on the here-and-now. Once they keep their focus on the issue of the moment, they were much happier.

## Writing for Working Life

Read the following letter written by an employee who is requesting a performance-based raise. Edit to ensure proper usage of the past tense. Use the chart on page 492 of this chapter or a dictionary to confirm the spellings of irregular verbs. Use your own paper.

Dear Ms. Diaz:

As the Webmaster for our company, I have created a record of hard work and achievement that qualifies me for a promotion and a raise. My accomplishments include the following. I make fourteen web sites for various departments. I turned words and art selected by each department into Internet sites that people were able to use. I check to see that employees with different computers can use the web sites. As the Webmaster, I also tryd to make the sites work faster. I keep the size of files small so that they do not take much time to download. I tested web sites, too. I watch people using a site to see if there were any parts that were hard to use. I also meet with designers, helping to decide how the sites should look and work. I also update web sites, and I fixed mistakes, such as broken links. Due to my expertise and hardwork as Webmaster, our Internet presence remain interesting and effective. Thank you for considering my request for a promotion and a raise based on my performance.

Respectfully,

Donald Malik

PORTFOLIO

# Academic Learning Log

## WHAT HAVE I LEARNED ABOUT THE PAST TENSE OF VERBS?

To test and track your understanding, answer the following questions.

**1.** What is the general rule for forming the past tense of regular verbs? Give an example.

---

---

---

**2.** What are three exceptions to the way in which regular verbs form the past tense? Give examples.

a. ______

______

b. ______

______

c. ______

______

**3.** What are two traits of irregular verbs?

---

---

---

**4.** What are the correct forms in the past tense of the following three irregular verbs: *to be, to have,* and *to do?*

---

**5.** List three often-confused helping verbs.

---

**6. How will I use what I have learned about the past tense?**
In your notebook, discuss how you will apply to your own writing what you have learned about the past tense of regular and irregular verbs.

**7. What do I still need to study about the past tense?**
In your notebook, describe your ongoing study needs by describing what, when, and how you will continue studying the past tense of regular and irregular verbs.

REVISING

# 26 The Past Participle

## Chapter Preview

- What's the Point of the Past Participle?
- Understanding the Point of the Past Participle: One Student Writer's Response
- Applying the Point: The Past Participle

A participle is a verb form that can be used to establish tenses or voices, or it can be used as a modifier, which describes, restricts, or limits other words in a sentence.

Thinking about a real-life situation helps us to understand the purpose of the past participle in our communication. The following photograph documents a bee keeper handling a colony of bees. Study the picture, complete the activity, and answer the question "What's the point of the past participle?"

# What's the Point of the Past Participle?

PHOTOGRAPHIC ORGANIZER: THE PAST PARTICIPLE

WRITING FROM LIFE

Practice 1

Assume you subscribe to a news blog, and that a correspondent has filed the following report, which contains misuses of the past participle. Where are the errors? What is the impact of the errors?

### Honey Bees Dropping Like Flies

Colony Collapse Disorder (CCD) has hurt bee colonies in Pennsylvania, North Carolina, Florida, Georgia, and California. So far, some bee keepers have loss up to 80 percent of their colonies to the mysterious disorder. Whatever kills the bees targets adult workers which die outside the colony. Few adults left inside, either alive or dead. The worker bee population wiped out in a matter of weeks by the disorder. Aside from making honey, honey bees are essential for the pollination of tens of million of dollars worth of cash crops all over the United States. That's why farmers across the country are worry. A fungus, virus, or a variety of microbes and pesticides are thought to be some of the possible causes.

**What's the point of the past participle?**

Adapted from Larry O'Hanlon, "Honey Bee Die-off Alarms Beekeepers," *Discovery News*, February 5, 2007

# Understanding the Point of the Past Participle: One Student Writer's Response

The following paragraph offers one writer's reaction to the paragraph "Honey Bees Dropping Like Flies."

*I thought this was a really interesting article, but there were some confusing errors. The verb "have loss" just doesn't sound right. I looked up the spelling for "loss," and the past participle form is "lost." The statement, "Few adults left inside, either alive or dead" is missing something. Maybe the helping verb "are" needs to be inserted so the verb is "are left." This same kind of error is in the sentence, "The worker bee population wiped out. . . ." The helping verb "is" needs to be inserted so the verb is "is wiped." Finally, "are worry" sounds wrong, too. "Worry" should be spelled "worried." The paragraph has too many misspelled words and is hard to follow.*

# Applying the Point: The Past Participle

A **participle** is a verb form that can be used to establish tenses or voices, or it can be used as a modifier, which describes, restricts, or limits other words in a sentence. The **past participle** of a verb joins with helping verbs to form the present perfect and past perfect tenses and the passive voice. In addition, the past participle can act as an adjective that describes another word. Just as with the simple past tense, the past participle takes on different forms for regular and irregular verbs.

## Past Participles of Regular Verbs

In general, regular verbs form the past participle by adding *-ed* to the base form of the verb. Just as with the simple past tense, there are several spelling exceptions for the past participle of regular verbs.

For more about the simple past tense, see Chapter 25.

| Base Form | Past Tense | Past Participle |
|---|---|---|
| live | liv***ed*** | liv***ed*** |
| cry | cr***ied*** | cr***ied*** |
| permit | permi***tted*** | permi***tted*** |

Practice 2

PAST PARTICIPLE OF REGULAR VERBS

Complete the following chart with the proper forms of the past tense and the past participle of each verb.

| Base | Past Tense | Past Participle |
|---|---|---|
| **1.** accept | accepted | accepted |
| **2.** agree | | |
| **3.** bang | | |
| **4.** bat | | |
| **5.** cheat | cheated | cheated |
| **6.** clip | | |
| **7.** hurry | | |
| **8.** relax | | |
| **9.** supply | | |
| **10.** whine | whined | whined |

More practice with the past participle of verbs: <www.mywritinglab.com>

## Past Participles of Irregular Verbs

As with the simple past tense, irregular verbs do not use *-ed* to form the past participle. Nor does the past participle of irregular verbs conform to uniform spelling rules with clear exceptions. In addition, the past participle forms of many irregular verbs vary from their past tense forms. The chart that follows Practice 3 lists the base form, past tense form, and past participle of some commonly used irregular verbs. It is not a comprehensive list, however. As with the simple past forms of irregular verbs, when in doubt, careful writers consult a dictionary to find the form and spelling of the past participle of an irregular verb. Throughout the rest of this chapter, the activities dealing with irregular verbs focus on those that, based on research, occur most frequently in English.

### Practice 3

PAST PARTICIPLE OF IRREGULAR VERBS

The following chart contains the top ten irregular verbs listed by frequency of use. Supply the proper forms of the past tense and the past participle of each verb. Consult a dictionary as necessary.

| Base | | Past Tense | Past Participle |
|---|---|---|---|
| **1.** | say | said | said |
| **2.** | make | made | made |
| **3.** | go | went | gone |
| **4.** | take | took | taken |
| **5.** | come | came | come |
| **6.** | see | saw | seen |
| **7.** | know | knew | known |
| **8.** | get | got | gotten |
| **9.** | give | gave | given |
| **10.** | find | found | found |

More practice with the past participle of verbs: <www.mywritinglab.com>

Study!

**Some Common Irregular Past Participles**

| se Form | Past Tense | Past Participle |
|---|---|---|
| | was, were | been |
| come | became | become |
| eak | broke | broken |
| ing | brought | brought |
| y | bought | bought |
| oose | chose | chosen |
| me | came | come |
| t | cut | cut |
| deal | dealt | dealt |
| dig | dug | dug |
| drink | drank | drunk |
| drive | drove | driven |
| eat | ate | eaten |
| fall | fell | fallen |
| feed | fed | fed |
| feel | felt | felt |
| find | found | found |
| fly | flew | flown |
| forget | forgot | forgotten |
| forgive | forgave | forgiven |
| freeze | froze | frozen |
| get | got | gotten |
| give | gave | given |
| go | went | gone |
| grow | grew | grown |
| hang | hung | hung |
| hang *(execute)* | hanged | hanged |
| have | had | had |
| hear | heard | heard |
| hide | hid | hidden |
| hold | held | held |
| hurt | hurt | hurt |
| keep | kept | kept |
| know | knew | known |
| lay *(to place)* | laid | laid |
| lead | led | led |
| leave | left | left |
| let | let | let |
| lie *(to recline)* | lay | lain |
| light | lit | lit |
| lose | lost | lost |
| make | made | made |
| mean | meant | meant |
| meet | met | met |
| pay | paid | paid |
| put | put | put |
| quit | quit | quit |
| read | read | read |
| ride | rode | ridden |
| ring | rang | rung |
| rise | rose | risen |
| run | ran | run |

**Some Common Irregular Past Participles**

| Base Form | Past Tense | Past Participle |
|---|---|---|
| say | said | said |
| see | saw | seen |
| sell | sold | sold |
| send | sent | sent |
| shake | shook | shaken |
| shine | shone *(shined)* | shone *(shined)* |
| sing | sang | sung |
| sit | sat | sat |
| sleep | slept | slept |
| speak | spoke | spoken |
| spend | spent | spent |
| swim | swam | swum |
| take | took | taken |
| teach | taught | taught |
| tear | tore | torn |
| tell | told | told |
| think | thought | thought |
| throw | threw | thrown |
| understand | understood | understood |
| wake | woke *(waked)* | woken *(waked)* |
| wear | wore | worn |
| win | won | won |
| write | wrote | written |

## Using the Present Perfect Tense

The **present perfect tense** connects the past to the present. The present perfect tense states the relationship of a past action or situation to a current, ongoing action or situation. The present perfect tense is formed by joining the helping verbs ***has*** or ***have*** with the past participle.

**The purposes of the present perfect tense are:**

- **to express change from the past to the present.**

PRESENT PERFECT "HAS IMPROVED" EXPRESSES CHANGE FROM THE PAST ACTION TO A PRESENT ONE

PAST ACTION

Jamel was sick for three weeks, but he has improved.

- **to express a situation or action that started in the past and continues to the present.**

PRESENT PERFECT "HAVE RACED" EXPRESSES AN ONGOING ACTION, WHICH STARTED IN THE PAST AND IS CONTINUING NOW

Carmen and Michelle have raced stock cars for several years.

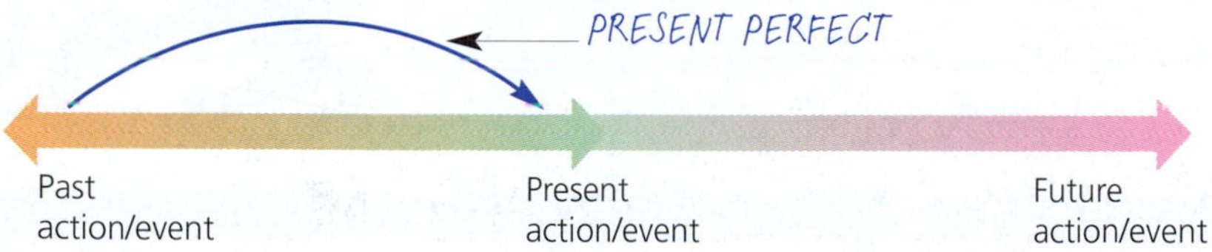

## Practice 4

Regular

### PRESENT PERFECT TENSE

Fill in the blanks with the present perfect tense of the **regular** verbs in the parentheses. Use the helping verbs *has* or *have* to form the present perfect tense.

**1.** NASA has remained *(remain)* a leading force in scientific research and in stimulating public interest in aerospace exploration, as well as science and technology in general.

**2.** Hospitals worldwide have used *(use)* image processing in CAT scanners and MRI machines based on the technology developed to computer-enhance pictures of the Moon for the Apollo programs.

**3.** Fetal heart monitors have developed *(develop)* from technology originally used to measure airflow over aircraft wings.

**4.** Space exploration has yielded *(yield)* advances in communications, weather forecasting, electronics, and countless other fields.

**5.** Write a sentence using the present perfect tense of a regular verb. Suggested topic: Space Exploration. ........................................

........................................

## Practice 5

Irregular

### PRESENT PERFECT TENSE

Fill in the blanks with the present perfect tense of the **irregular** verbs in the parentheses. Use the helping verbs *has* or *have* to form the present perfect tense.

**1.** I have thought *(think)* about adopting an animal from the humane society for several years.

**2.** My son, who works at the local animal shelter, has told *(tell)* me about some of the animals currently at the shelter.

**3.** At first, I didn't want to get involved, but I have become *(become)* attached to a particular greyhound named Pete, turned away from the racetrack.

**4.** When we brought Pete home, he was injured, malnourished, and anxious, but he has shown *(show)* remarkable improvement.

**5.** Write a sentence using the present perfect tense of an irregular verb. Suggested topic: Choosing a Pet.

........................................

........................................

More practice with the past participle of verbs: <www.mywritinglab.com>

# Using the Past Perfect Tense

The **past perfect** connects two past actions or situations. The past perfect is formed by joining the helping verb ***had*** with a past participle.

**The purposes of the past perfect tense are:**

- **to connect a previous action or event with a later action or event.**

PAST ACTION #2 → went

PAST ACTION #1: THE PAST PERFECT "HAD LEFT" SHOWS THAT THIS ACTION OCCURRED EVEN BEFORE THE OTHER PAST ACTION "SAMUEL WENT..."

Samuel went to Starbucks, but everyone had left.

- **to express an action or event that happened before a certain past time.**

PAST ACTION #2 → took

PAST ACTION #1: THE PAST PERFECT "HAD STUDIED" SHOWS THAT THIS ACTION OCCURRED EVEN BEFORE THE OTHER PAST ACTION "SHE TOOK..."

Before she took the test, Suzanne had studied for three weeks.

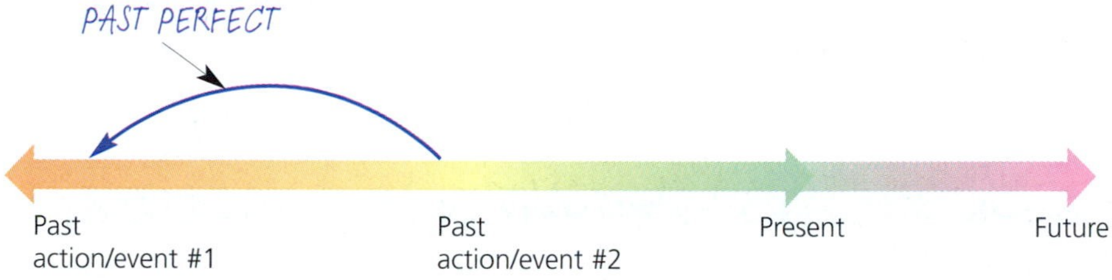


## Practice 6

PAST PERFECT TENSE

Fill in the blanks with the past perfect tense of the **regular** verbs in the parentheses. Use the helping verb *had* to form the past perfect tense.

1. In Texas, African Americans had waited (*wait*) a long time to hear the news brought to them on June 19, 1865.
2. On that day, Union soldiers had arrived (*arrive*) in Galveston, Texas, to announce freedom for slaves two years after Lincoln issued his Emancipation Proclamation.
3. On January 1, 1863, Lincoln had declared (*declare*) "that all persons held as slaves within the rebellious states are, and henceforward shall be free."
4. By 1979, Texas had proclaimed (*proclaim*) Emancipation Day, Juneteenth, an official state holiday.
5. Write a sentence using the past perfect tense of a regular verb. Suggested topic: A National Holiday. ........................................

........................................

Practice 7

**PAST PERFECT TENSE**

Fill in the blanks with the past perfect tense of the **irregular** verbs in the parentheses. Use the helping verb *had* to form the past perfect tense.

**1.** During my annual checkup, I discovered that my previous physician, Dr. Griffin, had held (*hold*) my records instead of sending them to my current physician, Dr. Doughney.

**2.** Six months before, I had written (*write*) Dr. Griffin to request the forwarding of my records to Dr. Doughney.

**3.** By the time I filled out all the required forms for a new patient and another form requesting my records, I had stood (*stand*) at the receptionist's window for 30 minutes.

**4.** I had heard (*hear*) from several friends that Dr. Doughney was an excellent doctor.

**5.** Write a sentence using the past perfect tense of an irregular verb. Suggested topic: An Annoying Event. ______________________________

______________________________

More practice with the past participle of verbs: <www.mywritinglab.com>

## Using the Passive Voice (*To Be* and the Past Participle)

In English, verbs establish two types of voices: the active voice and the passive voice. So far, you have only worked with the active voice. Expressing what the subject of a sentence does, action verbs establish the **active voice.** When the subject of a sentence receives the action (or is acted upon), the sentence is in the **passive voice.** The combination of *to be* with a past participle establishes the passive voice. In addition, the passive voice can be expressed in every tense.

**The purpose of the passive voice is to tell the reader what is done to a subject.**

**Active Voice**

SUBJECT "CONSTANCE" PERFORMS THE ACTION

Constance took herself to the hospital.

**Passive Voice**

SUBJECT "CONSTANCE" RECEIVES THE ACTION

Constance was taken to the hospital.

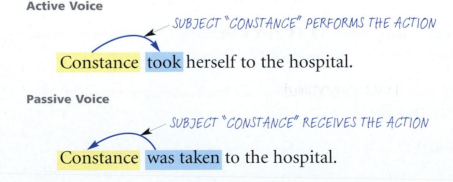

**Examples of the tenses of the passive voice**

**Present Tense**

SUBJECT — PRESENT TENSE OF "TO BE" — PAST PARTICIPLE OF "PACK"

The clothes are packed.

**Past Tense**

SUBJECT — PAST TENSE OF "TO BE" — PAST PARTICIPLE OF "STORE"

The furniture was stored.

**Present Perfect Tense**

SUBJECT — PRESENT PERFECT TENSE OF "TO BE" — PAST PARTICIPLE OF "WRAP"

The china has been wrapped in bubble pack.

**Past Perfect Tense**

SUBJECT — PAST PERFECT TENSE OF "TO BE" — PAST PARTICIPLE OF "BROKE"

Their possessions had been broken.

Practice 8

PASSIVE VOICE WITH REGULAR VERBS

Fill in the blanks with the passive voice of the **regular** verbs in the parentheses. Use the proper form of *to be* as a helping verb to form the passive voice.

**1.** The restaurant ________ *(open)* in 2006.

**2.** Before the restaurant opened, the market for Italian food ________ *(analyze)*.

**3.** After the owners had argued for months over the name for the restaurant, finally, the name Pantheon ________ *(agree)* upon.

**4.** To ensure high-quality customer service, the wait staff ________ *(train)* by experts in hospitality management.

**5.** Write a sentence using the passive voice of a regular verb. Suggested topic. A Consumer Complaint. ________

________

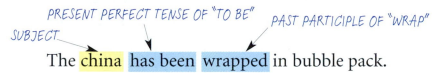

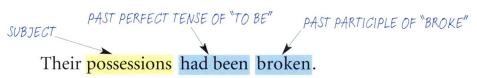

Practice 9

PASSIVE VOICE WITH IRREGULAR VERBS

Fill in the blanks with the passive voice of the **irregular** verbs in the parentheses. Use the proper form of *to be* with the past participle to form the passive voice.

**1.** Once again, Jeremy's peanut butter sandwich ............................ *(sit)* upon as it lay on the bench.

**2.** Before this, Jeremy ............................ *(speak)* to about leaving his lunch on the bench.

**3.** Jeremy's unopened lunch bag ............................ *(lie)* upon or sat upon at least once a week.

**4.** Every day after recess, the children ............................ *(lead)* inside for story time.

**5.** Write a sentence using the passive voice of an irregular verb. Suggested topic: A Routine Activity.

................................................................................................

................................................................................................

More practice with the past participle of verbs: <www.mywritinglab.com>

## Using the Past Participle as an Adjective

The past participle is often used as an adjective that modifies a noun or pronoun. Both regular and irregular forms of the past participle are used as adjectives.

**The purposes of the past participle as an adjective are:**

- **to describe a noun or pronoun with a word or phrase.**

PARTICIPLE "FALLEN" DESCRIBES NOUN "HEROES"

We honor our fallen heroes.

PARTICIPLE PHRASE

Destroyed by the wind, these houses will be raised again by hope.

PARTICIPLE "DESTROYED" DESCRIBES NOUN "HOUSES"

- **to describe the subject by completing a linking verb in the sentence.**

LINKING VERB

The vegetables are washed and peeled.

SUBJECT "VEGETABLES" IS DESCRIBED BY COMPOUND PAST PARTICIPLES "WASHED AND PEELED"

LINKING VERB

She seems worried.

SUBJECT "SHE" IS DESCRIBED BY PAST PARTICIPLE "WORRIED"

## Practice 10

### PAST PARTICIPLE AS AN ADJECTIVE

Fill in the blanks with the past participle forms of the verbs in parentheses.

**1.** At certain levels of success, some athletes become highly ______________ *(respect)* for their contributions to their sports.

**2.** David Beckham, an ______________ *(accomplish)* soccer player, enjoys worldwide recognition.

**3.** ______________ *(watch)* by 300 million fans, Yao Ming towers as a star in the National Basketball Association.

**4.** ______________ *(give)* to long hours of practice, Tiger Woods constantly breaks golf's longest-standing records.

**5.** Write a sentence using the past participle as an adjective. Suggested topic: A Sports Figure.

______________________________

______________________________

______________________________

______________________________

______________________________

______________________________

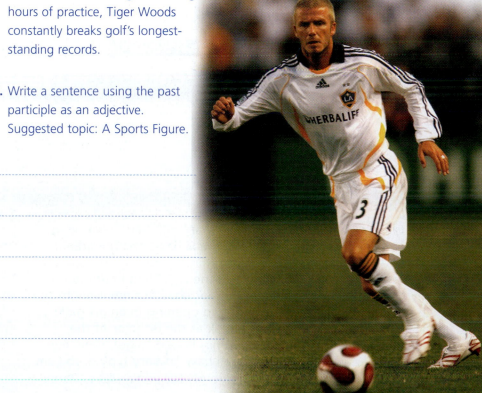

More practice with the past participle of verbs: <www.mywritinglab.com>

Practice 11

PAST PARTICIPLE REVIEW

Review what you have learned throughout this chapter by completing the following activity. Read the following short news release from the U.S. Department of Health and Human Services Website. Edit to ensure use of the appropriate form of the past participle to create proper, logical verb tenses.

**FDA Approves First ADHD Patch**

The first skin patch to treat attention-deficit hyperactivity disorder (ADHD) in children was gave the U.S. Food and Drug Administration's blessing late Thursday, the *Associated Press* reported.

Design to be worn for nine hours, the patch contains a methylphenidate, a stimulant that has been effective in treating ADHD for decades. Know as Daytrana and maked by Noven Pharmaceuticals Inc. in Miami, the wire service said the patch is consider an alternative treatment for children aged 6 to 12 with ADHD if taking pills is too difficult. The patch, which will be available in four doses, can also be remove immediately if side effects develop.

More than 3 million Americans under the age of 19 have use ADHD medications in the last year, according to Medco Health Solutions Inc., a prescription drug benefit program manager.

According to the *AP*, Daytrana's label will carry the same standard warnings of side effects as other methylphenidates, which have include insomnia, decreased appetite and nausea.

# Writing Assignments

## Writing for Everyday Life

Read the following blog. Edit the paragraph to ensure proper usage of the past participle. Use your own paper.

Here at last is the long promised summary of what I have be up to lately. Guess what? I have good news. I have find my dream job! I had gave up hope. I had even think about signing up as a temporary worker with an agency in the city. Then I ran into Caitlyn Myers who has graduated a year ahead of me. Delight to help a classmate, she told me about an opening in an art gallery near Central Park. I was hire last week as the director of the gallery. This is the very kind of job I has hoped to get. Well, my cell phone has rang the whole time I have sit here typing, so I am going to post my good news and sign off for now. – Ciao, Danni

## Writing for College Life

The following lab report was written by a student for a science class. The professor required the use of the passive voice. Edit to ensure proper usage of the past participle. Use your own paper.

LAB REPORT

| | | |
|---|---|---|
| | Cheri Jackson | May 15/24 |
| Lab 7: Responses to Abiotic Factors | (Name) | (Date/ Lab Section) |

**Overview**

This lab was design to understand the responses to abiotic factors by tracking transpiration by plants. Abiotic factors are made up of air, water, or temperature. Transpiration is known as the loss of water from a plant through evaporation. The behavior and structure of an organism are affect by the loss of water through evaporation.

**Procedure and Results**

A long branch with healthy leaves was select. Next, a clean cut at the base was made, the cut end was immediately transfer to a pan of water. The leaves were keep dry. A second cut was made a cm or so above the first. The cut end was not exposed to the air since an air bubble could form in plant's tissue. The cut end was kept under water, and the stem was carry through a rubber stopper. Petroleum jelly was spread at the top and bottom of the cork to seal and hold the stem in the stopper attached to a length of tubing. A bubble was introduced into the tubing. As water was took up by the plant, the bubble moved. Water uptake was measured by marking regular gradations on the tube. Next, the prepared plant leaf was placed under a lamp, and the movement of the air bubble were measured at one-minute intervals for five minutes. The light was turn off, and a small fan was move next to plant. This effect of wind was measured at one-minute intervals for five minutes. The results indicated that light and wind speed up transpiration of plants.

## Writing for Working Life

Read the following report written by a manager to be submitted at a meeting. Edit to ensure to ensure proper usage of the past participle. Use your own paper.

**BASIC WEB DESIGN**

**Prepared and Submitted by Diane Lipari**

As requested, I have analyze our website for its appeal and usability. The information I have gathers indicates a need for the application of basic Web design principles. Through a survey, our users have send us two messages. They don't care about new features. They just want easy usability. Before 2006, our Website has followed the basic guidelines of Web design. However, since our company's reorganization, we have not designate a person responsible for updating the Web. Two actions have recommended. The first recommendation has already occurred. Qualify and experience, Raul Mendez have taken responsibility for our company's Web design. He has promises to carry out the second recommendation, which is to follow these guidelines:

- Provide text they can read.
- Answer their questions with detailed information.
- Provide easy-to-use navigation and search options.
- Eliminate bugs, typos, corrupted data, dead links, and outdated content.

PORTFOLIO

# Academic Learning Log

## WHAT HAVE I LEARNED ABOUT THE PAST PARTICIPLE?

To test and track your understanding, answer the following questions.

**1.** The present perfect tense is formed by joining the helping verbs ………… or ………… with the past participle.

**2.** What are two purposes of the present perfect tense?

**a.** …………………………………………

**b.** …………………………………………

**3.** The past perfect tense is formed by joining the helping verb ………… with the past participle.

**4.** What are two purposes of the past perfect tense?

**a.** …………………………………………

**b.** …………………………………………

**5.** The passive voice is formed by the combination of ………… with a past participle.

**6.** The passive voice can be expressed in every ………….

**7.** What are two purposes of the passive voice?

**a.** …………………………………………

**b.** …………………………………………

**8.** What are two purposes of the past participle as an adjective?

**a.** …………………………………………

**b.** …………………………………………

**9. How will I use what I have learned about the past participle?**

In your notebook, discuss how you will apply to your own writing what you have learned about the past participle of regular and irregular verbs.

**10. What do I still need to study about the past participle?**

In your notebook, describe your ongoing study needs by describing what, when, and how you will continue studying the past participle of regular and irregular verbs.

REVISING

# 27

# Nouns and Pronouns

### Chapter Preview



## A noun names a person, animal, place, or thing. A pronoun stands in the place of a noun that has been clearly identified earlier in the text.

Thinking about a real-life situation helps us to understand the purpose of nouns and pronouns in our communication. The following photograph captures the essence of a controversial tourist attraction. Study the picture, complete the activity, and answer the question "What's the point of learning about nouns and pronouns?"

# What's the Point of Learning About Nouns and Pronouns?

WRITING FROM LIFE

Practice 1

PHOTOGRAPHIC ORGANIZER: NOUNS AND PRONOUNS

The following passage is adapted from a news story about the Skywalk bridge over the Grand Canyon that was built as a tourist attraction by the Hualapai tribe. All of the nouns and pronouns have been omitted from the passage. Work with a small group of your peers. Use the picture to help you fill in the blanks with nouns and pronouns that make the passage sensible. Answer the question "What's the point of learning about nouns and pronouns?"

**Skywalk**

An Indian .................. fastened a massive glass-bottomed .................. to the .................. of the .................. ................... The ambitious tourist .................. has angered .................................... and some tribal ................... The .................. (pronounced WALL-uh-pie) are an impoverished .................. of about 2,200 ................... .................. live at the canyon's remote western ................... A private .................. constructed the $30 million .................. to lure .................. to the ...................

**What's the point of learning about nouns and pronouns?**

........................................................................................................................

........................................................................................................................

# Understanding the Point of Learning About Nouns and Pronouns: One Student Writer's Response

The following paragraph offers one writer's reaction to the activity based on "Skywalk."

> I couldn't believe how hard this activity was! It was like trying to solve a riddle or a mystery. At least we had the picture to give us some clues. I was glad to be able to work with a group, too. Together we came up with more ideas, but we still couldn't figure out what all the words should be. This activity taught me that nouns and pronouns give really important information. You can't say what you want to say without using nouns and pronouns. I also learned that the words around pronouns and nouns can act like clues. Several times we chose a word that matched the word in front of it, like "the edge" and "an impoverished tribe."

# Applying the Point: Nouns

Often, nouns are the first words we learn to speak as we hear the names of people and things that we want or need. The word "noun" comes from the Latin word *nomen* which means "name." A **noun** names a person, animal, place, object, element, action, or concept.

| What a Noun Names | |
|---|---|
| **Person:** | Chris Rivers; a sales clerk |
| **Animal:** | Kitty; the cat |
| **Place:** | Lake Tahoe; a state park |
| **Object:** | Kleenex; tissue paper |
| **Element:** | water; air; gas |
| **Action:** | running |
| **Concept:** | Islam; a religion |

One type of noun is the proper noun. A **proper noun** names an individual person, place, or thing. A proper noun is always capitalized. The second type of noun is the common noun. A **common noun** is a general name for any member of a group or class. A common noun is not capitalized.

| Two Types of Nouns | |
|---|---|
| **Proper Noun** | **Common Noun** |
| Barnes & Noble | bookstore |
| Olive Garden | restaurant |
| Levi's | blue jeans |
| Batman | action hero |
| Polk County | county |

## Practice 2

TYPES OF NOUNS

Identify the following words as proper or common nouns. Edit to capitalize the proper nouns.

**1.** museum ______________________

**2.** smithsonian museum ______________________

**3.** basketball team ______________________

**4.** news anchor ______________________

**5.** katie couric ______________________

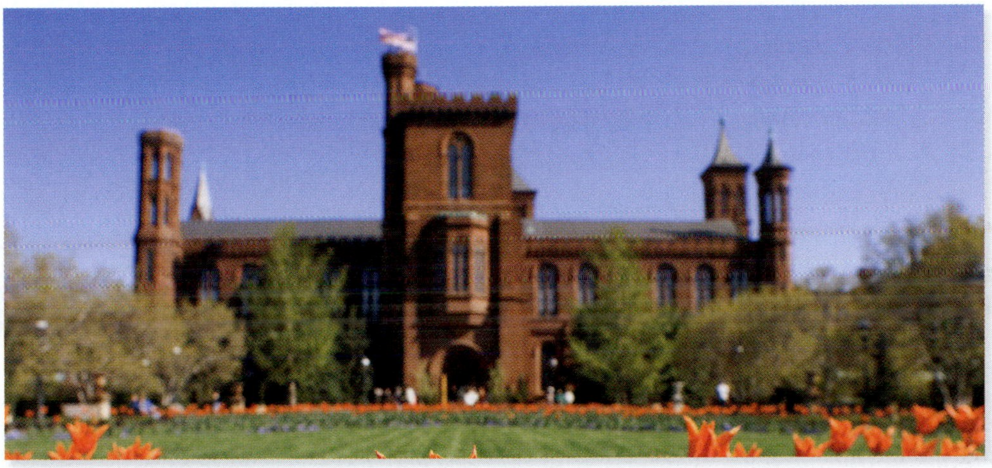

More practice with nouns and pronouns: <www.mywritinglab.com>

A proper or common noun can function in a sentence as a subject, an object of a verb, an object of a preposition, or an appositive (which describes another noun).

### Uses of a Noun

| Function in Sentence | Example |
|---|---|
| • Subject | PROPER NOUN AS SUBJECT<br>Roberto finished first. |

| Function in Sentence | Example |
|---|---|
| • Object of a verb | Maria drank coffee. (VERB → drank; COMMON NOUN AS OBJECT OF VERB "DRANK" → coffee) |
| • Object of a preposition | Justin went to AutoZone. (PREPOSITION → to; PROPER NOUN AS OBJECT OF PREPOSITION "TO" → AutoZone) |
| • Appositive (describes another noun) | Simon, the manager, has arrived. (SUBJECT (PROPER NOUN) → Simon; COMMON NOUN AS APPOSITIVE DESCRIBING "SIMON" → manager) |

## Practice 3

### USES OF A NOUN

Identify the following aspects of each of the nouns in the following sentences: the noun, what the noun names, type of noun, and function of the noun.

**1.** The Surgeon General filed a report with the following information.

---

**2.** In the United States, 11 million youths drink alcohol as underage drinkers.

---

**3.** Of the 11 million underage drinkers, 7.2 million drink as binge drinkers.

---

**4.** Alcohol may harm the development of the brain in adolescents.

---

**5.** Underage drinking, a disturbing trend, remains at high levels.

---

More practice with nouns and pronouns: <www.mywritinglab.com>

# Count and Noncount Nouns

For more information on irregular spellings, see Chapter 35, "Improving Your Spelling."

**Count nouns** name distinct individual units of a group or category. Count nouns usually refer to what we can see, hear, or touch. Count nouns are typically common nouns and can be plural or singular. Most singular count nouns are formed by adding *-s* or *-es*. However, many singular count nouns use irregular spellings in their plural form.

| Examples of Count Nouns | | |
|---|---|---|
| | **Singular** | **Plural** |
| **Regular** | age<br>baby<br>dress<br>garden | ages<br>babies<br>dresses<br>gardens |
| **Irregular** | calf<br>deer<br>man<br>person | calves<br>deer<br>men<br>people |

**Noncount nouns** name a nonspecific member of a group or category. Noncount nouns, which are typically common nouns, do not have plural forms. Noncount nouns name things that cannot be divided into smaller parts. Often, noncount nouns represent a group of count nouns. The following chart illustrates the differences between count and noncount nouns.

| Examples of Noncount Nouns and Corresponding Count Nouns | |
|---|---|
| **Noncount Noun** | **Count Noun** |
| air, oxygen, steam | gases |
| anger, happiness, grief | emotions |
| English, Spanish, Latin | languages |
| beauty, honesty, truth | concepts |

## Practice 4

COUNT AND NONCOUNT NOUNS

Read the following sentences. Identify the **boldfaced** nouns as a count or noncount noun.

**1.** A video **game** for **kids** offers the same sort of **humor** as watching a **cartoon**.

..............................................................................................

**2.** For example, **nose-picking** is a favorite **type** of **animation** found in both.

..............................................................................................

**3.** In addition, both offer the **act** of **shooting** bad **guys** with **guns** as **entertainment**.

..............................................................................................

Practice 4

**4.** In the game "Secret Rings," the **player** tries to win **rings** of **gold** floating in the **air**.

**5.** The **start** of the **game** begins slowly, but the **pace** picks up quickly.

## Articles and Nouns

An **article** is a type of adjective that describes a noun as being general or specific.

**Indefinite articles:** ***A*** and ***an*** are used before a singular noun that refers to any member of a larger group: ***a*** *cat,* ***an*** *umbrella.* These articles are often used to introduce a noun for the first time in the discussion. Use *a* before a noun that begins with a consonant: ***a*** *cat.* Use *an* before a noun that begins with a vowel: ***an*** *umbrella.*

**Definite article:** ***The*** is used before a singular or plural noun that refers to a specific member of the larger group: ***the*** *cat,* ***the*** *hat.* The article *the* is often used to indicate a noun that has already been introduced into the discussion. "A cat is at the front door; the cat looks hungry." *The* is the most commonly used word in the English language.

**Zero article:** No article is used before the noun. An example: *Time is money.* Use zero article to refer to general ideas.

- *A Chinese woman moves to a different country.*
- *The Chinese woman has a difficult time communicating.*
- *Chinese is a foreign language in her new country.*

Deciding which article to use with a noun can be a challenge. You must determine if the article refers to a count noun or a noncount noun, and you must determine if the noun is singular or plural. The following chart illustrates the proper combinations.

| Nouns and Their Articles | | |
|---|---|---|
| | **Count Nouns** | **Noncount Nouns** |
| **Singular** | A, An | The |
| **Plural** | The | — |

Practice 5

ARTICLES

Read the sentences below. Insert the correct article (*a*, *an*, or *the*) in the blanks provided.

(1) Dry, irritated skin is ........ threat to ........ person's well-being. (2) Well-moisturized skin offers ........ barrier against bacteria and viruses. (3) As........ individual ages, one's cell turnover slows down. (4) Weather damages ........ skin. (5) Water evaporates from ........ skin due to chilly temperatures and dry indoor heat. (6) Long, hot baths and

showers damage skin. (7) ........ natural protective layer of oil is stripped away by too much washing. (8) ........ lotion treatment can restore ........ protective barrier of moisture. (9) Many of ........ lotion treatments contain petrolatum, glycerin, or shea butter, ........ oil that prevents water loss.

More practice with nouns and pronouns <www.mywritinglab.com>

Homework! 523-534

# ★ Applying the Point: Pronouns

**Pronouns and antecedents** work closely together to communicate an idea. A **pronoun** refers to or stands in the place of a noun that has been clearly identified earlier in the discussion. An **antecedent** is the noun to which a pronoun refers. Every pronoun should refer clearly and specifically to one particular antecedent.

ANTECEDENT OF PRONOUN "IT" — PRONOUN "IT" REFERS TO ANTECEDENT "PACKAGE"

When the FedEx package arrived, the receptionist put it on the front counter.

In the preceding example, the pronoun "it" clearly refers to the antecedent "package."

For more information on using precision in drafting sentences, see Chapter 19, "Sentence Clarity: Point of View, Number, and Tense."

## How to Make Clear Pronoun References

Because a pronoun takes the place of a noun, careful writers make the relationship between a pronoun and its antecedent obvious and clear. Remembering a few guidelines can help you make clear pronoun references.

| Guidelines for Clear Pronoun Reference |
|---|
| • A pronoun refers clearly and unmistakably to one antecedent.<br>• The antecedent of a pronoun is clearly stated.<br>• A pronoun appears near its antecedent.<br>• A pronoun does not make a broad or sweeping reference to an entire group of words. |

Faulty pronoun references usually occur when the guidelines for clear reference are ignored. Once you understand why faulty pronoun references occur and how they can be corrected, you can avoid faulty pronoun references in your writing; then you can make clear pronoun references.

# How to Correct Faulty Pronoun References

## Faulty Pronoun Reference to More Than One Antecedent

**PROBLEM:**

The pronoun does not clearly and unmistakably refer to one specific antecedent.

PRONOUN "IT" REFERS TO ?

Jared threw the remote control at the television because it was broken.

ANTECEDENT OF "IT"?

**CORRECTION:**

Correct by replacing the pronoun with a noun.

Jared threw the remote control at the television because the remote control was broken.

ADDED NOUN REPLACES PRONOUN WITH NO CLEAR ANTECEDENT

## Faulty Pronoun Reference to Implied or Missing Antecedent

**PROBLEM:**

The antecedent is not stated or is missing.

ANTECEDENT OF PRONOUN "IT"? PRONOUN "IT" REFERS TO ?

The donut box is empty. Who ate it?

**CORRECTION #1:**

Correct by replacing the pronoun with a noun.

ADDED NOUN REPLACES PRONOUN WITH NO CLEAR ANTECEDENT

The donut box is empty. Who ate the last donut?

SUBJECT AND VERB IMPLY THAT "IT" IN THE ABOVE SENTENCE REFERS TO A DONUT

**CORRECTION #2:**

Correct by rewording to include a clear antecedent for the pronoun.

ANTECEDENT OF PRONOUN "IT" PRONOUN "IT" REFERS TO ANTECEDENT "DONUT"

The last donut is gone. Who ate it?

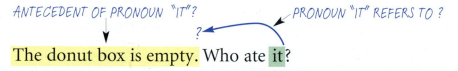

## Faulty Pronoun Reference due to Distant Pronoun Reference

**PROBLEM:**

The pronoun does not appear near its antecedent.

ACTUAL ANTECEDENT OF PRONOUN "WHO"

Saleem searched his apartment, his clothes, and his car, who misplaced the key to his apartment.

ANTECEDENT OF "WHO" ?

DISTANT PLACEMENT OF RELATIVE PRONOUN "WHO" FROM ITS ANTECEDENT "SALEEM" MAKES THE SENTENCE AWKWARD AND ITS ANTECEDENT UNCLEAR

**CORRECTION:**

Correct by rewording to place the pronoun closer to its antecedent.

ANTECEDENT OF PRONOUN "WHO"

PRONOUN "WHO" REFERS TO ANTECEDENT "SALEEM"

Saleem, who misplaced the key to his apartment, searched his apartment, his clothes, and his car.

## Faulty Pronoun Reference due to Broad Pronoun References

**PROBLEM:**

The pronoun refers to a group of words, such as an entire sentence.

ANTECEDENT OF PRONOUN "WHICH" ?

PRONOUN "WHICH" REFERS TO ?

Mick told Megan about his date with Kanesha, which annoyed Megan.

**CORRECTION:**

Correct by rewording to eliminate the pronoun.

Megan was annoyed because Mick told her about his date with Kanesha.

Practice 6

**CLEAR PRONOUN REFERENCE**

Revise the following sentences for clear pronoun reference.

1. Maxine spewed coffee into her food because it tasted terrible.

2. Colleen told Samantha that her dress was torn.

3. Employees must check with their managers who need sick-leave forms.

4. They say that college graduates earn more money than non-graduates.

5. Reading to children develops their minds which should be done daily.

More practice with nouns and pronouns: <www.mywritinglab.com>

## How to Make Pronouns and Antecedents Agree

A pronoun and its antecedent must agree with each other in three ways: person, number, and gender. The following chart presents pronouns based on these traits.

**Pronouns: Person, Number, and Gender**

| | **Singular** | **Plural** |
|---|---|---|
| **First Person** | I, me, my, mine | we, us, ours |
| **Second Person** | you, yours | you, yours |
| **Third Person** | he, him, his (**masculine**)<br>she, her, hers (**feminine**)<br>it, its (**neutral**) | they, their, theirs (**neutral**) |

**Pronoun agreement** makes the relationship between a pronoun and its antecedent obvious and clear. **Faulty pronoun agreement** reflects vague wording and results in reader confusion. Remembering a few guidelines can help you establish pronoun agreement.

| Guidelines for Clear Pronoun Reference |
|---|
| • Pronoun choice establishes consistent use of the person of pronouns.<br>• Singular pronouns refer to or replace singular nouns.<br>• Plural pronouns refer to or replace plural nouns.<br>• Feminine pronouns refer to or replace feminine nouns.<br>• Masculine pronouns refer to or replace masculine nouns.<br>• Use gender-neutral plural pronouns and antecedents to make statements that could apply to women or men. |

Faulty pronoun agreement usually occurs when the guidelines for clear agreement are ignored. Once you understand why faulty pronoun agreement occurs and how it can be corrected, you can avoid vague agreements in your writing; then you can create pronoun agreement based on person, number, and gender.

# How to Correct Faulty Pronoun Agreement

## Faulty Pronoun Agreement due to Shift in Person

### PROBLEM:

When the person of the pronoun differs from the person of the antecedent, it is called a faulty **shift in person**. In the example below, the faulty shift is from third person to second person.

THIS ANTECEDENT OF THE THIRD-PERSON PRONOUN "YOUR" IS A SECOND-PERSON NOUN

As soon as a contestant finishes a song, the judges evaluate your performance.

SECOND-PERSON PRONOUN "YOUR" DOES NOT AGREE WITH ITS THIRD-PERSON ANTECEDENT "CONTESTANT"

### CORRECTION #1:

Correct the shift in person by changing the antecedent to agree with the pronoun.

ADDED SECOND-PERSON ANTECEDENT AGREES WITH SECOND-PERSON PRONOUN

As soon as you finish a song, the judges evaluate your performance.

"-ES" IN VERB IS DELETED TO AGREE WITH ADDED PRONOUN "YOU" IN NUMBER

### CORRECTION #2:

Correct by changing the pronoun to agree with the antecedent.

THIRD-PERSON ANTECEDENT AGREES WITH ADDED THIRD-PERSON PRONOUN

As soon as a contestant finishes a song, the judges evaluate her performance.

## Faulty Pronoun Agreement due to Shift in Number

PROBLEM:

In a sentence with a faulty **shift in number,** the pronoun is a different number than the number of the antecedent. In the two examples below, the faulty shift is from singular to plural; the revised sentences show two different ways to correct the same problem.

SINGULAR ANTECEDENT

PLURAL PRONOUN DOES NOT AGREE WITH SINGULAR ANTECEDENT "ATHLETE"

A college athlete must keep their grades at a B average to be eligible to play.

CORRECTION:

Correct by making the antecedent the same number as the pronoun.

PLURAL ANTECEDENT AGREES WITH PLURAL PRONOUN

College athletes must keep their grades at a B average to be eligible to play.

PROBLEM:

SINGULAR ANTECEDENT

PLURAL PRONOUN DOES NOT AGREE WITH SINGULAR ANTECEDENT "EVERYONE"

Everyone on the women's soccer team has their gear loaded on the bus.

CORRECTION:

Correct by making the pronoun the same number as the antecedent.

SINGULAR ANTECEDENT AGREES WITH SINGULAR PRONOUN

Everyone on the women's soccer team has her gear loaded on the bus.

## Faulty Pronoun Agreement due to Shift in Gender

**PROBLEM:**

In a sentence with a faulty **shift in gender,** the pronoun is a different gender than the gender of the antecedent. Most often, gender agreement problems are due to using the masculine pronoun to refer to antecedents that could apply to either men or women.

SINGULAR PRONOUN ANTECEDENT IS NEUTRAL
("STUDENT" COULD BE EITHER MASCULINE OR FEMININE)

A student at Carleton College can buy his parking permit at the Campus Safety Office.

MASCULINE, SINGULAR PRONOUN "HIS" DOES NOT AGREE WITH NEUTRAL ANTECEDENT "STUDENT"

**CORRECTION #1:**

Correct by rewording to make the pronoun the same gender as the antecedent.

NEUTRAL, SINGULAR ANTECEDENT AGREES WITH NEUTRAL, SINGULAR PRONOUN "HIS OR HER"

A student at Carleton College can buy his or her parking permit at the Campus Safety Office.

If you reword the sentence by making the pronoun and its antecedent (neutral and) plural, make sure all other parts of the sentence are plural as necessary.

NEUTRAL, PLURAL ANTECEDENT AGREES WITH NEUTRAL, PLURAL PRONOUN

Students at Carleton College can buy their parking permits at the Campus Safety Office.

"-S" ADDED TO AGREE WITH PLURAL PRONOUN "THEIR" IN NUMBER

**CORRECTION #2:**

Correct by rewording to make the antecedent the same gender as the pronoun. In the instance below, this requires adding a masculine proper noun ("John") to match the masculine pronoun.

ADDED MASCULINE, SINGULAR ANTECEDENT

MASCULINE, SINGULAR PRONOUN "HIS" REFERS TO MASCULINE, SINGULAR ANTECEDENT "JOHN"

John, a student at Carleton College, can buy his parking permit at the Campus Safety Office.

ADDED COMMAS SET OFF NEW APPOSITIVE PHRASE

Practice 7

**PRONOUN AGREEMENT**

Edit the following sentences to create pronoun agreement. Cross out the faulty pronoun and insert the appropriate pronoun.

1. People should check their credit reports to find out if you have been victimized by identity theft.
2. A person can have his credit report sent to him for free.
3. A victim of identity theft loses more than money; they lose peace of mind.
4. A consumer should be diligent about paying bills; your payment history counts for 35 percent of your credit score.
5. Write a sentence that requires subject-verb agreement. Suggested topic: Physical Fitness.

---

---

**Pronoun case** identifies the function of a pronoun in a sentence. The definitions and examples of the three cases of pronouns are shown in the following chart.

More practice with nouns and pronouns: <www.mywritinglab.com>

**Pronoun Case**

| | **Subjective Case** | | **Objective Case** | | **Possessive Case** | |
|---|---|---|---|---|---|---|
| | **Singular** | **Plural** | **Singular** | **Plural** | **Singular** | **Plural** |
| **1st Person** | I | we | me | us | my, mine | our, ours |
| **2nd Person** | you | you | you | you | your, yours | your, yours |
| **3rd Person** | he, she, it<br>who<br>whoever | they | him, her, it<br>whom<br>whomever | them | his, his<br>her, hers<br>its, its<br>whose | their, theirs |

**Subjective case** pronouns act as subjects or predicate nouns. A **predicate noun** restates the subject, usually by completing a linking verb such as *is*.

SUBJECTIVE CASE PRONOUN

We are going to audition for a gig at the Comedy Club.

SUBJECT — SUBJECTIVE CASE PRONOUN RENAMES THE SUBJECT "COMEDIAN"

The funniest comedian is she.

**Objective case** pronouns act as an object of a verb or preposition. The **object** of a sentence is a noun or pronoun to which the action of a verb is directed or to which the verb's action is done.

VERB — OBJECTIVE CASE PRONOUN "THEM" IS THE OBJECT OF THE VERB "CAPTIVATED"

The comedian captivated them.

PREPOSITION — OBJECTIVE CASE PRONOUN "WHOM" IS THE OBJECT OF THE PREPOSITION "TO"

To whom are you speaking?

**Possessive case** pronouns show ownership.

POSSESSIVE CASE PRONOUN "HIS" INDICATES THAT THE GLASSES BELONG TO "TOM"

Tom put his glasses on the bookshelf.

POSSESSIVE CASE PRONOUN "THEIR" INDICATES THAT THE CAR BELONGS TO "JASON AND CINDY"

By the time Jason and Cindy parked their car, the baseball game was over.

## Practice 8

PRONOUN CASE

Underline the pronouns in each sentence. Then, identify the case of each pronoun.

1. The Library of Congress has added a popular Rolling Stones song to its archives.

2. The song "(I Can't Get No) Satisfaction" was first recorded in 1965; it was an instant hit.

3. The Library of Congress wants to preserve significant recordings because many of them have disappeared over the years.

4. The panel who choose the recording is made up of members of the public and a panel of music, sound, and preservation experts.

5. Write a sentence that requires the use of a subjective case pronoun. Suggested topic: Favorite Musical Group.

More practice with nouns and pronouns: <www.mywritinglab.com>

**Use of pronoun cases** relies upon understanding the function of the pronoun in the context of its use. Remembering a few guidelines can help you choose the appropriate case of a pronoun.

| **Guidelines for Use of Pronoun Cases** |
|---|
| • Choose the appropriate pronoun case in comparisons using *as* or *than* based on the meaning of the sentence. |
| • Use the appropriate pronoun case in compound constructions, such as compound subjects, compound objects of verbs, or compound objects of prepositions. |

**Misuse of pronoun case** usually occurs when the function of the pronoun is ignored or misunderstood. Once you understand why misuse of pronoun case occurs and how it can be corrected, you can choose the appropriate pronoun case based on the context of its use.

## How to Correct Faulty Use of Pronoun Case in Comparisons Using "as" or "than"

Pronouns in comparisons using "as" or "than" can be in the subjective, objective, or possessive case. Most writers have no difficulty using the possessive case correctly: *Sam's car is prettier than* ***mine***. However, writers often confuse the subjective and objective cases (for example, incorrectly substituting "I" for "me," "he" for "him," or "she" for "her") because they think it sounds more formal.

**PROBLEM:**

The objective case pronoun is being used as the subject of a clause.

DEPENDENT CLAUSE WITH UNSTATED VERB "IS"

Jerome is as concerned as her.

INCORRECT USE OF OBJECTIVE CASE PRONOUN

**CORRECTION:**

If the pronoun is a subject, correct by replacing the pronoun with a subjective case pronoun. To identify whether a pronoun in a comparison is a subject or an object, mentally complete the comparison by filling in the implied words and then choose the pronoun that matches it logically.

SUBJECTIVE CASE PRONOUN ACTS AS SUBJECT OF IMPLIED VERB "IS"

Jerome is as concerned as she [is].

IMPLIED VERB

**PROBLEM:**

The subjective case pronoun is being used as the object of a verb.

INCORRECT USE OF SUBJECTIVE CASE PRONOUN

The transit strike affected Marion as much as I.

**CORRECTION:**

If the pronoun is an object, correct by replacing the pronoun with an objective case pronoun. To identify whether a pronoun in a comparison is a subject or an object, mentally complete the comparison by filling in the implied words and then choose the pronoun that matches it logically.

OBJECTIVE CASE PRONOUN "ME" ACTS AS OBJECT OF IMPLIED, UNSTATED SUBJECT AND VERB PHRASE "IT AFFECTED"

The transit strike affected Marion as much as [it affected] me.

In some cases, the pronoun in a comparison could function as either a subject or an object and still make sense either way, but it would change the sentence's meaning. Both examples below are correct, but the first sentence means that Miguel respects Carlotta more than you respect her and the second sentence means that Miguel respects Carlotta more than he respects you.

SUBJECTIVE CASE PRONOUN "I" ACTS AS THE SUBJECT OF THE IMPLIED VERB AND OBJECT "RESPECT CARLOTTA"

Miguel respects Carlotta more than I [respect Carlotta].

OBJECTIVE CASE PRONOUN "ME" IS THE OBJECT OF THE UNSTATED SUBJECT AND VERB PHRASE "HE RESPECTS"

Miguel respects Carlotta more than [he respects] me.

## Faulty Use of Case in Compound Constructions

In some instances, a pronoun is joined with a noun or another pronoun to form a **compound.**

- **Joseph and I** went to a concert together.
- The mailman delivered the letter to **Joseph and me.**

To decide whether the subjective or objective case should be used for a pronoun in a compound, use the same rules that apply for a pronoun that is not in a compound. Use the subjective case for pronouns that function as subjects and the objective case for pronouns that function as objects.

**PROBLEM:**

The objective case pronoun is being used in a compound subject.

COMPOUND SUBJECT — VERB

Jim Yung and her earned large bonuses.

INCORRECT USE OF OBJECTIVE CASE PRONOUN IN COMPOUND SUBJECT

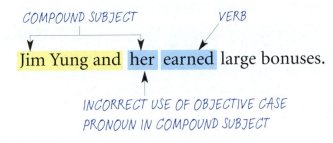

**CORRECTION:**

If the pronoun is a subject, correct by replacing the pronoun with the subjective case pronoun. To identify a pronoun as part of a compound subject, delete the other part of the compound so the pronoun stands alone, and see whether the sentence still makes sense. In the example below, you would delete "Jim Yung." The revised sentence, "Her earned large bonuses," does not make sense, which indicates that the pronoun used is part of a compound subject and should be subjective, not objective.

COMPOUND SUBJECTS OF VERB "EARNED" — VERB

Jim Yung and she earned large bonuses.

SUBJECTIVE CASE PRONOUN

**PROBLEM:**

The subjective case pronoun is being used in a compound object.

COMPOUND OBJECT — VERB

The supervisor told Bob and I the news.

MISUSED SUBJECTIVE CASE PRONOUN

**CORRECTION:**

If the pronoun is an object of either a verb or a preposition, correct by replacing the pronoun with the objective case pronoun. To identify a pronoun as part of a compound object, delete the other part of the compound so the pronoun stands alone, and see whether the sentence still makes sense. In the example, you would delete "Bob." The revised sentence, "The supervisor told I the news," does not make sense, which indicates that the pronoun used is part of a compound object and should be objective, not subjective.

VERB — COMPOUND OBJECTS OF THE VERB "TOLD"

The supervisor told Bob and me the news.

OBJECTIVE CASE PRONOUN

**Practice 9**

**PRONOUN AGREEMENT**

Edit the following sentences to ensure proper use of pronoun cases.

1. Michael, a highly skilled massage therapist, says that John is as effective as him.
2. In fact, many customers like John better than he.
3. Michael and him charge the same rates for a deep tissue massage.
4. Daniella strongly recommends both Michael and he as massage therapists.
5. Write a sentence that requires the proper use of pronoun case. Suggested topic: A Good Friend.

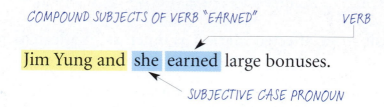

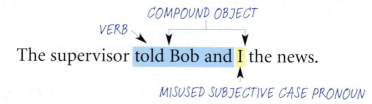

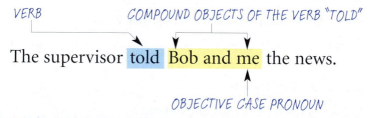

More practice with nouns and pronouns: <www.mywritinglab.com>

**Reflexive and intensive pronouns** include all the pronouns ending in *-self or -selves.* Often, in everyday, informal speech, the irregular forms of reflexive or intensive pronouns can be heard: *hisself, theirself,* and *theirselves.* However, these forms are to be avoided in standard, written English. The following chart lists the standard forms and uses of reflexive and intensive pronouns.

| Reflexive and Intensive Pronouns | | |
|---|---|---|
| **Person** | **Singular** | **Plural** |
| **First Person** | myself | ourselves |
| **Second Person** | yourself | yourselves |
| **Third Person** | himself, herself, itself | themselves |

**Reflexive pronouns** refer back to the subject.

REFLEXIVE PRONOUN "HERSELF" REFERS TO SUBJECT "JEANNIE"

Jeannie rewarded herself with a two-week cruise to the Bahamas.

**Intensive pronouns** add emphasis to another noun or pronoun.

INTENSIVE PRONOUN EMPHASIZES "DR. GILLON"

Dr. Gillon himself made a surprise appearance.

PROBLEM:

Because reflexive and intensive pronouns always refer to other nouns or pronouns, reflexive and intensive pronouns are never used on their own as the subject of a sentence.

REFLEXIVE PRONOUN MISUSED AS SUBJECT — VERB

Themselves went to the movies.

CORRECTION:

Correct by replacing the reflexive pronoun with a subjective pronoun.

ADDED SUBJECTIVE PRONOUN — VERB

They went to the movies.

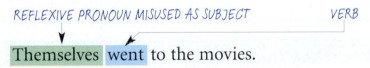

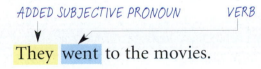

## Practice 10

**REFLEXIVE AND INTENSIVE PRONOUNS**

Complete each sentence by filling in the blank with the appropriate reflexive or intensive pronoun.

**1.** I do not need assistance; I can lift the weight by ____________.

**2.** Gil ____________ heard the diagnosis from the doctor.

**3.** Charlene gives ____________ a daily shot of her medicine for diabetes.

**4.** The President and the Vice President ____________ appeared at the rally.

**5.** You need to tell ____________ that success is possible.

## Practice 11

**NOUN AND PRONOUN REVIEW**

Test your understanding of nouns and pronouns by filling the blanks with the nouns, articles, and pronouns that best complete each idea.

(1) Cheating is often ____________ key to success for video gamers. (2) At some point in ______ game, everyone has gotten stuck. (3) Today's gamers use cheat sites to get unstuck and to learn how to master difficult games. (4) When ____________ pay $60 for ______ game, ____________ want to get ____________ money's worth. (5) While cheating can get ______ gamer blackballed in competitive video game play, solo cheating is widely practiced. (6) Still, few gamers want to admit that ____________ cheat. (7) This ________________________ has given rise to dozens of dedicated Web ____________.

More practice with nouns and pronouns: <www.mywritinglab.com>

# Writing Assignments

## Writing for Everyday Life

Assume you got into a fight last night with your significant other, and you are writing a note of apology. Edit the following apology to ensure proper use of nouns, articles, and pronouns. Use your own paper.

*Dear Jess,*

*Too often disagreement come between you and I. Yesterday, our arguing seemed to upset others more than it upset ourselves. As you know, the quick tempers run in my family. And your family is just as fiery as us. Yesterday, however, a faults was all me. I can't blame anyone but me. I should not have embarrassed you by arguing with your brother Jonathan, whose also full of the remorse. You and me have been together an long time. One hopes you can find within yourself to forgive Jonathan and me.*

*Regretfully, Pat*

## Writing for College Life

Assume you are taking a test for a unit in Interpersonal Communication 101. On the written portion of the test, you are asked to explain some of the differences between individualistic cultures and collective cultures. You have ten minutes left to proofread your response. Edit to ensure proper use of nouns, articles, and pronouns. Use your own paper.

**Exam question**: What are the major contrasting traits between individualistic and collective cultures?

*Individualistic and collective cultures differ in several aspect. Individualist cultures focus on the goales of an individual. You're responsible for yourself, and perhaps your immediate family. Your values are guided by your own consciences. A person's success is measured by surpassing other members of his group. Members of individualist culture are competitive, individualistic, and direct. Individualist cultures include American, Swedish, and German. In contrast, collective cultures focus on the goales of the group. Members of collective cultures are cooperative, submissive, and polite. You're responsible for a entire group and to group's values and rules. Collective cultures include Japaneses, Arabic, and Mexican.*

## Writing for Working Life

Assume you are a hairstylist who has recently opened a new salon. You have composed a letter to send to your customers to inform them about your move. Edit the letter to ensure proper use of nouns, articles, and pronouns. Use your own paper.

Dear Friends,

I would like to invite you to share in me new venture. I will now be at a following location: Waves & Day Spa, The Renaissance Center, 453 S. Oleander Street. We will offer your the same services at the same prices and also the addition of massage, facials, spa pedicures and manicures. There is also an selection of spa packages and escapes available. I will be working your same days Tuesday through Saturday with same flexible hours to accommodate yours schedule. I welcome you to join my new team and I at my new location and assure you that there will be same comfortable jovial atmosphere of a small salon with the offer of Day Spa services I appreciate your loyalty over the years and hope you will come see me at the new salon for a fresh new start to this new year.

Sincerely,

Denise Cossaboon

PORTFOLIO

# Academic Learning Log

## WHAT HAVE I LEARNED ABOUT NOUNS AND PRONOUNS?

To test and track your understanding, answer the following questions.

**1.** A noun names a ________, animal, place, object, action, or concept.

**2.** A ________ noun names an individual person, place, or thing; a ________ noun is a general name for any member of a group or class.

**3.** A noun can function as a ________, object of a verb, object of a ________, or appositive.

**4.** ________ nouns name distinct individual units of a group or category; noncount nouns name a nonspecific member of a group or category.

**5.** An ________ article is used before a singular noun that refers to any member of a larger group.

**6.** The definite article ______ is used before a singular or plural noun that refers to a specific member of a larger group.

**7.** A pronoun refers clearly and specifically to ______ antecedent.

**8.** An antecedent is the ________ to which a pronoun refers.

**9.** A pronoun and its antecedent must agree with each other in three ways: ________, ________, and ________.

**10.** The three pronoun cases are ________ case, ________ case, and ________ case.

**11.** A reflexive pronoun refers back to the ________.

**12.** An intensive pronoun adds ________ to another noun or pronoun.

**13. How will I use what I have learned about nouns and pronouns?**
In your notebook, discuss how you will apply to your own writing what you have learned about nouns and pronouns.

**14. What do I still need to study about nouns and pronouns?**
In your notebook, describe your ongoing study needs by describing what, when, and how you will continue studying pronouns and nouns.

REVISING

# 28 Adjectives and Adverbs

**Chapter Preview**

- What's the Point of Learning About Adjectives and Adverbs?
- Understanding the Point of Learning About Adjectives and Adverbs: One Student Writer's Response
- Applying the Point: Adjectives and Adverbs

## An adjective describes a noun or a pronoun. An adverb describes a verb, an adjective, or another adverb.

Thinking about a real-life situation helps us to understand the purpose of adjectives and adverbs in our communication. The following photograph captures the action of a highly skilled basketball player, Michael Jordan. Study the picture, complete the activity, and answer the question "What's the point of learning about adjectives and adverbs?"

# What's the Point of Learning About Adjectives and Adverbs?

WRITING FROM LIFE

Practice 1

**PHOTOGRAPHIC ORGANIZER: ADJECTIVES AND ADVERBS**

Assume you are a sports reporter for your college newspaper and you are featuring a series of articles on historic NBA basketball players. This week your column features Michael Jordan. Work with a small group of your peers. Use the picture to help you fill in the blanks with adjectives and adverbs that best describe the action in the photo.

*The Most Amazing Michael Jordan*

*Michael Jordan was an ______ basketball player.*
*He ______ leapt the ______ of all the*
*players on the court. When other players made*
*______ attempts to block Jordan's shots,*
*Jordan's jumps to the basket were ______ and*
*______ than those of his opponents. His*
*______ arms allowed him to make his*
*______ point ______ feet ______ from the basket.*
*Jordan remains one of the ______ players in the*
*history of the NBA.*

**What's the point of learning about adjectives and adverbs?**

______

______

# Understanding the Point of Learning About Adjectives and Adverbs: One Student Writer's Response

The following paragraph offers one writer's reaction to the paragraph about Michael Jordan.

> *This activity taught me how important adjectives and adverbs are. They paint a vivid picture so the reader can see the point of a topic or issue. I also noticed that each member of our group chose different words to describe Jordan and the action in the photograph. For example, one person in our group described Jordan as an "unbelievable basketball player" while another person said he was "an aggressive basketball player." So my choice of adjectives and adverbs helps me to get my own point across. I also noticed that adjectives describe people and things; while adverbs describe actions.*

# Applying the Point: Adjectives and Adverbs

Adjectives and adverbs are descriptive words that describe, modify, or limit the meaning of other words. Adjectives and adverbs have specific functions in a sentence and thus express precise meanings. Understanding the function and purpose of adjectives and adverbs allows a writer a thoughtful and effective expression of ideas.

An **adjective** modifies—in other words, it describes—a noun or a pronoun. It answers one or more of the following questions:

- What kind?
- Which one?
- How many?

ADJECTIVE "LOUD" DESCRIBES NOUN "VOICE"

Maya has a loud voice.

PRONOUN "SHE" DESCRIBED BY ADJECTIVE "HAPPY"

She is happy.

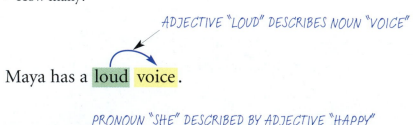

An **adverb** modifies, or describes, a verb, an adjective, or another adverb. It answers one or more of the following questions:

- How?
- Why?
- When?
- Where?
- To what extent?

VERB "TALKS" DESCRIBED BY ADVERB "LOUDLY"

Maya talks loudly.

NOUN "MAYA" DESCRIBED BY ADJECTIVE "HAPPY"

Maya is loudly happy.

ADVERB "LOUDLY" DESCRIBES ADJECTIVE "HAPPY"

## Practice 2

ADJECTIVES AND ADVERBS

Identify the **boldfaced** words in each sentence as adjectives or as adverbs.

**1.** Camping has **persistently** remained one of life's **greatest** bargains.

**2.** A couple can camp **inexpensively**.

**3.** An **entire** set of **high-quality** equipment can cost **less** than $500.

**4.** Nights in **many** areas can get **very** cold.

**5.** Sleeping bags are **widely** available in **various** weights at **reasonable** prices.

## Participles as Adjectives

Many adjectives are formed by adding *-ed* or *-ing* to verbs. These **participle adjectives** serve two purposes: The *-ed* form describes a person's reaction or feeling; the *-ing* form describes the person or thing that causes the reaction.

-ED PARTICIPLE ADJECTIVE DESCRIBES HOW THE "CROWD" FEELS

The amazed crowd watched the fireworks display.

-ING PARTICIPLE ADJECTIVE DESCRIBES THE "FIREWORKS" CAUSING THE REACTION

The amazing fireworks display lit up the entire sky.

The following chart lists some of the most common participles used as adjectives.

**Common Participles Used as Adjectives**

| | | | |
|---|---|---|---|
| alarmed | alarming | exhausted | exhausting |
| amused | amusing | fascinated | fascinating |
| annoyed | annoying | frightened | frightening |
| bored | boring | horrified | horrifying |
| concerned | concerning | irritated | irritating |
| confused | confusing | pleased | pleasing |
| depressed | depressing | satisfied | satisfying |
| discouraged | discouraging | shocked | shocking |
| encouraged | encouraging | stimulated | stimulating |
| engaged | engaging | terrified | terrifying |
| excited | exciting | worried | worrying |

Practice 3

PARTICIPLES AS ADJECTIVES

Complete the following ideas by filling in the blanks with the proper participle adjective. Create your participle adjectives from the following base words: *alarm*, *concern*, and *surprise*.

**1.** ______________ travelers worry about the effect of travel on global warming.

**2.** Every method of travel creates a ______________ amount of pollution.

**3.** Cruises, car trips, and airplane flights dump ______________ amounts of carbon dioxide into the environment.

**4.** ______________ researchers report that a round-trip flight between Los Angeles and New York produces 2.56 tons of carbon dioxide per passenger.

**5.** Due to the ______________ effect of travel on the environment, research into green energy is increasing.

## Nouns and Verbs Formed as Adjectives

More practice with adjectives and adverbs: <www.mywritinglab.com>

In addition to the *-ed* and *-ing* word endings, many adjectives are formed by other types of word endings. Just as a suffix transforms a verb into a specific type of adjective or adverb, a suffix can also create adjectives out of nouns. Adjectives come in so many forms that using a few carefully chosen adjectives can add power and interest to your writing. For your reference, the following chart lists a few frequently used adjectives by some of their word endings.

**Common Adjectives**

| **Word Endings** | ***-able*** ***-ible*** | ***-ful*** | ***-ic*** | ***-ish*** | ***-ive*** | ***-less*** | ***-ly*** ***-y*** | ***-ous*** |
|---|---|---|---|---|---|---|---|---|
| **Examples** | acceptable | bashful | alcoholic | boorish | abusive | cheerless | actually | ambiguous |
| | accessible | cheerful | aquatic | oafish | combative | jobless | cagy | auspicious |
| | capable | forgetful | dramatic | devilish | decisive | mindless | daffy | courageous |
| | honorable | graceful | erratic | elfish | instinctive | needless | earthy | glamorous |
| | laughable | joyful | gigantic | lavish | receptive | noiseless | lively | industrious |
| | obtainable | merciful | majestic | skittish | reflective | pointless | manly | malicious |
| | plausible | peaceful | melodic | snobbish | secretive | senseless | seemly | nervous |
| | tangible | rightful | organic | squeamish | selective | useless | smelly | righteous |

## Placement of Adjectives

A careful writer not only chooses the precise word for impact, but also arranges words in the most effective order for the greatest impact on the reader. As you work with adjectives, be aware that the placement of adjectives varies based on its relationship to other words.

Adjectives can appear before a noun.

ADJECTIVE "NERVOUS" DESCRIBES NOUN "SUSPECT"

The nervous suspect offered an alibi.

Adjectives can appear after **linking verbs** such as *is, are, were, seems,* and *appears.*

LINKING VERB "SEEMED" JOINS ADJECTIVE "PLAUSIBLE" TO NOUN "ALIBI"

The alibi seemed plausible.

NOUN "ALIBI" DESCRIBED BY ADJECTIVE "PLAUSIBLE"

Adjectives can appear after **sensory verbs**—those that describe physical senses—such as *look, smell, feel, taste,* and *sound.*

SENSORY VERB "LOOKED" JOINS ADJECTIVE "FRIGHTENED" TO NOUN "SUSPECT"

The suspect looked frightened.

NOUN "SUSPECT" DESCRIBED BY ADJECTIVE "FRIGHTENED"

Practice 4

**PLACEMENT OF ADJECTIVES**

Fill in the blanks by choosing the phrase that best completes the sentence's idea by appropriate placement of adjectives.

**1.** ______________________ in every aspect of daily life.

**a.** Needless conflicts arise **b.** Conflicts needless arise **c.** Conflicts arise needless

**2.** Many ______________________ after they are over.

**a.** senseless conflicts seem **b.** conflicts seem senseless **c.** conflicts senseless seem

**3.** Frequently, conflicts arise because ______________________ to the needs or wants of others.

**a.** people insensitive are **b.** are people insensitive **c.** people are insensitive

**4.** ______________________ often looks for conflict.

**a.** A boorish person **b.** A person boorish **c.** Boorish a person

**5.** In contrast a person ______________________ strives to resolve conflicts in everyone's best interest.

**a.** peaceful who is **b.** is peaceful who **c.** who is peaceful

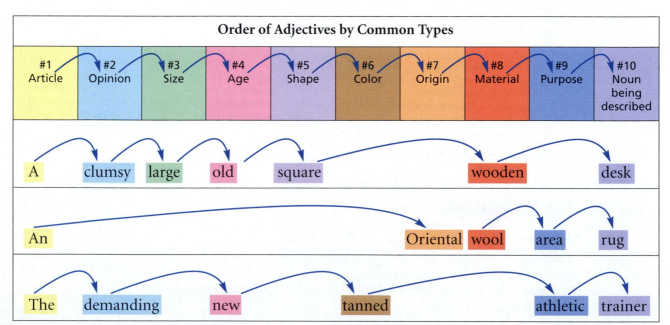

More practice with adjectives and adverbs: <www.mywritinglab.com>

## Order of Adjectives

Adjectives that appear before a noun follow a particular order. Effective writers use adjectives sparingly. Rarely are more than two or three used in one sequence. The chart below outlines the preferred order of adjectives in English arranged by common types and includes three examples of expressions that follow that order. Notice that the order moves from the subjective description of *opinion* to objective descriptions such as *material* and *purpose*.

**Order of Adjectives by Common Types**

| #1 Article | #2 Opinion | #3 Size | #4 Age | #5 Shape | #6 Color | #7 Origin | #8 Material | #9 Purpose | #10 Noun being described |
|---|---|---|---|---|---|---|---|---|---|
| A | clumsy | large | old | square | | | wooden | | desk |
| An | | | | | | Oriental | wool | area | rug |
| The | demanding | | new | | tanned | | | athletic | trainer |

## Practice 5

ORDER OF ADJECTIVES

**A.** Choose the option that best completes the idea by listing adjectives in appropriate order.

**1.** A ______________________ bird hopped on the birdfeeder.

**a.** small, brown, skittery **b.** brown, small, skittery **c.** skittery, small, brown

**2.** A ______________________ cat bounded into the backyard.

**a.** Siamese, young, silver **b.** young, silver Siamese **c.** young, Siamese, silver

**3.** The ______________________ creature sounded the alarm.

**a.** tiny, feathered **b.** feathered, tiny

**4.** As the bird chattered and hopped in alarm, it tipped the birdfeeder and spilled the ______________________ birdseed.

**a.** ample, fresh, organic **b.** fresh, ample, organic **c.** organic, ample, fresh

**5.** The scene remains a ______________________ memory.

**a.** fond, vivid childhood **b.** vivid, fond childhood **c.** childhood vivid, fond

**B.** Describe each noun with a set of two or more adjectives. List adjectives in proper order.

**1.** ______________________ iPod

**2.** ______________________ Website

**3.** ______________________ mother

**4.** ______________________ Johnny Depp

**5.** ______________________ *American Idol*

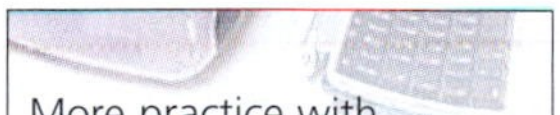

More practice with adjectives and adverbs: <www.mywritinglab.com>

# Adverbs

The most common use of adverbs is to describe verbs. In addition, adverbs modify other types of words such as adjectives and other adverbs. In purpose, adverbs answer the reporter's questions *When? Where?* and *How?*

Many adverbs are derived from adjectives, many adverbs end in *-ly*, and many adverbs are gradeable based on degree or quantity. In fact, adverbs provide very specific types of information. The following chart lists some of the most frequently used adverbs based on the type of information they provide.

| Common Adverbs | | | | |
|---|---|---|---|---|
| **Time, Frequency, or Sequence**<br>**When?** | **Place**<br>**Where?** | **Manner**<br>**How?** | **Certainty or Negation**<br>**How?** | **Degree or Quantity**<br>**How much?** |
| after | everywhere | automatically | certainly | absolutely |
| already | here | badly | clearly | almost |
| always | inside | beautifully | perhaps | a lot |
| at first | outside | cheerfully | probably | completely |
| consequently | somewhere | fast | maybe | enough |
| during | there | happily | obviously | entirely |
| early | | hard | surely | extremely |
| every | | quickly | | fully |
| finally | | seriously | not | hardly |
| often | | slowly | never | least |
| once | | well | | less |
| never | | | | little |
| next | | | | more |
| now | | | | most |
| rarely | | | | much |
| recently | | | | not |
| regularly | | | | partly |
| seldom | | | | rather |
| sometimes | | | | really |
| soon | | | | too |
| then | | | | too little |
| thus | | | | too much |
| tomorrow | | | | totally |
| usually | | | | very |
| when | | | | |
| while | | | | |
| yesterday | | | | |

ADVERBS

Practice 6

The following sentences tell a short story. Complete each sentence with the most appropriate adverb.

**1.** The Aimes family looked ________________ for their missing dog, Henry.
**a.** everywhere **b.** there **c.** somewhere

**2.** The family was alarmed because Henry ________________ leaves the yard.
**a.** recently **b.** never **c.** soon

**3.** The family found the gate open and thought that Henry ________________ just wandered off.
**a.** never **b.** slowly **c.** probably

**4.** Another family found Henry ________________ on a county road several miles away.
**a.** inside **b.** somewhere **c.** tomorrow

**5.** Henry's dog tags brought him ________________ home.
**a.** safely **b.** here **c.** partly

More practice with adjectives and adverbs: <www.mywritinglab.com>

# How to Use the Comparative and Superlative

A common error in using adjectives and adverbs occurs when a writer uses the wrong form to make degrees of comparisons between two things or among three things. Adjectives and adverbs take the form of three degrees: **absolute, comparative,** and **superlative.** The degrees of adverbs are formed by adding the suffixes *-er* or *-est* or by using *more* or *most*. For example, *more* or *most* establishes a degree of comparison with adverbs that end in *-ly*.

## Absolute

The absolute degree makes no comparison, or makes a one-to-one comparison (in which the adjective or adverb describes both things equally).

ABSOLUTE ADJECTIVE "SWEET" DESCRIBES COMPOUND SUBJECT "RAISINS AND PRUNES"

Raisins and prunes are sweet.

NOUNS "RAISINS" AND "PRUNES" ARE BEING COMPARED, BUT THE ABSOLUTE ADJECTIVE "SWEET" DESCRIBES BOTH EQUALLY

Raisins are as sweet as prunes.

## Comparative

The comparative degree compares and makes distinctions between two people or things, usually by using the adverb *more* or *less* or adding the suffix *-er*.

COMPARATIVE ADJECTIVE "SWEETER" COMPARES "RAISINS" WITH "PRUNES"

Raisins are sweeter than prunes.

COMPARATIVE ADVERB "MORE GENEROUSLY" DIRECTLY DESCRIBES VERB "ACTED" AND COMPARES THE ACTION OF NOUN "RIANA" (HOW RIANA ACTED) WITH THE ACTION OF NOUN "SISTER" (HOW HER SISTER ACTED)

Riana acted more generously than her sister [acted].

UNSTATED, IMPLIED VERB

## Superlative

The superlative degree makes distinctions among three or more people or things, usually by using the adverb *most* or *least* or adding the suffix *-est*.

SUPERLATIVE ADJECTIVE "SWEETEST" COMPARES NOUN "PRUNE" TO ALL THE OTHER PRUNES THE "I" HAS EATEN

This is the sweetest prune I have ever eaten.

SUPERLATIVE ADVERB "MORE GENEROUSLY" DESCRIBES VERB "ACTED" AND COMPARES THE ACTION OF NOUN "RIANA" (HOW RIANA ACTED) WITH THE ACTION OF NOUN "ALL THE STUDENTS ON THE DEBATE TEAM" (HOW ALL THE OTHER DEBATE TEAM STUDENTS ACTED)

Riana acted the most generously of all the students on the debate team.

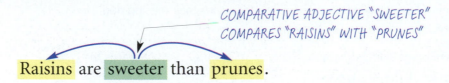

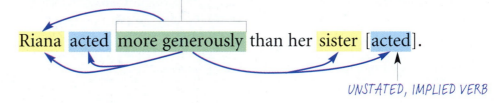

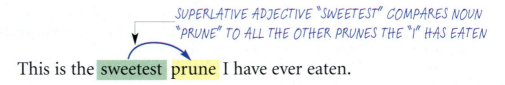

| Degrees of Adjectives and Adverbs | | | |
|---|---|---|---|
| **Degree of Comparison** | **Absolute:** One<br>as ________ as | **Comparative:** Two<br>*-er*<br>______ than | **Superlative:** Three or More<br>*-est*<br>the __________ |
| **Adjectives** | good | better | best |
| | bad | worse | worst |
| | large | larger | largest |
| | little | less | least |
| | much | more | most |
| | far | further/farther | furthest /farthest |
| **Adverbs** | busy | busier | busiest |
| | early | earlier | earliest |
| | carefully | more carefully | most carefully |
| | slowly | more slowly | most slowly |
| | well | better | best |

Practice 7

## USING COMPARATIVE AND SUPERLATIVES

Complete each of the following sentences with the appropriate comparative or superlative.

**1.** If the choice is between a diet and exercise to lose weight, exercise is the .......................... choice.

**a.** good **b.** better **c.** best

**2.** Lifting weights is a .......................... way to burn calories.

**a.** good **b.** better **c.** best

**3.** Working out instead of just dieting is a .......................... healthier way to control weight.

**a.** good **b.** more **c.** much

**4.** Dieters lose .......................... muscle mass than exercisers.

**a.** much **b.** more **c.** most

**5.** Write a sentence using a comparative or superlative. Suggested topic: A Day in Life.

..............................................................................................................................

..............................................................................................................................

More practice with adjectives and adverbs: <www.mywritinglab.com>

**Spelling Guidelines**
**Comparative and Superlative Adjectives and Adverbs**

| Number of Syllables | Word Ending | Comparative | Superlative |
|---|---|---|---|
| One-syllable adjectives or adverbs | any kind | add *-er* | add *-est* |
| Examples | fast<br>hard<br>young | faster<br>harder<br>younger | fastest<br>hardest<br>youngest |
| One-syllable adjectives | consonant-vowel-consonant | double last consonant add *-er* | double last consonant add *-est* |
| Examples | big<br>sad<br>wet | bigger<br>sadder<br>wetter | biggest<br>saddest<br>wettest |
| Two-syllable adjectives | ending in *-y* | change *-y* to *-i*; add *-er* | change *-y* to *-i*; add *–est* |
| Examples | busy<br>pretty<br>silly | busier<br>prettier<br>sillier | busiest<br>prettiest<br>silliest |
| Two- or more syllable adjectives or adverbs | not ending in *-y* | no change in spelling; use *more* | no change in spelling; use *most* |
| Examples | exciting<br>dangerous<br>difficult | more exciting<br>more dangerous<br>more difficult | most exciting<br>most dangerous<br>most difficult |

## Practice 8

### SPELLING COMPARATIVES AND SUPERLATIVES

Fill in the following chart with the correct spellings of each form of the comparatives and superlatives. Use *more* and *most* as needed.

| Absolute | Comparative | Superlative |
|---|---|---|
| 1. afraid | | |
| 2. chilly | | |
| 3. creepy | | |
| 4. fat | | |
| 5. handsome | | |

## Mastering *Good* and *Well*

More practice with adjectives and adverbs: <www.mywritinglab.com>

Two of the most often-confused words in the English language are *good* and *well*. One reason these two words are so often confused is that *well* can be used as either an adverb or an adjective to discuss health issues.

- ***Good*** is an **adjective** that describes a noun or pronoun.

NOUN "VOICE" IS DESCRIBED BY ADJECTIVE "GOOD"

Sally's singing voice sounds good.

NOUN "PERFUME" IS DESCRIBED BY ADJECTIVE "GOOD"

The perfume smells good.

ADJECTIVE "GOOD" DESCRIBES NOUN "JOB"

You did a good job.

- ***Well*** is an **adverb** that usually describes a **verb**.

VERB "DID" IS DESCRIBED BY ADVERB "WELL"

I did well on my test.

VERB "FINISHED" IS DESCRIBED BY ADVERB "WELL"

You finished your job well.

VERB "HEAR" IS DESCRIBED BY ADVERB "WELL"

You hear well with your hearing aid.

- Exception ***Well*** is an **adjective** when used to describe a person's health issues.

PRONOUN "I" IS DESCRIBED BY ADJECTIVE "WELL"

I feel well.

Practice 9

*GOOD* AND *WELL*

Fill in each blank with *good* or *well*.

**1.** The chocolate chip cookies smell ______________.

**2.** Jeremiah is not feeling ______________.

**3.** Donald Trump lives ______________.

**4.** My car has been a ______________ car.

**5.** Write a sentence that appropriately uses *good* or *well*. Suggested topic: The Condition of a Person or Thing.

______________________________________________

More practice with adjectives and adverbs: <www.mywritinglab.com>

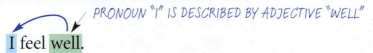

## Practice 10

### ADJECTIVES AND ADVERBS REVIEW

Complete the following sentences by filling in the blanks with the appropriate form or order of the adjective or adverb in parentheses.

**1.** The ______________ audience laughed at the antics of the performers. (amused/ amusing)

**2.** The ______________ performance entertained everyone. (amused/ amusing)

**3.** The ________________________ singer leapt about the stage with great energy. (athletic, youthful/ youthful, athletic)

**4.** The show ______________ sells out to a packed house. (quick/ quickly)

**5.** Some fans attend ______________ by traveling to each city where the group performs. (faithful/ faithfully)

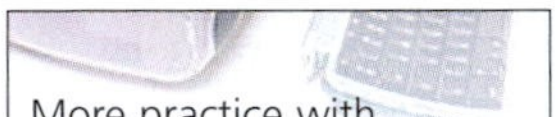

More practice with adjectives and adverbs: <www.mywritinglab.com>

# Writing Assignments

## Writing for Everyday Life

Assume you own a parrot whose behavior has been highly amusing. You want to share his antics with a friend so you have composed the following email. Edit the email to ensure proper use of adjectives and adverbs. Use your own paper.

Dear Jim,

You won't believe what Charlie, my African Grey large parrot, did to our family during this past month. For weeks, our doorbell rang every night in the middle of the night. I first angry blamed the neighbors. They repeatedly reassured me that they knew nothing about the situation. After several nights, we became frightened, so we called the police. The police seemed most skeptical than our neighbors about our story, yet they diligent watched our house every night. Derrick, finally my son, noticed Charlie. The whole time, Charlie had been mimicking the sound of our doorbell. That bird had never seemed happiest.

LOL, Jen

## Writing for College Life

Assume you are taking a study skills course, and you have been asked by your professor to reflect upon your progress as a learner as part of your midterm assessment. You are to describe what and how you have learned. Edit to ensure appropriate use of adjectives and adverbs. Use your own paper.

Self-Assessment Reflection:

Even though I have learned muchly this semester, I feel as if I have more to learn. One of the best important things I learned is that I am an auditory learner. I do my better when something is explained to me. So I now read out loud important information that I want to remember, or I pair up with a study buddy and talk about what we are studying. I need to hear information, so attendance is much important for me than it is for someone who isn't an auditory learner. Time management is another vital important skill that I am trying to apply. I then always have a study schedule. I want to do good in college. I have become a well student.

## Writing for Working Life

Assume you have written the following letter resigning from a job you really enjoy. Edit to ensure appropriate use of adjectives and adverbs. Use your own paper.

Dear Ms. Brown:

It is with great regret that I must submit my resignation due to my family's relocation to Texas. I have thorough enjoyed working as a team leader for the area's region. This area is the larger in the state, and our team has had the higher ratings for customer service and productivity. I remember as an exciting new employee how much I looked forward to all the wonderfully opportunities available under your leadership. I have not been disappointed in the least. My success is due to your encouraged mentorship. I thank you for your support, and I wish you and the company all the best.

Sincerely,

Sam Yoo

PORTFOLIO

# Academic Learning Log

## WHAT HAVE I LEARNED ABOUT ADJECTIVES AND ADVERBS?

To test and track your understanding, answer the following questions.

1. An adjective modifies a ______ or ______.
2. An adverb modifies a ______, an ______, or another ______.
3. Participle adjectives are formed by adding ______ or ______ to verbs.
4. Adjectives often appear in the following order: ______, opinion, size, age, shape, ______, origin, material, purpose.
5. Adverbs answer the questions ______, where, and ______.
6. Adjectives and adverbs take the form of three degrees: ______, ______, and ______.
7. The ______ degree makes distinctions between two things, usually by using the adverb *more* or *less* or by adding the suffix *-er*.
8. The ______ degree makes distinctions among three or more things, usually by using the adverb *most* or *least* or by adding the suffix *-est*.
9. *Good* is an ______.
10. Most often, *well* is an ______.

11. **How will I use what I have learned about adjectives and adverbs?**
    In your notebook, discuss how you will apply to your own writing what you have learned about adjectives and adverbs.
12. **What do I still need to study about adjectives and adverbs?**
    In your notebook, describe your ongoing study needs by describing what, when, and how you will continue studying adjectives and adverbs.

PART 7

# Punctuation and Mechanics

# 29 The Comma

**Chapter Preview**

- What's the Point of Commas?
- Understanding the Point of Commas: One Student Writer's Response
- Applying the Point: Commas

Homework
Nov 12
559–576

## A comma is a valuable, useful punctuation device because it separates the structural elements of a sentence into manageable segments.

Misuse of the comma ranks as one of the most common errors in punctuation. Thinking about a real-life situation helps us to understand the purpose of commas in our communication. Complete the following activity and answer the question "What's the point of commas?"

# What's the Point of Commas?

PHOTOGRAPHIC ORGANIZER: COMMAS

WRITING FROM LIFE

Practice 1

Assume you are working with a civic group to educate the public about pollution and the need for clean fuels. You have written the following paragraph to post on the group's Web blog. This draft does not include any commas. As you read the paragraph, think about where and why commas are needed.

**One Type of Clean Fuel: Alcohol**

(1) Pollution occurs when the air water or land become dirty through the actions of people. (2) Some types of pollution litter along the beach are easy to see. (3) Other types of pollution such as chemicals in the water or air are not as easy to see but can be even more harmful. (4) To reduce chemical pollution, we need to use clean fuels. (5) One type of clean fuel is alcohol and two types of alcohol fuel are ethanol and methanol. (6) Historically ethanol has been made from corn or sugarcane. (7) New processes can make ethanol from paper yard trimmings or sawdust. (8) Methanol is usually made from natural gas but it could also be made from wood or sugarcane. (9) Alcohol fuels produce less carbon monoxide.

**What's the point of commas?**

Adapted from "Hawaii's Fun-Fueled Activity Book: Clean Fuels," *Honolulu Clean Cities* Website, <www.hawaii.gov/dbedt/ert/cc/index.html>

# Understanding the Point of Commas: One Student Writer's Response

The following paragraph offers one writer's reaction to the paragraph "One Type of Clean Fuel: Alcohol."

> The paragraph "One Type of Clean Fuel: Alcohol" was confusing. I had to reread several sentences to make sense of what the writer was saying. One sentence that confused me was "Some types of pollution litter along the beach are easy to see." Another confusing sentence was "New processes can make ethanol from paper yard trimmings or sawdust." When I first read this sentence, my mind read "paper yard" as the name of something. It took a second to pick up on the word "trimmings." It would help to put a comma between "paper" and "yard trimmings." Now that I think about it, I guess, commas keep a reader from getting confused.

# Applying the Point: Commas

The primary purpose of the **comma** is to make a sentence easy to read by indicating a brief pause between parts of the sentence that need to be separated.

## Commas with Items in a Series

Use commas to separate a **series of items** in a list. A series of items in a list can be **three** or more words, phrases, or clauses. In addition, a series of items can be made up of subjects, verbs, adjectives, participles, and so on. Items in a series are parallel and equal in importance.

**Series of words**

COMMAS SET OFF SERIES OF WORDS

COMMAS SET OFF SECOND SERIES OF WORDS

Marissa, Evan, and Kanisha skate, swim, and ski.

COMMAS SET OFF SERIES OF WORDS

Marissa enjoys skating, swimming, and skiing.

**Series of phrases**

COMMAS SET OFF SERIES OF PHRASES

Marissa enjoys skating on ice, swimming in the ocean, and skiing down a snowy slope.

For more information about parallel structure, see Chapter 20, "Parallelism."

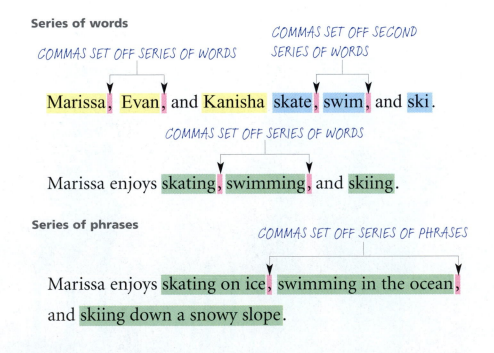

**Series of clauses**

Marissa is an athlete who trains consistently, who eats sensibly, and who competes well.

COMMAS SET OFF SERIES OF CLAUSES

**Note:** Journalists for newspapers and magazines often omit the comma before the coordinating conjunction that joins the last item in the series; however, in academic writing, this comma, which is called the **serial comma**, is usually included.

## Comma Misuses to Avoid with Items in a Series

- **Do not place a comma before the first item in a series.**

**Incorrect**

INCORRECT COMMA USE SEPARATES THE THREE OBJECTS IN THE SERIES BELOW FROM "DAMAGED," THE VERB THAT REFERS TO THEM

The storm damaged, the roof, the windows, and the carpet.

**Correct**

VERB

OBJECTS OF VERB "DAMAGED"

The storm damaged the roof, the windows, and the carpet.

COMMAS SEPARATE THREE OBJECTS OF VERB "DAMAGED"

- **Do not place a comma after the last item in a series.**

**Incorrect**

SUBJECT

INCORRECT COMMA USE SEPARATES THE ADJECTIVES IN THE SERIES BELOW FROM THE SUBORDINATE CLAUSE "BECAUSE OF FLOODING"

The carpet was soggy, moldy, and smelly, because of flooding.

**Correct**

SUBJECT

ADJECTIVES DESCRIBING SUBJECT "CARPET"

The carpet was soggy, moldy, and smelly because of flooding.

COMMAS SEPARATE THREE ADJECTIVES DESCRIBING SUBJECT "CARPET"

SUBORDINATE CLAUSE MODIFIES THE THREE ADJECTIVES DESCRIBING WHY THE CARPET BECAME SOGGY, MOLDY, AND SMELLY

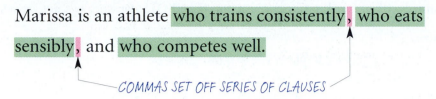

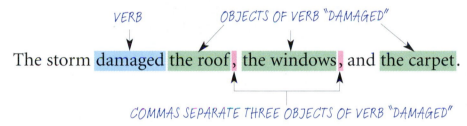

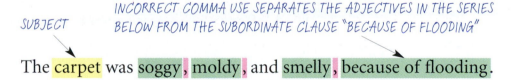

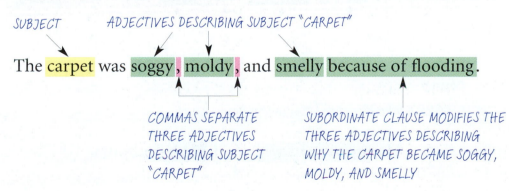

- **Do not place a comma between two words or phrases of equal importance joined with a coordinating conjunction** (FANBOYS: *for, and, nor, but, or, yet, so*).

**Incorrect**

INCORRECT COMMA USE DIVIDES COMPOUND SUBJECT AND SEPARATES PART OF IT FROM VERB "DESTROYED"

The twisting wind, and the unrelenting rain destroyed the house.

COMPOUND SUBJECT — VERB

**Correct**

COMPOUND SUBJECT [NO COMMA NEEDED] — VERB

The twisting wind and the unrelenting rain destroyed the house.

**Incorrect**

INCORRECT COMMA USE DIVIDES COMPOUND VERB AND SEPARATES PART OF IT FROM SUBJECT "WIND"

The wind lifted the car, and threw it across the street.

SUBJECT — COMPOUND VERB

**Correct**

COMPOUND VERB [NO COMMA NEEDED] — PREPOSITIONAL PHRASE

The wind lifted the car and threw it across the street.

SUBJECT — COMPOUND OBJECT (OF COMPOUND VERB)

**Incorrect**

INCORRECT COMMA USE DIVIDES COMPOUND ADJECTIVE AND SEPARATES PART OF IT FROM THE SUBJECT IT DESCRIBES, "WIND"

The strong, and wet wind blew for hours.

COMPOUND ADJECTIVE — SUBJECT — VERB

**Correct**

COMPOUND ADJECTIVE [NO COMMA NEEDED]

The strong and wet wind blew for hours.

SUBJECT — VERB

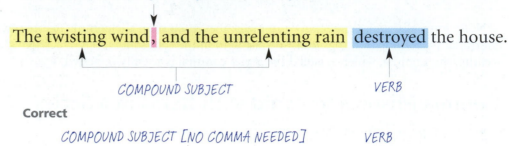

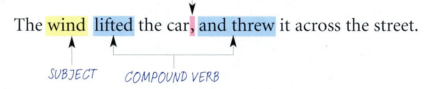

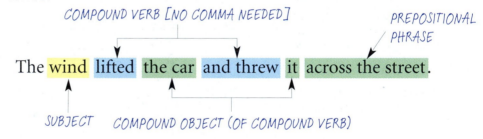

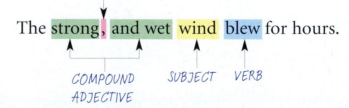

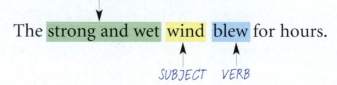

COMMAS FOR ITEMS IN A SERIES

Practice 2

Edit the following sentences by inserting commas to separate a series of items in a list. Cross out any incorrectly placed commas.

1. A graphic novel is, a type of comic is often long and complex and is written for mature audiences.
2. Graphic novels, and comic books are excellent reading materials because they assist poor readers connect with visual learners and engage adult readers.
3. Graphic novels spark interest make reading fun and develop the reading habit, for many.
4. Graphic novels address important themes such as acceptance rebellion prejudice injustice and personal growth.
5. Write a sentence that lists a series of items. Suggested topic: Your Favorite Possession.

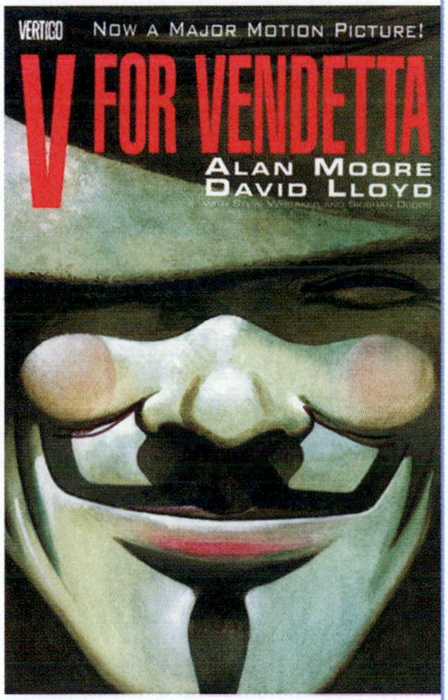


More practice with commas: <www.mywritinglab.com>

## Commas with Introductory Elements

Use commas to set off the introductory element of a sentence. **Introductory elements** are ideas that appear at the beginning of a sentence. Introductory elements come before a main clause. Introductory elements can be a word, phrase, or clause.

**Introductory Word**

COMMA SETS OFF INTRODUCTORY WORD

Overall, good health is achieved through wise choices.

**Introductory Phrase**

COMMA SETS OFF INTRODUCTORY PHRASE

To achieve good health, one should exercise on a regular basis.

**Introductory Dependent Clause**

COMMA SETS OFF INTRODUCTORY DEPENDENT PHRASE

As Maria increased her physical activity, her sense of well-being improved.

## COMMA MISUSES TO AVOID WITH INTRODUCTORY ELEMENTS

- An introductory element—a word, phrase, or clause—that precedes an independent (or main) clause must be followed by a comma.

**Incorrect**

*INTRODUCTORY PHRASE*

*ABSENCE OF COMMA MAKES IT DIFFICULT TO DISTINGUISH INTRODUCTORY PHRASE FROM MAIN CLAUSE*

After 21 years playing baseball Barry Bonds hit his 756th home run.

*MAIN CLAUSE*

**Correct**

*COMMA SETS OFF INTRODUCTORY PHRASE*

After 21 years playing baseball, Barry Bonds hit his 756th home run.

*MAIN CLAUSE*

DC, IC

### Practice 3

**COMMAS WITH INTRODUCTORY ELEMENTS**

Edit the following sentences by inserting commas to set off introductory elements.

1. When you are applying for a job over the Internet, take steps to avoid common mistakes that harm your chances of getting hired.

2. Before you click the send button, double check the recipient's address and your attached documents.

3. For example, one job applicant sent an email addressed to the wrong firm.

4. According to experts, providing clear and precise file names for attached documents creates a  professional impression.

5. Write a sentence that uses an introductory element. Suggested topic: Your Ideal Job.

--------------------------------------------------

--------------------------------------------------

More practice with commas: <www.mywritinglab.com>

## Commas to Join Independent Clauses

Use a comma with a coordinating conjunction to join two or more equally important and logically related independent clauses. An **independent clause** is a complete thought or sentence. To join sentences with a coordinating conjunction, place the comma before the conjunction. The acronym **FANBOYS** identifies the seven coordinating conjunctions: *for, and, nor, but, or, yet,* and *so.*  The following chart lists these conjunctions and the logical relationships they establish between ideas.

| Coordinating Conjunctions and the Relationships They Establish: **FANBOYS** | | | | | | |
|---|---|---|---|---|---|---|
| For | And | Nor | But | Or | Yet | So |
| reason, result | addition | negation | contrast | choice, condition, possibility | contrast | addition, result |

## Correct Use of a Comma to Join Independent Clauses

INDEPENDENT CLAUSE SUBJECT VERB COMMA ENDS FIRST CLAUSE

U2's lead singer Bono is a social activist, for he performs benefits to end AIDS.

SUBJECT VERB INDEPENDENT CLAUSE COORDINATING CONJUNCTION "FOR" COMBINES INDEPENDENT CLAUSES

### COMMA MISUSES TO AVOID WITH INDEPENDENT CLAUSES

- **Do not place a comma *after* the coordinating conjunction that joins independent clauses.**

**Incorrect**

INDEPENDENT CLAUSE SUBJECT VERB BECAUSE OF A MISPLACED COMMA, COORDINATING CONJUNCTION "SO" DOES NOT COMBINE INDEPENDENT CLAUSES

Alicia Keys wants to help children so, she donates to the organization Keep a Child Alive.

VERB SUBJECT INDEPENDENT CLAUSE MISPLACED COMMA DOES NOT END FIRST CLAUSE

**Correct**

SUBJECT VERB INDEPENDENT CLAUSE COMMA ENDS FIRST CLAUSE

Alicia Keys wants to help children, so she donates to the organization Keep a Child Alive.

VERB SUBJECT INDEPENDENT CLAUSE COORDINATING CONJUNCTION "SO" COMBINES INDEPENDENT CLAUSES

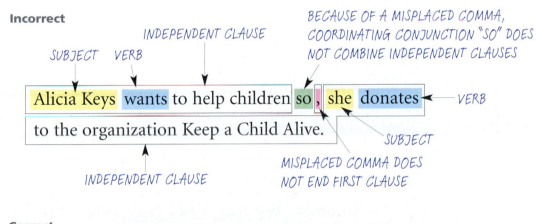

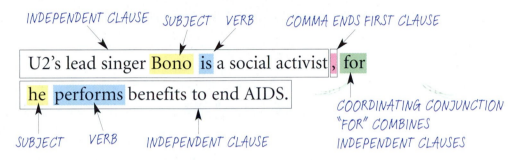

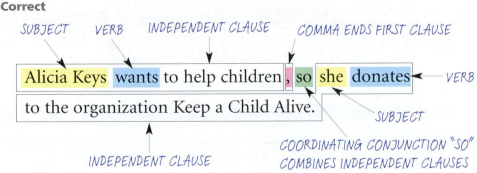

Practice 4

**COMMAS TO JOIN INDEPENDENT CLAUSES**

Edit the following sentences by inserting commas to join independent clauses with coordinating conjunctions. Cross out any incorrectly placed commas.

1. Darfur is a region in Western Sudan and, the vast majority of its population is black and Muslim.
2. Darfur is roughly the size of France yet it is home to around 8 million people.
3. The conflict in Darfur is often described as Arab against African blacks but conflicts in the region are really between herders and farmers over the use of Sudan's land.
4. African rebel groups in Darfur believe the government favors Arabs over non-Arabs so they accuse the government of Sudan of neglecting the Darfur region.
5. Write a sentence that contains two independent clauses properly joined with a coordinating conjunction and a comma. Suggested topic: Your Home Town.

More practice with commas: <www.mywritinglab.com>

## Commas with Parenthetical Ideas

Use commas to set off a parenthetical idea. A **parenthetical idea** is an idea that interrupts a sentence with information that is **nonessential** to the meaning of the sentence. Such an idea could be enclosed in parentheses. However, more often, a comma comes before and after such an idea. These interruptions can be words, phrases, or clauses.

**Parenthetical word**

COMMAS SET OFF PARENTHETICAL WORD

The demanding customer was, however, a generous tipper.

**Parenthetical phrase**

COMMAS SET OFF PARENTHETICAL PHRASE

The polite customer, surprisingly heartless, left no tip.

**Parenthetical clause**

COMMAS SET OFF PARENTHETICAL CLAUSE

Jennifer, who had been working a 12-hour shift, smiled at the sight of the generous tip.

**Note:** Two specific types of parenthetical ideas are the **nonessential appositive** (word or phrase) and the **nonessential clause**. The uses and misuses of commas with these specific types of words, phrases, and clauses are discussed in greater detail in the next two sections.

Practice 5

**COMMAS WITH PARENTHETICAL IDEAS**

Edit the following sentences by inserting commas to set off parenthetical ideas.

1. Prince Harry and Prince William who learned generosity from their mother have also founded charities to help many disadvantaged people.
2. Prince Harry as reported by the press has made some controversial decisions.
3. Prince William like his brother Prince Harry is an avid sportsman.
4. They inherited a competitive spirit often seen on the polo field from their father, Prince Charles.
5. Write a sentence that contains a parenthetical idea. Suggested topic: An Admirable Public Figure.

---

---

More practice with commas: <www.mywritinglab.com>

## Commas with Nonessential and Essential Clauses

A parenthetical idea, the **nonessential clause** offers additional and unnecessary information that does not change the meaning of the sentence. Often nonessential information appears in a relative clause introduced by the relative pronouns *who* or *which*. A nonessential relative clause gives information about a nearby noun.

Use commas to set off a nonessential clause. Commas come before and after a nonessential clause that interrupts a sentence. A single comma sets off a nonessential clause at the end of a sentence.

COMMAS SET OFF NONESSENTIAL CLAUSE DESCRIBING SUBJECT "GAYLE KING"

SUBJECT

Gayle King, who is Oprah Winfrey's best friend, is the editor at large of *O, The Oprah Magazine* in New York City.

NONESSENTIAL CLAUSE DESCRIBES SUBJECT "GAYLE KING," BUT COULD BE OMITTED WITHOUT CHANGING THE SENTENCE'S MEANING

COMMA SETS OFF NONESSENTIAL CLAUSE DESCRIBING NOUN "LARRY KING LIVE"

Celebrity interviews are the main attraction of Larry King Live, which is a one-hour show seen all over the world.

NOUN

NONESSENTIAL CLAUSE DESCRIBES NOUN "LARRY KING LIVE," BUT COULD BE OMITTED WITHOUT CHANGING THE SENTENCE'S MEANING

An **essential clause** also offers information about a nearby noun, but by contrast with a nonessential clause, it restricts or limits the meaning of a nearby noun and is necessary to the meaning of the sentence. Essential clauses should not be set off with commas. The following examples illustrate the differences between an essential and a nonessential clause.

**Essential Clause**

SUBJECT (COMMON NOUN) "ACTOR" IS DESCRIBED AND LIMITED IN MEANING BY ESSENTIAL CLAUSE

ESSENTIAL CLAUSE LIMITS THE MEANING OF SUBJECT "ACTOR" BY IDENTIFYING THE SPECIFIC ACTOR BEING REFERRED TO

The actor who fled the scene of the car accident was arrested.

NO COMMAS NEEDED BEFORE AND AFTER ESSENTIAL CLAUSE

**Nonessential Clause**

SUBJECT (PROPER NOUN) "LINDSAY LOHAN" IS UNALTERED IN MEANING BY NONESSENTIAL CLAUSE

ESSENTIAL CLAUSE GIVES EXTRA INFORMATION ABOUT SUBJECT "LINDSAY LOHAN," BUT THE SUBJECT'S MEANING WOULD NOT BE AFFECTED IF THE CLAUSE WERE OMITTED

Lindsay Lohan, who fled the scene of the car accident, was arrested.

COMMAS SET OFF NONESSENTIAL CLAUSE

## COMMA MISUSES TO AVOID WITH ESSENTIAL AND NONESSENTIAL CLAUSES

- **Do not set off an essential clause with commas.**

**Incorrect**

SUBJECT

ESSENTIAL CLAUSE LIMITS THE MEANING OF SUBJECT "PHOTOGRAPHERS" BY IDENTIFYING THE SPECIFIC PHOTOGRAPHERS BEING REFERRED TO

Photographers, who pursue stars in high-speed chases, are irresponsible.

INCORRECT COMMA USE DIVIDES ESSENTIAL CLAUSE FROM THE SUBJECT IT DESCRIBES "PHOTOGRAPHERS"

**Correct**

SUBJECT

Photographers who pursue stars in high-speed chases are irresponsible.

NO COMMAS NEEDED BEFORE OR AFTER ESSENTIAL CLAUSE

- **Do not omit the comma before or after the nonessential clause that interrupts an idea. Place a comma before and after a nonessential clause.**

**Incorrect**

CORRECT COMMA USAGE SETS OFF BEGINNING OF NONESSENTIAL CLAUSE

MISSING COMMA AFTER NONESSENTIAL CLAUSE

Scarlett Johansson, who tried to escape photographers had a minor car accident.

SUBJECT

NONESSENTIAL CLAUSE DESCRIBES SUBJECT "SCARLETT JOHANSSON," BUT COULD BE OMITTED WITHOUT CHANGING THE SENTENCE'S MEANING

**Incorrect**

MISSING COMMA BEFORE NONESSENTIAL CLAUSE

CORRECT COMMA USAGE SETS OFF END OF NONESSENTIAL CLAUSE

Scarlett Johansson who tried to escape photographers, had a minor car accident.

SUBJECT

**Correct**

COMMAS SET OFF NONESSENTIAL CLAUSE DESCRIBING SUBJECT "SCARLETT JOHANSSON"

Scarlett Johansson, who tried to escape photographers, had a minor car accident.

SUBJECT

## Practice 6

COMMAS WITH NONESSENTIAL CLAUSES

Edit the following sentences by inserting commas to set off nonessential clauses.

1. Chris Brown who is an R & B singer became the first male vocalist to have a single go straight to the top of the Billboard singles chart.
2. *Chris Brown* which is his debut album has sold three million copies worldwide.
3. Brown openly declares his love and respect for Joyce Hawkins who is his mother and his hero. Rule 9
4. Not many singers who have a flexible and emotional voice like Brown can also be an amazing dancer.
5. Write a sentence that contains a nonessential clause. Suggested topic: Your Hero.

More practice with commas: <www.mywritinglab.com>

## Commas with Appositives

Use commas to set off an appositive. An **appositive** is a word or phrase that renames a nearby noun. As a parenthetical idea, a **nonessential appositive** offers information that could be left out without changing the meaning of the sentence. A comma comes before and after a nonessential appositive when it interrupts an idea. A single comma sets off a nonessential appositive at the end of a sentence.

SUBJECT

NONESSENTIAL APPOSITIVE RENAMES THE SUBJECT "MOLE," BUT COULD BE OMITTED WITHOUT CHANGING THE SENTENCE'S MEANING

The star-nosed mole, a fast-eating mammal, can consume food in 120 milliseconds.

COMMAS SET OFF NONESSENTIAL APPOSITIVE DESCRIBING SUBJECT "MOLE"

COMMA SETS OFF NONESSENTIAL APPOSITIVE DESCRIBING NOUN "KOTETSU"

The *Guinness World Records* says the highest jump by a pig is 27.5 inches by Kotetsu, a pot-bellied pig.

NOUN

NONESSENTIAL APPOSITIVE RENAMES THE NOUN "KOTETSU," BUT COULD BE OMITTED WITHOUT CHANGING THE SENTENCE'S MEANING

An **essential appositive** restricts or limits the meaning of a nearby noun and is necessary to the meaning of the sentence. Essential appositives should not be set off with commas. The following examples show the differences between an essential and nonessential appositive.

**Essential Appositive**

SUBJECT

ESSENTIAL APPOSITIVE LIMITS THE MEANING OF SUBJECT "ACTOR" BY IDENTIFYING THE SPECIFIC ACTOR BEING REFERRED TO

The actor Daniel Radcliffe plays Harry Potter.

NO COMMAS NEEDED BEFORE AND AFTER ESSENTIAL APPOSITIVE

**Nonessential Appositive**

SUBJECT

NONESSENTIAL APPOSITIVE RENAMES THE SUBJECT "DANIEL RADCLIFFE," BUT COULD BE OMITTED WITHOUT CHANGING THE SENTENCE'S MEANING

Daniel Radcliffe, the actor, plays Harry Potter.

COMMAS SET OFF NONESSENTIAL APPOSITIVE

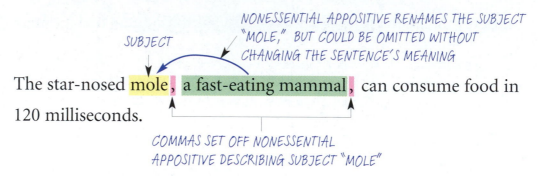

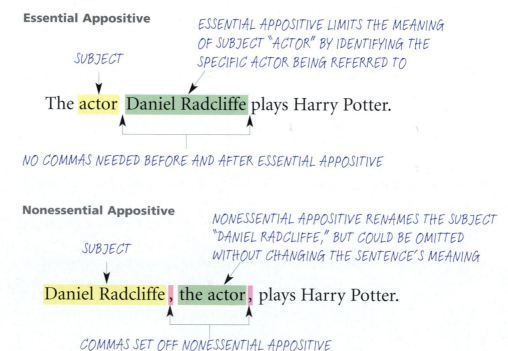

## COMMA MISUSES TO AVOID WITH APPOSITIVES

- **Do not set off an essential appositive with commas.**

**Incorrect**

ESSENTIAL APPOSITIVE LIMITS THE MEANING OF SUBJECT "PRESIDENT" BY IDENTIFYING THE SPECIFIC PRESIDENT BEING REFERRED TO

SUBJECT

The controversial former president, Bill Clinton, remains popular.

INCORRECT COMMA USE DIVIDES ESSENTIAL APPOSITIVE FROM THE SUBJECT IT DESCRIBES "PRESIDENT"

**Correct**

SUBJECT

The controversial former president Bill Clinton remains popular.

NO COMMAS NEEDED BEFORE OR AFTER ESSENTIAL APPOSITIVE

- **Do not omit the comma before or after the nonessential appositive that interrupts an idea. Place a comma before and after a nonessential appositive.**

**Incorrect**

CORRECT COMMA USAGE SETS OFF BEGINNING OF NONESSENTIAL APPOSITIVE

MISSING COMMA AFTER NONESSENTIAL APPOSITIVE

Andy Warhol, a pop artist designed art for mass production.

SUBJECT

NONESSENTIAL APPOSITIVE RENAMES SUBJECT "ANDY WARHOL," BUT COULD BE OMITTED WITHOUT CHANGING THE SENTENCE'S MEANING

**Incorrect**

SUBJECT

CORRECT COMMA USAGE SETS OFF END OF NONESSENTIAL APPOSITIVE

Andy Warhol a pop artist, designed art for mass production.

MISSING COMMA BEFORE NONESSENTIAL APPOSITIVE

**Correct**

SUBJECT

Andy Warhol, a pop artist, designed art for mass production.

COMMAS SET OFF NONESSENTIAL APPOSITIVE DESCRIBING SUBJECT "ANDY WARHOL"

Practice 7

**COMMAS WITH APPOSITIVES**

Edit the following sentences by inserting commas to set off appositives.

1. Bao Xishun, the world's tallest man, searched the entire world for a bride.
2. Bao, a herdsman, lives in Chifeng in Inner Mongolia.
3. His bride is Xia Shujian, a 5-foot-6 saleswoman, from his hometown.
4. Bao Xishun went through a long selection process, a grueling effort, to find a suitable bride.
5. Write a sentence that contains an appositive. Suggested topic: A Local Person of Interest.

..............................................................

..............................................................

More practice with commas: <www.mywritinglab.com>

## Commas with Dates and Addresses

Use commas to set off information in dates and addresses. When a date or address is made up of two or more parts, a comma separates the parts. When the parts of a date are both words or are both numbers, a comma separates the parts. And a comma follows the last item unless it is the final detail of a list or sentence.

- **Place commas after the day and year of a date.**

Beyoncé was born September 4, 1981, to Tina and Matthew Knowles.

COMMAS SET OFF THE DAY AND YEAR OF A DATE

- **When writing the day and the date, place a comma after the day.**

COMMA SETS OFF THE DAY FROM DATE

COMMAS SET OFF THE DAY AND YEAR OF A DATE

Beyoncé released the album *B'Day* on Tuesday, September 4, 2006, to coincide with the celebration of her 25th birthday.

- **Place commas after the street name, town or city, and state of an address.**

Jay-Z is part owner of an all-American sports bar and lounge at 6 West 25th Street, New York, New York that attracts many celebrities.

COMMAS SET OFF STREET, TOWN OR CITY, AND STATE OF AN ADDRESS

- **Separate two or more geographical names with a comma.**

Jay-Z is originally from a housing project in Brooklyn, New York, where he was abandoned by his father.

COMMAS SET OFF TWO OR MORE GEOGRAPHICAL NAMES

Practice 8

**COMMAS FOR DATES AND ADDRESSES**

Edit the following sentences by inserting commas to set off dates and addresses.

1. The Apollo 7 space vehicle was launched from Cape Kennedy, Florida, on October 11, 1968.
2. The first manned mission to the moon, Apollo 8 entered lunar orbit on Christmas Eve, December 24, 1968.
3. Man first stepped on the surface of the Moon on Sunday, July 20, 1969, during the Apollo 11 mission.
4. Explorer 1 was the first satellite launched by the United States on January 31, 1958.
5. Write a sentence that contains a date. Suggested topic: A Current Event.

---

---

More practice with commas: <www.mywritinglab.com>

# Other Uses of the Comma

Commas are also used in two additional ways.

1. Use commas to separate consecutive **coordinate adjectives** of equal importance. **Coordinate adjectives** are a series or two or more adjectives that could be arranged in any order or could be strung together with the word *and.* They each modify the noun directly. By contrast, **cumulative adjectives** are a series or two or more adjectives that accumulate before a noun, each adjective modifying the adjectives that follow. Cumulative adjectives must follow a certain order to make sense. Commas should not be used with cumulative adjectives.

2. Use commas to set off direct speech.

- **Commas between consecutive coordinate adjectives:** Use two questions to determine whether adjectives are coordinate.

  A. Can the word *and* be smoothly placed between the adjectives?

  B. Can the order of the adjectives be reversed?

  If the answer is *yes* to either of these questions, then separate these coordinate adjectives with a comma.

**Commas and Coordinate Adjectives**

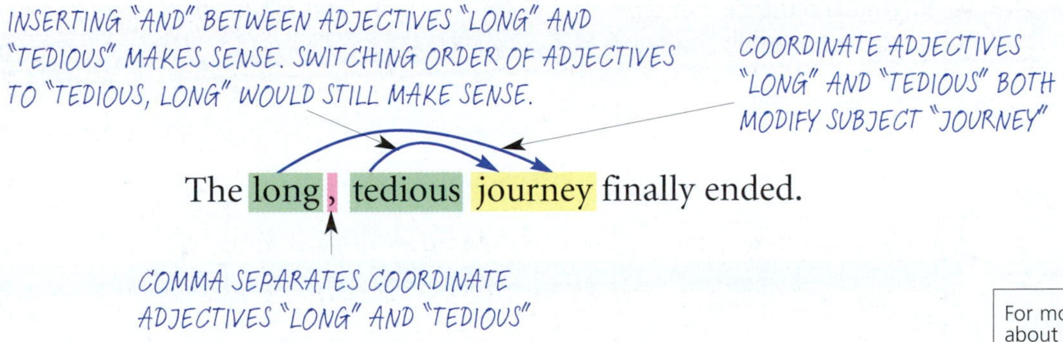

INSERTING "AND" BETWEEN ADJECTIVES "LONG" AND "TEDIOUS" MAKES SENSE. SWITCHING ORDER OF ADJECTIVES TO "TEDIOUS, LONG" WOULD STILL MAKE SENSE.
COORDINATE ADJECTIVES "LONG" AND "TEDIOUS" BOTH MODIFY SUBJECT "JOURNEY"
The long, tedious journey finally ended.
COMMA SEPARATES COORDINATE ADJECTIVES "LONG" AND "TEDIOUS"


For more information about the proper sequence of cumulative adjectives, see Chapter 28, "Adjectives and Adverbs."

For more information about proper use of quotation marks, see Chapter 31, "Quotation Marks."

**Commas and Cumulative Adjectives**

INSERTING "AND" BETWEEN ADJECTIVES "TEDIOUS" AND "PLANNING" MAKES NO SENSE.

ADJECTIVE "TEDIOUS" MODIFIES ENTIRE PHRASE "PLANNING SESSION" AND ADJECTIVE "PLANNING" MODIFIES SUBJECT "SESSION," SO THE ADJECTIVES ARE CUMULATIVE.

SWITCHING ORDER OF ADJECTIVES TO "PLANNING TEDIOUS" WOULD NOT MAKE SENSE.

The tedious planning session finally ended.

NO COMMA NEEDED BETWEEN CUMULATIVE ADJECTIVES "TEDIOUS" AND "PLANNING"

- **Commas after a verb that introduces a quotation:** The comma is used to set off the "said" clause, called the **speech tag**, and the comma is placed before the quoted information.

COMMA SEPARATES SPEECH TAG FROM THE QUOTATION, WHICH ENCLOSES THE EXACT WORDS OF THE SPEAKER

Mr. Newell said, "Let's begin the meeting promptly, please."

SPEECH TAG

QUOTATION MARKS ENCLOSE THE EXACT WORDS OF THE SPEAKER "MR. NEWELL"

Practice 9

**OTHER USES OF THE COMMA**

Edit the following sentences by inserting commas as needed to separate adjectives or to introduce a quotation.

1. The Net Generation is made up of curious, self-confident consumers.
2. The Net Generation will dominate their economic, social, and political worlds.
3. One member of the Net Generation says, "I go online for everything from shopping for running shoes to finding a job."
4. A study by the Department of Commerce said, "89.5% of all school-aged children between the ages of 5 and 17 use computers."
5. Write a sentence that separates adjectives or introduces a quotation. Suggested topic: You or Someone You Know as a Consumer.

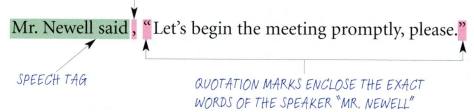

More practice with commas: <www.mywritinglab.com>

Practice 10

COMMA REVIEW

Write five sentences that illustrate five different comma rules. Identify the rule you used to write each sentence. Suggested topic: A Pleasant Memory.

1. ______________________________

______________________________

______________________________

2. ______________________________

______________________________

______________________________

3. ______________________________

______________________________

______________________________

4. ______________________________

______________________________

______________________________

5. ______________________________

______________________________

______________________________

More practice with commas: <www.mywritinglab.com>

# Writing Assignments

## Writing for Everyday Life

Assume you have been struggling with sleep issues, and you have decided to write and post your feelings about your experience on a blog about sleep disorders. Proofread and edit the posting to ensure appropriate use of commas. Use your own paper.

Dreams! I have them too. They plague me nightly. They swarm in on me as soon as I fall asleep and relentlessly tear through my mind until I wake. Always they are of pain loss suffering and violence. They often feature those people who are in my life. The cast is an unpredictable rotation through the night or from one night to the next. These dreams make me loathe sleep. They have though become the only companion that I can count on every night. Their fidelity is unsurpassed. Because of them there is no rest in my sleep. I wake more exhausted than I was the previous night.

Dreams! I know them too well. The word is usually associated with optimism hope for the future. I know the ugly truth behind the façade and it's a false promise to lull me into a false sense of security only to crush me from the inside out.

## Writing for College Life

Assume your government professor has asked you to write a one-paragraph report about a local person who takes an active role in civic life. Proofread and edit the report to ensure appropriate use of commas. Use your own paper.

**Billie Jean Young**

Billie Jean Young is a poet actor activist and educator. She lives in her rural Choctaw County Alabama hometown of Pennington from which she travels the world to teach work with young people and perform her one-woman play *Fannie Lou Hamer: This Little Light.* For nearly three decades Young has shared the life story of Fannie Lou Hamer a human rights activist and sharecropper from Sunflower County Mississippi. Billie Jean Young seeks to make change in the world in the spirit of Fannie Lou Hamer.

## Writing for Working Life

Assume you have written a letter of recommendation for a former employee who is seeking employment closer to her home. Proofread and edit the letter to ensure appropriate use of commas. Use your own paper.

**THE DENTAL CLINIC**
36 Big Buck Trail
Atlanta GA 30308

Dionne Brown Office Manager
The Aim Dental Group
2 Old Kings Road Suite 303
Atlanta GA 30301

June 15, 2007

Dear Ms. Brown:

As you requested in our phone conversation on June 10 2007 I am sending you this written recommendation to hire Sophia Larson as a full-time dental hygienist. Ms. Larson who has worked in our office for five years is a highly skilled personable hygienist. In addition you will find her to be an excellent educator advocate and manager. Ms. Larson a licensed clinician has 15 years of experience. I offer my strongest recommendation on behalf of Sophia Larson.

Sincerely,

Winston Ferrell

# Academic Learning Log

## WHAT HAVE I LEARNED ABOUT COMMAS?

To test and track your understanding, answer the following questions.

1. Use commas to separate a series of items in a list; a series of items in a list can be ________ or more words, phrases, or clauses.

2. Use commas to set off the ________ elements, ideas that appear at the beginning of a sentence.

3. Use commas in union with a coordinating conjunction to create a ________ sentence, which is a sentence made up of two or more independent clauses.

4. Use a pair of commas to set off a ________ idea, which is an idea that interrupts a sentence.

5. Use commas to set off a nonessential clause; often nonessential information appears in a relative clause introduced by ________ or ________.

6. Use commas for appositives, a word or phrase that ________ a noun.

7. When a date or address is made up of ________ parts, use a comma to separate the parts.

8. Use commas between ________ adjectives.

9. Ask two questions to determine whether adjectives are coordinate:

   **A.** ________________________________

   **B.** ________________________________

10. Use a comma ________ a verb that introduces a quotation.

11. **How will I use what I have learned about commas?**
    In your notebook, discuss how you will apply to your own writing what you have learned about commas.

12. **What do I still need to study about commas?**
    In your notebook, describe your ongoing study needs by describing what, when, and how you will continue studying commas.

REVISING

# 30 The Apostrophe

**Chapter Preview**

- What's the Point of the Apostrophe?
- Understanding the Point of the Apostrophe: One Student Writer's Response
- Applying the Point: The Apostrophe

## The apostrophe is used to show ownership and to form contractions by replacing omitted letters or numbers.

Thinking about a real-life situation helps us to understand the purpose of the apostrophe in our writing. Complete the following activity and answer the question "What's the point of the apostrophe?"

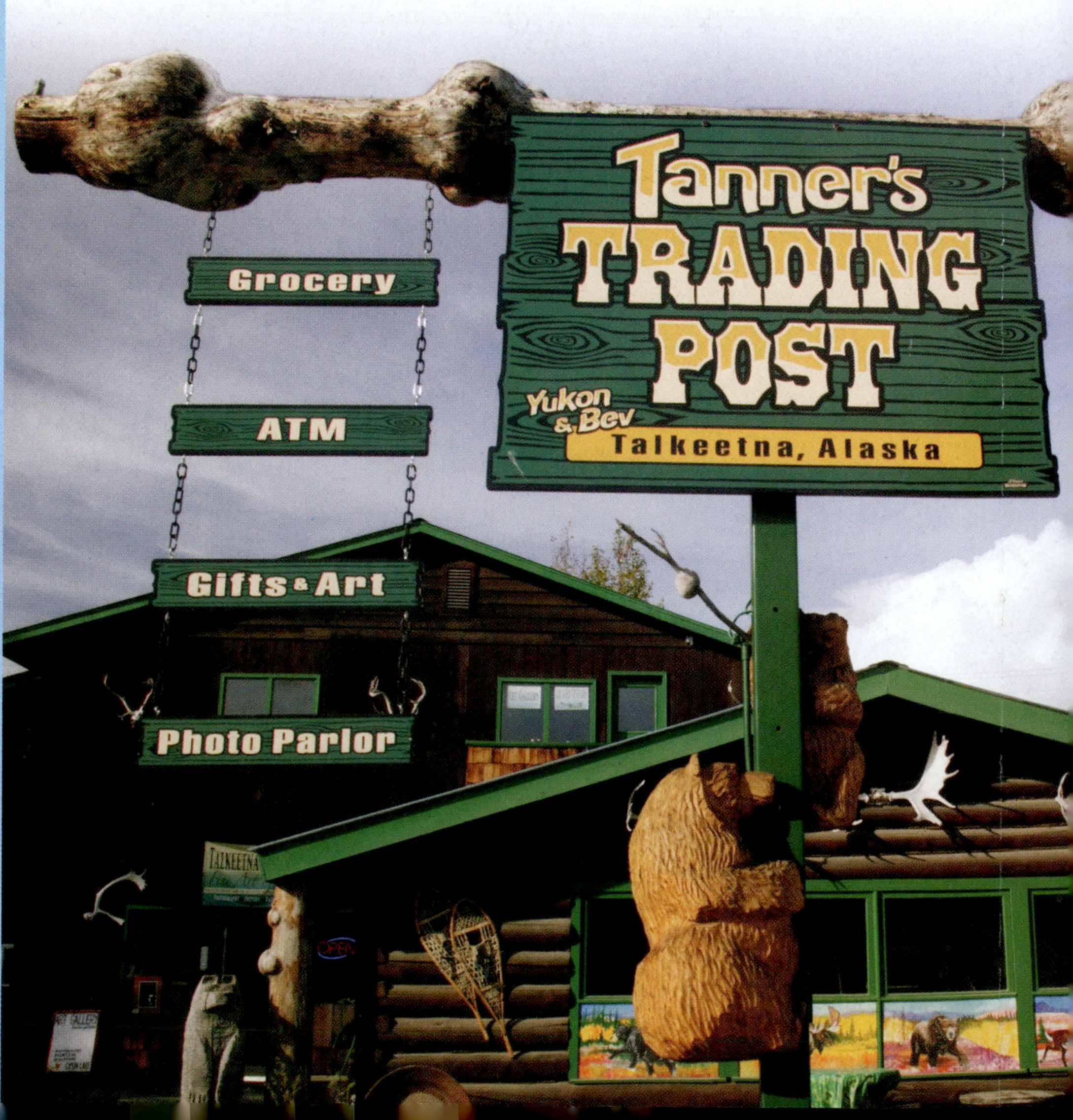

# What's the Point of the Apostrophe?

**Practice 1**

WRITING FROM LIFE

PHOTOGRAPHIC ORGANIZER: THE POINT OF THE APOSTROPHE

Apostrophes are often used in signs for businesses and in highway billboards. For example, the signs depicted in these photographs illustrate two different uses of the apostrophe. Study the signs shown in the photographs on pages 580–581 and explain why an apostrophe was used in each one.

------------------------------------------------------------

------------------------------------------------------------

------------------------------------------------------------

------------------------------------------------------------

------------------------------------------------------------

------------------------------------------------------------

------------------------------------------------------------

**What's the point of apostrophes?**

------------------------------------------------------------

------------------------------------------------------------

------------------------------------------------------------

# Understanding the Point of the Apostrophe: One Student Writer's Response

The following paragraph offers one writer's reaction to the pictures that use apostrophes.

> The sign for the trading post uses an apostrophe to show that Tanner owns the trading post. The sign about Oklahoma City uses an apostrophe to shorten a word. Some letters are left out of the word "national."

# Applying the Point: The Apostrophe

An **apostrophe** is used for two general purposes:

- To show ownership
- To form contractions

The apostrophe is often misused because words with apostrophes sound similar to other words, as in the following sentence:

INCORRECT USE OF APOSTROPHE

The cat loves it's toy mouse.

The use of the word *it's* in this sentence is incorrect because the contraction *it's* means *it is* or *it has*, as in the sentences *it's a shame* or *it's been a long time*. Instead, the correct word to use is the possessive pronoun *its* to state that the toy mouse belongs to the cat. Understanding the purposes of an apostrophe will help you reduce its misuse.

## The Apostrophe for Ownership

The **possessive form** of a noun and some pronouns is created by using an apostrophe followed, at times, by an *-s*. The possessive tells the reader that someone or something owns or possesses the next stated thing.

OWNER POSSESSION

George's Camry

OWNER POSSESSION

the Camry's front tire

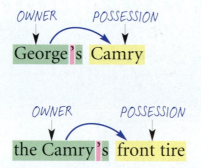

The following chart lists and illustrates the rules for using an apostrophe to show possession.

| Using the Apostrophe for Ownership | | |
|---|---|---|
| **To Show Possession for** | **Correct Use of Apostrophe** | **Example** |
| A singular noun | add ' | my husband's job<br>Henry's car |
| A singular noun ending with *-s* | add ' or add 's | the boss' memo<br>the boss's memo<br>James' home<br>James's home |
| A regular plural noun ending with *-s* | add ' | the writers' colony |
| An irregular plural noun | add 's | women's clothing |
| Compound words | add 's | vice president's speech<br>sister-in-law's business<br>(Note: Do not confuse the possessive form with the plural form, as in *sisters-in-law*) |
| Joint ownership of an item | add 's to the last noun | Abbott and Costello's comedy |
| Individual ownership | add 's to the end of both nouns | Clinton's and Bush's approaches to public speaking<br>(Each president has his own approach.) |
| Indefinite pronouns ending with "*one*" or "*body*" | add 's | someone's computer |

## Practice 2

APOSTROPHES AND POSSESSION

Change the phrases below into possessives by using *'s* or by adding an apostrophe.

1. the assignment of the day ____________

2. the duties of the police officers ____________

3. the house of my mother-in-law ____________

4. the car of Charles ____________

5. an agreement among gentlemen ____________

## Practice 3

APOSTROPHES AND POSSESSION

Edit the sentences for the correct use of the apostrophe to indicate possession.

1. Nelson R. Mandela's and Frederik Willem de Klerk's Nobel Peace Prize was given to them jointly to recognize their work to end apartheid in South Africa.
2. Nelson Mandela grandson became a tribal chief in 2007.
3. During a ceremony, Mandla Mandela was clothed in the lions skin of an African tribal chief.
4. The chiefs role is to act as head of the Mvezo Traditional Council in Mvezo, Eastern Cape, Africa.
5. Write a sentence that correctly uses an apostrophe to show possession. Suggested topic: An Important Ceremony.

____________

More practice with apostrophes: <www.mywritinglab.com>

## Practice 4

APOSTROPHES AND POSSESSION

Edit the paragraph for the correct use of the apostrophe to indicate possession.

My husbands family and I loved each other the moment we first met. My mother's-in-law Southern hospitality made me feel at home, and right away, my three future brothers-in-law began teasing me just like I was a little sister. Everyones sense of humor makes the family so much fun to be with. Some of my familys favorite memories are of Christmas at my in-laws house. Just like me, my childrens excitement always grows as we get ready to go to Pop's and Mimi's house on Christmas morning. One year, their cats mischievous nature created the days' excitement. Kitty, who liked to climb the Christmas tree, suddenly sprung out of the tree and toppled it over. Many of the gifts wrapping papers were soaked from the water in the tree stand. Everyone laughed, undisturbed by the mess.

Write a sentence that correctly uses an apostrophe to show possession. Suggested topic: An Item That Has Special Meaning.

## The Apostrophe for Contractions

An apostrophe is used to indicate the omission of letters to form a *contraction*. Most often, a **contraction** is formed to join two words to make one shorter word such as *don't* for *do not*. However, sometimes an apostrophe is used to form a one-word contraction such as *ma'am* for *madam* and *gov't* for *government*. An apostrophe ( ' ) takes the place of the letter or letters that are dropped to form the contraction.

The use of contractions gives a piece of writing an informal tone that records on paper the way we speak in general conversation. Writing for college courses usually requires a formal, academic tone. Thus, many professors discourage the use of contractions. Check with your professors about the required tone of your writing assignments. To ensure proper use of the apostrophe, the following chart illustrates how contracted verbs are formed.

**Apostrophe Use in Common Contractions**
The apostrophe replaces omitted letters.

| | |
|---|---|
| 'm APOSTROPHE REPLACES "A" IN "I AM"<br>I am = I'm | 's APOSTROPHE REPLACES "I" IN "IT IS"<br>it is = it's |
| 're APOSTROPHE REPLACES "A" IN "YOU ARE"<br>you are = you're | 've APOSTROPHE REPLACES "HA" IN "I HAVE"<br>I have = I've |
| n't APOSTROPHE REPLACES "O" IN "IS NOT"<br>is not = isn't | 'll APOSTROPHE REPLACES "WI" IN "I WILL"<br>I will = I'll |

Practice 5

APOSTROPHES IN CONTRACTIONS

Use apostrophes to form contractions for the following words.

**1.** I am ____________

**2.** he is ____________

**3.** could not ____________

**4.** let us ____________

**5.** they are ____________

**6.** should not ____________

**7.** he has ____________

**8.** it has ____________

**9.** it will ____________

**10.** they have ____________

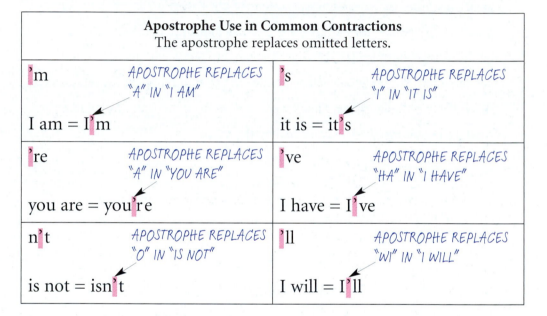

## Common Misuses of the Apostrophe

Quite often, the apostrophe is misused in several specific ways. The following chart lists and illustrates these common misuses of the apostrophe. Always base your use of an apostrophe on a specific rule. Proofread your writing for these common mistakes.

- **Do not use an apostrophe to form a plural noun.**

| Correct Plural | Incorrect Plural |
|---|---|
| homes<br>books | home's<br>book's |

- **Do not use an apostrophe to form a possessive pronoun.**

| Correct | Incorrect |
|---|---|
| ours<br>hers<br>theirs | our's<br>her's<br>their's |

- **Do not omit the apostrophe to form the possessive indefinite pronoun.**

| Correct | Incorrect |
|---|---|
| one's<br>everybody's | ones<br>everybodys |

- **Do not confuse contractions with similar sounding words.**

| Contraction | Possessive Pronoun |
|---|---|
| it's (it is)<br>who's (who is)<br>they're (they are) | its<br>whose<br>their |

## Practice 6

CORRECT USE OF THE APOSTROPHE

Edit the paragraph to ensure correct use of the apostrophe.

In 2005, Chevrolet unveiled it's retro HHR. The HHR blends element's of the 1949 Chevy Suburban with the look of the current SSR roadster pickup. Standard feature's include air conditioning, power windows and door locks, six-speaker CD stereo, and remote keyless entry. Carlotta loves Chevrolet's, and she really wanted to own an HHR. Finally in 2008, she bought her's at a great price from a previous owner.

Write a sentence that correctly uses the apostrophe. Suggested Topic: A Present You Would Like to Give to Someone.

---

---

---

More practice with apostrophes: <www.mywritinglab.com>

## Practice 7

REVIEW OF THE APOSTROPHE

Edit the paragraph to ensure correct use of the apostrophe.

The Hatfield's feud with the McCoys became one of the most infamous feuds in history. They're feud may be explained by a rare disease that may cause rage and violence. Dozens of the McCoys, who's symptoms have been documented, suffer from Hippel-Lindau disease. It's symptoms include headaches, excessive sweating, racing heart, anxiety, and excess adrenaline.

Write a sentence that correctly uses the apostrophe. Suggested Topic: The Causes or Effects of Road Rage.

---

---

---

More practice with apostrophes: <www.mywritinglab.com>

# Writing Assignments

## Writing for Everyday Life

Assume you have been having problems with a cell phone you just bought, and you are writing a letter of complaint to the manufacturer. Proofread and edit the body of the letter to ensure appropriate use of apostrophes. Use your own paper.

Recently, I purchased the Diamond Phone your currently advertising. Im writing to express my disappointment with you're product. I no longer use my phone for several reasons. First, the callers voice sounds muffled, or I cant hear someones voice message because of an echo in the phone. Im also disappointed in the quality of pictures taken with this phones camera. Bright colors looked washed out, and the prints didnt look crisp. In addition, the devices video feature isnt working. Overall, its been a disappointing purchase!

## Writing for College Life

Assume you have been required to write a one-paragraph summary about stress for your psychology class. Proofread and edit the paragraph to ensure appropriate use of apostrophes. Use your own paper.

Human action takes place within a persons' life space. Forces or demands within the life space cause ones movement from activity to activity. An individuals motivation leads to many demands. However, a human beings resources often cant meet those demands, so a person feels the strain to perform. Stress is the normal reaction. Its harmful to well-being and results in negative feelings and behaviors. Examples of stressors range from tolerating a neighbors loud music to losing a loved one. A natural disasters' impact, like a major earthquake, is so vast that it's known as a cataclysmic event. Demands or stressors cause an individual to make adjustments. An individual whose stressed needs to develop coping behaviors.

# Writing Assignments CONTINUED

## Writing for Working Life

Assume you must resign from your job. You have asked a colleague to proofread your letter, and she suggested that you eliminate all contractions to sound professional. In addition, she noticed several apostrophe errors. Edit the letter of resignation to ensure appropriate use of apostrophes and to eliminate contractions. Use your own paper.

218 Elm Drive
New Haven, GA 33215

Ms. Anna Rivers
Rivers Advertising Agency
2 Summit Drive
New Haven, GA 33215

July 6, 2007

Dear Ms. Rivers:

I'd like to inform you that I'm resigning from my position as an office assistant for the Rivers Advertising Agency, effective August 1. I'll be starting as Alcott Companys office manager in September. Thank you for the opportunities that you have provided me during the last five years. I've enjoyed working for your're agency and appreciate the support provided me during my time with the company. Even though I will miss my colleagues, I'm looking forward to this new challenge and to starting a new phase of my career. If I can be of any help during this transition, please don't hesitate to let me know.

Sincerely,

John Olarte

Academic Learning Log

PORTFOLIO

WHAT HAVE I LEARNED ABOUT THE APOSTROPHE?

To test and track your understanding, answer the following questions.

**1.** What are two general purposes of an apostrophe?

**a.** To show ............................................................

**b.** To form ............................................................

**3.** What are four common misuses of the apostrophe to avoid?

**a.** Using apostrophes to form ............................................................

**b.** Using apostrophe to form ............................................................

**c.** ............................................................ to form possessive indefinite pronouns

**c.** Confusing contractions with ............................................................

**How will I use what I have learned about the apostrophe?**

In your notebook, discuss how you will apply to your own writing what you have learned about the apostrophe.

**What do I still need to study about the apostrophe?**

In your notebook, describe your ongoing study needs by describing what, when, and how you will continue studying the apostrophe.

# 31 Quotation Marks

**Chapter Preview**

- What's the Point of Quotation Marks?
- Understanding the Point of Quotation Marks: One Student Writer's Response
- Applying the Point: Quotation Marks

## Quotation marks are used to set off exact words either written or spoken by other people or to set off titles of short works.

Quotation marks help us to record the ideas of other people. Thinking about a real-life situation helps us to understand the purpose of quotation marks in our communication. Complete the following activity and answer the question "What's the point of quotation marks?"

Jordin Sparks on *American Idol*

# What's the Point of Quotation Marks?

WRITING FROM LIFE

Practice 1

PHOTOGRAPHIC ORGANIZER: QUOTATION MARKS

Assume you are an avid fan of *American Idol*. You love the show so much that you have joined a blog about the competition, and you read the following posting on the blog about Jordin Sparks. As you read the paragraph, underline the ideas that you think should be in quotation marks.

American Idol

Blogs

**Sparks Sparkles**

***(1) Seventeen-year-old Jordin Sparks won the 2007*** **American Idol** ***television singing contest. (2) At the time, she became the youngest winner of the sought-after title. (3) According to one critic, Sparks captured the hearts of viewers with her bubbly personality and big voice. (4) Many praised her performance of the song Give Me One More Reason. (5) The show's host Ryan Seacrest announced that 74 million votes were cast. (6) Grateful and emotional, Sparks said, Thank you so much for everything—Mom and Dad, I love you! (7) We love you, too, Jordin. Congratulations!***

**What's the point of quotation marks?**

# Understanding the Point of Quotation Marks: One Student Writer's Response

The following paragraph offers one writer's reaction to the paragraph "Sparks Sparkles."

> *As I read the paragraph, I tried to figure out which ideas belonged to the writer of the paragraph and which ideas belonged to other people. This was hard! I underlined sentences 3 and 6. Both of these sentences mention other people. Sentence 3 gives credit for the idea to a critic, and sentence 6 is giving Jordin's exact words. I learned in another English class that song titles like "Give Me One More Reason" use quotation marks. I was unsure about sentences 5 and 7. Sentence 5 does give credit to Ryan Seacrest for the idea. But I think I remember that quotation marks are for someone's exact words. Does this sentence use Ryan's exact words? I don't know. I almost underlined sentence 7, but then I realized that's the writer talking.*

# Applying the Point: Quotation Marks

Use **quotation marks** (" ") to set off **direct quotes**—the exact words spoken by someone or quoted from another source—and for titles of short works. Always use quotation marks in pairs. The first quotation mark ("), also called the **opening quotation mark**, indicates the beginning of the quoted material. The second quotation mark ("), also called the **closing quotation mark**, indicates the end of the quoted material. Four general rules guide the use of quotation marks with other pieces of punctuation.

## General Guidelines for Using Quotation Marks

**1.** Place commas ( , ) and periods ( . ) inside the quotation marks ( " " ).

QUOTATION MARKS ENCLOSE EXACT WORDS OF THE JUSTICE DEPARTMENT

According to a recent article, the Justice Department promised to "combat gangs and guns," lower crime rates, and help local police in crimes involving juveniles.

COMMA GOES INSIDE QUOTATION MARK

The article also said gangs and guns contributed to "a nationwide crime spike."

PERIOD GOES INSIDE QUOTATION MARK

QUOTATION MARKS ENCLOSE EXACT WORDS FROM THE ARTICLE

**2**. Place semicolons ( ; ) and colons ( : ) outside the quotation marks.

QUOTATION MARKS ENCLOSE EXACT WORDS OF THE SPEAKER "WE"

We must say "no more violence"; we must strengthen gun control laws.

SEMICOLON GOES OUTSIDE QUOTATION MARK

QUOTATION MARKS ENCLOSE EXACT WORDS OF THE SPEAKER "WE"

There is one sure way we can say "no more violence": we can shut down violent media.

COLON GOES OUTSIDE QUOTATION MARK

**3**. Place a question mark ( ? ) inside quotation marks when it is part of the quotation. Place a question mark outside quotation marks when the larger sentence is a question, but the quotation included in it is not.

QUOTATION MARKS ENCLOSE EXACT WORDS OF THE SPEAKER "WE"

We should ask, "How does violence in movies and music affect youth?"

QUESTION MARK GOES INSIDE QUOTATION MARK BECAUSE IT IS PART OF THE QUOTATION. (THE QUOTATION IS A QUESTION.)

QUOTATION MARKS ENCLOSE EXACT WORDS OF THE SPEAKER "WE"

Did she really say "no more violence"?

QUESTION MARK GOES OUTSIDE QUOTATION MARK BECAUSE THE SENTENCE ITSELF IS A QUESTION, BUT THE QUOTATION INCLUDED IN IT IS NOT.

**4.** Use single quotation marks for quoted information—or titles of short works—that appear within direct quotation.

DOUBLE QUOTATION MARK INDICATES START OF QUOTED MATERIAL FROM NEWSPAPER

The *USA Today* article reports, "The Justice Department promises '$50 million this year to combat gangs and guns.' "

SINGLE QUOTATION MARK INDICATES START OF QUOTED MATERIAL FROM JUSTICE DEPARTMENT

SINGLE QUOTATION MARK INDICATES END OF QUOTED MATERIAL FROM JUSTICE DEPARTMENT. DOUBLE QUOTATION MARK INDICATES END OF QUOTED MATERIAL FROM NEWSPAPER.

Practice 2

QUOTATION MARKS WITH OTHER PUNCTUATION

Edit each sentence to ensure correct punctuation of quoted information and titles. Insert quotation marks and other punctuation as needed.

1. According to author Deborah Tannen, in her 2006 article in *The Los Angeles Times* Daughters and mothers agree on what the hurtful conversations are
2. I love your hair when it's combed back a mother says to her grown daughter.
3. The daughter snaps back Are you saying my hair looks unattractive this way
4. The teacher asked Do you agree with Tannen's statement Attention to hair reveals—and creates—intimacy
5. Write a quotation that records an idea stated by someone else. Suggested topic: An Opinion That Differs from Your Own.

Adapted from Deborah Tannen, "My Mother, My Hair"

More practice with quotation marks: <www.mywritinglab.com>

## Formatting and Punctuating Direct Quotations

One part of a direct quotation is the **speech tag** or the credit given to the source, the person who spoke or wrote an idea. A speech tag is formed by a subject (the speaker) and a verb that indicates the subject is speaking. The location of the speech tag affects the punctuation of a direct quotation. A speech tag can appear at the beginning, in the middle, or at the end of a quote. The following examples highlight the correct use of commas, periods, capitalization, and quotation marks based on the placement of the speech tag.

## Punctuating Direct Quotations

- **Speech tag at the beginning of quote**

COMMA SETS OFF SPEECH TAG

QUOTATION MARKS ENCLOSE EXACT WORDS OF THE SPEAKER "MOTHER"

Mother said, "Your brother is depressed."

SPEECH TAG

CAPITAL LETTER BEGINS QUOTED MATERIAL

PERIOD INSIDE QUOTATION MARK

- **Speech tag in the middle of quote**

**1 Quotation is stated in one sentence:**

QUOTATION MARKS ENCLOSE FIRST HALF OF THE SENTENCE OF THE SPEAKER "I"

QUOTATION MARKS ENCLOSE SECOND HALF OF THE SENTENCE OF THE SPEAKER "I"

LOWERCASE LETTER BEGINS SECOND PART OF INTERRUPTED QUOTE

"I think you're right," I replied, "because he isn't eating or sleeping."

COMMA INSIDE QUOTATION MARK

SPEECH TAG

COMMA SETS OFF SPEECH TAG

PERIOD INSIDE QUOTATION MARK

**2 Quotation is stated in two sentences:**

QUOTATION MARKS ENCLOSE FIRST SENTENCE OF THE SPEAKER "I"

PERIOD ENDS FIRST SENTENCE

QUOTATION MARKS ENCLOSE SECOND SENTENCE OF THE SPEAKER "I"

CAPITAL LETTER BEGINS SECOND SENTENCE OF QUOTE

"I think you're right," I replied. "He isn't eating or sleeping."

COMMA INSIDE QUOTATION MARK

SPEECH TAG ENDS FIRST SENTENCE OF QUOTE STATED IN TWO SENTENCES

OPENING QUOTATION MARK BEGINS SECOND SENTENCE OF QUOTE

PERIOD INSIDE QUOTATION MARK

- **Speech tag at the end of quote**

QUOTATION MARKS ENCLOSE EXACT WORDS OF THE SPEAKER "MOTHER"

"Do you think he would agree to get some professional help?" Mother asked.

SPEECH TAG

QUESTION MARK INSIDE QUOTATION MARK

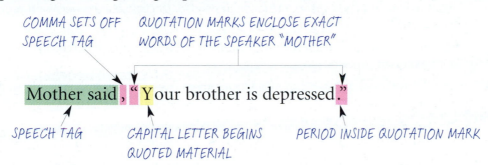

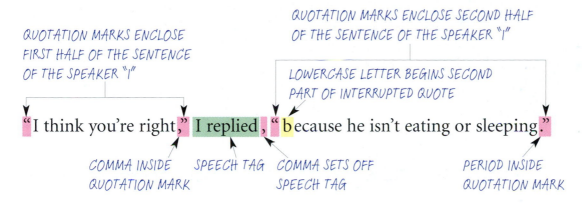

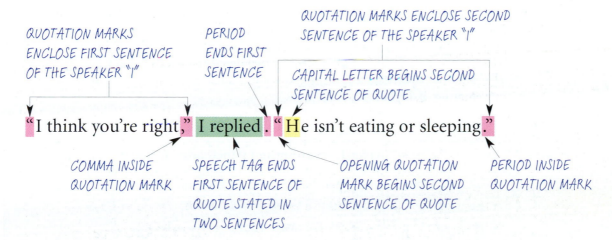

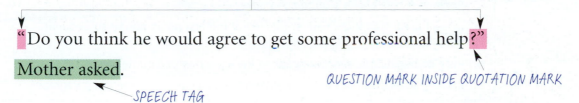

Practice 3

**PUNCTUATING DIRECT QUOTATIONS**

Edit each sentence to ensure correct punctuation of direct quotes and titles. Insert quotation marks and other punctuation as needed. Discuss your answers with your classmates.

**1.** According to *ConsumerReportsHealthGuide.org* Abuse of common cough suppressants may be increasing among teens

**2.** Dr. Suydam said Parents should educate themselves about the dangers of cough medicine abuse

**3.** High doses of cough suppressants can have serious side effects Dr. Gavin warns yet young people are not aware of the dangers

**4.** I can tell you firsthand that teens don't realize how dangerous the abuse of cough medications can be said Toren Volkmann, a former abuser of cough suppressants.

**5.** Write a direct quotation to record something someone else said. Suggested topic: Advice You Have Received.

More practice with quotation marks: <www.mywritinglab.com>

## Formatting and Punctuating Dialogue

Including dialogue in a piece of writing adds interest, details, and authenticity. Dialogue conveys action, time, place, and the traits and values of the speakers. Most often, dialogue is associated with creative writing, story telling, and journalism, but a well-crafted or carefully chosen piece of dialogue can effectively support a point in an academic paper. The following chart offers a few basic tips for formatting and punctuating dialogue.

**Tips for Formatting and Punctuating Dialogue**

- Follow the formatting and punctuation rules for direct quotations.
- Use quotation marks to indicate a speaker's exact words.
- Use speech tags to make sure the reader knows who is speaking.
- Vary the placement of speech tags.
- Begin a new paragraph to change speakers; record each person's turn at speaking, no matter how brief, in a separate paragraph.
- When a speaker's speech is longer than one paragraph:

  Begin the speech with a quotation mark.

  Do not use a quotation mark at the end of the first paragraph or subsequent paragraphs.

  Instead, begin each new paragraph in the speech with a quotation mark.

  End the speech with a closing quotation mark at the end of the last paragraph.

## Applying Appropriate Formatting

Note the ways in which the writer below applies appropriate formatting and punctuation rules for writing dialogue.

In *The Interpersonal Communication Book,* 10th edition, Joseph DeVito writes, "Many problems between people result from failure to recognize the distinction between the content and relationship dimensions of communication. Many couples argue because of the message communicated on the relationship level." He also points out that sensitivity can resolve conflicts. The following interchange, adapted from DeVito's book, illustrates DeVito's point.

He said, "I'm going bowling tomorrow night. The guys at the plant are starting a team."

"Why can't we ever do anything together?" she asked.

"We can do something together anytime," he replied. "Tomorrow's the day they're organizing the team."

"If it weren't a bowling team, there would be something else that you just had to do. You never make time to be with me."

He sat quietly for a while and then said, "Listen, I'd sure like to be on the team. And I should have asked if it would be a problem if I went to the meeting tomorrow. I know you were looking forward to having some fun and being together.

"Hey, why don't we meet at Joe's Pizza. We can have dinner after my meeting ends. Let's order the deep dish with extra cheese. You ought to think about taking up bowling, too. It would be fun to do something like that together."

She replied, "The pizza sounds great! I'm not so sure about the bowling, but I get your point. We should plan to do things together that we both enjoy."

**Comment:** New paragraphs signal changes in speakers.

**Comment:** Varied use of the speech tag.

**Comment:** No closing quotation mark because this one speech is two paragraphs long.

**Comment:** Quotation mark signals end of two paragraph speech.

Practice 4

### FORMATTING AND PUNCTUATING DIALOGUE

Write out the dialogue between Jeremy and his parents in this cartoon strip. Use appropriate formatting and punctuation.

©Zits Partnership, King Features Syndicate.

Practice 4

## Direct and Indirect Quotations

The spoken or printed words of other people are written in two ways: as a direct quotation or as an indirect quotation. So far, you have been learning about the **direct quotation**, which uses a pair of quotation marks to indicate someone else's exact words. In contrast, an **indirect quotation** rephrases or rewords what someone said or wrote. An indirect quotation is a **paraphrase** of someone else's words. Never use quotation marks with indirect quotations. To paraphrase a direct quotation into an indirect quotation, follow these steps:

| How to Paraphrase a Direct Quote into an Indirect Quote |
|---|
| 1. Remove quotation marks and internal capital letters. |
| 2. Add the word *that* to introduce the paraphrased idea. |
| 3. Revise verbs into past tense, except for actions continuing in the present. |
| 4. Revise verbs that command into infinitive form; revise speech tag for logical sense. |
| 5. Revise pronouns and signal words as needed. |

**Original Direct Quotation:**

QUOTATION MARKS ENCLOSE EXACT WORDS OF THE SPEAKER "HE"

He said, "Sit down, Shawn!"

SPEECH TAG

COMMA SETS OFF SPEECH TAG

SECOND-PERSON FORM OF "TO SIT" INDICATES A COMMAND

**Revised Indirect Quotation:**

QUOTATION MARKS REMOVED

He told Shawn to sit down.

SUBJECT

PAST-TENSE VERB

COMMAND REVISED TO INFINITIVE VERB

**Original Direct Quotation:**

SPEECH TAG

COMMA SETS OFF SPEECH TAG

QUOTATION MARKS SET OFF EXACT WORDS OF SPEAKER

Jackie Chan said, "I have been in tears when talking about my mother."

FIRST-PERSON PRONOUN

TENSE STATES ACTION IS ONGOING IN THE PRESENT.

**Indirect Quotation:**

QUOTATION MARKS REMOVED

SUBJECT

PAST-TENSE VERB

TENSE STATES ACTION IS ONGOING IN THE PRESENT.

Jackie Chan said that talking about his mom has made him cry.

INDICATES START OF PARAPHRASE

FIRST-PERSON PRONOUN REVISED TO THIRD-PERSON PRONOUNS

Practice 5

DIRECT OR INDIRECT QUOTATIONS

Identify each of the following statements as DQ for direct quotation or IQ for indirect quotation. Then, insert appropriate punctuation for direct and indirect speech.

........... **1.** Mark Twain said Man cannot be comfortable without his own approval

........... **2.** Mark Twain said that self acceptance is important to a person's peace of mind

........... **3.** A Chinese proverb teaches that one can learn from one's mistakes

........... **4.** A Chinese proverb states A fall into a ditch makes you wiser

........... **5.** According to Maya Angelou The honorary duty of a human being is to love

Practice 6

DIRECT AND INDIRECT QUOTATIONS

Paraphrase the following direct quotes into indirect quotes. Work with a classmate or small group of peers.

**1.** Speaking of drug addiction, Billie Holiday said, "A habit is hell for those you love."

---

---

**2.** "No passion so effectually robs the mind of all its powers of acting and reasoning as fear," according to Edmund Burke.

---

---

**3.** In 1933, President Franklin D. Roosevelt declared, "The only thing we have to fear is fear itself."

---

---

---

**4.** In his poem "Ulysses," Tennyson encouraged the weak "to strive, to seek, and not to yield."

---

---

**5.** Emily Dickinson wrote, "success is counted sweetest by those who ne'er succeed" in one of her better known poems.

---

---

# Titles

Quotation marks are also used to set off the titles of short works such as essays, short stories, short poems, songs, articles in magazines, TV episodes, and chapter titles in books.

- Follow the general rules for using quotation marks.
- Do not use quotation marks to set off titles of larger publications such as magazines, newspapers, and books. These larger publications are set off with italics or underlining.

**Poems**

QUOTATION MARKS SET OFF POEM TITLE

Maya Angelou read her poem "On the Pulse of Morning" at President Clinton's 1993 inauguration.

**Songs**

QUOTATION MARKS SET OFF SONG TITLE

Enrique Iglesias scored a big hit with the release of his single "Dimelo."

**Television Shows**

QUOTATION MARKS ARE NOT USED FOR THE TV SHOW TITLE

My favorite episode of the *George Lopez* show is "George's Mom Faces Hard Tambien."

QUOTATION MARKS SET OFF EPISODE TITLE OF A TV SHOW

## Practice 7

QUOTATION MARKS AND TITLES

Edit each sentence to ensure correct punctuation of titles.

1. Have you read Sandra Cisneros' short story Barbie-Q?
2. The *News Journal* article Barbie in Fatigues debates the role of women in combat.
3. The band Aqua mocked the Barbie doll as a role model in the song Barbie Girl.
4. In her poem Barbie Dolls, Marge Piercy expresses the anger women feel at being treated like sex objects.
5. Write a sentence that includes a title. Punctuate the title correctly. Suggested topic: A Popular Song.

---

More practice with quotation marks: <www.mywritinglab.com>

## Practice 8

REVIEW OF QUOTATION MARKS

Write a dialogue of five to ten sentences based on a recent conversation you have had or you have heard. Use appropriate format and punctuation. Work in pairs or with a small group of your classmates. Use your own paper.

More practice with quotation marks: <www.mywritinglab.com>

# Writing Assignments

## Writing for Everyday Life

Assume you have been in an automobile accident that is not your fault. The person who caused the accident denies that she is responsible. You have decided to make a written record of the event for your insurance company. Edit the following excerpt from the report. Insert quotation marks and other punctuation as needed. Use your own paper.

I was traveling north on Clyde Morris Avenue when I stopped for a red light. Once the light turned green, I began to accelerate and pulled out to cross over Highway 1. Suddenly, a 2006 white Ford pick-up truck slammed into the rear of the passenger's side of my 2008 Maxima. At the same time, my daughter cried out from the seat behind me, She ran a red light! The force of the impact sent me spinning. Before I could get out of my car, Roxanne DeVille, the driver who caused the accident, ran up to me. Are you all right? she asked. I am so sorry, she sobbed, because it's all my fault. I was trying to answer my cell phone and didn't notice the red light. I am so sorry!

## Writing for College Life

Assume you have written a summary paragraph about an article you read for a psychology course. Edit the paragraph. Insert quotation marks and other punctuation as needed. Use your own paper.

In the *Psychology Today* article How to Be Popular, Hara Estroff Marano talks about the eight traits that make people popular. Marano also argues that popularity is a trait that can be and should be learned. She writes having social contact and friends, even animal ones, improves physical health. Some of the traits of popular people include positive thinking and a good sense of humor.

# Writing Assignments CONTINUED

## Writing for Working Life

Assume you are working at the customer service desk of a retail store like Sears and you need to report a customer's complaint to your supervisor. Edit the paragraph. Insert quotation marks and other punctuation as needed. Use your own paper

Mr. Saul Richey was upset by the treatment he received from sales associate Martin Hawkins in the jewelry department. According to Richey, Hawkins refused to honor a discount coupon. Mr. Richey pointed out that the coupon was part of a promotion mentioned in the *Sunday Times* article A Jewelry Buyer's Dream: High Value at Low Cost. Mr. Richey said Your sales clerk was loud and rude; I was very embarrassed. I will never deal with that man again.

## Academic Learning Log

PORTFOLIO

### WHAT HAVE I LEARNED ABOUT QUOTATION MARKS?

To test and track your understanding, answer the following questions.

1. Quotation marks are used in pairs to indicate ________________ and ________________
2. ________________ and ________________ go inside the quotation marks.
3. Semicolons and colons go ________________ the quotation marks.
4. Use a pair of quotation marks to set off a ________________, which records the exact words of another person.
5. A ________________ is the credit given to the source of a quotation.
6. A speech tag can be placed ________________, ________________, or ________________.
7. **How will I use what I have learned about quotation marks?** In your notebook, discuss how you will apply to your own writing what you have learned about quotation marks.
8. **What do I still need to study about quotation marks?** In your notebook, describe your ongoing study needs by describing what, when, and how you will continue studying quotation marks.

# 32

# End Punctuation: Period, Question Mark, and Exclamation Point

**Chapter Preview**

- What's the Point of End Punctuation?
- Understanding the Point of End Punctuation: One Student Writer's Response
- Applying the Point: End Punctuation

## End punctuation marks the end of a complete thought.

Thinking about a real-life situation helps us to understand the purpose of end punctuation in our communication. Complete the following activity and answer the question "What's the point of end punctuation?"

# What's the Point of End Punctuation?

PHOTOGRAPHIC ORGANIZER: END PUNCTUATION

WRITING FROM LIFE

Practice 1

Assume you have witnessed the liftoff of the Space Shuttle *Discovery*. You have been asked by your college newspaper to write your eyewitness account. You quickly freewrite a draft with no concern for punctuation. As you read this early draft, think about the need for end punctuation. Also, think about the different types of end punctuation that could be used. How do you know when one complete thought ends and another begins? Try revising the draft below, inserting end punctuation where you think it is needed and changing capitalization of words as you see fit.

**An Awesome Sight**

Have you ever been at a concert so loud that the music made your heart vibrate was it so loud that you couldn't hear anyone talking around you as loud as a concert can be, it is nothing compared to the sound of the Space Shuttle lifting off the ground the sound of the Space Shuttle rattles both Earth and people what an awesome sight great plumes of smoke billow from a white-hot column of flame we all hold our breath as the shuttle soars into the blue sky.

**What's the point of end punctuation?**

................................................................................................

................................................................................................

................................................................................................

# Understanding the Point of End Punctuation: One Student Writer's Response

The following paragraph offers one writer's reaction to the paragraph "An Awesome Sight."

> *Without any end punctuation, I had to keep rereading to make sense of the ideas. I had to really stop and think about where one sentence ended and another one started. I am used to seeing capital letters at the beginning of a new idea. If I put a period to end a sentence, then I capitalize the first word of the next sentence. So both end punctuation and capital letters are needed. I also would use question marks to end the first two sentences because they are asking questions. All sentences end with some kind of punctuation mark.*

# Applying the Point: End Punctuation

A **sentence** is a complete thought that begins with a capital letter and ends with a specific type of end punctuation. The **punctuation marks** that indicate the end of a sentence (called **end punctuation**) are **the period**, **the question mark**, and **the exclamation point**. Each of these end punctuation marks indicates the purpose or type of a sentence. The following sections present a series of charts that show the relationship among end punctuation, the type of sentence, and the purpose of the sentence. Several sections also explain common end punctuation misuses to avoid.

## The Period

For more information on types and purposes of sentences, see Chapter 18, "Sentence Variety."

| End Punctuation | Type of Sentence | Purpose of Sentence |
|---|---|---|
| The Period ( . ) | Ends a declarative statement | To inform |
| | Ends an imperative statement | To command without urgency |

SUBJECT: light bulbs — VERB: waste — PERIOD ENDS DECLARATIVE STATEMENT: .

Incandescent light bulbs waste energy.

DECLARATIVE STATEMENT

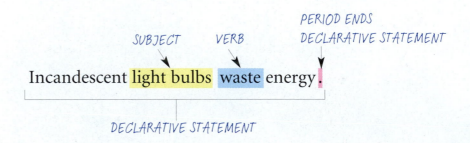

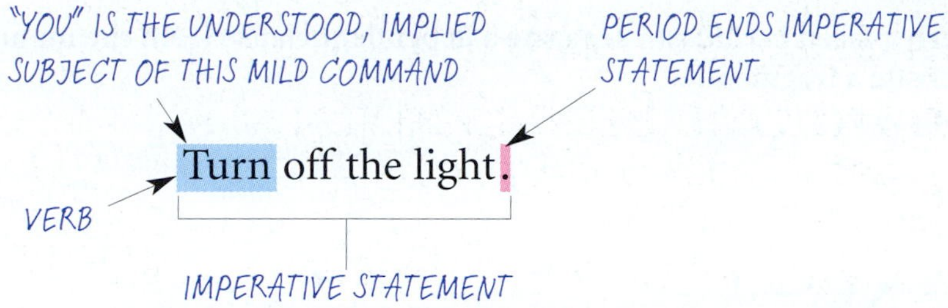


## Common Misuses of Periods

A complete sentence without a period to signal its end often becomes a **run-on sentence** or contains a **comma splice** error. Although there are several ways to correct these two errors, one simple correction for both is the insertion of the period. When you end a sentence with a period, capitalize the first word of the next sentence.

For more information on comma splices and run-on sentences and how to correct these errors, see Chapter 21, "Comma Splices and Run-Ons."

- **A run-on sentence occurs when two independent clauses are joined without any punctuation.**

**Incorrect**

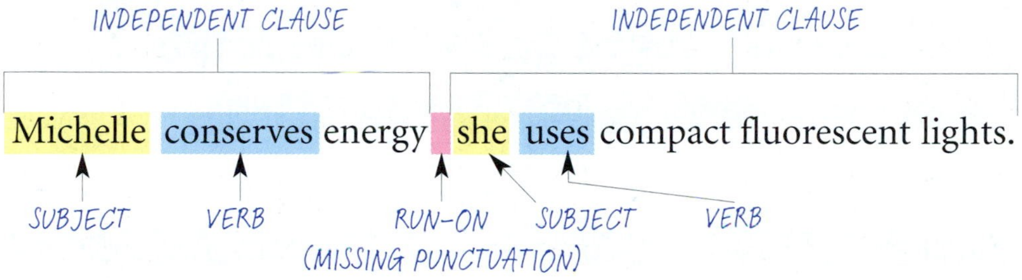


- **A comma splice occurs when a comma is used by itself (without a coordinating conjunction like *so*) to join two independent clauses.**

**Incorrect**

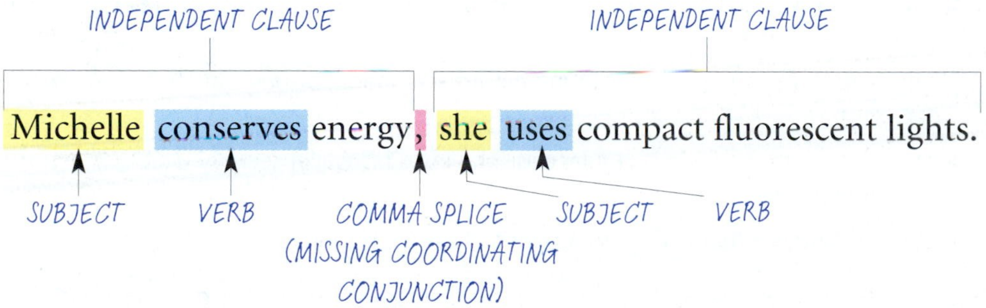


**Correct**

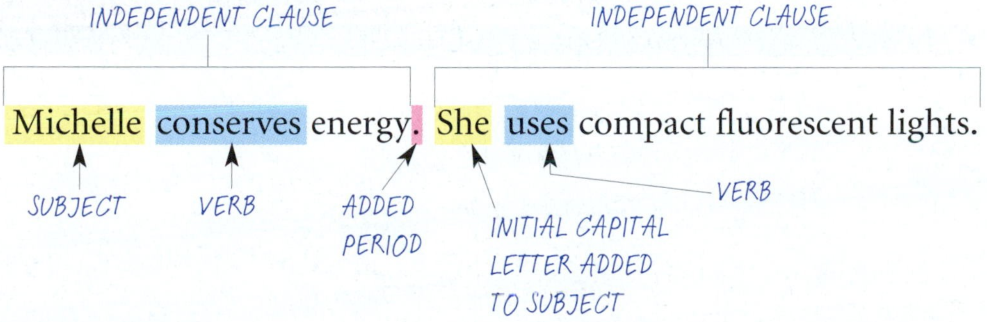

For more information on fragments and how to correct them, see Chapter 22, "Fragments."

- **An improperly placed period can separate a dependent clause from the main clause and create a fragment.**

**Incorrect**

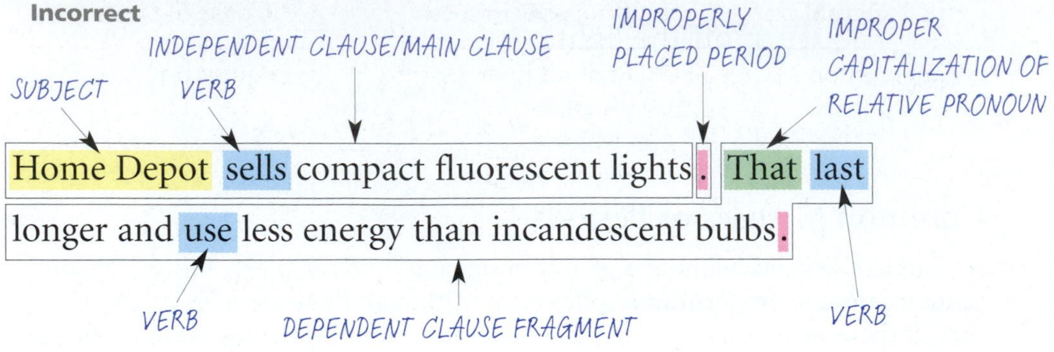

INDEPENDENT CLAUSE/MAIN CLAUSE
IMPROPERLY PLACED PERIOD
IMPROPER CAPITALIZATION OF RELATIVE PRONOUN
SUBJECT
VERB
Home Depot sells compact fluorescent lights. That last
longer and use less energy than incandescent bulbs.
VERB
DEPENDENT CLAUSE FRAGMENT
VERB


**Correct**

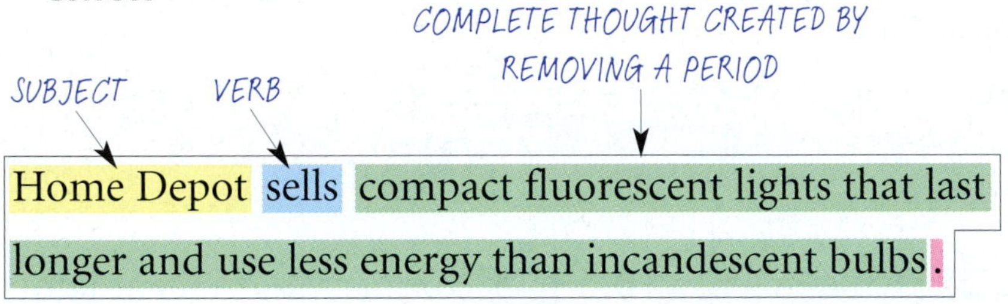

COMPLETE THOUGHT CREATED BY REMOVING A PERIOD
SUBJECT
VERB
Home Depot sells compact fluorescent lights that last
longer and use less energy than incandescent bulbs.


## Practice 2

**THE PERIOD**

Edit the following sentences to ensure appropriate use of capital letters and end punctuation.

1. Several factors can contribute to nightmares eating just before bed can increase brain activity.
2. Excessive alcohol intake may also contribute to nightmares. That cause poor sleep and health problems.
3. Stress may also play a role in causing nightmares Juan has them due to his fear of traveling.
4. One nightmare recurs on a regular basis, he loses his wallet security won't let him board the plane.
5. Write a sentence that ends with a period. Suggested topic: Effects of Stress.

..............................................................................................

..............................................................................................

More practice with end punctuation: <www.mywritinglab.com>

## The Question Mark

| End Punctuation | Type of Sentence | Purpose of Sentence |
|---|---|---|
| The Question Mark ( ? ) | Ends an interrogative statement | To question |
| | May invert order of subject and helping verb | To question |
| | May begin with *what*, *who*, or *how* | To ask a direct question |
| | Often uses a helping verb such as *do*, *can*, *will*, or *would* | To make a request |

SUBJECT

Why don't you turn off the lights?

VERB

QUESTION MARK ENDS INTERROGATIVE STATEMENT

SUBJECT

Is Justine still using incandescent light bulbs?

VERB

QUESTION MARK ENDS INTERROGATIVE STATEMENT

### Common Misuses of Question Marks

Do not use a question mark at the end of an indirect question. An **indirect question** tells about or reports a question asked by someone by paraphrasing it rather than reporting the exact words used. An indirect question usually begins with phrases like *I wonder if* or *he asked.* Place a period at the end of an indirect question.

**Incorrect**

QUESTION MARK SHOULD NOT END AN INDIRECT QUESTION

PHRASE INDICATES INDIRECT QUESTION

I wonder if I turned off the lights before I left the house this morning?

**Correct**

PERIOD ENDS INDIRECT QUESTION

I wonder if I turned off the lights before I left the house this morning.

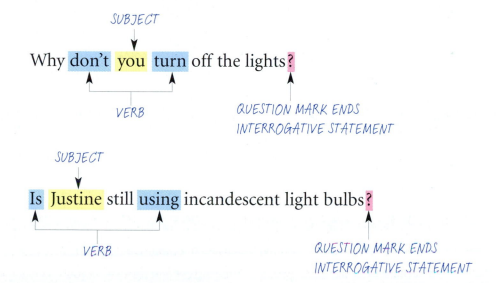

For more information on punctuating quotations, see Chapter 31, "Quotation Marks."

In direct quotations, writers often confuse what punctuation to use and where it should be placed. They often have particular trouble punctuating the **speech tag**, which is formed in the sentence by a subject and a verb (and an object, if any) and identifies the person speaking. To correctly punctuate a **direct question** asked by another person, follow these basic steps: (1) Set off the speech tag with a comma; (2) place a quotation mark before and after the exact words of the speaker's question; (3) capitalize the first letter of the first word in the quotation; and (4) place the question mark inside the end quotation mark.

**Incorrect**

SPEECH TAG

MISSING QUOTATION MARKS THAT SET OFF EXACT WORDS OF THE SPEAKER "DANNY"

Danny asked me did you turn off the lights before you left this morning.

MISSING COMMA SETTING OFF SPEECH TAG

INCORRECT USE OF INITIAL LOWERCASE "D" IN "DID," THE FIRST WORD IN THE QUOTATION

INCORRECT PERIOD USE IN DIRECT QUESTION

**Correct**

A PAIR OF QUOTATION MARKS SETS OFF THE EXACT WORDS OF THE QUESTION

Danny asked me, "Did you turn off the lights before you left this morning?"

SPEECH TAG SET OFF WITH COMMA

CAPITAL LETTER USED FOR FIRST WORD IN THE QUOTATION

QUESTION MARK GOES INSIDE THE QUOTATION MARK

## Practice 3

THE QUESTION MARK

Insert a period or a question mark as needed to appropriately end each idea.

1. What happened when you got to the airport and discovered you had lost your passport
2. Were the airline representatives helpful
3. Juan asked his doctor if nightmares are caused by stress
4. His doctor asked, "Are you having frequent nightmares"
5. Write a direct question. Suggested topic: Types of Identification That You Carry.

More practice with end punctuation: <www.mywritinglab.com>

# The Exclamation Point

| End Punctuation | Type of Sentence | Purpose of Sentence |
|---|---|---|
| The Exclamation Point ( ! ) | Ends an exclamatory statement | To express strong emotion |
| | Ends a strong imperative (command) | To express urgency, warning, or a forceful command |
| | Ends an interjection, a single word or phrase used as an exclamation that stands apart from the rest of a sentence | To cry out, to utter an emotion |
| | Used with interjections beginning with *how* or *what* | To emphasize an idea |

**Examples**

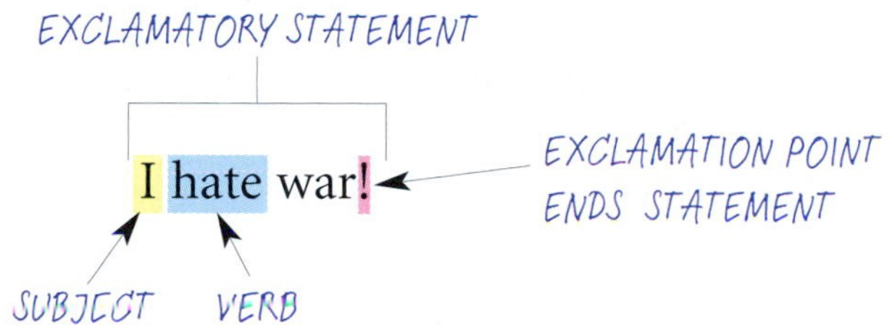


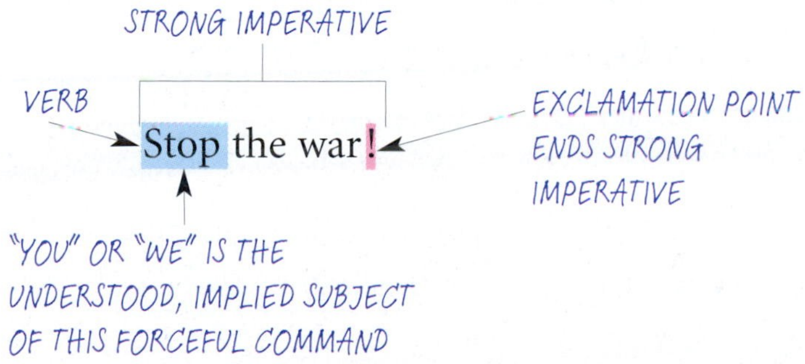


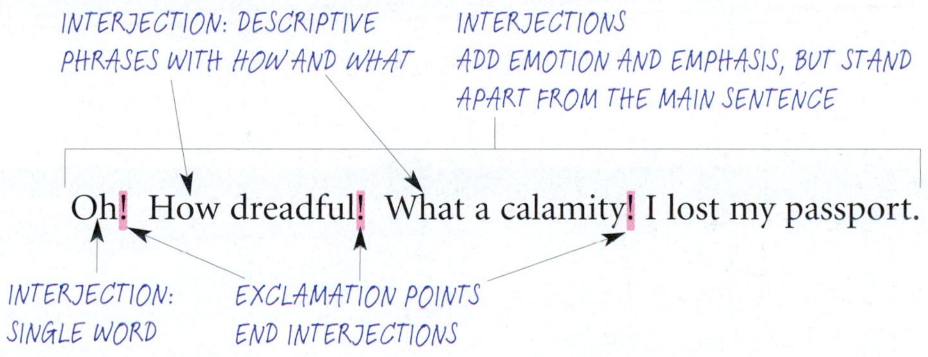

## Common Misuses of Exclamation Points

- Use the exclamation mark sparingly. Overuse makes the point less meaningful.
- Use only one exclamation mark for a sentence; avoid using several at a time to emphasize a point.

**Incorrect**

INCORRECT USAGE OF MULTIPLE EXCLAMATION POINTS FOR EACH SENTENCE

Save your life!!!!! Stop smoking, now!!!!!!

EXCLAMATION POINTS OVERUSED

**Correct**

USE OF PERIODS TO END IMPERATIVES MAKES USE OF EXCLAMATION POINT MORE EFFECTIVE

Save your life. Stop smoking. Now!

EXCLAMATION POINT ENDS SINGLE INTERJECTION

- Do not use exclamation marks in academic writing.

Practice 4

**THE EXCLAMATION POINT**

Insert a period or an exclamation mark as needed to appropriately end each idea. Use periods and capital letters as needed to make your point. Discuss your responses with your classmates.

1. Oh no my foot is broken
2. It's your fault you turned the light off before I was out of the room
3. What a nightmare I was just trying to conserve energy
4. I need to go to the emergency room hurry
5. Write a sentence of exclamation. Suggested topic: An Urgent Need.

---

---

More practice with end punctuation: <www.mywritinglab.com>

Practice 5

**END PUNCTUATION REVIEW**

Insert the appropriate end punctuation for each sentence. Capitalize words as needed.

**1.** Save the earth stop global warming

**2.** Is global warming a fact

**3.** The last two decades of the twentieth century were the hottest in 400 years arctic ice is rapidly disappearing

**4.** I still ask if global warming is a fact I wonder if it is too late to stop global warming

**5.** Write a sentence with a purpose of your own choosing. Use appropriate end punctuation. Suggested topic: The Local Climate.

---

---

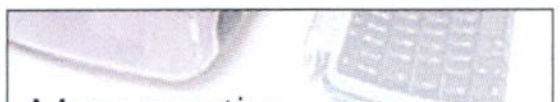

More practice with end punctuation: <www.mywritinglab.com>

# Writing Assignments

## Writing for Everyday Life

Assume you are writing an email to a family member about a travel experience. You write your first draft as a freewrite without concern for punctuation. You take time to proofread before you click the send button, and you see the need to insert end punctuation. Edit the email to insert appropriate end punctuation. Capitalize words as needed. Use your own paper.

Hi Aunt Jo,

You wouldn't believe what happened to me at the airport. When I tried to check in at the ticket counter, I couldn't find my wallet. I had left my new wallet with all my identification at home and had mistakenly picked up my old wallet. Now, you may be asking how that could have happened I know this was so avoidable an airline representative asked, "Do you have any government issued identification with you" Thank goodness I still had a library card in my old wallet she marked my ticket for "special screening" from security. Those folks took me aside, patted me down, and went through all my belongings. I got through security in time to board my plane I was so relieved. How stressful it all was

# Writing Assignments CONTINUED

## Writing for College Life

Assume you are working with a group of peers on a science project. You have been appointed the group recorder. You have started a rough draft of your group's lab report. Proofread and edit the report for correct use of end punctuation. Use your own paper.

**Airfare Price to Miles Traveled Correlation Report**

On Wednesday October 19, 2005 a research experiment was performed in order to detect whether or not there is a correlation between the price of a flight ticket and the actual mileage from origination to destination the three researchers conducting this research utilized the internet web sites Expedia.com and Mapquest.com to acquire the necessary data for the experiment. The following criteria were established in order to qualify the data for the experiment first, the flight must have at least, but not more than one layover second, the original flight must depart between six in the morning and noon. Third, the passenger must be an adult 19 to 64 years of age. Fourth, the flight must be for one adult in economy/coach class. Fifth, Delta Airlines must be the flight provider. Sixth, the data must be collected only from cities in the United States seventh, the flight must be a round trip airfare. The researchers randomly chose 25 cities in the United States to collect the required data for the experiment the researchers used Expedia.com to obtain the price of each of the 25 flights. The researchers then used Mapquest.com to collect the mileage data, from origination to destination. The researchers, by using data were able to determine that there is no correlation between the price of a flight ticket and the number of miles traveled

## Writing for Working Life

Assume you are working in a local restaurant to gain experience in the industry. You want to learn about running a small business because your long-term goal is to open your own restaurant. You notice a way to improve customer satisfaction, so on your break, you quickly write down your thoughts. As you read your first draft, you see the need for end punctuation. Edit this draft to insert appropriate end punctuation. Use your own paper.

*My First Thoughts: Ways to Improve Customer Satisfaction*

*In what ways can we improve customer satisfaction We need to improve our music and our napkins. Different age groups come at different times of the day the early crowd is older and quieter. The late evening crowd is younger and more active our music should be customized to meet their different tastes. I suggest classical or soft rock music to play quietly as background music for the early crowds the evening crowds are more likely to enjoy the hard-driving, party sound of hard rock or pop music. The quality of our napkins is another detail that needs improvement. I wonder how much we spend on our current small, thin paper napkins they need to be replaced with super-large, high quality paper napkins. Good napkins are well worth the money!!!!*

### WHAT HAVE I LEARNED ABOUT END PUNCTUATION?

Academic Learning Log

PORTFOLIO

To test and track your understanding, answer the following questions.

1. The ____________ ends a declarative or a mild ____________ statement.
2. The purpose of a declarative sentence is to ____________; the purpose of an imperative sentence is to ____________.
3. The question mark ends an ____________; the purpose of this sentence type is to ____________.
4. A question mark is not used at the end of an ____________ question.
5. An exclamation point ends an ____________ statement, a strong ____________, and an ____________.
6. The purpose of an exclamatory sentence is to express ____________, urgency, ____________, or a forceful ____________.
7. **How will I use what I have learned about end punctuation?** In your notebook, discuss how you will apply to your own writing what you have learned about end punctuation.
8. **What do I still need to study about end punctuation?** In your notebook, describe your ongoing study needs by describing what, when, and how you will continue studying end punctuation.

# 33 Capitalization

## Capitalization clearly identifies the beginning of a new idea or the names of specific people, places, and things.

**Chapter Preview**

- What's the Point of Capitalization?
- Understanding the Point of Capitalization: One Student Writer's Response
- Applying the Point: Capitalization

Thinking about a real-life situation helps us to understand the purpose of capitalization in our communication. Complete the following activity and answer the question "What's the point of capitalization?"

# What's the Point of Capitalization?

**PHOTOGRAPHIC ORGANIZER: CAPITALIZATION**

WRITING FROM LIFE

Practice 1

Many experts fear that excessive text messaging harms an individual's ability to write well. Other experts believe text messaging can teach students the appropriate use of language for different situations and audiences. For example, the use of capitalization in text messages differs from standard rules. The person in the photo is text messaging her family about a delay in her travel plans. Read her text message and consult the glossary of text message lingo, common expressions used in text messages. Explain how she uses capitalization in her message. Next, identify standard uses of capitalization you have seen in written language. Do you think text messaging harms an individual's ability to write well?

**Text Message Glossary**

**AFAIK** (As Far As I Know)

**BFN** (Bye for Now)

**CYA** (See You)

**FYI** (For Your Information)

**L8R** (Later)

**2NITE** (Tonight)

**What's the point of capitalization?**

# Understanding the Point of Capitalization: One Student Writer's Response

The following paragraph offers one writer's reaction to the text message.

*I do a lot of text messaging, so I know that some people capitalize everything in their messages while others don't capitalize anything. Just like the woman at the airport, I like to use capital letters in my messages because each group of caps makes up a word. Using capitals helps me see what I am writing. As I think about standard capitalization rules, I think of the names of people, places, days of the week, days of the month, and the first word of a sentence. I always follow these rules when I write for school or work, but I am not so sure about some capitalization rules, like people's titles. I can see how experts think text messaging hurts written language. Sometimes, if I'm in a hurry, I use text lingo like "4" for "four." I just make sure I proofread.*

# Applying the Point: Capitalization

**Capitalization** refers to writing letters (and sometimes words) in uppercase letters. The most frequent usage of capitalization, however, is writing a word with its first letter in uppercase (and the rest of its letters in lowercase) to indicate the beginning of a sentence.

Following seven basic rules will ensure proper use of capitalization in your writing.

### RULE 1: Capitalize the first word of every sentence.

INITIAL CAPITAL LETTERS IN THE FIRST WORD OF EVERY SENTENCE INDICATE THE START OF A NEW SENTENCE AND A NEW THOUGHT

Extreme horror films provide thrill rides for loyal fans. The core audience of horror is made up of 18- to 22-year-old males. Many criticize horror films for being too graphic.

## Practice 2

CAPITALIZATION

Edit the following paragraph for proper use of capitalization.

an unknown actress plays a tourist visiting a foreign country in a popular horror film. the tourist and her friends are terrorized in the cheap lodgings recommended by a beautiful model. the plot contains gruesome details. although horror films are very popular, some critics condemn them for showcasing violence against women. however, other experts say that watching horror films provides a healthy outlet for aggression.

Write a sentence that requires the appropriate use of capitalization. Suggested topic: Your Opinion about Horror Movies.

---

---

More practice with capitalization: <www.mywritinglab.com>

### RULE 2: Capitalize the pronoun *I*.

ALWAYS CAPITALIZE THE FIRST-PERSON SINGULAR PRONOUN "I"

I do not enjoy watching horror movies. Because I keep my eyes closed through most of a horror movie, I think they are a waste of my money.

## Practice 3

CAPITALIZATION

Edit the following paragraph for proper use of capitalization.

My boyfriend really enjoys horror movies, but i prefer romantic comedies. i enjoy movies that don't keep me awake all night with horrible images of dismembered bodies. i like to escape problems when i watch a movie. i don't want to think about murder, rape, and mayhem. i just want to watch a good love story. Most often, i have to watch the movies i like without my boyfriend. That's fine with me because he certainly has to watch horror movies without me.

Write a sentence that requires the appropriate use of capitalization. Suggested topic: Your Favorite Kind of Movie.

---

---

More practice with capitalization: <www.mywritinglab.com>

**RULE 3: Capitalize the first letter of the first words in written greetings and salutations (for example, *Dear friends,* or *Best regards*).**

ALWAYS CAPITALIZE THE FIRST LETTER OF THE FIRST WORDS IN WRITTEN GREETINGS OR CLOSINGS (IN LETTERS, MEMOS, EMAILS, ETC.)

Dear Mr. Sanchez:

I am writing to protest your support of horror films. As a sponsor of this type of film, you foster fear and violence in our culture. Until you stop sponsoring horror films, I will no longer buy items from your company.

Sincerely,

Dorothea Simmons

## Practice 4

CAPITALIZATION

Edit the following letter for proper use of capitalization.

dear Ms. Simmons:

our company appreciates your concern about horror films. we also appreciate the time you took to write to us about your concerns. our board of directors is taking this matter into consideration. we will make a public statement in the near future.

best regards,

Steve Sanchez

More practice with capitalization: <www.mywritinglab.com>

**RULE 4: In titles of publications, such as books, magazines, newspapers, songs, poems, plays, and articles, capitalize the first letter of the first and last words, the principal words, and the first word that comes after a semicolon or a colon.**

Do not capitalize the first letters of the following in titles, unless they are the first or last word or come after a semicolon or colon: articles (*a, an, the*), prepositions (such as *in, of,* and *with*), and conjunctions (such as *and, but,* and *for*). Keep in mind that capitalization styles for titles differ in certain academic disciplines, so always check with your teacher for style guidelines.

**Article:**

ALWAYS CAPITALIZE THE FIRST LETTER OF THE FIRST WORD IN A PUBLICATION TITLE

"Eight Top Jobs for Parents"

ALWAYS CAPITALIZE THE FIRST LETTER OF THE PRINCIPAL WORDS IN A PUBLICATION TITLE

**Book:**

ALWAYS CAPITALIZE THE FIRST LETTER OF THE PRINCIPAL WORDS IN A PUBLICATION TITLE

*The Grapes of Wrath*

**Magazine:**

*Sociology: The Journal of the British Sociological Association*

**Newspaper:**

*The New York Times*

**Play:**

UNLESS THEY ARE THE FIRST OR LAST WORD, DO NOT CAPITALIZE THE FIRST LETTER OF MINOR WORDS, ARTICLES, PREPOSITIONS, OR CONJUNCTIONS IN TITLES

*The Taming of the Shrew*

**Poem:**

"Death Be Not Proud"

**Song:**

"Dearly Beloved"

**Website:**

Health.gov

**Note:** Digital terms, such as Internet or the World Wide Web, use initial capitalization.

## Practice 5

CAPITALIZATION

Edit the following paragraph for proper use of capitalization.

In 2007, *harry potter and the deathly hallows* debuted to the delight of millions of fans. In the *washington post* article "where harry most enchants," Amy Gardner reported that the seventh and final novel easily sold more than all the previous books in the popular series about the young wizard and his friends. Some fans enamored with the story have written poems and songs in tribute. For example, on a *website* called *harry potter songs*, Mark Davis claims his song "*harry potter's school*" is the most popular Harry Potter song on the internet. Other fans post their praise on the official Harry Potter Scholastic Books website.

Write a sentence that requires the appropriate use of capitalization. Suggested topic: A Popular Movie, Song, or Website.

More practice with capitalization: <www.mywritinglab.com>

### RULE 5: Capitalize the first letters in all essential words in proper nouns.

**Proper nouns** name specific people, places, things, and events. Proper nouns include people's names; certain titles of people (see Rule 6 on page 626 for details), places, and regions; organizations and associations; and publications. Each of the examples in the chart below illustrates various rules for capitalizing proper nouns.

**Note** the capitalization of initials and abbreviations. Do not capitalize common nouns.

ALWAYS CAPITALIZE THE FIRST LETTER IN EACH PART OF A PERSON'S NAME

ALWAYS CAPITALIZE A PERSON'S INITIALS

THE FIRST LETTER OF THE TITLES OF FAMILY RELATIVES (PARENTS, AUNTS AND UNCLES, ETC.) REMAIN LOWERCASE AS COMMON NOUNS, BUT BECOME CAPITALIZED WHEN A SPECIFIC RELATIVE (THE SPEAKER'S) IS REFERRED TO

| | Common Nouns | Proper Nouns |
|---|---|---|
| **People** | a woman | Ms. Eileen Long |
| | a man | Mr. D. O. Nape |
| | a professor | Professor Walker |
| | an officer | Captain Rivera or Capt. Rivera |
| | a relative, an aunt | Aunt Jo |
| | a father, my mother | Father, Mother |
| | a believer of a religion | Christian, Catholic, Muslim |
| | member(s) of an organization | Republican(s), Boy Scout(s) |

| | Common Nouns | Proper Nouns |
|---|---|---|
| **Places and Regions** | a lake<br>a country<br>a street | Lake Tahoe<br>Mexico<br>Main Street |
| **Things** | a language<br>an academic course<br>a history course<br>a ship<br>south (a direction)<br>a religion<br>a sacred text<br>a god<br>a group/organization<br>a department, office, or institution<br>a monument<br>a company | English<br>Psychology 101<br>World History I<br>Titanic<br>the American South (a region)<br>Christianity, Judaism, Islam<br>the Koran, the Qur'an, the Bible<br>God, Christ, Allah, Buddha, Zeus<br>the Rolling Stones, the Kiwanis Club<br>the Senate, the Department of Commerce, Daytona Beach Community College<br>Lincoln Memorial<br>Apple, Inc. |
| **Events, Time Periods** | a day<br>a month<br>an era<br>a movement<br>a war<br>a holiday | Friday<br>January<br>the Middle Ages<br>the Civil Rights Movement<br>the Vietnam War<br>Easter, Passover, Thanksgiving, Ramadan |

## Practice 6

CAPITALIZATION

Edit the following paragraph for proper use of capitalization.

The enlightenment was a movement that started among a small group of people and slowly spread to influence society. In contrast, romanticism was more widespread in both its origins and its influence. Many experts believe that no other intellectual or Artistic Movement has had such influence since the end of the middle ages. Beginning in germany and england in the 1770s, by the 1820s

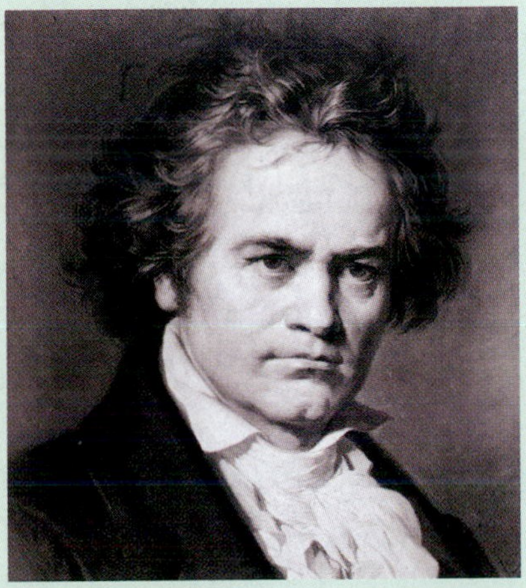

▲ *Beethoven*

More practice with capitalization: <www.mywritinglab.com>

## Practice 6

romanticism had swept through europe and traveled quickly to the western hemisphere. romanticism transformed poetry, the Novel, drama, painting, sculpture, and all forms of concert music. beethoven and mozart are two well-known composers from this era. The influence of Music from this romantic era is heard in the soundtracks for Epic Films such as *star wars*.

Write a sentence that requires the appropriate use of capitalization. Suggested topic: Person of Influence.

---

---

---

---

## RULE 6: Capitalize the first letter of the title of a person when the title precedes the person's name.

Some writers capitalize the first letter of a title of very high rank even when it follows a proper name. Capitalization of the first letter of a title is also common if it appears at the end of a letter, email, or other correspondence, following the person's name. Do not capitalize those titles when they appear on their own as common nouns (without modifying a particular person's name).

ALWAYS CAPITALIZE THE FIRST LETTER OF A PERSON'S TITLE WHEN IT APPEARS BEFORE THE PERSON'S NAME

WHEN A PERSON'S TITLE APPEARS AFTER THE PERSON'S NAME, THE INITIAL LETTER OF THE TITLE REMAINS LOWERCASE

| | |
|---|---|
| Doctor Kit Doughney | Kit Doughney, a medical doctor |
| Professor Rivers | Van Rivers, a professor of science |
| Senator Clinton | Hillary Clinton, the senator |

IN SOME CASES, IF IT'S A HIGH-RANKING TITLE, WRITERS WILL CAPITALIZE A TITLE EVEN IF IT APPEARS AFTER THE NAME

| | |
|---|---|
| Prime Minister Brown | Gordon Brown, Prime Minister of the United Kingdom of Great Britain and Northern Ireland |

CAPITALIZATION

Practice 7

Edit the following paragraph for proper use of capitalization.

Several people have influenced me and inspired me to be a better person. Some of these role models are close friends and family members; others are people I have only read about. One person who has inspired me is Margaret Basinger, a Medical Doctor who treats people who can't afford a Doctor. Another role model is professor Kibbens, who volunteers at a local soup kitchen on weekends. I have even been inspired by a Politician. Ronald Reagan, former president of the United States, showed me the importance of communication skills. He has inspired me to consider running for office; in particular, I am considering being a Senator or Congresswoman. All of these people showed me the importance of giving to society.

Write a sentence that requires the appropriate use of capitalization. Suggested topic: A Person You Admire.

---

---

---

---

More practice with capitalization: <www.mywritinglab.com>

**RULE 7: Capitalize proper adjectives. Proper adjectives are formed from proper nouns.**

| Proper Noun | Proper Adjective |
|---|---|
| Africa | Africans |
| America | Americans |
| Florida | Floridian |
| Japan | Japanese |
| Spain | Spanish |
| Shakespeare | Shakespearean |

Use and capitalize brand-name trademarks as proper adjectives:

Kleenex tissue

Scotch tape

## Practice 8

### CAPITALIZATION

Edit the following paragraph for proper use of capitalization.

> Heather and John enjoy going to foreign films. They particularly like french films although they also enjoy japanese animation films. They make a date once a week to go to a small theatre that shows the latest foreign film releases. Heather always gets a mountain dew soda and a pack of raisinets candy. John usually gets a cappuccino and a butterfinger candy bar.

More practice with capitalization: <www.mywritinglab.com>

## Practice 9

### CAPITALIZATION REVIEW

Write a five- to ten-sentence paragraph that requires the appropriate use of capitalization. Suggested topic: A Movie or Book Based on Real Life.

Practice 9

# Writing Assignments

## Writing for Everyday Life

Assume you are writing an email to a friend about a horror movie you just saw. Edit the paragraph for proper use of capitalization. Use your own paper.

i did not want to go see this movie. horror movies are not my thing, but I gave in and reluctantly went along to see *hostel ii.* i probably won't sleep soundly again for years. the motion picture association Of america gave it an r rating for "sadistic scenes of violence and torture." i have to say i didn't see a lot of the movie. i kept covering my eyes with my hands. but i heard every blood curdling sound. it was awful! i couldn't even enjoy my snacks; my coca-cola and twizzlers remained untouched. i would never recommend this movie.

# Writing Assignments CONTINUED

## Writing for College Life

Assume you are taking a health course and you have been assigned to write about the importance of sleep. Edit the paragraph for proper use of capitalization. Use your own paper.

according to the national sleep foundation, every person has Individual Sleep Needs, so there is no set number of hours that everyone needs. however, in general, an adult needs seven to eight hours of sleep each night. a constant lack of sleep can lead to several serious consequences. according to dr. dement, lack of sleep increases risk of motor vehicle accidents. lack of sleep may lead to a greater chance of obesity, diabetes, and heart problems. lack of sleep can also lessen a person's ability to pay attention or remember new information. dr. dement is a cofounder of the stanford sleep disorders clinic in stanford, california.

## Writing for Working Life

Assume you are working as a supervisor of the maintenance department for a small printing company. You are writing a letter that claims damages and payment for those damages. Edit this draft of the letter for proper use of capitalization. Use your own paper.

dear mr. rodriguez:

as someone who has used your services for several years, i am very disappointed with the quality of the work performed by your company, best electronic company, on thursday, may 18th of this year. during the repair, your crew damaged carpets, baseboards, and walls. as stated in the work order, you guarantee that you "leave no mess behind." i expect you to pay for the cost of the damages done by your workers denise brown and kevin allgood. photographs of the damages and an estimate of the repair cost are enclosed.

yours truly,

anna b. wright, supervisor
maintenance department
quality print shop

Academic Learning Log

PORTFOLIO

## WHAT HAVE I LEARNED ABOUT CAPITALIZATION?

To test and track your understanding, answer the following questions.

1. Capitalize the .............................. of every sentence.

2. Capitalize the pronoun ........................ .

3. Capitalize the first letter of the first words of ........................ and ........................ .

4. Capitalize the first letter of ........................ words in ........................ .

5. Capitalize the first letter of the ........................ of a person when the title

   ........................ the person's name.

6. Capitalize the first letter of ........................ nouns. Do not capitalize

   ........................ nouns.

7. Capitalize the first letter of ........................ adjectives.

8. **How will I use what I have learned about capitalization?**
   In your notebook, discuss how you will apply to your own writing what you have learned about capitalization.

9. **What do I still need to study about capitalization?**
   In your notebook, describe your ongoing study needs by describing what, when, and how you will continue studying capitalization.

# 34 Revising for Effective Expression

**Chapter Preview**

- What's the Point of Effective Expression?
- Understanding the Point of Effective Expression: One Student Writer's Response
- Applying the Point: Effective Expression

## Effective expression makes language clear and interesting.

Thinking about a real-life situation helps us understand the purpose and need for effective expression in our communication with others. Complete the following activity and answer the question "What's the point of effective expression?"

# What's the Point of Effective Expression?



WRITING FROM LIFE

Practice 1

PHOTOGRAPHIC ORGANIZER: EFFECTIVE EXPRESSION

Assume you received the following email from a coworker. What is your impression of the person based on the language used in the email?

**FROM:** Kendis Moore Kendis@ITsolutions.com
**Date:** January 15, 2008
**TO:** Dwayne <Dwayne@ITsolutions.com>
**SUBJECT:** FW: A Good Cause

FYI

--------Forwarded Message
**From:** "Douglas Whitten"
**Date:** January 15, 2008
**To:** All Employees of Clarke Photography & Printing
**Subject:** A Good Cause!

I know everyone is busy as a bee, so I am not going to beat around the bush. It's time to get the United Way Campaign under way. Last year, we let it fall through the cracks, but this year, we are going to hit the nail on the head and raise tons of money. You may think this is not important, but you're dead wrong. Now don't drop the ball. Be sure to give to the United Way.

**What's the point of effective expression?**

## Understanding the Point of Effective Expression: One Student Writer's Response

The following paragraph offers one writer's reaction to the email from the coworker.

> *I am not impressed with the coworker based on the sound of the memo. It's too informal; it doesn't sound professional at all. And it's boring and uninspiring. I would hit delete after the first sentence. It doesn't sound like the writer takes the campaign very seriously.*

# Applying the Point: Effective Expression

Effective expression is a result of thoughtful word choice. Mark Twain once said, "The difference between the almost right word and the right word is really a large matter—it's the difference between the lightning bug and the lightning." During early drafts, writers often relate thoughts and ideas without concern for word choice. Words or phrases are needlessly repeated, and clichés—overused expressions or ideas—are sometimes included in the draft. This rush to record ideas as they occur makes good use of the writing process *if* we take time to revise for effective expression after we have completed a draft. Effective expression involves concise, active, positive, concrete, creative, and fresh writing. Use the revision process to achieve effective expression.

## Use Concise Language

The most effective writing is concise and to the point. Concise language avoids wordiness—the use of unnecessary or redundant words and phrases that add nothing to the writer's meaning. The following example illustrates the difference between wordiness and concise writing.

**Wordy**

TWO ADJECTIVES THAT MEAN THE SAME THING DESCRIBE SUBJECT "COUNTY"

TWO-WORD VERB; USE OF PASSIVE VOICE

The whole, entire county was warned of flooding by the National Weather Service for the preparation of evacuations.

MULTIPLE, LONG PREPOSITIONAL PHRASES

**Concise**

SUBJECT — VERB; USE OF ACTIVE VOICE — ONE CLEAR ADJECTIVE DESCRIBES OBJECT "COUNTY"

The National Weather Service warned the entire county to prepare to evacuate due to flooding.

MORE CONCISE REVISION OF THE FOUR ORIGINAL PREPOSITIONAL PHRASES

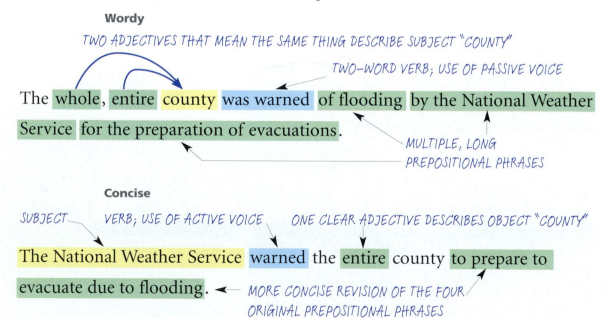

| Wordy Expressions with Revisions for Conciseness | |
|---|---|
| **Wordy** | **Concise** |
| absolutely certain | certain |
| advanced notice | notice |
| has the ability | can |
| he is a man who; she is a woman who | he; she |
| disappear from view | disappear |
| during the same time that | when |
| given the fact that | because |
| in an impatient manner | impatiently |
| in order to | to |
| in spite of the fact | although, though |
| in this day and age | today |
| in today's world | today, currently |
| personal opinion | opinion |
| personally, I think | I think |
| reason why is that | because |
| red in color | red |
| refer back | refer |
| repeat again | repeat |
| small in size | small |
| summarize briefly | summarize |
| there is no doubt but that | no doubt, doubtless |
| the fact that she had not succeeded | her failure |
| this is a topic which | this topic |
| very unique | unique |
| whole entire | whole; entire |

## Practice 2

### USE CONCISE LANGUAGE

Read each sentence and revise it using concise language.

**1.** A lake in southern Chile mysteriously disappeared from view.

**2.** The disappearance of a lake five acres in size is a situation that is puzzling in nature.

Practice 2

3. In March, the lake was exactly the same level as it had always been; by May the whole entire lake had vanished.

4. A river that flowed out of the lake was reduced to a trickle during the same time the lake vanished.

5. Experts suggest that the lake disappeared due to the fact that an earth tremor opened a crack in the ground that acted like a drain.

More practice with effective expression: <www.mywritinglab.com>

## Use Active and Positive Language

The most effective writing uses active, positive language to state ideas. The **active voice** states what somebody or something did. The **passive voice** states what was done to someone or something. Sentences written in the active voice are more concise because the active voice uses fewer words to state an action, and it clearly states the relationship between the subject and the action. In contrast, the passive voice uses more words to state an action, and the relationship between the subject and the action is less clear. The active voice is more direct and more powerful than the passive voice.

**Passive Voice**

THE SUBJECT "ANNA" RECEIVES THE ACTION PERFORMED BY SOMEONE ELSE.

Anna was surprised by her family.

**Active Voice**

THE SUBJECT "FAMILY" PERFORMS THE ACTION.

Anna's family surprised her.

Effective writing also involves stating ideas in the positive, which is more powerful than stating them in the negative. Too often, the use of a negative expression makes language seem unclear. The following chart offers some tips and examples for creating positive language.

| Tips for Creating a Positive Voice |
|---|
| • Say what something **is** instead of what it **is not**.<br>*Negative:* The diet does not allow you to eat as much as you want of such favorites as sweets, chips, and fried foods.<br>*Positive:* The diet allows you to eat your favorite foods in moderate amounts. |
| • Say what **can** be done instead of what **cannot** or **should not** be done.<br>*Negative:* Bridget should not consider auditioning for the singing competition because she has never sung in front of an audience.<br>*Positive:* Bridget can practice singing in front of friends and family to get used to singing in front of an audience; she will then be better prepared for the audition. |
| • Propose an **action** in addition to offering an **apology** or **explanation**.<br>*Negative:* I'm sorry I didn't call last night, but what do you expect? I worked all day and had school until 9:00 p.m.<br>*Positive:* I'm sorry I didn't call last night, but I was feeling overwhelmed with school and work. Perhaps we can meet for coffee when my schedule is less hectic. |

The following chart lists negative expressions in one column and positive revisions to those expressions in the other column.

**Negative Expressions with Revisions to the Positive**

| Negative Expression | Positive Expression |
|---|---|
| cannot lie | must tell the truth |
| cannot reconnect without | reconnect by |
| cannot waste resources | value resources |
| do not forget | remember |
| do not be late | be on time |
| do not be negative | be positive |
| never delay a response | respond quickly |
| never be rude | be polite |
| sorry, we cannot respond until | we will respond by |
| you misunderstood | let me clarify |

## USE ACTIVE AND POSITIVE LANGUAGE

Practice 3

Revise these sentences from passive voice to active voice or from negative statements to positive statements. Share and discuss your answers with a peer or your class.

**1.** Severe weather warnings must not be taken lightly by the public.

---

**2.** Severe weather alerts are issued by the National Weather Service (NWS), yet many do not pay attention to these official warnings.

---

---

Practice 3

3. No one in the warning zone of a weather alert is free from danger.

---

---

4. Minor flooding, moderate flooding, and major flooding are used by the NWS as flood severity categories.

---

---

5. Write a sentence that uses active, positive language. Suggested topic: A Weather Alert.

---

---

More practice with effective expression: <www.mywritinglab.com>

## Use Concrete Language

Another key to effective writing is using **concrete language**. When writers use concrete language, they give readers vivid descriptions that can be visualized. Concrete language is the result of the thoughtful choice of nouns, verbs, adjectives, and adverbs. Your choice of words can mean the difference between writing that is **abstract** (vague, nonspecific writing) and writing that is concrete. Let's look at the difference between abstract and concrete nouns, verbs, adjectives, and adverbs.

An **abstract noun** names an emotion, feeling, idea, or trait detached from the five senses. A **concrete noun** names an animal, person, place, or object that the reader can see, touch, taste, hear, or smell (sensory details). The following chart illustrates the difference between concrete and abstract nouns.

| Abstract Noun | Concrete Noun |
|---|---|
| beauty | rainbow |
| love | kiss |
| strength | steel |
| work | sweaty |

An **abstract verb** or verb phrase tells about a state of being or describes a general or nonspecific action. A **concrete verb** or verb phrase shows a specific action or creates a clear picture for the reader. The following chart illustrates the difference between abstract and concrete verbs and verb phrases.

| Abstract Verb | Concrete Verb |
|---|---|
| He is angry. | He spews curses. |
| I got an "A" on the exam. | I earned an "A" on the exam. |
| Jerome went in the room. | Jerome walked into the room. |
| Jerome went, "Hey." | Jerome said, "Hi." |

An **abstract adjective** is a broad and general description that is open to interpretation based on opinion. A **concrete adjective** shows a specific trait or sensory detail and is not open to interpretation. The best writing relies on the strength of concrete nouns and verbs, so use adjectives only when necessary.

| Abstract Adjective | Concrete Adjective |
|---|---|
| awesome sound | echoing canyon |
| good taste | salty ocean |
| weird behavior | quiet disposition |
| loud music | heavy-metal concert |

An **abstract adverb** is a broad and general description that is open to interpretation based on opinion. A **concrete adverb** shows a specific trait or sensory detail and is not open to interpretation. The best writing relies on the strength of concrete nouns and verbs, so use adverbs only when necessary.

| Abstract Adverb | Concrete Adverb |
|---|---|
| a lot | daily |
| kind of | quietly |
| sort of | gently |
| pretty much | most |
| really | intensely |
| very | extremely |

Practice 4

USE CONCRETE LANGUAGE

Revise these sentences from abstract language to concrete language. Share and discuss your answers with a peer or your class.

**1.** Pretty much all of us go to Lake Tahoe a lot.

---

**2.** Lake Tahoe is a beautiful place that we really enjoy visiting.

---

**3.** The children have a wonderful time and a lot of fun in the water.

**4.** It feels really good to get some rest on the beach.

**5.** Write a sentence that uses concrete language. Suggested topic: A Favorite Vacation Spot.

## Use Creative Expressions: Similes and Metaphors

Creative expressions deepen the reader's understanding of a writer's meaning. Similes and metaphors are two ways you can include creative expression in your writing. Similes and metaphors are figures of speech that compare two unrelated ideas.

A **simile** is an indirect comparison between two ideas that uses *like*, *as*, *as if*, or *as though.*

"LIKE" CREATES AN INDIRECT COMPARISON OF TWO NOUNS/IDEAS

"I put my hands in the pockets and flapped the jacket like a bird's wings."

—Gary Soto, "The Jacket"

A **metaphor** is a direct comparison between two ideas that does **not** use *like*, *as*, *as if*, or *as though.*

"OF" CREATES A DIRECT COMPARISON OF TWO NOUNS/IDEAS

"I returned to the sea of necessity."

—E. B. White, "The Sea and the Wind that Blows"

HELPING VERB "IS" CREATES DIRECT COMPARISON OF TWO NOUNS/IDEAS

"Poverty is an acid that drips on pride until all pride is worn away."

—Jo Goodwin Parker, "What is Poverty?"

*Note:* In the last two examples, the writers clarified or deepened the meaning of an abstract noun by connecting it to a concrete noun. To create similes and metaphors, make a logical connection between an abstract noun and a concrete noun.

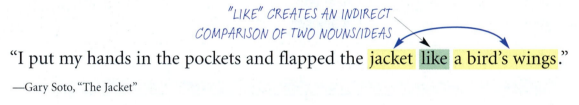

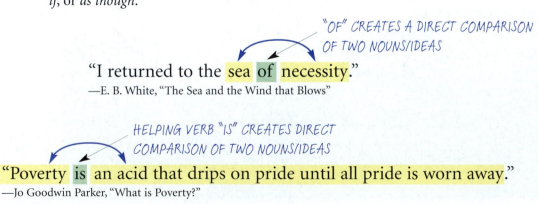

**USE CREATIVE EXPRESSIONS**

Practice 5

Complete the following sentences with a simile or a metaphor. Share and discuss your answers with a peer or your class.

**1.** Hope is like ______________________________

**2.** Addiction is ______________________________

**3.** ______________________________ struck like lightning.

**4.** The President's announcement was greeted with a blizzard of ______________________________

______________________________

**5.** Write a sentence that uses a simile or a metaphor. Suggested topic: A Mother's Love.

______________________________

______________________________

# Use Fresh Language

Effective writing also relies on using fresh language as opposed to clichés. Clichés are weak statements because they have lost their originality and forcefulness; see the example below.

More practice with effective expression: <www.mywritinglab.com>

**Cliché:**

OVERUSED NOUN PHRASE TO REPRESENT NATURE

OVERUSED PHRASE TO DESCRIBE SNOWY WEATHER

Mother Nature covered the ground with a snowy white blanket.

**Fresh language:**

STRONG, ORIGINAL NOUNS AND ADJECTIVES DESCRIBE SNOWY WEATHER IN VIVID DETAIL

"On top of this ice were as many feet of snow. It was all pure white, rolling in gentle undulations where the ice-jams of the freeze-up had formed."

—Jack London, "To Build a Fire"

The following chart lists popular clichés and their meanings.

| Clichés and Their Meanings | |
|---|---|
| **Cliché** | **Meaning** |
| a needle in a haystack | hard to find |
| all thumbs | clumsy |
| as easy as pie | easy |
| beat around the bush | to speak indirectly about something |
| backstabber | an untrustworthy or deceitful person |
| busy as a bee | always working, very busy |
| drop the ball | to fail at a task |
| fall between the cracks | overlooked, not attended to |
| fit to be tied | angry |
| hidden agenda | sneaky |
| hit the nail on the head | to be correct about something |
| like a bull in china shop | tactless, clumsy |
| like a chicken with its head cut off | inefficient, erratic |
| never a dull moment | exciting |
| off your rocker | crazy, poor judgment |
| one foot in the grave | terminally ill |
| one in a million | rare; well-liked |
| splitting hairs | focusing on unimportant details |
| wishy-washy | lack of conviction, unclear |
| water over the dam | a past event that cannot be changed |

Instead of relying on clichés such as the ones presented here, use fresh language as you revise your writing. When logical, create your own similes and metaphors to express your meaning.

Practice 6

USE FRESH LANGUAGE

Revise the following sentences by eliminating the clichés and replacing them with fresh, creative language. Share and discuss your answers with a peer or your class.

**1.** Gerald dropped the ball when he decided to stay in his house during the hurricane.

**2.** Devastating several coastal communities, the tsunami was one in a million.

3. After the storm, emergency rescuers ran around like chickens with their heads cut off.

4. When Tamika saw the water rushing toward her, she thought she had one foot in the grave.

5. Many people were fit to be tied because of the poor response from the Federal Emergency Management Agency (FEMA).

More practice with effective expression: <www.mywritinglab.com>

Practice 7

## EFFECTIVE EXPRESSION REVIEW

Revise the following sentences for effective expression. Remember to use the key ingredients of effective expression—concise, active, positive, concrete, creative, and fresh language.

1. In this day and age, global warming is a topic that is accepted as absolutely the truth.

2. In today's society, the science behind global warming is still thought of as not proven by many.

3. Al Gore is a knight in shining armor fighting the dragon of global warming.

4. Our earth is harmed due to the fact that we do not pay attention to pollution.

5. Write a sentence using effective expression. Suggested topic: Global Warming.

More practice with effective expression: <www.mywritinglab.com>

# Writing Assignments

## Writing for Everyday Life

Assume you are writing a thank-you letter for a graduation gift you received from a relative. Revise this letter using effective expression. Use your own paper.

Dear Grandfather,

Thank you for the wallet and money I got from you. I personally think that you are a man who is very generous and thoughtful. I am as happy as a lark with my new wallet, and the hundred dollars you put inside it made my day. I have always been supported by you. I am filled with gratitude.

## Writing for College Life

Assume you are taking a sociology class and you are studying current events. You are required to write a paragraph discussing the impact on society of a new technological invention. Revise this draft for effective expression. Use your own paper.

The "brain-machine interface" has been developed by Hitachi, Inc. This development has the ability to totally change the way we use technology. The device can be controlled by brain activity, so you don't have to lift a finger to make anything happen. Slight changes in the brain's blood flow are analyzed, and the brain motion is converted to electrical signals. To demonstrate, a reporter was given a cap to wear that was also connected with optical fibers to a toy train. When she did simple math in her head, the train moved. A TV remote controller is being developed by Hitachi's scientists. Soon we may be able to turn on any electrical device with a simple thought.

## Writing for Working Life

Assume you are working at an entry-level position for a firm that offers opportunities for advancement. You need to schedule a week off for personal reasons. Revise the following memo using effective expression. Use your own paper.

> To: Mr. Gordon
>
> From: Raul Estevez
>
> RE: Request for Personal Leave
>
> I am writing you to request personal leave due to the fact that surgery must be performed on my knee that will require a week's recovery time. I wanted to give you advanced notice given the fact that we are short on staff, but I absolutely must be off on the days of July 1 through July 8.

## Academic Learning Log

### WHAT HAVE I LEARNED ABOUT USING EFFECTIVE EXPRESSION?

To test and track your understanding, answer the following questions.

**What have I learned about effective expression?**

1. The most effective writing is __________ and to the point.
2. __________ avoids wordiness.
3. __________ is the use of unnecessary or redundant words and phrases that add nothing to the writer's meaning.
4. The __________ voice states what somebody or something did.
5. The __________ voice states what was done to somebody or something.
6. Stating ideas in the __________ is much more powerful than stating them in the __________.
7. __________ language is the result of the thoughtful choice of nouns, __________, adjectives, and adverbs.
8. A __________ is an indirect comparison between two apparently unrelated ideas.
9. A __________ is a direct comparison between two apparently unrelated ideas.
10. A __________ is a trite or overused expression.
11. **How will I use what I have learned about effective expression?**
    In your notebook, discuss how you will apply to your own writing what you have learned about effective expression. When during the writing process will you apply this knowledge?
12. **What do I still need to study about effective expression?**
    In your notebook, describe your ongoing study needs by describing what, when, and how you will continue studying effective expression.

# 35 Improving Your Spelling

**Chapter Preview**

- What's the Point of Improving Your Spelling?
- Understanding the Point of Improving Your Spelling: One Student Writer's Response
- Applying the Point: Improving Your Spelling

## To spell correctly is to understand the rules for properly arranging letters in a word.

Do you have trouble spelling words? If so, you are not alone. Many people have trouble spelling. Despite these difficulties, it is important to work toward accurate spelling because it is an important part of effective expression. Complete the following activity and answer the question "What's the point of improving your spelling?"

# What's the Point of Improving Your Spelling?

WRITING FROM LIFE

Practice 1

PHOTOGRAPHIC ORGANIZER: IMPROVING YOUR SPELLING

Assume a friend of yours has applied for an internship as a nurse at your local hospital. He is going to send a follow-up letter to express his interest in the position. He has asked you to proofread the first few sentences of the letter he wants to send. Can you find the ten misspelled words in this draft? What impact would misspelled words in this follow-up letter have on your friend's chances of getting the internship?

> I submited a letter of aplication and a résumé earler this month for a nurseing internship with Memrial Hospital. To date, I have not herd from your office. I would like to confirm reciept of my leter and agian state my intrest in the job.

**What's the point of improving your spelling?**

---

---

---

# Understanding the Point of Improving Your Spelling: One Student Writer's Response

The following paragraph offers one writer's reaction to the spelling in the follow-up letter for the nursing internship.

> *Too many misspellings makes the writer of the letter seem uneducated or careless. I would say his poor spelling could cost him the internship. I mean he is probably competing against people who will make a better first impression. It's a good thing he asked someone to read over his letter. I don't know if my spelling is as bad as the writer of the letter, but I do seem to misspell a lot of words. I would love to be a better speller. I want to make a good impression on paper. I mean if it's worth my time to write, it's worth my time to do it correctly, right?*

# Applying the Point: Improving Your Spelling

You can improve your spelling by identifying and correcting patterns of misspellings in your writing. Each writer develops his or her own system for learning and using correct spelling. For example, some writers keep a vocabulary journal of new words or difficult-to-spell words, and most writers use a spell checker as a last step before publishing a piece of writing. The steps, rules, and practices in this chapter are designed to help you develop a system to improve your spelling.

## Five Steps to Improve Your Spelling

Five of the best ways to improve your spelling are to use a spell checker, dictionary, mnemonics, spelling error tracking, and the writing process.

### 1. Use a Spell Checker

Word processing programs such as Microsoft Word provide spell checkers to verify the spellings of words in a document. Beware, however, because spell checkers seldom catch all the errors in a text. In particular, spell checkers fail to spot words that sound alike but differ in meaning, such as *to*, *too*, and *two*. In addition, spell checkers sometimes flag proper nouns (nouns that name specific people, places, and things) as misspellings even though they may be spelled correctly. Thus, carefully consider the reason the spell checker highlights a word. Be cautious about clicking the "change" or "change all" button too quickly. With thoughtful use, a spell checker offers helpful assistance in catching commonly misspelled words.

### 2. Use a Dictionary

Look up misspelled words in a dictionary. Place a dot next to each word you look up in your dictionary to flag it as a word for further study.

Most print dictionaries have guide words at the top of each page to help you locate a word. For each entry, the spelling of the main word is given first in bold type. The word is also divided into syllables. The function or part of speech and the etymology, the history of the word, are also given. It is often helpful to understand the origin of a word since many words in the English language came from other languages. Additional spellings of the word appear at the end of the entry. This listing is especially helpful when letters are dropped or added to create a new word.

Online dictionaries locate words through a search box instead of using guide words. If you misspell a word during your search, online dictionaries usually offer alternate spellings to help you find the word you are looking for. As you study the example shown on the next page from the *Merriam-Webster Online Dictionary*, think about how you will use the information in a dictionary to improve your spelling.

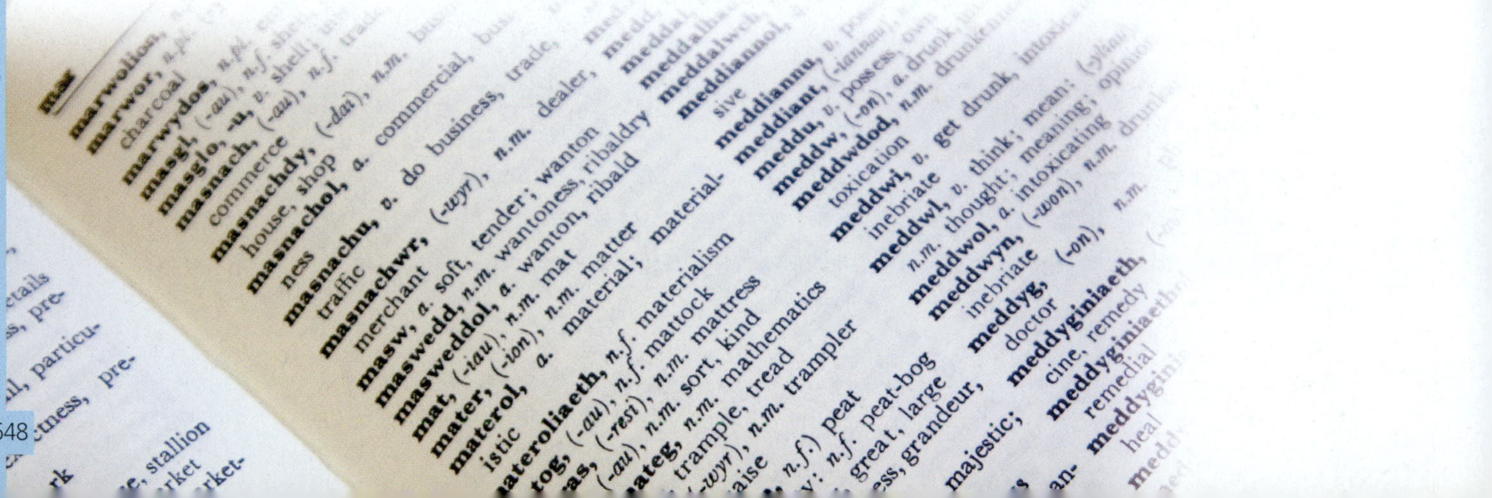

jealous

Main Entry: **jeal·ous**

Pronunciation: \ˈje-ləs\

Function: *adjective*

Etymology: Middle English *jelous*, from Anglo-French *gelus*, from Vulgar Latin **zelosus*, from Late Latin *zelus* zeal — more at ZEAL

Date: 13th century

**1 a:** intolerant of rivalry or unfaithfulness **b:** disposed to suspect rivalry or unfaithfulness

**2:** hostile toward a rival or one believed to enjoy an advantage

**3:** vigilant in guarding a possession <new colonies were *jealous* of their new independence — Scott Buchanan>

— **jeal·ous·ly** *adverb*

— **jeal·ous·ness** *noun*

Source: *Merriam-Webster Online Dictionary* copyright © 2007 by Merriam-Webster, Incorporated http://mw1.merriam-webster.com/dictionary/jealous.

## 3. Use Mnemonics

Mnemonics are different types of memory tricks that can help you remember the correct spelling of words. For example:

- Create a mental or visual image: Picture a person screaming **"e-e-e"** as he passes a cemetery.
- Chunk a word into visual parts: unforgettable = un for get table
- Color-code trouble spots in a word: rec**ei**ve (***not*** recieve).
- Create a silly saying using each letter of the word: The first letter of each word in the following sentence combines to spell ***geography***: **G**eorge's **E**lderly **O**ld **G**randfather **R**ode **A** **P**ig **H**ome **Y**esterday.

## 4. Track Spelling Errors

Identify your misspellings through teacher feedback, peer edits, or a spell checker. In a journal, create a list of words that you have misspelled. Contrast the way you misspell the word with the rule and the correct spelling. Identify information that helps you remember the correct spelling such as the word's function or etymology. Create a memory trick as needed. Choose from the headings in the following example to create your own journal system for improving your spelling.

| Correct Spelling | Function | Etymology | My Misspelling | Spelling Rule | Memory Trick |
|---|---|---|---|---|---|
| argument | noun | Latin *argumentum* (from the verb *arguere*) | arguement | Drop the silent e when a vowel comes right before it. | I lost an "e" in my argument. |

## 5. Use the Writing Process to Improve Your Spelling

As you write, use these tips to ensure accurate spelling:

- [ ] **Decide when during the writing process you will identify and correct misspellings.**
  Some writers who compose as they type or write pause frequently to revise and edit what they just wrote. Others prefer to complete a draft and then check for misspellings during the revision and proofreading phases of the writing process.
- [ ] **Identify and study specialized or difficult words that are connected to your writing assignment.**
  Verify the spelling and etymology (how the word originated) of these words before you begin writing. Find correctly spelled synonyms (words that have similar meanings) for these words. Use this group of correctly spelled words to brainstorm additional details for your writing.
- [ ] **Use one proofreading session to focus only on spelling accuracy**.
  By devoting time to proofreading your spelling, you are more likely to catch errors.
- [ ] **During the proofreading phase, edit on a printed copy of your writing if you are using a word processor.**
  It's easy to overlook errors in text on a computer screen.
- [ ] **Decide how you will track your misspelling patterns as you write.**
  Will you make a list as you go, or will you list troubling words after you have completed your final edit?

Commit to improving your spelling by creating an individual study process.

### Practice 2

**STEPS TO IMPROVING YOUR SPELLING**

Write out the steps you will take to improve your spelling. When possible, tie your steps to the writing process: Prewriting, Drafting, Revising, and Editing. Include additional steps if necessary. Share and discuss your responses with your class or a classmate.

**Step 1** ______________________________

______________________________

**Step 2**

______________________________

**Step 3** ______________________________

______________________________

**Step 4** ______________________________

______________________________

**Step 5** ______________________________

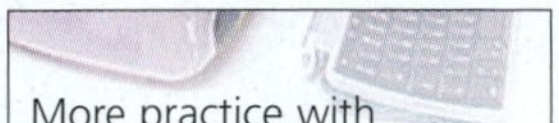

More practice with improving your spelling: <www.mywritinglab.com>

# Rules for Improving Your Spelling

Improving your spelling involves understanding rules about vowel and consonant patterns, as well as rules about the use of suffixes and prefixes.

## Recognize Vowel and Consonant Patterns

Many spelling rules are based on the use of vowels and consonants to form words, so to improve your spelling, take note of the patterns of vowels and consonants in words. Take a moment to look at the following examples to refresh your memory about consonant (c) and vowel (v) patterns in words.

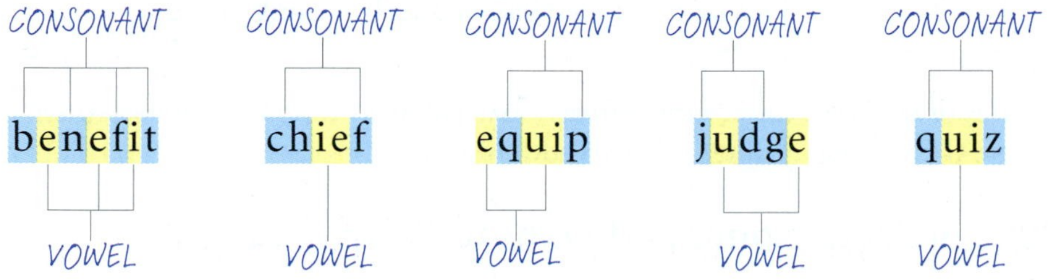


## Understand How Suffixes Are Used

A **suffix** is added to the end of a **base word** (a word's original meaning) to change the use or meaning of the word. For example, the suffixes *-ing* or *-ed* can either change the tense of a verb or change the verb into a noun or an adjective. For example, *walk* is a verb, but adding *-ing* creates the present participle *walking*; adding *-ed* creates the past participle *walked*. The present and past participles can function as verbs, adjectives, or nouns depending on the context in which they are used.

Suffixes begin with either a vowel or a consonant, which affects the spelling rules for adding them to base words. You will learn about the specific ways in which vowels and consonants impact spelling throughout this chapter. The following chart lists a few common vowel and consonant suffixes, along with their meanings and examples.

| **Vowel Suffix** | **Meaning** | **Example** |
|---|---|---|
| -able -ible | able to | touchable, visible |
| -ed | past tense of a verb | talked, walked |
| -en | present or past participle | bitten, written |
| -er | one who is or does | player, adopter |
| -er | comparison | bigger, smaller |
| -es | plural of a noun | dresses, boxes |
| -es | singular present tense of a verb | washes, finishes |
| -ous | full of | dangerous, luxurious |

| Consonant Suffix | Meaning | Example |
|---|---|---|
| -ful | full of | wonderful, careful |
| -ly or -y | like | gently, weekly |
| -ness | state of being | happiness, faithfulness |
| -ment | state of | government, statement |
| -s | plural of a noun | doctors, workers |
| -s | singular present tense of a verb | runs, quits |

The rules of spelling words with suffixes vary. The next several sections explain and illustrate the various spelling rules for adding suffixes.

## Add -*s* or -*es* to Nouns and Verbs to Form the Plural

- **Add -*s* to form the plural of most regular nouns, including those that end with *o*.**

  book + s ⟶ books

  video + s ⟶ videos

- **Add -*es* to nouns that end with a consonant immediately before a final *o*.**

  hero + es ⟶ heroes

- **Add -*s* to most regular verbs to form the singular present tense in the third person.**

  ask + s ⟶ asks

- **Add -*es* to form the plural of nouns and to third person present tense verbs that end in *ch*, *sh*, *s*, *x*, or *z*.**

| **Nouns** | | **Verbs** | |
|---|---|---|---|
| watch + es | watches | catch + es | catches |
| marsh + es | marshes | wash + es | washes |
| bus + es | buses | pass + es | passes |
| mix + es | mixes | buzz + es | buzzes |

## Practice 3

**ADD -*S* OR -*ES* TO NOUNS AND VERBS TO FORM THE PLURAL**

Complete the chart by choosing the appropriate suffix to each of the following base words. Consult a dictionary to check your answers.

| **Base Words** | **Suffixes** | |
|---|---|---|
| | ***-s*** | ***-es*** |
| **1.** church | | |
| **2.** girl | | |
| **3.** potato | | |
| **4.** fax | | |
| **5.** echo | | |
| **6.** embargo | | |
| **7.** glass | | |
| **8.** studio | | |
| **9.** mock | | |

More practice with improving your spelling: <www.mywritinglab.com>

## Double the Final Consonant in Words with One Syllable

Many **one syllable** words end in a **consonant** with a **vowel** immediately **before** it. (*Hint*: Remember **CVC**.) For a word with one syllable, one consonant, and one vowel, double the final consonant when adding a vowel suffix. The final consonant is *not* doubled when adding a consonant suffix.

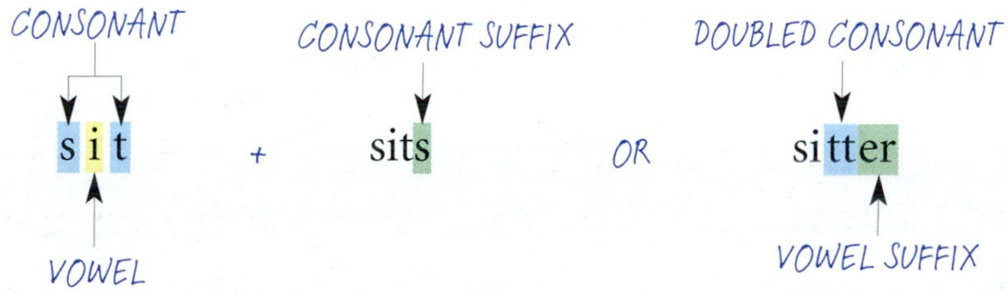


*Exception:* Do not double the final consonant of words that end in *w*, *x*, or *y* as in the following examples: snowing, boxer, obeys.

Practice 4

DOUBLE THE FINAL CONSONANT IN WORDS WITH ONE SYLLABLE

Complete the chart by adding each of the suffixes to the base words. Consult a dictionary to check your answers.

| Base Words | Suffixes | | | |
|---|---|---|---|---|
| | *-s* or *-es* | *-er* | *-ed* | *-ing* |
| **1.** fit | | | | |
| **2.** hop | | | | |
| **3.** flip | | | | |
| **4.** fix | | | | |
| **5.** plan | | | | |

More practice with improving your spelling: <www.mywritinglab.com>

## Double the Final Consonant in Words with More Than One Syllable

Words with more than one syllable often end with a vowel immediately before a **consonant**. (*Hint*: Remember **VC**.) If the final syllable is stressed or emphasized in its pronunciation, **double the final consonant**.

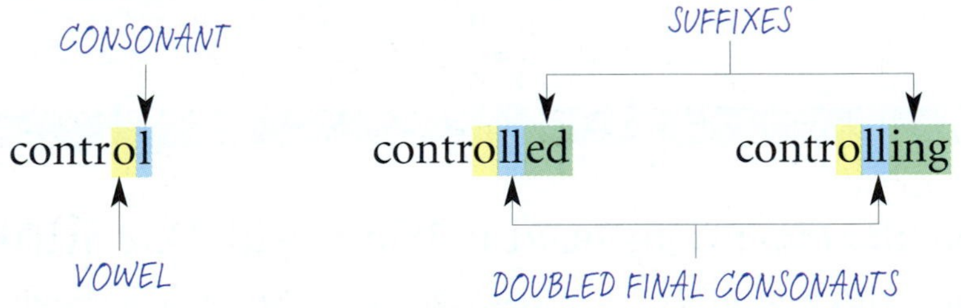


Practice 5

DOUBLE THE FINAL CONSONANT IN WORDS WITH MORE THAN ONE SYLLABLE

Complete the chart by adding the appropriate suffixes to the base words. Consult a dictionary to check your answers.

| Base Words | Suffixes | | | |
|---|---|---|---|---|
| | *-s* | *-ed* | *-er* | *-ing* |
| **1.** acquit | | | — — — | |
| **2.** begin | | — — — | | |
| **3.** infer | | | | |
| **4.** propel | | | | |
| **5.** submit | | | | |
| **6.** transmit | | | | |

More practice with improving your spelling: <www.mywritinglab.com>

## Drop or Keep the Final *E*

- **Drop the *e* when the base *word ends* with a *silent e* and the *suffix begins* with a *vowel.***

advance + -ing ⟶ advancing

- **Drop the *e* when a *vowel comes immediately before* the silent *e*.**

true + -ly ⟶ truly

- **Keep the *e* when the base *word ends* with a silent *e* and the *suffix begins* with a *consonant.***

advance + -ment ⟶ advancement

Practice 6

DROP OR KEEP THE FINAL *E*

Complete the chart by adding the appropriate suffixes to the base words. Consult a dictionary to check your answers.

| Base Words | Suffixes | | | | |
|---|---|---|---|---|---|
| | *-s* | *-ful* | *-ing* | *-ly* | *-ment* |
| **1.** hope | | | | ——— | ——— |
| **2.** live | | ——— | | | ——— |
| **3.** manage | | ——— | | ——— | |
| **4.** state | | ——— | | | |
| **5.** use | | | | ——— | ——— |

More practice with improving your spelling: <www.mywritinglab.com>

## Change or Keep the Final *Y*

- **When a *consonant* appears before the final *y*, change the *y* to *i*.**

supply + -ies ⟶ supplies

- **When a *vowel* appears before the final *y*, keep the *y*.**

obey + -ed ⟶ obeyed

- **Keep the *y* when adding the suffix *-ing*.**

cry + -ing ⟶ crying

Practice 7

CHANGE OR KEEP THE FINAL *Y*

Complete the chart by adding each of the suffixes to the base words. Consult a dictionary to check your answers.

| Base Words | Suffixes | | | | | |
|---|---|---|---|---|---|---|
| | *-es* | *-ed* | *-er* | *-ier* | *-est* | *-ing* |
| **1.** bury | | | — — — | — — — | — — — | |
| **2.** dry | | | | | | |
| **3.** carry | | | — — — | | — — — | |
| **4.** hurry | | | — — — | — — — | — — — | |
| **5.** play | | | | — — — | — — — | |

More practice with improving your spelling: <www.mywritinglab.com>

## Understand How Prefixes Are Used

A prefix added to the beginning of a base word changes the word's meaning, but it does not change the word's spelling. The following chart lists a few common prefixes, their meanings, and example words.

| Prefix | Meaning | Example |
|---|---|---|
| bi- | two | bicycle |
| de- | not | deregulated |
| dis- | not | disagree |
| im- | not | impossible |
| mis- | not | misunderstood |
| pre- | before | preview |
| re- | again | rewrite |
| un- | not | unknown |

Adding a prefix to a word does not alter its spelling.

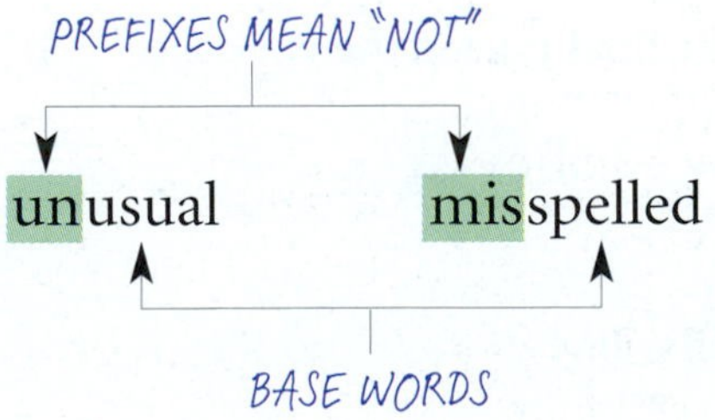

## Practice 8

**USE PREFIXES TO BUILD AND CORRECTLY SPELL NEW WORDS**

Use your dictionary to match words to the correct prefix. Complete the chart by writing the new words created by adding the appropriate prefixes. Consult a dictionary to check your answers.

| **Base Words** | **Prefixes** | | | | |
|---|---|---|---|---|---|
| | ***dis-*** | ***pre-*** | ***pro-*** | ***re-*** | ***un-*** |
| **1.** active | ___ | ___ | | | ___ |
| **2.** qualified | | | ___ | | |
| **3.** satisfied | | ___ | ___ | ___ | |
| **4.** view | ___ | | ___ | | ___ |

More practice with improving your spelling: <www.mywritinglab.com>

## Choose *ie* or *ei*

A helpful way to remember how to use *ie* and *ei* in spelling is to think of the following rhyme:

"***i*** before ***e*** except after ***c*** or when sounds like *ay* as in *neighbor* or *weigh*"

I BEFORE E...

achieve brief chief

... EXCEPT AFTER C ...

receive receipt ceiling

... OR WHEN SOUNDS LIKE "AY"

eight feign vein

There are, however, some exceptions to the *ie*, *ei* rule that should be memorized:

***ie***: species, science, conscience

***ei***: height, either, neither, leisure, seize, counterfeit, foreign, forfeit, sleight, weird

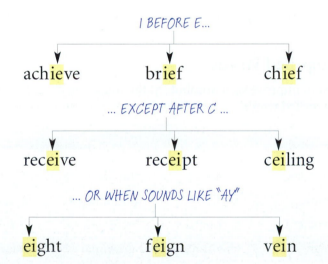

Practice 9

CHOOSE *IE* OR *E*

Underline the correctly spelled word in each pair of words. Consult a dictionary to check your answers.

1. believe ______ beleive ______
2. conceited ______ concieted ______
3. frieght ______ freight ______
4. mischeivous ______ mischievous ______
5. mischief ______ mischeif ______
6. perceive ______ percieve ______
7. recieve ______ receive ______
8. reign ______ riegn ______
9. relieve ______ releive ______
10. veiw ______ view ______

More practice with improving your spelling: <www.mywritinglab.com>

## Commonly Misspelled Words

To aid in your efforts to improve your vocabulary, the following chart lists 120 of the most commonly misspelled words.

**120 Commonly Misspelled Words**

| | | | | |
|---|---|---|---|---|
| absence | calendar | easily | finally | interruption |
| accommodate | ceiling | eight | fundamental | invitation |
| acquire | cemetery | embarrass | generally | irritable |
| across | chief | environment | grammar | island |
| advertise | coming | exaggerate | guarantee | judgment |
| advice | criticize | excellent | humorous | knowledge |
| apparent | definite | except | imaginary | laboratory |
| argument | describe | exercise | imitation | length |
| becoming | develop | experience | incidentally | license |
| beginning | difference | experiment | independent | loneliness |
| believe | dilemma | explanation | intelligent | losing |
| business | disappoint | fascinating | interesting | mathematics |

### 120 Commonly Misspelled Words (continued)

| | | | | |
|---|---|---|---|---|
| medicine | peculiar | prejudice | repetition | succeed |
| minute | perceive | privilege | restaurant | surely |
| miscellaneous | permanent | probably | ridiculous | surprise |
| naturally | persevere | promise | sacrifice | temporary |
| necessary | persuade | proof | scissors | through |
| noticeable | picture | quiet | secretary | twelfth |
| occasion | piece | quit | separate | unusual |
| occurred | planning | quite | shining | using |
| omission | political | receive | sincerely | village |
| optimism | possess | recognize | soldier | weird |
| original | possible | recommend | stopping | whether |
| parallel | prefer | reference | studying | writing |

More practice with improving your spelling: <www.mywritinglab.com>

## Practice 10

### CORRECT MISSPELLED WORDS

Edit the following sentences to correct misspelled words. Cross out each misspelled word and write the correct spelling above it.

1. *Staphylococcus aureus* or a Staph skin infection developes pimples or boils that are ususaly swollen, painful, and filled with pus.

2. People are more likly to aquir a Staph infection thruogh skin-to-skin contact with someone who has a Staph infection.

3. Most Staph skin infections are minor and may be easyly treated.

4. Generaly, a doctor prescribes an antibiotic and drains the infection if necesary.

5. Surly, one way of stoping the spread of Staph infections is to avoid sharing personal items like towels or razors.

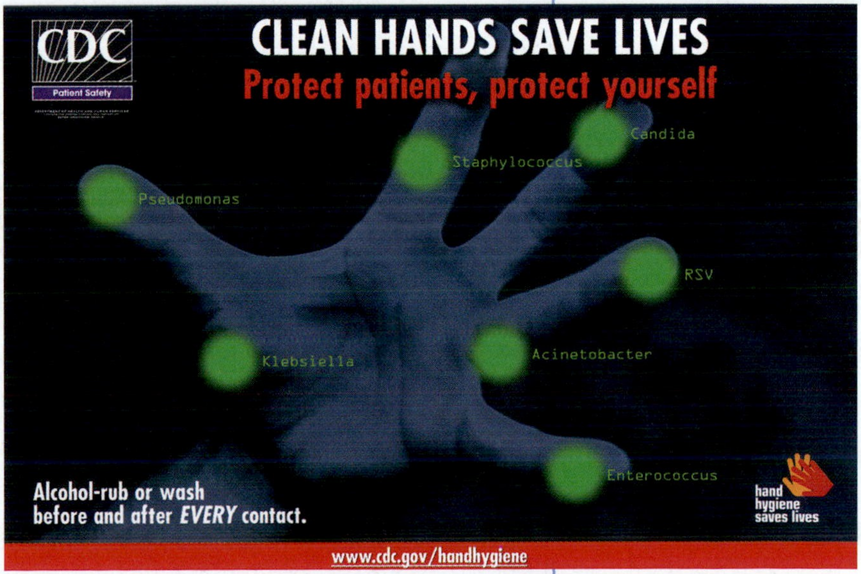

## Practice 11

**SPELLING REVIEW**

Edit the following sentences to correct misspelled words. Cross out each misspelled word and write the correct spelling above it.

**1.** Poor hand hygeine is a sure way of transmiting Staph infections.

**2.** The Centers for Disease Control recomends hand washing and the use of alcohol-based hand rubbs by health care providers.

**3.** Even with the use of gloves, excelent hand hygeine is still necesary.

**4.** An ethical health care provider changes gloves and washs his hands before and after each pateint.

**5.** Simple tasks, such as takeing a person's blood pressure, contaminate the hands of nurses, doctors, and other health care workers.

More practice with improving your spelling: <www.mywritinglab.com>

# Writing Assignments

## Writing for Everyday Life

Assume you recently visited an emergency clinic to get stitches in your foot. You believe you have contracted a Staph infection from one of the clinic's health care providers. You are writing to officially document your complaint against the clinic. Edit the misspellings in the following draft. Use your own paper.

To Whom It May Concern:

On September 24 of this year, I recieve stitchs at your clinic for a deep cut on the bottom of my left foot. While I waited in the examination room for the doctor, a nurse took my blood pressure and my temperature. Then she closly examined my foot. As I lay down to be examined, she lifted my foot onto the table. Much later, it occured to me that she had not washed her hands. I beleive she is the source of the Staph infection that I developed within days of that visit. By writting, I am hopeing to persuade all the staff members of your clinic to remember to wash thier hands.

Sincerly, Jean Martinez

## Writing for College Life

Assume you are taking a college health class. You have been assigned to write a report about the importance of hand washing. Edit the misspellings in the following draft. Use your own paper.

*A recent survey of people in restrooms confirms that the spread of at least some infectious deseases could be curbbed if greater attention were spent on hand washing after going to the bathroom. Dirty hands can spread deseases such as colds and diarrhea and other intestinal problems. Experts say that the problem occurres across the country. According to research, only 60 percent of people useing the restrooms at Pennsylvania Station in New York City washed up. Other cityes have higher rates: 71 precent washed up at a casino in New Orleans, 69 precent at the Golden Gate Park in San Francisco, and 64 precent at a Braves game in Atlanta. Apparantly, women washed up more than men; however, men used soap more often than women did.*

## Writing for Working Life

Assume you are working as a health care provider for a hospital in a small community. You have been asked to research ways to improve the quality of care in your area. You are to present your recommendations in a PowerPoint presentation. Edit the misspellings in the following slide created for the presentation. Use your own paper.

**Monitoring Hand Hygeine Monitoring**

A hand hygeine audit determines health care worker (HCW) compliance with hand hygeine practice. Each department appointes a quality controler. The quality controler observes and records missed opportunites to carry out hand hygeine. Examples of hand hygeine opportunities include:

- Before and after touching a pateint
- After handleing body fluids
- After touching objects involved in the pateint's care
- After removeing gloves

A total of 10 observations should be performmed each month. Completed forms will be submited to the Infection Control Department by the 5th of each month.

PORTFOLIO

# Academic Learning Log

## WHAT HAVE I LEARNED ABOUT IMPROVING SPELLING?

To test and track your understanding, answer the following questions.

**1.** Add .................... to form the plural of regular nouns and regular verbs in the present tense for the singular third person.

**2.** Add .................... to nouns that end with a consonant immediately before a final *o*.

**3.** Add .................... to form the plural of nouns and to the third person present tense of verbs that end in *ch, sh, s, x,* or *z*.

**4.** When a word has one syllable, one consonant and one vowel, .................... the final consonant before adding the suffix.

**5.** When words with more than one syllable end with a .................... immediately before a consonant and the final syllable is stressed, double the final consonant.

**6.** Drop the *e* when the base word ends with a .................... *e* and the suffix begins with a vowel.

**7.** Drop the *e* when a .................... comes immediately before the silent *e*.

**8.** Keep the *e* when the word ends with a silent *e* and the suffix begins with a ....................

**9.** When a .................... appears before the final *y*, change the *y* to *i*.

**10.** When a .................... appears before the final *y*, keep the *y*.

**11.** Keep the *y* when adding the suffix ....................

**12.** Adding a .................... to a word does not alter its spelling.

**13.** "*I* before *e* except after *c* or sounds like .................... as in n*ei*ghbor or w*ei*gh."

**14. How will I use what I have learned about improving spelling?**
In your notebook, discuss how you will apply to your own writing what you have learned about improving spelling.

**15. What do I still need to study about improving spelling?**
In your notebook, write down your ongoing study needs by describing how you will continue to improve your spelling.

PART 8

# Reading Selections

## What's the Connection Between Reading and Writing?

## Understanding the Connection Between Reading and Writing

## Applying the Point: The Connection Between Reading and Writing

## Nineteen Reading Selections

# Reading Selections

## Reading and writing are mirror reflections of the thinking process.

The connection between reading and writing is a natural one. Effective writers are often avid readers. They know that reading and studying well-written pieces by other writers is one way to become a better writer. To begin your thinking about the connection between reading and writing, complete the following activity.

# What's the Connection Between Reading and Writing?

Practice 1

**YOUR COLLEGE EXPERIENCE REQUIRES THAT YOU READ AND WRITE.**

Many students agree that reading and writing are related, but often, they do not actively make use of the connection. To gauge your own understanding and use of the connection between reading and writing, answer the following questions in your notebook. Brainstorm or share your answers in a small group discussion.

- Do you enjoy reading? Why or why not?
- Do you think reading is an important activity? Why or why not?
- Do you enjoy writing? Why or why not?
- Do you think writing is an important activity? Why or why not?
- What do you read for school? For work? For personal enjoyment? For general information?
- If you don't read much, what could or should you read for school, work, personal enjoyment, or general information?
- How often do you write? Why? What kind of writing do you do: journal writing, creative writing, academic assignments, business reports and letters, electronic emailing or blogging?
- What are some specific ways you think reading can help a writer?

# Understanding the Connection Between Reading and Writing

Reading benefits a writer in many ways. For example, by reading, a writer gains the following:

- New vocabulary
- Different opinions on a topic
- Additional facts about a topic
- Details that support an opinion
- Varying ways to apply writing techniques
    - Ways to use punctuation
    - Ways to use fresh or creative expressions
    - Ways to write sentences
    - Ways to organize ideas
    - Ways to open and close an essay

The more you read, the more you know and the more you have to write about.

A major similarity between reading and writing is that each is a thinking process best accomplished in specific stages; careful thought before, during, and after reading a selection or writing a piece improves your ability to do both. The following chart correlates the stages of the reading and the writing processes by listing the similarities between each of their phases.

## The Connection Between Reading and Writing

| | Reading | Writing |
|---|---|---|
| Phase 1: | Preread: Ask questions and skim details to discover the writer's purpose and point | Prewrite: Ask questions to generate details to discover your purpose and point for writing; read for information to use in your writing |
| Phase 2: | Read: Comprehend the writer's purpose and point; take note of key words, main ideas, major supports | Draft: Communicate your purpose and point with the use of key words, main ideas, and supporting details |
| Phase 3: | Review and Reflect: Achieve and reinforce clear understanding of the writer's purpose and point; adjust your views based on new information gained through reading | Revise: Rephrase or reorganize ideas to clearly support your point; ensure reader's understanding of your purpose and point |
| Phase 4: | Record: Discuss changes in your thinking based on new information learned through reading; respond to writer's ideas with your new insights based on new understandings; use all the phases of the writing process | Edit: Create an error-free draft that reflects your new insights and skills as a writer |

As you can see, reading and writing mirror each other. Becoming strong in one makes you strong in the other.

### Practice 2

Working together with a small group of your peers, use the reporter's questions (*Who? What? When? Where? How? Why?*) to generate prereading and prewriting questions. Create general questions about the writer's purpose, main idea, supporting details, logical order, or word choice. Use your own paper.

# Applying the Point: The Connection Between Reading and Writing

The fundamental connection between reading and writing is thinking: thinking about the meaning of what you read and what you say, and thinking about the connection between what you read and what you write. To fully realize the connection between reading and writing, you need to be an active and focused thinker. Two active thinking-reading-writing tasks are annotating a text and writing a summary. The following discussions take you through several steps that show you how to think, read, think again, reread, and then write—as a strategy to improve your writing.

## How to Annotate a Text

Use your writing skills throughout the reading process to ensure that you are an active thinker. Annotate the text, take notes, and write journal entries, summaries, and critical responses to what you read. Annotating the text before and during reading is an active thinking-reading-writing strategy. You have been taught to ask questions as a prereading thinking task. When you read, annotate your text as you find the answers to your questions.

The word *annotate* suggests that you "take notes" on the page of the text. Writing notes in the margin of the page as you read focuses your attention and improves your concentration. Annotating also will improve your understanding of the writer's purpose and point. You can note questions or answers quickly where they occur, move on in your reading, and later return to those details for clarification. In addition to writing notes, you can underline, circle, or highlight important terms, definitions, examples, or other key ideas. After reading, a review of your annotations will make responding to the material easier and more efficient. The following techniques are often used to annotate a text. Use these as guidelines to develop your own system for annotating a text.

| Annotation Techniques |
|---|
| • Underline the main idea once. |
| • Underline major supporting details twice. |
| • Circle or highlight key words or special terms. |
| • Place small question marks above unknown words. |
| • Signal steps in a process or list by using numbers. |
| • Point out important concepts with symbols such as a star or a check. |
| • Write recall questions in the margin where the answer is found. |
| • Write a statement for an implied idea. |
| • Write a summary. |

Use your annotations to guide your written response to a piece of writing. The following selection has been annotated for you as an illustration.

Implied Main Idea: Lincoln preserved the UNION of the states; both he and the United States are immortal.

**The Death of President Lincoln**

*By Walt Whitman*

*April 16, '65.*—I find in my notes of the time, this passage on the death of Abraham Lincoln: He leaves for America's history and biography, so far, not only its most dramatic reminiscence ^memories —he leaves, in my opinion, the greatest, best, most characteristic, artistic, moral personality. Not but that he had faults, and show'd them in the Presidency; but honesty, goodness, shrewdness, conscience, and (a new virtue, unknown to other lands, and hardly yet really known here, but the foundation and tie of all, as the future will grandly develop,) UNIONISM ^keeping the United States undivided! in its truest and amplest sense, form'd the hard-pan of his character. These he seal'd with his life. The tragic splendor of his death, purging, illuminating all, throws round his form, his head, an aureole ^?crown? that will remain and will grow brighter through time, while history lives, and love of country lasts. By many has this Union been help'd; but if one name, one man, must be pick'd out, he, most of all, is the conservator ^legal guardian or keeper of it, to the future. He was assassinated—but the Union is not assassinated—*ca ira!* ^?French expression for "it will be fine" One falls, and another falls. The soldier drops, sinks like a wave—but the ranks of the ocean eternally press on. Death does its work, obliterates ^? literates ^? a hundred, a thousand—President, general, captain, private—but the Nation is immortal.

—Whitman, Walt. *Prose Works*. Philadelphia: David McKay, 1892; Bartleby.com, 2000. www.bartleby.com/229/. 12 August 2007.

Practice 3

Choose a selection from the 19 reading selections. Annotate the text. After you have annotated the text, recall and record in your notebook what you remember about the selection.

## How to Write a Summary

A summary includes only the most important points of a text. A summary is a restatement of the main idea and the major supporting details. The length of the summary should reflect the length of the passage you are trying to understand. For example, a paragraph might be summarized in a sentence or two; an article might be summarized in a paragraph, and a much longer document may be summarized in several paragraphs.

Writing a summary by relying on the annotations you make during reading is an excellent way to check your understanding of what you read. Always use the writer's name and the title of the text in your summary. The following summary is based on the annotations of the Walt Whitman piece about Abraham Lincoln's death.

*In his short note "The Death of President Lincoln," dated April 16, 1865, Walt Whitman honors the memory of the fallen president for his devotion to "Unionism," for being a faithful keeper of the future, for ensuring that it will be fine and that the "Nation is immortal."*

**Practice 4**

Write a summary based on the annotations you made for the reading selection you used in Practice 3. Use your own paper.

## A Reading Strategy for a Writer

As you read the 19 selections included in this section, use the following reading strategy to make the connection between reading and writing. Read each selection three times. Read it once just to enjoy the writing. Then, reread the piece to annotate it for understanding. Then, read a third time to study the piece more closely to prepare for a written response. The following steps are a guide to how to get the most out of your reading.

### Reading Like a Writer

**Before Reading** Write a journal entry about the topic, title, and vocabulary. What do you already know, believe, or feel about the topic? Skim the text to identify and look up new or difficult words.

**During Reading** Annotate the text. Underline or highlight key terms, definitions, and main ideas. Generate questions to guide your thinking as you read; these questions will help you recall information after you read. Look for the answers to these questions and annotate the text when you come across the answers. Many college textbooks provide comprehension questions after a section of information. Feel free to use these after reading questions to focus your attention as you read.

**After Reading** Think, discuss, and write about what you read. Each of the 19 reading selections has four discussion questions about the writer's main idea, relevant details, logical order, and effective expression. These directed thinking activities are called "After Reading Discussion Questions: Meaning, Structure, and Expression." Your writing will improve as you learn how other writers handle these elements.

**Discuss it** Use your annotations to compare your views about a text with those of your classmates. Be open to ideas you had not considered. Add information to your notes. Discuss possible written responses.

**Write about it** Respond in writing to the text. Each of the 19 reading selections has three activities called "Thinking Prompts to Move from Reading to Writing."

# Nineteen Reading Selections

## Description

### Snow

**JOHN HAINES**

John Haines, born in Norfolk, Virginia, in 1924, spent more than twenty years homesteading in Alaska. He is also an award-winning author of more than ten collections of poetry and has published a book of essays entitled *Fables and Distances: New and Selected Essays* (1996). The following essay is an excerpt from *The Stars, the Snow, the Fire: Twenty-five Years in the Northern Wilderness.*

**Before Reading** Write a journal entry about your experience with the outdoors. Do you enjoy being outdoors? Why or why not? What is your favorite season?

To one who lives in the snow and watches it day by day, it is a book to be read. The pages turn as the wind blows; the characters shift and the images formed by their combinations change in meaning, but the language remains the same. It is a shadow language, spoken by things that have gone by and will come again. The same text has been written there for thousands of years, though I was not here, and will not be here in winters to come, to read it. These seemingly random ways, these paths, these beds, these footprints, these hard, round pellets in the snow: they all have meaning. Dark things may be written there, news of other lives, their sorties and excursions, their terrors and deaths. The tiny feet of a shrew or a vole make a brief, erratic pattern across the snow, and here is a hole down which the animal goes. And now the track of an ermine comes this way, swift and searching, and he too goes down that white-shadow of a hole. 1

A wolverine, and the loping, toed-in track I followed uphill for two miles one spring morning, until it finally dropped away into another watershed and I gave up following it. I wanted to see where he would go and what he would do. But he just went on, certain of where he was going, and nothing came of it for me to see but that sure and steady track in the snowcrust, and the sunlight strong in my eyes. 2

Snow blows across the highway before me as I walk—little, wavering trails of it swept along like a people dispersed. The snow people—where are they going? Some great danger must pursue 3 them. They hurry and fall, the wind gives them a push, they get up and go on again.

4 I was walking home from Redmond Creek one morning late in January. On a divide between two watersheds I came upon the scene of a battle between a moose and three wolves. The story was written plainly in the snow at my feet. The wolves had come in from the west, following an old trail from the Salcha River, and had found the moose feeding in an open stretch of the overgrown road I was walking.

5 The sign was fresh, it must have happened the night before. The snow was torn up, with chunks of frozen moss and broken sticks scattered about; here and there, swatches of moose hair. A confusion of tracks in the trampled snow—the splayed, stabbing feet of the moose, the big, furred pads and spread toenails of the wolves.

6 I walked on, watching the snow. The moose was large and alone, almost certainly a bull. In one place he backed himself into a low, brush-hung bank to protect his rear. The wolves moved away from him—those moose feet are dangerous. The moose turned, ran on for fifty yards, and the fight began again. It became a running, broken flight that went on for nearly half a mile in the changing, rutted terrain, the red morning light coming across the hills from the sun low in the south. A pattern shifting and uncertain; the wolves relenting, running out into the brush in a wide circle, and closing again: another patch of moose hair in the trodden snow.

7 I felt that I knew those wolves. I had seen their tracks several times before during that winter, and once they had taken a marten from one of my traps. I believed them to be a female and two nearly grown pups. If I was right, she may have been teaching them how to hunt, and all that turmoil in the snow may have been the serious play of things that must kill to live. But I saw no blood sign that morning, and the moose seemed to have gotten the better of the fight. At the end of it he plunged away into thick alder brush. I saw his tracks, moving more slowly now, as he climbed through a low saddle, going north in the shallow, unbroken snow. The three wolves trotted east toward Banner Creek.

8 What might have been silence, an unwritten page, an absence, spoke to me as clearly as if I had been there to see it. I have imagined a man who might live as the coldest scholar on earth, who followed each clue in the snow, writing a book as he went. It would be the history of snow, the book of winter. A thousand-year text to be read by a people hunting these hills in a distant time. Who was here, and who has gone? What were their names? What did they kill and eat? Whom did they leave behind?

## Vocabulary

Before, during, and after reading the selection, annotate the text and write in your journal. Create a list of vocabulary words, along with their definitions, and give examples of their use from the selection you just read.

## After Reading Discussion Questions: Meaning, Structure, and Expression

1. **Main Idea:** Work as a group to write a summary that answers the following questions: What purpose did John Haines have for writing this essay? Who is his intended audience? What is the main idea of the essay?
2. **Relevant Details:** Haines states "To one who lives in the snow and watches it day by day, it is a book to be read." How does the incident with the moose support this point?
3. **Logical Order:** Paragraphs 1 through 3 and paragraph 8 focus on the snow, and paragraphs 4 through 7 tell about the wolves and the moose. Would the essay be

just as effective if it began with the incident about the wolves and the moose and then made the point about snow? Why or why not?

4. **Effective Expression:** According to a *Washington Post Book World* review, "Haines is a poet who crafts each sentence piece by piece … slowly, carefully, each word examined meticulously for rightness before being slid into place." Identify three examples of Haines's use of words that you find particularly effective. Discuss the reasons for your selections.

## Thinking Prompts to Move from Reading to Writing

1. Haines uses vivid sensory details in his descriptions of the snow, the wolves, and the moose to create strong visual images in his reader's mind. No doubt, he wrote what he had closely observed through experience. Use vivid sensory details to describe a place or event in nature that you have experienced. Choose details that make a point about the scene such as *nature soothes in times of trouble* or *nature teaches harsh lessons.*
2. Haines effectively describes the nature or temperament of the wolves and the moose based on their physical traits and behaviors. Write a description of a pet or animal that reveals its personality, temperament, or nature.

# Maya Lin's Design Submission to the Vietnam Memorial Competition

MAYA LIN

Born in 1959 in Athens, Ohio, Maya Lin, as a senior at Yale University, submitted the winning design in a national competition for the Vietnam Veterans Memorial that now stands in Washington, D.C. Lin, a Chinese American, designs spaces that make room for individuals within the landscape.

**Before Reading** Write a journal entry about the Vietnam Memorial. What do you know about it? Have you seen it? What was its impact on you? If you have not seen it, do you want to? Why or why not? Why are monuments and memorials important?

Walking through this park-like area, the memorial appears as a rift in the earth—a long, polished black stone wall, emerging from and receding into the earth. Approaching the memorial, the ground slopes gently downward, and the low walls emerging on either side, growing out of the earth, extend and converge at a point below and ahead. Walking into the grassy site contained by the walls of the memorial we can barely make out the carved names upon the memorial's walls. These names, seemingly infinite in number, convey the sense of overwhelming numbers, while unifying those individuals into a whole. For this memorial is meant not as a monument to the individual but rather, as a memorial to the men and women who died during this war, as a whole. 1

The memorial is composed not as an unchanging monument, but as a moving composition, to be understood as we move into and out of it; the passage itself is gradual, the descent to the origin slow, but it is at the origin that the meaning of the memorial is to be fully understood. At the intersection 2 of these walls, on the right side, at the wall's top, is carved the date of the first death. It is followed by the names of those who have died in the war, in chronological order. These names continue on this wall, appearing to recede into the earth at the wall's end. The names resume on the left wall, as the wall emerges from the earth, continuing back to the origin, where the date of the last death is carved, at the bottom of this wall. Thus the war's beginning and end meet; the war is "complete," coming full circle, yet broken by the earth that bounds the angle's open side, and contained within the earth itself. As we turn to leave, we see these walls stretching into the distance, directing us to the Washington Monument, to the left, and the Lincoln Memorial, to the right, thus bringing the Vietnam Memorial into an historical context. We the living are brought to a concrete realization of these deaths.

Brought to a sharp awareness of such a loss, it is up to each individual to 3
resolve or come to terms with this loss. For death, is in the end a personal and private matter, and the area contained with this memorial is a quiet place, meant for personal reflection and private reckoning. The black granite walls, each two hundred feet long, and ten feet below ground at their lowest point (gradually ascending toward ground level) effectively act as a sound barrier, yet are of such a height and length so as not to appear threatening or enclosing. The actual area is wide and shallow, allowing for a sense of privacy, and the sunlight from the memorial's southern exposure along with the grassy park surrounding and within its walls, contribute to the serenity of the area. Thus this memorial is for those who have died, and for us to remember them.

The memorial's origin is located approximately at the center of the site; its 4
legs each extending two hundred feet towards the Washington Monument and the Lincoln Memorial. The walls, contained on one side by the earth, are ten feet below ground at their point of origin, gradually lessening in height, until they finally recede totally into the earth, at their ends. The walls are to be made of hard, polished black granite, with the names to be carved in simple Trajan letter. The memorial's construction involves recontouring the area within the wall's boundaries, so as to provide for an easily accessible descent, but as much of the site as possible should be left untouched. The area should remain as a park, for all to enjoy.

## Vocabulary

Before, during, and after reading the selection, annotate the text and write in your journal. Create a list of vocabulary words, along with their definitions, and give examples of their use from the selection you just read.

## After Reading Discussion Questions: Meaning, Structure, and Expression

1. **Main Idea:** Work as a group to write a summary that answers the following questions: What purpose did Maya Lin have for writing this essay? Who is her intended audience? What is the main idea of the essay?
2. **Relevant Details:** Lin writes, "For death, is in the end a personal and private matter, and the area contained with this memorial is a quiet place, meant for personal reflection and private reckoning." Based on the details in her description, how does the memorial represent this belief?
3. **Logical Order:** As Lin gives her physical description of the memorial, she explains the significance of each detail. Do her explanations help create a mental image of the memorial? Would it have been just as effective to give an uninterrupted physical description and then explain the purpose of each detail in a separate section? Why or why not?

4. **Effective Expression:** Of the 1,421 essays submitted in the design competition for the Vietnam Memorial, this essay won. In what ways did Lin use effective expression to communicate her vision? Identify three effective expressions in the essay. Discuss the reasons for your selections.

## Thinking Prompts to Move from Reading to Writing

1. Just as the memorials erected in Washington, D.C. represent people and events of historical significance, many communities build memorials to honor local individuals, groups of people, or events. Describe such a memorial in your community. Use your description to convey the significance of the memorial.
2. Identify a person, place, or event that is worthy of a memorial. Design a memorial and write an essay that describes your design and the significance of the honor.

# Narration

## New Directions

MAYA ANGELOU

An acclaimed poet, award-winning writer, activist, performer, director, and teacher, Maya Angelou was born on April 4, 1928, in St. Louis and raised in Stamps, Arkansas. Dr. Angelou has authored twelve bestselling books including *I Know Why the Caged Bird Sings* and her current bestseller *A Song Flung Up to Heaven.* In January 1993, she became only the second poet in U.S. history to have the honor of writing and reciting her original work at a Presidential Inauguration. Angelou is hailed as one of the great voices of contemporary literature. The following essay is an excerpt from her book *Wouldn't Take Nothing for My Journey Now* (1993).

**Before Reading** Write a journal entry about making a life change. Have you ever made a significant change in your life? What were the advantages or disadvantages of making the change? Was it easy? If life has not changed for you, what would you change about your life if you could?

In 1903 the late Mrs. Annie Johnson of Arkansas found herself with two toddling sons, very little money, a slight ability to read and add simple numbers. To this picture add a disastrous marriage and the burdensome fact that Mrs. Johnson was a Negro. 1

When she told her husband, Mr. William Johnson, of her dissatisfaction with their marriage, he conceded that he too found it to be less than he expected and had been secretly hoping to leave and study religion. He added that he thought God was calling him not only to preach but to do so in Enid, Oklahoma. He did not tell her that he knew a minister in Enid with whom he could study and who had a friendly, unmarried daughter. They parted amicably, Annie keeping the one-room house and William taking most of the cash to carry himself to Oklahoma. 2

Annie, over six feet tall, big-boned, decided that she would not go to work as a domestic and leave her "precious babes" to anyone else's care. There was no possibility of being hired at the town's cotton gin or lumber mill, but maybe there was a way to make the two factories work for her. In her words, "I looked up the road I was going and back the way I come, and since I wasn't satisfied, I decided to step off the road and cut me a new path." She told herself that she wasn't a fancy cook but that she could "mix groceries well enough to scare hunger away from a starving man." 3

She made her plans meticulously and in secret. One early evening to see if she was ready, she placed stones in two five gallon pails and carried them three miles to the cotton gin. She rested a little, and then, discarding some rocks, she walked in the darkness to the saw mill five miles farther along the 4 dirt road. On her way back to her little house and her babies, she dumped the remaining rocks along the path.

That same night she worked into the early hours boiling chicken and 5
frying ham. She made dough and filled the rolled-out pastry with meat. At last she went to sleep.

The next morning she left her house carrying the meat pies, lard, an iron 6
brazier, and coals for a fire. Just before lunch she appeared in an empty lot behind the cotton gin. As the dinner noon bell rang, she dropped the savors into boiling fat, and the aroma rose and floated over to the workers who spilled out of the gin, covered with white lint, looking like specters.

Most workers had brought their lunches of pinto beans and biscuits or 7
crackers, onions and cans of sardines, but they were tempted by the hot meat pies which Annie ladled out of the fat. She wrapped them in newspapers, which soaked up the grease, and offered them for sale at a nickel each. Although business was slow, those first days Annie was determined. She balanced her appearances between the two hours of activity.

So, on Monday if she offered hot fresh pies at the cotton gin and sold the 8
remaining cooled-down pies at the lumber mill for three cents, then on Tuesday she went first to the lumber mill presenting fresh, just-cooked pies as the lumbermen covered in sawdust emerged from the mill.

For the next few years, on balmy spring days, blistering summer noons, 9
and cold, wet, and wintry middays, Annie never disappointed her customers, who could count on seeing the tall, brown-skin woman bent over her brazier, carefully turning the meat pies. When she felt certain that the workers had become dependent on her, she built a stall between the two hives of industry and let the men run to her for their lunchtime provisions.

She had indeed stepped from the road which seemed to have been chosen 10
for her and cut herself a brand-new path. In years that stall became a store where customers could buy cheese, meal, syrup, cookies, candy, writing tablets, pickles, canned goods, fresh fruit, soft drinks, coal, oil, and leather soles for worn-out shoes.

Each of us has the right and the responsibility to assess the roads which lie 11
ahead, and those over which we have traveled, and if the future road looms ominous or unpromising, and the roads back uninviting, then we need to gather our resolve and, carrying only the necessary baggage, step off that road into another direction. If the new choice is also unpalatable, without embarrassment, we must be ready to change that as well.

## Vocabulary

Before, during, and after reading the selection, annotate the text and write in your journal. Create a list of vocabulary words, along with their definitions, and give examples of their use from the selection you just read.

## After Reading Discussion Questions: Meaning, Structure, and Expression

1. **Main Idea:** Work as a group to write a summary that answers the following questions: What purpose did Maya Angelou have for writing this piece? Who is her intended audience? What is the main idea of the essay? What is the significance of the title of the book from which the selection was taken? How does this piece reflect that title?

2. **Relevant Details:** Angelou captures the reality of daily life in1903 for Annie Johnson and her community. List the details that paint this realistic picture; consider organizing your list based on sensory details. Describe the society or type of community in which Johnson lived. Are any of the details of this story similar to or different from today's society or parts of your community? In what ways?
3. **Logical Order:** Angelou ends her essay with a paragraph that explains the lesson she wants her reader to learn from Johnson's life. What is the impact of this paragraph on you as a reader? Is the concluding paragraph necessary? Why or why not? Why do you think Angelou waits to the end of the essay to explain her point? Would the essay be as effective if she began by stating this point? Why or why not?
4. **Effective Expression:** A key statement in the essay is made by Annie Johnson, "I looked up the road I was going and back the way I come, and since I wasn't satisfied, I decided to step off the road and cut me a new path." Explain the meaning of the metaphors "road" and "path." What "road" was Johnson on? What "path" did she cut for herself? Are these metaphors effective? Why or why not?

## Thinking Prompts to Move from Reading to Writing

1. Think of an important lesson you have learned, or a truth about life that you think everyone needs to know. Write a narrative essay that illustrates this lesson or important truth about life.
2. Have you or someone you know made a decision to make a major life change? Was the change positive or negative? Was the change difficult to make? In the end, was the change worth the effort? Write a narrative that illustrates the significance of making a decision to change.

# Confessions

AMY TAN

Born in 1952 to immigrant parents from China, Amy Tan is the award-winning author of several novels, including her widely popular and critically acclaimed novel *The Joy Luck Club*. Tragically, Tan's father and oldest brother both died of brain tumors within a year of each other, and Tan was in constant conflict with her mother. Tan's work has been translated into 35 languages, including Spanish, French, Chinese, Arabic, and Hebrew. The following selection is an excerpt from her autobiographical collection of essays *The Opposite of Fate*.

**Before Reading** Write a journal entry about the conflicts within a family. Have you ever had a terrible fight with a family member? How did it make you feel? Do mothers and daughters or fathers and sons experience a particular kind of conflict?

My mother's thoughts reach back like the winter tide, exposing the wreckage of a former shore. Often she's mired in 1967, 1968, the years my older brother and my father died. 1

1968 was also the year she took me and my little brother—Didi—across the Atlantic to Switzerland, a place so preposterously different that she knew she had to give up grieving simply to survive. That year, she remembers, she was very, very sad. I too remember. I was sixteen then, and I recall a late-night hour when my mother and I were arguing in the chalet, that tinderbox of emotion where we lived. 2

She had pushed me into the small bedroom we shared, and as she slapped me about the head, I backed into a corner, by a window that looked out on the lake, the Alps, the beautiful outside world. My mother was furious because I had a boyfriend. She was shouting that he was a drug addict, a bad man who would use me for sex and throw me away like leftover garbage. 3

"Stop seeing him!" she ordered. 4

I shook my head. The more she beat me, the more implacable I became, and this in turn fueled her outrage. 5

"You didn't love you daddy or Peter! When they die you not even sad." 6

I kept my face to the window, unmoved. What does she know about sad? 7

She sobbed and beat her chest. "I rather kill myself before see you destroy you life!" 8

Suicide. How many times had she threatened that before? 9

"I wish you the one die! Not Peter, not Daddy." 10

She had just confirmed what I had always suspected. Now she flew at me with her fists. 11

"I rather kill you! I rather see you die!" 12

And then, perhaps horrified by what she had just said, she fled the room. Thank God that was over. I wished I had a cigarette to smoke. Suddenly she was back. She slammed the door shut, latched it, then locked it with a key. I saw the flash of a meat cleaver just before she pushed me to the wall and brought the blade's edge to within an inch of my throat. Her eyes were like a wild animal's, shiny, fixated on the kill. In an excited voice she said, "First, I kill you. Then Didi and me, our whole family destroy!" She smiled, her chest heaving. "Why you don't cry?" She pressed the blade closer and I could feel her breath gusting. 13

Was she bluffing? If she did kill me, so what? Who would care? While she rambled, a voice within me was whimpering, "This is sad, this is so sad." 14

For ten minutes, fifteen, longer, I straddled these two thoughts—that it didn't matter if I died, that it would be eternally sad if I did—until all at once I felt a snap, then a rush of hope into a vacuum, and I was crying, I was babbling my confession: "I want to live. I want to live." 15

For twenty-five years I forgot that day, and when the memory of what happened surfaced unexpectedly at a writers' workshop in which we recalled our worst moments, I was shaking, wondering to myself, Did she really mean to kill me? If I had not pleaded with her, would she have pushed down on the cleaver and ended my life? 16

I wanted to go to my mother and ask. Yet I couldn't, not until much later, when she became forgetful and I learned she had Alzheimer's disease. I knew that if I didn't ask her certain questions now, I would never know the real answers. 17

So I asked. 18

"Angry? Slap you?" she said, and laughed. "No, no, *no.* You always good girl, never even need to spank, not even one time." 19

How wonderful to hear her say what was never true, yet now would be forever so. 20

## Vocabulary

Before, during, and after reading the selection, annotate the text and write in your journal. Create a list of vocabulary words, along with their definitions, and give examples of their use from the selection you just read.

## After Reading Discussion Questions: Meaning, Structure, and Expression

1. **Main Idea:** Work as a group to write a summary that answers the following questions: What purpose did Amy Tan have for writing this essay? Who is her intended audience? What is the main idea of the essay? What is the significance of the title?
2. **Relevant Details:** Tan often implies a main idea through the use of well-chosen details that draw a vivid picture. Paragraph 13 describes a shocking scene. What point is Tan making with these details? How do these details fulfill her purpose and support her main idea? Why would Tan reveal so much personal and painful information?
3. **Logical Order:** Tan sets her narrative up as a flashback to an unpleasant memory. Later, in paragraph 16, she tells us she remembered this incident in a writing workshop 25 years after it occurred. Why do you think she waited to tell us why or how she remembered the incident? Would the essay be as effective if she had begun the narrative from the moment she recalled the incident in the workshop? Why or why not?
4. **Effective Expression:** Tan begins the essay with a simile, an indirect comparison between two things using *like* or *as*: "My mother's thoughts reach back like the winter tide, exposing the wreckage of a former shore." How are her mother's thoughts similar to the *winter tide*? To what do *wreckage* and *former shore* refer?

## Thinking Prompts to Move from Reading to Writing

1. The conflict between parent and child is age-old and universal. In her essay, Tan shows us how this timeless conflict affected her relationship with her mother. Write a narrative about a conflict between a parent and child that shows the impact of the conflict.
2. "Confessions" is a painful admission of a "worst moment" in both Amy Tan's life and her mother's life. Her confession reveals personal and potentially embarrassing information. Often, we gain wisdom and understanding through conflict and suffering. However, not every writer feels comfortable making a point through a personal confession. Find a story in the news about a "worst moment" in someone's life. Write a narrative that makes a point about the incident.

# Process

## How to Write a Personal Letter

GARRISON KEILLOR

Born in Anoka, Minnesota, in 1942, Garrison Keillor is the host and writer of *A Prairie Home Companion* and *The Writer's Almanac* heard on public radio stations across the country and the author of more than a dozen books, including *Lake Wobegon Days, The Book of Guys, Love Me, Homegrown Democrat,* and *Pontoon: A Novel of Lake Wobegon.*

**Before Reading** Write a journal entry about letter writing. Do you or does anyone you know write letters? Why do you think letter writing is declining? How is writing a personal letter different from other kinds of writing?

1 We shy people need to write a letter now and then, or else we'll dry up and blow away. It's true. And I speak as one who loves to reach for the phone, dial the number, and talk. The telephone is to shyness what Hawaii is to February; it's a way out of the woods. *And yet* a letter is better.

2 Such a sweet gift—a piece of handmade writing, in an envelope that is not a bill, sitting in our friend's path when she trudges home from a long day spent among savages and wahoos, a day our words will help repair. They don't need to be immortal, just sincere. She can read them twice and again tomorrow: "You're someone I care about, Corinne, and think of often, and every time I do, you make me smile."

3 We need to write; otherwise, nobody will know who we are. They will have only a vague impression of us as "A Nice Person" because, frankly, we don't shine at conversation, we lack the confidence to thrust our faces forward and say, "Hi, I'm Heather Hooten; let me tell you about my week." Mostly we say "Uh-huh" and "Oh really." People smile and look over our shoulder, looking for someone else to meet.

4 So a shy person sits down and writes a letter. To be known by another person—to meet and talk freely on the page—to be close despite distance. To escape from anonymity and be our own sweet selves and express the music of our souls. The same thing that moves a giant rock star to sing his heart out in front of 123,000 people moves us to take ballpoint in hand and write a few lines to our dear Aunt Eleanor. *We want to be known.* We want her to know that we have fallen in love, that we have quit our job, that we're moving to New York, and we want to say a few things that might not get said in casual conversation: "Thank you for what you've meant to me. I am very happy right now."

5 The first step in writing letters is to get over the guilt of *not* writing. You don't "owe" anybody a letter. Letters are a gift. The burning shame you feel when you see unanswered mail makes it harder to pick up a pen and makes for a cheerless letter when you finally do. "I feel bad about not writing, but I've been so busy," etc. Skip this. Few letters are obligatory and they are "Thanks for the wonderful gift" and "I am terribly sorry to hear about George's death" and "Yes, you're welcome to stay with us next month." Write these promptly if you

want to keep your friends. Don't worry about other letters, except love letters, of course. When your true love writes, "Dear Light of My Life, Joy of My Heart, O Lovely Pulsating Core of My Sensate Life," some response is called for.

Some of the best letters are tossed off in a burst of inspiration, so keep your 6
writing stuff in one place where you can sit down for a few minutes, and—"Dear Roy, I am in the middle of an essay but thought I'd drop you a line. Hi to your sweetie too"—dash off a note to a pal. Envelopes, stamps, address book, everything in a drawer so you can write fast when the pen is hot. A blank white 8" × 11" sheet can look as big as Montana if the pen's not so hot; try a smaller page and write boldly. Get a pen that makes a sensuous line, get a comfortable typewriter, a friendly word processor—whichever feels easy to the hand.

Sit for a few minutes with the blank sheet of paper in front of you, and 7
meditate on the person you will write to; let your friend come to mind until you can almost see him or her in the room with you. Remember the last time you saw each other and how your friend looked and what you said and what perhaps was unsaid between you, and when your friend becomes real to you, start to write. Write the salutation, "Dear You," and take a deep breath and plunge in. A simple declarative sentence will do, followed by another and another. Talk about what you're doing and tell it like you were talking to us. Don't think about grammar, don't think about style, don't try to write dramatically, just give us your news. Where did you go, who did you see, what did they say, what do you think?

If you don't know where to begin, start with the present: "I'm sitting at the 8
kitchen table on a rainy Saturday morning. Everyone is gone, and the house is quiet." Let your description of the present moment lead to something else; let the letter drift gently along. The toughest letter to crank out is one that is meant to impress, as we all know from writing job applications; if it's hard work to write a letter to a friend, maybe you're trying too hard to be terrific. A letter is only a report to someone who already likes you for reasons other than your brilliance. Take it easy.

Don't worry about form. It's not a term paper. When you come to the end of 9
one episode, just start a new paragraph. You can go from a few lines about the sad state of pro football to the fight with your mother to your cat's urinary tract infection to a few thoughts on personal indebtedness and on to the kitchen sink and what's in it. The more you write, the easier it gets, and when you have a true friend to write to, a *compadre*, a soul sibling, then it's like driving a car; you just press on the gas.

Don't tear up the page and start over when you write a bad line; try to write 10
your way out of it. Make mistakes and plunge on. Let the letter cook along and let yourself be bold. Outrage, confusion, love—whatever is in your mind, let it find a way to the page. Writing is a means of discovery, always, and when you come to the end and write "Yours ever" or "Hugs and Kisses," you'll know something that you didn't when you wrote "Dear Pal."

Probably your friend will put your letter away, and it'll be read again a few 11
years from now, and it will improve with age. And forty years from now, your friend's grandkids will dig it out of the attic and read it, a sweet and precious relic that gives them a sudden clear glimpse of you and her and the world we old-timers knew. Your simple lines about where you went, who you saw, what they said, will speak to those children, and they will feel in their hearts the humanity of our times.

You can't pick up a phone and call the future and tell them about our times. 12
You have to pick up a piece of paper.

**Vocabulary** Before, during, and after reading the selection, annotate the text and write in your journal. Create a list of vocabulary words, along with their definitions, and give examples of their use from the selection you just read.

## After Reading Discussion Questions: Meaning, Structure, and Expression

1. **Main Idea:** Work as a group to write a summary that answers the following questions: What purpose did Garrison Keillor have for writing this essay? Who is his intended audience? What is the main idea of the essay?
2. **Relevant Details:** Keillor's advice about how to write a personal letter does not begin until the fifth paragraph. How are the details in the first four paragraphs related to his main point? Would the essay be as effective without these paragraphs? Why or why not?
3. **Logical Order:** Keillor describes a step-by-step process for writing a personal letter. Map out the steps in the order he suggests them. Do you agree with his advice? Would you change the order of any of the steps? Would you add or delete any steps? Why or why not?
4. **Effective Expression:** Keillor is often praised for his light-hearted, easy-to-read style. Find three expressions that are amusing in tone. Explain the reasons for your selections.

## Thinking Prompts to Move from Reading to Writing

1. This essay offers clear instructions about how to write a letter based on Keillor's expertise in and understanding of the writing process. Think of a task or process that you understand or have mastered through experience. Write an essay that explains the significance of the task or process and the steps necessary to successfully accomplish it.
2. Keillor advises in paragraph 9, "Don't worry about form. It's not a term paper." His statement indicates differences among writing a personal letter for everyday life, writing a term paper for college life, and writing letters and reports for working life. How might the writing process change for each of these situations? Write an essay that describes how to write a term paper or a letter of application for a job. Use Keillor's essay as a model.

# Old Age

MARK TWAIN

Born in Florida, Missouri, in 1835, Samuel Clemens (alias Mark Twain) was a humorist, writer, lecturer, and journalist whose literature has endured for more than a century. He is known for his keen wit and sharp satires. His many publications include the world classics *The Adventures of Tom Sawyer* and *Huckleberry Finn*.

**Before Reading** Write a journal entry about your experiences with getting older. Are you enjoying growing older? Do you know an elderly person? Is that person enjoying being older? What do you think about being old? How are the elderly viewed in your culture?

I think it likely that people who have not been here will be interested to know what it is like. I arrived on the thirtieth of November, fresh from care-free and frivolous 69, and was disappointed. 1

There is nothing novel about it, nothing striking, nothing to thrill you and make your eye glitter and your tongue cry out, "Oh, but it *is* wonderful, perfectly wonderful!" Yes, it is disappointing. You say, "Is *this* it?—*this?* after all this talk and fuss of a thousand generations of travelers who have crossed this frontier and looked about them and told what they saw and felt? why, it looks just like 69." 2

And that is true. Also it is natural; for you have not come by the fast express, you have been lagging and dragging across the world's continents behind oxen; when that is your pace one country melts into the next one so gradually that you are not able to notice the change: 70 looks like 69; 69 looked like 68; 68 looked like 67—and so on, back, and back, to the beginning. If you climb to a summit and look back—ah, then you see! 3

Down that far-reaching perspective you can make out each country and climate that you crossed, all the way up from the hot equator to the ice-summit where you are perched. You can make out where Infancy merged into Boyhood; Boyhood into down-lipped Youth; Youth into indefinite Young-Manhood; indefinite Young-Manhood into definite Manhood; definite Manhood with aggressive ambitions into sobered and heedful Husbandhood and Fatherhood; these into troubled and foreboding Age, with graying hair; this into Old Age, white-headed, the temple empty, the idols broken, the worshippers in their graves, nothing left but You, a remnant, a tradition, belated fag-end of a foolish dream, a dream that was so ingeniously dreamed that it seemed real all the time; nothing left but You, centre of a snowy desolation, perched on the ice-summit, gazing out over the stages of that long *trek* and asking Yourself "would you do it again if you had the chance?" 4

## Vocabulary

Before, during, and after reading the selection, annotate the text and write in your journal. Create a list of vocabulary words, along with their definitions, and give examples of their use from the selection you just read.

## After Reading Discussion Questions: Meaning, Structure, and Expression

1. **Main Idea:** Work as a group to write a summary that answers the following questions: What purpose did Mark Twain have for writing this essay? Who is his intended audience? What is the main idea of the essay?
2. **Relevant Details:** Twain is describing the process of reaching "old age," yet he does not offer many concrete details about old age from his or any particular person's life. Why do you think he chose to leave "real life" details out of this essay? Do you think examples from life would make his point stronger? Why or why not?
3. **Logical Order:** What are the stages of life he describes? Create a timeline that illustrates the phases of life as he describes them. About how old would a person be in each of the stages Twain describes?
4. **Effective Expression:** Based on Twain's choice of words, how would you describe the tone of this essay? Is it optimistic, flattering, disappointed, disrespectful, or does it communicate some other attitude about old age? Identify three expressions that illustrate the tone of the piece. Explain the reasons for your selections.

## Thinking Prompts to Move from Reading to Writing

1. When Twain describes how a person reaches old age, he is describing the steps taken to reach an end result. Think of a desirable or undesirable end result, such as a passing or failing grade on an exam or in an academic course. Write an essay that describes the process that led to the end result.
2. Twain talks about "*perching*" on a "*summit*" and looking back at what has been accomplished. Identify an accomplishment that makes you or someone you know proud. Write an essay that describes how you reached your accomplishment.

# Illustration

## Don't Call Me a Hot Tamale

JUDITH ORTIZ COFER

Born in 1952 in Puerto Rico and raised in Paterson, New Jersey, Judith Ortiz Cofer is an acclaimed poet, novelist, and essayist. Her writings explore the experiences of being a minority as a Hispanic woman. She is currently the Regents' and Franklin Professor of English and Creative Writing at the University of Georgia.

**Before Reading** Write a journal entry about your experiences with stereotypes. Have you ever been stereotyped? Describe the incident. What are some common stereotypes in our culture? How are these stereotypes harmful?

On a bus to London from Oxford University, where I was earning some graduate 1
credits one summer, a young man, obviously fresh from a pub, approached my seat. With both hands over his heart, he went down on his knees in the aisle and broke into an Irish tenor's rendition of "Maria" from *West Side Story.* I was not amused. "Maria" had followed me to London, reminding me of a prime fact of my life: You can leave the island of Puerto Rico, master the English language, and travel as far as you can, but if you're a Latina, especially one who so clearly belongs to Rita Moreno's gene pool, the island travels with you.

Growing up in New Jersey and wanting most of all to belong, I lived in two 2
completely different worlds. My parents designed our life as a microcosm of their *casas* on the island—we spoke in Spanish, ate Puerto Rican food bought at the *bodega,* and practiced strict Catholicism complete with Sunday mass in Spanish.

I was kept under tight surveillance by my parents, since my virtue and 3
modesty were, by their cultural equation, the same as their honor. As teenagers, my friends and I were lectured constantly on how to behave as proper *señoritas.* But it was a conflicting message we received, since our Puerto Rican mothers also encouraged us to look and act like women by dressing us in clothes our Anglo schoolmates and their mothers found too "mature" and flashy. I often felt humiliated when I appeared at an American friend's birthday party wearing a dress more suitable for a semiformal. At Puerto Rican festivities, neither the music nor the colors we wore could be too loud.

I remember Career Day in high school, when our teachers told us to come 4
dressed as if for a job interview. That morning, I agonized in front of my closet, trying to figure out what a "career girl" would wear, because the only model I had was Marlo Thomas on TV. To me and my Puerto Rican girlfriends, dressing up meant wearing our mother's ornate jewelry and clothing.

At school that day, the teachers assailed us for wearing "everything at 5
once"—meaning too much jewelry and too many accessories. And it was painfully obvious that the other students in their tailored skirts and silk blouses thought we were hopeless and vulgar. The way they looked at us was a taste of the cultural clash that awaited us in the real world, where prospective employers

and men on the street would often misinterpret our tight skirts and bright colors as a come-on.

6 It is custom, not chromosomes, that leads us to choose scarlet over pale pink. Our mothers had grown up on a tropical island where the natural environment was a riot of primary colors, where showing your skin was one way to keep cool as well as to look sexy. On the island, women felt freer to dress and move provocatively since they were protected by the traditions and laws of a Spanish/Catholic system of morality and machismo, the main rule of which was: *You may look at my sister, but if you touch her I will kill you.* The extended family and church structure provided them with a circle of safety on the island; if a man "wronged" a girl, everyone would close in to save her family honor.

7 Off-island, signals often get mixed. When a Puerto Rican girl who is dressed in her idea of what is attractive meets a man from the mainstream culture who has been trained to react to certain types of clothing as a sexual signal, a clash is likely to take place. She is seen as a Hot Tamale, a sexual firebrand. I learned this lesson at my first formal dance when my date leaned over and painfully planted a sloppy, overeager kiss on my mouth. When I didn't respond with sufficient passion, he said in a resentful tone: "I thought you Latin girls were supposed to mature early." It was only the first time I would feel like a fruit or vegetable—I was supposed to *ripen,* not just grow into womanhood like other girls.

8 These stereotypes, though rarer, still surface in my life. I recently stayed at a classy metropolitan hotel. After having dinner with a friend, I was returning to my room when a middle-aged man in a tuxedo stepped directly into my path. With his champagne glass extended toward me, he exclaimed, "Evita!"

9 Blocking my way, he bellowed the song "Don't Cry for Me, Argentina." Playing to the gathering crowd, he began to sing loudly a ditty to the tune of "La Bamba"—except the lyrics were about a girl named Maria whose exploits all rhymed with her name and gonorrhea.

10 I knew that this same man—probably a corporate executive, even worldly by most standards—would never have regaled a white woman with a dirty song in public. But to him, I was just a character in his universe of "others," all cartoons.

11 Still, I am one of the lucky ones. There are thousands of Latinas without the privilege of the education that my parents gave me. For them every day is a struggle against the misconceptions perpetuated by the myth of the Latina as whore, domestic worker or criminal.

12 Rather than fight these pervasive stereotypes, I try to replace them with a more interesting set of realities. I travel around the U.S. reading from my books of poetry and my novel. With the stories I tell, the dreams and fears I examine in my work, I try to get my audience past the particulars of my skin color, my accent or my clothes.

13 I once wrote a poem in which I called Latinas "God's brown daughters." It is really a prayer, of sorts, for communication and respect. In it, Latin women pray "in Spanish to an Anglo God/with a Jewish heritage," and they are "fervently hoping / that if not omnipotent, / at least He be bilingual."

## Vocabulary

Before, during, and after reading the selection, annotate the text and write in your journal. Create a list of vocabulary words, along with their definitions, and give examples of their use from the selection you just read.

## After Reading Discussion Questions: Meaning, Structure, and Expression

1. **Main Idea:** Work as a group to write a summary that answers the following questions: What purpose did Judith Ortiz Cofer have for writing this essay? Who is

her intended audience? What is the main idea of the essay? What is the significance of the title?

2. **Relevant Details:** Cofer relies mostly on personal experience to make her point about stereotypes based on race or gender. Does she provide enough details to make her point convincingly? Would the use of facts or expert opinions strengthen her point? Why or why not?
3. **Logical Order:** Cofer opens her essay with an example from her personal life. Is this an effective opening for the essay? Why or why not? Compare the introduction of the essay to the conclusion of the essay. How does the conclusion relate to the introduction? Is this an effective conclusion? Why or why not? What other ways could Cofer have opened or closed her essay?
4. **Effective Expression:** Based on Judith Ortiz Cofer's choice of words, how would you describe the tone of this essay? Is it angry, embarrassed, disappointed, confrontational, or candid, or does it communicate some other attitude about stereotypes? Identify three expressions that illustrate the tone of the piece. Explain the reasons for your selections.

## Thinking Prompts to Move from Reading to Writing

1. Cofer makes a connection between culture and fashion. According to her description, Hispanic fashion for women is "flashy," "mature," and "sexy" with "ornate jewelry" and "tight skirts and bright colors." Write an essay in which you illustrate how fashion represents a particular culture. For example, illustrate fashion in the Hip-Hop culture.
2. Cofer's essay illustrates the stereotypes she faces as a Hispanic woman. Identify and exemplify a stereotype that you or someone you know has encountered. For example, what are some stereotypes that elderly people face?

# My Own Style

NIKI GIOVANNI

Born in 1943 in Knoxville, Tennessee, and raised in Lincoln Heights, an all-black suburb of Cincinnati, Ohio, Nikki Giovanni, a world-renowned poet, writer, activist, and educator, prides herself on being "a Black American, a daughter, a mother, a professor of English." Giovanni is a determined and committed champion of civil rights and equality.

**Before Reading** Write a journal entry about your definition of personal style. What is personal style? What are some examples? Describe your personal style.

I want to be a modern woman. I still have a nostalgic Afro, though it's stylishly short. I apologize to the hair industry, but frankly, I like both my kinks and my gray strands. Plus, being a sixties person, glowing in the dark carries negative implications for me. Most of my friends do wear base, pancake, powder, eye make-up, lipstick and always keep their nails in perfectly ovaled shapes with base, color, sealer and oil for the cuticles. Do I use these things? No. But neither do I put them down nor try to make my friends feel guilty for not being natural. There is something to be said for improvement. I've been known to comment: "Wow, you look really good. Who does your nails?" Why, I even have a dear friend who is a few months younger than I and uses a night cream to 1 guard against wrinkles. Do I laugh? No, ma'am. I say: "Well, your face is very, very smooth," which (1) makes her feel good about her efforts and (2) keeps the friendship intact.

2 My major contribution to cosmetics is soap. I love soap . . . in pretty colors . . . hand milled . . . in interesting shapes . . . with the names of good perfumers on them . . . preferably French. I use it to bathe, of course, but it's also so pretty on my open shelves. Plus it smells good and when properly arranged, is more or less sculpture. No one in my immediate family, and few who have ever used my bathroom, ever wonders what to give me for my birthday, Christmas, Valentine's Day, Mother's Day, the Fourth of July, Labor Day, Martin Luther King Jr.'s Birthday or Lincoln Heights Day. The way I figure, ask for what you want.

3 I really like useful things. You never know. Take candles. I really like a candle. I'm a Democrat, so I have a donkey. I'm a Delta, so I have an elephant. I'm a woman, so I have an apple. (Well, maybe I don't have to justify that.) I also have candle candles. Just tall, pretty candles in little holders. If the house gets hit by lightning, I'm ready. Like all modern women, I like to be ready.

4 Without raising a hair on my chinny-chin-chin I can turn three cans of anything and a quarter cup of dry white wine into a gourmet meal in 15 minutes flat. Give me an ounce of cognac and I really raise hell. I've been known to make the most wicked bean soup with warm croutons and garlic zwieback (the secret is a dabble of sherry) the world has known. People say: "How can you be a full-time mother, full-time professional, and still cook like this?" I smile sweetly, indicating that perhaps the very best is yet to come. Or as the old folks liked to say: "It ain't what you do; it's the way you do it."

5 In observing the younger women, that seems to be the one thing that they are missing: the ability to take nothing and make everybody think that something is there. Know what I mean? The younger women like to brag that they can't cook, as if that makes them modern. What is really modern is that you can throw it together from cans and frozen food and pretend that it was easy. Half of life is not avoiding what you don't like but doing it with no sweat.

6 I must congratulate the twentieth-century woman on her internationalism. You go into practically any house these days and they have Nigerian art, Egyptian cotton throws, French water, Hawaiian fruit, Japanese televisions, California wines, Polish crystal, Haitian lace curtains, Lesothoan rugs and Dutch flowers sitting on grandmother's handmade quilts draped across an Early American table. I remember when you could go by the apartment of any guy and find stale beer in the refrigerator. Nowadays even *their* places are perking up. Everybody wants to make a statement.

7 Oh sure, I've heard all the jokes about BUMP's (Black Upwardly Mobile Professionals), but I like a BUMP. Hell, I am one. The modern woman is a BUMP who is not a grind. And we could use a little ambition in our community. Every time somebody wants to trade their Toyota for a BMW, it means they have to have more people to supervise, a bigger budget to spend. If they're in business for themselves, they have to sell more, do more, 'cause everybody knows you don't get big in business by saving; you get big by spending, by expansion.

8 We are only 15 years away from the twenty-first century! The Black community is 40 percent teenage unemployed, social security froze, Medicaid stopped, unwed, underemployed, unpromoted and generally a not-appreciated-at-all community in America. Who we gonna call—Honkeybusters? No! We're gonna climb out on the BUMP's. We can do it 'cause we've done everything else. And hey, even though my body will be old, sitting on a porch in some home (unless I can convince my son, now 15, to let me live with him), I'll be surrounded by the good feeling that I am a modern woman, 'cause even if I'm old, I'm sure to be positive—and that's our ace in the hole.

**Vocabulary** Before, during, and after reading the selection, annotate the text and write in your journal. Create a list of vocabulary words, along with their definitions, and give examples of their use from the selection you just read.

## After Reading Discussion Questions: Meaning, Structure, and Expression

1. **Main Idea:** Work as a group to write a summary that answers the following questions: What purpose did Niki Giovanni have for writing this essay? Who is her intended audience? What is the main idea of the essay? What is the significance of the title?
2. **Relevant Details:** In paragraph 3, Giovanni discusses her collection of candles. How do the details in this paragraph support her main point about personal style?
3. **Logical Order:** According to the title, "My Own Style," this essay is about Giovanni's personal style; however, in paragraph 8, she focuses on the traits of the black community in the twentieth century. Explain the logic of her thinking. Why does she include these details? Why did she place these details at the end of the essay? In what ways do you think the black community influenced her personal style?
4. **Effective Expression:** In this essay, Giovanni uses an informal tone to make a point for a general audience. Identify three examples of her use of informal language. Explain the reason for your selections. How does her choice of words illustrate her personal style?

## Thinking Prompts to Move from Reading to Writing

1. In paragraph 5, Giovanni states, "Half of life is not avoiding what you don't like but doing it with no sweat." Do you agree with this opinion? Write an essay in which you agree or disagree, and use examples to illustrate your point.
2. Write an essay that describes your personal style or the personal style of someone you know. Use examples to illustrate your point.

# Classification

## The Ways of Meeting Oppression

MARTIN LUTHER KING, JR.

During the Civil Rights Movement, Martin Luther King, Jr. preached and lived out the philosophy of nonviolent resistance to overcome oppression and create a just society. Through his leadership, he proved the power of this method to combat racial segregation. King defines his philosophy of nonviolent resistance in this essay.

**Before Reading** Write a journal entry about your experiences with oppression. Have you or someone you know ever been treated unfairly? How does unfair treatment make you feel? What is the natural reaction to unfair treatment?

Oppressed people deal with their oppression in three characteristic ways. One way is acquiescence: the oppressed resign themselves to their doom. They tacitly adjust themselves to oppression, and thereby become conditioned to it. In every movement toward freedom some of the oppressed prefer to remain oppressed. Almost 2800 years ago Moses set out to lead the children of Israel from the slavery of Egypt to the freedom of the promised land. He soon discovered that slaves do not always welcome their deliverers. They become accustomed to being slaves. They would rather bear those ills they have, as Shakespeare pointed out, than flee to others that they know not of. They prefer the "fleshpots of Egypt" to the ordeals of emancipation. 1

There is such a thing as the freedom of exhaustion. Some people are so worn down by the yoke of oppression that they give up. A few years ago in the slum areas of Atlanta, a Negro guitarist used to sing almost daily: "Been down so long that down don't bother me." This is the type of negative freedom and resignation that often engulfs the life of the oppressed. 2

But this is not the way out. To accept passively an unjust system is to cooperate with that system; thereby the oppressed become as evil as the oppressor. Noncooperation with evil is as much a moral obligation as is cooperation with good. The oppressed must never allow the conscience of the oppressor to slumber. Religion reminds every man that he is his brother's keeper. To accept injustice or segregation passively is to say to the oppressor that his actions are morally right. It is a way of allowing his conscience to fall asleep. At this moment the oppressed fails to be his brother's keeper. So acquiescence—while often the easier way—is not the moral way. It is the way of the coward. The Negro cannot win the respect of his oppressor by acquiescing; he merely increases the oppressor's arrogance and contempt. Acquiescence is interpreted as proof of the Negro's inferiority. The Negro cannot win the respect of the white people of the South or the peoples of the world if he is willing to sell the future of his children or his personal and immediate comfort and safety. 3

A second way that oppressed people sometimes deal with oppression is to resort to physical violence and corroding hatred. Violence often brings about momentary results. Nations have frequently won their independence in battle. But in spite of temporary victories, violence never brings permanent peace. It solves no social problem; it merely creates new and more complicated ones. 4

Violence as a way of achieving racial justice is both impractical and immoral. 5
It is impractical because it is a descending spiral ending in destruction for all. The old law of an eye for an eye leaves everybody blind. It is immoral because it seeks to humiliate the opponent rather than win his understanding; it seeks to annihilate rather than to convert. Violence is immoral because it thrives on hatred rather than love. It destroys community and makes brotherhood impossible. It leaves society in monologue rather than dialogue. Violence ends by defeating itself. It creates bitterness in the survivors and brutality in the destroyers. A voice echoes through time saying to every potential Peter, "Put up your sword." History is cluttered with the wreckage of nations that failed to follow this command.

If the American Negro and other victims of oppression succumb to the 6
temptation of using violence in the struggle for freedom, future generations will be the recipients of a desolate night of bitterness, and our chief legacy to them will be an endless reign of meaningless chaos. Violence is not the way.

The third way open to oppressed people in their quest for freedom is the way 7
of nonviolent resistance. Like the synthesis in Hegelian philosophy, the principle of nonviolent resistance seeks to reconcile the truths of two opposites—the acquiescence and violence—while avoiding the extremes and immoralities of both. The nonviolent resister agrees with the person who acquiesces that one should not be physically aggressive toward his opponent; but he balances the equation by agreeing with the person of violence that evil must be resisted. He avoids the nonresistance of the former and the violent resistance of the latter. With nonviolent resistance, no individual or group need submit to any wrong, nor need anyone resort to violence in order to right a wrong.

It seems to me that this is the method that must guide the actions of the 8
Negro in the present crisis in race relations. Through nonviolent resistance the Negro will be able to rise to the noble height of opposing the unjust system while loving the perpetrators of the system. The Negro must work passionately and unrelentingly for full stature as a citizen, but he must not use inferior methods to gain it. He must never come to terms with falsehood, malice, hate, or destruction.

Nonviolent resistance makes it possible for the Negro to remain in the South 9
and struggle for his rights. The Negro's problem will not be solved by running away. He cannot listen to the glib suggestion of those who would urge him to migrate en masse to other sections of the country. By grasping his great opportunity in the South he can make a lasting contribution to the moral strength of the nation and set a sublime example of courage for generations yet unborn.

By nonviolent resistance, the Negro can also enlist all men of good will in his 10
struggle for equality. The problem is not a purely racial one, with Negroes set against whites. In the end, it is not a struggle between people at all, but a tension between justice and injustice. Nonviolent resistance is not aimed against oppressors but against oppression. Under its banner consciences, not racial groups, are enlisted.

**Vocabulary** Before, during, and after reading the selection, annotate the text and write in your journal. Create a list of vocabulary words, along with their definitions, and give examples of their use from the selection you just read.

## After Reading Discussion Questions: Meaning, Structure, and Expression

1. **Main Idea:** Work as a group to write a summary that answers the following questions: What purpose did Martin Luther King, Jr. have for writing this essay? Who is his intended audience? What is the main idea of the essay? What is the significance of the title?
2. **Relevant Details:** What are the three ways that people deal with oppression, according to King? Which way does King recommend people deal with oppression? Do you agree with his opinion? Why or why not?
3. **Logical Order:** King presents these three ways of dealing with oppression in a specific order. Why did he choose this order? Would the essay be as effective if he changed the order of these three major details? Why or why not?
4. **Effective Expression:** Throughout the essay, King refers to African Americans as Negroes. Why do you think he used this term? What is the tone of this essay, based on King's use of language? Is the tone angry, disillusioned, hopeful, spiritual, or some other tone? Identify three expressions that illustrate the tone of the piece. Explain the reasons for your selections.

## Thinking Prompts to Move from Reading to Writing

1. In his essay, King discusses a particular social problem: oppression of the African American before and during the Civil Rights Movement. Identify and discuss three types of current social problems of great importance.
2. King opens his essay with the statement, "Oppressed people deal with their oppression in three characteristic ways." Identify a specific group of people who face particular challenges, and discuss the characteristic ways in which they deal with the situation. Consider the following suggestions: the ways students typically deal with the demands of pursuing an education; the ways one deals with a disability or handicap; the ways people react to death or loss.

# The Truth about Lying

JUDITH VIORST

Judith Viorst was born in Newark, New Jersey, in 1931. As the author of several works of fiction and nonfiction, for children as well as adults, she has been honored with various awards for her journalism and psychological writings.

**Before Reading** Write a journal entry about your experiences with lying. Have you ever told a lie or been lied to? Why was the lie told? How do you feel when you lie or are lied to? Is lying necessary sometimes? If so, when?

I've been wanting to write on a subject that intrigues and challenges me: the subject of lying. I've found it very difficult to do. Everyone I've talked to has a quite intense and personal but often rather intolerant point of view about what we can—and can never *never*—tell lies about. I've finally reached the conclusion that I can't present any ultimate conclusions, for too many people would promptly disagree. Instead, I'd like to present a series of moral puzzles, all concerned with lying. I'll tell you what I think about them. Do you agree? 1

### *Social Lies*

Most of the people I've talked with say that they find social lying acceptable and necessary. They think it's the civilized way for folks to behave. Without these little white lies, they say, our relationships would be short and brutish and nasty. It's arrogant, they say, to insist on being so incorruptible and so brave that you cause other people unnecessary embarrassment or pain by compulsively assailing them with your honesty. I basically agree. What about you? 2

Will you say to people, when it simply isn't true, "I like your new hairdo," "You're looking much better," "It's so nice to see you," "I had a wonderful time"? 3

Will you praise hideous presents and homely kids? 4

Will you decline invitations with "We're busy that night—so sorry we can't come," when the truth is you'd rather stay home than dine with the So-and-sos? 5

And even though, as I do, you may prefer the polite evasion of "You really cooked up a storm" instead of "The soup"—which tastes like warmed-over coffee—"is wonderful," will you, if you must, proclaim it wonderful? 6

There's one man I know who absolutely refuses to tell social lies. "I can't play that game," he says; "I'm simply not made that way." And his answer to the argument that saying nice things to someone doesn't cost anything is, "Yes, it does—it destroys your credibility." Now, he won't, unsolicited, offer his views on the painting you just bought, but you don't ask his frank opinion unless you want *frank,* and his silence at those moments when the rest of us liars are muttering, "Isn't it lovely?" is, for the most part, eloquent enough. My friend does not indulge in what he calls "flattery, false praise, and mellifluous comments." When others tell fibs, he will not go along. He says that social lying is lying, that little white lies are still lies. And he feels that telling lies is morally wrong. What about you? 7

### *Peace-Keeping Lies*

Many people tell peace-keeping lies; lies designed to avoid irritation or argument; lies designed to shelter the liar from possible blame or pain; lies (or so it is rationalized) designed to keep trouble at bay without hurting anyone. 8

I tell these lies at times, and yet I always feel they're wrong. I understand why we tell them, but still they feel wrong. And whenever I lie so that someone won't disapprove of me or think less of me or holler at me, I feel I'm a bit of a coward, I feel I'm dodging responsibility, I feel . . . guilty. What about you? 9

Do you, when you're late for a date because you overslept, say that you're late because you got caught in a traffic jam? 10

Do you, when you forget to call a friend, say that you called several times but the line was busy? 11

Do you, when you didn't remember that it was your father's birthday, say that his present must be delayed in the mail? 12

And when you're planning a weekend in New York City and you're not in the mood to visit your mother, who lives there, do you conceal—with a lie, if you must—the fact that you'll be in New York? Or do you have the courage—or is it the cruelty?—to say, "I'll be in New York, but sorry—I don't plan on seeing you"? 13

(Dave and his wife Elaine have two quite different points of view on this very subject. He calls her a coward. She says she's being wise. He says she must assert her right to visit New York sometimes and not see her mother. To which she always patiently replies: "Why should we have useless fights? My mother's too old to change. We get along much better when I lie to her.") 14

Finally, do you keep the peace by telling your husband lies on the subject of money? Do you reduce what you really paid for your shoes? And in general do you find yourself ready, willing, and able to lie to him when you make absurd mistakes or lose or break things? 15

"I used to have a romantic idea that part of intimacy was confessing every dumb thing that you did to your husband. But after a couple of years of that," says Laura, "have I changed my mind!" 16

And having changed her mind, she finds herself telling peace-keeping lies. And yes, I tell them too. What about you? 17

*Protective Lies*

Protective lies are lies folks tell—often quite serious lies—because they're convinced that the truth would be too damaging. They lie because they feel there are certain human values that supersede the wrong of having lied. They lie, not for personal gain, but because they believe it's for the good of the person they're lying to. They lie to those they love, to those who trust them most of all, on the grounds that breaking this trust is justified. 18

They may lie to their children on money or marital matters. 19

They may lie to the dying about the state of their health. 20

They may lie about adultery, and not—or so they insist—to save their own hide, but to save the heart and the pride of the men they are married to. 21

They may lie to their closest friend because the truth about her talents or son or psyche would be—or so they insist—utterly devastating. 22

I sometimes tell such lies, but I'm aware that it's quite presumptuous to claim I know what's best for others to know. That's called playing God. That's called manipulation and control. And we never can be sure, once we start to juggle lies, just where they'll land, exactly where they'll roll. 23

And furthermore, we may find ourselves lying in order to back up the lies that are backing up the lie we initially told. 24

And furthermore—let's be honest—if conditions were reversed, we certainly wouldn't want anyone lying to us. 25

Yet, having said all that, I still believe that there are times when protective lies must nonetheless be told. What about you? 26

If your Dad had a very bad heart and you had to tell him some bad family news, which would you choose: to tell him the truth or lie? 27

If your former husband failed to send his monthly child-support check and in other ways behaved like a total rat, would you allow your children—who believed he was simply wonderful—to continue to believe that he was wonderful? 28

If your dearly beloved brother selected a wife whom you deeply disliked, would you reveal your feelings or would you fake it? 29

And if you were asked, after making love, "And how was that for you?" would you reply, if it wasn't too good, "Not too good"? 30

Now, some would call a sex lie unimportant, little more than social lying, a simple act of courtesy that makes all human intercourse run smoothly. And some would say all sex lies are bad news and unacceptably protective. Because, says Ruth, "a man with an ego that fragile doesn't need your lies—he needs a psychiatrist." Still others feel that sex lies are indeed protective lies, more serious than simple social lying, and yet at times they tell them on the grounds that when it comes to matters sexual, everybody's ego is somewhat fragile. 31

"If most of the time things go well in sex," says Sue, "I think you're allowed to dissemble when they don't. I can't believe it's good to say, 'Last night was four stars, darling, but tonight's performance rates only a half.'" 32

I'm inclined to agree with Sue. What about you? 33

*Trust-Keeping Lies*

34 Another group of lies are trust-keeping lies, lies that involve triangulation, with *A* (that's you) telling lies to *B* on behalf of *C* (whose trust you'd promised to keep). Most people concede that once you've agreed not to betray a friend's confidence, you can't betray it, even if you must lie. But I've talked with people who don't want you telling them anything that they might be called on to lie about.

35 "I don't tell lies for myself," says Fran, "and I don't want to have to tell them for other people." Which means, she agrees, that if her best friend is having an affair, she absolutely doesn't want to know about it.

36 "Are you saying," her best friend asks, "that if I went off with a lover and I asked you to tell my husband I'd been with you, that you wouldn't lie for me, that you'd betray me?"

37 Fran is very pained but very adamant. "I wouldn't want to betray you, so . . . don't ask me."

38 Fran's best friend is shocked. What about you?

39 Do you believe you can have close friends if you're not prepared to receive their deepest secrets?

40 Do you believe you must always lie for your friends?

41 Do you believe, if your friend tells a secret that turns out to be quite immoral or illegal, that once you've promised to keep it, you must keep it?

42 And what if your friend were your boss—if you were perhaps one of the President's men—would you betray or lie for him over, say, Watergate?

43 As you can see, these issues get terribly sticky.

44 It's my belief that once we've promised to keep a trust, we must tell lies to keep it. I also believe that we can't tell Watergate lies. And if these two statements strike you as quite contradictory, you're right—they're quite contradictory. But for now they're the best I can do. What about you?

45 Some say that truth will out and thus you might as well tell the truth. Some say you can't regain the trust that lies lose. Some say that even though the truth may never be revealed, our lies pervert and damage our relationships. Some say . . . well, here's what some of them have to say.

46 "I'm a coward," says Grace, "about telling close people important, difficult truths. I find that I'm unable to carry it off. And so if something is bothering me, it keeps building up inside till I end up just not seeing them any more."

47 "I lie to my husband on sexual things, but I'm furious," says Joyce, "that he's too insensitive to know I'm lying."

48 "I suffer most from the misconception that children can't take the truth," says Emily. "But I'm starting to see that what's harder and more damaging for them is being told lies, is *not* being told the truth."

49 "I'm afraid," says Joan, "that we often wind up feeling a bit of contempt for the people we lie to."

50 And then there are those who have no talent for lying.

51 "Over the years, I tried to lie," a friend of mine explained, "but I always got found out and I always got punished. I guess I gave myself away because I feel guilty about any kind of lying. It looks as if I'm stuck with telling the truth."

52 For those of us, however, who are good at telling lies, for those of us who lie and don't get caught, the question of whether or not to lie can be a hard and serious moral problem. I liked the remark of a friend of mine who said, "I'm willing to lie. But just as a last resort—the truth's always better."

"Because," he explained, "though others may completely accept the lie I'm telling, I don't." 53

I tend to feel that way too. 54

What about you? 55

**Vocabulary** Before, during, and after reading the selection, annotate the text and write in your journal. Create a list of vocabulary words, along with their definitions, and give examples of their use from the selection you just read.

## After Reading Discussion Questions: Meaning, Structure, and Expression

1. **Main Idea:** Work as a group to write a summary that answers the following questions: What purpose did Judith Viorst have for writing this essay? Who is her intended audience? What is the main idea of the essay? What is the significance of the title?
2. **Relevant Details:** Viorst describes four types of lies. Examine the examples she gives for each type of lie. Do you agree that she chose the best examples? Why or why not?
3. **Logical Order:** Throughout the essay, Viorst poses questions directly to the audience. Locate those questions. Why did she place these questions where she did? What impact do the questions have on the effectiveness of the essay?
4. **Effective Expression:** Based on her word choice, who is the intended audience for this essay? Identify several expressions that you used as clues to identify the audience. Does the point of the essay have meaning for other audiences? What changes in words or examples would you recommend to make this essay appealing to a specific audience that is different from the one Viorst intended?

## Thinking Prompts to Move from Reading to Writing

1. Throughout the essay, Viorst asks her readers if they agree with her. Discuss your views about these four types of lies. Write a classification essay that answers the questions she poses to the reader.
2. Lying is an act that leads to a variety of emotional reactions for both the one who lies and the one who is lied to. How do you feel when you lie? How do you feel when you know you have been lied to? Write an essay that classifies and explains the types of reactions people have in response to lying.

# Comparison–Contrast

## The Ugly Truth about Beauty

DAVE BARRY

Born in Armonk, New York, in 1947, Dave Barry is a humor columnist. For 25 years, he was a syndicated columnist whose work appeared in more than 500 newspapers in the United States and abroad. In 1988, he won the Pulitzer Prize for Commentary. Barry has also written a total of 30 books.

**Before Reading** Write a journal entry about your beliefs about beauty. What makes a man or woman attractive? How does the media define beauty for women or attractiveness for men? Is the media version of attractiveness different from reality? If so, how?

If you're a man, at some point a woman will ask you how she looks. 1

"How do I look?" she'll ask. 2

You must be careful how you answer this question. The best technique is to form an honest yet sensitive opinion, then collapse on the floor with some kind of fatal seizure. Trust me, this is the easiest way out. Because you will never come up with the right answer. 3

The problem is that women generally do not think of their looks in the same way that men do. Most men form an opinion of how they look in the seventh grade, and they stick to it for the rest of their lives. Some men form the opinion that they are irresistible stud muffins, and they do not change this opinion even when their faces sag and their noses bloat to the size of eggplants and their eyebrows grow together to form what appears to be a giant forehead-dwelling tropical caterpillar. 4

Most men, I believe, think of themselves as average-looking. Men will think this even if their faces cause heart failure in cattle at a range of 300 yards. Being average does not bother them; average is fine, for men. This is why men never ask anybody how they look. Their primary form of beauty care is to shave themselves, which is essentially the same form of beauty care that they give to their lawns. If, at the end of his four-minute daily beauty regimen, a man has managed to wipe most of the shaving cream out of his hair and is not bleeding too badly, he feels that he has done all he can, so he stops thinking about his appearance and devotes his mind to more critical issues, such as the Super Bowl. 5

Women do not look at themselves this way. If I had to express, in three words, what I believe most women think about their appearance, those words would be: "not good enough." No matter how attractive a woman may appear to be to others, when she looks at herself in the mirror, she thinks: woof. She thinks that at any moment a municipal animal-control officer is going to throw a net over her and haul her off to the shelter. 6

Why do women have such low self-esteem? There are many complex psychological and societal reasons, by which I mean Barbie. Girls grow up playing with a doll proportioned such that, if it were human, it would be seven feet tall and weigh 81 pounds, of which 53 pounds would be bosoms. This is a difficult appearance standard to live up to, especially when you contrast it with the standard set for little boys by their dolls . . . excuse me, by their action 7 figures. Most of the action figures that my son played with when he was little were hideous-looking. For example, he was very fond of an action figure (part of the He-Man series) called "Buzz-Off," who was part human, part flying insect. Buzz-Off was not a looker. But he was extremely self-confident. You could not imagine Buzz-Off saying to the other action figures: "Do you think these wings make my hips look big?"

But women grow up thinking they need to look like Barbie, which for most women is impossible, although there is a multibillion-dollar beauty industry devoted to convincing women that they must try. I once saw an Oprah show wherein supermodel Cindy Crawford dispensed makeup tips to the studio audience. Cindy had all these middle-aged women applying beauty products to their faces; she stressed how important it was to apply them in a certain way, using the tips of their fingers. All the women dutifully did this, even though it was obvious to any sane observer that, no matter how carefully they applied these products, they would never look remotely like Cindy Crawford, who is some kind of genetic mutation. 8

I'm not saying that men are superior. I'm just saying that you're not going to get a group of middle-aged men to sit in a room and apply cosmetics to themselves under the instruction of Brad Pitt, in hopes of looking more like him. Men would realize that this task was pointless and demeaning. They would find some way to bolster their self-esteem that did not require looking like Brad Pitt. They would say to Brad: "Oh YEAH? Well what do you know about LAWN CARE, pretty boy?" 9

Of course many women will argue that the reason they become obsessed with trying to look like Cindy Crawford is that men, being as shallow as a drop of spit, WANT women to look that way. To which I have two responses: 10

1. Hey, just because WE'RE idiots, that does not mean YOU have to be; and 11

2. Men don't even notice 97 percent of the beauty efforts you make anyway. Take fingernails. The average woman spends 5,000 hours per year worrying about her fingernails; I have never once, in more than 40 years of listening to men talk about women, heard a man say, "She has a nice set of fingernails!" Many men would not notice if a woman had upward of four hands. 12

Anyway, to get back to my original point: If you're a man, and a woman asks you how she looks, you're in big trouble. Obviously, you can't say she looks bad. But you also can't say that she looks great, because she'll think you're lying, because she has spent countless hours, with the help of the multibillion-dollar beauty industry, obsessing about the differences between herself and Cindy Crawford. Also, she suspects that you're not qualified to judge anybody's appearance. This is because you have shaving cream in your hair. 13

**Vocabulary** Before, during, and after reading the selection, annotate the text and write in your journal. Create a list of vocabulary words, along with their definitions, and give examples of their use from the selection you just read.

## After Reading Discussion Questions: Meaning, Structure, and Expression

1. **Main Idea:** Work as a group to write a summary that answers the following questions: What purpose did Dave Barry have for writing this essay? Who is his intended audience? What is the main idea of the essay? What is the significance of the title?
2. **Relevant Details:** Barry begins his concluding paragraph (13) with the statement, "Anyway, to get back to my original point." Do you agree that he strayed off point? Why or why not? If you agree, which details are not relevant to his point?

3. **Logical Order:** In this essay, Barry contrasts a woman's view of her beauty to a man's view of his attractiveness. Does he organize these contrasting views point by point or by presenting one block of ideas (the woman's) and then another (the man's)? Do you think he chose the more effective method for ordering his details? Why or why not?
4. **Effective Expression:** This essay showcases Barry's distinct sense of humor through the use of exaggerations. Identify three examples of his humorous use of exaggeration. Why are these exaggerations funny?

## Thinking Prompts to Move from Reading to Writing

1. Barry contrasts the Barbie dolls for girls with the action figures for boys to illustrate the differences between females and males. What other examples have you observed that illustrate the differences between women and men? For example, do men and women prefer different types of movies, sports, books, cars? Write an essay using your own examples that discusses another important difference between women and men.
2. Barry states that the Barbie doll damages the self-esteem of girls. Many believe that boys are also negatively influenced by some of their toys, such as toy guns and soldiers. What are some toys for boys or girls that have positive influences? Write a contrast essay to convince parents to replace toys that could be harmful to a girl or boy with toys that foster positive values.

# A Fable for Tomorrow

RACHEL CARSON

Born in Springfield, Pennsylvania, in 1902, Rachel Carson lived the rugged life of a farmer's daughter. A biologist, environmentalist, and nature writer, Carson became a foreleader in the environmental movement. Her book *Silent Spring* raised the alarm and instigated change in national attitudes and policies about pesticides. She was awarded the Presidential Medal of Freedom.

**Before Reading** Write a journal entry about your views about the environment. Are you concerned about the environment? Why or why not? What do you think is the greatest threat to our environment? Why? What should be done?

There was once a town in the heart of America where all life seemed to live in harmony with its surroundings. The town lay in the midst of a checkerboard of prosperous farms, with fields of grain and hillsides of orchards where, in spring, white clouds of bloom drifted above the green fields. In autumn, oak and maple and birch set up a blaze of color that flamed and flickered across a backdrop of pines. Then foxes barked in the hills and deer silently crossed the fields, half hidden in the mists of the fall mornings. 1

Along the roads, laurel, viburnum and alder, great ferns and wildflowers delighted the traveler's eye through much of the year. Even in winter the roadsides were places of beauty, where countless birds came to feed on the berries and on the seed heads of the dried weeds rising above the snow. The countryside was, in fact, famous for the abundance and variety of its bird life, and when the flood of migrants was pouring through in spring and fall people 2 traveled from great distances to observe them. Others came to fish the streams, which flowed clear and cold out of the hills and contained shady pools where trout lay. So it had been from the days many years ago when the first settlers raised their houses, sank their wells, and built their barns.

Then a strange blight crept over the area and everything began to change. 3
Some evil spell had settled on the community: mysterious maladies swept the flocks of chickens; the cattle and sheep sickened and died. Everywhere was a shadow of death. The farmers spoke of much illness among their families. In the town the doctors had become more and more puzzled by new kinds of sickness appearing among their patients. There had been several sudden and unexplained deaths, not only among adults but even among children, who would be stricken suddenly while at play and die within a few hours.

There was a strange stillness. The birds, for example—where had they gone? 4
Many people spoke of them, puzzled and disturbed. The feeding stations in the backyards were deserted. The few birds seen anywhere were moribund; they trembled violently and could not fly. It was a spring without voices. On the mornings that had once throbbed with the dawn chorus of robins, catbirds, doves, jays, wrens, and scores of other bird voices there was now no sound; only silence lay over the fields and woods and marsh.

On the farms the hens brooded, but no chicks hatched. The farmers 5
complained that they were unable to raise any pigs—the litters were small and the young survived only a few days. The apple trees were coming into bloom but no bees droned among the blossoms, so there was no pollination and there would be no fruit.

The roadsides, once so attractive, were now lined with browned and withered 6
vegetation as though swept by fire. These, too, were silent, deserted by all living things. Even the streams were now lifeless. Anglers no longer visited them, for all the fish had died.

In the gutters under the eaves and between the shingles of the roofs, a white 7
granular powder still showed a few patches; some weeks before it had fallen like snow upon the roofs and the lawns, the fields and streams.

No witchcraft, no enemy action had silenced the rebirth of new life in this 8
stricken world. The people had done it themselves.

This town does not actually exist, but it might easily have a thousand 9
counterparts in America or elsewhere in the world. I know of no community that has experienced all the misfortunes I describe. Yet every one of these disasters has actually happened somewhere, and many real communities have already suffered a substantial number of them. A grim specter has crept upon us almost unnoticed, and this imagined tragedy may easily become a stark reality we all shall know.

## Vocabulary

Before, during, and after reading the selection, annotate the text and write in your journal. Create a list of vocabulary words, along with their definitions, and give examples of their use from the selection you just read.

## After Reading Discussion Questions: Meaning, Structure, and Expression

1. **Main Idea:** Work as a group to write a summary that answers the following questions: What purpose did Rachel Carson have for writing this essay? Who is her intended audience? What is the main idea of the essay? What is the significance of the title?
2. **Relevant Details:** When Carson begins her concluding paragraph by stating, "This town does not actually exist," she admits that she has used a fictitious example to

make her point. Does she provide enough details to make her point convincingly? Would the use of facts or expert opinions strengthen her point? Why or why not? What is the effect of her sudden admission of using a fictitious example?

3. **Logical Order:** Carson contrasts two descriptions of a fictional place: what the place was like before it was damaged by pesticides and what the place looked like after the damage occurred. Does she organize these contrasting views point by point or by presenting one block of ideas (description of the place before it was damaged) and then another (description of the place after it was damaged)? Do you think she chose the more effective method for ordering her details? Why or why not?
4. **Effective Expression:** To make her point, Carson describes sensory details of sights and sounds to create vivid mental images in the reader's mind. Identify four sensory details: two that depict the town before it changed and two that depict the town after it changed. What impact do these details have on the reader?

## Thinking Prompts to Move from Reading to Writing

1. Carson uses sensory details to describe the change of seasons in this fictitious town, such as "in spring, white clouds of bloom drifted above the green fields." Write an essay that contrasts the seasons as they occur in a particular place. Use sensory details to depict the contrast of sights, sounds, aromas, or textures among the seasons.
2. "A Fable for Tomorrow" is a story that warns the reader about the negative effects of pesticide by contrasting before and after images. Identify a specific problem such as gangs, graffiti, drug abuse, alcoholism, an eating disorder, or obesity. Write a fable that warns against this problem by contrasting before and after situations.

# Definition

## What is Poverty?

JO GOODWIN-PARKER

The following selection was published in *America's Other Children: Public Schools Outside Suburbs*, by George Henderson in 1971 by the University of Oklahoma Press. The author specifically requests the right to her privacy and offers no additional information about herself for public use. In her essay, a personal testimony about living in poverty, she speaks directly to the reader.

**Before Reading** Write a journal entry about your response to poverty. How would you define poverty? Why are people poor? How does society react to the poor? Do you think our government does enough to help poor people? What can be done to fight poverty?

1 You ask me what is poverty? Listen to me. Here I am, dirty, smelly, and with no "proper" underwear on and with the stench of my rotting teeth near you. I will tell you. Listen to me. Listen without pity. I cannot use your pity. Listen with understanding. Put yourself in my dirty, worn out, ill-fitting shoes, and hear me.

2 Poverty is getting up every morning from a dirt- and illness-stained mattress. The sheets have long since been used for diapers. Poverty is living in a smell that never leaves. This is a smell of urine, sour milk, and spoiling food sometimes joined with the strong smell of long-cooked onions. Onions are cheap. If you have smelled this smell, you did not know how it came. It is the smell of the outdoor privy. It is the smell of young children who cannot walk the long dark way in the night. It is the smell of the mattresses where years of "accidents" have happened. It is the smell of the milk which has gone sour because the refrigerator long has not worked, and it costs money to get it fixed. It is the smell of rotting garbage. I could bury it, but where is the shovel? Shovels cost money.

3 Poverty is being tired. I have always been tired. They told me at the hospital when the last baby came that I had chronic anemia caused from poor diet, a bad case of worms, and that I needed a corrective operation. I listened politely—the poor are always polite. The poor always listen. They don't say that there is no money for iron pills, or better food, or worm medicine. The idea of an operation is frightening and costs so much that, if I had dared, I would have laughed. Who takes care of my children? Recovery from an operation takes a long time. I have three children. When I left them with "Granny" the last time I had a job, I came home to find the baby covered with fly specks, and a diaper that had not been changed since I left. When the dried diaper came off, bits of my baby's flesh came with it. My other child was playing with a sharp bit of broken glass, and my oldest was playing alone at the edge of a lake. I made twenty-two dollars a week, and a good nursery school costs twenty dollars a week for three children. I quit my job.

Poverty is dirt. You can say in your clean clothes coming from your clean house, "Anybody can be clean." Let me explain about housekeeping with no money. For breakfast I give my children grits with no oleo or cornbread without eggs and oleo. This does not use up many dishes. What dishes there are, I wash in cold water and with no soap. Even the cheapest soap has to be saved for the baby's diapers. Look at my hands, so cracked and red. Once I saved for two months to buy a jar of Vaseline for my hands and the baby's diaper rash. When I had saved enough, I went to buy it and the price had gone up two cents. The baby and I suffered on. I have to decide every day if I can bear to put my cracked sore hands into the cold water and strong soap. But you ask, why not hot water? Fuel costs money. If you have a wood fire it costs money. If you burn electricity, it costs money. Hot water is a luxury. I do not have luxuries. I know you will be surprised when I tell you how young I am. I look so much older. My back has been bent over the wash tubs every day for so long, I cannot remember when I ever did anything else. Every night I wash every stitch my school age child has on and just hope her clothes will be dry by morning. 4

Poverty is staying up all night on' cold nights to watch the fire knowing one spark on the newspaper covering the walls means your sleeping child dies in flames. In summer poverty is watching gnats and flies devour your baby's tears when he cries. The screens are torn and you pay so little rent you know they will never be fixed. Poverty means insects in your food, in your nose, in your eyes, and crawling over you when you sleep. Poverty is hoping it never rains because diapers won't dry when it rains and soon you are using newspapers. Poverty is seeing your children forever with runny noses. Paper handkerchiefs cost money and all your rags you need for other things. Even more costly are antihistamines. Poverty is cooking without food and cleaning without soap. 5

Poverty is asking for help. Have you ever had to ask for help, knowing your children will suffer unless you get it? Think about asking for a loan from a relative, if this is the only way you can imagine asking for help. I will tell you how it feels. You find out where the office is that you are supposed to visit. You circle that block four or five times. Thinking of your children, you go in. Everyone is very busy. Finally, someone comes out and you tell her that you need help. That never is the person you need to see. You go see another person, and after spilling the whole shame of your poverty all over the desk between you, you find that this isn't the right office after all—you must repeat the whole process, and it never is any easier at the next place. 6

You have asked for help, and after all it has a cost. You are again told to wait. You are told why, but you don't really hear because of the red cloud of shame and the rising cloud of despair. 7

Poverty is remembering. It is remembering quitting school in junior high because "nice" children had been so cruel about my clothes and my smell. The attendance officer came. My mother told him I was pregnant. I wasn't, but she thought that I could get a job and help out. I had jobs off and on, but never long enough to learn anything. Mostly I remember being married. I was so young then. I am still young. For a time, we had all the things you have. There was a little house in another town, with hot water and everything. Then my husband lost his job. There was unemployment insurance for a while and what few jobs I could get. Soon, all our nice things were repossessed and we moved back here. I was pregnant then. This house didn't look so bad when we first moved in. Every week it gets worse. Nothing is ever fixed. We now had no money. There were a few odd jobs for my husband, but everything went for food then, as it does now. I don't know how we lived through three years and three babies, but we did. I'll tell you something, after the last baby I destroyed 8 my marriage. It had been a good one, but could you keep on bringing children in this dirt? Did you ever think how much it costs for any kind of birth control? I knew my husband was leaving the day he left, but there were no goodbye between us. I hope he has been able to climb out of this mess somewhere. He never could hope with us to drag him down.

9 That's when I asked for help. When I got it, you know how much it was? It was, and is, seventy-eight dollars a month for the four of us; that is all I ever can get. Now you know why there is no soap, no needles and thread, no hot water, no aspirin, no worm medicine, no hand cream, no shampoo. None of these things forever and ever and ever. So that you can see clearly, I pay twenty dollars a month rent, and most of the rest goes for food. For grits and cornmeal, and rice and milk and beans. I try my best to use only the minimum electricity. If I use more, there is that much less for food.

10 Poverty is looking into a black future. Your children won't play with my boys. They will turn to other boys who steal to get what they want. I can already see them behind the bars of their prison instead of behind the bars of my poverty. Or they will turn to the freedom of alcohol or drugs, and find themselves enslaved. And my daughter? At best, there is for her a life like mine.

11 But you say to me, there are schools. Yes, there are schools. My children have no extra books, no magazines, no extra pencils, or crayons, or paper and most important of all, they do not have health. They have worms, they have infections, they have pink-eye all summer. They do not sleep well on the floor, or with me in my one bed. They do not suffer from hunger, my seventy-eight dollars keeps us alive, but they do suffer from malnutrition. Oh yes, I do remember what I was taught about health in school. It doesn't do much good.

12 In some places there is a surplus commodities program. Not here. The country said it cost too much. There is a school lunch program. But I have two children who will already be damaged by the time they get to school.

13 But, you say to me, there are health clinics. Yes, there are health clinics and they are in the towns. I live out here eight miles from town. I can walk that far (even if it is sixteen miles both ways), but can my little children? My neighbor will take me when he goes; but he expects to get paid, one way or another. I bet you know my neighbor. He is that large man who spends his time at the gas station, the barbershop, and the corner store complaining about the government spending money on the immoral mothers of illegitimate children.

14 Poverty is an acid that drips on pride until all pride is worn away. Poverty is a chisel that chips on honor until honor is worn away. Some of you say that you would do something in my situation, and maybe you would, for the first week or the first month, but for year after year after year?

15 Even the poor can dream. A dream of a time when there is money. Money for the right kinds of food, for worm medicine, for iron pills, for toothbrushes, for hand cream, for a hammer and nails and a bit of screening, for a shovel, for a bit of paint, for some sheeting, for needles and thread. Money to pay in money for a trip to town. And, oh, money for hot water and money for soap. A dream of when asking for help does not eat away the last bit of pride. When the office you visit is as nice as the offices of other governmental agencies, when there are enough workers to help you quickly, when workers do not quit in defeat and despair. When you have to tell your story to only one person, and that person can send you for other help and you don't have to prove your poverty over and over and over again.

16 I have come out of my despair to tell you this. Remember I did not come from another place or another time. Others like me are all around you. Look at us with an angry heart, anger that will help.

**Vocabulary** Before, during, and after reading the selection, annotate the text and write in your journal. Create a list of vocabulary words, along with their definitions, and give examples of their use from the selection you just read.

## After Reading Discussion Questions: Meaning, Structure, and Expression

1. **Main Idea:** Work as a group to write a summary that answers the following questions: What purpose did Jo Goodwin-Parker have for writing this essay? Who is her intended audience? What is the main idea of the essay?
2. **Relevant Details:** Parker offers her own life experiences to define poverty. Does she provide enough details to make her point convincingly? Would the use of facts or expert opinions strengthen her point? Why or why not?
3. **Logical Order:** Parker defines poverty with a series of seven statements that begin with "Poverty is." Summarize her definition of poverty using these seven statements. Do you agree with the order in which she presents these statements? Why or why not?
4. **Effective Expression:** Based on Parker's choice of words, how would you describe the tone of this essay? Is it angry, embarrassed, disappointed, reflective, sad, or optimistic, or does it communicate some other attitude about poverty? Identify three expressions that illustrate the tone of the piece. Explain the reasons for your selections.

## Thinking Prompts to Move from Reading to Writing

1. Often, people do not understand what they have not experienced. Parker defines poverty for people who have never experienced it. In the last sentence in the first paragraph, she commands her readers to step into her shoes so they can learn from her experiences. Assume the view of one who understands an issue such as depression, addiction, or prejudice based on experience. Write an essay that defines the issue so that someone who has not experienced it can better understand the problem.
2. In her essay, Parker defines the problem of poverty, but she does not offer a solution, other than to say "look at us with an angry heart, anger that will help." What kind of anger will help this situation? Respond to Parker by writing an essay that defines this kind of anger. Consider using a phrase like "Anger that will help is" to reply to specific points she raises in her essay.

# Siena, Burnt and Raw

MARY PAUMIER JONES

Writer and editor, Mary Paumier Jones, along with Judith Kitchen, coined the term "short" for creative nonfiction pieces that are artistic and typically brief as "a way of seeing the world." Jones, who teaches creative nonfiction, has a degree in library science.

**Before Reading** Write a journal entry about your reaction to color. Do you have a favorite color? If so, what is it and why is it your favorite color? Why is color important? What is the significance of a particular color such as red, gold, or purple?

1 Obscured by thick cloud cover, the Tuscan sun is nowhere in evidence. Rain falls; stops. It sprinkles again. The air holds maximum moisture, softening edges, making distance and form palpable if sometimes deceptive. In this light the buildings ringing the famous piazza are not the bright color we have been conditioned to expect by travel guides and postcards. Still the bricks are a shade so distinctive as to have taken its name from this place: Siena, sienna. The stones of Florence are gray and masculine in comparison; the marble of Carrera, unearthly white.

2 The name for the color sienna did not come into use until later, but the iron oxide limonite clay from which it comes was abundant from antiquity in Italy and other places. Cave painters at Lascaux extracted and used it, creating forms that take our breath away today, 15,000 years later. Yellow-brown in its raw state, sienna clay reddens when its water is removed by heating. Burnt sienna: color of Tuscan sun even in cloudy shade. Remember it from crayon boxes?

3 Natural pigments naturally vary tremendously from one place to another. The sienna from terra di Sienna was particularly valued through the ages for its rich hue and jewel-like transparency, caused by the silicates in the clay. Leonardo used transparent sienna in the delicate gradations of his *sfumato* technique, Caravaggio to achieve the depth of his chiaroscuro. But clay mines, sadly, are finite resources. Those in the Siena hills that yielded the pigments of Michelangelo, Botticelli, Rembrandt, Vermeer, and on and on are used up now. Since the 1940s, natural sienna has come mainly from Sardinia and Sicily, and from the Appalachian Mountains. Still called sienna, no longer Sienese.

4 At Lascaux the fungal "green and white sickness" caused by so many visitors endangered the paintings and necessitated closing the cave. History turns. An exact replica, painstakingly built, still inspires our awe while saving the original.

5 High-quality earth pigments become rarer every year. Purists and standard makers insist on the superiority of the natural. Many experts, however, say that lower-quality natural pigments are really inferior to the high-quality new synthetics. To get the look of the sienna of the old masters, they say, you'd be better off using a rich-hued transparent synthetic iron oxide paint, first developed by—what else?—the auto industry.

6 Nor is the crayon box sacred. Last year burnt sienna was one of five hues Crayola nominated for retirement to make way for new colors. The others—blizzard blue, teal blue, mulberry, and magic mint were voted off the island, and have been replaced by jazzberry jam, wild blue yonder, inch worm, and mango tango—names not without a certain poetry perhaps, but a little lacking in historical resonance. Loyal fans of burnt sienna, however, raised the hue and cry. Prevailing in their Internet vote, they kept burnt sienna in the box.

## Vocabulary

Before, during, and after reading the selection, annotate the text and write in your journal. Create a list of vocabulary words, along with their definitions, and give examples of their use from the selection you just read.

## After Reading Discussion Questions: Meaning, Structure, and Expression

1. **Main Idea:** Work as a group to write a summary that answers the following questions: What purpose did Mary Paumier Jones have for writing this essay? Who is her intended audience? What is the main idea of the essay? What is the significance of the title?
2. **Relevant Details:** Jones makes references to several artists, geographical locations, and skills or methods artists use to paint. What is the impact of these details on the reader? What does Jones assume about her audience?

3. **Logical Order:** Jones uses time order to organize the details of her definition of the color sienna. She begins with the color's historical background, its origin, and examples of its use throughout time; then, she discusses its current status of being replaced by man-made or newly developed shades. Finally, she ends with the triumph of the fan's attempt to keep sienna in the Crayola crayon boxes. Why did she choose to order her ideas in this way? How does this ordering of details support her point about the historical significance of the color? Would another order be more effective or interesting for the reader? Why or why not?
4. **Effective Expression:** Jones uses words that are scientific or specific to the art world. Based on her word choice, who is the intended audience for this essay? What changes in words or examples would you recommend to make this essay appealing to a specific audience different from the audience Jones intended? For example, how would the essay change had she written it for sixth- to eighth-grade children?

## Thinking Prompts to Move from Reading to Writing

1. Choose a your favorite color from a crayon box. Assume that Crayola is going to get rid of this color. Write an essay that defines the color and its significance in order to convince Crayola to keep it in the crayon box.
2. Create a new color that you would like Crayola to include in its crayon box. Define your new color by naming it, describing its origin (or your inspiration for its creation), giving examples of it, and describing its value to an artist.

# Cause–Effect

## Hunger

E. B. WHITE

Essayist and early *New Yorker* writer E. B. White (1899–1985) also wrote the children's classics *Stuart Little*, *Charlotte's Web*, and *The Trumpet of the Swan*, and updated *The Elements of Style*. He lived in Maine and New York City.

**Before Reading** Write a journal entry about your experience with food safety. Have you or someone you know experienced food poisoning? If so, describe the incident. Do you worry about food poisoning? Do you worry about the food industry's use of artificial additives? Why or why not?

Yesterday in the graybar building I bumped into my friend Philip Wedge, 1
looking like the devil. The sight of him gave me a start—he was horribly thin, nothing but skin and bones.

"Hello, Wedge," I said. "Where is the rest of you?" 2

He smiled a weak smile. "I'm all right." 3

We chatted for a few moments, and he admitted he had lost almost forty 4
pounds; yet he seemed disinclined to explain. Had it been anybody but Philip Wedge, I would have dropped the subject, but this queer skeleton fascinated me and I finally persuaded him to come along to lunch. At table, we got to the root of the thing quickly enough, for when the waiter appeared Wedge simply shook his head.

"I don't want anything." 5

"Good Lord," I said, "why not?" 6

Wedge fixed his eyes on me, the hollow gaze of a death's-head. "Look here," 7
he said, sharply, "you think I'm broke, or sick. It happens I'm neither. I can't eat food, and I'm going to tell you why."

So while I listened he poured it out, this amazing story. I shall set it down as 8
it came from him, but I cannot describe his utter emaciation of body, his moribundity of spirit, as he sat there opposite me, a dying man.

"It wasn't so bad," he began, "while I still had coffee. Up to a few weeks ago I 9
used to get along pretty well on coffee. Practically lived on it. Now even coffee is gone."

"Gone?" I asked. 10

"Full of rancid oil," said Wedge, drearily. "In its natural state the coffee bean 11
contains a certain amount of oil. This gets rancid, same as any oil." He drew from his pocket an advertisement telling about rancid oil in coffee. When I had read it, he folded it and returned it to his pocket.

"I haven't always been this way," he continued. "I used to eat what was set 12
before me. I believe it all started when I learned about marmalade's being made out of bilgewater."

"Out of what?" I gasped. 13

"Bilgewater. I was only fourteen. A friend of my father's, visiting at our 14
house, told us. The oranges are brought to Scotland from Spain in the holds of ships. During the voyage the oranges float around in the bilge, and when they

are unloaded the bilgewater is dumped out with them. The manufacturers find that it gives the marmalade a rich flavor."

15 "Holy Moses," I murmured. Wedge raised his hand.

16 "I could never eat marmalade after that. Wouldn't have mattered, of course, but soon other foods began to be taken from me. A year later I learned about wormy pork. Saw an item in the paper. Whole family wiped out, eating underdone pork. Awful death. I haven't had a mouthful since."

17 I glanced down at my plate and gently pushed it to one side.

18 "Used to be crazy about cheese," Wedge went on. "Did you ever see the bulletin that the Department of Agriculture issued in regard to mold? If you sniff mold it starts to grow in your lungs, like seaweed. Sometimes takes years but finally gets you. I gave up everything that might be moldy, even bread. One night I was opening a bottle of French vermouth, and the top of the cork was alive with mold. I haven't had a peaceful moment since. Jove, it seems as though every day I learned something awful about food. Ripe olives—every time I opened a newspaper, one or two dinner parties poisoned, people dying like rats. Sometimes it was éclairs. In 1922 I learned about what happens if you eat spinach from a can."

19 Wedge looked at me steadily.

20 "The vaguest rumors used to prey on my mind: casual remarks, snatches of overheard conversation. One time I came into a room where a radio was going. A speaker was ending his talk: '. . . or sulphuric acid from dried apricots, or the disintegration of the spleen from eating a poor grade of corn syrup.' That was all I heard. Haven't touched any dried fruit or any syrup since.

21 "Maybe you recall the track meet some years ago in Madison Square Garden, when Paavo Nurmi collapsed. Put his hand to his side, threw back his head, and collapsed. That was veal. Still, even with wormy pork and veal gone, my diet wasn't so bad until I found out about protein poisoning: somebody ate meat and eggs and nuts, and swelled up. I gave up all meat and all eggs, and later all nuts. At meals I began to see not the food that was actually before me—I'd see it in its earlier stages: oysters lying at the mouths of typhoid rivers, oranges impregnated by the citrus fly, gin made from hospital alcohol, watercress in drainage ditches, bottled cherries dipped in aniline dyes, marshmallows made of rotten eggs, parsley vines covered with green caterpillars, grapes sprayed with arsenate of lead. I used to spend hours in my kitchenette testing cans of foodstuffs to see if the cans sat flat. If a can doesn't sit flat, it has an air bubble in it, and its contents kill you after a few hours of agony.

22 "I grew weaker right along, hardly took a mouthful of anything from day to day. I weigh ninety-five now. All I've had since yesterday morning is a graham cracker. I used to drink quite a lot—alcohol kept me going. Had to quit. Fragmentary bits of gossip I picked up: '. . . lay off the Scotch in the West Forties,' 'The liqueurs contained traces of formaldehyde,' '. . . she died of fusel oil in homemade wine.' I even gave up cigars when I heard how they were made. You know how the ends of cigars are sealed?"

23 I nodded.

24 "Life is hell these days. I'm wasting away fast, but it's better than eating things you're scared of. Do you know what happens inside the human stomach when fruit is eaten in combination with any of the root-vegetables such as carrots, turnips . . . ?" Wedge's voice was failing. His eyelids drooped.

25 I shook my head.

26 "Enough gas is formed to inflate a balloon the size of . . ."

27 Wedge swayed in his chair, then slumped down. The poor chap had fainted. When he came to, I held a glass of water to his lips, but he motioned it away.

"Not potable," he murmured. "Reservoirs . . . too low." Then he fainted again. In the sky over Forty-third Street a buzzard wheeled and wheeled on motionless wings. 28

**Vocabulary** Before, during, and after reading the selection, annotate the text and write in your journal. Create a list of vocabulary words, along with their definitions, and give examples of their use from the selection you just read.

## After Reading Discussion Questions: Meaning, Structure, and Expression

1. **Main Idea:** Work as a group to write a summary that answers the following questions: What purpose did E. B. White have for writing this essay? Who is his intended audience? What is the essay's main idea? What is the significance of the title?
2. **Relevant Details:** White makes up a conversation with a fictitious character to support his point about the causes and effects of fear, using hunger that results from fear of food poisoning as an example. Does he provide enough details to make his point convincingly? Would the use of expert opinions strengthen his point? Why or why not?
3. **Logical Order:** The character Philip Wedge is explaining his reasons for being so hungry. Make a list of the reasons he gives for not eating. Do you find his reasons logical? Give examples to support your view. Does Wedge seem to ramble, or does he present his reasons in an order that is easy to follow? Give examples to support your view?
4. **Effective Expression:** Like Dave Barry in his essay "The Ugly Truth about Beauty," White creates a humorous tone through the use of exaggerations. Identify three examples of his humorous use of exaggeration. Why are these exaggerations humorous? Both writers rely on humor to make a point about serious topics. Why is humor an effective technique to use to make a serious point?

## Thinking Prompts to Move from Reading to Writing

1. In "Hunger," the character Wedge refers to several sources of information as reasons for his choices: advertisements, government warnings, pieces of conversations overheard, and rumors. Write an essay that warns readers about the dangers of relying on bad information or the improper use of information. Feel free to use examples from "Hunger" to support your point.
2. As depicted in the essay, Wedge could be considered an illustration of someone suffering from an eating disorder. Use his situation to identify a few possible causes and effects of an eating disorder. Write an essay that explains the causes and effects you identified. Use current examples to support your point, or feel free to use examples from "Hunger."

# Why We Crave Horror Movies

STEPHEN KING

Stephen King, born in Portland, Maine in 1947, has been writing full-time since the 1973 publication of his novel *Carrie*. He has since published over 40 books and has become one of the world's most successful writers.

**Before Reading** Write a journal entry about your reaction to horror movies. Do you enjoy horror movies? Why or why not? Why do you think horror movies are so popular? Do graphically violent horror movies have a harmful effect on society? Explain your reasons.

I think that we're all mentally ill: those of us outside the asylums only hide it a 1
little better—and maybe not all that much better, after all. We've all known people who talk to themselves, people who sometimes squinch their faces into horrible grimaces when they believe no one is watching, people who have some hysterical fear—of snakes, the dark, the tight place, the long drop . . . and, of course, those final worms and grubs that are waiting so patiently underground.

When we pay our four or five bucks and seat ourselves at tenth-row center in 2
a theater showing a horror movie, we are daring the nightmare.

Why? Some of the reasons are simple and obvious. To show that we can, that 3
we are not afraid, that we can ride this roller coaster. Which is not to say that a really good horror movie may not surprise a scream out of us at some point, the way we may scream when the roller coaster twists through a complete 360 or plows through a lake at the bottom of the drop. And horror movies, like roller coasters, have always been the special province of the young; by the time one turns 40 or 50, one's appetite for double twists or 360-degree loops may be considerably depleted.

We also go to re-establish our feelings of essential normality; the horror 4
movie is innately conservative, even reactionary. Freda Jackson as the horrible melting woman in *Die, Monster, Die!* confirms for us that no matter how far we may be removed from the beauty of a Robert Redford or a Diana Ross, we are still light-years from true ugliness.

And we go to have fun. 5

Ah, but this is where the ground starts to slope away, isn't it? Because this is a 6
very peculiar sort of fun indeed. The fun comes from seeing others menaced—sometimes killed. One critic has suggested that if pro football has become the voyeur's version of combat, then the horror film has become the modern version of the public lynching.

It is true that the mythic, "fairytale" horror film intends to take away the 7
shades of gray. . . . It urges us to put away our more civilized and adult penchant for analysis and to become children again, seeing things in pure blacks and whites. It may be that horror movies provide psychic relief on this level because this invitation to lapse into simplicity, irrationality and even outright madness is extended so rarely. We are told we may allow our emotions a free rein . . . or no rein at all.

If we are all insane, then sanity becomes a matter of degree. If your insanity 8
leads you to carve up women like Jack the Ripper or the Cleveland Torso Murderer, we clap you away in the funny farm (but neither of those two amateur-night surgeons was ever caught, heh-heh-heh); if, on the other hand your insanity leads you only to talk to yourself when you're under stress or to pick your nose on the morning bus, then you are left alone to go about your business . . . though it is doubtful that you will ever be invited to the best parties.

The potential lyncher is in almost all of us (excluding saints, past and 9
present; but then, most saints have been crazy in their own ways), and every now and then, he has to be let loose to scream and roll around in the grass. Our emotions and our fears form their own body, and we recognize that it demands its own exercise to maintain proper muscle tone. Certain of these emotional muscles are accepted—even exalted—in civilized society; they are, of course,

the emotions that tend to maintain the status quo of civilization itself. Love, friendship, loyalty, kindness—these are all the emotions that we applaud, emotions that have been immortalized in the couplets of Hallmark cards. . . .

When we exhibit these emotions, society showers us with positive 10
reinforcement; we learn this even before we get out of diapers. When, as children, we hug our rotten little puke of a sister and give her a kiss, all the aunts and uncles smile and twit and cry, "Isn't he the sweetest little thing?" Such coveted treats as chocolate-covered graham crackers often follow. But if we deliberately slam the rotten little puke of a sister's fingers in the door, sanctions follow—angry remonstrance from parents, aunts and uncles; instead of a chocolate-covered graham cracker, a spanking.

But anticivilization emotions don't go away, and they demand periodic 11
exercise. We have such "sick" jokes as, "What's the difference between a truckload of bowling balls and a truckload of dead babies?" (You can't unload a truckload of bowling balls with a pitchfork . . . a joke, by the way, that I heard originally from a ten-year-old.) Such a joke may surprise a laugh or a grin out of us even as we recoil, a possibility that confirms the thesis: If we share a brotherhood of man, then we also share an insanity of man. None of which is intended as a defense of either the sick joke or insanity but merely as an explanation of why the best horror films, like the best fairy tales, manage to be reactionary, anarchistic, and revolutionary all at the same time.

The mythic horror movie, like the sick joke, has a dirty job to do. It 12
deliberately appeals to all that is worst in us. It is morbidity unchained, our most base instincts let free, our nastiest fantasies realized . . . and it all happens, fittingly enough, in the dark. For those reasons, good liberals often shy away from horror films. For myself, I like to see the most aggressive of them—*Dawn of the Dead,* for instance—as lifting a trap door in the civilized forebrain and throwing a basket of raw meat to the hungry alligators swimming around in that subterranean river beneath.

Why bother? Because it keeps them from getting out, man. It keeps them 13
down there and me up here. It was Lennon and McCartney who said that all you need is love, and I would agree with that.

As long as you keep the gators fed. 14

**Vocabulary** Before, during, and after reading the selection, annotate the text and write in your journal. Create a list of vocabulary words, along with their definitions, and give examples of their use from the selection you just read.

## After Reading Discussion Questions: Meaning, Structure, and Expression

1. **Main Idea:** Work as a group to write a summary that answers the following questions: What purpose did Stephen King have for writing this essay? Who is his intended audience? What is the essay's main idea?
2. **Relevant Details:** In paragraphs 10 and 11, King uses children as examples to support his point. Why do you think he uses these examples? Do you think these examples are typical of most children? Do you agree that these examples effectively support his point? Why or why not?
3. **Logical Order:** King declares his thesis in paragraph 11. Locate his thesis statement. Why do you think King waited until this late in the essay to state his thesis? Reread his introduction. What is his opening point? Why do you think he opened his essay with this idea? How would the impact of the essay change if King had stated his thesis in the opening paragraph?

4. **Effective Expression:** To make his point, King appeals to our senses and prior experiences with references to roller coasters, Jack the Ripper, lynching, and alligators. Discuss how each of these images supports his point.

## Thinking Prompts to Move from Reading to Writing

1. King offers reasons that explain the positive effects of horror movies. However, many disagree with this view and see the violence in horror movies as a negative factor in our society. Write an essay that explains the negative impact of horror movies.
2. King claims that we are "all mentally ill" and that horror movies appeal to the "worst in us." However, many believe that humans are basically good. The famous American essayist Emerson once encouraged us "to look into yourselves and do good because you are good." Write an essay that illustrates the goodness and positive impact of human nature. Consider, for example, the reasons and effects of Habitat for Humanity or other charities or volunteer organizations.

# Persuasion

## Let's Tell the Story of All America's Cultures

YUH JI-YEON

Yuh Ji-Yeon, born in 1965, immigrated with her parents to Chicago from Seoul, Korea. She is best known for her book *Beyond the Shadow of Camptown* that examines the experiences of Korean women who immigrated to this country as brides of U.S. soldiers. She currently teaches history at Northwestern University.

**Before Reading** Write a journal entry about the positive contributions of minorities to the culture of the United States. For example, how have African Americans, Asians, or Latinos affected music, movies, fashion, or politics? Identify a particular person who has made a specific contribution. Do you think history books adequately record the contributions made by minorities? Explain your reasons.

I grew up hearing, seeing and almost believing that America was white—albeit with a little black tinge here and there—and that white was best. 1

The white people were everywhere in my 1970s Chicago childhood: Founding Fathers, Lewis and Clark, Lincoln, Daniel Boone, Carnegie, presidents, explorers and industrialists galore. The only black people were slaves. The only Indians were scalpers. 2

I never heard one word about how Benjamin Franklin was so impressed by the Iroquois federation of nations that he adapted that model into our system of state and federal government. Or that the Indian tribes were systematically betrayed and massacred by a greedy young nation that stole their land and called it the United States. 3

I never heard one word about how Asian immigrants were among the first to turn California's desert into fields of plenty. Or about Chinese immigrant Ah Bing, who bred the cherry now on sale in groceries across the nation. Or that plantation owners in Hawaii imported labor from China, Japan, Korea and the Philippines to work the sugar cane fields. I never learned that Asian immigrants were the only immigrants denied U.S. citizenship, even though they served honorably in World War I. All the immigrants in my textbook were white. 4

I never learned about Frederick Douglass, the runaway slave who became a leading abolitionist and statesman, or about black scholar W.E.B. Du Bois. I never learned that black people rose up in arms against slavery. Nat Turner wasn't one of the heroes in my childhood history class. 5

I never learned that the American Southwest and California were already settled by Mexicans when they were annexed after the Mexican-American War. I never learned that Mexico once had a problem keeping land-hungry white men on the U.S. side of the border. 6

So when other children called me a slant-eyed chink and told me to go back where I came from, I was ready to believe that I wasn't really an American because I wasn't white. 7

America's bittersweet legacy of struggling and failing and getting another 8
step closer to democratic ideals of liberty and equality and justice for all wasn't for the likes of me, an immigrant child from Korea. The history books said so.

Well, the history books were wrong. 9

Educators around the country are finally realizing what I realized as a 10
teenager in the library, looking up the history I wasn't getting in school. America is a multicultural nation, composed of many people with varying histories and varying traditions who have little in common except their humanity, a belief in democracy and a desire for freedom.

America changed them, but they changed America too. 11

A committee of scholars and teachers gathered by the New York State 12
Department of Education recognizes this in their recent report, "One Nation, Many Peoples: A Declaration of Cultural Interdependence."

They recommend that public schools provide a "multicultural education, 13
anchored to the shared principles of a liberal democracy."

What that means, according to the report, is recognizing that America was 14
shaped and continues to be shaped by people of diverse backgrounds. It calls for students to be taught that history is an ongoing process of discovery and interpretation of the past, and that there is more than one way of viewing the world.

Thus, the westward migration of white Americans is not just a heroic settling 15
of an untamed wild, but also the conquest of indigenous peoples. Immigrants were not just white, but Asian as well. Blacks were not merely passive slaves freed by northern whites, but active fighters for their own liberation.

In particular, according to the report, the curriculum should help children 16
"to assess critically the reasons for the inconsistencies between the ideals of the U.S. and social realities. It should provide information and intellectual tools that can permit them to contribute to bringing reality closer to the ideals."

In other words, show children the good with the bad, and give them the skills 17
to help improve their country. What could be more patriotic?

Several dissenting members of the New York committee publicly worry that 18
America will splinter into ethnic fragments if this multicultural curriculum is adopted. They argue that the committee's report puts the focus on ethnicity at the expense of national unity.

But downplaying ethnicity will not bolster national unity. The history of 19
America is the story of how and why people from all over the world came to the United States, and how in struggling to make a better life for themselves, they changed each other, they changed the country, and they all came to call themselves Americans.

*E pluribus unum.* Out of many, one. 20

This is why I, with my Korean background, and my childhood tormentors, 21
with their lost-in-the-mist-of-time European backgrounds, are all Americans.

It is the unique beauty of this country. It is high time we let all our children 22
gaze upon it.

**Vocabulary** Before, during, and after reading the selection, annotate the text and write in your journal. Create a list of vocabulary words, along with their definitions, and give examples of their use from the selection you just read.

## After Reading Discussion Questions: Meaning, Structure, and Expression

1. **Main Idea:** Work as a group to write a summary that answers the following questions: What purpose did Yuh Ji-Yeon have for writing this essay? Who is her intended audience? What is the essay's main idea?
2. **Relevant Details:** Yuh blends details from her personal experiences with expert opinions. Identify the details based on her experiences. Are the personal details she provides convincing enough to persuade her reader to agree with her? Identify the details based on expert opinions. Does Yuh provide enough expert opinions and factual details to make her point? Why did she choose to include both personal experiences and expert opinions? Is the mixture persuasive? Why or why not?
3. **Logical Order:** An effective persuasive technique is to answer the concerns of the opposing view. Yuh waits to address the opposing view until paragraph 18. Why did she choose to do so at this point in her essay? Would her point be better made if she addressed the opposing view earlier in the essay? Why or why not?
4. **Effective Expression:** In paragraphs 1 through 6, Yuh repeats the parallel phrases "I never heard" or "I never learned." What is the impact of repeating these phrases and other parallel expressions on the essay's effectiveness? Explain your answer.

## Thinking Prompts to Move from Reading to Writing

1. Yuh identifies and argues against one problem in education that she sees as particularly troubling. What problems have you noticed in our country's educational system or at your institution? For example, some suggest school uniforms as a solution to behavior problems and underachievement in public education. Another example is the acute problem of binge drinking on college campuses. Identify a problem or a solution to a problem in education. Take a stand on the issue. Write an essay that convinces others to agree with your stand; be sure to answer the opposing view.
2. Yuh calls for educators to "tell the story of all America's cultures," and she offers several examples of important historical figures that she never learned about in school. Identify a person, place, or event that students should study. Write an essay to convince your teacher, school board, or community to include this person, place, or event in the curriculum. Anticipate and answer the opposing view.

# Statement of Senator Joe Lieberman on Rating the Ratings System

JOE LIEBERMAN

Born on February 24, 1942 in Stamford, Connecticut, Joe Lieberman is now serving his fourth term representing Connecticut in the United States Senate. According to his official website, Joe Lieberman is "dedicated to strengthening America's families and renewing our common values by working with parents to improve the culture in which they raise their children." This essay was submitted to the United States Committee on Government Affairs in 2001.

**Before Reading** Write a journal entry about graphic material and the government's role in censorship. Are some movies, music, and video games are too sexually or violently explicit? Why is graphic material so popular? Do you pay attention to the various media rating systems? Are the current rating systems effective? Should government be more involved in controlling graphic material? Explain your thinking.

Good morning. We are here today to revisit an issue that parents repeatedly raise with just about anyone who will listen—the challenge they face in raising healthy children in today's 500-channel, multiplexed, videogamed, discmanned universe. 1

That is a reflection of the quantity of time children spend consuming and using media—an average of 6-1/2 hours a day, according to the Annenberg Public Policy Center. But it is even more a reflection of the quality of the messages about sex and violence kids are being exposed to by the entertainment media—messages which too often reject rather than reflect the basic values parents are trying to instill—and the growing sense that the totality of these messages is having a harmful influence on the attitudes and behaviors of our children, and therefore on the safety and moral condition of our country. 2

There are limits to what we in government can do to respond to these concerns—because of our devotion to the First Amendment, and because governments don't raise children, parents do. At the same time, though, there are some things that we can do—hopefully with the movie, music, video game, and television industries—to empower parents and make the hard job of raising healthy children a little easier. 3

One way to empower is to inform. Over the years, the major entertainment media have developed rating and labeling systems, largely at the urging of public advocates, to offer parents and consumers information about the content of their products and help parents exercise more informed control over their children's media diets. And over that time, these ratings, particularly those of the movie industry, have become cultural icons. 4

But as the content and marketing practices of the entertainment media have become worse, we have been hearing more and more concerns about how these ratings systems work. There have been specific criticisms about their reliability, visibility, and understandability. And there have been general complaints that the ratings do not provide parents with enough information about content—about the levels of sex, violence, and vulgarity in each product—to make the right choice for their children. Last year, for example, a Gallup survey found that 74 percent of parents said the movie, music and television ratings were inadequate on that count. 5

Those concerns culminated in a letter sent to policymakers last month by a distinguished coalition of researchers, medical groups, and child development experts, which recommended a complete overhaul of media ratings. That letter, initiated by the National Institute on Media and the Family, argued that the different ratings are often applied inconsistently, that many parents find the multiplicity of rating icons confusing, and, as a result, that the ratings are not adequately serving their purpose—helping parents or protecting kids. To fix this problem, the signers of the letter called for replacing the existing formats with a new uniform rating system, monitored by an independent oversight committee and grounded in sound research. 6

I thought this was an important statement with a provocative proposal that deserved more public discussion. I believe that is one critical way in which we in government can help parents, to provide a platform, facilitate a dialogue, and ideally build common ground. That is the aim of our hearing today—to flesh 7 out the concerns raised in the NIMF's letter and explore the merits of their recommendations, to hear the response of industry keepers of these rating systems, and see if there is any agreement on ways to improve the ratings to better inform parents.

I have expressed interest in the idea of uniform ratings before—as have others in Congress, including Senators McCain and Clinton, and in the entertainment industry, notably Disney President Robert Iger—and I remain interested in it. Many parents appear interested as well—a survey by the Kaiser Family Foundation being released today found that 40 percent of parents believe that a uniform rating system would be more useful than the current approach, and only 17 percent think it would be less useful. So today we will hear the arguments in favor of switching to a single system, as well as the industry's objections to it. 8

I hope the entertainment industry witnesses come with an equally open mind, particularly on the question of providing more and better information. For some time now many of us have voiced dissatisfaction with the recording industry's one size-fits-all parental advisory program, which provides a solitary stickered warning to parents of "explicit content." We have urged the major record companies to expand and clarify their system and tell parents what kinds of explicit content are in the lyrics. Those same criticisms and calls for change were repeated vociferously at a hearing before the House Telecommunications Subcommittee last week, as I understand it, and Ms. Rosen ruled out adding any content descriptions to the recording industry's labeling system. I hope in our discussion today that Ms. Rosen will reconsider that position. 9

I also hope that Mr. Valenti will alter the outrageous suggestion he makes in his response to the aforementioned letter from the NIMF that there is serious doubt about whether violence in the media poses a risk of harm to our children. 10

If we are looking for an industry model, I would point to the video game rating system, which is administered by the independent Electronic Software Ratings Board (ESRB). The ESRB system, which was a response to Congressional hearings, pairs age-based icons with detailed content descriptors in a clear, concise, and informative format. I believe it is the best media rating system in existence. 11

Ultimately any potential reforms in the ratings will be meaningless if parents don't use them. We need to remind parents of their responsibilities as we renew our call for more and better information in the ratings. 12

One last word about the First Amendment, which is one thing all of us seem to support. We are not talking about any legislation or government regulation today. But I want to warn the industry again that the best way to invite censorship is to disengage from this discussion and tune out the larger concerns of millions of American parents about media influence on our kids and our country. Indeed, the most striking finding of the Kaiser survey to me was that 48 percent of parents would support government regulations to limit the amount of violent and sexual content in early evening TV shows. That is an outcry that begins to express just how frustrated and angry America's parents are about the state of our culture and its impact on our children. 13

**Vocabulary** Before, during, and after reading the selection, annotate the text and write in your journal. Create a list of vocabulary words, along with their definitions, and give examples of their use from the selection you just read.

## After Reading Discussion Questions: Meaning, Structure, and Expression

1. **Main Idea:** Work as a group to write a summary that answers the following questions: What purpose did Joe Lieberman have for writing this essay? Who is his intended audience? What is the essay's main idea?
2. **Relevant Details:** Lieberman relies on several outside sources for details to support his point, such as the Annenberg Public Policy Center, a Gallup survey, the National Institute on Media and the Family, a Kaiser Family Foundation survey, and the Electronic Software Ratings Board. Identify the details provided by each of these sources. Is the information from each source objective or biased? Are these details convincing enough to persuade his audience to agree with him? Why or why not?
3. **Logical Order:** Lieberman addresses opposing views in paragraphs 3, 10, and 13. What are these opposing views? Why do you think he spaced them in separate parts of his essay instead of addressing them all in one paragraph? Would his point be more effective if he had discussed those points in one paragraph? Why or why not?
4. **Effective Expression:** Lieberman uses the first person pronoun "I" around a dozen times in this essay. Find these first person statements. Why does he use the first person pronoun? Is his use of first person effective in his effort to convince the audience to agree with him? Why or why not?

## Thinking Prompts to Move from Reading to Writing

1. Locate a copy of a rating system such as the ones provided by the Motion Picture Association of America (mpaa.org) or the Electronic Software Ratings Board (www.esrb.org). Write an essay that supports or opposes a particular rating system. Use examples from the media and address opposing views to convince your reader to agree with you.
2. Write a letter about the ratings system to an elected representative from your area. Ask your representative or senator to support or oppose a government-sponsored rating system for the entertainment industry. To find your elected representative, go to the government website *Thomas: Legislative Information on the Internet* at thomas.loc.gov.

# The Hip-Hop Summit Action Network Statement for the Senate Committee on Governmental Affairs Hearing on Entertainment Ratings, July 25, 2001

RUSSELL SIMMONS

Born in 1957 and raised in Hollis, Queens, New York City, Russell Simmons, rap record producer and artist manager, is credited with the explosive entry of rap music onto the national music scene in the late 1980s. He is the co-owner and founder of the rap label Def Jam Records and head of Rush Artist Management, the largest black-owned music business in the United States. This essay was submitted as testimony to the United States Committee on Government Affairs in 2001.

**Before Reading** Write a journal entry about the values and role models provided by the music industry. For example, does Hip Hop provide positive or negative content and role models for youth? Explain your opinion. Should graphic material be banned or censored? Why or why not?

1 My name is Russell Simmons and I am submitting this statement on behalf of the Hip Hop Summit Action Network and its Executive Director, Minister Benjamin Muhammad. I am Chairman of the Hip Hop Summit Action Network and I have worked in the music and entertainment industry for more than twenty-five years. Minister Benjamin is the former Executive Director and CEO of the NAACP and has over thirty-five years of experience in civil and human rights.

2 The Hip Hop Summit Action Network is the broadest national coalition of Hip Hop artists, entertainment industry executives, civil rights and community leaders. Established this year, the mission of the Hip Hop Summit Action Network is to support Hip Hop and freedom, justice, equality and empowerment for all based on the principles of freedom of speech, music and art creativity, and the universality of humanity.

3 I regret that despite our request to the Committee there is neither space nor time for me to testify today. Not simply because I, both individually and on behalf of the Hip Hop generation have some important things to say about these issues, but also because many of us feel that these hearings are really about us, and it would be better in our view to hear from us and speak to us directly before you pass judgment and deny our fundamental rights.

4 But let me start with something positive. The Hip Hop community has decided to take a leadership position toward the evolution of our artistic destiny and responsibility. We convened an historic summit last month in New York and we are planning others In Los Angeles and Miami in August to explore questions related to violence in our own communities, racial profiling, police brutality, representation of women, and the profanity of poverty . . . and how we can work from within our industry to expand and elevate the artistic presentation of our culture and experience.

5 Although we know that the harsh underlying social realities that some of our music exposes have not changed much in our communities, we are committed to speaking the truth. We believe that we must continue to tell the truth about the street if that is what we know and we must continue to tell the truth about God if that is who we have found. Part of telling the truth is making sure that you know, and talk more about what you know than to speak or do music to appease those who are in power. Hip Hop represents truth telling, speaking the truth to ourselves and speaking the truth to power out of the context and condition of our community.

6 The Congress of the United States should not censor free speech nor artistic expression. It is unconstitutional for government intrusion or dictation concerning "labeling of music" or "rating of music" that has the effect of denying free speech.

7 What is offensive is any attempt by the government to deny the expression of words and lyrics that emerge out of a culture that has become the soul of America. In fact Hip Hop has now grown to become a global cultural and artistic phenomena.

8 Congress should not attempt to legislate preferences in music, art and culture.

9 My final point is that this is often largely about race. And it makes some of us very concerned that few will publicly admit that this effort to censure Hip

Hop has deep seated racial overtones. Hip Hop emerged out of the African American experience. Eminem is a successful white Hip Hop artist who, power to him, has excelled and profited from the genre of black music. He stands on the shoulders of other originators of Hip Hop. The Federal Trade Commission's report on explicit content disproportionately focused on black Hip Hop artists. This report flawed scientifically as well as morally and culturally and should not, therefore, be used as a basis for constructing a system of "ratings" in regard to music and other forms of entertainment.

Simply put, we conclude by appealing to the Senate Committee on 10
Government Affairs to refrain from censoring, labeling, or rating our music and culture in the absence of understanding and appreciation of our artistic work which represents the genius of our culture and talent of our youth, in fact all youth of today . . . black, white, Latino, Asian and all others.

Thank you.

## Vocabulary

Before, during, and after reading the selection, annotate the text and write in your journal. Create a list of vocabulary words, along with their definitions, and give examples of their use from the selection you just read.

## After Reading Discussion Questions: Meaning, Structure, and Expression

1. **Main Idea:** Work as a group to write a summary that answers the following questions: What purpose did Russell Simmons have for writing this essay? Who is his intended audience? What is the essay's main idea?
2. **Relevant Details:** Who does Simmons rely on as an expert opinion? What factual details does he provide to support his point? In paragraph 9, Simmons claims the Federal Trade Commission's report on explicit content is "flawed scientifically as well as morally and culturally and should not, therefore, be used." What evidence does he offer to support this claim? Overall, does Simmons offer enough details to convince his audience to agree with him? Why or why not?
3. **Logical Order:** Simmons says, "My final point is that this is often largely about race." What does he mean by this statement? Why did he wait to introduce race as his final point? Would his overall message be stronger if he addressed the issue of race earlier in his essay? Why or why not?
4. **Effective Expression:** Simmons uses a number of emotionally laden expressions such as "racial profiling," "police brutality," and "genius." Identify other instances of his use of emotional language. What effect does Simmons hope to have on his audience? Explain your reasons. Do you think he achieved the effect he wanted? Why or why not?

## Thinking Prompts to Move from Reading to Writing

1. Create a ratings system that gives parents enough information about the contents of a movie, song, video game, or television show. Write an essay that convinces Russell Simmons and the entertainment industry to accept your ratings system.
2. Simmons describes Hip Hop as exposing and "speaking the truth" about "harsh underlying social realities." He goes on to say that the music "must continue to tell the truth about the street." Do you agree or disagree with this view? What are the "harsh realities" and the "truth of the street" to which he refers? Does the music encourage change or reinforce these "truths"? Write a letter to Simmons in which you offer support for or opposition to his view. Use examples from his essay and Hip Hop music to support your stand.

# Text Credits

Angelou, Maya, "New Directions," from *Wouldn't Take Nothing for My Journey Now.* New York: Random House, Inc., 1993.

Barry, Dave. "The Ugly Truth About Beauty," from *The Miami Herald,* February 1, 1998.

Campbell, Neil A., Reece, Jane B., Taylor, Martha R., and Simon, Eric J. *Biology: Concepts and Connections,* 5th ed. Copyright © 2008 Benjamin Cummings.

Carson, Rachel. "A Fable for Tomorrow" from *Silent Spring.* Copyright © 1962 by Rachel L. Carson, renewed 1990 by Roger Christie. Reprinted by permission of Houghton Mifflin Company. All rights reserved.

Centers for Disease Control and Prevention. "Women and Smoking: A Report of the Surgeon General—2001," January 31, 2004.

Cofer, Judith Ortiz "Don't Call me a Hot Tamale" or "The Myth of the Latin Woman: I Just Met a Girl Named Maria," from *The Latin Deli: Prose and Poetry.* University of Georgia Press.

Crosby, Olivia. "Associate Degree: Two Years to a Career or a Jump Start to a Bachelor's Degree." Washington, D.C.: U.S. Department of Labor.

De Vito, Joseph A. *The Interpersonal Communication Book,* 10th ed. Boston: Allyn and Bacon, 2004.

De Vito, Joseph A. *Messages: Building Interpersonal Communication Skills,* 4th ed. Boston: Allyn and Bacon, 1999.

Giovanni, Nikki. "My Own Style." *Essence,* 16 (May 1985): 60, 62. By permission of the Author © 1988 from Sacred Cows and Other Edibles.

Goodwin-Parker, Jo. "What is Poverty?" in *America's Other Children: Public Schools Outside Suburbia,* by George Henderson. Copyright © 1971 by University of Oklahoma Press, Norman. Reprinted by permission of the publisher. All rights reserved.

Haines, John. "Snow," from *The Stars, the Snow, the Fire: Twenty-Five Years in the Alaska Wilderness.* Minneapolis: Graywolf Press, 2000.

Hasselstrom, Linda M. "A Peaceful Woman Explains Why She Carries a Gun," *UTNE Reader,* May-June 1991.

"Hawaii's Fun-Fueled Activity Book: Clean Fuels." Honolulu Clean Cities Website. www.hawaii.gov/dbedt/ert/cc/index.html

Jaffe, Michael L. *Understanding Parenting,* 2nd ed. Boston: Allyn and Bacon, 1997, figure on p. 241.

Jones, Mary Paumier. "Siena, Burnt and Raw," from *Short Takes: Brief Encounters with Contemporary Nonfiction,* edited by Judith Kitchen. New York: Norton 2005.

Keillor, Garrison. "How to Write a Personal Letter," from *We Are Still Married.* Copyright © 1987 by International Paper Company. Reprinted by permission of Garrison Keillor.

King, Martin Luther Jr. "Ways of Meeting Oppression," from *Stride Towards Freedom.*

King, Stephen. "Why We Crave Horror Movies." Reprinted with permission. © Stephen King. All rights reserved. Originally appeared in *Playboy* (1982).

Lieberman, Joe. "Statement on Rating the Ratings System."

O'Connor, Sabato, and Haig, Keith. *American Government: Continuity and Change, 2004.* Texas Edition. Copyright © 2004 by Pearson.

O'Hanlon, Larry. "Honey Bee Die-off Alarms Beekeepers," *Discovery News,* February 5, 2007.

Simmons, Russell. "The Hip-Hop Summit Action Network Statement for the Senate Committee on Governmental Affairs Hearing on Entertainment Ratings," July 25, 2001.

Swetlow, Karen. "Children at Clandestine Methamphetamine Labs: Helping Meth's Youngest Victims." *OVC Bulletin,* U.S. Department of Justice, June 2003.

Tan, Amy. "Confessions." Copyright © 1997 by Amy Tan. Reprinted by permission of the author and the Sandra Dijkstra Literary Agency.

Twain, Mark. "Old Age."

United States Department of Agriculture. "Balance the Food You Eat with Physical Activity—Maintain or Improve Your Weight." *Nutrition and Your Health: Dietary Guidelines for Americans,* December 1995.

United States Department of Health and Human Services. "Stroke," Women's Health.gov. The National Women's Health Information Center, March 26, 2006.

United States Equal Employment Opportunity Commission. "Facts about Sexual Harassment," March 13, 2006.

United States Park Service. "Maya Lin's Design Submission to the Vietnam Memorial Competition."

Viorst, Judith. "The Truth About Lying." Copyright © 1981 by Judith Viorst. Originally appeared in *Redbook.* Reprinted by permission of Lescher & Lescher, Ltd. All rights reserved.

White, E. B. "Hunger." From *E. B. White, Writings from The New Yorker: 1927–1976* (edited by Rebecca M. Dale), copyright 1990 by Joel White and Rebecca Dale, HarperCollins. Reprinted by permission © E. B White. Originally published in *The New Yorker.* All rights reserved.

Yuh, Ji-Yeon. "Let's Tell the Story of All America's Cultures." From *The Philadelphia Inquirer,* June 30, 1991. Used by permission of the author.

# Photo Credits

**Contents:** iii (top) David Buffington/Corbis; iii (bottom) ©David Pollack/Corbis; iv (top) Hans Neleman/Corbis; iv (bottom) Wesley Hitt/ Alamy; v (top) © Bojan Brecelj/Corbis; v (bottom) M;L; Sinibaldi/Corbis; vi (top) Peter Dazeley/Corbis; vi (bottom) Dallas and John Heaton/Corbis; vii Image Select/Getty Images RF; viii (top) Richard Cummins/Corbis; viii (bottom) Fotosearch;

**Chapter 1:** 2 David Buffington/Corbis; 3 (top) Helene Rogers/Alamy; 3 (top center) ©fotofresh/Alamy; 3 (bottom center) ©Myrleen Ferguson Cate/PhotoEdit, Inc; 3 (bottom) ©Gary Conner/PhotoEdit, Inc; 5 (all) Dorling Kindersley Media Library; 7 (all) Dorling Kindersley Media Library;

**Chapter 2:** 14 RF Comstock/Corbis; 15 (top left) Chuck Savage/Corbis; 15 (top right) Image Source/Getty Images RF; 15 (bottom left) AP/Wide World Photos; 15 (bottom right) Royalty-Free/Corbis; 16 Michigan Board of Education 1994; 18 (bottom left) Merry Alpern/Corbis; 18 (bottom right) Royalty-free/Corbis; 18 (top left) Myrleen Ferguson/ PhotoEdit, Inc; 18 (top right) Jessica Rinaldi/Reuters/Corbis; 20 (left)Aristide Economopoulos/Star Ledger/Corbis; 20 (right) Royalty-Free/Corbis; 21 (left) Royalty-Free/Corbis; 21 (right) Bettmann/Corbis; 22 (left) Aristide Economopoulos/Star Ledger/Corbis; 22 (center left) Royalty-Free/Corbis; 22 (center right) Royalty-Free/Corbis; 22 (right) Bettmann/Corbis; 24 Michigan State Board of Education 1994; 26 ©2004 David Farley; 28 Courtesy TRIMSPA; 30 Buddy Mays/Corbis; 32 Jose Luis Pelaez, Inc./Corbis; 38 Kevin Cooley/Stone/Getty Images.

**Chapter 3:** 50 ©Trains and Planes/Alamy; 52 (top) ©Bob Krist/Corbis; 52 (center) RF ©Image Source/Corbis; 52 (bottom left) ©Steve Chenn/Corbis; 52 (bottom right) ©Jerome Sessini/Corbis; 54 (top) ©David Muench/Corbis; 54 (bottom) ©Gene Blevins/LA Daily News/Corbis; 57 (left) ©Jeff Greenberg/PhotoEdit, Inc.; 57 (center) ©Michael Newman/ PhotoEdit, Inc.; 57 (right) ©Bill Varie/Corbis; 63 ©David Wells/Corbis; 64 ©John Miller/Robert Harding World Imagery/Corbis.

**Chapter 4:** 68 ©David Pollack/Corbis; 69 Corbis/Bettmann; 70 (all) Corbis/Bettmann 71 (both) Corbis/Bettmann; 73 Corbis/Bettmann; 78 Tom & Dee Ann McCarthy/Corbis 80 Joseph Sohm/Corbis

**Chapter 5:** 88 (all) Douglas Kirkland/Corbis; 89 (top) Frank Micelotta/Getty Images; 89 (center) Dreamworks/David James/The Kobal Collection; 89 (bottom) Mike Blake/Corbis; 98 Dorling Kindersley Media Library.

**Chapter 6:** 106 © Rebecca Emery/Corbis; 107 (all) Dorling Kindersley Media Library; 109 (all) Dorling Kindersley Media Library; 112 Richard Hutchings/PhotoEdit, Inc.; 114 (far left) David Young-Wolff/PhotoEdit, Inc.; 114 (center left) Michael Newman/PhotoEdit, Inc.; 114 (center) Elizabeth Lippman/Corbis Sygma; 114 (center right) Jeff Greenberg/Alamy; 114 (far right) Tom Grill/Corbis; 115 (top) Gregor Schuster/zefa/Corbis; 115 (bottom) Ray Coleman/Photo Researchers, Inc; 116 (top) Larry Lilac/Alamy RF; 116 (bottom) Superstock.

**Chapter 7:** 124 Richard Drury/The Image Bank/Getty Images; 125 (left) Henry Diltz/Corbis; 125 (center) Eric Gaillard/Reuters/Corbis; 125 (right) Frank Trapper/Corbis; 127 (top) Henry Diltz/Corbis; 127 (center) Eric Gaillard/ Reuters/Corbis; 127 (bottom) Frank Trapper/Corbis; 132 (left) David Young-Wolff/PhotoEdit, Inc.; 132 (center) George Shelley/Corbis; 132 (right) Blend Images/Alamy; 135 Radius Images/Alamy; 136 (top) ©Envision/Corbis; 136 (top center) Dynamic Graphics Group/Creatas/Alamy; 136 (bottom center) Edward Kinsman/Photo Researchers, Inc.; 136 (bottom) Jose Luis Pelaez, Inc./Corbis.

**Chapter 8:** 144 Hans Neleman/Corbis; 145 (left) John Gress/ Reuters/Corbis; 145 (center) Carlos Barria/Reuters/Corbis; 145 (right) Zack Seckler/Corbis; 148 (top) John Gress/ Reuters/Corbis; 148 (center) Carlos Barria/Reuters/Corbis; 148 (bottom) Zack Seckler/Corbis; 152 Mauro Fermariello/ Photo Researchers, Inc.; 154 ©David Turnley/Corbis.

**Chapter 9:** 166 (left) AP/Wide World; 166 (right) RF/Mick Roessler/Corbis; 167 (top left) NASA/Corbis; 167 (top right) NOAA/Corbis; 167 (center left) Robert Galbraith/Reuters/ Corbis; 167 (center right) Smiley N. Pool/Dallas Morning News/Corbis; 167 (bottom left) AP/Wide World Photos; 167 (bottom right) Smiley N. Pool/Dallas Morning News/Corbis; 169 (top to bottom)NASA/Corbis, NOAA/Corbis, Robert Galbraith/Reuters/Corbis, Smiley N. Pool/Dallas Morning News/Corbis, Smiley N. Pool/Dallas Morning News/Corbis, AP/Wide World Photos; 173 (left) ©Disney Enterprises; 173 (right) Private Collection/Scala/Art Resource, NY ©2007 Estate of Marc Chagall/Artists Rights Society (ARS), NY; 175 ©Tony Freeman/PhotoEdit, Inc.; 176 (top) ©Robert W; Ginn/PhotoEdit, Inc.; 176 (bottom) ©Richard M; Abarno/Corbis.

**Chapter 10:** 184 Chloe Johnson/Alamy; 185 (left) Mike Powell/Corbis; 185 (top right) Kapoor Baldev/Sygma/ Corbis; 185 (right center) Reuters/Corbis; 185 (bottom right) Jehad Nga/Corbis; 187 (top) Mike Powell/Corbis; 187 (center top) Kapoor Baldev/Corbis Sygma;187 (bottom center) Reuters/Corbis; 187 (bottom) Jehad Nga/Corbis; 193 (left) Chloe Johnson/Alamy; 193 (center) Art Kowalsky/ Alamy; 193 (right) ©Thunderdog Studios, Inc;/Thunderdog Collective/Corbis; 195 Gene Blevins/ La Daly News/Corbis; 202 Dorling Kindersley Media Library.

**Chapter 11:** 204 George Diebold/Corbis; 205 (top left) Joseph Sohm/ChromoSohm Inc;/Corbis; 205 (all other photos) Courtesy Habitat for Humanity; 207 (top) Joseph Sohm/ChromoSohm Inc./Corbis; 211 (left) Patrik Giardino/Corbis; 211 (top right)©Hill Street Studios/Blend Images/Corbis RF; 211 (bottom right) RF ©LWA-Dann Tardif/Corbis; 212 Michael Newman/PhotoEdit, Inc.; 213 (top) Michael Newman/PhotoEdit, Inc.; 213 (bottom) Tony Freeman/PhotoEdit, Inc.

**Chapter 12:** 222 Chris Stowers/Dorling Kindersley Media Library; 223 (top) National Library of Medicine National Institute of Health; 223 (bottom) The Advertising Archives, London; 225 (top) National Library of Medicine National Institute of Health; 225 (bottom) The Advertising Archives, London; 229 Alamy; 231 Michael Newman/Photo Edit, Inc.

**Chapter 13:** 242 Dorling Kindersley Media Library; 245 Wesley Hitt/Alamy; 250 Buzz Pictures/Alamy; 252 (top) David Young-Wolff/PhotoEdit, Inc.; 252 (bottom left) © Image100/Corbis RF; 252 (bottom center) Andrew Fox/Alamy; 252 (bottom right) Jose Luis Pelaez, Inc;/Alamy; 262 Kent Wood/Peter Arnold, Inc.; 264 Alex Wong/Getty Images; 265 (top) ©Rainer Jensen/epa/Corbis; 265 (center top) Pinellas County Department of Environmental Management; 265 (center bottom) Pinellas County Department of Environmental Management; 265 (bottom) Pinellas County Department of Environmental Management; 266 (all) David Young-Wolff/PhotoEdit, Inc.

**Chapter 14:** 278 Dorling Kindersley Media Library; 279 (left) Thomas & Pat Leeson/Photo Researchers, Inc.; 279 (center) Explorer/Photo Researchers, Inc.; 279 (right) Calvin Larsen/Photo Researchers, Inc.

**Chapter 15:** 288 Dorling Kindersley Media Library; 289 (left) Steve Lewis ©2005 Getty Images Royalty-Free; 289 (middle) ©Michael S. Yamashita/Corbis; 289 (right) © Bojan Brecelj/Corbis; 291 © Dennis Hallinan/Alamy; 295 Reinhard Dirschert/Peter Arnold, Inc; 299 ©Jeff Greenberg/PhotoEdit, Inc.; 305 © Richard Melloul/Sygma Corbis; 309 (top) © Rune Hellestad/Corbis; 309 (center) Hulton Archive/Getty Images; 309 (bottom) © Goss Images/Alamy; 314 Courtesy of the author; 315 Courtesy of the author; 319 Aly Song/Reuters; 324 Brand X Pictures/Alamy; 325 ©Brian Sytnyk/Masterfile; 330 © Thinkstock/Corbis RF; 336 David Young-Wolff/PhotoEdit, Inc.

**Chapter 16:** 342 M;L; Sinibaldi/Corbis; 343 Myrleen Ferguson/PhotoEdit, Inc.; 350 ©2007 AP/Wide World Photos.

**Chapter 17:** 356 Creatas Images (RF)/Jupiter Images; 357 Dorling Kindersley Media Library; 367 Envision/Corbis.

**Chapter 18:** 374 Comstock Images/Picturequest/Jupiter Images; 375 Peter Dazeley/Corbis; 379 Comstock Images/Picturequest/Jupiter Images; 388 Bettmann/Corbis.

**Chapter 19:** 394 Sharie Kennedy/Corbis; 395 ©Myrleen Ferguson Cate/PhotoEdit, Inc.; 397 David King/Dorling Kindersley Media Library; 398 Lon Diehl/PhotoEdit, Inc.; 407 Dorling Kindersley Media Library.

**Chapter 20:** 410 Rough Guides/Dorling Kindersley Media Library; 411 (all) Library of Congress; 413 Museo Nacional de Antropologia, Mexico City, Mexico/Index/The Bridgeman Art Library; 416 ©Richard A; Cooke/Corbis.

**Chapter 21:** 422 Doug Armand/Getty Images; 423 Dallas and John Heaton/Corbis; 428 Bettmann/Corbis.

**Chapter 22:** 438 Amy Etra/PhotoEdit, Inc.; 439 ©Rolf Bruderer/Corbis; 444 Davis Barber/PhotoEdit, Inc.; 446 Bill Bachmann/PhotoEdit, Inc.; 448 The Advertising Archive, London; 449 David Young-Wolff/PhotoEdit, Inc.; 451 Cassy Cohen/PhotoEdit, Inc.; 453 Alfred Pasieka/Photo Researchers, Inc.; 455 Dorling Kindersley Media Library.

**Chapter 23:** 458 Reuters/Corbis; 459 AFP/Getty Images.

**Chapter 24:** 468 Image Select/Getty Images RF; 469 RF Masterfile; 474 Apple Handout/Corbis.

**Chapter 25:** 488 Age fotostock/Superstock; 495 ©Erik Freeland/Corbis.

**Chapter 26:** 500 AGE Fotosearch; 501 Frank Greenway/Dorling Kindersley Media Library; 506 Dorling Kindersley Media Library; 511 Stephen Dunn/Getty Images.

**Chapter 27:** 516 David Kadlubeowski/Corbis; 517 David Kadlubeowski/Corbis; 519 MedioImages (RF)/Jupiter Images; 531 Bettmann/Corbis.

**Chapter 28:** 540 NBAE/Getty Images; 543 Comstock/Jupiter Images.

**Chapter 29:** 558 Foodpix/Jupiter Images; 559 Radius Images RF/Jupiter Images; 563 *V is for Vendetta* by Alan Moore and David Lloyd Cover and Compilation © 1990 DCComics; All Rights Reserved.

**Chapter 30:** 580 Terry Eggers/Corbis; 581 Richard Cummins/Corbis; 581 (left) Terry Eggers/Corbis; 584 Anthony Kaminju/Reuters; 585 Ariel Shelley/Blend Images/Getty Images RF.

**Chapter 31:** 592 Fred Prouser/Reuters/Corbis; 599 ©Zits Partnership, King Features Syndicate.

**Chapter 32:** 606 Roger Ressmeyer/Corbis; 607 Roger Ressmeyer/Corbis; 612 Wink/Jupiter Images.

**Chapter 33:** 618 Jack Hollingsworth/Corbis RF; 619 Dorling Kindersley Media Library; 621 Don Hammond/Design Pics/Corbis; 625 Lebrecht Music and Arts Photo Library.

**Chapter 34:** 632 Fotosearch; 639 Visions of America/Alamy.

**Chapter 35:** 646 ©Kristy-Anne Glubish/Design Pics/Corbis RF; 648 Dorling Kindersley Media Library; 659 Center for Disease Control Public Health Foundation.

# Index